BEIHEFTE ZUM TÜBINGER ATLAS
DES VORDEREN ORIENTS

herausgegeben im Auftrag des Sonderforschungsbereichs 19
von Heinz Gaube und Wolfgang Röllig

Reihe B
(Geisteswissenschaften)
Nr. 47

Aharon Oppenheimer

Babylonia Judaica in the Talmudic Period

WIESBADEN 1983
DR. LUDWIG REICHERT VERLAG

Babylonia Judaica in the Talmudic Period

by

Aharon Oppenheimer

in collaboration with

Benjamin Isaac and Michael Lecker

WIESBADEN 1983
DR. LUDWIG REICHERT VERLAG

CIP-Kurztitelaufnahme der Deutschen Bibliothek

Oppenheimer, Aharon:
Babylonia Judaica in the Talmudic period / by Aharon Oppenheimer. [Diese Arbeit ist im Sonderforschungsbereich 19, Tübingen, entstanden]. – Wiesbaden : Reichert, 1983.
(Beihefte zum Tübinger Atlas des Vorderen Orients : Reihe B, Geisteswiss. ; Nr. 47)
ISBN 3-88226-174-9
NE: Tübinger Atlas des Vorderen Orients / Beihefte / B

The preparation of this volume was made possible by a grant from the Memorial Foundation for Jewish Culture

Diese Arbeit ist im Sonderforschungsbereich 19, Tübingen, entstanden und wurde auf seine Veranlassung unter Verwendung der ihm von der Deutschen Forschungsgemeinschaft zur Verfügung gestellten Mittel gedruckt.

Gesamtherstellung: Hubert & Co., Göttingen · Printed in Germany

To Nili

Table of Contents

Abbreviations

AAB	*Abhandlungen der Deutschen Akademie der Wissenschaften zu Berlin*
AE	*Année Épigraphique*
AFO	*Archiv für Orientforschung*
AJA	*American Journal of Archaeology*
ANRW	*Aufstieg und Niedergang der römischen Welt*
APAW	*Abhandlungen der Preussischen Akademie der Wissenschaften*
ASTI	*Annual of the Swedish Theological Institute*
Bab. Env.	Babylonia and Its Environs (map)
B-a-ḥ	*Bayit Ḥadash* (a commentary on *Ṭur* by Joel Sirkes)
BE	*Bulletin Épigraphique*, in *REG*
BGA	*Bibliotheca Geographorum Arabicorum*
BMC	*British Museum Catalogue: Syria* (Worth); *Arabia* (Hill)
BSOAS	*Bulletin of the School of Oriental and African Studies*
CIG	*Corpus Inscriptionum Graecarum*
CIJ	*Corpus Inscriptionum Iudaicarum* (J.-B. Frey)
CIS	*Corpus Inscriptionum Semiticarum*
Cl. Ph.	*Classical Philology*
CRAI	*Comptes-rendus de l'Académie des Inscriptions et Belles-Lettres*
CSCO	*Corpus Scriptorum Christianorum Orientalium*
DAFI	*Cahiers de la Délégation Archéologique Française en Iran*
Diq. Sof.	*Diqduqei Soferim*
EI[1]	*Enzyklopaedie des Islam*, 1913–1938
EI[2]	*The Encyclopaedia of Islam*, 1960ff.
FHG	*Fragmenta Historicorum Graecorum* (C. Müller)
GAL	*Geschichte der arabischen Literatur* (C. Brockelmann)
GAS	*Geschichte des arabischen Schrifttums* (F. Sezgin)
HTR	*Harvard Theological Review*
HUCA	*Hebrew Union College Annual*
ICIT	Institute for the Complete Israeli Talmud
ILS	*Inscriptiones Latinae Selectae* (H. Dessau)
IOS	*Israel Oriental Studies*
JEA	*Journal of Egyptian Archaeology*
JESHO	*Journal of the Economic and Social History of the Orient*
JHS	*Journal of Hellenic Studies*
JNES	*Journal of Near Eastern Studies*
JPK	*Jahrbuch der Preußischen Kunstsammlungen*
JQR	*Jewish Quarterly Review*
JRAS	*Journal of the Royal Asiatic Society*
JRGS	*Journal of the Royal Geographical Society*
JRS	*Journal of Roman Studies*
KP	*Der kleine Pauly* (K. Ziegler & W. Sontheimer)
LCL	The Loeb Classical Library
MAMA	*Monumenta Asiae Minoris Antiqua*
MDP	*Mémoires de la Délégation en Perse*

MGWJ	*Monatsschrift für Geschichte und Wissenschaft des Judentums*
MMFP	*Monuments et Mémoires Fondation Piot*
NNM	*Numismatic Notes and Monographs*
OGIS	*Orientis Graeci Inscriptiones Selectae* (W. Dittenberger)
PAAJR	*Proceedings of the American Academy for Jewish Research*
R-a-b-a-d	R. Abraham b. David
R-a-ḥ	R. Ḥananel b. Ḥushiel
Rashi	R. Shelomo Yitzḥaqi
RE	*Realencyclopädie der classischen Altertumswissenschaft* (Pauly-Wissowa)
REA	*Revue des Études Anciennes*
REG	*Revue des Études Grecques*
R-i-f	R. Yitzḥaq Alfasi
R-o-sh	R. Asher (b. Yeḥiel)
SAWM	*Sitzungsberichte der k.b. Akademie der Wissenschaften zu München*
SEG	*Supplementum Epigraphicum Graecum*
SHA	*Scriptores Historiae Augustae*
Tal. Bab.	Talmudic Babylonia (map)
T.B.	Babylonian Talmud
T.J.	Jerusalem Talmud
TUP	Trinity University Press
UVB	*Vorläufiger Bericht über die Ausgrabungen in Uruk-Warka*
WZKM	*Wiener Zeitschrift zur Kunde des Morgenlandes*
YCS	*Yale Classical Studies*
ZA	*Zeitschrift für Assyriologie und verwandte Gebiete*
ZDMG	*Zeitschrift der Deutschen Morgenländischen Gesellschaft*
ZGEB	*Zeitschrift der Gesellschaft für Erdkunde zu Berlin*
ZPE	*Zeitschrift für Papyrologie und Epigraphik*

Transcription

Hebrew	Arabic	Persian
א = ʾ	ا = ʾ	ا = ʾ
בּ = b; ב = v	ب = b	ب = b
ג = g	ت = t	پ = p
ד = d	ث = ṯ	ت = t
ה = h	ج = ǧ	ث = s̱
ו = w	ح = ḥ	ج = ǧ
ז = z	خ = ḫ	چ = č
ח = ḥ	د = d	ح = ḥ
ט = ṭ	ذ = ḏ	خ = ḫ
י = y	ر = r	د = d
כּ = k; כ = ḵ	ز = z	ذ = ẕ
ל = l	س = s	ر = r
מ = m	ش = š	ز = z
נ = n	ص = ṣ	ژ = ž
ס = s	ض = ḍ	س = s
ע = ʿ	ط = ṭ	ش = š
פּ = p; פ = f	ظ = ẓ	ص = ṣ
צ = ṣ	ع = ʿ	ض = ż
ק = q	غ = ġ	ط = ṭ
ר = r	ف = f	ظ = ẓ
שׂ = ś	ق = q	ع = ʿ
שׁ = š	ك = k	غ = ġ
ת = t	ل = l	ف = f
	م = m	ق = q
	ن = n	ك = k
	ه = h	گ = g
	و = w	ل = l
	ي = y	م = m
		ن = n
		ه = h
		و = v
		ي = y

Because the vocalisation of Hebrew and Aramaic place-names in general and those outside of Eretz Israel in particular presents problems, the transcription makes no attempt to differentiate between long and short vowels. Non-geographic Hebrew items, including titles of books and articles, are rendered in a simplified transcription.

Preface

The subject of this study is the Jewish communities in Babylonia in the talmudic period, and its point of departure is the information on those communities in talmudic literature, first of all, naturally, the Babylonian Talmud. Further data are found in classical literature in Greek and Latin; and for new proposals for the identification of the places, Geographical and historiographical works in Arabic were consulted in particular.
The classical sources as well as the archaeological material and related subjects were covered by Prof. Benjamin Isaac of the Department of Classics of Tel Aviv University. The Arabic material was covered by Dr. Michael Lecker of the Arabic Department of the Hebrew University in Jerusalem. The interdisciplinary nature of this study may be ascribed to the collaboration of these two scholars.
It is a privilege to thank the many individuals and institutions who helped us: Prof. S. Safrai of the Hebrew University in Jerusalem encouraged me to embark upon the research on this subject. It was carried out within the framework of Tel Aviv University's Diaspora Institute, and at all stages benefited from the assistance of its director, Prof. S. Simonsohn. The Tübinger Atlas des Vorderen Orients (TAVO) financed the translation into English of the book, and accepted it for publication, on the recommendation of Prof. M. Hengel, head of the Institut für Antikes Judentum und Hellenistische Religionsgeschichte at Tübingen University. Prof. H. Halm kindly advised on matters concerning the Arabic sources. TAVO scholars gave me all possible help. Their spokesman, Prof. W. Röllig, provided active assistance and valuable comments on the text. I am especially indebted to Dr. F. Hüttenmeister, who was generous with advice based on experience, and undertook to edit the manuscript in accordance with TAVO norms.
Throughout, I was aided by the supportive advice of Prof. M. Stern of the Hebrew University, Prof. M. Gil, Prof. I. Eph'al, Dr. N. Na'aman, and Dr. R. Zadok of Tel Aviv University. Special thanks are due Dr. I. Ben-Shalom for his active assistance in organizing the talmudic material.
Prof. Isaac completed his work on the book in 1980–81 while on leave at the Institute for Advanced Study at Princeton, where he had access to the libraries of both the Institute and the University, and to the counsel of Prof. M. Morony of UCLA, Dr. J. Matthews of the Queen's College, Oxford, and Prof. S. Humphreys of the University of Wisconsin. Dr. Lecker was aided in the course of his work by a grant from the Ben-Zvi Institute. The research as a whole was made possible by a grant from the Memorial Foundation for Jewish Culture.

Thanks are extended to the Carta Publishing Co. in Jerusalem and its staff, in particular Ms. P. Cohen, for their fine work in drawing the maps. I am especially grateful to Mr. M. Kosovsky for kindly allowing me to consult the material he is compiling for a concordance of the Jerusalem Talmud. My deep appreciation goes to Ms. Naomi Handelman of the English Department at Tel Aviv University for the thought and effort she applied to the translation. I should like also to thank Hubert & Co. and Dr. Ludwig Reichert for the pains they took in the printing and publication of this book.
My wife Nili participated in all the tasks needed to complete the research—collecting material, checking and preparing it for the press, and compiling the bibliography and indexes. Without her contribution this book could not have been published.

Aharon Oppenheimer

Tel Aviv University, June 1981.

Introduction

The Jews of ancient Babylonia left their mark on the history on the Jewish people more than those of any other country in the Diaspora. During the Sassanian period Babylonia gradually superseded Eretz Israel as the leading Jewish center. The Babylonian Talmud established the way of life not only of the Jews of Babylonia in the period in which it was produced; more than any other work it shaped the entire Jewish people, its thinking, its way of life, its relationship with the world around, its law and rules through the ages.

A number of factors combined to enhance the particularity and importance of the Jewish community in Babylonia: it was the oldest of the Diaspora, in continuous existence since the first deportation of Jews in biblical times. According to Josephus, the Jewish community there totaled "countless myriads whose number cannot be ascertained" (*Antiquities* XI, 133).

During the Parthian period, Babylonian Jewry acquired a considerable degree of autonomy, thanks to the feudal and decentralized nature of the regime. Its development and prestige saw progress in particular when Eretz Israel was under Roman rule. The traumatic events that took place then—the destruction of Jerusalem and the Temple (in A.D. 70), the failure of the Bar Kokhva revolt (135), the economic depression during the period of anarchy (235–284), the adoption of Christianity as the Roman state religion (313) and the abolition of the Patriarchate (429)—led to a gradual decline of the community in Eretz Israel and a concomitant growth in Babylonia until the latter largely took the place of the former in Jewish life. The crucial impetus for the rise of Babylonian Jewry came in the first half of the second century when the suppression of the revolt in the Diaspora during Trajan's reign (A.D. 117) and the defeat of Bar Kokhva in Eretz Israel set in motion a wave of immigration to Babylonia, which contained the only significant Jewish community outside the borders of the Roman Empire.

The relatively salutary political and economic conditions obtaining in Babylonia and the gradual emancipation of the Jewish community there from its subordination to Eretz Israel enabled it to evolve a life style and creativity of its own. Life centered around the leadership institutions of the community, the Exilarch and the main yeshivas. The Exilarch was the political head of Babylonian Jewry, deriving his authority on the one hand from the status accorded him by the government, and on the other from his recognition by the people, who acknowledged him as a descendant of the House of David. Although the Patriarchate in Eretz Israel was likewise related to the House of David, the Exilarch's lineage was deemed superior. The first Exilarch whose name is known—Rav Huna, a contemporary of Rabbi Judah ha-Nasi—occupied the post in about A. D. 200, but the institution was far older than that. It was the yeshivas that shaped spiritual and cultural life and determined the rules and customs of Babylonian Jewry. The establishment of the yeshivas was connected with the return from Eretz Israel in A. D. 219 of Rav, who together with Samuel headed the first generation of Babylonian amoras. Rav set up a yeshiva at Sura, and Samuel took over the Torah center at Nəhardəʻa and made it a great yeshiva. The learning of Eretz Israel as represented by the Mishnah and the study methods Rav brought along, combined with the Babylonian heritage and creativity, laid the foundations for the Babylonian Talmud and the process of its formation in the Babylonian yeshivas which lasted until its redaction and completion in the fifth century.

Babylonian Jews considered themselves not only responsible for the inculcation of Jewish tradition, but also charged with preserving pure Jewish lineage. They preserved it by exercising extremely meticulous care in matrimonial matters, involving the rejection of people with various genealogical defects. They avoided intermarriage with individuals who had been converted not according to the halakhic practice, with offspring of priests married to unsuitable women (such as divorcees), Gentile slaves improperly emancipated, *mamzerim* and the like. Tradition places the start of this strictness as far back as Ezra, who did not leave Babylonia for Eretz Israel until he "made her like pure sifted flour" (T. B. Qiddushin 69b). While admitting that the Jews of Eretz Israel were also punctilious about pure lineage, the Babylonian Jews considered themselves paramount in that respect: "All countries are an admixture (with impure lineage) for Eretz Israel, and Eretz Israel is an admixture for Babylonia" (ibid. and parallels). The source (Qiddushin 71b) tells of the friction between the Babylonian amora Zeʻiri, an immigrant to Eretz Israel, and Rabbi Yoḥanan who was head of the Sanhedrin in Tiberias in the third century: "Zeʻiri used to evade Rabbi Yoḥanan, who told him, Marry my daughter. One day they were walking on the road, came to a puddle, and he took Rabbi Yoḥanan on his shoulders and carried him over. He said, Our learning is fit and our daughters are not fit?!" The fact that Babylonian Jews made safeguarding their lineage the core of their value system also undoubtedly helped them to maintain their identity and particularity.

Eretz Israel was distinguished by the application of precepts connected with the produce of the land, and its boundaries were set accordingly, separating it from "eretz ha-ʻamim" (the land of the nations) whose inhabitants were not required to fulfill such precepts as the *terumot*, the tithes and the sabbatical year. For the Babylonian sages, the preservation of pure lineage was the criterion determining the borders, separating "healthy Babylonia," where great strictness was observed, from adjacent lands considered "dead," "dying," or "sick" in regard to their lineage. However, determination of the boundaries of Eretz Israel was presumably based not only on the applicability of the precepts connected with the soil, but also on political, economic and social factors; in the same way the amoraitic decisions on the boundaries of the Babylonia of pure lineage went beyond purely religious considerations: they demarcate regions with a large Jewish population in contrast to scattered communities, and reflect the sages' attitudes to and relations with the authorities and the Jewish community. It is therefore no accident that the borders of Babylonia of pure lineage coincide in a number of localities with those of the Sassanian empire. The cornerstone of any research on the geography and history of the Jewish community in Babylonia must be the identification and location of the borders of the Babylonia of pure lineage.

This work takes as its point of departure the places in Babylonia mentioned in talmudic literature, and its aim is to identify those places and from the testimony on them glean information on their history, economy, social life and culture and on the daily life of Babylonian Jews from the Hellenistic period to the Arab conquest. A talmudic reference to a place may be fortuitous, for certainly not all Babylonian places with Jewish inhabitants appear in the Talmud. On the other hand such references, especially a number of references to the same place, are often an indication of its importance and prestige.

The Talmud does not abound in information that is of assistance in determining the location of the places it names. In order to identify them, it is necessary to have recourse to Latin and Greek sources of the period, to gaonic literature, and to the works of Arab geographers and historians of later times.

Except for Maḥoza, Opis (Akšak), Ctesiphon, Seleucia and Be-Ardəšir-Koḵe—which are grouped together under the heading "The Maḥoza Area"—the entries appear in alphabetical order. They comprise all the places for which the sources provide information contributing to their identification and/or to knowledge of the life of the inhabitants. Additional places which could not be identified and on which the available data are devoid of historical importance are listed in the appendix. Doubtful names (which may or may not apply to places in Babylonia, or which may not designate places at all) and other geographical names (of rivers, mountains, etc.) do not figure among the entries.

Each entry begins with the talmudic sources mentioning the place concerned (from the Babylonian Talmud unless otherwise noted). As a rule all such sources are included for each entry, first in the original language and then in an English translation prepared for this book (quotation marks indicate a biblical verse). Exceptions to this rule are the places where the great yeshivas were located—Nəhardəʿa, Sura, Pumbədita and Maḥoza—concerning which the sources given are limited to those having some bearing on matters discussed further on in the entry. Footnotes indicate variants mainly of the name of the place and the sages mentioned. Testimony on sages and on Babylonian Jewish life where no reference is made to a specific place is omitted.

Where a place is mentioned in classical literature—which provides us with most of the hard facts available on the communities dealt with—Latin and/or Greek sources follow those from the Talmud. There is no attempt to list all the relevant classical sources; the selection made consists of texts which appear to be particularly informative. These too are given in both the original language and in English; where the source of the translation is not indicated, we ourselves are responsible. Other references are given in the footnotes, but here again the material represents a selection, since this book is concerned first and foremost with talmudic sources. In principle the sources cited are those relating to the period dealt with, i.e., from Hellenistic times to the Muslim conquest. In some cases important inscriptions are cited together with the literary sources.

Nineteenth century travelers and scholars consulted classical literature extensively because they knew the languages and had easy access to the texts. Consequently most of the relevant sources are familiar and often cited in secondary literature. A comprehensive treatment presenting "western" evidence together with that of talmudic literature, however, has heretofore been unavailable. The combination may help to promote a better understanding of the mixed culture concerned. On a more practical level it is hoped that scholars with diverse backgrounds will find here a convenient compilation of material which is otherwise widely scattered.

Texts in Syriac are relevant mainly for the periphery of Jewish Babylonia, notably for the christianization of the area. We have included references which seemed important, without claiming independent research, since they are accessible to us only through secondary literature. The same must be said of works in Pahlavi.

After the sources in each entry comes a discussion of the identification of the place, headed by a short definition of its location, with referral to one of the maps in the book. These discussions are variously captioned, depending on whether the location is definite, was previously proposed, or is first proposed in the present work. For some entries the data available are not sufficient to make identification possible.

The basis for the identification of the places is mainly the material in Arabic geographical and historical works. The first to employ these was Jacob Obermeyer, in *Die Landschaft Babylonien* (Frankfurt am Main, 1929). Combining a first-hand acquaintance with Iraq with familiarity with Arab sources, he sharply criticized his predecessors for relying exclusively on classical literature and talmudic exegetes, and provided a new basis and guide lines for research on the location of Jewish communities in Babylonia. Some of his proposals have been adopted, others re-examined in the light of the rich Arabic literature that has appeared in the fifty years since the publication of his book.

Doubts as to the identification made by Obermeyer and others arose in particular concerning places located far from the Babylonia of pure lineage.

The boundaries of the Jewish community in Babylonia do not necessarily coincide with those of the Babylonia of pure lineage, for of course there were Jews living beyond them. As Jewish settlement was clearly concentrated within the latter boundaries, however, they are a likely indication for the identification and location of places. It is consequently our practice in this study to favor where possible identification within the boundaries of the Babylonia of pure lineage, although not, of course, in connection with well-known districts and sites such as Mesene, Be Ḥozai, Adiabene, etc. outside Babylonia.

Thereafter a number of sections in each entry deal with matters reflected in the relevant sources such as the history of the place, the sages associated with it, relations with leadership institutions, with Gentiles and with other places, the economy, social structure, material culture, etc. A bibliography completes each entry.

Due to circumstances beyond our control, we unfortunately have no first-hand knowledge of the region. We have however attempted to present the findings of archaeological exploration in the form of brief discussions and references to other literature and archaeological reports. Such discussions focus on conclusions regarding the history of the sites, and extensive descriptions have been avoided.

The book contains two maps—one of talmudic Babylonia indicating the boundaries of the Babylonia of pure lineage as established in this study, and the other of Babylonia and its environs showing places outside Babylonia in adjacent regions mentioned in talmudic literature. A plan of the Maḥoza Area appears in the relevant entry. The map of talmudic Babylonia seems to show the concentrations of Jewish settlements in Babylonia. It may not necessarily be accurate, and errors may have arisen from reliance on Arabic sources in regard to many places. Arabic historical literature which abounds in geographic data, and even purely geographical literature, naturally focus on the regions where dramatic events took place during the Muslim period, which do not encompass all the populated areas of Iraq. The Kūfa area in southwest Iraq, for instance, which was the scene of turbulent events during several centuries of Muslim history, is fully documented in Arabic literature, making possible quite well-founded proposals for identification in that region of a number of Jewish communities referred to in the Talmud. These may indeed have been located there, and Kūfa and its environs may have already been important in Jewish life in talmudic times, but it is also possible that many Jewish communities lay in adjacent regions, while the lack of documentation prevents their locations from being established.

The transcription from languages using other than the Latin alphabet is a combination of various systems. Place names from the Talmud are rendered according to the system of the Tübinger Atlas des Vorderen Orients (see Key to Transcriptions, p. 11). Other proper names from ancient or modern Hebrew follow a modified system easier for English speakers to read. The same modified system is used for Hebrew bibliographical references and quotations, unless the author concerned has himself made another choice. The transcription from Arabic and other languages follows the Tübinger Atlas system. Non-English terms are unitalicized if they so appear in the Random House Dictionary.

This book does not claim to be the last word on Jewish communities in Babylonia. Naturally, study of the manuscripts of talmudic literature, systematic review of gaonic literature, extensive perusal of Arabic geographical and historical literature, and archaeological exploration in Iraq will certainly further research, enrich it with additional identifications, and expand knowledge of life in the Jewish communities of Babylonia. It is hoped that this work will point the way for subsequent studies also based on the interdisciplinary use of talmudic, classical and Arabic literature.

Gazetteer

Adiabene (Ḥadyav) חדייב

A. *Sources*

1. Qiddushin 72a

... דאמר רבי אבא בר כהנא מאי דכתיב "וינחם בחלח ובחבור נהר גוזן וערי מדי", חלח זו חלזון[1] חבור זו הדייב[2]... "ותלת עלעין בפומה בין שיניה", אמר רבי יוחנן זו חלזון הדייב ונציבין, שפעמים בולעתן ופעמים פולטתן.

... For Rabbi Abba b. Kahana said, What is meant by "And he settled them in Ḥalaḥ and along the Ḥavor and the River Gozan and in the towns of Media" (II Kings 18:11); Ḥalaḥ is Ḥelzon,[1] Ḥavor is Hadyav[2] ...; "It had three ribs in its mouth between its teeth" (Dan. 7:5) said Rabbi Yoḥanan, That is Ḥelzon, Hadyav and Nisibis which she [Rome] sometimes swallows and sometimes spits out.

2. Yevamot 16b–17a

... דאמר רבי אבא בר כהנא "וינחם בחלח ובחבור נהר גוזן וערי מדי", חלח זה חלזון,[3] וחבור זו חדייב.[4]

... For Rabbi Abba b. Kahana said, "And he settled them in Ḥalaḥ along the Ḥavor and the River Gozan and in the towns of Media" (II Kings 18:11); Ḥalaḥ is Ḥelzon,[3] and Ḥavor is Ḥadyav.[4]

3. Shabbat 121b[5]

מתיב רב יוסף חמשה נהרגין בשבת, ואלו הן זבוב שבארץ מצרים וצירעה שבנינוה ועקרב שבחדייב[6] ונחש שבא"י וכלב שוטה בכל מקום.

Rav Joseph argued, Five may be killed on the Sabbath, and they are the fly that is in the land of Egypt, the hornet that is in Nineveh, the scorpion that is in Ḥadyav,[6] the snake that is in Eretz Israel and a mad dog anywhere.

---

[1] The Venice printing has חלזיון, further on as well.

[2] The Munich MS has חדייב.

[3] The Munich MS and *Ginzei Talmud* have חלזיון; the Venice printing has 'חלוא; the Vatican 111 MS has חליין.

[4] The Munich MS has הדייב, the Vatican 111 MS has חדיאב.

[5] Similarly the T. J. Shabbat XIV 1–14b, 60–61.

[6] The T. J. parallel has הדיית.

4. Mo'ed Qaṭan 28a

תנא להו זוגא[7] דמהדייב . . .

The pair of scholars[7] from Hadyav taught them ...

5. Niddah 21b

כי אתא זוגא דמן חדייב, אתא ואייתי מתניתא בידיה.

When a pair of scholars came from Ḥadyav they came and brought a *baraita* with them ...

6. Bava Batra 26b

בעא מיניה יעקב הדייבא[8] מרב חסדא . . .

Jacob Hadyava[8] asked Rav Ḥisda.

7. See Josephus, *Antiquities*, XX, 17–96.

8. Ammianus, XXIII 6, 20–22
Intra hunc circumitum Adiabena est Assyria priscis temporibus uocitata longaque assuetudine ad hoc translata uocabulum ea re, quod inter Onam et Tigridem sita nauigeros fluuios adiri uado numquam potuit; transire enim diabenin dicimus Graeci, et ueteres quidem hoc arbitrantur, nos autem didicimus, quod in his terris amnes sunt duo perpetui, quos transiimus, Diabas et Adiabas, iunctis naualibus pontibus, ideoque intellegi Adiabenam cognominatam ut a fluminibus maximis Aegyptos Homero auctore et India et Euphratensis ante hoc Commagena itidemque Hiberia ex Hibero, nunc Hispania, et a Baeti amne insigni prouincia Baetica.
In hac Adiabena Ninus est ciuitas, quae olim Persidis regna possiderat, nomen Nini potentissimi quondam regis, Semiramidis mariti, declarans et Ecbatana et Arbela et Gaugamela, ubi Dareum Alexander post discrimina uaria proeliorum incitato Marte prostrauit.

Within this area is Adiabena, called Assyria in ancient times, but by long custom changed to this name because, lying between the navigable rivers Ona and Tigris it could never be approached by a ford; for we Greeks for *transire* say διαβαίνειν. At least, this is the opinion of the ancients. But I myself say that there are two perpetually flowing rivers to be found in these lands, the Diabas and Adiabas, which I myself have crossed, and over which there are bridges of boats; and therefore it is to be assumed that Adiabena was named from them, as from great rivers Egypt was named, according to Homer, as well as India, and the Euphratensis, before my time called Commagena; likewise from the Hiberus, Hiberia (now Hispania), and the province of Baetica from the noble river Baetis.

---

[7] The Munich B MS has ההוא מרבנן. On *zuga* as a pair of sages rather than the name of a sage, see Epstein, *Mavo le-Nusaḥ ha-Mishnah*, pp. 16–17.

[8] The Hamburg MS has חידייבא, the Pesaro printing has חדיאבא, and see *Diq. Sof.*

In this Adiabena is the city of Ninus, which once possessed the rule over Persia, perpetuating the name of Ninus, once a most powerful king and the husband of Semiramis; also Ecbatana, Arbela and Gaugamela, where Alexander, after various other battles, overthrew Darius in a hot contest. (trans.: J. C. Rolfe, LCL)

B. *Location*

A region between the two Zāb rivers, whose capital was Arbela; later the name was also applied to the Nisibis area (see Bab. Env. map).

C. *History*

Adiabene was the Greek name of the Seleucid eparchy which occupied the region of Ḥadyav between the two rivers Zāb, east of the Tigris. The name is sometimes also used for the territory further north[9] and Latin sources consider it the equivalent of the older Assyria.[10] In the first century A. D. it was ruled by its own kings, vassals of the Parthians.[11] As a consequence it became involved in many of the wars with Rome and internal quarrels of the Parthians.[12] Because of its geographical position, Roman armies repeatedly overran the country on their way to Babylonia,[13] as suggested by Rabbi Yoḥanan in Source 1.[14] The major town of the region was Arbela (q.v. for its position on one of the most important trade routes between Babylonia and the west, and for the penetration of Christianity). Adiabene was eventually absorbed into the Sassanian Empire. The name Ḥadyav has survived in the place name Ḥazza that figures in Arabic sources.

According to Ṭabarī, Ardashīr b. Bābak built in Mosul (i.e. in its vicinity) the town of Būḏ Ardašīr which is Ḥazza.[15] Of the two places by that name mentioned by Yāqūt, the second is a place between the Greater Zāb and the Lesser Zāb: "a small town near Irbil, in the Mosul region, after which rough

---

[9] Philostratus, *Life of Apollonius* I 31, 37, describes Nineveh as part of Adiabene.

[10] E.g., Pliny, *Natural History* V 66; VI 41; Source 8.

[11] See Josephus (Source 7) for their conversion to Judaism (and see below). See also Tacitus, *Annals* XII 13, 14; XV 1.

[12] Tacitus, *loc.cit.*; Josephus, Source 7; Cassius Dio LXII 20; LXVIII 28; Debevoise, *A Political History of Parthia*, passim.

[13] See Debevoise for Adiabene during the wars under Trajan, Severus and Caracalla.

[14] That sermon was explicated in Pirqoi Ben Baboi as follows: שפעמים פלטתן (צ"ל בולעתן) רומי הרשעה שהן מולכין במדינות הללו, ופעמים פולטתן שהן באין פרסיים וטורדין אותן ושולטין מלכי פרסיים על אדום ... (= Sometimes evil Rome swallows them that ruled those countries and sometimes spits them out when the Persians come and annoy them and the Persian kings rule Edom [= Rome]...; *Ginzei Schechter*, vol. 2, p. 563; *Otzar ha-Geonim* for Qiddushin, *ha-Teshuvot*, p. 178, and n. א there.)

[15] Ṭabarī, vol. 2, p. 41 (= vol. 1, p. 820); Nöldeke, *Perser und Araber*, p. 20, n. 4; see also Ḥamza, *Ta'rīḫ*, pp. 46, 47; Ibn Ḫurdāḏbih, p. 17; Ibn al-Faqīh, p. 131.

priestly vestments are called, in the past the capital of the province of Irbil."[16] In a later period the name was applied to the Nisibis area. Cf the location of the other Ḥazza listed by Yāqūt: "A place between Nisibis and Ra's al-ʿAin, on the Ḫābūr, etc."[17]

D. *The Royal Converts*

Source 7 contains the famous story of the conversion of the kings of Adiabene. The ruler between A.D. 35 and A.D. 60 was Izates II who with his mother Helena had adopted Judaism even before his accession to the throne. He was succeeded by his brother Monobazus who likewise converted. Monobazus transported the bones of his mother and brother to Jerusalem for burial there, and his deeds and generosity left their mark on talmudic literature.[18] During the great revolt against the Romans in Eretz Israel (A.D. 66–70) the kings of Adiabene dispatched reinforcements to Jerusalem who conducted themselves with outstanding bravery.

The conversion of the Adiabene royal family to Judaism is indicative of a general trend in Babylonia.[19] There is no doubt that the increase in the number of Jews there was in part due to conversions. It should be noted that the conversion of the Adiabene kings was the outcome of a common practice at the time of Jews traveling to various places and persuading the inhabitants "to worship God according to the custom of the forefathers of the Jews" (cf. the section on Economy in the entry on "Mesene").[20]

Beer, *Rashut ha-Golah* (1970), p. 138
Beer, *Amora'ei Bavel* (1974), p. 22
Eshel, *Yishuvei ha-Yehudim* (1979), p. 118
Fiey, *Assyrie Chrétienne* (1965), vol. 1, part 1
Funk, *Monumenta* (1913), p. 31
Hirschenson, *Sheva Ḥokhmot* (1883), p. 101
Jastrow, *Dictionary* (1950³), p. 333
Kohut, *Arukh ha-Shalem* (1878–1892), vol. 3, p. 183; *Tosefot* (1937), p. 156
Levy, *Wörterbuch* (1924²), vol. 1, p. 453; vol. 2, p. 16
Neubauer, *Géographie* (1868), pp. 374, 423
Neusner, *History* (1965–1970), 5 vols. passim
Newman, *Agricultural Life* (1932), p. 12
Obermeyer, *Landschaft* (1929), pp. 10, 12, 91, 123, 132f.
Wiesner, *Scholien* (1862), vol. 2, pp. 240–241

---

16 Yāqūt, s.v. "Ḥazza." See on it also Bakrī, s.v. "Ḥazza"; Ibn Ḥauqal, p. 217; Morony, *Iran* 14 (1976): 55; *Ta'rīḫ al-Mauṣil*, pp. 313, 423; al-Aḫṭal, *Dīwān*, vol. 1, pp. 114, 269; Streck, *EI*¹, s.v. "Irbil." In the opinion of Streck, (*ibid.*) the Adiabene region which was also called Arbelitis after its capital, Arbela (q.v.) is equivalent to the district (*arḍ*) of Irbil of the Arab geographers. Cf. perhaps Yāqūt, s.v. "Kafr ʿIzzā."

17 Yāqūt, s.v. "Ḥazza." Many sources refer to the scorpions of Nisibis whose bite was bad. On an original way to deal with the scorpion problem in the period of the caliph ʿUṯmān b. ʿAffān, see *Futūḥ al-buldān*, p. 178; Yāqūt, s.v. "Naṣībīn," and see Source 3.

18 See e.g. Mishnah Yoma III 10; Bava Batra 11a.

19 See Josephus, *Jewish War*, II, 520; VI, 355–356.

20 For the phenomenon of conversion, see Neusner, *History*, vol. 1, pp. 58–64 and the bibliography there.

Afsaṭya אפסטיא

See the entry on "Sura and Mata Məḥasya."

Agama אגמא

See the entry on "Damim."

Aluš אלוש

A. *Source*

Yoma 10a (= Soṭah 34b)

"ושם אחימן ששי ותלמי ילידי הענק" . . . אחימן בנה ענת,[1] ששי בנה אלוש,[2] תלמי בנה תלבוש.[3]

"And there Aḥiman, Sheshai, and Talmai, the Anaqites lived" (Num. 13:22)... Aḥiman built ʿAnat,[1] Sheshai built Aluš,[2] Talmai built Talbuš.[3]

B. *Already Proposed Location*

On an island in the Euphrates between Ihi də-Qira and Talbuš (on Bab. Env. map).

C. *Identification*

The legend interpreting the verse in the source lists Aluš together with ʿAnat and Talbuš (qq.v.), all of which were built by one of the three Anaqites, i.e., offspring of the *ʿanaq* (= giant).[4] All three are mentioned by Arab geographers as places on islands in the Euphrates.[5]

---

[1] The Venice printing of Soṭah has אנת, and see Soṭah in the ICIT edition.

[2] The Soṭah parallel has אלש, but the Munich and Vatican 110 MSS and *Ein Yaʿaqov* have אלוש as Yoma does.

[3] The Munich MS has תלביש, and see Soṭah in the ICIT edition.

[4] Care must be taken to distinguish between Aluš in the Euphrates which is not far from ʿAnat and Talbuš, and the Aluš in the Sinai desert mentioned in connection with the wanderings of the Israelites in the desert ("in Aluš the Sabbath was given" etc. in the T. J. Betzah II 1–61a, 63; or "the Aluš desert" in Genesis Rabbah XLVII 12, Theodor-Albeck ed., p. 490). There is no sense either in identifying the Aluš in the source with any place in Eretz Israel (as did, e.g. Horowitz, *Eretz Israel u-Shekhenoteha*, p. 46, and see n. 9 in the entry on "ʿAnat").

[5] On Aluš see "Alūs" in Yāqūt, *Marāṣid*; see "ʿĀnāt" in *ar-Rauḍ al-miʿṭār*; *BGA*, passim; Le Strange, "Ibn Serapion," pp. 10, 15; Suhrāb, p. 119; cf. Péres, *EI*², s.v. "al-Ālūsī," and see Musil, *The Middle Euphrates*, index, s.v. "Alūš," etc.

For the Arab tradition somewhat resembling the talmudic legend in the source above regarding the establishment of those towns, see the entries on "ʿAnat" and "Talbuš."

ESHEL, *Yishuvei ha-Yehudim* (1979), p. 20
HIRSCHENSON, *Sheva Ḥokhmot* (1883), pp. 186–187 ("ענת")
JASTROW, *Dictionary* (1950³), p. 68
KOHUT, *Arukh ha-Shalem* (1878–1892), vol. 1, p. 107
LEVY, *Wörterbuch* (1924²), vol. 1, p. 83
OBERMEYER, *Landschaft* (1929), pp. 36, 102

ʿAnat ענת

A. *Sources*

1. Yoma 10a (= Soṭah 34b)

"ושם אחימן ששי ותלמי ילידי הענק" ... אחימן בנה ענת,[1] ששי בנה אלוש,[2] תלמי בנה תלבוש.[3]

"And there Aḥiman, Sheshai, and Talmai, the Anaqites, lived" (Num. 13:22) ... Aḥiman built ʿAnat,[1] Sheshai built Aluš,[2] Talmai built Talbuš.[3]

2. Ammianus XXIV 1,6–10[4]

Exin dierum quattuor itinere leui peracto, uespera incedente, cum expeditis mille inpositis nauibus, Lucillianus comes imperatu principis mittitur Anathan munimentum expugnaturus, quod (ut pleraque alia) circumluitur fluentis Eufratis. et nauibus (ut praeceptum est) per oportuna dispersis, obsidebatur ... insula, nebulosa nocte obumbrante impetum clandestinum. sed postquam aduenit lux certa, aquatum quidam egressus, uisis subito hostibus, ululabili clamore sublato, excitos tumultuosis uocibus propugnatores armauit. et mox a specula quadam altissima explorato situ castrorum, quam ocissime cum duarum praesidio nauium, amnem supermeat imperator, pone sequentibus nauigiis multis, quae obsidionales machinas aduehebant. iamque muris propinquans, cum non absque discriminibus multis consideraret esse certandum, sermone cum leni tum aspero et minaci, hortabatur ad deditionem defensores qui ad conloquium petito Ormizda, promissis eius et iuramentis inlecti, multa sibi de lenitudine Romana spondebant. denique prae se bouem coronatum agentes, quod est apud eos susceptae pacis indicium, descendere suppliciter, et statim munimento omni incenso, Pusaeus eius praefectus, dux Aegypti postea, honore tribunatus adfectus est. reliqui uero cum caritatibus suis et supellectili, humaniore cultu ad Syriacam ciuitatem Chalcida transmissi sunt.

---

[1] The Venice printing of Soṭah has אנת, and see Soṭah in the ICIT edition.

[2] The Soṭah parallel has אלש, but the Munich and Vatican 110 MSS and *Ein Yaʿaqov* have אלוש as Yoma does.

[3] The Munich MS has תלביש, and see Soṭah in the ICIT edition.

[4] Julian's campaign, A. D. 363.

inter hos miles quidam, cum Maximianus perrupisset quondam Persicos fines, in his locis aeger relictus, prima etiam tum lanugine iuuenis, ut aiebat, uxores sortitus gentis ritu conplures, cum numerosa subole tunc senex incuruus ...

Then, after completing a leisurely march of four days, just as evening was coming on Count Lucillianus, with a thousand light-armed troops embarked in ships, was sent, by the emperor's order, to capture the fortress of Anatha, which, like many others, is girt by the waters of the Euphrates. The ships, according to orders, took suitable positions and blockaded the island, while a misty night hid the secret enterprise. But as soon as daylight appeared, a man who went out to fetch water, suddenly catching sight of the enemy, raised a loud outcry, and by his excited shouts called the defenders to arms. Then the emperor, who from an elevated point had been looking for a site for a camp, with all possible haste crossed the river, under the protection of two ships, followed by a great number of boats carrying siege-artillery. But on drawing near the walls he considered that a battle must be accompanied by many dangers, and accordingly, partly in mild terms, partly in harsh and threatening language, he urged the defenders to surrender. They asked for a conference with Ormizda, and were induced by his promises and oaths to expect much from the mercy of the Romans. Finally, driving before them a garlanded ox, which with them indicates the acceptance of peace, they came down in suppliant guise. At once the whole fortress was set on fire; Pusaeus, its commander, later a general in Egypt, was given the rank of tribune. As for the rest, they were treated kindly, and with their families and possessions were sent to Chalcis, a city of Syria. Among them was a soldier who, when in former times Maximianus made an inroad into the Persian territory, had been left behind because of illness; he was then a young man, whose beard was just beginning to grow. He had been given several wives (as he told us) according to the custom of the country, and was on our arrival a bent old man with numerous offspring. (trans.: J. C. Rolfe, LCL)

3. Theophylactus Simocatta V 1, 2[5]

καὶ οὖν τὸν Μιραδουρὶν ἐς τὸ 'Ανάθων φρούριον τὸ πρὸς τῷ Κιρκησίῳ παρὰ τὸν Εὐφράτην ᾠκοδομημένον ἐξέταττεν μετὰ πλήθους δυνάμεως.

. . . and he (Vahram) sent Miradouris to the fort Anatha built on the Euphrates near Circension with a large force.

B. *Location*

On an island in the Euphrates between Ihi də-Qira and Dura Europos, today 'Āna (on Bab. Env. map).

---

[5] V 2, 3 relates that the soldiers killed their commander and declared for Khusro II (in the campaign of 591).

C. *History*

Musil[6] notes that the center of the ʿAnat settlement originally lay on the islands, which were always very fertile and formerly surely not so eroded as they are today. The inhabitants were not only safe from the nomads, but were even able to subjugate the surrounding settlements. For that reasons the Assyrians usually had the political district of Sūḫi administered by the lords of ʿAnat. Stephanus citing Arrian (*Parthica* X) mentions Anatha, which Arrian calls Tyros, in connection with Trajan's Parthian campaign.

After converting to Christianity, Muʿajh, commander under the Sassanian king, Shapur II (309–379), built ninety-six monasteries, churches, and other sanctuaries; he also ordained priests and other clergy at Šiggar (Sinğār). Afterwards he went to ʿAnat, and two miles away on the banks of the Euphrates built himself a hermitage where he lived for seven years. He healed the sick with such success that his fame spread all over Persia. Mebārak, a contemporary of Mar Bar-ʿIdtā' in the middle of the sixth century, was a native of ʿAnat.[7]

From 629 onwards, ʿAnat is referred to as the see of the Monophysite bishopric of the Banū Ṭaġlib.[8] Mention is made also of a monastery of Saint Sergios at ʿAnat. Occupied by monks but alas also surrounded by vineyards, this monastery was one of the centers where the famous ʿAnat wine was produced, and attracted all kinds of unwanted visitors from Hīt and elsewhere. Another monastery at ʿAnat was built by Prince Muʿīn, of the family of Mundir, the famous general of Shapur II.

The legend interpreting the verse in Source 1 lists ʿAnat together with Aluš and Talbuš (qq. v.) each built by one of the three Anaqites, i.e. offspring of the ʿ*anaq* (= giant).[9] All three are referred to by Arab geographers as places on islands in the Euphrates.[10] An Arab tradition seeks to explain by popular etymology how the place got its name, in a manner somewhat resembling the

---

[6] Musil, *The Middle Euphrates*, pp. 345–346; see also Hoffmann, *Auszüge*, p. 30; Wright, *Catalogue of the Syriac Manuscripts*, p. 1135, col. 1.

[7] Musil, *ibid.*, p. 346 cites Budge, *Histories*, vol. 1, p. 127.

[8] Cf., Fiey, *Assyrie Chrétienne*, vol. 3, pp. 239–242.

[9] There have been attempts, on the basis of the context in the scriptural verse to which the interpretation in the source relates, to identify ʿAnat with places in Eretz Israel (see e.g. Neubauer, p. 154; *Arukh ha-Shalem*, vol. 6, p. 227; Horowitz, *Eretz Israel u-Shekhenoteha*, pp. 46, 148), but such an approach is basically untenable, especially since the source comes from the Babylonian Talmud.

[10] On ʿAnat see "ʿĀnāt" and "ʿĀna" in Yāqūt, *Marāṣid*; "ʿĀnāt" in Bakrī and in *ar-Rauḍ al-miʿṭār*; *BGA*, passim (according to Ibn al-Faqīh, the "length" of Iraq stretched from ʿĀna to Baṣra); Mustaufī, vol. 2, p. 49; Idrīsī, vol. 6, p. 658; *Ḥudūd al-ʿālam*, pp. 76, 141; and see also Le Strange, "Ibn Serapion," pp. 10, 52; Suhrāb, p. 119; Ibn Saʿīd, *Geography*, p. 155; Musil, *The Middle Euphrates*, index, s. v. "ʿĀna," etc. especially Appendix XVI, pp. 345–349.

talmudic legend on the establishment of ʿAnat, Aluš and Talbuš.[11] According to that tradition, the villages of ʿĀnāt (i.e., the forts, which are built on islands), were named after three brothers of the ʿĀd tribe[12] who fled for their lives (*ḫarağū hurrāban*) and settled there, and were called Alūs, Sālūs and Nāwūs (see the entries on "Aluš," "Talbuš" and "Na'usa"). When the Arabs looked at the villages, they said they resembled *ʿānāt*, that is, herds of deer.
A more modern reference states that "The ancient town of Ana is . . . at the point where the Euphrates changes direction south-eastwards. It lies among palm trees and marks the northern limit of the ripening of the date."[13]

Eshel, *Yishuvei ha-Yehudim* (1979), pp. 207–208
Fiey, *Assyrie Chrétienne* (1968), vol. 3, pp. 234–242
Hirschenson, *Sheva Ḥokhmot* (1883), pp. 186–187
Hoffmann, *Auszüge* (1880), p. 30
Jastrow, *Dictionary* (1950³), p. 1097
Musil, *The Middle Euphrates* (1927), pp. 19–20, 345–349
Neusner, *History* (1965–1970), vol. 4, p. 10
Obermeyer, *Landschaft* (1929), pp. 26 n. 1, 68, 76, 78, 101–104

Apamea אפמייא

A. *Sources*

1. Qiddushin 71b

עד היכן היא בבל . . . לתחתית בדיגלת עד היכא אמר רב שמואל[1] עד אפמייא[2] תתאה. תרתי אפמייא[3] הויין, חדא עיליתא וחדא תתייתא, חדא כשירה וחדא פסולה, ובין חדא לחדא פרסה וקא קפדי אהדדי ואפילו נורא לא מושלי אהדדי. וסימניך דפסולתא הא דמישתעיא מישנית.[4]

How far does Babylonia extend? ... on the lower Tigris, how far? Said Rav Samuel,[1] To Lower Apamea.[2] There are two Apameas,[3] the Upper and the Lower, one fit and one unfit, and between one and the other one parasang, and they are particular with each other and do not even lend each other fire. And your sign of the unfit, the one that speaks Mesenean.[4]

---

[11] See "ʿĀnāt" in Yāqūt who quotes al-Kalbī (*GAS*, vol. 1, pp. 34–35; *GAL*, Suppl. vol. 1, pp. 331–332).

[12] On it see Buhl, *EI*[1,2] s.v. "ʿĀd."

[13] *The British Admiralty Handbook of Iraq and the Persian Gulf* (1944), p. 27.

[1] The Munich and Vatican 111 MSS have "Rav Papa b. Samuel," which seems correct, for Samuel did not have the title of "Rav."

[2] The Munich MS has **אפומי'**, the Vatican 111 MS has **אפמיית**, and the Oxford MS has **פומייתא**.

[3] The Munich MS has **אפומיית'** and the Vatican 111 MS has **אפומיית'**.

[4] The source has **מישנית**; the Vatican 111 MS has **משונית**.

2. Ptolemy V 17,6

Ἀπάμεια οϑ' λ'' λδ'γ''
ὑφ' ἣν ἡ τοῦ βασιλείου ποταμοῦ
πρὸς τὸν Τίγριν συμβολή.

Apamea 19° 50'' 34° 20''
below this (town) is the confluence of the Royal River and the Tigris.

3. Pliny, *Natural History*, VI 31, 129

Tigris . . . lustratis montibus Gordyaeorum circa Apamiam Mesenes oppidum, citra Seleuciam Babyloniam CXXV M. passuum divisus in alveos duos.[5]

The Tigris then traverses the mountains of the Gurdiaei, flowing round Apamea, a town belonging to Mesene, and 125 miles short of Babylonian Seleucia splits into two channels.[5] (trans.: H. Rackham, LCL)

4. Pliny, *Natural History*, VI 31, 132

item Apamea, cui nomen Antiochus matris suae imposuit; Tigri circumfunditur haec, dividitur Archoo.[6]

. . . and also Apamea, which Antiochus named after his mother; the town is surrounded by the Tigris, and the Archous intersects it.[6] (trans.: H. Rackham, LCL)

5. Pliny, *Natural History*, VI 32, 146

nostri negotiatores dicunt Characenorum regi parere et Apamean, sitam ubi restagnatio Euphratis cum Tigri confluat, itaque molientes incursionem Parthos operibus obiectis inundatione arceri.[7]
Our merchants say that the king of the Characeni also rules over Apamea, at the confluence of the overflow of the Euphrates with the Tigris; and that con-

---

[5] Herzfeld (*Samarra*, p. 56) comments that the stream is considered to flow from West to East . . . only for the *lacus chaldaici* would one expect the sea, for the Choaspes of Susa reached the sea below the marshes. Mesene—Syriac, Middle Persian, *mēšān*, *mēšūn*, Arabic *maisān*—is sometimes limited to the very southern part of the delta, and sometimes includes even Wāsiṭ. Mesene, however, does not lie beyond the point where the Tigris divides into two streams, nowadays near Kūt al-Imāra. Apamea must have been near Kūt, not near southern Sāmarrā, (see below).

[6] The king referred to is Antiochus I (294–261). The river Archous cannot be identified. The city is mentioned after Sittace (near Dair al-ʿĀqūl) and Sabdata (Sābāṭ al-Madā'in) as a town of Sittacene (Herzfeld, *Samarra* p. 56), For the river Archous Herzfeld (*ibid.*, n. 2) suggests a connection with Aram. ארכויא [Ezra 4:9] ὀρχοή Warka. Schaeder, *Der Islam* 14 (1924): 15ff. identifies the Archous with the Šaṭṭ-al Hai and the Seleias-Sellas with the Nahr aṣ-Ṣilḥ. Herzfeld (*Samarra*, p. 58) says that this river is the Δίγλαϑ in Josephus (*Antiquities* I, 39) and the Diglit(o) in Pliny (*Natural History* VI 31, 127) and is the Tigris itself which flows through Wāsiṭ and reaches the marshes or the sea further south.

[7] The location of Apamea according to this passage would be further to the south. See below on this difficulty.

sequently when the Parthians threaten an invasion they are prevented by the construction of dams across the river, which cause the country to be flooded.[7] (trans.: H. Rackham, LCL)

6. Stephanus Byzantius, s.v. "Ἀπάμεια"

ἔστι καὶ ἄλλη ἐν τῇ Μεσηνῶν γῇ "τῷ Τίγρητι περιεχομένη, ἐν ᾗ σχίζεται ὁ Τίγρης ποταμός, καὶ ἐν μὲν τῇ δεξιᾷ μοίρᾳ περιέρχεται ποταμὸς Σέλλας, ἐν δὲ τῇ ἀριστερᾷ Τίγρης ὁμώνυμος τῷ μεγάλῳ."[8]

There is yet another Apameia in the land of Mesene around which the Tigris flows. The Tigris splits there so that on the right the river Sellas flows around the town, on the left the Tigris, having the same name as the great river.[8]

7. Inscription (Kern, *Inschriften aus Magnesia*, No. 61, 11. 110 = *OGIS* 233)[9]

Ἀπαμεῦσιν τοῖς [π]ρὸς τῷ Σελείᾳ.[10]

Apamea on the Seleia[10]

8. Ammianus XXIII 6, 23

In omni autem Assyria, multae sunt urbes. Inter quas Apamia eminet, Mesene cognominata, et Teredon et Apollonia et Vologessia, hisque similes multae.[11]

But in all Assyria there are many cities, among which Apamia, also named Mesene, and Teredon, Apollonia and Vologessia, and many similar ones are conspicuous.[11] (trans.: J. C. Rolfe, LCL)

B. *Already Proposed Location*

Fāmiya, on the east bank of the Tigris, near Kūt al-Imāra (F4 on the Tal. Bab. map).

C. *Identification*

Source 1 notes that there were two places named Apamea located a parasang (about $4^1/_2$ kilometers) apart, and that the boundary of the Babylonia of pure lineage passed between them (see below). There were many towns named Apamea in antiquity. One of them, known only from literary sources, was in southern Mesopotamia. Various authors have interpreted these sources as

[8] See also Stephanus, s.v. "Μεσσηνή" where it appears that the source for this region is Asinius Quadratus, who himself used older material (cf. Herzfeld, *Samarra*, p. 57).

[9] Cf. Robert, *Hellenica* 7 (1949): 20, n. 1. This inscription is dated ca. 205 B.C.

[10] The Sellas of Stephanus and the Seleias of the inscription are undoubtedly identical. The inscription thus refers to the town discussed here. The town appears as "Apameia on the Silhu" in a cuneiform text of 141/140 B.C. (Olmstead, *Cl. Ph.* 32 [1937]: 13; Le Rider, *Suse*, pp. 355–356). See also n. 15 below.

[11] For Ammianus, Assyria encompasses Babylonia as well as Mesene (cf. Le Rider, *Suse*, p. 260, n. 2 with references).

referring to two towns named Apamea in southern Mesopotamia.[12] Others do not agree with this view.[13] Sources 2, 3, 6 and 7 have been explained as referring to a northern Apamea, while the other Greek and Latin excerpts cited above have been taken as referring to an Apamea further south. None of these sources, however, actually refers to two towns of that name, and the existence of two has been inferred from geographical inconsistencies. These can very well be explained by the fact that Apamea was situated in the border land between Mesene and Sittacene. Great precision cannot be expected of the Greek and Latin sources, and only one Apamea, near Kūt al-Imāra, can be shown to have existed beyond a doubt. That Apamea appears to be identifiable with Fāmiya mentioned in Arabic sources (see below).

D. *The Borders of Babylonia*

The Talmud (Source 1) mentions Apamea, or rather two neighboring Apameas, in order to demarcate the border on the Tigris to the south of Babylonia as regards purity of lineage. The source notes that the two places are distinguishable as one of them "speaks Mesenean," an indication that the border in question separated Babylonia and Mesene, being the northern border of Mesene. According to the Arabic sources, that border did indeed pass near two Apameas as stated in the Talmud, and perhaps between the two. The information in the Arabic sources relating to one of the two Apameas, called Fāmiya, and to a river known as Nahr Maisān that flowed near by makes it possible to formulate a clear impression of the border of Babylonia in that place.

Mešan (Arabic Maisān) in the sources refers variously to a region, a district, and a city, the capital of the region (see the entry on "Mesene"). In regard to the Babylonia-Mesene border near Apamea, it is the region called Mesene that is meant.

Yāqūt describes Fāmiya as follows: "One of the Wāsiṭ villages in the Fam aṣ-Ṣilḥ district."[14] An unsuccessful attempt has been made to identify a place called Zurfāmiya or Zurfāniya that is mentioned with Fāmiya, as the second of the two Apameas of the Talmud.[15] There remains thus only Fāmiya, whose

---

[12] Thus Schwartz, in Kern, *Inschriften aus Magnesia*, pp. 171–173; Fischer in Müller's edition of Ptolemy (Paris 1901), p. 1007; Droysen, *Hellenismus*, vol. 2, p. 149; Tscherikower, *Städtegründungen*, p. 171.

[13] Saint-Martin, *Recherches*, pp. 118–119; de Goeje, *ZDMG* 39 (1885): 3; Schaeder, *loc.cit.* in n. 6 above; Herzfeld, *Samarra*, pp. 55–58; Le Rider, *Suse*, p. 260, n. 2. See also Weissbach, *RE*, vol. 15, s.v. "Mesene," cols. 1085–1086.

[14] Yāqūt, s.v. "Fāmiya" ("neighborhood" might be understood instead of "district"; but cf. Yāqūt, s.v. "Ṣilḥ": "a large region").

[15] de Goeje (*loc.cit.* in n. 13) suggested identifying lower Apamea with the Zurfāmiya or Zūrfaniya mentioned in Yāqūt. In his view the syllable *zur* meant "lower." According to Yāqūt, Zurfāmiya (q.v. in Yāqūt) was a large village in the Qūsān, i.e. the Greater Zāb, area between Wāsiṭ and Baghdad on the west bank of the Tigris. It was already in ruins in Yāqūt's time and only some remnants were left where the Greater Zāb joins the

identity with one of the two, and it is not clear which, seems definite. It was certainly in the Fam aṣ-Ṣilḥ district.[16] A description of the course of the Tigris

Tigris. This Zurfāmiya was located in the neighborhood of Nuʿmānīya (see F 4 on the Tal. Bab. map) as the latter was the provincial capital of Greater Zāb (see Yāqūt, s.v. "Zāb," p. 124; cf. Streck, *Die alte Landschaft*, vol. 1, p. 32; vol. 2, p. 305). Streck (*ibid.*, pp. 305–306) convincingly refutes de Goeje's opinion of the prefix *zur*. In his own view, the northernmost of the two Apameas was called Zurfāmiya in order to distinguish it from the Fāmiya near Wāsiṭ, so that *zur* could not mean "lower." In any case, Streck is of the opinion (p. 306) that as both Apameas are in Mesene (Fraenkel, *RE* vol. 1, s.v. "Apameia," col. 2664), Fāmiya or Zurfāmiya cannot be connected with the talmudic Apameas. Streck's explanation of the prefix *zur* (p. 306, n. 2) was justifiably rejected by Schaeder (*loc. cit.* in n. 6) who believes that Zurfāniya, the other version of the place name according to Yāqūt, was the original form, and not a variant or garble (as Streck proposed). Schaeder believes that Fāmiya was south of Fam aṣ-Ṣilḥ, between it and Wāsiṭ, and that it was the Lower Apamea of the Talmud. In support he cites an anecdote told by Yāqūt, s.v. "Fāmiya" (see also Ibn Ṭaifūr, *Baġdād*, p. 44) saying that the residents of Fāmiya were "Nabateans," i.e., Arameans, and in Lower Apamea Mesenean was spoken. As to Upper Apamea, Schaeder (p. 16) assumed it should be identified with Fam aṣ-Ṣilḥ. Since according to Yāqūt (s.v. "Ṣilḥ") Fam aṣ-Ṣilḥ was also called just aṣ-Ṣilḥ, "*Fam* is simply an abbreviation of (A)fāmiya," that is, "the mouth of the river aṣ-Ṣilḥ at the Tigris." Fam aṣ-Ṣilḥ is in his view "the Apamea of the province of Ṣilḥ." Thus he proposes (*ibid.*, n. 1) that Fam Furāt Bādaqlā mentioned in Ṭabarī, vol. 3, p. 359 (= vol. 1, pp. 2037–2038) suggests another Apamea across from Zeugma on the Euphrates. The transition Apamea > Fam proposed by Schaeder was adopted by Hartmann, *EI*[1], s.v. "Didjla," p. 970. Hartmann wonders whether the Fam aṣ-Ṣilḥ canal is Apamea on the Sellas or whether Fam is a popular abbreviation of Fāmiya near Wāsiṭ, and refers to Herzfeld (*Memnon* 1 [1907]: 140). See Source 6 and the remarks in n. 10 above.

There does not seem to be any proof that the Fāmiya mentioned in Arabic sources is the lower city as Schaeder believes, and information on "Nabateans" in Fāmiya is no proof. The transition from Apamea to Fam does not seem likely either. It should be remembered that Fam Furāt Bādaqlā was in the Ḥīra area, and not as Schaeder speculated (see Nöldeke, *ZDMG* 28 [1874]: 97).

Fam, "the mouth of the river," that is, the point where it flowed out of another, was a topographic term quite common in Iraq. Cf., e.g., Fam al-Furāt, mentioned in Ṭabarī, vol. 7, p. 413 (= vol. 3, p. 13) as the place where the Umayyad army camped. From there a branch of the Euphrates flowed out of the main stream. Cf. Ḫalīfa b. Ḫayyāṭ, *Taʾrīḫ*, vol. 2, pp. 605–606, who mentions the dam (*musannāt*) of the Euphrates as the camping place of the Umayyad army. And Fam Furāt Bādaqlā is the "mouth" of the canal called Furāt Bādaqlā, for it was there that the flow of water to the Euphrates was stopped and diverted to the canals, according to Ṭabarī (vol. 3, p. 359 = [vol. 1, pp. 2037–2038]). Cf. Streck, *ibid.*, vol. 1, pp. 16, 20. Obermeyer (p. 88) proposes a complicated Persian etymology for the prefix *zur* which in his opinion means "upper." Since the distance between Zurfāmiya near Nuʿmānīya and Fāmiya (= lower Apamea in his view) is about twelve parasangs, he suggests that the Talmud should be corrected to twelve parasangs. That distance would in his opinion explain the linguistic difference between the two Apameas, as well as the difference in purity of lineage. Such a correction would however invalidate the talmudic assertion that the Apameas did not even lend each other fire, and in any case there is no support for Obermeyer's proposal.

[16] See n. 14 above. Samʿānī, *Ansāb*, s.v. "Fāmī"; *Taʾrīḫ Baġdād*, vol. 11, p. 254. On Fam aṣ-Ṣilḥ, see Le Strange, p. 38 and the sources there; Streck, *Die alte Landschaft*,

in the area indicates the location of Fāmīya within the district; Toward the end of the reign of Khusro II Parwez (590/1–628) the Tigris carved itself a new course, straight south to Kaskar rather than in a broad curve far east of it (see Šaṭṭ al-Ġarrāf, F4 on the Tal. Bab. map).[17] Mas'ūdī notes several places where in his time remnants of the eastern bed of the Tigris were still visible.[18] He lists five places—Fam aṣ-Ṣilḥ, Bahandaf, Bādarāyā, Bākusāyā and Fāmiyat al-'Irāq (to distinguish it from Fāmiya in Syria). (After that Mas'ūdī jumps south of Wāsiṭ.) Thus from the description it appears that Fam aṣ-Ṣilḥ was the closest to the point where the new course of the Tigris started, in the neighborhood of Kūt al-Imāra (see the map). The three places Mas'ūdī lists between Fam aṣ-Ṣilḥ and Fāmiya (see Yāqūt s.vv.) were possibly between them, all in the lower Nahrawān district. They were not necessarily on the bank of the Nahrawān canal, and may merely have gotten their water supply from it. Fāmiya, one of the two talmudic Apameas, should therefore be sought along the old course of the Tigris (which is its course at present as well) not far from the starting point of the straight course that was the main one during the Middle Ages.

Thus the Mesene region evidently extended northwards to a point north of Wāsiṭ, not far from Fam aṣ-Ṣilḥ. According to Yāqūt, Maisān was the name of a large region between Baṣra and Wāsiṭ;[19] though it does not necessarily follow from these words that it occupied that entire area, that becomes clear from the designation of the northern border of Mesene as north of Wāsiṭ.

Supporting evidence for this appears in the geographical dictionary, *ar-Rauḍ al-mi'ṭār*, s.v. "Fam aṣ-Ṣilḥ": "Nahr Maisān of the Wāsiṭ surroundings," and then "aṣ-Ṣilḥ - Nahr Maisān." On the other hand Bakrī says that "aṣ-Ṣilḥ is a 'Nahr in Maisān'." It is hard to determine whether the correct version should be "aṣ-Ṣilḥ is Nahr Maisān" (and in that case Nahr Maisān is another name for Nahr aṣ-Ṣilḥ), or perhaps Bakrī's version is to be preferred. In any case, clearly the Mesene region stretched to Fam aṣ-Ṣilḥ north of Wāsiṭ.[20] Consequently

---

vol. 2, p. 310ff., esp. pp. 315–317; Mustaufī, vol. 2, p. 166; *Ḥudūd al-'ālam*, p. 138; Ibn Ḫallikān, *Wafayāt al-a'yān*, vol. 1, p. 290; Sam'ānī, *Ansāb*, s.v. "Ṣilḥī"; Ibn Ṭaifūr, *Baġdād*, Index.

[17] See Streck, *ibid.*, vol. 2, p. 312; de Goeje, *op.cit.* in n. 13, p. 9; Schaeder, *op.cit.* in n. 6, p. 21f.; Le Strange, pp. 27–28; idem, "Ibn Serapion," p. 310; Streck, *EI*[1], s.v. "Baṭīha," p. 676; Streck, al-Alī, *EI*[2], s.v. "Baṭīḥa," p. 1094; Streck, *EI*[1], s.v. "Maisān," p. 150.

[18] Mas'ūdī, *Tanbīh*, pp. 53–54: *wa-āṯār 'amūd Diġla ilā waqtinā hāḏā*, etc.

[19] S.v. "Maisān," and see Qazwīnī, *Bilād*, p. 464.

[20] *ar-Rauḍ al-mi'ṭār*, s.v. "Fam aṣ-Ṣilḥ" (under "Ṣilḥ"). The assertion "aṣ-Ṣilḥ—Nahr Maisān" is cited from *Muḫtaṣar al-'ain*, that is, an abridgement of *Kitāb al-'ain* by al-Ḫalīl b. Aḥmad. The author of the *Muḫtaṣar* is Muḥammad b. al-Ḥasan az-Zubaidī (d. 989; see *GAL*, vol. 1, pp. 100, 132). The title of the parallel entry in Bakrī is "'Ain aṣ-Ṣilḥ" (under "Ṣilḥ"). Apparently "'*Ain*" here is just the "'Ain" in the title of the book quoted, that is, *Kitāb al-'ain* or its abridgement *Muḫtaṣar al-'ain*. The form "Nahr in Maisān" appears in *Lisān*, s.v. "ṣlḥ." The fact that there was a canal called Nahr Maisān

the talmudic description of the southeastern border of Babylonia for genealogical purposes reaching on the Tigris up to the two Apameas, and of one Apamea distinguishable from the other by its Mesenean speech, is authentic also in regard to the Sassanian administrative borders between Babylonia and Mesene.[21]

BEER, *Rashut ha-Golah* (1970), pp. 23–24
BERLINER, *Beiträge* (1883), pp. 19, 22
ESHEL, *Yishuvei ha-Yehudim* (1979), pp. 24–25
FUNK, *Juden* (1902–1908), vol. 1, p. 12; vol. 2, pp. 150–151
FUNK, *Monumenta* (1913), pp. 23, 288
DE GOEJE, *ZDMG* 39 (1885): 3
GRAETZ, *MGWJ* 2 (1853): 195–196
GRAETZ, *Geschichte* (1908⁴), vol. 4, p. 249
GRAETZ, *Das Königreich Mesene* (1879), pp. 27–28
HERZFELD, *Samarra* (1948), pp. 55–58
HIRSCHENSON, *Sheva Ḥokhmot* (1883), p. 40
JASTROW, *Dictionary* (1950³), p. 105
JÖEL, *MGWJ* 16 (1867): 336–337
KOHUT, *Arukh ha-Shalem* (1878–1892), vol. 1, p. 218
KRAUSS, *Qadmoniot ha-Talmud* (1923–1945), vol. 1A, pp. 37, 130
LEVY, *Wörterbuch* (1924²), vol. 1, p. 145
NEUBAUER, *Géographie* (1868), pp. 325–326
NEUSNER, *History* (1965–1970), vol. 2, pp. 241–243
NEWMAN, *Agricultural Life* (1932), p. 7
OBERMEYER, *Landschaft* (1929), pp. 86–90, 93, 97–98, 183–184
SCHAEDER, *Der Islam* 14 (1924): 14–16, 19, 25
TSCHERIKOWER, *Städtegründungen* (1927), p. 171
WEISSBACH, *RE*, vol. 15, col. 1085f., s.v. "Mesene"

Aqra də-Agama אקרא דאגמא

See the entry on "Damim."

Aqra də-Koke אקרא דכוכי

See the entry on "Be Ardəšir-Koke" under "Maḥoza Area."

Aqra di-Səlequm אקרא דסליקום

See the entry on "Seleucia" under "Maḥoza Area."

---

which flowed out of the Tigris south of Wāsiṭ (Yāqūt, s.v. "Diğla," p. 441; Mustaufī, vol. 2, p. 207; Streck, *Die alte Landschaft*, vol. 1, p. 39f.; idem, *EI*¹, s.v. "Maisān," p. 150, and see Yāqūt, s.v. "Bazzāz") should not tip the scale in favor of the "in Maisān" version. Cf. Dimašqī, *Nuḫbat ad-dahr*, p. 113: Fam aṣ-Ṣilḥ (*sic*), a river flowing in the Sawād.

[21] On the question of to what extent Mesene and Kaskar overlap, see the entry on "Mesene."

Aqra də-Tulbanqe אקרא דתולבנקי

A. *Sources*

1. Qiddushin 71b

עד היכן היא בבל... לעיל בפרת עד היכא, רב אמר עד אקרא דתולבקני,[1] ושמואל אמר עד גישרא דבי פרת,[2] ורבי יוחנן אמר עד מעברת דגיזמא.[3]

How far does Babylonia extend? ... On the upper Euphrates, how far? Rav said, To Aqra də-Tulbanqe;[1] and Samuel said, To Gišra də-Be Pərat;[2] and Rabbi Yoḥanan said, To the Gizma crossing.[3]

2. Megillah 6a[4]

והאמר רבה בר בר חנה אמר רבי יוחנן, לדידי חזי לי זבת חלב ודבש דכל ארעא דישראל, והויא כמבי כובי[5] עד אקרא דתולבקני,[6] עשרין ותרתין פרסי אורכא ופותיא שיתא פרסי.

... since Rabbah b. Bar Ḥana said, Rabbi Yoḥanan said: I have myself seen the flow of milk and honey of the whole land of Israel, and it is as from Be Kube[5] to Aqra də-Tulbanqe,[6] [which area is] twenty-two parasangs in length and in width six parasangs.

3. Ketubot 111b–112a (parallel to Source 2)

אמר רבה בר בר חנה... והויא כמבי מיכסי[7] עד אקרא דתולבנקי...

Rabbah b. Bar Ḥana said, ... and it is as from Be Mikse[7] to Aqra də-Tulbanqe ...

B. *Proposed Location*

Niqyā, a village in the vicinity of Anbār (see the entry on "Pumbədita") (C2 on the Tal. Bab. map).

---

[1] The source has אקרא דתולבקני; the Venice printing has עקרא דתולבקני.

[2] The Vatican 111 MS has גירש דבי פרת (corrected interlinearly to גישרא) and גירשא דפרת further on.

[3] The Venice printing has מעברת דגידמ'; the Vatican 111 MS has מעברא דגימא.

[4] The T. B. Ketubot parallel (see Source 3) and *Midrash ha-Gadol* to Genesis, *wa-yeḥi*, 49:13 (Margulies ed., p. 846) have: והויא כי מבי מכסי עד אקרא דתולבוקני; *Midrash ha-Gadol* to Deuteronomy, *wa-etḥanan* 6:3. (Fisch ed., p. 125) has: והויא כי מבי מכסא לאקרא דתולבקני; *Yalquṭ ha-Makhiri*, Psalms 107 (Buber ed., p. 176) has: הוי כמבי מכסא עד אקרא דתולבנקי. See also the entries on "Be Kube" and "Be Mikse."

[5] The Munich, London and Parma MSS have כמבי כסי; the Munich B MS has כמבי כאסי; the Oxford MS has כמבי מכסא; *Aggadot ha-Talmud* has כמבי מכסי.

[6] The source has אקרא דתולבקני; the Parma MS has עקרא דתולבנקי; the Munich B, Oxford and London MSS have עקרא דתולבקני; *Aggadot ha-Talmud* has אקרא דקולבנכי.

[7] The Munich and Vatican 130 MSS have כמבי כסי; the Vatican 113 MS has כמיבי מכסי. For additional variants see Ketubot in the ICIT edition, and nn. 1–3 there.

C. *Identification*

Obermeyer proposed identifying Aqra də-Tulbanqe with a place called Bāniqyā.[8] Although reasonable linguistically, that identification must be rejected on several geographical grounds:

a) Aqra də-Tulbanqe is referred to in Source 1 as a border point of the Babylonia of pure lineage on the upper Euphrates (according to Rav). That does not fit in with the location of Bāniqyā which Obermeyer places on the west bank of the right branch of the Euphrates (today the Hindīya canal) between Ḥīra in the south and Anbār in the north. Such a location would put Pumbədita outside the borders of the Babylonia of pure lineage, which is hard to imagine.[9]

b. In any case Bāniqyā was not on the Hindīya canal, but near Nağaf in the Kūfa region (see the entry on "Tarbiqna"), that is, much further south.

c. The points marking the borders of the Babylonia of pure lineage as posited by Rav and Samuel were not very far apart, a few kilometers at most.[10] Samuel sets the border on the upper Euphrates at Be Pərat, identified with Bait Fāriṭ which is one parasang from Anbār (see the entry on "Gišra də-Be Pərat").

Thus Aqra də-Tulbanqe too must be sought in the vicinity of Anbār, keeping Pumbədita within the Babylonia of pure lineage, and at a spot not far from Bait Fāriṭ. An administrative unit called Bāniġyā that was in the Anbār district seems suitable, although more precise information on its location is unavailable. Bāniġyā seems to be identical with Niġyā (with the deletion of the Aramaic prefix *ba* = "house"),[11] which according to Yāqūt was a village near Anbār.[12] Al-Qifṭī says that at the time of Gallienus (A.D. 253–268) a village called Niqyā in the Anbār district marked the border between the Persians and the Romans. The village was in fact a garrison post where the Persian and Roman armies and their scouts came in contact.[13] According to

---

[8] Obermeyer, pp. 94–96.

[9] Obermeyer believes that Abbaye's and Rav Joseph's anger at Rav (see the continuation of the passage) was the reaction of those two Pumbədita sages to the exclusion of Pumbədita from the Babylonia of pure lineage.

[10] See the entries on "Apamea," "ʿUḇbara," "Awana" and "Moškani."

[11] Similarly Ardəšir is found along with Be Ardəšir (see "Be Ardəšir-Koḵe" in the entry on the "Maḥoza Area") and Argiza along with Be Argiza (see the entry on "Ḥarta də-Argiz").

[12] See the entry in Yāqūt (another place with the same name is a district between Wāsiṭ and Baṣra). One of two people called by the place name (meaning that they came from there) was the vizier of the caliph Muʿtazz (866–869), Aḥmad b. Isrāʾīl, on whom see Ṭabarī, index. Ṣābī, *Wuzarāʾ*, p. 191, calls him *al-Anbārī*. Cf. Anbār as a border of Babylonia in the entry on "Ihi də-Qira."

[13] al-Qifṭī, *Taʾrīḫ al-ḥukamāʾ*, p. 136: *wa-ḏukira anna ḥadda r-Rūm kāna fī ayyām Gālīnūs min nāḥiyati l-mašriq mimmā yalī l-Furāta l-qarya l-maʿrūfa bi-Niqyā min ṭassūği l-Anbār, wa-kānat maslaḥa yağtamiʿu ğund Fāris wa-r-Rūm wa-nawāẓiruhumā fīhā.*

Yāqūt, Niqyā was "a village in the vicinity of Anbār in the Sawād of Iraq (literally, 'of Baghdad')."[14] That Niqyā seems to be identical with Niġyā/Bāniġyā.[15] The fact that a point on the border between Persian and Roman territory is identical with one on the border of the Babylonia of pure lineage is not fortuitous, and there are additional instances of such coincidence with some administrative border.[16] At the same time, the coincidence here is of limited significance, because the Persian-Roman border was variable, and because the reasons for locating the border in one place or another were not necessarily the same for the two categories. (On the distance between Aqra də-Tulbanqe and Be Kube [or Be Mikse, see Source 2 and note 4]; see the entries on "Be Kube" and "Be Mikse").

Berliner, *Beiträge* (1883), pp. 19, 23
Eshel, *Yishuvei ha-Yehudim* (1979), p. 33
Funk, *Jahrbuch*, 6 (1908/9): 328–329
Funk, *Juden* (1902–1908), vol. 1, p. 13; vol. 2, p. 151
Funk, *Monumenta* (1913), pp. 4, 24, 278
Gil, *Tarbiẕ* 48 (1979): 51–52
de Goeje, *ZDMG* 39 (1885): 1, 4
Goldhaar, *Admat Qodesh* (1913), pp. 22, 74
Graetz, *MGWJ* 2 (1853): 196–197
Graetz, *Geschichte* (1908⁴), vol. 4, p. 249
Hirschenson, *Sheva Ḥokhmot* (1883), p. 43
Horowitz, *Eretz Israel u-Shekhenoteha* (1923), p. 74
Jastrow, *Dictionary* (1950³), p. 1653
Klein, *Tarbiẕ* 1 (1930): B 130–131
Kohut, *Arukh ha-Shalem* (1878–1892), vol. 1, p. 260; vol. 8, p. 231
Krauss, *Qadmoniot ha-Talmud* (1923–1945), vol. 1A, p. 38
Krauss, *Paras we-Romi* (1948), p. 21
Levy, *Wörterbuch* (1924²), vol. 1, p. 568
Neubauer, *Géographie* (1868), pp. 330, 352
Obermeyer, *Landschaft* (1929), pp. 94–96
Rapoport, *Erekh Millin* (1914), vol. 2, pp. 10–11

Arbela (Arbel) ארבל

A. *Source*

T. J. Soṭah IV 4–19d, 2–3

רבי מר עוקבא[1] הורי בארבלי[2] עשרים וארבעה חדש ואפילו מת התינוק.

---

[14] Yāqūt, s.v. "Niqyā." He also says it was the birthplace of the traditionist Yaḥya b. Maʿīn. See also Samʿānī, *Ansāb*, s.v. "Niqyāʾī": "after Niqyā, of the Anbār (villages) twelve parasangs from Baghdad"; Ibn al-Aṯīr, *Lubāb*, s.v. "Niqyāʾī"; *Taʾrīḫ Baġdād*, vol. 14, pp. 177–178.

[15] The editor of *Taʾrīḫ al-ḥukamāʾ* lists the variants bi-n.f.y.sā/bi-n.q.y.sā/*bi-nifyā*/*bi-niġyā* (from Ibn Abī Uṣaibiʿa, *Ṭabaqāt al-aṭibbāʾ*, vol. 1, p. 77, where the source has *bi-niqyā*). In the opinion of the editor of al-Qifṭī, Niqyā is Nicephorion near Raqqa (see *EI*¹, s.v. "Raḳḳa") which does not seem likely, and see already Ibn Abī Uṣaibiʿa in notes to *loc. cit.*

[16] See e.g. the entry on "Moškani."

[1] The Vatican 133 MS has מן עוקבן; and see Epstein, *Mevoʾot le-Sifrut ha-Amoraʾim*, p. 342, n. 38.

[2] The source has בארבלי, the Vatican 133 MS has בארבאל.

Rabbi Mar ʿUqba[1] ruled in Arbela,[2] twenty-four months even though the baby died.

B. *Location*

East of the Tigris between the Greater Zāb and the Lesser Zāb (on Bab. Env. map).

C. *History*

Arbela was one of the most important towns in Assyria. It is called Arba-ilu in Babylonian and Assyrian documents, and Arbira in Old Persian cuneiform. Arbela controlled part of the ancient Royal Road that was the shortest route between Babylon and Nineveh, and later between Baghdad and Mosul. Other caravan routes led from it to the north and northeast.[3]
Although the plain surrounding it is very fertile, Arbela was not on a river, and water was supplied to it through underground channels.[4] Being at a crossroads, Arbela was on the path of the numerous armies that invaded Mesopotamia in ancient times,[5] and the crucial 331 B.C. battle of Gaugamela between Alexander and Darius III took place nearby.
Arbela was an important cult center of the goddess Ishtar. In the fourth century Christians were persecuted there, and produced a number of martyrs, among them a priest of the goddess Arbela and the Sassanian governor, Kardaġ, both of whom had converted in the middle of the fourth century.[6] After A.D. 410 Arbela was one of the five metropolitanates.[7]
Yāqūt describes Arbela (s.v. Irbil) as a strong fort and large city located on a broad plain. Surrounded by a deep moat, the fort is at one side of the city and interrupts the city wall (in Yāqūt's time). It is located on a huge tell with a broad top, and contains markets, houses and a mosque. It resembles but is larger than the Aleppo fort. Streck notes that Arbela is not mentioned in the Muslim period before the later Abbasids.[8] Ṭabarī does not refer to it at all in his *Annals*, and among the Arab geographers only Ibn Ḫurdāḏbih and Qudāma mention it as a district in Ḥulwān province.[9]

---

[3] On the roads, see Sarre & Herzfeld, *Archäologische Reise*, vol. 2, p. 326; Dillemann, *Haute Mésopotamie*, pp. 103, 147, 160 and n. 3, index p. 328.

[4] Streck, *loc.cit.*; Sarre & Herzfeld, *ibid.*, p. 313. Herzfeld reports that the subterranean channels (= *qanāte*) that carry water to the place start a considerable distance away. He notes that the place did not develop much because of the shortage of water.

[5] Among them Trajan (Cassius Dio, LXVIII 26) and Caracalla (Cassius Dio LXXIX 1).

[6] Labourt, *Le Christianisme*, pp. 55, 74, 76–77.

[7] Labourt, *ibid.*, p. 98.

[8] Streck, *EI*¹, s.v. Irbil; Sourdel, *EI*², s.v. Irbil.

[9] Streck, *op.cit.*, p. 15; Ibn Ḫurdāḏbih, p. 6; Qudāma, Ḫarāǧ, p. 235; and see Mustaufī, vol. 2, p. 102 who devotes a separate entry to Irbil.

Arbela has not been systematically excavated.[10] Sarre and Herzfeld made a sketch plan of the tell and the lower city.[11] In their opinion the tell resembles those of Aleppo, Ḥamāt and Ḥimṣ but is much larger, being about 40 meters high and having an area of 10–12 hectares.

D. *The Exilarch and Arbela*

The source above deals with a case in which "Rabbi Mar ʿUqba" ruled the halakhah in Arbela regarding when a nursing mother who is widowed may remarry. This source, like others in which Rabbi Mar ʿUqba figures, presents some difficulties in regard to the identity of the sage. For example, what is the significance of the double title, rabbi and mar, or perhaps it should be corrected on the basis of other versions (cf. note 1 above). Is he the Exilarch Mar ʿUqba who was active in the first generation of Babylonian amoras, or a member of the Exilarch's family? Did he teach in Babylonia or Eretz Israel, or did he leave Babylonia for Eretz Israel? If an amora of Eretz Israel is meant, the source may refer to Arbel in lower Galilee rather than Arbela east of the Tigris.[12] The data in this source and in other places in talmudic literature do not appear sufficient to solve these problems definitively. At the same time, it seems reasonable to suppose that if he was not the Exilarch himself, then, as Epstein proposes (note 12), he was a member of the exilarchal family. Another source reports a visit of Mar ʿUqba to Ginzaq (q.v.) and that may tip the scale toward the Arbela east of the Tigris. Indeed the reference may be to a single journey of the Exilarch or member of his family, in the course of which he visited both Ginzaq and Arbela, and ruled halakhah in both places.

Obermeyer believes that the Exilarch Hezekiah was buried in Arbela but Seder Olam Zuṭa on which he bases this belief speaks explicitly of Arbel in Eretz Israel,[13] and there are no grounds for resorting to a secondary source suggesting that the place was the Arbela near the Tigris.

Dillemann, *Haute Mésopotamie* (1962), pp. 103, 147, 160 and n. 3, index p. 328
Eshel, *Yishuvei ha-Yehudim* (1979), p. 35
Fiey, *Assyrie Chrétienne* (1965), vol. 1, pp. 39–97
Funk, *Monumenta* (1913), pp. 24, 289
Hirschenson, *Sheva Ḥokhmot* (1883), p. 43
Jastrow, *Dictionary* (1950³), p. 114 ("ארבלי")

[10] Abu al-Soof and Es-Siwwani, *Sumer* 22 (1966): 77–82; 23 (1967): 69–75. The authors excavated at Tall Qalinğ Aġa and report on the discovery of early material.

[11] Sarre & Herzfeld, *ibid.*, p. 313f.; figs. 293–294.

[12] See Rapoport, *Erekh Millin*, vol. 2, pp. 12–13; Obermeyer, p. 139; Epstein, *Tarbiẓ* 5 (1934): 267–269; Albeck, *Mavo la-Talmudim*, p. 346; Beer, *Rashut ha-Golah*, p. 71, n. 54. In any case, deducing from this source that there was a study house in Arbela (as e.g. Segal, *Sefer Segal* p. 35*; Eshel, p. 35) is far-fetched.

[13] Obermeyer, pp. 139–140; and cf. Seder Olam Zuṭa, IX, Grossberg ed., p. 35; and see Rapoport, *op.cit.*, pp. 11–12.

Kohut, *Arukh ha-Shalem* (1878–1892), vol. 1, p. 268
Levy, *Wörterbuch* (1924²), vol. 1, p. 157
Neubauer, *Géographie* (1868), p. 374
Obermeyer, *Landschaft* (1929), pp. 138–139
Rapoport, *Erekh Millin* (1914), vol. 2, pp. 12–13
Sarre & Herzfeld, *Archäologische Reise* (1920), vol. 2, pp. 313–318
Segal, *Sefer Segal* (1964), p. 35*

Argiza ארגיזא

See the entry on "Ḥarta də-Argiz."

Arṭivna ארטיבנא

A. *Source*

ʽEruvin 51b–52a

רבה בר רב חנן[1] הוה רגיל דאתי מארטיבנא[2] לפומבדיתא, אמר תהא שביתתי בצינתא.[3]

Rabbah b. Rav Ḥanan[1] used to come [on the Sabbath] from Arṭivna[2] to Pumbədita; he said, My camp will be in Ṣinta.[3]

B. *Location*

Near Pumbədita (q.v., C2 on the Tal. Bab. map).

C. *Identification*

The source testifies that Rabbah (or Rava) b. Rav Ḥanan, of the fourth generation of Babylonian amoras, was accustomed to go to Pumbədita on the Sabbath from his home in Arṭivna, apparently in order to hear the sermon in the Pumbədita yeshiva.[4] The distance exceeded the permitted Sabbath walk of two thousand cubits (about one kilometer) but was less than four thousand. Consequently, before the Sabbath Rabbah b. Rav Ḥanan would establish a camp, that is, place an *ʽeruv teḥumim* in Ṣinta (q.v.) which was between Arṭivna and Pumbədita. In the same way the Mavrakta people who wished to walk to Maḥoza on the Sabbath used to place an *ʽeruv* in Be Govar (see the

[1] The Munich and Oxford MSS have "Rava b. Rav Ḥanin."

[2] The Munich MS has מארטוניא; the Oxford MS has מארטביא; the Salonika printing has מארטבינא, and Rashi there has מארטבניא.

[3] For variants see the entry on "Ṣinta."

[4] Cf. R-a-ḥ: "רבא בר חנן רגיל דאתא מאנטוכיא לפומבדיתא לפירקיה דרב יוסף ..." (= Rava b. Ḥanan used to come from Antokya to Pumbədita to the *pirqa* of Rav Joseph . . .) ("Antokya" is a garble).

entries on "Mavrakta" and "Be Govar"). Obermeyer's proposal that Arṭivna was named after one of the Parthian kings called Artabanus, of the Arsacid dynasty, seems reasonable.[5] The variations in the name of the place (see n. 2) suggest that the place may well have had a name such as Arṭabanya more closely resembling the king's.

Beer, *Amora'ei Bavel* (1974), p. 95
Berliner, *Beiträge* (1883), p. 24
Eshel, *Yishuvei ha-Yehudim* (1979), p. 37
Funk, *Monumenta* (1913), pp. 25, 289
Hirschenson, *Sheva Ḥokhmot* (1883), p. 44
Jastrow, *Dictionary* (1950³), p. 118
Kohut, *Arukh ha-Shalem* (1878–1892), vol. 1, p. 280
Levy, *Wörterbuch* (1924²), vol. 1, p. 163
Neubauer, *Géographie* (1868), p. 363
Obermeyer, *Landschaft* (1929), p. 232

Astunya אסתוניא

See the entry on "Pumbədita."

Awana אוונא

A. *Source*

Qiddushin 71b

עד היכן היא בבל . . . לעיל בדיגלת עד היכא, רב[1] אמר עד בגדא (כ"י ואטיקאן 111: עכברא) ואוונא,[2] ושמואל אמר עד מושכני.[3]

How far does Babylonia extend? . . . Upstream, how far on the Tigris? Rav[1] said, To Bagda (the Vatican 111 MS has ʿUkbara) and Awana.[2] And Samuel said, To Moškani.[3]

B. *Location*

Awānā opposite ʿUkbarā (q.v.) on the west bank of the Tigris (D1 on the Tal. Bab. map).[4]

---

[5] Obermeyer, p. 232, and see also Eshel, pp. 37–38.

[1] The Vatican 111 MS has "Rava," but as the difference of opinion is with Samuel, the correct version is most likely "Rav," the former being a scribal error produced by the addition of the letter *alef* to "Rav" under the influence of the initial *alef* in the next word (רב[א] אמר).

[2] The Munich MS has עד נגד' וחוונא; the Vatican 111 MS has עד עכברא ואוינא as does the *Arukh* (see *Arukh ha-Shalem*, vol. 1, p. 45, s.v. "אונא" and *Tosefot*, p. 13 of the entry.

[3] The Venice printing and Vatican 111 MS have משכני.

[4] Awānā is well known from Arabic literature, and Obermeyer (pp. 80–81) already identified it with a place of that name referred to in the Talmud. The poet Ǧaḥẓa al-

C. *History*

Awānā is generally mentioned together with ʿUkbarā and Buṣrā. The three were in the same region on the main route northwards from Baghdad. During the Muslim period, they were all resorts for the inhabitants of Baghdad. Awānā was on the west bank of the Tigris across the river a little downstream from ʿUkbarā.[5] In the thirteenth century the course of the Tigris moved a few kilometers eastwards[6] so that it no longer separated the two places.
The word *'awāna* means hostel.[7] Possibly the place originally developed around an inn designed to serve wayfarers and caravans traveling north from Baghdad.[8]
The remains of Awānā, still called *Tulūl Wāna*, are near Tall Kaff al-Imām ʿAlī, close to a place called Tall Šaniṯ or Tall aṣ-Ṣaḫr.[9]

D. *The Borders of Babylonia*

The above source is part of a passage dealing with the borders of Babylonia in respect to acceptable lineage, and notes the northeastern extremity of the border on the Tigris, in the opinions of Rav and Samuel (and see in detail in the entry on "ʿUḵbara").

Adams, *Land Behind Baghdad* (1965), pp. 90–91
Berliner, *Beiträge* (1883), p. 18
Eshel, *Yishuvei ha-Yehudim* (1979), pp. 12–13
Funk, *Juden* (1902–1908), vol. 1, p. 12; vol. 2, pp. 149, 150
Funk, *Monumenta* (1913), pp. 4, 277
Graetz, *MGWJ* 2 (1853): 193–194
Herzfeld, *Samarra*, p. 32, n. 1
Hirschenson, *Sheva Ḥokhmot* (1883), pp. 58–60
Jastrow, *Dictionary* (1950³), p. 28
Kohut, *Arukh ha-Shalem* (1878–1892), vol. 1, p. 45; *Tosefot* (1937), p. 13
Levy, *Wörterbuch* (1924²), vol. 1, pp. 41, 279
Neubauer, *Géographie* (1868), p. 331

Barmakī (died 936) asks two of his friends to take him to the Awānā vineyard and give him old wine made by Jews. ʿUkbarā and Awānā were a similar distance from Baghdad (Streck, *Die alte Landschaft*, vol. 2, p. 227). When the muezzin of Ṣarīfūna summoned the faithful to prayer, he was heard in ʿUkbarā and Awānā (see Yāqūt, s.v. "Ṣarīfūna"). On Awānā see also Yāqūt, *Marāṣid*, s.v. "Awānā"; Samʿānī, *Ansāb*, s.v. "Awānī"; Mustaufī, vol. 2, p. 48, (Wāna); *BGA*, passim; Le Strange, "Ibn Serapion," pp. 9, 39; Suhrāb, p. 118, and see the entry on "ʿUḵbara" and n. 9 in particular. See also Musil, *The Middle Euphrates*, pp. 138–139 and n. 76.

[5] Obermeyer's opinion was that Awānā was on the east bank of the Tigris in the talmudic period, but this seems unlikely. See the detailed discussion on this in the entry on ʿUḵbara.

[6] Adams, *Land Behind Baghdad*, p. 90.

[7] E.g., Bava Metziʿa 79b, and see the talmudic dictionaries. See also Krauss, *Qadmoniot ha-Talmud*, vol. 1A, p. 131, n. 2 and p. 140, n. 3. According to Herzfeld, *Samarra*, p. 32, n. 1, Awānā is derived from old Persian *avahana*, meaning "post station." There was another Awānā near Gaugamela.

[8] See Eshel, p. 13.

[9] Sūsa, *Rayy Sāmarrā*, vol. 1, pp. 192–194.

NEUSNER, *History* (1965–1970), vol. 2, pp. 241–242
NEWMAN, *Agricultural Life* (1932), p. 6
OBERMEYER, *Landschaft* (1929), pp. 81–85, 105 n. 1, 144, 155
RAPOPORT, *Erekh Millin* (1914), p. 51
STRECK, *Die alte Landschaft*, vol. 2, p. 217

Babylon (Bavel) בבל

A. *Sources*

1. Berakhot 57b[1]

דרש רב המנונא הרואה בבל הרשעה[2] צריך לברך חמש ברכות, ראה בבל אומר ברוך שהחריב בבל הרשעה, ראה ביתו של נבוכדנצר אומר ברוך שהחריב ביתו של נבוכדנצר הרשע, ראה גוב של אריות או כבשן האש אומר ברוך שעשה נסים לאבותינו במקום הזה . . . ראה מקום שנוטלין ממנו עפר אומר ברוך אומר ועושה גוזר ומקיים. רבא כי הוה חזי חמרי דשקלי עפרא, טריף להו ידא על גבייהו ואמר רהוטו צדיקי למעבד רעותא דמרייכו. מר בריה דרבינא כי הוה מטי לבבל הוה שקיל עפרא בסודריה ושדי לברא, לקיים מה שנאמר "וטאטאתיה במטאטא השמד". אמר רב אשי אנא הא דרב המנונא לא שמיע לי אלא מדעתאי בריכתינהו לכולהו.

Rav Hamnuna preached, A person seeing wicked[2] Babylon must pronounce five blessings. Seeing Babylon, he says, Blessed be He who destroyed wicked Babylon; seeing Nebuchadnezzar's house, he says, Blessed be He who destroyed wicked Nebuchadnezzar's house. Seeing the lions' den or the fiery furnace, he says, Blessed be He who wrought miracles for our ancestors in this place . . . On seeing the place dust is carried away from he says, Blessed be He who says and does, who decrees and carries out. When seeing asses carrying dust away, Rava slapped them on their backs and said, Run, righteous ones, to do your Master's will. When arriving in Babylon, Mar son of Ravina took some dust in his scarf and threw it away, to comply with the verse "I will sweep it with a broom of extermination" (Isa. 14:23). Rav Ashi said, This [of] Rav Hamnuna I did not hear but of my own sense made all those blessings.

2. ʿAvodah Zarah 11b

אמר רב חנן בר רב חסדא אמר רב, ואמרי לה א"ר חנן בר רבא אמר רב חמשה בתי עבודת כוכבים קבועין הן, אלו הן בית בל בבבל, בית נבו בכורסי,[3] תרעתא שבמפג, צריפא שבאשקלון, נשרא שבערביא.

---

[1] Rav Hamnuna's interpretation appears in T. J. Berakhot IX 1–12d, 30–35 unattributed. The Tower of Babel and the wall of Babylon are mentioned in *midrashim* but these sources provide no historical evidence.

[2] The Munich MS has "seeing the wicked Babylonian kingdom" which might be construed as referring to Babylonia rather than Babylon, but the rest of the passage mentions only places within the city.

[3] The source has "Korsi" but the manuscripts make it clear that the intention is Borsif (q.v.).

Rav Ḥanan b. Rav Ḥisda said, Rav said, and some have it that Rav Ḥanan b. Rava said Rav said: Five heathen temples are long established. They are that of Bel in Babylon, Nebo in Borsif,[3] Tarʿata in Mapag, Ṣərifa in Ašqəlon, Nišra in ʿArabia.

3. Berakhot 59b

ואמר רמי בר אבא א״ר יצחק הרואה פרת אגשרא דבבל אומר ברוך עושה מעשה בראשית.

Rami b. Abba said, Rabbi Isaac said, A person who sees the Euphrates at Gišra də-Bavel (= the bridge of Babylon) says, Blessed is the Doer of the work of creation.

4. Shabbat 36a (= Sukkah 34a)

אמר רב אשי[4] אף אנו נאמר בבל בורסיף בורסיף בבל.

Rav Ashi[4] said, We too will say, Babylon [is] Borsif, Borsif Babylon.

5. Sanhedrin 109a

אמר רב יוסף בבל ובורסיף סימן רע לתורה.[5]

Rav Joseph said, Babylon and Borsif are an evil omen for the Torah.[5]

6. Ketubot 54a

אתמר רב אמר הלכה כאנשי יהודה, ושמואל אמר הלכה כאנשי גליל. בבל וכל פרוודהא[6] נהוג כרב, נהרדעא וכל פרוודהא נהוג כשמואל. ההיא בת מחוזא דהות נסיבא לנהרדעא, אתו לקמיה דרב נחמן שמעה לקלה דבת מחוזא היא, אמר להו בבל וכל פרוודהא נהוג כרב, אמרו ליה והא לנהרדעא נסיבא, אמר להו אי הכי נהרדעא וכל פרוודהא נהוג כשמואל. ועד היכא נהרדעא, עד היכא דסגי קבא דנהרדעא.

It was stated Rav said, The halakhah is like the men of Judaea, and Samuel said, The halakhah is like the men of Galilee. Babylon and all its surroundings[6] acted according to Rav, Nəhardəʿa and all its surroundings acted according to Samuel. That woman of Maḥoza who was married to a [man of] Nəhardəʿa they came before Rav Naḥman, who heard from her voice that she was a Maḥozan and said to them, Babylon and all its surroundings acted according to Rav. They said to him, But she is married to Nəhardəʿa. He said to them, If so, Nəhardəʿa and all its surroundings acted according to Samuel. And how far is Nəhardəʿa? As far as the *qav* of Nəhardəʿa extends.

---

[4] In the Sukkah parallel the statement is attributed to Rava b. Joseph and the reference is apparently simply to Rava. But the Munich B MS has "Rav Ashi" as in the Shabbat source; see also *Diq. Sof.*

[5] The Munich MS has in addition "Babylon because there the Lord confounded the speech of all the earth," as do other manuscripts; see also *Diq. Sof.*

[6] This word appears in different forms in the manuscripts; see Ketubot in the ICIT edition, and see "פרוור" in *Arukh ha-Shalem* and in Geiger's supplements in *Tosefot Arukh ha-Shalem.*

7. Megillah 22a

ת"ש דרב איקלע לבבל בתענית צבור, קם קרא בסיפרא פתח בריך, חתים ולא בריך . . .

Come and hear, happening to be in Babylon during a public fast, Rav rose and read the scroll; he began with a blessing, finished and did not make a blessing . . .

8. Ta'anit 28b

רב איקלע לבבל חזינהו דקא קרו הלילא בריש ירחא, סבר לאפסוקינהו, כיון דחזא דקא מדלגי דלוגי אמר שמע מינה מנהג אבותיהם בידיהם.

Happening to be in Babylon, Rav saw them reciting the *Hallel* at the New Moon, and thought to stop them. As he saw they were omitting parts, he said, Conclude from this that it is the custom of their ancestors.

9. Bava Batra 22a

הנהו דיקולאי דאייתו דיקלאי לבבל, אתו בני מתא קא מעכבי עלויהו, אתו לקמיה דרבינא, אמר להם מעלמא אתו ולעלמא ליזבנו.

Basket-makers having brought baskets to Babylon, the townspeople hindered them, and they came before Ravina. He said to them, They have come from the outside and they can sell to outsiders.

10. Qiddushin 45a

הנהו בי תרי דהוו קא שתו חמרא תותי ציפי בבבל, שקל חד מינייהו כסא דחמרא יהב ליה לחבריה, אמר מיקדשא לי ברתיך לברי, אמר רבינא . . .

Of those two men drinking wine under willows in Babylon, one took a goblet of wine, gave it to his companion and said, Let your daughter be betrothed to my son. Ravina said . . .

11. 'Eruvin 63a

רבינא סר סכינא בבבל, א"ל רב אשי מאי טעמא עבד מר הכי, א"ל והא רב המנונא אורי בחרתא דארגיז[7] בשני דרב חסדא, אמר ליה לאו אורי אתמר, אמר ליה אתמר אורי ואתמר לא אורי, בשני דרב הונא רביה הוא דלא אורי, ואורי בשני דרב חסדא דתלמיד חבר דיליה הוה, ואנא נמי תלמיד חבר דמר אנא.

Ravina having examined a knife in Babylon, Rav Ashi said to him, Why does the master do this? He said, Did not Rav Hamnuna rule at Ḥarta də-Argiz[7] in the days of Rav Ḥisda? He said to him, It was stated that he did not rule. He (Ravina) said to him, It was said that he ruled and that he did not rule. During the time of Rav Huna, his master, he did not rule, and he ruled during the time of Rav Ḥisda who was a disciple and colleague of his, and I too am a disciple and colleague of the master's.

---

[7] The Munich and Oxford MSS have בחדתא דארגיז, and see the entry on "Ḥarta də-Argiz."

12. Giṭṭin 65a

... דאמרה ליה התקבל לי גיטא במתא מחסיא וזימנין דמשכחת ליה בבבל.

... She said to him, Obtain my bill of divorcement for me in Mata Məḥasya, but sometimes you will find him in Babylon.

13. Berakhot 31a (= Soṭah 46b)

כי הא דרב כהנא[8] אלוייה לרב שימי בר אשי[9] מפום נהרא[10] עד בי צניתא דבבל, כי מטא להתם א"ל מר ודאי דאמרי אינשי הני צניתא דבבל איתנהו מאדם הראשון ועד השתא.

... Rav Kahana[8] escorted Rav Shimi b. Ashi[9] from Pum Nahara[10] to the place of the palms in Babylon. When he got there he said to him, Sir, it is known that people say these palms of Babylon have been from the time of the first Adam up to now.

14. Strabo XVI 1,5–6 (738–739)

Ἡ δὲ Βαβυλὼν καὶ αὐτὴ μέν ἐστιν ἐν πεδίῳ, τὸν δὲ κύκλον ἔχει τοῦ τείχους τριακοσίων ἐξήκοντα πέντε σταδίων, πάχος δὲ τοῦ τείχους ποδῶν δύο καὶ τριάκοντα, ὕψος δὲ τῶν μὲν μεσοπυργίων πήχεις πεντήκοντα τῶν δὲ πύργων ἐξήκοντα, ἡ δὲ πάροδος τοῖς ἐπὶ τοῦ τείχους ὥστε τέθριππα ἐναντιοδρομεῖν ἀλλήλοις ῥᾳδίως· διόπερ τῶν ἑπτὰ θεαμάτων λέγεται καὶ τοῦτο καὶ ὁ κρεμαστὸς κῆπος ἔχων ἐν τετραγώνῳ σχήματι ἑκάστην πλευρὰν τεττάρων πλέθρων· συνέχεται δὲ ψαλιδώμασι καμαρωτοῖς ἐπὶ πεττῶν ἱδρυμένοις κυβοειδῶν ἄλλοις ἐπ' ἄλλοις· οἱ δὲ πεττοὶ κοῖλοι πλήρεις γῆς ὥστε δέξασθαι φυτὰ δένδρων τῶν μεγίστων, ἐξ ὀπτῆς πλίνθου καὶ ἀσφάλτου κατεσκευασμένοι καὶ αὐτοὶ καὶ αἱ ψαλίδες καὶ τὰ καμαρώματα. ἡ δ' ἀνωτάτω στέγη προσβάσεις κλιμακωτὰς ἔχει, παρακειμένους δ' αὐταῖς καὶ κοχλίας δι' ὧν τὸ ὕδωρ ἀνῆγον εἰς τὸν κῆπον ἀπὸ τοῦ Εὐφράτου συνεχῶς οἱ πρὸς τοῦτο τεταγμένοι. ὁ γὰρ ποταμὸς διὰ μέσης ῥεῖ τῆς πόλεως σταδιαῖος τὸ πλάτος, ἐπὶ δὲ τῷ ποταμῷ ὁ κῆπος. ἔστι δὲ καὶ ὁ τοῦ Βήλου τάφος αὐτόθι, νῦν μὲν κατεσκαμμένος, Ξέρξης δ' αὐτὸν κατέσπασεν, ὥς φασιν· ἦν δὲ πυραμὶς τετράγωνος ἐξ ὀπτῆς πλίνθου καὶ αὐτὴ σταδιαία τὸ ὕψος, σταδιαία δὲ καὶ ἑκάστη τῶν πλευρῶν· ἣν Ἀλέξανδρος ἐβούλετο ἀνασκευάσαι, πολὺ δ' ἦν ἔργον καὶ πολλοῦ χρόνου (αὐτὴ γὰρ ἡ χοῦς εἰς ἀνακάθαρσιν μυρίοις ἀνδράσι δυεῖν μηνῶν ἔργον ἦν), ὥστ' οὐκ ἔφθη τὸ ἐγχειρηθὲν ἐπιτελέσαι· παραχρῆμα γὰρ ἡ νόσος καὶ ἡ τελευτὴ συνέπεσε τῷ βασιλεῖ, τῶν δ' ὕστερον οὐδεὶς ἐφρόντισεν. ἀλλὰ καὶ τὰ λοιπὰ ὠλιγωρήθη καὶ κατήρειψαν τῆς πόλεως τὰ μὲν οἱ Πέρσαι τὰ δ' ὁ χρόνος

---

[8] Some of the manuscripts of the two parallels have "Rav Huna" but this seems to be a garble resulting from the deletion of the *kaf* and the addition of a *waw*. "Ravina" too is sometimes given, and see Soṭah, ICIT edition. The *Midrash ha-Gadol* to Genesis has "Rav Mordecai escorted Rav Shimi b. Ashi from Pum Nahara to the *ṣiniata* (= stone palms) of Babylon. Rav Kahana escorted Rav Ashi ..." (*Midrash ha-Gadol* to Genesis, 18:16, Margulies ed., p. 303; cf. *ibid.*, 2:19—Margulies ed., p. 86); and cf. the testimony on Rav Mordecai in the rest of the passage in Berakhot and Soṭah. See also the entry on "Pum Nahara."

[9] The Vatican 110 MS of Soṭah has "Rav Sheshet."

[10] The Oxford MS has "from Pum Bədita" in Soṭah and see Soṭah in the ICIT edition.

καὶ ἡ τῶν Μακεδόνων ὀλιγωρία περὶ τὰ τοιαῦτα, καὶ μάλιστα ἐπειδὴ τὴν Σελεύκειαν ἐπὶ τῷ Τίγρει πλησίον τῆς Βαβυλῶνος ἐν τριακοσίοις που σταδίοις ἐτείχισε Σέλευκος ὁ Νικάτωρ. καὶ γὰρ ἐκεῖνος καὶ οἱ μετ' αὐτὸν ἅπαντες περὶ ταύτην ἐσπούδασαν τὴν πόλιν καὶ τὸ βασίλειον ἐνταῦθα μετήνεγκαν· καὶ δὴ καὶ νῦν ἡ μὲν γέγονε Βαβυλῶνος μείζων ἡ δ' ἔρημος ἡ πολλή, ὥστ' ἐπ' αὐτῆς μὴ ἂν ὀκνῆσαί τινα εἰπεῖν ὅπερ ἔφη τις τῶν κωμικῶν ἐπὶ τῶν Μεγαλοπολιτῶν τῶν ἐν Ἀρκαδίᾳ "ἐρημία μεγάλη 'στὶν ἡ Μεγάλη πόλις." διὰ δὲ τὴν τῆς ὕλης σπάνιν ἐκ φοινικίνων ξύλων αἱ οἰκοδομαὶ συντελοῦνται καὶ δοκοῖς καὶ στύλοις· περὶ δὲ τοὺς στύλους στρέφοντες ἐκ τῆς καλάμης σχοινία περιτιθέασιν, εἶτ' ἐπαλείφοντες χρώμασι καταγράφουσι, τὰς δὲ θύρας ἀσφάλτῳ· ὑψηλαὶ δὲ καὶ αὗται καὶ οἱ οἶκοι καμαρωτοὶ πάντες διὰ τὴν ἀξυλίαν· ψιλὴ γὰρ ἡ χώρα καὶ θαμνώδης ἡ πολλὴ πλὴν φοίνικος· οὗτος δὲ πλεῖστος ἐν τῇ Βαβυλωνίᾳ, πολὺς δὲ καὶ ἐν Σούσοις καὶ ἐν τῇ παραλίᾳ [τῇ] Περσίδι καὶ ἐν τῇ Καρμανίᾳ. κεράμῳ δ' οὐ χρῶνται· οὐδὲ γὰρ κατομβροῦνται. παραπλήσια δὲ καὶ τὰ ἐν Σούσοις καὶ τῇ Σιτακηνῇ.

Ἀφώριστο δ' ἐν τῇ Βαβυλῶνι[11] κατοικία τοῖς ἐπιχωρίοις φιλοσόφοις τοῖς Χαλδαίοις προσαγορευομένοις, οἳ περὶ ἀστρονομίαν εἰσὶ τὸ πλέον· προσποιοῦνται δέ τινες καὶ γενεθλιαλογεῖν, οὓς οὐκ ἀποδέχονται οἱ ἕτεροι.[12]

Babylon, too, lies in a plain; and the circuit of its wall is three hundred and eighty-five stadia. The thickness of its wall is thirty-two feet; the height thereof between the towers is fifty cubits; that of the towers is sixty cubits; and the passage on top of the wall is such that four-horse chariots can easily pass one another; and it is on this account that this and the hanging garden are called one of the Seven Wonders of the World. The garden is quadrangular in shape, and each side is four plethra in length. It consists of arched vaults, which are situated, one after another on checkered, cube-like foundations. The checkered foundations, which are hollowed out, are covered so deep with earth that they admit of the largest trees, having been constructed of baked brick and asphalt—the foundations themselves and the vaults and the arches. The ascent to the uppermost terrace-roofs is made by a stairway; and alongside these stairs there were screws, through which the water was continually conducted up into the garden from the Euphrates by those appointed for the purpose. For the river, a stadium in width, flows through the middle of the city; and the garden is on the bank of the river. Here too is the tomb of Belus, now in ruins, having been demolished by Xerxes, as it is said. It was a quadrangular pyramid of baked brick, not only being a stadium in height, but also having sides a stadium in length. Alexander intended to repair this pyramid, but it would have been a large task and would have required a long time (for merely the clearing away of the mound was a task for ten thousand men for two months), so that he could not finish what he had attempted; for

---

[11] Ed. Groskurd & Meineke. The manuscripts have in Soṭah "in Babylon."

[12] I.e., to be astrologers, or to know how to cast horoscopes (H. L. Jones' note).

immediately the king was overtaken by disease and death. None of his successors cared for this matter; and even what was left of the city was neglected and thrown into ruins, partly by the Persians and partly by time and by the indifference of the Macedonians to things of this kind, and in particular after Seleucus Nicator had fortified Seleuceia on the Tigris near Babylon, at a distance of about three hundred stadia therefrom. For not only he, but also all his successors, were strongly interested in Seleuceia and transferred the royal residence to it. What is more, Seleuceia at the present time has become larger than Babylon, whereas the greater part of Babylon is so deserted that one would not hesitate to say what one of the comic poets said in reference to the Megalopolitans in Arcadia: "The Great City is a great desert." On account of the scarcity of timber their buildings are finished with beams and pillars of palmwood. They wind ropes of twisted reed round the pillars; and then they plaster them and paint them with colours, though they coat the doors with asphalt. Both these and the private homes are built high, all being vaulted on account of the lack of timber; for, with the exception of the palm tree, most of the country is bare of trees and bears shrubs only. The palm is most abundant in Babylonia, and is found in abundance in Susa and on the coast of Persis and in Carmania. They do not use tiles much on their houses, for they get no rain; and this is likewise the case both in Susa and Sitacene.
In Babylonia[11] a settlement is set apart for the local philosophers, the Chaldaeans, as they are called, who are concerned mostly with astronomy; but some of these, who are not approved by the others, profess to be genethlialogists.[12] (trans.: H. L. Jones, LCL)

15. Livy XXXVIII 17,11

Macedones, qui Alexandriam in Aegypto, qui Seleuciam ac Babyloniam quique alias sparsas per orbem terrarum colonias habent, in Syros, Parthos, Aegyptios degenerarunt.[13]

The Macedonians who hold Alexandria in Egypt, who hold Seleucia and Babylonia and other colonies scattered throughout the world, have degenerated into Syrians, Parthians, Egyptians.[13] (trans.: F. G. Moore, LCL)

16. Pliny, *Natural History*, VI 26, 123

sunt etiamnum in Mesopotamia oppida Hipparenum, Chaldaeorum doctrina et hoc, sicut Babylon.

In Mesopotamia there exist even at this time the towns of Hipparenum—this is also a school of Chaldaean learning, like Babylon. (trans.: H. Rackham, LCL)

---

[13] It should be noted that this is taken from Livy's version of a speech made by a Roman consul in 189 B.C.

17. Iamblichus[14] in Photius, *Bibliotheca*, 75

Λέγει δὲ καὶ ἑαυτὸν Βαβυλώνιον εἶναι ὁ συγγραφεύς, καὶ μαθεῖν τὴν μαγικήν, μαθεῖν δὲ καὶ τὴν Ἑλληνικὴν παιδείαν, καὶ ἀκμάζειν ἐπὶ Σοαίμου τοῦ Ἀχαιμενίδου τοῦ Ἀρσακίδου,[15]

The author says that he himself is a Babylonian, that he studied the magic arts and also acquired a Greek education. He says that he was in his prime under Soaimos the Achaemenid and Arsacid.[15]

Scholia according to A[1] (fol. 72 R)

Οὗτος ὁ Ἰάμβλιχος Σύρος ἦν γένος πατρόθεν καὶ μητρόθεν. Σύρος δὲ οὐχὶ τῶν ἐπῳκηκότων τὴν Συρίαν Ἑλλήνων, ἀλλὰ τῶν αὐτοχθόνων, γλῶσσαν δὲ σύραν εἰδὼς καὶ τοῖς ἐκείνων ἔθεσι ζῶν ἕως αὐτὸν τροφεύς, ὡς αὐτός φησι, βαβυλώνιος λαβών, βαβυλωνίαν τε γλῶσσαν καὶ ἤθη καὶ λόγους μεταδιδάσκει, ὧν ἕνα τῶν λόγων εἶναί, φησι, καὶ ὃν νῦν ἀναγράφει. Αἰχμαλωτισθῆναι δὲ τὸν Βαβυλώνιον καθ' ὃν καιρὸν Τραιανὸς εἰσέβαλεν εἰς Βαβυλῶνα, καὶ πραθῆναι Σύρῳ ὑπὸ τῶν λαφυροπώλων. Εἶναι δὲ τοῦτον σοφὸν τὴν βάρβαρον σοφίαν ὡς καὶ τῶν βασιλέως γραμματέων τῇ πατρίδι διάγοντα γεγενῆσθαι. Ὁ μὲν οὖν Ἰάμβλιχος οὗτος Σύραν τὴν πάτριον γλῶσσαν εἰδώς, ἐπιμαθὼν καὶ τὴν βαβυλωνίαν μετὰ ταῦτα καὶ τὴν ἕλληνά φησιν ἀσκήσει καὶ χρήσει λαβεῖν ὡς ἀγαθὸς ῥήτωρ γένοιτο.

This Iamblichus was a Syrian by birth on both his father's and his mother's side. He was a Syrian who did not belong to the Greeks who had settled in Syria, but to the local inhabitants. He knew the Syrian tongue and lived according to their customs until, as he himself says, he received a Babylonian tutor who taught him the Babylonian language, customs and tales, and it is one of these tales, he says, which he now records. He says that when Trajan came to Babylon the Babylonian was made captive and sold to a Syrian by the sellers of booty. This man was learned in the barbarian wisdom as he had been one of the king's secretaries when he lived in his own country. This Iamblichus now, knew Syriac as his native tongue and later also learned Babylonian and says that he learned Greek by practice and use, so that he might be a good rhetorician.

18. Cassius Dio LXVIII 26,4 (Xiph. 238)[16]

καὶ μετὰ ταῦτα καὶ μέχρι τῆς Βαβυλῶνος αὐτῆς ἐχώρησαν κατὰ πολλὴν τῶν κωλυσόντων αὐτοὺς ἐρημίαν, ἅτε καὶ τῆς τῶν Πάρθων δυνάμεως ἐκ τῶν ἐμφυλίων πολέμων ἐφθαρμένης καὶ τότε ἔτι στασιαζούσης.

After this they advanced as far as Babylon itself (i.e. Trajan and his troops) being quite free from molestation, since the Parthian power had been de-

[14] Author of a Greek novel called *Babyloniaca* or *Rhodanes and Sinonis*; ca. A.D. 160.

[15] It is further mentioned that Iamblichus claimed to have predicted the war between Rome and Parthia under Marcus Aurelius and Lucius Verus, A.D. 162–166.

[16] Referring to A.D. 116.

stroyed by civil conflicts and was still at this time a subject of strife. (trans.: E. Cary, LCL)

19. Cassius Dio LXVIII 27,1 (Xiph. 238)

ἔνθα μέντοι τήν τε ἄσφαλτον εἶδε Τραϊανὸς ἐξ ἧς τὰ τείχη Βαβυλῶνος ᾠκοδόμητο (τοσαύτην γὰρ ἀσφάλειαν πλίνθοις ὀπταῖς ἢ καὶ λίθοις λεπτοῖς συμμιχθεῖσα παρέχεται ὥστε καὶ πέτρας καὶ σιδήρου παντὸς ἰσχυρότερα αὐτὰ ποιεῖν), καὶ τὸ στόμιον ἐθεάσατο ἐξ οὗ πνεῦμα δεινὸν ἀναδίδοται, ὥστε πᾶν μὲν ἐπίγειον ζῷον πᾶν δὲ πετεινὸν ἀποφθείρειν, εἰ καὶ ἐφ' ὁποσονοῦν ὄσφροιτό τι αὐτοῦ...

Here, moreover, Trajan saw the asphalt out of which the walls of Babylon had been built. When used in connexion with baked bricks or small stones this material affords so great security as to render them stronger than any rock or iron. He also looked at the opening from which issues a deadly vapour that destroys any terrestrial animal and any winged creature that so much as inhales a breath of it, etc. (trans.: E. Cary, LCL)

20. Cassius Dio LXVIII 30,1

μαθὼν δὲ ταῦτα ὁ Τραϊανὸς ἐν Βαβυλῶνι (καὶ γὰρ ἐκεῖσε ἦλθε κατά τε τὴν φήμην, ἧς οὐδὲν ἄξιον εἶδεν ὅ τι μὴ χώματα καὶ λίθους καὶ ἐρείπια, καὶ διὰ τὸν Ἀλέξανδρον, ᾧ καὶ ἐνήγισεν ἐν τῷ οἰκήματι ἐν ᾧ ἐτετελευτήκει)

Trajan learned of this at Babylon (namely, of the revolt in A.D. 116); for he had gone there both because of its fame—though he saw nothing but mounds and stones and ruins to justify this—and because of Alexander, to whose memory he offered sacrifice in the room where he had died. (trans.: E. Cary, LCL)

21. Cassius Dio LXXV 9,3[17]

ταχέως τήν τε Σελεύκειαν καὶ τὴν Βαβυλῶνα ἐκλειφθείσας ἔλαβε. καὶ μετὰ τοῦτο καὶ τὴν Κτησιφῶντα ἑλὼν ἐκείνην τε πᾶσαν διαρπάσαι τοῖς στρατιώταις ἐφῆκε, φόνον τε ἀνθρώπων πλεῖστον εἰργάσατο, καὶ ζῶντας ἐς δέκα μυριάδας εἷλεν.

Thus he soon seized Seleucia and Babylon, both of which had been abandoned. Later, upon capturing Ctesiphon, he permitted the soldiers to plunder the entire city, and he slew a vast number of people, besides taking as many as a hundred thousand captives. (trans.: E. Cary, LCL)

22. Jerome, in *Isaiam* V 14 in Migne, *Patrologiae Series Latina*, vol. 24, col. 163

Didicimus a quodam fratre Elamita, qui de illis finibus egrediens, nunc Hierosolymis vitam exigit monachorum, venationes regias esse in Babylone, et omnis generis bestias murorum eius tantum ambitu coerceri.

I learned from a certain Persian brother who came from that region and now leads a monk's life in Jerusalem that there are royal hunting parties in Babylon and that nothing but animals of every kind are kept within its walls.

[17] The passage refers to Septimius Severus' Parthian campaign in A.D. 198.

23. Jerome, in *Isaiam* V 14 in Migne, *Patrologiae Series Latina*, vol. 24, col. 168

. . . exceptis enim muris coctilibus, qui propter bestias concludendas post annos plurimos instaurantur, omne in medio spatium solitudo est.

. . . for apart from those walls which have been restored after very many years in order to confine the animals, the whole space in the middle (namely, of the city of Babylon) is deserted.

B. *Location*

In the Sura-Mata Məḥasya region, near the site of ancient Babylon which was on the east bank of the Euphrates, eighty-seven kilometers south of Baghdad (D4 on the Tal. Bab. map).

C. *History*

Alexander intended to make Babylon a royal capital, and planned to restore the sanctuary of the chief god, Marduk.[18] Restoration of the Esagila sanctuary was indeed begun and went on after Alexander's death in Babylon.[19] Seleucus I, however, transferred the royal residence to the new city of Seleucia (q.v.) on the Tigris, though not from any desire to destroy Babylon. Probably Babylon could no longer function as the metropolis of southern Babylonia because the Pallacottas branch of the Euphrates had become marshy. There is, in fact, evidence of a friendly royal policy towards the city of Babylon. A cuneiform inscription of Antiochus I records building activity in 287 B.C. in the sanctuary of Esagila at Babylon and of Ezida at Borsippa (Inscription 1 below).[20] For the first time since the Persians destroyed the statue of Marduk in 479 B.C., the king was called *šar Bābili*, king of Babylon. Stamped tiles were produced for the rebuilding of Esagila.[21] In 275/4 land was taken over from Babylon, Kuta and Borsippa, apparently due to the exigencies of the first Syrian war (Inscription 2 below),[22] and under Antiochus II (in 238/237) land was reallocated to them (Inscription 3 below).[23] It appears from the document on the

[18] Strabo XV 3, 9 (731); Source 14; Arrian, *Anabasis* III 16, 4; VII 17, 2.

[19] For the Babylonian sources referring to the reconstruction of Esagila between 323 and ca. 315 B.C. see Wetzel et al., *Das Babylon der Spätzeit*, p. 71; Rostovtzeff, *Social and Economic History of the Hellenistic World*, vol. 3, p. 1427, n. 234. For Alexander's death in Babylon see Arrian, *Anabasis* VII 17; 19, 4; 21, 1; 25; 26; Plutarch, *Alexander* 73–76.

[20] Weissbach, *Keilinschriften der Achämeniden*, p. 132f., col. I; cf. Wetzel, *ibid.*, p. 29.

[21] Sarkisian, in Diakonoff (ed.), *Ancient Mesopotamia*, p. 316f.; Smith, *Babylonian Historical Texts*, p. 157; Wetzel, *op cit.*, p. 72.

[22] Smith, *ibid.*, pp. 154–157; Sarkisian, *ibid.*, pp. 315–319; Doty, *Mesopotamia* 13/14 (1978–1979): 96–97.

[23] Sarkisian, *op.cit.*, pp. 321–327; Lehmann, *ZA* 7 (1892): 330–332. See further bibliography in Doty, *op.cit.*, n. 15; Oelsner, *Klio* 60 (1978): 101–116; Sherwin-White, *ZPE* 47 (1982): 51–70.

land restoration that Babylon, like Orchoi and Kuta, had an assembly linked with the temple, which recorded its deliberations in Accadian, and had its own officers, including some Greeks. There is thus good evidence to show that under the Seleucids Babylon enjoyed favorable treatment and an absence of religious or cultural interference. Antiochus IV Epiphanes, the Hellenizer of the Jews, appears on an inscription from Babylon as θεὸς σωτῆρ τῆς Ἀσίας κτίστης τῆς πόλεως (= god, savior of Asia, founder of the city).[24]

In 141 the Parthians first conquered Babylon[25] only to lose it again in 130 to Antiochus VII Sidetes (138–129).[26] From 129 to 124 Hyspaosines of Characene (see the entry on "Mesene") ruled the country,[27] and then Mithridates II (123–87) reconquered it.[28] It was then governed by the oppressive Himeros, who set part of the city of Babylon on fire and deported its inhabitants.[29] Inscriptions dated 122/1 and 111/110 B.C. mention Mithridates II.[30] During a civil war in 55 B.C. between Mithridates III and Orodes II, the city suffered a protracted siege and eventually capitulated.[31]

Writing in the reign of Augustus but using older sources, Strabo (Source 14) describes Babylon as a city slowly declining, the greater part of it having been deserted: "Seleucia at the present time has become larger than Babylon." Pliny the Elder knew of the existence there in his time of a school of Chaldean learning (Source 16). Trajan visited Babylon in 116 (Source 20) but "saw nothing but mounds and stones and ruins" to justify its fame. These gloomy descriptions may be exaggerated, however, as the Dioscorides inscription proves that the theatre was in use.

Two inscriptions—one of them certainly, the other almost certainly—show that in A.D. 19 and 24 there was an organization of Palmyran merchants in the city of Babylon, as pointed out by Rostovtzeff (see Inscription 10 and the entry on "Mesene"). Such organizations are known from later inscriptions to have existed also in Vologesias (see the entry on "Walašpaṭ") and in Mesene. They were responsible for the caravan trade between those centers and Palmyra (see the entry on "Tadmor"). It is important to know that in the first three decades of the first century A.D. at least part of the east-west trade still passed through the city of Babylon, along the Euphrates. The

---

24 Below, Inscription No. 4, in the section on Inscriptions.

25 Justinus XXXVIII 9, 5; Debevoise, *A Political History of Parthia*, p. 23.

26 Debevoise, *ibid.*, p. 31f.

27 Pinches, *The Babylonian and Oriental Record* 4 (1889/1890): 131–135; idem, *The Old Testament*², pp. 481–484; Bellinger, *YCS* 8 (1942): 58; Debevoise, *op.cit.*, pp. 38–40.

28 Bronze coins of Hyspaosines overstruck with a type of Mithridates II dated 121/120 show that by that time Characene had become a vassal state of the Parthians. See the entry on "Mesene."

29 Justinus XLV 1, 3; Diodorus Siculus XXXIV 21; Athenaeus XI 466b; cf. Le Rider, *Suse*, pp. 368, 382.

30 Below, Inscriptions Nos. 6 and 7, in the section on Inscriptions.

31 Justinus XLV 4, 2; cf. Debevoise, *op.cit.* (in n. 25), pp. 77–78.

inscriptions of the second half of the first century and later all mention Charax and Vologesias (from 142 on, Forat; see the entry on "Pərat də-Mešan"). It is very likely that by that time Babylon had ceased to attract foreign merchants.

Severus, in 198, found Babylon abandoned, but that was in wartime. Iamblichus and his scholia (see Source 17) indicate the kind of mixed community that inhabited Babylon in the second century A. D. Jerome (Source 22) states that he learned from a Persian monk that Babylon was deserted (fourth-fifth century).

D. *Archaeological Finds*

Nebuchadnezzar's summer palace (Babil) was in use until the Parthian period, to which belong the Hellenistic roof tiles and fragments of painted plaster found. Under the Parthians, the palace appears to have been transformed into a fort.[32] A citadel of the Persian and early Hellenistic period was found on the so-called Qaṣr. Though still occupied in the Parthian period, it was perhaps no longer a palace. In the Arab period, this part of town was used only as a quarry for building materials.[33] Fourth century and Seleucid efforts to reconstruct the old sanctuary of Babylon, Esagila, have been mentioned above.[34] It is considered improbable that Esagila was still in use as a temple in the Parthian period. In the second century B.C. a wall was built round the old ziggurat, Etemenanki. It may have served as a fort, like the ziggurats at Nippur and Orchoi/Warka.

A large Parthian villa was found between the two sanctuaries.[35] First built with a courtyard in the old Babylonian style, it later had a peristyle court, like the villa found at Nippur. A Parthian town quarter was found on the Amran hill, south of Esagila, with houses of this type and colonnaded streets.[36] These date to the first and especially the second centuries A. D., but it is possible that they were still inhabited in Sassanian and early Arab times.

Further east excavations have uncovered a Greek theatre and palaestra. Various stages have been observed. The original structure dates to the third or even the fourth century B.C.[37]

At various places in the city Jewish incantation bowls have been found in Parthian and later layers.[38] Other small finds are published by Wetzel et al. in the volume on Babylon after the neo-Babylonian period.

---

[32] Wetzel, *op.cit.* (in n. 19), pp. 24–25, Pl. 13; 23c, d; 31; 32; 33b, c; 34.

[33] *Ibid.*, pp. 25–27; Pl. 12; 24c; 27f.

[34] See further Wetzel, *ibid.*, pp. 29–33; 71f.; Pl. 14.

[35] *Ibid.*, pp. 31–32; Pl. 15; 25.

[36] *Ibid.*, p. 32f.; Pl. 24d; 25b, c.

[37] *Ibid.*, pp. 3–22; Pl. 2–11b.

[38] Layard, *Discoveries in the Ruins of Nineveh and Babylon*, pp. 509–526 (six complete bowls and fragments of others, with drawings, transcription and English translation).

Finally an important coin hoard of nine thousand pieces has recently come to light; 441 of them have been published. The majority date from the period of the caliphs.[39]

E. *Inscriptions*

1. F. H. Weissbach, *Die Keilinschriften der Achämeniden* (Leipzig 1911), p. 132, Appendix II, col. 1.

[1]^{m}*An-ti-ʾu-ku-us šarru rabu-ú* [2]*šarru dan-nu šar kiššati šar Bābìli šar mātāte* [3]*za-ni-in É-sag-íla ù É-zi-èd* [4]*aplu ašarīdu ša* ^{m}*Si-lu-uk-ku šarri* [5]^{lú}*Ma-ak-ka-du-na-a-a šar Bābìli* [6]*a-na-ku*
i-nu-ma a-na e-pé-eš$_{15}$ [7]*É-sag-íla ù É-zi-èd* [8]*lìb-bi ub-lam-ma libnat*^{há} [9]*É-sag-íla ù É-zi-èd* [10]*i-na māt Ḫa-at-tim ina qāte*^{II}*-i̯á el-li-ti* [11]*ina šaman ru-uš-ti al-bi-in-ma* [12]*a-na na-di-e uš-šu ša É-sag-íla* [13]*ù É-zi-èd ub-bi-x*(ḪI+DU$_{6}$)*-il ina arḫi Addari umi* XX^{kam} [14]*šatti* XLIII^{kam} *uš-šu ša É-zi-èd* [15]*bīti ki-i-ni bīt* ^{d}*Nabû šá qé-reb Bar-zip*^{ki} [16]*ad-di-e uš-ši-šu*

Antiochus, the great king, the mighty king, king of the universe, king of Babylon, king of the lands, provider of Esagila and Ezida, first son of Seleucus, the king, the Macedonian, King of Babylon, I am.
After my heart had decided to build Esagila and Ezida, after I had made the bricks for Esagila and Ezida in the land of Ḫatti, with my pure hands, with the finest oil and after I had transported them to lay the foundations of Esagila and Ezida, I laid, on the twentieth of Addar of the year 43, the foundations of Ezida, the eternal house, the temple of Nabu, which stands in Borsippa.

2. G. Kh. Sarkisian, "City Land in Seleucid Babylonia," *Ancient Mesopotamia*, ed. I. M. Diakonoff (Moscow 1969), p. 316.

šatti 37^{kam} ^{m}*An-ti u* ^{m}*Si-lu* ^{iti}*Addari 9* ^{lú}*mu-ma-ʾi-ir* ^{kur}*Akkadī u* ^{lú}*paq-du*^{meš} *ša šarri ša ina šatti 36*^{kam} *ana* ^{kur}*Sa-par-du ana muḫḫi šarri illiku-uʾ a-na* ^{uru}*Si-lu-ku-u-ʾa āl šarru-tu šá ina muḫḫi*^{id} *Idiglat itūrū*^{meš}*-ni* ^{kuš}*ši-piš-t*[*a-š*]*ú-nu ana muḫ-ḫi* ^{lú}*mārē*^{meš} *Bābili*^{ki} *tat*($^{!}$ for *šaṭ*)*-ri Tašrīti ūmi 12*^{kam} ^{lú}*mārē*^{meš} *Bābìli*^{ki} *ana* ^{uru}*Si-lu-ku-uʾ-a ušēṣū*^{meš} *arḫi šiʾāti* ^{lu}*mu-ma-ʾi-ir* ^{kur}*Akkadī*^{ki} ŠE.NUMUN *šá ina šatti 32*^{kam} *ina ṭēmi ša šarri ana kurummāt*^{há} ^{lú}*Bābilāia*^{meš} ^{lú}*Bar*[*sippāia*]^{meš} *u* ^{lú}*Kutāia*^{meš} *innadnu*^{meš} *alpē*^{há} *ṣēnē*^{há} *mimma gab-bi ša* [*ina ṣēri*]^{meš} *u ma-ḫa-zi*^{meš} *ina ṭēmi ša šarri la-pa-ni* ^{lú}*mārē*^{meš} [*Bābili*^{ki} *išū*^{meš} *ina muḫ*]*-ḫi bīt šarri ēpuš*^{uš} *šatti šiʾāti libnāti*^{há} *maʾdūtum*^{tum} *a-na e-peš ša É-sag-*[*íla*] *eliš Bābili*^{ki} *u šapliš Bābili*^{ki} *li-ib-*[*nu-ni*]

37th year of Anti(ochus) and Sele(ucus). On the 9th of Addar the ruler of Akkad and the royal officials who in the 36th year had gone to the king in Lydia, came back to Seleucia, the royal city on the Tigris, (and) their message

---

39 Simon, *Acta Iranica* 12 (1977): 149–337.

to the inhabitants of Babylon was written(?). On the 12th of Tishri they led out the inhabitants of Babylon to Seleucia. In the same month the ruler of Akkad assigned [to] the royal house the arable lands which in the 32nd year had been granted by the king's decision for subsistence of the Babylonians, Bor[sippans], and Cutheans, the cattle and the sheep, all that the inhabitants of Babylon [had in the open country] and in the cities by the decision of the preceding king. In that year many bricks for the building of Esag[il] were produc[ed] above and below Babylon.

3. *Ibid.*, p. 321.

^{iti}*Addaru ūmu 8 šattu 75* ^{m}*Si-lu-ku šarru ša* ^{m}*Nergal-teši-eṭir* ^{lú}*šà-tam* [*É-sag-íl*] *aplu ša* ^{m}*Bēl-ibni* ^{lú}*Bābilāia* ^{lú}*ṭupšarru ša Esagil iqbū um-*[*ma-a*] ^{m}*An-ti-'u-uk-su šarru ṣi-bu-ta da-mi-iq-⟨ta⟩ i-te-ep-ša an-na šu-*[*u*] *mimma ša* ^{m}*An-ti-'u-uk-su abu-šu u* ^{m}*Si-lu-ku abu abi-šu šarru ı-šaṭ-ṭ*[*a*(?)*-ru*(?)] ŠE.NUMUN^{meš} *ša bīt ra-ma-ni-šu-*[*nu*(?)] *ša*(?) *ana le-met Bābili*^{ki} *u Bar-zip*$^{\text{ki(!)}}$ *ša ina imitti u šumēli ša* ^{id}*Puratti u* ŠE.NUMUN^{meš} *ša a-na ku-mu ṣib-tum ša bīt šarri u mimma ša ina*(?) [ŠE.NUMUN^{meš} *šu-ātunu*] *šu-qu-ra-a' a-na* ^{f}*Lu-da-ke-e aššati-šu* ^{m}*Si-lu-ku u* ^{m}*An-ti-'u-uk-su aplē-šu id-din-nu* ^{f}*Lu-da-ke-e aššatu-šu* ^{m}*Si-lu-ku u* ^{m}*An-ti-'u-uk-su aplē-šu ana* ^{lú}*Bābilāia* ^{lú}*Barsippāia* ^{lú}*Kutāia id-din-nu-u' u iš-ṭu-ru-u'*.

The 8th of Addar of the 75th year of Seleucus the king. (This is) what Nergal-teši-eṭir, the steward [of Esagil], son of Bēlibni the Babylonian, the scribe of Esagil, said: "King Antiochus fulfilled a good wish. This is it. Everything that his father Antiochus and his grandfather Seleucus regi[stered]—the arable land of h[is (their?)] own house (pertaining) to the environs of Babylon and Borsippa which is in the right and the left of the Euphrates, as well as the arable land which (has been given?) instead of the tribute(?) of the royal house, as well as everything that is valuable on [these arable lands]—he gave to Laodice, his wife, to Seleucus and Antiochus, his sons. Laodice, his wife, Seleucus and Antiochus, his sons, gave (all this) and assigned in writing to (= registered with) the Babylonians, Borsippans and Cutheans."

4. W. Dittenberger, *Orientis Graeci Inscriptiones Selectae* (Leipzig 1903), No. 253. Revised text in M. Zambelli, *Rivista di Filologia* 38 (1960): 363–398, esp. p. 378.

Dedication of 169/8 B.C. to Antiochus IV Epiphanes, savior of Asia and founder of the city. The provenance of this inscription and of Nos. 5 and 8 (below) is not certain; see Sherwin-White, *op.cit.* (in n. 23), p. 52ff.

5. *OGIS*, No. 254.

Dedication by the city to Democrates, son of Byttakos, commander of the garrison in the citadel (2nd century B.C.).
(On the *strategos* and *epistates* see the entry on "Nineveh.")

6, 7. B. Haussoulier, *Klio* 9 (1909): 352ff.; *SEG*, vol. 7, No. 39 (111/110 B.C.) and No. 40 (122/121 B.C.).

Two Greek inscriptions referring to a gymnasium in which games were held. No. 39 lists the *ephebes* who were victorious in the various games. (Haussoulier's reading according to *SEG*, with corrections in lines 2 and 3.)

[Βα]σιλεύοντος [Μεγάλου Ἀρσάκου]
Ἐπιφανοῦς Φιλέλλην[ος, ἔτους]
ζλ' καὶ ρ' ὡς ὁ βασιλεύς, [ὡς δὲ τὸ πρότερον]
βσ', γυμνασιαρχοῦντος
εἰσὶν οἱ νενικηκότες ὅλωι τ[ῶι ἐνιαυτῶι,]
τεθέντων τῶν χρημάτων ὑπὸ Δι[ογένου τοῦ]
Ἀρτεμιδώρου, ὁ γενόμενος ταμ[ίας ἐν τῶι]

B ϙ καὶ P ἔτει·

Τ ῶ ν μ ὲ ν	ἐφήβ[ων·]
Τόξωι	Δίκαιος Διοδώρου·
Ἀκοντίωι	Ἀρτεμίδωρος Ἀνδρονείκου·
Ὁπόλωι κοίλωι	Καστυρίδης Κεφάλωνος·
Θυρεῶι	Δημήτριος Ἀθηνογένου·
Δολίχωι	Ἀριστείδης Ἀρτεμιδώρου·
Σταδίωι	Νικάνωρ Ἑρμολάου·
Τῶν δὲ	νέων·
Τόξωι	Δίκαιος Νικοστράτου·
Ἀκ[οντίωι]	Ἡρακ[λ]έων Ἡρακλέωνος·
	. . . . ς Ἀπολλοδώρου·
	ο]γένου

8. Haussoulier, *op. cit.*, p. 362; *SEG* vol. 7, No. 38.

Greek inscription on a clay jar cover mentioning "Aristeas also named Ardubelteos".

9. E. Schmidt in F. Wetzel, et al., *Das Babylon der Spätzeit*, pp. 49–50, Pl. 40a.

Found in the ruins of the peristyle house south of the theatre. The editor dates the shape of the lettering between A. D. 130 and 200. This might be the date, but the material for comparison is inadequate.

Διοσκουρ[ίδης - - -]
ὁ φιλόδοξ[ος - - -]
τὸ θέατρο[ν - - -]
καὶ σκην[ήν - - -]

The inscription records the repair of the theater and its skene at the expense of one Dioscorides.

10. J. Cantineau, *Syria* 12 (1931): 122–123, No. 4.

Inscription set up at Palmyra by Palmyran tradesmen in Babylon, A. D. 24.

ב[יר]ח כנון שנת cccxxxvi צלמא דנה די מלכו
בר נשא בר בולחא די מתקרא חשש די מן בני
כמרא די אקימו לה ת[ג]ריא כלהון די במדינת
בבל מן די שפר להון בכל גנס כלה ועדר בנ[ינ]א
די ה[י]כלא די בל ויהב מן כיסה די לא עבדה
אנש בדיל כות אקימו לה צלמא דנה ליקרה

Μάλιχον Νεσᾶ τοῦ Βωλάα τοῦ ἐπικαλο-
υμένου Ἀσάσου, φυλῆς Χομαρηνῶν, Παλ-
μυρηνῶν ὁ δῆμος, εὐνοίας ἕνεκα.

Translation of the Palmyrene Text

In the month Kanun 336. This statue of Malikho son of Neše, son of Bolḥa, also named Ḥašaš, of the Bene Komara, was set up by the merchants who are in the city of Babylon because he favored them in every possible way and because he gave assistance for the construction of the temple of Bel and gave from his own purse, which no one else has done; because of this they erected this statue in his honor.

Translation of the Greek Text

To Malikhos the son of Nesa, the son of Bola, also named Asases, of the tribe of the Khomarenians, the people of Palmyra, out of gratitude.

Cf. *CIS*, II 3, No. 3924 and the comments by M. I. Rostovtzeff, *Mélanges Gustave Glotz*, vol. 2, pp. 796–798. As pointed out by Rostovtzeff, this inscription shows that there was an organization of Palmyran merchants in the city of Babylon. Malikhos must have been their leader. Rostovtzeff further notes that it is of interest that the merchants in Babylon appear only in the Palmyrene version, while the Greek mentions the people of Palmyra.

11. A. Dumont, *Revue Archéologique*, n. s. 20 (1869): 192; *Mélanges d'archéologie et d'épigraphie* (Paris 1892), p. 136f.; R. H. McDowell, *Stamped and Inscribed Objects from Seleucia on the Tigris* (Ann Arbor 1935), pp. 146; 256–257.

A rectangular Greek weight found at Ḥilla:

Obverse:	Θεοδο / σίου τοῦ / Ἀνδρο / μάχου
Reverse:	Ἀγορα / νομοῦν / τος
On the four sides:	χρυσοὶ / δύο / ἔτους / ζνσ'.

Obverse:	Under Theodosios the son of Andromachos
Reverse:	agoranomos
On the four sides:	two gold, the year 257

The editor notes that the unit was the stater, an Attic weight. The year 257 of the Seleucid era was 55 B.C. It was part of the duties of the agoranomos to certify weights.
There can be no doubt that this must have been an official at Babylon, since Ḥilla (near Babylon) did not have a polis-type organization in the first century B.C.

12. A Greek ostracon of the early third century B.C. is now extensively discussed by Sherwin-White, *op.cit.* (in n. 23). It is evidence of the presence of a (Seleucid) military unit in town.

F. *Babylon and Its Environs*

Since Hebrew uses the same term—Bavel—for both the city and country, it is not always possible to determine which was meant in some of the talmudic sources. Cited here are sources where, because of the content or context, it is certain or probable that the reference is to the city.[40]
A number of sources mention places near Babylon, such as "Be Kəništa də-Daniel" (ʿEruvin 21a) and see the entry on "Barneš." Source 5 mentions Babylon and Borsif together and Source 4 even notes that the names are sometimes interchanged (see the entry on "Borsif"). The Arabic sources report pilgrimages by Jews and Christians to Daniel's pit (*ǧubb*) in Babylon on their festivals.[41]

---

[40] E.g. the phrase "Bavel is regarded as a border town, and that meant Nəhardəʿa" (see Sources 7 and 8 in the entry on "Nəhardəʿa") may mean that Nəhardəʿa is an example of a border town in Babylonia, or alternatively, that Babylon, like Nəhardəʿa, is a border town. On Babylon see e.g. Yāqūt, Bakrī, *Marāṣid* and *ar-Rauḍ al-miʿṭār*, s.v. "Bābil"; Yāqūt, s.v. "Ṣarḥ"; Idrīsī, vol. 6, p. 670; Masʿūdī, *Murūǧ*, vol. 1, p. 265 (= vol. 2, p. 115); idem, *Tanbīh*, p. 35; Zuhrī, pp. 249–250; *Ḥudūd al-ʿālam*, p. 139; Qazwīnī, *Bilād*, pp. 304–306; *BGA*, passim; Mustaufī, vol. 2, p. 162; Muqaddasī, p. 121. See also ʿAwwād, *Sumer* 5 (1949): 72–73; Fransīs & ʿAwwād, *Sumer* 8 (1952): 253; Awad, *EI*², s.v. "Bābil"; Herzfeld, *EI*¹, s.v. "Bābil"; al-ʿAli, *Sumer* 21 (1965): 232. Hinting at a Jewish settlement, which Benjamin of Tudela said was a mile away from ancient Babylon, *Ta'rīḫ al-Ḥilla*, vol. 1, p. 13, notes that it was called al-Yahūdīya because of its Jewish inhabitants. See also p. 154 there. According to a well-known Shīʿite tradition, the earth of Babylon was cursed (variant: a place which the earth opened its mouth and swallowed), and it is forbidden to pray there: Yāqūt, s.v. "Bābil," p. 310; Dīnawarī, *Aḫbār ṭiwāl*, vol. 1, p. 177; Bakrī, vol. 1, pp. 218–219; Naṣr b. Muzāḥim, *Kitāb Ṣiffīn*, p. 135; Abū Dāwūd, *Sunan*, vol. 1, p. 114; *Šarḥ nahǧ al-balāġa*, vol. 1, p. 277.

[41] See Masʿūdī, *Murūǧ*, vol. 1, p. 265 (= vol. 2, p. 115); Qazwīnī, *Bilād*, p. 304; al-Qurṭubī, *al-Masālik wa-l-mamālik*, Nur Osmaniya MS, fol. 59a; cf. Qazwīnī, *ʿAǧā'ib*, p. 235; Mustaufī, vol. 2, p. 44; *Ṯimār al-qulūb*, p. 233; *Taḏkirat al-ḥuffāẓ*, vol. 1, pp. 92–93. On the pit see especially *Masālik al-abṣār*, p. 232. For the pit, see also Source 1.

G. *Physical Features*

Talmudic sources note various physical features relating to Babylon and its environs. The ruins of ancient Babylon are mentioned in Source 1, including "Nebuchadnezzar's house" probably meaning the remains of the Nebuchadnezzar palace at the site of ancient Babylon.[42] (See also above, the section on Archaeological Remains.)

At or near Babylon was Gišra də-Bavel, referred to in Source 3, from which the Euphrates could be seen. If the name is taken literally, this was a bridge across the Euphrates near Babylon.[43] The talmudic wording, however, clearly suggests a connection beetwen the blessing and the diversion of the Euphrates (by means of a dam). Thus Obermeyer's explanation of the passage must be rejected, as it posits an irregular flow of the river below Babylon which made canals necessary. For before the Persians shifted the course of the Euphrates at Be Šabur (see the entry on "Pumbədita"), they had already constructed canals above Babylon. Both classical and talmudic sources speak of the palm trees abounding in the city and its surroundings.[44] Source 13 mentions "*be ṣanita də-Bavel,*" apparently a particular type of palm common in the area.[45] The popular tradition holding that those palm trees survived from the time of Adam probably developed because they grew at the site of ancient Babylon. It is of course possible that "Be Ṣanita" itself represents a place in which case "də-Bavel" would refer to either Babylonia or the city.[46]

H. *Sages and Babylon*

Amoras belonging to several generations are connected with Babylon, but there is no evidence of sages having been born there or been long resident there. Rav, of the first generation of Babylonian amoras and founder of the Sura yeshiva, is mentioned in connection with Babylon. Source 6 covers a case of residents of Babylon and its environs following the rulings of Rav in regard to a woman's *ketubah.*[47] What is interesting is that the area is described as

---

[42] Cf. also Pirqe Rabbi Eliezer, II, Appendices to Seder Eliahu Zuṭa, Friedmann ed., p. 31.

[43] Obermeyer, pp. 52–53. He refers to Muqaddasī, p. 121. The text there does not include the phrase "the bridge of Babylon." A more explicit reference to the bridge appears in Ibn Ḥabīb, *Kitāb al-muḥabbar*, p. 482. Cf. Mas'ūdī, *Murūǧ*, vol. 1, p. 265 (= vol. 2, p. 115) who mentions a town called Ǧisr Bābil from which the village called Babylon, on the bank of a canal of the Euphrates, is an hour's distance.

[44] On the palm trees in Babylon, see Eustathius, *Commentaries* 1010, Müller ed., *Geographi Graeci Minores*, vol. 2, pp. 25, 60.

[45] See *Arukh ha-Shalem*, vol. 7, pp. 27–28, s.v. "צני" and cf. "ציניתא" in the dictionaries of Jastrow (p. 1278) and Levy (vol. 4, p. 202). On the type of palm trees see Löw, *Die Flora*, vol. 2, p. 313.

[46] See Berliner, p. 60. See Beer, *Amora'ei Bavel*, p. 95, n. 35, but "Ṣinta" (q.v.) should be distinguished from "*be ṣanita də-Bavel.*"

[47] See Beer, *Rashut ha-Golah*, pp. 74–75.

Babylon and its environs rather than Sura and its environs which would be expected. Sources 7 and 8 deal with cases in which Rav "happened to be in Babylon." If indeed the city is meant, as Source 7 in particular implies, this group of sources (6, 7, 8) indicates that Rav had a special connection with Babylon.[48] The statement in Source 2 as well, on heathen temples in various places including Babylon, is attributed to Rav.
Another amora who at times got to Babylon was Ravina, of the fifth generation of Babylonian amoras, a resident of Mata Məḥasya. Sources 9–11 cover various cases arising in Babylon which Ravina ruled on. On the one hand they show that Babylon was subject to Mata Məḥasya (q.v.) in halakhic matters, and on the other, in Source 11, Ravina proffers the excuse that he was ruling in Babylon and not Mata Məḥasya itself to explain why he acted independently without submitting the case to Rav Ashi, then head of the Mata Məḥasya yeshiva.

I. *Economy*

Source 9 provides some idea of the economy of Babylon and the daily life of its Jewish residents. The case involves weavers of palm-leaf baskets who tried to sell their wares in the Babylon market.[49] The citizens wished to prevent "foreign" merchants from operating in the local market and applied to Ravina. He ruled in favor of the outsiders, explaining that since out-of-town buyers patronized the market, out-of-town merchants would be allowed to sell there. The importance of the Babylon market and the existence of a sizeable Jewish community in the town can be inferred from the case described. Strabo (in Source 14) mentions the use of palm wood in building.

Awad, *EI*², s.v. "Bābil"
Beer, *Amora'ei Bavel* (1974), pp. 91, 95 n. 35
Beer, *Rashut ha-Golah* (1970), p. 75
Berliner, *Beiträge* (1883), pp. 25, 60
Ellis, *Mesopotamian Archaeological Sites* (1972), pp. 9–11
Eshel, *Yishuvei ha-Yehudim* (1979), pp. 44–45, 69
Funk, *Monumenta* (1913), pp. 6, 8, 21, 22, 25, 81, 287, 323
Getzow, *Al Neharot Bavel* (1887), p. 20
al-Haik, *Key Lists* (1968), No. 99
Herzfeld, *EI*¹, s.v. "Bābil"
Hirschenson, *Sheva Ḥokhmot* (1883), pp. 57–65
Jastrow, *Dictionary* (1950³), pp. 136–137
Kohut, *Arukh ha-Shalem* (1878–1892), vol. 2, p. 8
Koldewey, *Das Wiedererstehende Babylon* (1925)
Krauss, *Qadmoniot ha-Talmud* (1923–1945), vol. 1, p. 162
Layard, *Discoveries in the Ruins of Nineveh and Babylon* (1853), pp. 509–526
Levy, *Wörterbuch* (1924²), vol. 1, p. 190
Neubauer, *Géographie* (1868), pp. 344–345

---

[48] There are mentions of various amoras "happening to be in Bavel" (איקלע לבבל) where the context indicates that Babylonia and not Babylon is meant (e.g., Rosh ha-Shanah 21a: "Levy happened to be in Bavel . . .").

[49] *Metivot* (p. 82) has בשוקא דבבל in Source 9, instead of בבל alone. Thus the source there explicitly mentions the Babylon market.

OBERMEYER, *Hamagid* 20 (1876), passim
OBERMEYER, *Landschaft* (1929), pp. 52–59, 251–252, 301–306
PIGULEVSKAJA, *Les Villes* (1963), Chapter 2
REUTHER, *Die Innenstadt von Babylon* (1926)
SARKISIAN, in *Ancient Mesopotamia*, ed., Diakonoff (1969), pp. 312–331
SHERWIN-WHITE, *ZPE* 47 (1982): 51–70
SIMON, *Acta Iranica* 12 (1977): 149–337
WETZEL, SCHMIDT & MALLWITZ, *Das Babylon der Spätzeit* (1957)
ZURI, *Shilton* (1939), pp. 233–234, 237–238

Bagda בגדא

See the entry on "'Uḵbara."

Bagdat (Baghdad?) בגדת

A. *Sources*

1. Shabbat 147b[1]

אמר רב חנא בגדתאה אמר שמואל . . .

Rav Ḥana Bagdata'a said, Samuel said . . .

2. ʿEruvin 81b; 95a[2]

אמר ליה רב חנא בגדתאה לרב יהודה אמר שמואל . . .

Rav Ḥana Bagdata'a said to him to Rav Judah, Samuel said . . .

3. Ketubot 10b[3]

אמר רב חנא בגדתאה.

Rav Ḥana Bagdata'a said.

B. *Already Proposed Location*

Baghdad (D2 on the Tal. Bab. map).

C. *Identification*

Obermeyer and others before him already assumed that Rav Ḥana Bagdata'a, of the second generation of Babylonian amoras, mentioned in the sources

[1] Rav Ḥana Bagdata'a citing Samuel and with Samuel figures also in Shabbat 148a, Yevamot 67a, Ketubot 7b, Bava Batra 142b and Zevaḥim 92a.

[2] Rav Ḥana Bagdata'a is mentioned together with Rav Judah also in Berakhot 54b.

[3] The parallel in *Midrash ha-Gadol* Leviticus 21:14 (Steinsalz ed., p. 602) has "Rav Huna Bagdata'a." A question of Rav Ḥana Bagdata'a's appears also in Zevaḥim 9a.

above came from Baghdad.[4] Rashi too identified Bagdat with Baghdad,[5] and this identification seems well founded.[6]
The name Bagdadu appears in Babylonian documents of 1200[7] and 900 B.C.[8] The Arabs give as the oldest form, in 13A.H. (= A.D. 635), "*sūq Baġdād.*" The "*sūq al-ʿatīqa*" or "*maḥalla al-ʿatīqa*" of west Baghdad was later included in the metropolis. The detailed description available of old Baghdad makes it possible to locate this quarter near the presentday Shīʿite sanctuary of Mašhad al-Minṭaqa. An analogous name is "Sūq al-Ahwāz," today Ahwāz (see the entry on "Be Ḥozai").[9]

Berliner, *Beiträge* (1883), p. 25
Duri, *EI*², s.v. "Baġdād," p. 894
Eshel, *Yishuvei ha-Yehudim* (1979), pp. 48–49
Funk, *Juden* (1902–1908), vol. 2, p. 150
Funk, *Monumenta* (1913), pp. 25, 277, 279
Herzfeld, *Samarra* (1948), pp. 28, 33
Herzfeld, *The Persian Empire* (1968), pp. 38–40
Hirschenson, *Sheva Ḥokhmot* (1883), p. 65
Jastrow, *Dictionary* (1950³), p. 137
Kohut, *Arukh ha-Shalem* (1878–1892), vol. 2, pp. 10–11; *Tosefot* (1937), p. 74
Levy, *Wörterbuch* (1924²), vol. 1, p. 190
Musil, *The Middle Euphrates* (1927), index
Neubauer, *Géographie* (1868), p. 360
Neusner, *History* (1965–1970), vol. 2, pp. 247, 256, 263; vol. 3, p. 164
Newman, *Agricultural Life* (1932), pp. 6, 19, 37
Nöldeke, *ZDMG* 36 (1882): 183
Nöldeke, *SAWW phil. hist. Klasse* 128, 9 (1893), p. 28
Obermeyer, *Landschaft* (1929), passim

Barneš ברניש

A. *Sources*

1. ʿEruvin 21a

אמר ליה רב חסדא למרי בריה דרב הונא[1] בריה דרב ירמיה בר אבא אמרי אתיתו מברנש[2] לבי כנישתא דדניאל דהוה תלתא פרסי בשבתא, אמאי סמכיתו אבורגנין, הא

[4] Obermeyer, pp. 148–150, and see already Berliner, p. 25; Funk, *Monumenta*, p. 25. For the form "Bagdata'a" in the T. J. see Nöldeke, *ZDMG* 36 (1882): 183.

[5] Rashi on Berakhot 54b, says re Bagdata'a: "The name of his city is Baghdad, the most important city in Babylonia since Babylon was destroyed."

[6] In a passage dealing with the boundary of Babylonia in regard to purity of lineage, "Bagda" appears as the northern border point on the Tigris. This is certainly a scribal error, and the preferred version is the one in the Vatican 111 MS citing ʿUḵbara (q.v.).

[7] The *kudurru* of Marduk-apla-iddina I, Scheil, *MDP* VI, p. 32ff.

[8] Fragmentary *kudurru* from Susa, Scheil *MDP* VI, p. 46, undated and the *Synchron. Geschichte* III, p. 12 of 900 B.C.: *Reall. Assyr.* I, p. 390. Herzfeld refutes the view of Nöldeke (*loc.cit.* in n. 4 above), who considers Baghdad related to an Iranian personal name *Bagdata* and denies that it occurs in pre-Persian times.

[9] Herzfeld, *Samarra*, pp. 28, 33; idem, *The Persian Empire*, pp. 38–40. On old Baghdad, see also the entry on "Šunya."

[1] The Munich MS has "Rav Mari b. Rav Huna"; see also *Diq. Sof.*

[2] The Oxford MS has **מבדמש**, the Munich MS has **מבי נכיש דברניש**. See Abramson, *Rav Nissim Gaon*, p. 123, esp. n. 54.

אמר אבוה דאבוה[3] משמיה דרב אין בורגנין בבבל, נפק ואחוי ליה הנהו מתוותא דמבלען בשבעים אמה ושיריים.

Rav Ḥisda said to Mari son of Rav Huna[1] son of Rav Jeremiah b. Abba, They say that you came from Barneš[2] to Daniel's synagogue on the Sabbath, that was three parasangs away. What do you rely upon, upon the isolated huts? But your father's father[3] said in the name of Rav that there are no isolated huts in Babylonia. He went out and showed him certain [ruined] settlements that were within seventy cubits and a fraction [from each other].

2. Shabbat 28a[4]

אמר ליה רבא מברניש לרב אשי . . .

Rava from Barneš said to Rav Ashi . . .

B. *Already Proposed Location*

Presentday Ḫān Bīrnūs, in the vicinity of Ḥilla (see D4 on the Tal. Bab. map).

C. *Identification*

Neubauer logically proposed identifying Barneš with Ḫān Bīrnūs in the Ḥilla region.[5] Source 1 mentions Daniel's synagogue which is not far from the place (see the entry on "Babylon").

Beer, *Amora'ei Bavel* (1974), p. 79
Berliner, *Beiträge* (1883), p. 28
Eshel, *Yishuvei ha-Yehudim* (1979), p. 79–80
Funk, *Monumenta* (1913), p. 28
Hirschenson, *Sheva Ḥokhmot* (1883), pp. 83–84
Jastrow, *Dictionary* (1950³), p. 196
Kohut, *Arukh ha-Shalem* (1878–1892), vol. 2, p. 196; *Tosefot* (1937), p. 107
Levy, *Wörterbuch* (1924²), vol. 1, p. 269
Neubauer, *Géographie* (1868), p. 345
Neusner, *History* (1965–1970), vol. 2, p. 248; vol. 3, p. 246; vol. 5, p. 277
Newman, *Agricultural Life* (1932), p. 19
Obermeyer, *Landschaft* (1929), pp. 297, 300
Wiesner, *Scholien* (1867), vol. 3, pp. 17–18

Be Ardəšir בי ארדשיר

See the entry on "Be Ardəšir-Koḵe" under "Maḥoza Area."

---

[3] The Munich MS like other manuscripts and printings has אבא דאבוך; and see *Diq. Sof.*

[4] And in many other places. Thus Rava of Barneš who was in touch with Rav Ashi (see the entry on "Sura") belonged to the sixth generation of Babylonian amoras.

[5] In regard to the connection proposed by Obermeyer (p. 297) between Barneš and the Borniṣ river, see the section on Physical Features in the entry on "Sura."

Be Bire בי בירי

A. *Sources*

1. Soṭah 10a

כתיב "וירד שמשון תמנתה," וכתיב "הנה חמיך עולה תמנתה," ... ר' שמואל בר נחמני אמר שתי תמנאות היו, חדא בירידה וחדא בעליה. רב פפא אמר חדא תמנה הואי, דאתי מהאי גיסא ירידה ודאתי מהאי גיסא עליה כגון ורדוניא[1] ובי בארי[2] ושוקא דנרש.[3]

It is written "Samson went down to Timnah" (Jud. 14: 1) and it is written "Your father-in-law is coming up to Timnah" (Gen. 38: 13) ... Rabbi Samuel b. Naḥmani said, There were two Timnahs, one down and one up. Rav Papa said, There is one Timnah, Whoever came from one direction went down, and whoever came from another direction went up, such as Wardunya,[1] Be Bire[2] and the market of Nareš.[3]

2. ʿEruvin 56a

אמר רב יהודה אמר רב כל עיר שיש בה מעלות ומורדות אדם ובהמה שבה מתים בחצי ימיהן, מתים ס"ד, אלא אימא מזקינים בחצי ימיהן. אמר רב הונא בריה דרב יהושע הני מולייתא דבי בירי ודבי נרש[4] אזקנון.

Rav Judah said Rav said, Every town that has ascents and descents, man and beast die in the prime of life. Die, would you say? Rather say, they age in the prime of life. Rav Huna the Son of Rav Joshua said, Those ascents at Be Bire and Be Nareš[4] have made us old.

3. Yoma 81b

דתניא רבי אומר חומץ משיב את הנפש. דרש רב גידל בר מנשה[5] מבירי דנרש[6] אין הלכה כרבי.

It was taught Rabbi says, Vinegar refreshes the soul. Rav Giddal b. Manasseh[5] of Bire də-Nareš[6] expounded, The halakhah is not like Rabbi.

4. Yevamot 85a

בעו מיניה בני בירי[7] מרב ששת שניה לבעל ולא שניה ליבם יש לה כתובה מיבם או לא ... אמר להו רב ששת תניתוה ...

---

[1] For variations in the name, see the entry on "Wardina."

[2] The source has ובי בארי; the Venice printing has וביבארי (as one word), the Oxford MS has ובי ברי; and see Soṭah in the ICIT edition.

[3] For variations in the name, see the entry on "Nareš."

[4] The Munich MS has דבי בארי דנרש, the Oxford MS has דבי בירי ונרש and the Salonika printing has דבי בירי דנרש.

[5] The Munich MS has רב גידל בר מניו', the Oxford and London MSS have רב גידל בר מנשיא, and the Munich B MS has גדול בר מנשי.

[6] The Munich B MS has בביברי דנרש, and the Oxford MS does not have the place name at all; see *Diq. Sof.*

[7] The Venice printing has בני באירי.

The men of Be Bire[7] asked Rav Sheshet, Is [a woman of] the second [grade of kinship] to her husband, but not second to her levir, entitled to claim her *ketubah* from the levir or not ... Rav Sheshet said to them, You have learned this ...

(5. Ḥullin 127a)[8]

B. *Already Proposed Location*

Near Nareš (q.v., D4 on the Tal. Bab. map).

C. *Identification*

Rav Papa, head of the Nareš yeshiva, indicates in Source 1 that Be Bire (or Be Bare), Wardina and Nareš (qq.v.) were in the same area, which unlike most of Babylonia, was rather hilly. Rav Huna the son of Rav Joshua, also of Nareš, likewise refers (Source 2) to the terrain of Be Bire and Nareš, and the physical difficulties it presents.

D. *Sages and Be Bire*

As noted above, sages from Nareš make references to Be Bire, which was evidently a kind of suburb of Nareš. According to Source 3, one of these sages, Rav Giddal b. Manasseh, apparently resided in Be Bire.[9]
Source 4 has the Be Bire people addressing a halakhic question to Rav Sheshet, of the third generation of Babylonian amoras. That source does not, however, say it was the Be Bire near Nareš, so that the reference may be to another place bearing the same name.
Other places in the Talmud mention Rabbi Dostai of Bire,[10] evidently an amora of Eretz Israel, who came from a Bire in that country.[11]

Beer, *Amora'ei Bavel* (1974), p. 152
Berliner, *Beiträge* (1883), pp. 26–27
Eshel, *Yishuvei ha-Yehudim* (1979), pp. 54, 73
Funk, *Juden* (1902–1908), vol. 2, p. 156
Funk, *Monumenta* (1913), pp. 26, 290
Hirschenson, *Sheva Ḥokhmot* (1883), p. 71
Jastrow, *Dictionary* (1950³), p. 165

[8] In the entry on "Nareš" see Source 5, nn. 6 and 41; and see the *Arukh ha-Shalem*, vol. 2, p. 9, under "ביברי".

[9] On Rav Giddal see, in the entry on "Nareš," the section on Sages and Nareš, and nn. 5 and 6 above.

[10] See 'Eruvin 45a, Bava Qamma 83a, Sanhedrin 107a, 'Avodah Zarah 40a, and cf. T. J. 'Avodah Zarah II 10–42a.

[11] Funk (*Monumenta*, p. 290), Eshel (p. 73), Hyman (pp. 326–327) and others believe the reference is to a place in Babylonia, but cite no grounds. Since the sage involved is an amora from Eretz Israel, and places called Bire are known there, it seems much more likely that the references are to one of those. See also Albeck, *Mavo la-Talmudim*, p. 232 and n. 163, and cf. Klein, *Sefer ha-Yishuv*, vol. 1, p. 11, under "בירי."

Kohut, *Arukh ha-Shalem* (1878–1892), vol. 2, p. 9 ("בי ברי")
Krauss, *Qadmoniot ha-Talmud* (1923–1945), vol. 1A, pp. 37, 52
Levy, *Wörterbuch* (1924²), vol. 1, p. 217 ("ביבר II")
Neubauer, *Géographie* (1868), p. 365
Neusner, *History* (1965–1970), vol. 3, p. 279; vol. 5, p. 205
Obermeyer, *Landschaft* (1929), pp. 308–309

Be Dura בי דורא

A. *Source*

Soṭah 46b; Berakhot 31a

רב מרדכי אלויה לרב אשי[1] מהגרוניא[2] ועד בי כיפי[3] ואמרי לה עד בי דורא.[4]

Rav Mordecai escorted Rav Ashi[1] from Hagrunya[2] to Be Kife,[3] or, as some say, to Be Dura.[4]

B. *Proposed Location*

Not far from Hagrunya (q.v., C3 on the Tal. Bab. map) in the direction of Sura.

C. *Identification*

The source relates that according to a certain tradition, Rav Mordecai escorted his master, Rav Ashi,[5] from Hagrunya (q.v.) to Be Dura, rather than to Be Kife (q.v.). It may be deduced from this that Be Dura[6] too was not far from Hagrunya and probably in the direction of Mata Məḥasya (q.v.) which was near Sura and was Rav Ashi's place of residence.
Obermeyer proposed identifying Be Dura with Bādūrāyā west of Baghdad.[7] Although perfectly acceptable from the linguistic point of view, this identi-

[1] The Berakhot parallel has "Rav Shimi b. Ashi" as does *Ein Ya'aqov* for Soṭah. See also Source 13 in the entry for "Babylon" and the notes there.

[2] See the entry for "Hagrunya" for various versions.

[3] See the entry for "Be Kife" for various versions.

[4] The Munich MS has דורת, the Oxford MS has דרדיא, and the Vatican 100 MS has זיראת. For the Berakhot parallel the Munich MS has דייריא, the Oxford MS has דראי, and the Florence MS has דירא. See also Soṭah in the ICIT edition, and *Diq. Sof.* for Berakhot. The *Midrash ha-Gadol* to Genesis version is רב כהנא אלוייה לרב אשי מגרוניא ועד ביקיפי ואמרי לה עד דירא = "Rav Kahana escorted Rav Ashi from Gərunya to Beqife and some say to Dira." (*Midrash ha-Gadol* Genesis 18:16, Margulies ed., p. 303).

[5] The Berakhot parallel has "Rav Shimi b. Ashi," but Rav Mordecai was definitely Rav Ashi's disciple, so that the Soṭah version is more likely (see Albeck, *Mavo la-Talmudim*, pp. 437–438).

[6] For the meaning of the word "Dura" and the many place names it forms part of see the entry for "Dura də-Ra'awata."

[7] Obermeyer, p. 268, and see the entry for Bādūrāyā in Yāqūt.

fication is untenable for two reasons. First of all, Bādūrāyā is too far away from Hagrunya for a sage to have provided a courtesy escort to, and secondly, Mata Məḥasya, the site of the yeshiva Rav Ashi headed, was southeast of Hagrunya, while Baghdad and Bādūrāyā were northwest of it.[8]

BERLINER, *Beiträge* (1883), p. 30
ESHEL, *Yishuvei ha-Yehudim* (1979), p. 56
FUNK, *Monumenta* (1913), pp. 26, 290
HIRSCHENSON, *Sheva Ḥokhmot* (1883), p. 101 "הגרוניא"
JASTROW, *Dictionary* (1950³), p. 289
KOHUT, *Arukh ha-Shalem* (1878–1892), vol. 2, p. 35 "בזתא"
LEVY, *Wörterbuch* (1924²), vol. 1, p. 214
NEUBAUER, *Géographie* (1868), p. 347
OBERMEYER, *Landschaft* (1929), p. 268
ZURI, *Shilton* (1938), pp. 227–228, 242

Be Govar בי גובר

A. *Sources*

1. ʿEruvin 61b

מר יהודה אשכחינהו לבני מברכתא דקא מותבי עירובייהו בבי כנישתא דבי אגובר,[1] אמר להו גוו ביה טפי כי היכי דלישתרי לכו טפי, אמר ליה רבא פלגאה בעירובין לית דחש להא דרבי עקיבא.

Mar Judah found the people of Mavrak̲ta putting their *ʿeruv* in the Be Govar[1] synagogue. He said to them, Put it further in, so that you will be allowed [to walk] further, Rava said to him, Disputer, in regard to *ʿeruv*, no one bothers about Rabbi ʿAqiva's ruling.

2. Taʿanit 26a

. . . והא רב פפא איקלע לבי כנישתא דאבי גובר[2] וגזר תענית וירדו להם גשמים עד חצות ואמר הלל ואחר כך אכלו ושתו, שאני בני מחוזא דשכיחי בהו שכרות.

. . . For Rav Papa happened to be in the synagogue of Be Govar[2] and ordained a fast, and rains fell before noon, and he said *Hallel* and afterwards they ate and drank. The Maḥoza people are different, for drunkenness is common among them.

---

[8] See Eshel, p. 56, in whose opinion Be Dura was near Babylon, to the east, "perhaps on the upper Sura river, that is north of the Dura valley/plain mentioned in Daniel 3:1." The identification does not seem likely because the Book of Daniel, as well as Benjamin of Tudela who is also quoted by Eshel, cannot constitute evidence for the identification of talmudic Be Dura, aside from the fact that the name there is "the plain of Dura" and not Be Dura.

[1] The source has **דבי אגובר**, the Munich MS and Venice printing have **דאבי גובר**, and see *Diq. Sof.* The *She'iltot* has **דאבי גוברי** in *beshallaḥ she'ilta* 48.

[2] The source has **דאבי גובר**, the Munich B MS has **דאבי גבר**, and Rashi in the Pesaro printing has **דאבר גובר**.

3. Megillah 21b

רב פפא איקלע לבי כנישתא דאבי גובר[3] וקרא ראשון ארבעה, ושבחיה[4] רב פפא.

Rav Papa happened to be in the Be Govar[3] synagogue and the first read four [verses], and Rav Papa praised[4] him.

4. Berakhot 50a

רפרם בר פפא איקלע לבי כנישתא דאבי גיבר,[5] קם קרא בספרא ואמר ברכו את ה׳ ואשתיק ולא אמר המבורך אוושו כ״ע ברכו את ה׳ המבורך אמר רבא פתיא אוכמא בהדי פלוגתא למה לך, ועוד הא נהוג עלמא כרבי ישמעאל.

Rafram b. Papa happened to be in the Be Govar[5] synagogue. He rose, read in the Book and said "Bless the Lord" and was silent and did not say ,,who is to be blessed." They all shouted and said, "Bless the blessed Lord." Rava said, You black pot, why should you [intervene] in the dispute, for the world acts like Rabbi Ishmael.

B. *Location*

In the vicinity of Mavrakta (q.v.) near Maḥoza (q.v.) (D 3 on the Tal. Bab. map).

C. *Identification*

Be Govar was near Mavrakta and Maḥoza as appears from Sources 1 and 2. According to Source 1, Be Govar was within the Sabbath walking distance (2,000 cubits) of Mavrakta. The Mavrakta people probably put their *'eruv* in the Be Govar synagogue so as to be able on the Sabbath to go through Be Govar to Maḥoza to hear some sage preach.[6] Obermeyer proposes identifying Be Govar with Nahr Ğaubar[7] but this seems unlikely because the latter is far from Maḥoza,[8] and even Obermeyer himself agrees that Be Govar was in the Maḥoza area.

All the sources mention the Be Govar synagogue. Although that may be a coincidence, it is also possible that the synagogue was an exceptional institution around which the community formed. Govar or Agovar may originally have been the name of a person who founded the synagogue.[9]

---

[3] The source has **דאבי גובר**, the Munich MS has **דבי עסיא**, the R-i-f has **דאבי גזר**, the R-i-f MS has **דאביגבר**.

[4] The British Museum MS of *Seder Rav 'Amram Gaon* has "And Be Govar praised Rav Papa" (Goldschmidt ed., pp. 73–74), and see below.

[5] The source has **דאבי גיבר**, the Munich MS has "to the house of the synagogue head of Abe Govar," and see *Diq. Sof.*

[6] See Obermeyer, pp. 177–178.

[7] Obermeyer, p. 178; Eshel notes only the resemblance to the name Nahr Ğaubar (p. 9).

[8] Cf. e.g. Ṭabarī, vol. 3, p. 451 (= vol. 1, pp. 2169–2170).

[9] Neubauer already has this, p. 358, and see Yudelevitz, *Maḥoza*, pp. 90–91. The same emerges also from the *Seder Rav 'Amram Gaon* MS mentioned in n. 4 above, but that version does not seem likely.

D. *Sages and Be Govar*

The sages referred to in connection with Be Govar are not local, but amoras who happened to go to the Be Govar synagogue. The matters mentioned in the source relating to them are connected with synagogue ritual or religious life, as follows: the community of Sabbath limits (Source 1), the order of prayer on a day a rain fast was ordained and rain fell in the same day (Source 2), the number of Torah verses that should be read on Monday, Thursday and the Sabbath *minḥah* service (Source 3), and the text of the Torah blessing (Source 4).

The points are related to Mar Judah of the third generation of Babylonian amoras, Rafram b. Papa of the fourth, and Rav Papa of the fifth. In Sources 1 and 4 Rava, head of the Maḥoza yeshiva in the fourth generation of Babylonian amoras, comments on things that happened in the Be Govar synagogue and sages who were active there. In Source 1 he decides that Mar Judah's proposal is superfluous and calls him a "controversialist,"[10] and in Source 4 he is critical of the blessing approved by Rafram b. Papa whom he dubs a "black pot," which may be an allusion to the man's complexion.[11]

BERLINER, *Beiträge* (1883), pp. 21–22
ESHEL, *Yishuvei ha-Yehudim* (1979), pp. 8–9
FIEY, *Sumer* 23 (1967): p. 32f.
FUNK, *Juden* (1902–1908), vol. 2, p. 160
FUNK, *Monumenta* (1913), pp. 22, 288
HERZFELD, *Samarra* (1948), p. 15
KOHUT, *Arukh ha-Shalem* (1878–1892), vol. 2, p. 48
LEVY, *Wörterbuch* (1924²), vol. 1, p. 214
NEUBAUER, *Géographie* (1868), p. 358
NEUSNER, *History* (1965–1970), vol. 4, pp. 327–328; vol. 5, pp. 264, 277
OBERMEYER, *Landschaft* (1929), pp. 177–178
PINELES, *Darkah shel Torah* (1861), pp. 27–28
YUDELEVITZ, *Maḥoza* (1947), pp. 90–91

Be Ḥozai בי חוזאי

A. *Sources*

1. Taʿanit 21b

אמרו ליה לשמואל איכא מותנא בי חוזאי, גזר תעניתא, א״ל והא מרחק, אמר ליכא מעברא הכא דפסיק ליה[1] . . . והא אמרו ליה לשמואל איכא מותנא בי חוזאי גזר תעניתא, שאני התם כיון דאיכא שיירתא דלווי ואתיא בהדיה.[2]

---

[10] Cf. Qiddushin 58a (where Rabbah is credited with the epithet).

[11] A number of sages were so nicknamed, and see Brand, *Kelei ha-Ḥeres*, pp. 445–446; cf. also the section on Material Culture on the entry on "Be Mikse."

[1] The Munich MS has וכי מברא פסקו ליה; and see *Diq. Sof.*

[2] The Munich MS has דשכיחי שיירתא דאזלי להתם מילוו בהדייהו ואתו; and see *Diq. Sof.*

They said to him to Samuel, There's a plague in Be Ḥozai, and he ordered a fast. They said to him, But it's far away. He said, There's no crossing here that separates it[1] . . . And they said to him to Samuel, There's a plague in Be Ḥozai, and he ordered a fast . . . because there are caravans it attaches to and comes with.[2]

2. Bava Qamma 112b

. . . ואי מירחק ואיכא קרובים אי נמי איכא שיירתא דאזלי ואתו התם משהינן ליה תריסר ירחי שתא עד דאזלא ואתי שיירתא, כי הא דרבינא שהא למר אחא[3] תריסר ירחי שתא עד דאזלא ואתייא שיירתא מבי חוזאי.

. . . And if he's far and he has relatives, and even if there are caravans that go and come there, we leave him [the lender who has not recovered his debt and seeks to posses his debtor's property] twelve months until a caravan goes and comes. Just as Ravina made Mar Aḥa[3] stay twelve months till a caravan went to Be Ḥozai and returned.

3. Pesaḥim 50b

בני חוזאי[4] נהגי דמפרשי חלה מארוזא, אתו ואמרו ליה לרב יוסף, אמר להו ניכלה זר באפייהו[5] . . .

The people of Ḥozai[4] used to set aside a *ḥallah* (the priests' share of dough) made of rice. They came and told Rav Joseph. He said to them, Let a non-priest eat it in their presence[5] . . .

4. Shabbat 51b

לוי שדר זוזי לבי חוזאי למיזבן ליה חמרא לובא, צרו שדרו ליה שערי, למימר דניגרי דחמרא שערי.

Levi sent money to Be Ḥozai to buy him a Libyan ass. They packed and sent him some barley, meaning, an ass's steps are [dependent on] barley.

5. Bava Qamma 104b; Bava Metzi'a 46a; Bava Batra 77b, 150b

כי הא דרב פפא הוה מסיק[6] תריסר אלפי זוזי בי חוזאי, אקנינהו ניהליה לרב שמואל בר אבא[7] אגב אסיפא דביתיה, כי אתא נפק לאפיה עד תואך[8].

As in the case when Rav Papa was owed[6] twelve thousand *zuz* [in] Be Ḥozai, transferred them to Rav Samuel b. Abba[7] by means of the threshold of his house. When he (Samuel) came, he went out to Tawaḵ[8] to meet him.

---

[3] The Munich MS has "Mar Aḥa b. Sama"; and see *Diq. Sof.*

[4] The Munich B MS has "the people of Be Ḥozai"; and see *Diq. Sof.*

[5] The Munich MS has ניכלינהו באנפייהו; and see *Diq. Sof.*

[6] The parallels have הוו ליה (= he had).

[7] The Munich MS and the parallels have "Rav Samuel b. Aḥa" which seems more likely; and see the section below on Sages and Be Ḥozai.

[8] For variations see the entry on "Tawaḵ."

6. Ketubot 80a

ההיא איתתא דנפלו לה ארבע מאה זוזי בי חוזאי,[9] אזיל גברא אפיק שית מאה אייתי ארבע מאה, בהדי דקאתי איצטריך ליה חד זוזא ושקל מנייהו, אתא לקמיה דר׳ אמי,[10] א״ל מה שהוציא הוציא ומה שאכל אכל . . .

The woman who acquired four hundred *zuz* in Be Ḥozai,[9] her husband spent six hundred, brought back [the] four hundred. On his way back, he needed one *zuz* and took from them. He came before Rabbi Ammi[10] who said to him, What he spent he spent and what he ate he ate . . .

7. Ketubot 85a

אבימי בריה דרבי אבהו הוו מסקי ביה זוזי בי חוזאי, שדרינהו ביד חמא בריה דרבה בר אבהו,[11] אזל פרעינהו.

Avimi the son of Rabbi Abbahu owed money [in] Be Ḥozai. He sent it with Ḥama b. Rabbah b. Abbahu,[11] who went and paid it.

8. Ketubot 27b; Bava Metziʿa 39b

כי הא דמרי בר איסק, ואמרי לה חנא בר איסק,[12] אתא ליה אחא מבי חוזאה,[13] א״ל פלוג לי בנכסי דאבא, א״ל לא ידענא לך, אתא לקמיה דרב חסדא . . .

As in the case of Mari b. Isaq, and some say Ḥana b. Isaq,[12] a brother from Be Ḥozai[13] came to him and said, Share the property of father with me. He said to him, I don't know you. He came before Rav Ḥisda . . .

9. Ketubot 111a

ההוא גברא דנפלה ליה יבמה בי חוזאה,[14] אתא לקמיה דר׳ חנינא, א״ל מהו למיחת וליבמה, א״ל אחיו נשא כותית ומת ברוך המקום שהרגו והוא ירד אחריו.

The man who had a brother's widow without issue [in] Be Ḥozai[14] came before Rabbi Ḥanina, and asked whether to go down there and marry her. He replied, His brother married a Cuthean (a Gentile) and died, blessed be the Omnipresent who killed him, and this one would go down after him.

---

9 The Munich MS has בי חזאי, and see Ketubot in the ICIT edition.

10 The Munich and Vatican 487 MSS have "Rabbi Assi" but they too have "Rabbi Ammi" later in the passage.

11 The Vatican 113 and Leningrad MSS have "Rava bar Avuha", and see Ketubot in the ICIT edition.

12 The Bava Metziʿa parallel and some of the MSS do not have "and some say Ḥana b. Isaq."

13 The source has בי חוזאה but the Bava Metziʿa parallel and some of the MSS have "Be Ḥozai."

14 The source has בי חוזאה but some of the MSS have "Be Ḥozai." Cf. *Midrash ha-Gadol* to Leviticus 25:38 (Steinsalz ed., p. 713): ההוא גברא דנפלא ליה יבמה בי הוזאי אתא לקמיה דרבי חנינה אמר ליה מהוא למנחת יבומה. אמר ליה אחיך נשא גויה, ברוך המקום שהרגו, ואתה תרד אחריו.

10. Giṭṭin 89a

ההיא דנפק עלה קלא דאיקדשה לבר בי רב, אתייה רב חמא לאבוה אמר ליה אימא לי היכי הוה עובדא, אמר ליה על תנאי קדיש אדעתא דלא אזיל לבי חוזאי[15] ואזל . . .

The one who was reported to have become betrothed to a rabbinical student, Rav Ḥama sent for his father and said to him, Tell me what happened. He told him he arranged the betrothal on condition he would not go to Be Ḥozai[15] and he went . . .

11. Ḥullin 45b

רב דימי בר יצחק[16] הוה קא בעי למיזל לבי חוזאי,[17] אתא לקמיה דרבי[18] יהודה אמר ליה ליחוי לי מר בין הפרשות היכא, א״ל זיל אייתי לי גדי ואחוי לך.

Rav Dimi b. Isaac[16] wanted to go to Be Ḥozai.[17] He came before Rabbi[18] Judah and said to him, Will my master show me where [the place] between the "ramifications" is? He said to him, Bring me a kid and I will show you.

12. Nedarim 22a

עולא במיסקיה לארעא דישראל איתלוו ליה תרין בני חוזאי בהדיה, קם חד שחטיה לחבריה . . .

When ʿUlla went to Eretz Israel, two residents of Ḥozai accompanied him; one rose and slaughtered his friend . . .

13. Bava Metziʿa 97a

מרימר בר חנינא[19] אוגר כודנייתא בי חוזאי, נפק לדלויי טעונה בהדייהו, פשעו בה ומית, אתו לקמיה דרבא חייבינהו.

Maremar b. Ḥanina[19] rented his mule [to residents of] Be Ḥozai. He went out to load it with them, they mistreated it and it died. They came before Rava; he held them liable.

14. Taʿanit 22a

ר׳ ברוקא[20] חוזאה הוה שכיח בשוקא דבי לפט.[21]

Rabbi Beroqa[20] Ḥoza'a was in the market at Be Lapaṭ.[21]

---

[15] The Vatican 140 MS has לבי חיוואי.

[16] The MSS have "Rav Dimi b. Joseph;" and see *Diq. Sof.*, n. ו. But the Munich MS has "Rav Dimi b. Isaac" like the printing.

[17] The Soncino printing has לבי חיואי.

[18] All the MSS have "Rav Judah" which seems more correct; and see *Diq. Sof.*

[19] The Munich MS has "Mar b. Ḥanina"; for other variations see *Diq. Sof.*

[20] The Munich MS has "Rav Beroqa"; and see *Diq. Sof.*

[21] For variations see the entry on "Be Lapaṭ." See there also for details of what happened to Rabbi Beroqa in the Be Lapaṭ market.

15. Mo'ed Qaṭan 20a

רב חנינא[22] אתיא ליה שמועה דאבוה מבי חוזאי, אתא לקמיה דרב חסדא, אמר ליה שמועה רחוקה אינה נוהגת אלא יום אחד. רב נתן בר אמי אתא ליה שמועה דאימיה מבי חוזאי, אתא לקמיה דרבא, אמר ליה הרי אמרו שמועה רחוקה אינה נוהגת אלא יום אחד בלבד.

Rav Ḥanina[22] heard news of [the death of] his father in Be Ḥozai. He came before Rav Ḥisda; he said, In distant news [mourning] is customary for only one day. Rav Nathan b. Ammi heard news of [the death of] his mother at Be Ḥozai. He came before Rava; he said to him, But they said that in distant news [mourning] is customary for only one day.

16. Ḥullin 95b

רב חנינא חוזאה איתבד ליה גבא דבשרא, אתא לקמיה דרב נחמן, א"ל אית לך סימנא בגויה, אמר ליה לא, אית לך טביעות עינא בגויה, אמר ליה אין, אם כן זיל שקול.

Rav Ḥanina Ḥoza'a lost [and located] a side of meat. He came before Rav Naḥman. He said to him, Do you have a sign on it? He said, No. Do you recognize it? He said, Yes. If you do, go take it.

17. Shabbat 130b

אמר ליה רב חנינא חוזאה[23] לרבה ...

Rav Ḥanina Ḥoza'a[23] said to Rabbah ...

18. Yevamot 111b[24]

אמר רבי חנינא חוזאה ...

Rabbi Ḥanina Ḥoza'a said ...

19. Niddah 5b

והא כי אתא אבימי[25] מבי חוזאי אתא ואייתי מתניתא בידיה מעת לעת שבנדה משכבה ומושבה כמגעה ... והא אבימי מבי חוזאי מתניתא קאמר ...

For when Avimi[25] from Be Ḥozai came, he came and brought a *baraita* that during the twenty-four hours preceding the discovery of her menstrual flow, a woman's bed and seat are [as unclean] as the object she touches ... but Avimi of Be Ḥozai said a *baraita* ...

20. Ḥullin 68b

והא כי אתא אבימי מבי חוזאי אתא ואייתי מתניתא בידיה פרסה החזיר אכול, פרסות החזיר אכול.

---

[22] The Munich MS has "Rav Ḥinena Ḥoza'a," the Munich B MS has "Rabbi Ḥanina Ḥoza'a"; and see *Diq. Sof.*

[23] The Munich MS has just "Rav Ḥinena"; the Oxford MS has "Rav Ḥinena Ḥozna'a said to Rav."

[24] Rav/Rabbi Ḥanina Ḥoza'a is quoted also in 'Eruvin 32a (and its parallels: Pesaḥim 9a, 'Avodah Zarah 41b, Niddah 15b) and in Bava Metzi'a 88a.

[25] A Geniza fragment has "Avdimi of Be Ḥozai" but later in the passage "Avimi of Be Ḥozai" as well; and see *Ginzei Talmud*, vol. 2, p. 153.

For when Avimi from Be Ḥozai came, he brought with him a *baraita*: If it withdrew one hoof within you may eat, if it withdrew two hoofs within you may eat.

21. Giṭṭin 50a

והתני אברם חוזאה אין נפרעין מנכסי יתומים אלא מן הזיבורית ואפילו הן ניזקין.

Abram Ḥoza'a taught that, except for the poorest land, orphans' property cannot be claimed against even for damages.

22. Giṭṭin 7a

א"ל רב הונא בר נתן לרב אשי מאי דכתיב "קינה ודימונה ועדעדה" . . . רב אחא מבי חוזאה[26] אמר בה הכי כל מי שיש לו צעקת לגימא על חבירו ודומם שוכן בסנה עושה לו דין.

Rav Huna b. Nathan said to Rav Ashi, What is the meaning of "Qinah, Dimonah, ʿAdʿadah" (Jos. 15:22) . . . Rav Aḥa of Be Ḥozai[26] said thus, Anyone who has a complaint against his fellow regarding his livelihood and keeps quiet, the Dweller in the bush provides justice for him.

23. Betzah 15b–16a

תני רב תחליפא אחוה דרבנאי חוזאה[27] כל מזונותיו של אדם קצובים לו מראש השנה ועד יום הכפורים, חוץ מהוצאת שבתות והוצאת י"ט והוצאת בניו לתלמוד תורה שאם פחת פוחתין לו ואם הוסיף מוסיפין לו.

Rav Taḥlifa, the brother of Rabbannai Ḥoza'a[27] taught, All a man's sustenance is fixed between the New Year and the Day of Atonement, except for expenditures for Sabbaths and holidays and the instruction of his children in the law. For if he reduced these, he is reduced [in income] and if he increased them, he is increased.

24. Strabo XV 3,10,11

See Source 6 in the entry on "Susa."

B. *Location*

The Ḫūzistān district of modern Iran, east of southern Iraq[28] (on Bab. Env. map).

---

[26] The Vatican 140 and Vatican 127 MS have "Rav Aḥai." The source has מבי חוזאה; but the Munich and Vatican 127 MSS have מבי חוזאי. *Iggeret Rav Sherira Gaon* has ורב אחא(י) מבי ח(א)תים . . . ובי ח(א)תים היא עיר בסביבי נהרדעא (Lewin ed., p. 70). Cf. also *Otzar ha-Geonim* for Giṭṭin, *ha-Perushim*, p. 218.

[27] The Munich MS has "Rabbannai Ḥoza'a taught"; and see *Diq. Sof.*

[28] See Obermeyer, p. 204ff.; Eshel, pp. 58–59. On Ḫūzistān see Yāqūt, *ar-Rauḍ al-miʿṭār* and *Marāṣid*; see also Yāqūt, *ar-Rauḍ al-miʿṭār*, *Marāṣid* and Bakrī, s.v. "Ahwāz"; Streck, *EI*[1], s.v. "Ahwāz"; Huart, *ibid.*, s.v. "Khūzistān"; Savory, *EI*[2], s.v. "Khūzistān"; *BGA*, passim; Mustaufī, vol. 2, pp. 107–110, and especially the detailed description in Muqaddasī, pp. 402–420; and see Schwarz, *Iran im Mittelalter*, Index (Ahwāz, Ḫūzistān). See also the entries on "Be Lapaṭ" and "Hurmiz Ardəšir."

C. *Economy*

The hot climate of Ḫūzistān made irrigation necessary, but as long as water was supplied, the land produced a great variety of crops (see the entry on "Šuštar"), such as cereals, grapes, rice, dates and sesame.[29] It was also known for the excellent sugar produced in Ǧundaisābūr[30] (see the entry on "Be Lapaṭ"). Oil producing today, the region provided its inhabitants even in antiquity with liquid asphalt (naphtha).[31] Coins indicate that horses were bred there,[32] and there is evidence that bronze statues were produced for export in the Hellenistic town of Susa (q.v.) in the district.[33]

Susa was an important road station. The "royal road" described by Herodotus (V 52) linked it with Sardis in Asia Minor, and other roads led westwards to Babylon and Seleucia and northwards to Ecbatana. Southeastwards roads branched to Kāzarūn and Fīrūzābād on the one hand, and to Persepolis and Pasargadae on the other. From Persepolis the trade continued overland to Kandahar and the lower Indus. As the Eulaeus was navigable as far as Susa,[34] the Persian Gulf was also accessible.

The great number of coins found at Susa provide valuable insights into the economic history of the region. Especially remarkable are the quantities of bronze coins from Seleucia and Charax found at the Susa excavations.[35] They could have been brought to Susa by Seleucians coming there to buy local products and goods in transit, most likely from the Persian Gulf, or overland through Persepolis. Le Rider in fact assumes that part of the traffic from the Gulf to Seleucia passed through Susa, and as the Seleucian coins found there are not offset by Susa coins found at Seleucia, presumably the Seleucians traveled to Susa to buy their goods. The relative number of such coins are thus by and large thought to reflect the intensity of this traffic throughout the period discussed. The Seleucian coins found at Susa, in other words, serve

---

[29] Le Rider, *Suse*, pp. 271–272; Arrian, *de Indica* 42,5; Strabo, Source 24; Diodorus XIX 13, 6; on coins see Le Rider, *Suse*, nos. 140, 163, 175, 186.

[30] "... To the west it is bordered by the Dklat (Tigris) which separates Babylonia from Ḫūzistān, to the south by the Persian Gulf and to the north by Asorestan. It has three rivers; it has five Ostane, i.e. provinces, in which the following cities are: Ormšir, Sulura, Šōš, which is mentioned by Daniel, Gundir-Šapuh, where excellent sugar is made ... It has three rivers, five towns, i.e. Gundir-Šapuh where excellent sugar is made ..." (Ptolemy, in Moses of Khorene (31, 37); see Marquart ed., *Ērānšahr*).

[31] Strabo, XVI 1, 15; Pliny, *Natural History*, VI 26, 99.

[32] And perhaps asses as well (see source 4). See Le Rider, *Suse*, Index, p. 465. For Susiane as a horse-breeding country, see Herzfeld, *The Persian Empire*, pp. 1–2, 8, 11.

[33] Le Rider, *Suse*, p. 272.

[34] Pliny, *Natural History*, VI 26, 99, on the navigability of the river; for the roads around Susa see Herzfeld, *op.cit.* (in n. 32 above), pp. 11, 178; Le Rider, *Suse*, pp. 267–271; Tarn, *The Greeks*, p. 29f.

[35] Le Rider, *Suse*, pp. 446–448, gives a resume of conclusions based on the detailed analysis elsewhere in his book.

to delineate the role of Susa as an intermediary in the eastern trade. The first Seleucid rulers are hardly represented. Since under Antiochus III the situation changed completely, especially from 205/4 B.C. on, Le Rider infers that Antiochus III succeeded in stimulating caravan trade on an unprecedented scale (cf. the entries on "Mesene" and "Mašmahig"). This activity seems to have diminished under Seleucus IV and Antiochus IV and ceased almost completely thereafter. It was resumed under Mithridates II at the beginning of the first century B.C., on a scale comparable to that under Seleucus IV and Antiochus IV, and lasted till the final quarter of the first century B.C. For the years up to the beginning of the second century A.D. a total of 152 isolated Seleucian coins have been found (compared with 1281 Seleucian coins altogether and 1519 coins struck at Susa itself for the whole period of activity of that mint). Thereafter numbers again decline.

Shapur II settled captives in the H̱ūzistān region, in the new town of Erānšahr-Šāpūr (al-Karẖa, modern Ivān-e Karẖa)[36] and the re-founded Susa. The Roman captives carried out various engineering works, some of which have been studied, in the area. They built bridges—one at Dezfūl, a second across the Karẖe at Pā-ye Pul, and a third across the Karun, near Šuštar—and constructed several dams at Šuštar as well.[37]

The ramified economy of H̱ūzistān described explains the numerous commercial contacts between that district and the Jewish population centers in Babylonia, far to the north.

Source 3 suggests that Be Ḥozai people ate rice bread,[38] and indeed Arab geographers too have noted the baking of bread from rice in the H̱ūzistān district.[39] Yāqūt reports that the residents of the rural district of Kaskar (see the entry for "Kaškar") in the Wāsiṭ region ate such food as well.[40] Thus Rav Ashi's indication of places where the staple food was rice (cited later in the Pesaḥim passage) is based on the actual practice in Be Ḥozai.[41]

---

[36] For the name and identification see Nöldeke, *Perser und Araber*, p. 57, cf. Altheim & Stiehl, *Ein asiatischer Staat*, p. 28–29. The town has been excavated by Ghirshman, *Campagnes*, vol. 1 (1952), pp. 10–12; see also vanden Berghe, *Archéologie de l'Iran ancien*, p. 67. The function of this town was among others to serve as base of operations against the Arabs of southern Iraq. It was a rectangular, strongly fortified town. Bīšapūr was established further southeast, in the region of Šīrāz.

[37] Dieulafoy, *L'art antique de la Perse*, vol. 5, pp. 105–109, Pls. X, XI (bridge near Dezfūl); *ibid.*, vol. 1, p. 3 and vol. 5, p. 60, Pl. XII (bridge near Šuštar); Stein, *Old Routes of Western Iran*, pp. 171–174 (bridge near Pā-ye Pul); see also vanden Berghe, *loc. cit.* (in n. 36 above). The connection with captives taken by Shapur I and his victory over Valerian in 260 is proven by Ṭabarī's remarks (vol. 2, p. 47 [= vol. 1, p. 827]), and by the present name of the dam near Šuštar: Bend-e Kaiser (= Caesar's dam).

[38] See Krauss, *Qadmoniot ha-Talmud*, vol. 1B, p. 188; Newman, *Agricultural Life*, p. 90.

[39] See Muqaddasī, p. 416; and see Obermeyer, p. 207.

[40] See Yāqūt, s.v. "H̱ūzistān."

[41] See Pesaḥim 51a.

D. *Connections with Be Ḥozai*

The relatively large number of sources in talmudic literature referring to Be Ḥozai testify to the close ties between the areas of dense Jewish settlement in Babylonia and the Jews living in the Be Ḥozai district. These ties are indicated by evidence on caravans (Sources 1 and 2), commercial relations (Source 4), financial transactions (Sources 5, 6 and 7), family connections (Sources 8, 9 and 15) and sages and other people from Be Ḥozai arriving in the centers of concentrated Jewish inhabitation in Babylonia (Sources 13, 15–23, and see the section below on Sages and Be Ḥozai).
Some scholars have deduced from Source 2 that it took a year for a caravan to go from Jewish Babylonia to Be Ḥozai and back.[42] Obermeyer already noted that the journey would, in his opinion, require no more than three weeks.[43] The statement in Source 2 can be explained in various ways, such as that at least one caravan a year could be counted on to leave for Be Ḥozai and return to Mata Məḥasya (q.v.) where Ravina was.
That there were also ties between Be Ḥozai and Eretz Israel emerges from Sources 19 and 20 reporting that Avimi brought *baraitot* from Be Ḥozai to the Babylonian yeshivas. For that meant that tannaitic traditions unknown in Babylonia reached Be Ḥozai from Eretz Israel. Source 12 tells of two men from Be Ḥozai who in fact joined ʿUlla, a *naḥota*,[44] on one of his journeys to Eretz Israel.

E. *Sages and Be Ḥozai*

The sources testify to a number of sages who were active in Be Ḥozai, went from there to the Babylonian yeshivas, or from the mainly Jewish part of Babylonia to Be Ḥozai. Rav Beroqa (see n. 20) of Be Ḥozai is reported in Source 14 in the market of Be Lapaṭ (q.v.), one of the main towns of Be Ḥozai.[45]
Rav Ḥanina of Be Ḥozai, of the third generation of Babylonian amoras, asks Rav Ḥisda in Source 16 how he should observe the mourning ceremony upon receipt of the news of his father's death in Be Ḥozai. He also checks with Rav Naḥman in Source 16 on whether he is permitted to repossess a lost item that he recognizes as his but cannot point to any signs it can be identified by. Other problems and decisions of Rav Ḥanina's on halakhic matters appear in Sources 17, 18 and n. 24.

---

[42] Berliner, p. 35; Eshel, p. 59 and others. See Rashi for Shabbat 51b, s. v. "צרו שדרו ליה שערי"; and Rav Hai Gaon in *Otzar ha-Geonim* for Bava Qamma, *ha-Teshuvot*, p. 96. In quotations from the Talmud Rav Hai Gaon calls the place בי הוזאי.

[43] Obermeyer, pp. 206–207.

[44] The *naḥote* were amoras of Eretz Israel whose task was to travel constantly between that country and Babylonia in order to carry the law of Eretz Israel abroad.

[45] For details of the case see the entry on "Be Lapaṭ."

Avimi of Be Ḥozai, of the fourth generation of Babylonian amoras, is twice reported as bearing *baraitot* from Be Ḥozai to the Babylonian yeshivas (and see above). The *baraitot* are dealt with by Rava in the continuation of Source 19, and by Rav Naḥman b. Isaac in that of Source 20. Source 21 mentions Abram of Be Ḥozai as disagreeing with Rava, head of the Maḥoza yeshiva in the fourth generation of Babylonian amoras. Rav Nathan b. Ammi in Source 15, asks how to observe mourning upon hearing of his mother's death in Be Ḥozai.

Rav Dimi b. Isaac (or b. Joseph, see n. 16) is mentioned in Source 11 as about to go to Be Ḥozai, and applying to Rav Judah, head of the Pumbədita yeshiva in the second generation of Babylonian amoras, for guidance in matters of the fitness of food. Rav Samuel b. Aḥa (see n. 7) of the fifth generation of Babylonian amoras is reported in Source 5 as setting out for Be Ḥozai and collecting money there as agent for Rav Papa.[46]

Source 22 mentions Rav Aḥa of Be Ḥozai interpreting a verse from the Book of Joshua, but Rav Sherira Gaon refers to him as Rav Aḥa of Be Ḥatim (see n. 26), and describes him as a savora. Source 23 has Rav Taḥlifa, the brother of Rabbannai Ḥoza'a, quoting a *baraita*, but according to the Munich MS it was Rabbannai himself who quoted it.[47]

Adams, *Science* 136 (1962): 109–122
Beer, *Amora'ei Bavel* (1974), pp. 197–198
Berliner, *Beiträge* (1883), pp. 35–36
Eshel, *Yishuvei ha-Yehudim* (1979), pp. 58–59
Funk, *Juden* (1902–1908), vol. 2, p. 159
Funk, *Monumenta* (1913), pp. 34, 292–293
Graetz, *Geschichte* (1908⁴), vol. 4, pp. 248–250
Herzfeld, *The Persian Empire* (1968), pp. 1–2, 8, 11, 178
Hirschenson, *Sheva Ḥokhmot* (1883), pp. 68–69
Huart, *EI*¹, s.v. "Khūzistān"
Jastrow, *Dictionary* (1950³), p. 430
Kohut, *Arukh ha-Shalem* (1878–1892), vol. 2, p. 49; vol. 3, p. 356; *Tosefot* (1937) p. 85
Krauss, *Qadmoniot ha-Talmud* (1923–1945), vol. 1, pp. 76, 124
Krauss, *Paras we-Romi* (1948), p. 26
Le Rider, *Suse* (1965), pp. 267–272, 446–448
Levy, *Wörterbuch* (1924²), vol. 1, p. 214
Neubauer, *Géographie* (1968), p. 390
Newman, *Agricultural Life* (1932), pp. 90, 126
Markwart, *Catalogue* (1931), pp. 95–96
Obermeyer, *Landschaft* (1929), pp. 204–209, passim
Rapoport, *Kerem Chemed* 5 (1841): pp. 218–229
Rapoport, *Erekh Millin* (1914), vol. 2, pp. 179–181
Savory, *EI*², s.v. "Khūzistān"
Tarn, *The Greeks* (1950), p. 29f.
Wenke, *Mesopotamia* 10–11 (1975–1976): 31–221

[46] See Beer, *Amora'ei Bavel*, pp. 197–198.

[47] See n. 27. According to *Aggadot ha-Talmud*, Rav Taḥlifa was the father of Rabbannai Ḥoza'a; and see *Diq. Sof.*

Be Katil בי כתיל

A. *Sources*

1. Betzah 23a

דרש רב גביהא מבי כתיל אפתחא דבי ריש גלותא קטורא שרי, אמר ליה [1] אמימר מאי קטורא ... אמר ליה רב אשי ... איכא דאמרי אמר ליה אמימר ... אמר רב אשי אנא אמריתה נהליה ...

Rav Geviha from Be Katil preached at the gate of the Exilarch's house, *Qiṭṭura* is allowed [on a festival]. Ameimar said to him,[1] What is *Qiṭṭura*? ... Rav Ashi said to him ... some say Ameimar said to him ... Rav Ashi said, I said it about him ...

2. Bava Batra 83a (twice); Menaḥot 8a; Ḥullin 64b

אמר ליה רב גביהה מבי כתיל לרב אשי ...

Rav Geviha from Be Katil said to him to Rav Ashi ...

3. Meʿilah 10a

אמר רב גביהא דבי כתיל [2] לרב אשי ...

Rav Geviha of[2] Be Katil said to Rav Ashi ...

4. Yevamot 60a; Ḥullin 26b

אזל רב גביהה מבי כתיל אמרה לשמעתא קמיה דרב אשי ...

Rav Geviha from Be Katil went and issued a halakhah before Rav Ashi ...

5. Bava Qamma 82a

רב גביהה מבי כתיל מתני לה בהדיא ...

Rav Geviha from Be Katil taught it specifically ...

6. ʿAvodah Zarah 22a

רב גביהה מבי כתיל אמר ...

Rav Geviha from Be Katil said ...

B. *Location*

None can be proposed due to insufficient data.

C. *Attempts at Identification*

On the basis of linguistic similarity, Obermeyer sought to connect Be Katil with the Qāṭūl canal.[3] There were three canals by that name starting from the

---

[1] The Munich MS has "Ameimar said" (without "to him") and thereafter as well.
[2] The Munich MS has "from."
[3] Obermeyer, pp. 143–144.

east bank of the Tigris near Sāmarrā, and one was actually called al-Qāṭūl al-Yahūdī.[4]

The proposal does not bear critical examination. For one, while the name al-Qāṭūl al-Yahūdī indicates that at some time or other Jews lived in the vicinity of that canal, all three canals were a considerable distance from the centers of Jewish settlement. Moreover, although the absence of the "Be" element in the Arabic name, the fact that one applies to a settlement and the other to a canal, and the substitution of q-ṭ for k-t can be accounted for, in Arabic the *fa'īl* form is much more common than the *fā'ūl* form, so that a shift from the former to the latter is not likely.

D. *Sages and Be Katil*

All references to Be Katil are connected with Rav Geviha of Be Katil. In most of them that sage appears in halakhic discussion before Rav Ashi who was the head of the yeshiva at Mata Məḥasya (q.v.) in the sixth generation of Babylonian amoras. The contents of the passages referred to indicate that Rav Geviha took part in Rav Ashi's work of redacting the Babylonian Talmud. Source 1 has Rav Geviha preaching at the gate of the Exilarch's house on a topic connected with festival rules while Rav Ashi and Ameimar consider his remarks. This reflects the custom of the great amoras of gathering at the Exilarch's home, apparently on holidays, to deal there with halakhic matters.[5]

According to Rav Sherira Gaon, Rav Geviha of Be Katil headed the yeshiva at Pumbədita (q.v.) and died in 432.[6] At that time, the Pumbədita yeshiva was subordinate to the one at Mata Məḥasya, and that would fit in with the connection between Rav Geviha and Rav Ashi.

BEER, *Rashut ha-Golah* (1970), p. 80
BERLINER, *Beiträge* (1883), p. 38
ESHEL, *Yishuvei ha-Yehudim* (1979), pp. 65–66
FUNK, *Juden* (1902–1908), vol. 2, p. 102
KOHUT, *Arukh ha-Shalem* (1878–1892), vol. 2, p. 50
LEVY, *Wörterbuch* (1924²), vol. 1, p. 215
NEUBAUER, *Géographie* (1868), p. 388
OBERMEYER, *Landschaft* (1929), pp. 143–144

[4] On these canals, see Yāqūt, the entry for "al-Qāṭūl"; Suhrāb, p. 127; Le Strange, "Ibn Serapion," p. 19. On al-Qāṭūl al-Yahūdī see Suhrāb, p. 128; Le Strange, "Ibn Serapion," pp. 19–20, 267.

[5] See Funk, *Juden*, vol. 2, p. 102; Beer, *Rashut ha-Golah*, p. 80.

[6] *Iggeret Rav Sherira Gaon*, Lewin ed., p. 96, and see the variants there.

Be Kife בי כיפי

A. *Sources*

1. Soṭah 46b; Berakhot 31a

רב מרדכי אלויה לרב אשי[1] מהגרוניא[2] ועד בי כיפי[3] ואמרי לה עד בי דורא.[4]

Rav Mordecai escorted Rav Ashi[1] from Hagrunya[2] to Be Kife[3] or, as some say, to Be Dura.[4]

2. Bava Batra 24a

הנהו זיקי דחמרא דאשתכחן בי קופאי,[5] שרנהו רבא.

The wineskins that were found in Be Qufai[5] were allowed by Rava.

B. *Proposed Location*

Not far from Hagrunya (q.v., C 3 on the Tal. Bab. map) in the direction of Sura.

C. *Identification*

Source 1 says that Rav Mordecai accompanied Rav Ashi,[6] his master, from Hagrunya (q.v.) to Be Kife. Consequently Be Kife was probably not far from Hagrunya and in the direction of Mata Məḥasya (q.v.; near Sura) where Rav Ashi resided.

Obermeyer proposed identifying Be Kife with ʿAqr Qūf which according to Yāqūt (q.v.) was four parasangs west of Baghdad.[7] That identification is untenable for two reasons: a) the distance between ʿAqr Qūf and Hagrunya is too great to justify a purely courtesy escort, and b) Mata Məḥasya, the site of Rav Ashi's yeshiva, was southeast of Hagrunya, so there would be no sense in Rav Mordecai's escorting him northeast toward Baghdad.[8]

---

[1] The Berakhot parallel has "Rav Shimi b. Ashi," as does *Ein Yaʿaqov* for Soṭah; see also the entry for "Babylon", Source 13 and the notes there.

[2] For the various versions see "Hagrunya".

[3] The Oxford MS and *Ein Yaʿaqov* have "*Be Qifai*" as does the Florence MS for Berakhot; The Vatican 110 MS has קיפאי; The Munich MS for Berakhot has בי קופאי (Be Qufai); and see Soṭah, ICIT ed., and *Diq. Sof.* for Berakhot. The *Midrash ha-Gadol* to Genesis version is רב כהנא אלוייה לרב אשי מגרוניא ועד ביקיפי ואמרי לה עד דירא (= Rav Kahana escorted Rav Ashi from Gərunya to Beqife [the MSS have Be Qife] and some say to Dira [*Midrash ha-Gadol* to Genesis 18:16, Margulies ed., p. 303]).

[4] See "Be Dura" for the various versions.

[5] The Florence MS has בי קפאי, the *Arukh* has בי קיפאי.

[6] Although the Berakhot parallel has Rav Shimi b. Ashi, Rav Mordecai was definitely Rav Ashi's disciple, so that the Soṭah version is preferable (see Albeck, *Mavo la-Talmudim*, pp. 437–438).

[7] Obermeyer, pp. 267–268.

[8] See also the entry for "Be Dura."

D. *Sages and Be Kife*

Source 2 testifies that Rava, head of the Maḥoza yeshiva in the fourth generation of Babylonian amoras, allows drinking from the wineskins found in Be Qufai; the place should apparently be identified with Be Kife, especially since some manuscripts of Source 1 too have Be Qufai.[9] The absence of suspicion that the wine might be libation wine indicates that the Be Kife people, at least those who dealt in wine, were Jews.[10]

Beer, *Amora'ei Bavel* (1974), p. 169
Berliner, *Beiträge* (1883), p. 38
Eshel, *Yishuvei ha-Yehudim* (1979), pp. 62–63
Funk, *Juden* (1902–1908), vol. 2, p. 156
Funk, *Monumenta* (1913), p. 26
Hirschenson, *Sheva Ḥokhmot* (1883), pp. 70, 101 "הגרוניא"
Jastrow, *Dictionary* (1950³), p. 635
Kohut, *Arukh ha-Shalem* (1878–1892), vol. 2, p. 50; vol. 7, pp. 157–158 "קפאי"
Levy, *Wörterbuch* (1924²), vol. 1, p. 215
Neubauer, *Géographie* (1868), p. 347
Obermeyer, *Landschaft* (1929), pp. 267–268

Be Kube בי כובי

A. *Sources*

1. Qiddushin 70b

אמר רב יוסף, האי בי כובי דפומבדיתא כולם דעבדי.

Rav Joseph said, That Be Kube [in the vicinity] of Pumbədita, all of them are from slaves.

2. Giṭṭin 4a

ואמר רבה בר בר חנה, לדידי חזי לי ההוא אתרא והוי כמבי כובי לפומבדיתא.

And Rabbah b. Bar Ḥana said, I myself saw the place and it was as [far as] from Be Kube to Pumbədita.

3. Sukkah 26b

אמר רב אסור לאדם לישן ביום יותר משינת הסוס . . . אביי הוה ניים כדמעייל [1] מפומבדיתא לבי כובי, קרי עליה רב יוסף, "עד מתי עצל תשכב מתי תקום משנתך".

---

[9] That is the version in the Munich MS of Berakhot, and see n. 3. It is also possible that "Be Qufai" is not a place name at all, and means simply "among the vines" (as Rashi says) or is the name of a family (cf. Yevamot 15b: ומשפחת בית קופאי מבן מקושש = and the family of the house of Qufai of Ben Meqoshesh); and see in *Arukh ha-Shalem*, vol. 7, pp. 156–158, the entries for "קף 10" and "קפאי."

[10] The Talmud there explains that Rava, who was usually strict in regard to wines of unknown provenance as they might be libation wines, in this case allowed the wine because דרובא דשפוכאי ישראל נינהו, that is, most of the people who poured the wine from the barrels into the skins were Jews; and see the entire passage in the Talmud. See also Beer, *Amora'ei Bavel*, p. 169, n. 43.

[1] The source has כדמעייל; the Munich B MS has כדמיזל (= going) rather than "going up." See also *Diq. Sof.*

Rav said, A man must not sleep by day more than the sleep of a horse . . . Abbaye slept [by day] like a person going up[1] from Pumbədita to Be Kube, and Rav Joseph called at him, "How long, sluggard, will you lie, when will you rise from your sleep?" (Prov. 6: 9).

4. Ketubot 111a[2]

אמר רב יהודה אמר שמואל, כשם שאסור לצאת מארץ ישראל לבבל כך אסור לצאת מבבל לשאר ארצות. רבה ורב יוסף דאמרי תרוייהו, אפילו מפומבדיתא לבי כובי. ההוא דנפק מפומבדיתא לבי כובי שמתיה רב יוסף.

Rav Judah said, Samuel said, Just as it is forbidden to leave Eretz Israel for Babylonia, so it is forbidden to leave Babylonia for other countries. Rabbah and Rav Joseph both said, Even from Pumbədita to Be Kube. A man who left Pumbədita for Be Kube was banned by Rav Joseph.

5. Megillah 6a

והאמר רבה בר בר חנה אמר רבי יוחנן, לדידי חזי לי זבת חלב ודבש דכל ארעא דישראל, והויא כמבי כובי,[3] עד אקרא דתולבקני,[4] עשרין ותרתין פרסי אורכא ופותיא שיתא פרסי.

. . . Rabbah b. Bar Ḥana said: Rabbi Yoḥanan said, I myself saw the flow of milk and honey of the whole land of Israel, and it is as from Be Kube[3] to Aqra də-Tulbanqe,[4] which area is twenty-two parasangs in length and in width six parasangs.

B. *Proposed Location*

A village close to Pumbədita (q.v., C2 on the Tal, Bab. map).

C. *Identification*

The talmudic sources clearly indicate the propinquity of Be Kube to Pumbədita, and Source 1 even uses the phrase "Be Kube of Pumbədita." Consequently scholars are in agreement on the location, though no proposals have been made as to the exact site.[5] Despite the sources suggesting that Be Kube

---

[2] There is a parallel in *Midrash ha-Gadol* to Leviticus, *be-har* 25: 38, Steinsalz ed., p. 713.

[3] The Oxford MS has כמבי מכסא, *Aggadot ha-Talmud* has כמבי מכסי, the Munich MS and others have כמבי כסי, and see *Diq. Sof.* All the parallel texts (Ketubot 111b–112a; *Midrash ha-Gadol* to Genesis, *wa-yeḥi*, 49:13 [Margulies ed., p. 846]; *Midrash ha-Gadol* to Deuteronomy, *wa-etḥanan*, 6:3 [Fisch ed., p. 125]; *Yalquṭ ha-Makhiri*, Psalms 107 [Buber ed., p. 176]) have "Be Mik̲se" and not "Be Kube." See the entries on "Aqra də-Tulbanqe" and „Be Mik̲se."

[4] The source has אקרא דתולבקני; for variants see note 6 in the entry on "Aqra də-Tulbanqe."

[5] See Neubauer, p. 350; Berliner, p. 27; Obermeyer, pp. 229–230. From "going up . . . to Be Kube" in Source 3 Obermeyer infers that Be Kube was north of Pumbədita. That

was near Pumbədita, Rashi notes that the distance between them was six parasangs (27 kilometers). In his commentary on the Source 3 sentence "going up from Pumbədita to Be Kube," he says "which elsewhere is explained as six parasangs." The "elsewhere" is most certainly Source 5, which in the version available to Rashi must have had "Be Kube."[6] It is true that Source 5 notes the distance between Be Kube and Aqra də-Tulbanqe (q.v.) rather than Pumbədita. Aqra də-Tulbanqe, however, has been identified with a place near Anbār, that is, in the Pumbədita area, so that difficulty is resolved. Thus it was the width of the strip that was marked by those two places, Be Kube and Pumbədita, from which the region probably extended southwards for the twenty-two parasangs specified. It should be noted that the most fertile areas west of the Euphrates lay in that direction.[7]

D. *Sages and Be Kube*

Most of the sources connected with Be Kube mention Rav Joseph. Rav Joseph b. Ḥiyya belonged to the third generation of Babylonian amoras. He was a friend of Rabbah's and headed the Pumbədita yeshiva after the latter's death. The other sages mentioned in connection with Be Kube—Rabbah, Rabbah b. Bar Ḥana and Abbaye—are all Pumbədita sages. It is quite natural, given the propinquity of the two places, that the sages referring to Be Kube as well as those referred to in connection with it should be associated with Pumbədita. All of them belong to the third generation of Babylonian amoras, including Abbaye who was active in the fourth but is mentioned here as still a pupil of Rav Joseph. Thus all the evidence on Be Kube dates from early in the fourth century.[8]

E. *The Inhabitants*

Despite the short distance between the center of learning and Jewish life at Pumbədita and Be Kube, there were obviously reservations in regard to the inhabitants of the latter place. Rav Joseph in Source 1 states that there is a defect in the lineage of the Be Kube Jews and they are considered slaves. That may be the reason Rabbah and Rav Joseph in Source 4 stress that a person should not move from Pumbədita to Be Kube, though they might

---

may be so, but the phrase can also be interpreted to mean that Be Kube was at a higher elevation than Pumbədita. Furthermore, some versions have כדמיזל (= going) rather than כדמעייל (= going up) and thus provide no indication at all of the relative positions of Be Kube and Pumbədita.

6 See n. 3 above. Possibly Rashi had "Be Kube" rather than "Be Miḵse" in the Ketubot 112a parallel as well, which is the case in Rashi in the Oxford MS of the parallel.

7 Cf. Musil, *Arabia Deserta*, p. 364.

8 However, the Vatican 111 MS of Qiddushin 8a mentions Be Kube in connection with Rav Ashi of the fifth century; see "Qube" in the appendix.

mean that a person should not abandon a place of learning to move even a short distance away. Most likely the underlying motive comprises both the dubious ancestry of the people of Be Kube and the lack of learning there.

Berliner, *Beiträge* (1883), p. 27
Eshel, *Yishuvei ha-Yehudim* (1979), p. 61
Funk, *Monumenta* (1913), p. 26
Goldhaar, *Admat Qodesh* (1913), pp. 86, 89
Hirschenson, *Sheva Ḥokhmot* (1883), pp. 69, 70
Jastrow, *Dictionary* (1950³), p. 616
Kohut, *Arukh ha-Shalem* (1878–1892), vol. 2, p. 50
Krauss, *Qadmoniot ha-Talmud* (1923–1945), vol. 1, p. 37
Levy, *Wörterbuch* (1924²), vol. 1, pp. 214–215; vol. 4, p. 543
Neubauer, *Géographie* (1868), p. 350
Neusner, *History* (1965–1970), vol. 2, p. 248; vol. 4, p. 389
Obermeyer, *Landschaft* (1929), pp. 229–230

Be Lapaṭ בי לפט

A. *Sources*

1. Ta'anit 22a

ר׳ ברוקא חוזאה[1] הוה שכיח בשוקא דבי לפט[2] הוה שכיח אליהו גביה, א״ל איכא בהאי שוקא בר עלמא דאתי, א״ל לא. אדהכי והכי חזא לההוא גברא דהוה סיים מסאני אוכמי ולא רמי חוטא דתכלתא בגלימיה א״ל האי בר עלמא דאתי הוא. רהט בתריה א״ל מאי עובדך, א״ל זיל האידנא ותא למחר א״ל למחר א״ל מאי עובדך, א״ל זנדוקנא אנא ואסרנא גברי לחוד ונשי לחוד ורמינא פורייאי בין הני להני כי היכי דלא ליתו לידי איסורא, כי חזינא בת ישראל דיהבי נכרים עלה עינייהו, מסרנא נפשאי ומצילנא לה, יומא חד הוות נערה מאורסה גבן דיהבו בה נכרים עינייהו שקלי דורדייא דחמרא ושדאי לה בשיפולה ואמרי דיסתנא היא. א״ל מאי טעמא לית לך חוטי ורמית מסאני אוכמי, א״ל עיילנא ונפיקנא ביני נכרים כי היכי דלא לידעו דיהודאה אנא, כי הוו גזרי גזירתא מודענא להו לרבנן ובעו רחמי ומבטלי לגזירתייהו. ומאי טעמא כי אמינא לך אנא מאי עובדך ואמרת לי זיל האידנא ותא למחר, א״ל בההיא שעתא גזרי גזירתא ואמינא ברישא איזיל ואשמע להו לרבנן דלבעי רחמי עלה דמילתא. אדהכי והכי אתו הנך תרי א״ל הנך נמי בני עלמא דאתי נינהו. אזל לגבייהו אמר להו מאי עובדייכו, אמרו ליה אינשי בדוחי אנן מבדחינן עציבי, אי נמי כי חזינן בי תרי דאית להו תיגרא בהדייהו טרחינן ועבדינן להו שלמא.

Rabbi Beroqa Ḥoza'a[1] was often in the market of Be Lapaṭ[2] where Elijah often appeared to him. He said to him, Is there anyone in this market [worthy] of the next world? He said to him, No. Meanwhile he saw a man who was wearing black shoes and had no blue thread in his garment. He said to

[1] The Munich MS has "Rav" rather then "Rabbi" which seems correct; and see *Diq. Sof.*

[2] The first printing of *Ein Ya'aqov* has דבילפט (in one word), *Aggadot ha-Talmud* has דביל שפט and see *Diq. Sof.* See also the various versions in the entry on "Walašpaṭ" some of which resemble "Be Lapaṭ."

him [Elijah to Rav Beroqa Ḥoza'a], That one is of the next world. He ran after him and said to him, What do you do? He said, Go now and come tomorrow. On the morrow he said to him, What do you do? He said to him, I am a prison guard, and I imprison men separately and women separately, I place my bed between them so that they do not come to the forbidden; when I see a daughter of Israel the Gentiles look at, I risk my life and save her. One day there was a betrothed girl at our place that the Gentiles looked at. I took wine lees and threw it on her lower parts and said she was menstruating. He said to him, What's the reason you have no threads and are wearing black shoes? He said to him, I go in and out among Gentiles so they won't know I'm a Jew. When a harsh decree is issued I inform them, the sages, and they pray for mercy, and the decrees are annulled. And for what reason when I asked you what you do, did you tell me go now and come tomorrow? He said to him, Just then they issued a decree, and I said, first I'll go and inform them, the sages, so they can pray for mercy about it. Meantime those two came; he said to him [Elijah to Rav Beroqa], Those are also of the next world. He went to them and said to them, What do you do? They said to him, We are entertainers. We entertain the sorrowful, or also when we see two fighting, we take the trouble and make peace between them.

2. Procopius, *Wars* VIII 10,9 (*The Gothic War* IV 10,9)

ἔστι δέ τις ἐν Πέρσαις Οὐαζαΐνη χώρα, ἀγαθὴ μάλιστα, οὗ δὴ πόλις Βηλαπατῶν καλουμένη οἰκεῖται, ἑπτὰ ἡμερῶν ὁδῷ Κτησιφῶντος διέχουσα.

Now there is a certain land in Persia called Vazaine, an exceedingly good country in which the city named Belapaton is situated, seven day's journey distant from Ctesiphon.

B. *Location*

Ğundaisābūr, one of the cities of Be Ḥozai (q.v.) which is Ḫūzistān, northwest of Šuštar (on Bab. Env. map).

C. *History*

The town was founded by Shapur I, who settled in it Roman captives taken in the battle against Valerian (A.D. 259–260)[3] and established a royal residence

[3] On Ğundaisābūr see Yāqūt, s.v. "Ğundaisābūr" and "Ğundaišahbūr"; Bakrī, *ar-Rauḍ al-mi'ṭār*, s.v. "Ğundāsābūr"; Ṭabarī, vol. 8, p. 432 (= vol. 3, p. 852); *BGA*, passim; Ṯa'ālibī, *Ġurar*, p. 494. Cf. *ibid.*, p. 527, which states it was rebuilt by the Byzantines in the reign of Shapur II. Mustaufī, vol. 2, p. 109 (who reports that Shapur I built it, and Shapur II added beautiful buildings); Ḥamza, *Ta'rīḫ*, p. 49; *Ḥudūd al-'ālam*, index s.v. "Gundē Shāpūr"; Huart-Sayili, *EI*², s.v. "Gondēshāpur." See Herzfeld, *Der Islam* 11

there. According to Mas'ūdī,[4] Ǧundaisābūr was the Sassanian royal residence until the reign of Hormizd II, while according to Ḥamza[5] it was that until Shapur II was thirty, after which he lived in Madā'in till he died.
Be Lapaṭ was known for its fine sugar. The area in general was celebrated for its fertility, and in particular for its excellent sugar.[6]
The town was an important center of learning.[7] When its founder Shapur I married the daughter of the Roman emperor Aurelian, she brought with her two Greek physicians, who began to teach medicine. In general, the activity of scholars and physicians was encouraged. The population grew and became cosmopolitan, and Aramaic became the language of the cultured. Shapur II further enlarged the city and founded an academy there for the teaching of astronomy, theology and medicine.
In the fifth century Be Lapaṭ was one of the five Persian cities that were metropolitanates.[8] In 484 it was the site of the crucial synod that confirmed the schism between Melchites, Monophysites and Nestorians.[9] After the Nestorians were expelled from Edessa in 489, many of them settled in Be Lapaṭ and became an important element in its cultural life.

(1921): 149. On the establishment of the city by Shapur I who named it Palāpāt see Markwart, *Catalogue*, § 48 and p. 98.

On Shapur II's settlement in Ǧundaisābūr of captives from the cities of Syria see *ar-Rauḍ al-mi'ṭār*, s.v. "al-Ḥaḍr"; Dīnawarī, *Aḫbār ṭiwāl*, vol. 1, pp. 48–49. On the phenomenon in general, s.v. "Be Ḥozai."

The people of Ahwāz (= Be Ḥozai) called Ǧundaisābūr Bīl, after the man Shapur I entrusted its construction to (Ṭabarī, vol. 2, pp. 50–51 [= vol. 1, pp. 830–831]); Nöldeke, *Perser und Araber*, pp. 40–41, esp. p. 41, n. 2, comments on further garblings of the name: Nīlāb (see Yāqūt, s.v. who says "The name of Ǧundaisābūr; and it was once Nīlāṭ"; and see Yāqūt, s.v. "Nīlāṭ" [who adds nothing new]). According to Dīnawarī, in the language of Ḫūzistān, Ǧundaisābūr is called Nīlāṭ, and the residents call it Nīlāb (*Aḫbār ṭiwāl*, vol. 1, pp. 48–49). The names Nīlāb and Nīlāṭ seem to be garbles of Bīlāb and Bīlāṭ, as in Arabic *bā'* and *nūn* are distinguished only by the placement of the diacritical dot. The form Bīlāṭ is more likely as a garble of Be Lapaṭ; cf. the entry on "Šum Ṭəmaya" (Šum Ṭəmaya becomes Šumyā).

[4] Mas'ūdī, *Murūǧ*, vol. 1, p. 295 (= vol. 2, p. 175).

[5] Ḥamza, *Ta'rīḫ*, p. 52.

[6] See Marquart ed., *Ērānšahr*, pp. 31, 137 and note on p. 145; see also the entry on "Be Ḥozai."

[7] Information on culture and science in Ǧundaisābūr comes from Abbott, in Adams, *Ars Orientalis* 7 (1968): 70–73.

[8] Christensen, *L'Iran*, p. 271, and n. 62. The city became a metropolitanate after the synod of Seleucia in 410; see Labourt, *Le Christianisme*, p. 98. There is no archaeological evidence on the settlement of the city or its environs before the Sassanian period; see also Adams & Hansen, *Ars Orientalis* 7 (1968): 53–54; Wenke, *Mesopotamia*, 10–11 (1975–1976): 71–73. This fact refutes the statement in the chronicle of Arbela that the city became the seat of a bishop in 224 (Sachau, *APAW philos. hist. Klasse*, [1915] No. 6, pp. 17, 61–62) and indicates that the document should be considered unreliable even on places where no archaeological or other evidence can be resorted to for support. See now Fiey, *L'Orient Syrien* 12 (1967): 265–302.

[9] Labourt, *Le Christianisme*, pp. 138f., 142f.

D. *Physical Features*

Adams and Hansen note that "the ruins of Jundī Shāhpūr lie south of the village of Shahabad, three kilometers below the last of the low ridges marking the northern limit of the Khuzestan plain. The rectangular outline of the city is immediately apparent on aerial photographs although within the low wall-like embankment presently marking the outer boundary on three sides the visitor today encounters only sprawling, indistinct clusters of low mounds. A grid pattern suggesting regularly spaced intersecting streets within the wall is also strikingly apparent on aerial photographs . . ."
The two authors found that evidence of an earlier occupation than the Sassanian period was wholly lacking. They conclude that "physical remains" are those of a city newly founded in the early Sassanian period, even though much of the population—and hence also much of its urban structure—may have been physically transferred to it from another locality. They conclude that by the late Abbasid period the place had been reduced to a small impoverished village. This contradicts statements by contemporary Arab geographers. The survey also included the monumental Siāh Mansūr siphon-bridge west of the town.[10]

E. *Sages and Be Lapaṭ*

Source 1 testifies to the presence in Be Lapaṭ of Rav Beroqa Ḥoza'a (see note 1 and the entry on "Be Ḥozai"). The source does not, however, indicate clearly whether he was a resident of the town or only made frequent trips to its market.

F. *Relations with Gentiles*

The story of the Jewish prison guard in Source 1[11] is one of the rare pieces of evidence on Jewish officials in the royal service.[12] The case itself illustrates the relations between Jews and Gentiles, as well as the strains involved. The prison guard speaks to Rav Beroqa of his habit of dressing like the Gentiles so as to mix with them without being identified as a Jew and thus hear of anti-Jewish measures about to be adopted and inform the sages of them. Without doubt the story as a whole that emerges in the conversation between Rav Beroqa and the prophet Elijah has a legendary tinge. Its main purpose is to demonstrate that sometimes people whose appearance and status seem remote

---

[10] See Adams & Hansen, *Ars Orientalis* 7 (1968): 53–70, plan (fig. 1); Abbott, *ibid.*, 70–73.

[11] On the term זנדוקנא meaning "prison guard" see *Tosefot Arukh ha-Shalem*, p. 174.

[12] There is no evidence at all on Jewish high officials, and cf., in T.B. Ta'anit 20a, Rav Judah who expresses satisfaction that the Jews are not appointed to certain high posts. See also Widengren, *Iranica Antiqua* 1 (1961): 151f.

from Judaism—such as the prison guard and the pair of clowns[13]—merit the world to come by their deeds. At the same time, the testimony on a Jewish prison guard in Be Lapaṭ seems authentic, reflecting the relations between Jews and Gentiles that the prison guard's own story depicts.

ADAMS, *Science* 136 (1962): 109–122
ADAMS & HANSEN, *Ars Orientalis* 7 (1968): 53–70
BEER, *Amora'ei Bavel* (1974), p. 198
BERLINER, *Beiträge* (1883), p. 38
CHRISTENSEN, *L'Iran* (1944²), p. 271
ESHEL, *Yishuvei ha-Yehudim* (1979), pp. 66–67
FUNK, *Monumenta* (1913), pp. 27, 290
HIRSCHENSON, *Sheva Ḥokhmot* (1883), p. 70
KOHUT, *Arukh ha-Shalem* (1878–1892), vol. 2, p. 50; *Tosefot* (1937), p. 85
KRAUSS, *Paras we-Romi* (1948), p. 157
LABOURT, *Le Christianisme* (1904²), pp. 98, 138f., 142f.
NEUBAUER, *Géographie* (1868), p. 380
NEUSNER, *History* (1965–1970), vol. 4, pp. 50–51, 357; vol. 5, p. 45
NÖLDEKE, *Perser und Araber* (1879), pp. 40–41
OBERMEYER, *Landschaft* (1929), pp. 209–232, 290 n. 2

Be Mikse בי מיכסי

A. *Sources*

1. Ketubot 111b–112a[1]

אמר רבה בר בר חנה, לדידי חזי לי זבת חלב ודבש של כל ארץ ישראל והויא כמבי מיכסי[2] עד אקרא דתולבנקי, כ״ב פרסי אורכא ופותיא שיתא פרסי.

Rabbah b. Bar Ḥana said, I have myself seen the flow of milk and honey of the whole land of Israel, and it is as from Be Mikse[2] to Aqra də-Tulbanqe, [which area is] twenty-two parasangs in length, and in width six parasangs.

---

[13] A case similar to that of the clowns who excelled in making peace between people is that of the meeting of Rabbi Yannai of the first generation of Eretz Israel amoras with an *'am ha-aretz*; see also Leviticus Rabbah, IX 3, Margulies ed., pp. 176–178. This was contrary to the common view of the tannas from the destruction of the Second Temple on, that lofty qualities notwithstanding, an ignoramus is considered worthless and cannot attain the world to come. See also Oppenheimer, *'Am ha-Aretz*, pp. 170–195.

[1] This phrase also figures in Megillah 6a. Although the printing has והויא כמבי כובי עד אקרא דתולבקני (= and it is as from Be Kube to Aqra də-Tulbaqne), the Oxford MS has כמבי מכסא, *Aggadot ha-Talmud* has כמבי מכסי, while the Munich MS and others have כמבי כסי; and see *Diq. Sof.* Other parallels in *Midrash ha-Gadol* to Genesis, *wa-yeḥi*, 49:13 (Margulies ed., p. 846): והויא כי מבי מכסי עד אקרא דתולבוקני; *Midrash ha-Gadol* to Deuteronomy, *wa-etḥanan*, 6:3 (Fisch ed., p. 125): והויא כי מבי מכסא לאקרא דתולבקני; *Yalquṭ ha-Makhiri*, Psalms 107 (Buber ed., p. 176): הוי כמבי מכסא עד אקרא דתולבנקי. See also the entries on "Aqra də-Tulbanqe" and "Be Kube."

[2] The Munich and Vatican 130 MSS have כמבי כסי; the Vatican 113 MS has כמיבי מכסי; for other versions see Ketubot in the ICIT edition.

2. Giṭṭin 46b

הנהו בני בי מיכסי,[3] דיזפי זוזי מעובדי כוכבים ולא הוה להו למפרעינהו, אתו וקא גרבי להו, אתו לקמיה דרב הונא,[4] אמר להו מאי איעביד לכו, דתנן המוכר את עצמו ואת בניו לעובדי כוכבים אין פודין אותו, אמר ליה רבי אבא[5] לימדתני רבינו והוא שמכר ושנה ושילש, אמר ליה הני מרגל רגילי דעבדי הכי.

Certain men of Be Mikse[3] borrowed money from idol worshipers and when they could not repay were taken as slaves. They went before Rav Huna[4] who said, What can I do for you? For it was taught, If a man sells himself and his children to idol worshipers, he is not to be ransomed. Then Rabbi Abba[5] said to him, You have taught us, Master, that this is a man who sold himself a second and third time. He [Rav Huna] said to them, They do this habitually.

3. ʿAvodah Zarah 33b

אמר רב פפי הני פתוותא דבי מיכסי[6] כיון דלא בלעי טובא משכשכן במים ומותרין.

Rav Papi said, Those clay vessels from Be Mikse[6] may be used after being rinsed in water, as they do not absorb much.

4. Ketubot 67a

אמר רב פפי[7] הני תותבי דבי מכסי[8] אשה גובה פרנא מהם.

Rav Papi[7] said, The clothes from Be Mikse[8] a woman can claim her *ketubah* from them.

5. Yevamot 45a

שלחו ליה בני בי מיכסי[9] לרבה,[10] מי שחציו עבד וחציו בן חורין הבא על בת ישראל מהו, א"ל השתא עבד כולו אמרי' כשר, חציו מיבעיא.

The men of Be Mikse[9] sent [a query] to Rabbah:[10] A person half slave and half free who cohabits with a Jewish woman, what of him? He said, Now a full slave is considered fit, there is no question of a half one.

B. *Location*

None can be proposed due to insufficient data.

---

[3] The Munich MS has הנהו בי מיכסי, the Vatican 140 and Oxford MSS have הנהו בני מיכסי.

[4] The Oxford MS has "Rav Judah."

[5] Some manuscripts have "Rabbi Abbahu" (Vatican 130), "Rav Aḥai" (Oxford), and "Rav Aḥa" (Vatican 140).

[6] A Spanish MS (Abramson ed., p. 58) has דבי מכסי.

[7] A Geniza fragment has "Rav Papa," and see Ketubot in the ICIT edition on that, and n. 28 there.

[8] The Munich MS has דכי(?) מיכסי, and see Ketubot, ICIT edition, n. 29.

[9] The Munich MS has בני בר מיכסי, the Oxford MS has בני בי מכסי.

[10] The Venice printing has "to Rava."

C. *Attempts at Identification*

Attempts to identify Be Mikse fall into two categories. One seeks to identify it on the basis of phonetic similarity, particularly with Makesin on the Ḫābūr River.[11] The other, based on meaning (*mekes* = customs), has led scholars to suggest it was a customs station on the border between Babylonia and Arabia.[12] At first glance, Source 1 seems to provide sufficient data to locate Be Mikse, since it gives the dimensions of the area between it and Aqra də-Tulbanqe (q.v.) which can be identified with a place near Anbār. But it does not make clear whether the distance between the two places is twenty-two parasangs (the length) or six (the width). Furthermore, in the printing of Megillah 6a Be Kube (q.v.) is cited instead of Be Mikse.

D. *Relations with Gentiles*

The Babylonian Jews had commercial contacts of various kinds with Gentiles, including monetary ones involving loans. Sassanian Persian law stipulated that if a debt was unrepaid, the borrower could be taken into slavery. Source 2 covers a case of this kind of enslavement for debt, involving the Jews of Be Mikse. They ask Rav Huna, of the second generation of Babylonian amoras and head of the Sura yeshiva, whether the precept to ransom captives could be applied to such slaves. Rav Huna forbids redeeming such a captive, on the grounds that it was well known that a person who did not repay his debts risked being made a slave by the Gentile moneylenders. That responsum shows that enslavement for debt was not a unique instance, but a custom accepted both legally and socially.[13] The Be Mikse people pose a question involving slaves in Source 5 as well.

E. *Material Culture*

Source 3 mentions *patwata,* clay pots used primarily to draw water from wells. The Be Mikse pots had the unusual property of being non-absorbant.[14]
Source 4 refers to *totave də-Be Mikse,* that is, clothing manufactured there.[15] According to the halakhah personal effects cannot be pledged for a marriage contract or debt. In exceptional cases, however, where the inhabitants of a

---

[11] Thus Berliner and in his wake de Goeje, and Kohut in *Arukh ha-Shalem,* and cf. also Neubauer in the bibliography below.

[12] Thus Obermeyer, without additional evidence, and in his wake Krauss in *Tosefot Arukh ha-Shalem* (see bibliography below).

[13] See Elon, *Ḥerut ha-Perat,* p. 15; Urbach, *Zion* 25 (1960): 188; Beer, *Amora'ei Bavel,* pp. 207, 329.

[14] *Teshuvot ha-Geonim,* Harkavy, § 47; "*Patwata də-Be Mikse*—pitchers used to measure wine, etc." and see Brand, *Kelei ha-Ḥeres,* pp. 445–446.

[15] See Krauss, *Qadmoniot ha-Talmud,* vol. 2B, p. 177.

certain place deal in those effects or goods, debts or pledges can be collected in kind. An instance of such a case is represented by the clothing industry of Be Mik̲se, indicating that those items were typical of the place.

BEER, *Amora'ei Bavel* (1974), pp. 307, 329
BERLINER, *Beiträge* (1883), p. 43
BRAND, *Kelei ha-Ḥeres* (1953), pp. 445–446
ELON, *Ḥerut ha-Perat* (1964), p. 15
ESHEL, *Yishuvei ha-Yehudim* (1979), pp. 67, 68, 147
FUNK, *Monumenta* (1913), p. 294
DE GOEJE, *ZDMG* 39 (1885): 10
GOLDHAAR, *Admat Qodesh* (1913), pp. 86, 89
GRAETZ, *MGWJ* 2 (1853): 197
HIRSCHENSON, *Sheva Ḥokhmot* (1883), p. 70
JASTROW, *Dictionary* (1950[3]), p. 616: "II כובא"; p. 784
KOHUT, *Arukh ha-Shalem* (1878–1892), vol. 1, p. 260: "אקרא"; vol. 2, p. 51; *Tosefot* (1937), p. 85
KRAUSS, *Qadmoniot ha-Talmud* (1923–1945), vol. 2B, p. 177
NEUBAUER, *Géographie* (1868), p. 388
OBERMEYER, *Landschaft* (1929), p. 344–345
URBACH, *Zion* 25 (1960): 188

Ben ha-Nəharot בין הנהרות

See the entry on "Šuṭ Mišuṭ."

Be Pərat בי פרת

See the entry on "Gišra də-Be Pərat."

Be Rav בי רב

A. *Source*

Pesaḥim 52a

רב נתן בר אסיא[1] אזל מבי רב[2] לפומבדיתא בי"ט שני של עצרת, שמתיה רב יוסף.

Rav Nathan b. Assia[1] went from Be Rav[2] to Pumbədita on the second holy day of the Feast of Weeks; Rav Joseph banned him.

B. *Proposed Location*

Ar-Rabb on the bank of the Euphrates, between Ihi də-Qira (q.v.) and Anbār (see the entry on "Pumbədita") (B2 on the Tal. Bab. map).

---

[1] The Munich and Oxford MSS have „Bar Nathan Assia."

[2] The Munich MS has from בירם as do the Munich B MS (but corrected to בי רב) and also the R-o-sh; the Oxford MS has from בירא.

C. *Identification*

The source above indicates that Be Rav was at most a day's distance from Pumbədita. This distance applies to ar-Rabb on the Euphrates which is mentioned by the Arab geographers. According to Muqaddasī, it was a day's distance from Anbār to ar-Rabb, and two day's distance from the latter to Hīt.[3] The prefix "Be" is sometimes already deleted in Aramaic, and names beginning with it often occur without it as well.
Obermeyer preferred the form "Biram" (see note 2) to Be Rav.[4] Although he was aware of the existence of ar-Rabb, he did not pay attention to the possible connection between it and Be Rav.[5] He rejected that form because he construed it as denoting the residence of the amora Rav, which was in Sura, much more than a day's distance from Pumbədita, or as meaning a study house in general, rather than a particular place. However, Biram (q. v.) was evidently not exactly on the Euphrates, and Be Rav must be viewed as the name of the actual settlement.

JASTROW, *Dictionary* (1950³), p. 158
KOHUT, *Arukh ha-Shalem* (1878–1892), vol. 2, p. 53
LEVY, *Wörterbuch* (1924²), vol. 1, p. 215
OBERMEYER, *Landschaft* (1929), p. 98 n. 2

Be Šabur בי שבור

See the entry on "Pumbədita."

[3] Musil, *The Middle Euphrates*, p. 248, identifies ar-Rabb with presentday aš-Šaiḫ Ḥadīd opposite ar-Rumādī. On ar-Rabb see also Idrīsī, vol. 6, pp. 654–656 and Streck, *Die alte Landschaft*, vol. 1, pp. 8, 24; vol. 2, p. 221; see also Muqaddasī, p. 134. According to Ibn Ḫurdāḏbih, p. 72, and Qudāma, *Ḫarāǧ*, p. 217, it was seven parasangs from Anbār to ar-Rabb and twelve from ar-Rabb to Hīt. Cf. Le Strange, "Ibn Serapion," p. 10, who says that the Euphrates flows below Hīt *bi-l-ġarbi l-Anbār*. That is Le Strange's correction of *bi-l-ʿarab wa-l-Anbār* of the manuscript, and see also his translation, p. 47: ". . . it flows to the westward of al-Anbār." The text was properly corrected by the editor of Suhrāb, p. 119 (*ṯumma yamurru bi-r-Rabb wa-l-Anbār*) according to Muqaddasī.

[4] Obermeyer, pp. 24–25, 98.

[5] Obermeyer, pp. 232–233. Obermeyer identified ar-Rabb with the Ruv referred to in *Iggeret Rav Sherira Gaon* (Lewin ed., pp. 70–71) and consequently proposed vocalizing the Arabic name as Rubb. The identification does not seem likely, for the *Iggeret* implies that Ruv was very close to Nəhardəʿa. In any case, no vowel change need be proposed, for even if the original form was Ruv, it could well have been garbled to ar-Rabb (= the Lord) through popular etymology (and see Le Strange, "Ibn Serapion," p. 14; Suhrāb, p. 123). Eshel, s. v. "Ruv" (p. 232) followed Le Strange's mistake ("Ibn Serapion," p. 14, and the translation, p. 68, and see the map there), and placed ar-Rabb on the Tigris north of ʿUkbarā. Obermeyer does not identify Ruv with ar-Rabb that was supposedly on the Tigris, but with ar-Rabb which he properly locates on the Euphrates, north of Anbār.

Be Tarbu בי תרבו

A. *Sources*

1. Yoma 77b

רב יוסף שרא להו לבני בי תרבו[1] למיעבר במיא למיתי לפירקא.

Rav Joseph allowed the people of Be Tarbu[1] to cross the water [on the Day of Atonement so as] to come to the *pirqa*.

2. Bava Qamma 23b

הנהו עיזי דבי תרבו[2] דהוו מפסדי ליה לרב יוסף, א"ל לאביי זיל אימא להו למרייהו דליצנעינהו.

[Of] those goats of Be Tarbu[2] that damaged him, Rav Joseph. He said to him, to Abbaye, Tell them, the owners, to keep them inside.

B. *Already Proposed Location*

A place near Pumbədita (q.v., C2 on the Tal. Bab. map) within the Sabbath walking distance (about one kilometer) from it.

C. *Identification*

Rav Joseph was one of the major Pumbədita sages in the third generation of Babylonian amoras, and for two and a half years headed the Pumbədita yeshiva.[3] In Source 1 he allows the people of Be Tarbu to cross the water on the Day of Atonement (despite the prohibition against washing) in order to attend the public lecture (*pirqa*)[4] probably held at the yeshiva on that day. It is thus evident that the distance between Be Tarbu and Pumbədita (q.v.) did not exceed two thousand cubits (about a kilometer), the permitted out-of-town walking distance on the Sabbath and holidays. Source 2 indicates that Rav Joseph owned fields in or near Be Tarbu.

Berliner, *Beiträge* (1883), p. 65
Eshel, *Yishuvei ha-Yehudim* (1979), p. 71
Funk, *Monumenta* (1913), pp. 54, 300
Gafni, *Ha-Yeshivah be-Bavel* (1978), p. 115
Goodblatt, *Rabbinic Instruction* (1975), pp. 179, 183
Jastrow, *Dictionary* (1950³), p. 1694
Kohut, *Arukh ha-Shalem* (1878–1892), vol. 2, p. 54; *Tosefot* (1937), p. 86
Levy, *Wörterbuch* (1924²), vol. 1, p. 216
Neubauer, *Géographie* (1868), p. 363
Neusner, *History* (1965–1970), vol. 2, p. 247; vol. 4, pp. 164, 248
Obermeyer, *Landschaft* (1929), p. 181 note, 230f.

[1] The Munich MS has בתרבו, the Munich B MS has ביתרכו, and the London MS has בתרכו.

[2] The Hamburg MS has בי תרכו.

[3] Berakhot 64a, and see Albeck, *Mavo la-Talmudim*, pp. 291–293.

[4] On the *pirqa* see the entry on "Hagrunya." Cf. the permission to cross canals on the Sabbath which Rava granted the inhabitants of ʻEver Yamina (Yoma 77b).

Be Torta בי תורתא

See the entry on "Pumbədita."

Biram בירם

A. *Sources*

1. Qiddushin 72a

אמר ליה אביי לרב יוסף להא גיסא דפרת עד היכא, אמר ליה מאי דעתיך משום בירם,[1] מייחסי דפומבדיתא מבירם נסבי.

Abbaye said to him, to Rav Joseph, How far [does Babylonia extend] on this side of the Euphrates? He said to him. What is your opinion [that you came to ask] about Biram?[1] Those of pure lineage from Pumbədita, they marry [women] from Biram.

2. Rosh ha-Shanah 23a–b

מאי בית בלתין,[2] אמר רב זו בירם.[3]

What is Bet Biltin,[2] Rav said it is Biram.[3]

3. ʿAvodah Zarah 57a

ההוא עובדא דהוה בבירם דההוא עובד כוכבים דהוה קא סליק בדיקלא ואייתי לוליבא, בהדי דקא נחית נגע בראשה דלוליבא בחמרא שלא בכוונה, שרייה רב לזבוניה לעובדי כוכבים.

That case that was in Biram, when that heathen who climbed the palm and brought the branch, when he came down he inadvertently touched its end to wine, Rav allowed it to be sold to heathens.

B. *Already Proposed Location*

West of the Euphrates in the area of Pumbədita (q. v., C 2 on the Tal. Bab. map).

C. *Identifications*

Source 1 deals with the boundary of Babylonia for genealogical purposes, and explains the extent of the zone of pure lineage from the northwestern corner. The northernmost point was established earlier in the passage so that the

---

[1] The Munich MS has ביראם, and later בירם; the Vatican 111 MS has בים and later בירם.

[2] The Munich MS has בית בילתי, the Munich B MS has בית בלתי and the London MS has בית בילתין.

[3] The London MS has בירס.

intention here is to clarify further, how far westward the zone stretches (cf. the entry on "Nəhar Yo'ani" in regard to the zone from the Tigris eastward). A Pumbədita sage in the third generation of Babylonian amoras, and head of the Pumbədita yeshiva for a time, Rav Joseph believes that Biram falls within the zone of pure lineage, for Pumbədita men of impeccable lineage married women from there. Thus it appears that Biram was in the Pumbədita area and west of the Euphrates, though a precise identification is not yet possible. Obermeyer proposed placing Biram some eight parasangs (ca. forty kilometers) north of Pumbədita, west of the Euphrates.[4] That distance, however, is based on a source in Pesaḥim most versions of which refer to Be Rav, and only a few to Biram. There is thus no reason to prefer Biram, nor any to identify Biram with Be Rav (q.v.).[5] In Source 2, Rav identifies Biram with Bet Biltin, which was the last of the signal fire stations from which the new moon used to be announced.[6] Source 3 indicates that there were palm trees at Biram. In Sanhedrin 108a Rabbi Yoḥanan mentions a Biram in connection with water sources, but as the other places listed are Tiberias and Gader probably a Biram in Eretz Israel is meant.

Berliner, *Beiträge* (1883), pp. 16, 27
Eshel, *Yishuvei ha-Yehudim* (1979), pp. 73–74
Funk, *Monumenta* (1913), pp. 27, 28
Hirschenson, *Sheva Ḥokhmot* (1883), p. 72
Jastrow, *Dictionary* (1950³), p. 166
Kohut, *Arukh ha-Shalem* (1878–1892), vol. 2, pp. 58–59; *Tosefot* (1937), p. 86
Levy, *Wörterbuch* (1924²), vol. 1, p. 223
Neubauer, *Géographie* (1868), p. 354
Obermeyer, *Landschaft* (1929), pp. 24f., 28 n. 2, 98f.

Birta בירתא

A. *Sources*

1. Ta'anit 24a

אלעזר איש בירתא[1] כד הוו חזו ליה גבאי צדקה הוו טשו מיניה, דכל מאי דהוה גביה יהיב להו.

Eleazar of Birta,[1] when collectors for charity saw him, they hid from him, because everything he had he would give them.

---

[4] Obermeyer, pp. 24–25, 98.

[5] See the source from Pesaḥim 52a, in the entry on "Be Rav."

[6] See Mishnah Rosh ha-Shanah II 4; T. J. Rosh ha-Shanah II 2 – 58a, 18, and the passage referred to in Source 2, in its entirety.

[1] The Munich MS has רבי אלעזר איש כפר ברתותא (= Rabbi Eleazar of the village of Bartuta) and see *Diq. Sof.*, note ז. If this version is accepted, the place is not Birta at all. Bartuta is most probably in Eretz Israel though its location has not been clarified (cf. Mishnah Ṭevul Yom III 4; T. J. Demai V 1 – 24c, 3; Ḥallah II 3 – 58c, 17; T. B. Pesaḥim 13a; see also Klein, *Eretz ha-Galil*, pp. 81, 205 and n. 11 there).

2. Soṭah 38b

והתני רב שימי מבירתא[2] דשיחורי בית הכנסת שכולה כהנים מקצתן עולין ומקצתן עונין אמן.

Rav Shimi of Birta[2] də-Šiḥori taught, In a synagogue all of *kohanim*, some of them ascend [the platform] and some of them respond Amen.

3. Qiddushin 72a

כי הוה ניחא נפשיה דרבי אמר . . . בירקא[3] איכא בבבל שני אחים יש שמחליפים נשותיהם זה לזה, בירתא דסטיא איכא בבבל היום סרו מאחרי המקום, דאקפי פירא בכוורי בשבתא ואזיל וצדו בהו בשבתא ושמתינהו ר׳ אחי ברבי יאשיה ואישתמוד.

When Rabbi was dying he said . . . There is Birqa[3] in Babylonia [where] two brothers interchange wives; there is Birta də-Saṭya in Babylonia, today they turned away from the Omnipresent, for they flooded the fishpond on the Sabbath, and they went and caught them on the Sabbath, and Rabbi Aḥi b. Rabbi Josiah pronounced a ban against them and they renounced Judaism.

B. *Location*

"Birta" means a fortified locality or a fort.[4] There were a number of places with that name, and not enough data are available for identifying the place (or places) called Birta mentioned in talmudic literature.

C. *Attempts at Identification*

The sources above deal with various places known as Birta, Source 3 with two of them (see note 3). Obermeyer proposes identifications for Birta də-Saṭya and Birta də-Nida (as per the Oxford manuscript) referred to in that source. He identifies Birta də-Saṭya with Barāṯā, a village near Baghdad that eventually became part of the city,[5] and Birta də-Nida with another Barāṯā in the Nahr al-Malik area.[6] However, as the name Barāṯā is derived from the Syriac word *baraiṯa* which means "outer,"[7] and has no connection with Birta

---

[2] The Munich MS has מברת׳; it was missing in the Oxford MS and inserted in the margin. See also Soṭah, ICIT ed.

[3] The Oxford MS has בירתא דנדה, the Vatican 111 MS has (?)בירתא דנראי, and the Munich MS has ביותא. In any case, "Birta" and not "Birqa" seems to be the correct version, the letter ת having been miswritten as ק.

[4] See *Arukh ha-Shalem*, vol. 2, pp. 57–58 ("בירה"); Levy, *Wörterbuch*, vol. 1, p. 223 ("II בירה"); Jastrow, *Dictionary*, p. 167 ("בירתא"). The name "Birta" is equivalent to the Greek τεῖχος on which see also Dillemann, *Haute Mésopotamie*, pp. 92–93; Townsend, *JNES* 13 (1954): 52f.

[5] Obermeyer, p. 73, n. 2. On the place see Streck, *EI*[1], s.v. "Barāṯā"; Awad. *EI*[2], s.v. "Barāṯā" and the bibliography there.

[6] Obermeyer, *ibid.* On the place see Yāqūt, at the end of the entry on "Barāṯa."

[7] Fraenkel, *Fremdwörter*, p. XX.

which means "fort," those identifications are untenable. There are a number of places called Birta. One of them was in Osrhoëne on the Euphrates,[8] and another was likewise on the Euphrates, apparently below Thapsacus. A third Birta, by far the most important one, is the fort of the ancient city of Takrīt and it is first mentioned in documents of the seventh century.[9] Takrīt was on the Tigris, between Sāmarrā and the diffluence of the Lesser Zāb and the Tigris. Herzfeld described the ruins of that city[10] which stretch over several hills, two of them near the river, the highest of the two being the site of the fort.

D. *Sages and Birta*

Source 2 has Rav Shimi of Birta də-Šiḥori citing a *baraita*. This sage is mentioned nowhere else in talmudic literature.

E. *The Inhabitants*

The term *šiḥori* in "Birta də-Šiḥori" means "black" and may be a reference to some feature of the site or to the complexion of the local people.
Source 3 has Rabbi Judah ha-Nasi[11] referring critically to residents of places called Birta. The first Birta (or Birqa) is castigated for an offense in the area of sex, and the second for a desecration of the Sabbath[12] causing Rabbi Aḥi b. Rabbi Josiah to proclaim a ban, to which the Birta people responded by converting. The names Birta də-Nida (= uncleanness) and Birta də-Saṭya (= deviation) commemorate Rabbi's reproaches. These criticisms are by no means intended to imply that residents of all places called Birta are sinners,[13] as in fact Source 1 lauds a resident of Birta for his eagerness to give all his money to charity and the collectors for their efforts to restrain him.

---

[8] Müller, *RE*, vol. 3, cols. 498–499; s.v. "Birtha"; Musil, *The Middle Euphrates*, p. 333ff.

[9] Musil, *ibid.*, p. 363. It has been suggested that the Kainai mentioned by Xenophon is Takrīt (*Anabasis*, II 4,28) see Herzfeld, *Samarra*, pp. 34–35; Winckler, *Altorientalische Forschungen*, II vol. 1, p. 526f.; Ptolemy V 18: Βίρϑα (approximately where Takrīt is located). It may be the "Virta" mentioned by Ammianus (XX 7,17–18). See also Georgius Cyprius, *Descriptio Orbis Romani*, Gelzer ed., p. 937: Κάστρον Βίρϑα. Birta was an important Monophysite community. Nestorians appear only after the Muslim conquest (Fiey, *Assyrie Chrétienne*, vol. 3, p. 110, and idem, *L'Orient Syrien* 8 (1963): 289–342).

[10] Sarre & Herzfeld, *Archäologische Reise*, vol. 1, pp. 219–231. Herzfeld notes that in his day the people in the region called the place "Burṯa" (Herzfeld, *Samarra*, p. 35).

[11] On Rabbi Judah ha-Nasi's attitude to places in Babylonia see Source 5 and the section on Sages and Šəḵanṣiv in the entry on "Šəḵanṣiv." See also Neusner, *PAAJR* 31 (1963): 192f.

[12] The Sabbath sin was flooding a fishpond and thus catching a large number of fish. See Beer, *Amora'ei Bavel*, pp. 151–152; and cf. the source, note 1, and the section on Economy in the entry on "Ləvai."

[13] Thus Eshel, p. 75.

BEER, *Amora'ei Bavel* (1974), pp. 151–152
BERLINER, *Beiträge* (1883), p. 28
DILLEMANN, *Haute Mésopotamie* (1962), pp. 92–93
ESHEL, *Yishuvei ha-Yehudim* (1979), pp. 74–76, 240
FUNK, *Juden* (1902–1908), vol. 1, p. 42
FUNK, *Monumenta* (1913), pp. 27, 52, 290
HERZFELD, *Samarra* (1948), pp. 34–35
HIRSCHENSON, *Sheva Ḥokhmot* (1883), p. 72
JASTROW, *Dictionary* (1950³), p. 167
KOHUT, *Arukh ha-Shalem* (1878–1892), vol. 2, pp. 57–58 "בירה"
KRAUSS, *Qadmoniot ha-Talmud* (1923–1945), vol. 1 A, p. 50
LEVY, *Wörterbuch* (1924²), vol. 1, pp. 223, 569
MÜLLER, *RE*, vol. 3, s.v. "Birtha", cols. 498–499
MUSIL, *The Middle Euphrates* (1927), pp. 333ff., 363
NEUBAUER, *Géographie* (1868), p. 399
NEUSNER, *History* (1965–1970), vol. 4, p. 46
NEWMAN, *Agricultural Life* (1932), pp. 13, 138
OBERMEYER, *Landschaft* (1929), p. 73, n. 2
SARRE & HERZFELD, *Archäologische Reise* (1911), vol. 1, pp. 218–231
TOWNSEND, *JNES* 13 (1954): 52ff.
WIDENGREN, *Iranica Antiqua* 1 (1961): 132 and n. 1, 2
WINCKLER, *Altorientalische Forschungen* II vol. 1 (1898): 526f.

Borsif בורסיף

A. *Sources*

1. Sanhedrin 109a

אמר רב יוסף, בבל ובורסיף סימן רע לתורה[1], מאי בורסיף, אמר ר׳ אסי בור שאפי[2].

Rav Joseph said, Babylon and Borsif are an evil omen for the Torah.[1] What is Borsif? Rabbi Assi said, It is *bor šafe*.[2]

2. Shabbat 36a (= Sukkah 34a)

אמר רב אשי[3], אף אנו נאמר בבל בורסיף בורסיף בבל.

Rav Ashi[3] said, We too will say Babylon [is] Borsif, Borsif Babylon.

3. ʿAvodah Zarah 11b

אמר רב חנן בר רב חסדא אמר רב, ואמרי לה א״ר חנן בר רבא אמר רב: חמשה בתי עבודת כוכבים קבועין הן, אלו הן בית בל בבבל, בית נבו בכורסי[4], תרעתא שבמפג, צריפא שבאשקלון, נשרא שבערביא.

---

[1] The Munich MS goes on to say "Babylon, for there the Lord confounded the speech of the whole earth" as do other MSS, and see *Diq. Sof.*

[2] A kind of popular etymology for Borsif, meaning "a smooth (or, empty) pit"; for other versions see *Diq. Sof.*, n. ה as well as the talmudic dictionaries.

[3] The Sukkah parallel has Rava b. Joseph making the statement, apparently meaning Rava. But the Munich B MS has "Rav Ashi" like the Shabbat version, and see *Diq. Sof.*

[4] The source has כורסי. The Munich MS has בורסין, and see *Diq. Sof.*; the Spanish MS (Abramson ed.) has כורסיף; *Halakhot Gedolot, Hilkhot* ʿAvodah Zarah, has בורסיף. There does not seem to be any doubt that Borsif is meant. On the Temple of Nebo see also Inscription 1 in the entry on "Babylon."

Rav Ḥanan b. Rav Ḥisda said Rav said, and some have it that Rav Ḥanan b. Rava said Rav said, Five heathen temples are long established. They are that of Bel in Babylon, Nebo in Borsif,[4] Tarʿata in Mapag, Ṣərifa in Ašqəlon, Nišra in ʿArabia.

4. Genesis Rabbah, XXXVIII 11 (Theodor-Albeck ed., pp. 360–361)

חד תלמיד מדר׳ יוחנן הוה יתיב קומיה, הוה מסבר ליה ולא סבר, אמר ליה מאי האי, אמר ליה דאנא גלי מאתרי, אמר ליה מן הידן אתר את, אמר ליה מן בורסיף, אמר ליה לא כן אלא בולסיף[5] ״כי שם בלל ה׳ שפת״.

A pupil of Rabbi Yoḥanan was sitting before him. He explained and he did not understand. He said, What is it? He said, That I've been exiled from my place. He said, What place are you from? He said, From Borsif. He said, Not that, but Bolsif,[5] because "there the Lord confounded (*balal*) the speech of the whole earth" (Gen. 11:9).

Pərat də-Borsif

5. Yoma 10a

... תני רב יוסף אשור זה סילק.[6] ״ויבן את נינוה ואת רחובות עיר ואת כלח,״ נינוה כמשמעו, רחובות עיר זו פרת דמישן, כלח זו פרת דבורסיף.

... Rav Joseph taught, Aššur is Sileq.[6] "and built Nineveh, Rəḥovot-ʿir, Kalaḥ" (Gen. 10:11). Nineveh is what it says, Reḥovot-ʿir is Pərat də-Mešan, Kalaḥ is Pərat də-Borsif.

6. Qiddushin 72a

מאי חביל ימא, אמר רב פפא, זו פרת דבורסי.[7]

What is Ḥavel Yama? Rav Papa said, It is Pərat də-Borsif.[7]

7. Strabo XVI 1,6 (739)

ἔστι δὲ καὶ τῶν Χαλδαίων τῶν ἀστρονομικῶν γένη πλείω· καὶ γὰρ Ὀρχηνοί τινες προσαγορεύονται καὶ Βορσιππηνοὶ καὶ ἄλλοι πλείους ὡς ἂν κατὰ αἱρέσεις ἄλλα καὶ ἄλλα νέμοντες περὶ τῶν αὐτῶν δόγματα.

There are also several tribes of the Chaldaean astronomers. For example, some are called Orcheni, others Borsippeni, and several others by different names,

---

[5] Manuscripts and printings also have בול סוף, and see Genesis Rabbah (Theodor-Albeck ed.) for variants. The parallel in *Yalquṭ Shimʿoni* also has the version "Not that, but Babylon, for it is said because the Lord confounded ..." (*Yalquṭ Shimʿoni* for Genesis § 62 according to the Oxford MS, Mossad Harav Kook ed., p. 236; in the printing the version is like that of Genesis Rabbah). It should be kept in mind that Rabbi Yoḥanan habitually reproached pupils from Babylonia. Cf. Bacher, *Palästinensische Amoräer*, vol. 1, pp. 212–213.

[6] See the entry on "Seleucia" under "Maḥoza Area."

[7] Although the source has פרת דבורסי, the Munich MS has פרת דבורסיף, which is what seems correct (the Vatican 111 MS has דבורציף, and interlinearly דבורסיף).

as though divided into different sects which hold to various dogmas about the same subjects. (trans.: H. L. Jones, LCL)

8. Strabo XVI 1,7 (739)

Τὰ δὲ Βόρσιππα ἱερὰ πόλις ἐστὶν Ἀρτέμιδος καὶ Ἀπόλλωνος, λινουργεῖον μέγα. πληθύουσι δὲ ἐν αὐτῇ νυκτερίδες μείζους πολὺ τῶν ἐν ἄλλοις τόποις· ἁλίσκονται δ' εἰς βρῶσιν καὶ ταριχεύονται.

Borsippa is a city sacred to Artemis and Apollo, and it manufactures linen in great quantities. It abounds in bats, much larger in size than those in other places; and these bats are caught and salted for food. (trans.: H. L. Jones, LCL)

B. *Location*

Presentday Birs Nimrūd, southwest of the site of Babylon (q.v.) (D4 on the Tal. Bab. map).

C. *Identification*

The identification of Borsif with the Burs mentioned in Arabic sources (presentday Birs Nimrūd) does not seem to present any difficulties.[8] Some information is available on Burs: Yāqūt says that it is a place in the neighborhood of Babylon where there are remains of Nebuchadnezzar's palace and a very high tell called Ṣarḥ al-Burs.[9] There was a lake (*ağama*) at Burs known as Ağamat Burs. It was near Ṣarḥ Nimrūd in Babylon, and had a deep bed that was said to be a pit from which the mortar to build the Tower was taken, and some say the earth opened up there (cf. note 2).[10] Bakrī reports that Burs was a well-known lake whose water was the sweetest in al-Ğāmiʿ.[11] On textile manufacture in Burs see the entry on "Nareš." Compare also the entry on "Nəhar Abba" and its proposed identification with Tall Aba, which is in the same neighborhood as Burs.[12]

---

[8] See already Obermeyer, p. 314. On the Burs-Nars confusion common in Arabic sources see the entry on "Nareš." On a village called Bursuf east of Baghdad, see Yāqūt, s.v. "Bursuf."

[9] Yāqūt, s.v. "Burs." Sometimes it is said that the Tower was in Babylon. See, e.g., Ṭabarī, *Tafsīr* (Būlāq), vol. 3, pp. 16–17. This may indicate a confusion between Babylon and Borsif (cf. Source 2).

[10] *Futūḥ al-buldān*, p. 247. Balāḏurī sums up "God knows better." The lake in Burs is mentioned in connection with taxation; see *Futūḥ al-buldān, loc.cit.*; Yāqūt, s.v. "Ağamat Burs" (quoting *Futūḥ al-buldān*); Yaḥyā b. Ādam, *Ḫarāğ*, p. 31; Abū Yūsuf, *Ḫarāğ*, pp. 95, 112.

[11] Bakrī, s.v. "Burs." Al-Ğāmiʿ is al-Ğāmiʿain, later Ḥilla (see the entries on "Nareš" and "Dəruqart").

[12] On Burs in the conquest of Iraq, see e.g. *Futūḥ al-buldān*, p. 255; Ṭabarī, vol. 3, pp. 619–620 (= vol. 1, pp. 2420–2421). Cf. Gil, *Tarbiẓ* 48 (1979): 51. See also Herzfeld, *EI*[1,2], s.v. "Birs"; ʿAwwād, *Sumer* 5 (1949): 74–75; Fransīs & ʿAwwād, *Sumer* 8 (1952): 256; Scoville, *Gazetteer*, vol. 1, p. 536, s.v. "Birs Nimrūd"; Morony, *Iran* 14 (1976): 44–45, 54.

D. *History*

Borsif was a Babylonian town that was destroyed by Xerxes I, partly rebuilt in the third century B.C. and finally abandoned before the Middle Ages. Obermeyer indicates that the Parthian-Sassanian Pərat də-Borsif was near Borsif.[13] Gibson observes that the pottery found in the vicinity of the old excavations at Borsif were exclusively neo-Babylonian, except for a very slight admixture of later Parthian types and Islamic ones.[14] The Parthian-Sassanian town may not be on the site of the earlier one, but al-Haik notes that the remains found there stem from various periods up to Arab times.[15] The site has not been excavated since 1902.

A cuneiform inscription of Antiochus I records building activity in 287 B.C. in the sanctuary of Esagila at Babylon and of Ezida at Borsippa. Land was taken over at the time from Borsippa, Babylon and Kuta, but under Antiochus II land was donated to these cities (see the entries on "Babylon" [and Inscriptions 2 and 3 there], "Seleucia" and "Kuta"). Greek and Latin sources indicate that in the first centuries B.C. and A.D. there was a flourishing town there.[16]

E. *Borsif and Its Environs*

Borsif was in the immediate vicinity of ancient Babylon, and the two appear together in Source 1. In Source 2, Rav Ashi, head of the Mata Məḥasya yeshiva in the sixth generation of Babylonian amoras, notes that the names Borsif and Babylon are used interchangeably. He does so in the course of discussing pairs of concepts whose meanings have come to overlap. Further on he says that it is of practical importance to distinguish between Babylon and Borsif in designating the place in a divorce decree.

Borsif was identified as the site of the Tower of Babel. The Tower is mentioned in the context of Source 1, with the words of Rav Joseph preceded by the comment of Rav on the air of the Tower having the power to make people forget to study the Torah. Sources 1 and 4 both note the defective learning of the Borsif people. There is no way of knowing whether the Borsif people were in fact guilty of ignorance which was attributed to the fact that their town was the site of the Tower. Their reputation may, on the contrary, have been an attempt of attach unfavorable features to the supposed site of the Tower, with no actual grounds. There may also be some connection between the mention of Borsif as the site of a heathen temple (in Source 2) and the emphasis on ignorance of the Torah there.

---

[13] Obermeyer, p. 315.

[14] Gibson, *The City and Area of Kish,* No. 233.

[15] See al-Haik, *Key Lists,* No. 105.

[16] In addition to the sources above, Borsif and its inhabitants are also mentioned in Stephanus Byzantius; Josephus, *Against Apion* I, 152, and in Ptolemy V 19.

Source 5 mentions Pərat də-Borsif,[17] apparently a settlement near Borsif which was given the name of a Parthian king, Phraates,[18] and designated Pərat də-Borsif to distinguish it from Pərat də-Mešan. Rav Joseph's proposal to identify it with Kalaḥ is untenable. Kalaḥ (Kalḫu in Assyrian) was the Assyrian empire's second capital (after Assur and before Nineveh) and was located some 500 kilometers north of Borsif (northeast of the mouth of the Greater Zāb River, thirty kilometers south of Mosul). The identification apparently reflects the habitual desire of the amoras to relate places mentioned in the Bible to their own neighborhood.[19]
Pərat də-Borsif is mentioned in Source 6 by Rav Papa in connection with the boundaries of the Babylonia "of pure lineage" (see Introduction). It is possible that the reference here is not to the settlement but to the section of the Euphrates (Pərat) River at Borsif.[20]

BERLINER, *Beiträge* (1883), pp. 26, 61
ELLIS, *Mesopotamian Archaeological Sites* (1972), pp. 61–62
ESHEL, *Yishuvei ha-Yehudim* (1979), pp. 50–51, 218
FEUCHTWANG, *MGWJ* 42 (1898): 153–154
FUNK, *Juden* (1902–1908), vol. 1, p. 13; vol. 2, p. 157
FUNK, *Monumenta* (1913), p. 289
GIBSON, *The City and Area of Kish* (1972), No. 233
AL-HAIK, *Key Lists* (1968), No. 105
HIRSCHENSON, *Sheva Ḥokhmot* (1883), pp. 66–67
JASTROW, *Dictionary* (1950³), p. 151
KOHUT, *Arukh ha-Shalem* (1878–1892), vol. 2, pp. 197–198; vol. 3, p. 477; *Tosefot* (1937), p. 108
KRAUSS, *MGWJ* 39 (1895): 59
KRAUSS, *Lehnwörter* (1898–1899), vol. 2, pp. 146
LEVY, *Wörterbuch* (1924²), vol. 1, p. 204
NEUBAUER, *Géographie* (1868), p. 346
NEUSNER, *History* (1965–1970), vol. 4, p. 389
OBERMEYER, *Landschaft* (1929), pp. 118–127, 314–315

Ctesiphon אקטיספון

See the entry under "Maḥoza Area."

---

[17] In Obermeyer's opinion (p. 315) Pərat də-Borsif was a town near Borsif, so named in order to distinguish it from Pərat də-Mešan. On the other hand he believes that the Pərat də-Borsi in Source 6 is a river, and suggests the right branch of the Euphrates that flowed before the town of Borsif, the Hindīya canal of today (and see Obermeyer, p. 119). The distinction seems reasonable, for in Source 6 Pərat də-Borsi figures as an explanation of Ḥavel Yama which is a region, and it appears that the name of the region was the same as that of the river that flowed through it. In any case, this identification as well as that of Ḥavel Yama (q.v.) requires further investigation.

[18] See Obermeyer, p. 315.

[19] See Pərat də-Borsif (p. 218) and Kalaḥ (p. 131) in Eshel.

[20] See Obermeyer, p. 315.

Damharya דמהריא

A. *Sources*

1. Rosh ha-Shanah 21a

רב נחמן[1] יתיב בתעניתא כוליה יומי דכיפורי, לאורתא אתא ההוא גברא אמר ליה למחר[2] יומא רבה במערבא, אמר ליה מהיכא את,[3] אמר ליה מדמהריא,[4] אמר ליה דם תהא אחריתו, קרי עליה[5] "קלים היו רודפינו."

Rav Naḥman[1] sat fasting all of the Day of Atonement. In the evening that man came and said to him, Tomorrow[2] is the Day of Atonement in Eretz Israel. He said to him, Where are you from?[3] He said to him, From Damharya.[4] He said to him, Blood (= *dam*) will be your end. He read about him,[5] "Swift were our pursuers" (Lam. 4:19).

2. ʿEruvin 6a

... וכן אמר ליה רב הונא לרב חנן בר רבא[6] לא תפלוג עלאי, דרב איקלע לדמחריא[7] ועבד עובדא כוותי, אמר ליה רב בקעה מצא וגדר בה גדר.

... And thus said to him Rav Huna to Rav Ḥanan b. Rava,[6] Do not dispute me, for Rav happened to come to Damharya[7] and did as I did. He said to him, Rav found an open field and fenced it in.

3. Sanhedrin 29b

רבינא איקלע לדמהריא, אמר ליה רב דימי בר רב הונא מדמהריא לרבינא מטלטלי ואיתנהו בעינייהו מאי ...

Ravina happened to come to Damharya. Rav Dimi b. Rav Huna of Damharya said to Ravina, Movables that are intact, what is [the rule] ...?

4. Menaḥot 81a

רבינא איקלע לדמהוריא[8] אמר ליה רב דימי בריה דרב הונא מדמהוריא[9] לרבינא ולייתי בהמה ולימא הרי עלי ...

---

[1] The Munich and London MSS have "Rav Naḥman b. Isaac"; and see *Diq. Sof.*

[2] The Munich, Oxford and London MSS have האידנא (= now) which is more likely since the man got to Rav Naḥman in the evening, that is, when the Day of Atonement had already begun by his count; and see *Diq. Sof.*

[3] The Munich MS has אתית (= Where did you come from) as do the other MSS; and see *Diq. Sof.*

[4] The Munich MS has מדניהריא, the Oxford MS has מדמתריא, the Munich B MS has מדמהרוניא; and see *Diq. Sof.*

[5] The Munich MS has "Rav read about him," a scribal error.

[6] The Munich and Oxford MSS have "Rav Ḥanin b. Abba"; and see *Diq. Sof.* See also Albeck, *Mavo la-Talmudim*, p. 198, n. 107.

[7] The source has לדמחריא, the Munich and Oxford MSS and the Salonika printing have לדמהריא and the Pesaro printing has לדחמריא; and see *Diq. Sof.*

[8] The source has לדמהוריא, the Munich, Vatican 118, and Vatican 123 MSS have לדמהריא, the Cairo MS has לדמהדיא; and see *Diq. Sof.*

[9] The source has מדמהוריא, the Munich, Vatican 118 and Vatican 123 MSS have מדמהריא, the Cairo MS has לדמהדיא; and see *Diq. Sof.*

Ravina happened to come to Damharya[8] and Rav Dimi b. Rav Huna of Damharya[9] said to Ravina, Let him bring an animal and say, I take upon myself . . .

B. *Already Proposed Location*

Ḏamār, southwest of Sura (D4 on the Tal. Bab. map).

C. *Identification*

Obermeyer proposed identifying Damharya with a place called Ḏamār that appears in Ibn Rusta.[10] That identification seems reasonable, even though it is based on only one source. According to Ibn Rusta, Ḏamār was a station on the Baghdad-Kūfa road southwest of the Sūrā bridge. The distance from the Sūrā bridge[11] to Ḏamār is nine miles, and from Ḏamār, through a number of other stations, to Kūfa fifty-six miles, along the route described by Ibn Rusta.[12]

D. *Sages and Damharya*

Source 2 contains Rav Huna's testimony on a visit in Damharya of Rav, the founder of the Sura yeshiva in the first generation of Babylonian amoras.
Rav Dimi b. Rav Huna was active in Damharya in the fifth generation of Babylonian amoras[13] and Sources 3 and 4 mention two questions on halakhic matters he submitted to Ravina when the latter happened to be in Damharya.

BERLINER, *Beiträge* (1883), p. 30
ESHEL, *Yishuvei ha-Yehudim* (1979), pp. 96–97
FUNK, *Monumenta* (1913), pp. 29, 291
JASTROW, *Dictionary* (1950³), p. 312
KRAUSS, *Tosefot Arukh ha-Shalem* (1937), p. 144
NEUBAUER, *Géographie* (1868), p. 390
NEUSNER, *History* (1965–1970), vol. 2, p. 247; vol. 3, p. 319
OBERMEYER, *Landschaft* (1929), pp. 42–43; 48–49, 298
ZURI, *Shilton* (1938), p. 237

---

[10] Obermeyer, p. 298, and see Ibn Rusta, p. 182.

[11] Ibn Rusta has "the Sūrān bridge." See de Goeje, *ZDMG* 39 (1885): 11. Obermeyer's explanation for the derivation of the name Sūrān (*loc.cit.*, n. 7) is not tenable. Cf. *Futūḥ al-buldān*, pp. 359–369; Muqaddasī, pp. 412–413.

[12] The name "Ḏamār" is mentioned twice in Ibn Rusta, and in the first instance the editor, de Goeje, notes that it can be read "Ḏamād"; and see also his article (*op.cit.* in n. 11). If the form Ḏamār is admissible, it may have developed by analogy with a place in Yemen by the same name (q.v. in Yāqūt and Bakrī). According to one of the versions in Yāqūt, "Ḏimār" is another name for Ṣan'ā'. Yāqūt adds that traditionists call the place in Yemen by the name Ḏimār. In Rashi, on Sanhedrin 29b, the form is לדימהריא (= Dimharya), but as Rav Naḥman in Source 1 derives the word "blood" (= *dam*) from the place name, the vowel could not have been *i*. See also "Ḏamār" in *Muštarik*, *ar-Rauḍ al-mi'ṭār*, and Streck, *Die alte Landschaft*, vol. 1, p. 11.

[13] See Albeck, *Mavo la-Talmudim*, p. 406.

Damim דמים

A. *Source*

Bava Metzi'a 86a

אמר רב כהנא[1] אישתעי לי רב חמא[2] בר ברתיה דחסא רבה בר נחמני אגב שמדא נח נפשיה. אכלו ביה קורצא בי מלכא, אמרו איכא חד גברא ביהודאי דקא מבטל תריסר אלפי[3] גברי מישראל ירחא בקייטא וירחא בסתוא מכרגא דמלכא.[4] שדרו פריסתקא דמלכא בתריה ולא אשכחיה. ערק ואזל מפומבדיתא לאקרא[5] מאקרא לאגמא[6] ומאגמא לשחין[7] ומשחין לצריפא[8] ומצריפא לעינא דמים[9] ומעינא דמים לפומבדיתא . . .

Rav Kahana[1] said, Rav Ḥama[2] the son of Ḥasa's daughter told me: Rabbah b. Naḥmani's soul expired through persecution. He was informed against at the king's court, and they said, There is a person among the Jews who exempts twelve thousand[3] men of Israel a month in the summer and a month in the winter of the *karga* (= poll tax) of the king.[4] They sent an envoy of the king's after him and he did not find him. He fled and went from Pumbədita to Aqra[5], from Aqra to Agama,[6] from Agama to Šaḥin,[7] and from Šaḥin to Ṣərifa,[8] and from Ṣərifa to 'Ena Damim,[9] and from 'Ena Damim to Pumbədita . . .

B. *Already Proposed Location*

Dimimmā near Anbār (see the entry on "Pumbədita") near the diffluence of the Nahr 'Īsā and the Euphrates.

---

[1] The Florence MS has "Ravina."

[2] The Munich, Hamburg, Florence and Vatican 117 MSS have "Ḥama" (without "Rav"). *Ein Ya'aqov* has "Ḥama" further on as well (instead of Ḥasa); see *Diq. Sof.*

[3] The Munich, Florence and Vatican 117 MSS have "thirteen thousand."

[4] The Hamburg MS has שית ירחי בקיטא ושית ירחי בסיתוא. The word שית (= six) is erased in both places, and the plural ירחי is corrected interlinearly to the singular ירחא. All manuscripts have *karga* without the addition "of the king." See also *Diq. Sof.*

[5] The Munich, Vatican 116, Vatican 117, Florence and Hamburg MSS do not have "Aqra" at al.

[6] The Munich, Vatican 116, and Vatican 117 MSS have "Agama" as the last place in the escape route.

[7] The Munich MS has שהי', the Florence MS has שיחא, the Hamburg MS has אפדנא דשוחא, the Vatican 116 MS has אפדנא דשיזהא, the Vatican 117 MS has אפדנא דשיהיא and אפדנא דשיסתנא further on.

[8] The Munich, Florence, Hamburg, Vatican 116 and Vatican 117 MSS have צריפא דעינא some printings also have the form צריכא.

[9] "'Ena Damim" occurs only in the printing; see n. 8 and *Diq. Sof.* The name Damim may have been dropped because of the odd meaning of 'En Damim (= spring of blood). Perhaps, however, the name should be vocalized as 'Ena də-Mayim or 'Ena də-Maya (= the spring of water).

C. *Identification*

The source above describes the escape route of Rabbah, head of the Pumbədita yeshiva in the third generation of Babylonian amoras. According to that testimony, Rabbah had to flee the wrath of the authorities, because he was reported to be contributing to non-payment of the poll tax by Jews on a massive scale. That situation came about because thousands of Jews left their places of residence (where the tax was levied) and streamed into Pumbədita in the *yarḥei kallah*, the "conference" months (Adar and Elul when the yeshiva was open to all).[10] The passage goes on to describe Rabbah's death as a result of the affair.

Starting out from Pumbədita, Rabbah eventually ended up there, indicating in Obermeyer's view that the route described was circular. ʿEna Damim, the last place before Rabbah's return to Pumbədita, was identified by Obermeyer with Dimimmā near Anbār, adjacent to Pumbədita (q.v.).[11] Dimimmā is a large village south of Anbār, near the diffluence of the Nahr ʿĪsā and the Euphrates, a place where the Euphrates was spanned by a stone bridge likewise known as Dimimmā.[12] The name may be an abridgement of the earlier Aramaic name of the place, Damim Mata (*mata* = place).[13] Obermeyer's identification seems well founded, and the propinquity of Dimimmā to Pumbədita is a conclusive reason for adopting it, if the form ʿEna Damim is indeed correct.[14]

The identification of the other places along Rabbah's escape route is harder, the more so since their names occur in a number of variants in the manuscripts.[15] Obermeyer claims that the first two places, Aqra and Agama, are actually one place—Aqra də-Agama—and in fact a place of that name is mentioned

---

[10] On the historical background to this affair see e.g. Beer, *Tarbiẓ* 33 (1964): 349–357; Urbach, *Tarbiẓ* 34 (1965): 156–161; Beer, *Rashut ha-Golah*, pp. 210–224. On the institution of the *kallah* in the amoraic period, see Gafni, *Ha-Yeshiva be-Bavel*, pp. 131–144; Goodblatt, *Rabbinic Instruction*, pp. 155–170.

[11] Obermeyer, pp. 236–238.

[12] On Dimimmā see Abū l-Fidā', p. 47; Yāqūt, *Marāṣid*, s.v. "Dimimmā"; Yāqūt, s.v. "Nahr ʿĪsā"; Idrīsī, vol. 6, p. 667; Dīnawarī, *Aḫbār ṭiwāl*, vol. 1, p. 366; Abū l-Fidā' has "Dahamā," which Streck (*Die alte Landschaft*, vol. 1, pp. 25–26) miscorrected to "Dimmimā" (instead of "Dimimmā," as the second *mim* has the *šadda*). See also Iṣṭaḫrī, p. 84; Ibn Ḥauqal, p. 242; Muqaddasī, pp. 54, 115; Ṭabarī, vol. 7, pp. 410, 412 (= vol. 3, pp. 10, 13). Cf. *Ḥudūd al-ʿālam* (p. 76), who says Nahr ʿĪsā branches off from the Euphrates "after," i.e. south of, Anbār. Near Dimimmā is an estate known as Fallūǧa; Yāqūt, s.v. "Dimimmā." The two are mentioned together also in Ibn al-Aṯīr, *Kāmil*, vol. 9, p. 602. See also Le Strange, p. 66; al-ʿAlī, *Sumer* 21 (1965): 234; Le Strange, "Ibn Serapion," p. 14; Suhrāb, p. 123; Ǧāḥiẓ, *Buldān*, p. 198. See also the entries on "Nəhar Anaq" and "Pumbədita."

[13] Obermeyer, p. 237, n. 3.

[14] See n. 9.

[15] See nn. 5 to 9.

in various other passages in the Talmud.[16] Still, further on, the passage states that Rabbah was in Agama (without "Aqra") another time. In any case, various proposals have been made for the identification of Aqra, Agama (or Aqra də-Agama), Šaḥin and Ṣərifa, but the available data are insufficient to permit either their acceptance or rejection.[17]

Eshel, *Yishuvei ha-Yehudim* (1979), p. 205
Krauss, *Paras we-Romi* (1948), p. 155, n. 28
Neubauer, *Géographie* (1868), p. 368
Neusner, *History* (1965–1970), vol. 4, p. 41
Obermeyer, *Landschaft* (1929), p. 237

Dəruqart דרוקרת

A. *Sources*

1. Taʿanit 21b

בדרוקרת[1] הוות דליקתא ובשיבבותיה דרב הונא לא הוות דליקתא.

In Dəruqart[1] there was a fire, and in the neighborhood of Rav Huna there was no fire.

2. Taʿanit 21b

דרוקרת[2] עיר המוציאה חמש מאות רגלי הוה ויצאו ממנה שלשה מתים ביום אחד, גזר רב נחמן בר רב חסדא תעניתא. אמר רב נחמן בר יצחק כמאן, כרבי מאיר, דאמר ריחק נגיחותיו חייב, קירב נגיחותיו לא כל שכן. אמר ליה רב נחמן בר רב חסדא לרב נחמן בר יצחק ליקום מר ליתי לגבן, אמר ליה תנינא רבי יוסי אומר לא מקומו של אדם מכבדו, אלא אדם מכבד את מקומו . . . אמר ליה אי הכי ניקום אנא לגבי מר, אמר ליה מוטב יבא מנה בן פרס אצל מנה בן מנה, ואל יבא מנה בן מנה אצל מנה בן פרס.

In Dəruqart,[2] a city that supplies five hundred foot soldiers, and had three deaths in ony day, Rav Naḥman b. Rav Ḥisda ordained a fast. Rav Naḥman

[16] Rabbi says, in Qiddushin 72a: אקרא דאגמא יש בבבל אדא בר אהבה יש בה (= There is an Aqra də-Agama in Babylonia, and Adda b. Ahavah in it); in Sanhedrin 38b: אמר רב אחא מאקרא דאגמא אמר רבי יוחנן בר חנינא (= Rav Aḥa of Aqra də-Agama said that Rabbi Yoḥanan b. Ḥanina said); in Bava Batra 127a: שלחו ליה בני אקרא דאגמא לשמואל (= The people of Aqra də-Agama sent [it] to him to Samuel); in ʿAvodah Zarah 39a: רבה בר בר חנה איקלע לאקרא דאגמא (= Rabbah b. Bar Ḥana happened to come to Aqra də-Agama).

[17] See e.g. Neubauer, p. 368; Berliner, p. 22; Funk, *Monumenta*, pp. 23, 288; Obermeyer, p. 237; Eshel, according to the entries.

[1] The name occurs in MSS in various forms, such as דיוקרת (Munich MS) and דרדקת (Munich B MS). See *Diq. Sof.*

[2] MSS and printings have other forms of the name (see n. 1). Rashi has the additional form דיוקרא but his comment implies the form יו"ד קרת, and cf. Qiddushin 16b.

b. Isaac said, This must be in accordance with the view of Rabbi Meir who declared, If for goring at long intervals [during three days] there is [full] liability, how much more so for goring at short intervals [in one day]. Said Rav Naḥman b. Rav Ḥisda to Rav Naḥman b. Isaac, Pray, take a seat nearer us. The latter replied, We have taught, Rabbi Yose says: It is not the place that honors the man but the man who honors the place . . . The former retorted, If so, I will come nearer to you; whereupon the latter replied, It is more fitting that a scholar who is the son of an ordinary man should go to the one who is a scholar and the son of a scholar, than that the latter should go to the former.

3. Shabbat 94b

ההוא שכבא דהוה בדרוקרא[3] שרא רב נחמן בר יצחק לאפוקיה לכרמלית.

A dead body was lying in Dəruqart[3] which Rav Naḥman b. Isaac allowed to be carried out into a *karmelit*.

4. Niddah 58b

אמר רב נחמן בר יצחק והא דדוקרת[4] כעיר שיש בה חזירים דמיא.

Rav Naḥman b. Isaac stated, The condition of Dəruqart[4] is like that of a town in which there are pigs.

5. Ta'anit 23b–24a

רבי יוסי בר אבין הוה שכיח קמיה דר׳ יוסי דמן יוקרת,[5] שבקיה ואתא לקמיה דרב אשי . . . אמר ליה ולאו קמיה דר׳ יוסי דמן יוקרת הוה שכיח מר, אמר ליה הן. אמר ליה ומ״ט שבקיה מר ואתא הכא, אמר ליה גברא דעל בריה ועל ברתיה לא חס עלי דידי היכי חייס . . .

Rabbi Yose b. Avin used to be with Rabbi Yose of Dəruqart,[5] left him and came to Rav Ashi . . . [who] said to him, Didn't you use to [study] with Rabbi Yose of Dəruqart? He said, Yes. He said, What's the reason for leaving him and coming here? He said, A person who doesn't spare his son and daughter, how will he spare me . . .

B. *Proposed Location*

Durqaiṭ on the Sura River, in the vicinity of Sura (D4 on the Tal. Bab. map).

---

[3] The source has דרוקרא. The R-i-f has בדרוקרת while a MS of the R-i-f has בדיוקרת. See *Diq. Sof.*

[4] The source has דדוקרת; the Munich MS has דרוקר׳.

[5] The source has יוקרת, the Munich MS and *Aggadot ha-Talmud* has יוקדת (later too); the Munich B MS has ידקרת (later too); Rashi has דיוקרת. All seem to mean Dəruqart, but see the comments of *Diq. Sof.* on this, n. כ; and Klein, who locates it in Eretz Israel (*Eretz ha-Galil*, pp. 37, 128; *Sefer ha-Yishuv* [addenda], vol. 1, p. 177, s. v. ״יוקרת״).

C. *Identification*

Obermeyer identified Dəruqart with Darauqara in the Mesene region of southern Babylonia.[6] This identification seems doubtful because it would place Dəruqart with its considerable Jewish population outside the Babylonia "of pure lineage,"[7] and also because Dəruqart is mentioned as the home of Rav Huna who headed the Sura yeshiva. It is more reasonable to place Dəruqart on the Sura River, as is done by Rav Naṭronai Gaon in a statement quoted in *Otzar ha-Geonim* in reference to Source 1: "Dəruqart is a place in Babylonia situated on the River Sura, as Rav Naṭronai Gaon has written."[8]

The location of Dəruqart in relation to Sura is clearly shown in a statement of Ṭabarī's dealing with two consecutive battles in the Sura area.[9] In the first, an army from Qaṣr Ibn Hubaira, after crossing the Sura by ferry, fought an army encamped at the start of the al-Ǧāmiʿ canal (*Fam al-ǧāmiʿ*). Then, when the army from Qaṣr Ibn Hubaira had reformed with reinforcements that reached it at the village of al-Ǧāmiʿ (on the right bank of the al-Ǧāmiʿ canal), a second battle was fought between that village and Nahr Durqaiṭ. The name al-Ǧāmiʿ—of the canal and village—suggests al-Ǧāmiʿain, the ancient name of Ḥilla.[10]

D. *Sages and Dəruqart*

Source 1, which tells of a fire that broke out in Dəruqart but did not spread to the neighborhood of Rav Huna, the head of the Sura yeshiva, is evidence that he lived in Dəruqart.

Referring to a fast which Rav Naḥman b. Rav Ḥisda, of the fourth generation of Babylonian amoras, ordered the inhabitants of Dəruqart to observe when it was feared that an epidemic was imminent, Source 2 implies the existence of a fairly large Jewish community in the place. Rav Naḥman b. Rav Ḥisda lived there and following an argument between him and Rav Naḥman b.

---

[6] Obermeyer, p. 197. The identification with Darauqara or Dauqara had previously been proposed by Funk, *Juden*, vol. 1, p. 111, n. 1. See also *Maǧallatu l-maǧmaʿi l-ʿilmī l-ʿarabī*, 10 (1930): 480; al-Qāḍī at-Tanūḫī, *Nišwār al-muḥāḍara*, vol. 8, p. 100; Yaʿqūb Sarkīs, *Mabāḥiṯ ʿirāqīya*, vol. 1, pp. 295, 297. The reading should apparently be ad-Darauqara instead of al-Ḥarāuqala; Yāqūt, s.v. "Darauqara" and "Dauqara" as well as "Wāsiṭ," p. 349.

[7] See Introduction.

[8] דרקרת פי' מאתא בבבל על נהר סורא מותבא, כך כתב רב נטרונאי גאון *Otzar ha-Geonim*, Taʿanit, *ha-Perushim*, § 149.

[9] Ṭabarī, vol. 8, p. 436 (= vol. 3, pp. 857–858). The letter *dāl* is vocalized Durqaiṭ in the Cairo and Leiden editions. Cf. perhaps *Futūḥ al-buldān*, p. 271; Yāqūt, *Marāṣid*, s.v. "Darqaiṭ"; Ṭabarī, vol. 2, p. 41 (= vol. 1, p. 819); Nöldeke, *Perser und Araber*, p. 16 (Darqīṭ); Ibn Ḫurdāḏbih, pp. 7, 9 (Durqīṭ); Qudāma, *Ḫarāǧ*, pp. 236, 237.

[10] Lassner, *EI*², s.v. "Ḥilla"; Yāqūt, s.vv. "Ḥilla," "Ǧāmiʿaini"; cf. perhaps Ibn al-Faqīh, p. 183.

Isaac, the latter came there. Sources 3 and 4 confirm that Rav Naḥman b. Isaac was associated with Dəruqart. If the place noted in Source 5 is properly construed as Dəruqart, it was the home of another sage, Rabbi Yose *de-min* Yuqart, who belonged to the sixth generation of Babylonian amoras. According to the continuation of the Taʿanit passage, that sage engaged in such extreme Hassidic practices that he caused the death of his son and daughter. His disciple, Rabbi Yose b. Avin, left him because of that extremism and went to study with Rav Ashi.[11]

Albeck, *Mavo la-Talmudim* (1969), pp. 370–371, 395–396
Beer, *Amora'ei Bavel* (1974), pp. 231–232
Berliner, *Beiträge* (1883), pp. 30, 31
Eshel, *Yishuvei ha-Yehudim* (1979), pp. 101–102
Funk, *Jahrbuch* 9 (1911/12): 209, n. 2
Funk, *Juden* (1902–1908), vol. 1, p. 111, n. 1; vol. 2, p. 158
Funk, *Monumenta* (1913), pp. 30, 291
Graetz, *Geschichte* (1908⁴), vol. 4, p. 289
Hirschenson, *Sheva Ḥokhmot* (1883), pp. 100, 125
Hyman, *Toledot Tanaim we-Amoraim* (1964), pp. 338, 941, 943
Jastrow, *Dictionary* (1950³), pp. 332, 568
Kohut, *Arukh ha-Shalem* (1878–1892), vol. 3, p. 162; vol. 4, pp. 112–113; *Tosefot* (1937), pp. 135, 153, 212
Krauss, *Qadmoniot ha-Talmud* (1923–1945), vol. 1, pp. 39, 43
Levy, *Wörterbuch* (1924²), vol. 1, pp. 428, 571
Neubauer, *Géographie* (1868), p. 390
Neusner, *History* (1965–1970), vol. 4, pp. 176, 289
Neusner, *Talmudic Judaism* (1976), p. 69
Newman, *Agricultural Life* (1932), p. 24
Obermeyer, *Landschaft* (1929), p. 197
Wiesner, *Scholien* (1862), vol. 2, p. 193
Zuri, *Shilton* (1938), pp. 163, 212 n. 4, 224

Difte דפתי

A. *Sources*

1. Berakhot 8b[1]; Shabbat 142b[2]

תנא ליה[4] חייא בר רב מדפתי.[3]

Ḥiyya b. Rav of Difte[3] taught him.[4]

---

[11] See Albeck, *Mavo la-Talmudim*, pp. 395–396.

[1] Parallels are Shabbat 10a, Pesaḥim 68b, Yoma 81b, Rosh ha-Shanah 9a, Yevamot 74a, Ketubot 68a, Bava Batra 10a.

[2] The Munich MS has "Rav Aḥa of Difte," but as the matter concerns a *baraita*, the version in the printing is to be preferred, and see the section below on Sages and Difte.

[3] Some of the sources have מדפתי and some have מדיפתי.

[4] This is the version in Berakhot 8b. One wording or another referring to the citing of a *baraita* figures in all the sources listed in n. 1 except for Bava Batra 10a which has אמר ליה (= said to him) although a *baraita* is cited thereafter in the passage.

2. Shabbat 18b (twice)[5] Berakhot 25a (the printing has "Rav Judah of Difte");[6] Shabbat 22a (the printing has "Rav Samuel of Difte");[7] 146b (the printing has "Rav Yemar of Difte");[8] Yoma 42a;[9] Sanhedrin 27a;[10] Zevaḥim 99b[11]

רב ירמיה מדפתי.[3]

Rav Jeremiah of Difte.[3]

3. Berakhot 45b; Bava Qamma 80b (twice); Bava Batra 12b

רב אחא מדפתי.[3]

Rav Aḥa of Difte.[3]

4. Shabbat 139b;[12] Bava Qamma 26a;[13] Sanhedrin 42a[14]

אמר ליה רב אחא מדפתי[3] לרבינא . . .

Rav Aḥa of Difte[3] said to him, to Ravina . . .

5. Ketubot 104b (as per the Munich MS)

חמתיה דרב חייא אריכא מדפתי.[15]

The mother-in-law of Rav Ḥiyya Arika of Difte.[15]

---

[5] Parallels are Shabbat 74a, 82a, 109b, 155b; ʿEruvin 24a; Yoma 63a; Megillah 18b; Nedarim 22b; Qiddushin 33a; Bava Qamma 73a; Bava Batra 52a; 171b; Sanhedrin 69a; ʿAvodah Zarah 22b, 40a; Zevaḥim 15b, 18b, 34b (twice); Menaḥot 31b, 42a; Ḥullin 35b, 87b; Niddah 20a, 23a, 30a, 57b, 69a.

[6] The Munich and Florence MSS have "Rav Jeremiah of Difte," and see *Diq. Sof.*

[7] The Munich and Oxford MSS have "Rav Jeremiah of Difte," and see *Diq. Sof.* (whose author believes Rav Samuel [= שמואל] is a garble of the word משמאל that appears in the sentence).

[8] The Munich and Oxford MSS have "Rav Jeremiah of Difte," and see *Diq. Sof.*

[9] The Munich, Munich B and Oxford MSS have "Ravina said, Rav Jeremiah of Difte said to me"; the London MS has "Rav Joseph of Difte said."

[10] The Munich and Florence MSS have "Rav Judah of Difte said," and see *Diq. Sof.*

[11] The Vatican 118 and Cairo MSS do not have "Difte." *Diq. Sof.* accepts just "Rav Jeremiah" on the grounds that it is not logical that Rav Jeremiah of Difte who is a later amora should appear before Rav Assi who is mentioned subsequently in the passage. Albeck, however, rejects this claim on the assumption that the Rav Assi there is Rav Assi (or Atti) of the sixth generation of Babylonian amoras, so that he would naturally follow Rav Jeremiah of Difte who was of the fifth generation (and see *Diq. Sof.* for the place, note צ, and Albeck, *Mavo la-Talmudim*, p. 413, n. 415).

[12] Parallels are Betzah 21b; Yevamot 8a, 54a; Nedarim 23a, 66b; Nazir 42a; Giṭṭin 69b, 73a; Qiddushin 45b; Bava Qamma 14a, 25b, 96a, 105a, 116a; Bava Metziʿa 5b, 7a, 7b, 35b, 55a, 65a, 66b, 103a, 104b; Bava Batra 116a, 169a; Sanhedrin 15a, 53a, 61a, 66b; Shevuʿot 32a; Makkot 6a; Zevaḥim 4b, 58a, 88a; Menaḥot 5b, 8b; Ḥullin 109a; Bekhorot 19b.

[13] The Munich MS does not have the place-name.

[14] The Munich MS has "Rava of Difte said to Ravina" which *Diq. Sof.* believes was a case of רב א׳ being garbled to רבא.

[15] The Vatican 113 and Leningrad MSS have מדיפתי; the printed version does not have מדפתי at all. On this source, see Rosenthal, *Sefer Yalon*, p. 336.

B. *Location*

None can be proposed due to insufficient data.

C. *Attempts at Identification*

Obermeyer sought to identify Difte with Dibṯa in the vicinity of Wāsiṭ,[16] but that identification is unlikely because it would place Difte in Mesene, far from the main Jewish centers in Babylonia (see "Gifte" in the Appendix).

D. *Sages and Difte*

The Talmud mentions a number of sages from Difte. An examination of the various versions[17] makes it possible to establish that three amoras definitely had some connection with Difte, although their regular activity was at the main yeshivas. The three are Rav Ḥiyya b. Rav of Difte, Rav Jeremiah of Difte and Rav Aḥa of Difte.

Rav Ḥiyya b. Rav of Difte, of the third generation of Babylonian amoras, generally appears as teaching *baraitot*. Rav Jeremiah of Difte, of the fifth generation of Babylonian amoras, takes part in various halakhic discussions. Rav Aḥa of Difte,[18] of the seventh generation of Babylonian amoras, appears in a variety of halakhic discussions, in all of which he submits questions to Ravina. The T. B. Bava Batra contains indications that some sages wished to appoint Rav Aḥa of Difte head of the yeshiva at Mata Məḥasya (q. v.) but were stopped by Mar b. Rav Ashi.[19]

Eshel, *Yishuvei ha-Yehudim* (1979), pp. 99–100
Gafni, *Ha-Yeshiva be-Bavel* (1978), pp. 64, 169–174
Hirschenson, *Sheva Ḥokhmot* (1883), p. 99
Jastrow, *Dictionary* (1950³), p. 304
Kohut, *Arukh ha-Shalem* (1878–1892), vol. 3, p. 114
Neubauer, *Géographie* (1868), p. 390
Obermeyer, *Landschaft* (1929), p. 197
Zuri, *Shilton* (1938), pp. 238–239

16 Obermeyer, p. 197, and see in Yāqūt the entries for "Dibṯā" and "Dabaiṯā." See also Zuri (*Shilton*, p. 239, n. 22c), who doubted Obermeyer's identification and sought to fix the site of Difte according to the *Midrash ha-Gadol* version: "Rabbi Yoḥanan said from Nəhar Ešel to Rifte" (*Midrash ha-Gadol* to Exodus 9:33, Margulies ed., p. 140), believing that "Rifte" was supposed to be "Difte" (but see Sanhedrin 92b which says "from Nəhar Ešel to Rabbat Biq'at Dura" and the Munich MS which has "to Duḵte Biq'at Dura" there, and see *Diq. Sof.* for the place.

17 See nn. 2, 6–8, and 14.

18 On Rav Aḥa of Difte and the traditions on him in gaonic literature, and their significance, see Neusner, *History*, vol. 4, p. 82; vol. 5, passim.

19 Bava Batra 12b. On Rav Aḥa of Difte's frustration at not obtaining the appointment see also Bava Qamma 80b. On the attempt to have Rav Aḥa of Difte appointed head of the Mata Məḥasya yeshiva see Gafni, *Ha-Yeshiva be-Bavel*, pp. 169–174, and the bibliography there.

Disqarta דיסקרתא

A. *Sources*

1. Shabbat 93a; Nazir 52a; Soṭah 6b, 25a; Giṭṭin 28b; Niddah 55b

אמר רב יהודה מדיסקרתא.[1]

Rav Judah of Disqarta[1] said.

2. Nazir 35a; Yevamot 87b; Niddah 35a

אמר ליה רב יהודה מדיסקרתא[2] לרבא.

Rav Judah of Disqarta[2] said to Rava.

3. Bava Metziʿa 47a

אמר ליה רב הונא[3] מדסקרתא[4] לרבא.

Rav Huna[3] of Disqarta[4] said to Rava.

4. Niddah 39a

אמר רב פפא אמריתא לשמעתא קמיה רב יהודה מדסקרתא[5] . . . אישתיק ולא א״ל ולא מידי.

Rav Papa said, I spoke of that tradition before Rav Judah of Disqarta[5] . . . he kept silent and said nothing to me.

Disqarta də-Reš Galuta

5. ʿEruvin 59a

היכי דמי עיר של יחיד ונעשית של רבים, אמר רב יהודה כגון דאיסקרתא[6] דריש גלותא. א״ל רב נחמן מאי טעמא,[7] אילימא משום דשכיחי גבי הרמנא מדכרי אהדדי, כולהו ישראל נמי בצפרא דשבתא שכיחי גבי הדדי, אלא אמר רב נחמן, כגון דיסקרתא דנתזואי.[8]

---

[1] Giṭṭin 28b and Niddah 55b have מדסקרתא. The MSS also have מאיסקרתא (see the Munich MS for Shabbat 93a, and cf. also the Munich MS for Soṭah 6b (מדאיסקרת׳); in some places the Oxford MS has מדסקרתא. In the context of all the passages considered, Rav Judah of Disqarta's remarks always appear in connection with Rava's, and see Albeck, *Mavo la-Talmudim*, p. 365.

[2] Yevamot 87b has מדאסקרתא, Niddah 35b has מדסקרתא.

[3] The Munich MS and others have "Rav Judah"; the Vatican 117 MS has "Rav Huna," like the printing. See also *Diq. Sof.*

[4] The source has מדסקרתא, the Munich MS and others have מדיסקרתא, the Vatican 115 MS has מדסקיתא.

[5] The source has מדסקרתא, the Munich MS has מדיסקרתא.

[6] The source has דאיסקרתא, the Munich MS and others have דסקרתא; see also *Diq. Sof.*

[7] The Munich MS has א״ל רב נחמן דיסקרתא דריש גלותא מאי טעמא and see additional versions in *Diq. Sof.*

[8] The Munich MS has דסקרתא דנשואר, the Oxford MS has דסקרתא דנאתידוור, and see other versions in *Diq. Sof.*

How [it is possible to describe the condition of] a town of an individual that becomes one of many? Rav Judah said, Like Disqarta[6] də-Reš Galuta [the Exilarch's place]. What's the reason?[7] said Rav Naḥman. If you say it because those meeting at the ruler's remind each other, every Saturday morning too all Jews can be found with each other. Rather, said Rav Naḥman, like the *disqarta* of Nitzoi.[8]

B. *Proposed Location*

Daskara, a village in the Nahr al-Malik district southwest of Baghdad (D 3 on the Tal. Bab. map).

C. *Identification*

The identification of Disqarta with a place called Daskara is not new. A number of scholars have proposed identifying Disqarta with the Daskara on the road to Ḫurāsān, some hundred kilometers northeast of Baghdad,[9] but that location is far from the centers of Jewish settlement in Babylonia. Furthermore, the close ties between Rav Judah of Disqarta and Rava, head of the Maḥoza yeshiva, also make questionable the location of Disqarta at any great distance from Maḥoza. In addition, it should be noted that if the settlements of Disqarta and Disqarta də-Reš Galuta are identical, it is more reasonable to suppose that the place was near the seat of the Exilarch, which was then at Maḥoza (see below).

Yāqūt, under "Daskara" (q.v.), lists a number of places with this name, the first of which is "a large village with a pulpit in the neighborhood of Nahr al-Malik west[10] of Baghdad."[11] It is reasonable to suppose that it is that place that is to be identified with the talmudic Disqarta.

D. *Sages and Disqarta*

In all the texts where Disqarta appears, it is referred to as the place of residence of Rav Judah of Disqarta, of the fourth generation of Babylonian amoras. He is generally mentioned in connection with Rava in the context of discussions on various halakhic points. It may thus be inferred that there were close ties between Rav Judah of Disqarta and the Maḥoza yeshiva which Rava headed.[12]

---

[9] See Neubauer, p. 389, and Funk, *Jahrbuch* 9 (1911/12): 208; Obermeyer, p. 146, and others in his wake.

[10] Actually, southwest.

[11] Samʿānī, *Ansāb*, s.v. "ad-Daskarī," notes that it is five parasangs from Baghdad. See also *Marāṣid*, s.v. "Daskira": "a large village, resembling a little township, in the vicinity of Nahr al-Malik, on the bank of Nahr al-Malik."

[12] It might be said that Rav Judah of Disqarta was so named on the basis of his birthplace and not his residence, but in that case the connection between Rav Judah and Rava would have no bearing on the identification of Disqarta.

Source 4 implies that Rav Papa of the fifth generation of Babylonian amoras—a disciple of Rava's—also studied with Rav Judah of Disqarta.
Source 3 mentions Rav Huna of Disqarta, but it appears that the version in the manuscripts, where this source too refers to Rav Judah of Disqarta, is to be preferred, the more so since the discussion there is likewise conducted with Rava.

E. *Disqarta də-Reš Galuta*

Disqarta is not only the name of a place, but also a word meaning "estate" or "holding."[13] Thus the Talmud contains expressions like the "*disqarta* of *reš galuta* (= the Exilarch)" and the "*disqarta* of Nitzoi"—that is, an estate owned by a person of that name—and the "*disqarta* of slaves" (Giṭṭin 40a). At the same time, there seems to be an identity between the "Disqarta də-Reš Galuta" cited in Source 5 and the place called Disqarta.
The sage making the sole reference to "*disqarta də-reš galuta*" is Rav Judah. Taking into account the fact that in Rava's time the Exilarch resided in Maḥoza,[14] it may be assumed that this Rav Judah is Rav Judah of Disqarta, and "*disqarta də-reš galuta*" is identical with the Disqarta that was the place of residence of the Rav Judah who conducted frequent discussion with Rava (see the entry for "Sikra").

ALBECK, *Mavo la-Talmudim* (1969), p. 365
BEER, *Rashut ha-Golah* (1970), pp. 110, n. 37; 151
BERLINER, *Beiträge* (1883), p. 30
ESHEL, *Yishuvei ha-Yehudim* (1979), pp. 95–96, 98
FUNK, *Jahrbuch* 9 (1911/12): 208
FUNK, *Monumenta* (1913), pp. 29, 30, 291
GEIGER, *WZKM* 42 (1935): 126
GOODBLATT, *Rabbinic Instruction* (1975), pp. 218–219
HIRSCHENSON, *Sheva Ḥokhmot* (1883), p. 98
JASTROW, *Dictionary* (1950³), p. 303
KOHUT, *Arukh ha-Shalem* (1878–1892), vol. 3, p. 104; *Tosefot* (1937), p. 146
KRAUSS, *Qadmoniot ha-Talmud* (1923–1945), vol. 1, pp. 36, 68
KRAUSS, *Paras we-Romi* (1948), p. 148
LEVY, *Wörterbuch* (1924²), vol. 1 p. 415
NEUBAUER, *Géographie* (1868), p. 389
NEUSNER, *History* (1965–1970), vol. 2, p. 247
OBERMEYER, *Landschaft* (1929), p. 146

Dura də-Raʿawata דורא דרעותא

A. *Sources*

1. Bava Batra 54b

... אמר ליה אנא לא ידענא, עובדא הוה בדורא דרעותא[1] בישראל דזבן ארעא מעובד כוכבים ואתא ישראל אחרינא רפיק בה פורתא, אתא לקמיה דרב יהודה, אוקמה בידא

[13] See Eshel, s.v. "Disqarta də-Nitzoi" and the bibliography there (pp. 95–96).
[14] See, e.g., Beer, *Rashut ha-Golah*, p. 103, n. 31.

[1] The Florence MS has **דורא דרעוותא**, and further on as well; the Munich MS has **דורא דרעוותא**, but the same form as the printing further on.

דשני, א״ל לדורא דרעותא קאמרת, התם באגי מטמרי הוו, דאינהו גופייהו לא הוו יהבי טסקא למלכא, ומלכא אמר מאן דיהיב טסקא ליכול ארעא.

... He said to him (Rav Joseph to Abbaye), I don't know, there was a case in Dura də-Raʿawata[1] of a Jew who bought a field from a Gentile and another Jew came, dug in it a bit. He came before Rav Judah; he assigned it to the latter. He said to him (Abbaye to Rav Joseph), Dura də-Raʿawata, you say, there were hidden valleys for which they themselves (the Gentiles) did not give the *ṭasqa* (= harvest tax) to the king. The king said, Whoever gives the *ṭasqa* shall eat of the field.

2. Bava Batra 82b–83a

... א״ל אנא לא ידענא אלא עובדא הוה בדורא דרעותא, ואתו לקמיה דרב יהודה, וא״ל זיל הב ליה כמלא[2] בקר וכליו.

... He said to him (Rav Joseph to Abbaye), I don't know. But there was a case in Dura də-Raʿawata, and they came before Rav Judah, and he said to him, Go give him for a team[2] of oxen and their equipment.

3. ʿEruvin 12a

... אמר ליה ואנא לא ידענא דעובדא הוה בדורה דרעותא לשון ים הנכנס לחצר הוה ואתא לקמיה דרב יהודה ולא אצרכיה אלא פס אחד.

... He said to him (Rav Joseph to Abbaye), I don't know. There was a case in Dura də-Raʿawata, a tongue of the sea entered the courtyard, and it came before Rav Judah and he required only one strip.

4. ʿEruvin 7b

... אמר ליה אנא לא ידענא, עובדא הוה בדורא דרעותא מבוי שכלה לרחבה הוא ואתא לקמיה דרב יהודה ולא אצרכיה ולא מידי.

... He said to him (Rav Joseph to Abbaye), I don't know. There was a case in Dura də-Raʿawata, an alley ending in a backyard, and it came before Rav Judah, and he required nothing.

B. *Location*

None can be proposed due to insufficient data.

C. *Attempts at Identification*

The identification proposed by Obermeyer, with Dūr which lies between Takrīt and Sāmarrā, is doubtful because of the remoteness of that Dūr from

---

[2] The manuscripts have כדי שיעבור בקר וכליו (= so that cattle and equipment can pass).

the centers of Jewish settlement in Babylonia.[3] The name Dūr is very common in Iraq, so that additional evidence is needed before the location of Dura də-Raʿawata[4] can be specified.

D. *Economy*

The name Dura də-Raʿawata was already explained by Rashi as "village of shepherds." If so, the name itself points to one of the sources of livelihood of its residents. Sources 1 and 2 indicate that some of the villagers were landowners engaging in agriculture. Source 1 deals with a case in which one Jew purchased land from a Gentile and another Jew tried to establish a *ḥazaqah* in it. Source 2 considers the question of how far from the edge of a field a man must plant a tree so that he can cultivate it without encroaching on his neighbor's field.[5]

Both sources, as well as Sources 3 and 4 dealing with *ʿeruv*, involve discussions between Abbaye and Rav Joseph, which were probably conducted in Pumbədita where they both lived. In all four instances Rav Joseph replies to Abbaye citing cases that took place in Dura də-Raʿawata and were submitted to Rav Judah, who founded the Pumbədita yeshiva in the second generation of Babylonian amoras.

ESHEL, *Yishuvei ha-Yehudim* (1979), p. 94
FUNK, *Juden* (1902–1908), vol. 2, p. 148
FUNK, *Monumenta* (1913), pp. 29, 30
HALEVY, *Dorot ha-Rishonim* (1897–1939), vol. 5, pp. 493, 506
HIRSCHENSON, *Sheva Ḥokhmot* (1883), p. 97
JASTROW, *Dictionary* (1950³), p. 289
KOHUT, *Arukh ha-Shalem* (1878–1892), vol. 7, p. 228
KRAUSS, *Paras we-Romi* (1948), p. 148
LEVY, *Wörterbuch* (1924²), vol. 1, p. 387
NEUSNER, *History* (1965–1970), vol. 4, pp. 40, 170,
NEWMAN, *Agricultural Life* (1932), pp. 6, 162, 165, 198
OBERMEYER, *Landschaft* (1929), pp. 142–143

---

3 Obermeyer, pp. 142–143.

4 Herzfeld explains that Assyrian *dūru* and Aramaic *dūrā* mean "wall" in place names. In Arabic the word is considered to be the plural of *dār* (= house). Yāqūt, s.v. "Dūr," has seven places in Iraq alone by that name (see Herzfeld, *Samarra*, p. 37, n. 3, and Treidler, *Kleine Pauly*, vol. 2, cols. 179–181 s.v. "Dura"). Aside from Dura də-Raʿawata, the Talmud has Be Dura (q.v.), Biqʿat Dura (Sanhedrin 92b and mentioned in Daniel 3:1); Dura də-Be Bar Ḥašu (Pesaḥim 40a; cf. "a man named Yemar Bar Ḥašu" [Ketubot 84b]), Dura di-Netinai (Qiddushin 70b) in the Munich and Vatican 111 MSS, Durnunita in the printing, see also Rashi there. The latter name appears in the sentence beginning "Guvai Givʿonai" (see the entry on "Guvai") in which Rav Judah indicates the unfitness of the inhabitants of that Dura in regard to lineage by describing them as *netinim*. Outside of Babylonia was another Dura, Dura Europos (q.v.) where Jews lived.

5 See Beer, *Amora'ei Bavel*, p. 88; Felix, *Ha-Ḥakla'ut be-Eretz Israel*, pp. 58–59 and n. 239. The same passage mentions a place called Ṣalmon which may however be a reference to the one in Eretz Israel.

Dura Europos

While not mentioned in talmudic literature, Dura Europos (Ṣāliḥīya), located on the Euphrates about sixty kilometers southeast of Circesium (on Bab. Env. map), is the site of an ancient synagogue, noted for the murals on its inside walls, which has been excavated.

Frey, *CIJ* (1952), vol. 2, Nos. 825–845
Du Mesnil du Buisson, *Les peintures de la synagogue de Doura-Europos* (1939)
Goodenough, *Jewish Symbols in the Greco-Roman Period*, vol. 9–11 (1964)
Hopkins, in *The Discovery of Dura Europos*, ed. Goldman (1979), and references on pp, 295–300
Kraeling, *The Excavations of Dura Europos. Final Reports*, vol. 8, 1, The Synagogue (1956)
Rostovtzeff et al., *The Excavations. Preliminary Reports* (1929–1956)
Rostovtzeff et al., *Final Reports* (1943–1952) and (1977)
Schneid, *Tziurei Bet ha-Keneset be-Dura Europos* (1946)
Sukenik, *Bet ha-Keneset shel Dura Europos we-Tziuraw* (1947)

ʿEn Damim עין דמים

See the entry on "Damim."

Ginzaq גינזק

A. *Sources*

1. ʿAvodah Zarah 39a

רבי עקיבא[1] איקלע לגינזק, אייתו לקמיה ההוא נונא דהוה דמי לחיפושא, חפייה בדיקולא, חזא ביה קלפי ושרייה.

Rabbi ʿAqiva[1] happened to visit Ginzaq. They set before him a fish resembling the mud-fish; he covered it over with a basket, noticed scales on it, and allowed it.

2. ʿAvodah Zarah 34a; Taʿanit 11b

רבי עקיבא[2] איקלע לגינזק, בעו מיניה מתענין לשעות או אין מתענין לשעות, לא הוה בידיה, קנקנים של עובדי כוכבים אסורין או מותרין, לא הוה בידיה, במה שימש משה כל שבעת ימי המלואים, לא הוה בידיה.

[1] The Spanish MS published by Abramson has "Rav ʿAqavya."

[2] The Spanish MS published by Abramson has "Rav ʿAqavya" in ʿAvodah Zarah. The Taʿanit parallel has "Mar ʿUqba," while the Munich B MS of Taʿanit has "Rabbi ʿAqiva"; and see *Diq. Sof.*

Rabbi ʿAqiva[2] happened to visit Ginzaq. He was asked, Does one fast just for hours or not. He did not have any [answer]. Are containers of idolators forbidden or allowed? He did not have any. What did Moses use throughout the seven days after the inauguration [of the priest]? He did not have any.

3. Genesis Rabbah XXXIII 5, Theodor-Albeck ed., p. 310

דרש רבי עקיבה מעשה דור המבול בגינזך[3] ולא בכו כיון שהזכיר מעשה עורב בכו ...

Rabbi ʿAqiva preached the story of the flood generation in Ginzaq[3] and they did not cry. When he mentioned the story of the raven, they cried ...

4. Moʿed Qaṭan 20a; Nazir 44a; Semaḥot XII, 2 ed. Higger, p. 194

דתניא מעשה ומת אביו של רבי צדוק[4] בגינזק[5] והודיעוהו לאחר שלש שנים ובא ושאל את אלישע בן אבויה[6] וזקנים שעמו ואמרו נהוג שבעה ושלשים.

It has been taught, It happened that the father of Rabbi Ṣadoq[4] died at Ginzaq[5] and he was informed three years later. He went and asked Elisha b. Avuya[6] and the elders with him, and they said, Observe seven [days of mourning] and thirty.

5. T. J. Berakhot II 6–5b, 15

בנימן גנזכייה נפק ומור משמיה דרב מותר ...

Benjamin Ginzak̲ya went out and said in Rav's name, It is permitted [to cohabit with a virgin on the Sabbath].

6. Yevamot 16b–17a; Qiddushin 72b

דאמר רבי אבא בר כהנא "וינחם בחלח ובחבור נהר גוזן וערי מדי"... נהר גוזן זו גינזק ...

For Rabbi Abba b. Kahana said, "And he settled them in Ḥalaḥ and along the Ḥavor and the River Gozan and in the towns of Media" (II Kings 18:11) ... the River Gozan is Ginzaq ...

7. Strabo XI 13, 3 (c. 523)

Βασίλειον δ' αὐτῶν θερινὸν μὲν ἐν πεδίῳ ἱδρυμένον Γάζακα, [χειμερινὸν δὲ] ἐν φρουρίῳ ἐρυμνῷ Οὐέρα, ὅπερ 'Αντώνιος ἐπολιόρκησε κατὰ τὴν ἐπὶ Παρθυαίους στρατείαν. διέχει δὲ τοῦτο τοῦ 'Αράξου ποταμοῦ τοῦ ὁρίζοντος τήν τε 'Αρμενίαν καὶ τὴν 'Ατροπατηνὴν σταδίους δισχιλίους καὶ τετρακοσίους, ὥς φησιν ὁ Δέλλιος ὁ τοῦ 'Αντωνίου φίλος, συγγράψας τὴν ἐπὶ Παρθυαίους αὐτοῦ στρατείαν ἐν ᾗ παρῆν καὶ αὐτὸς ἡγεμονίαν ἔχων.

---

[3] The source has גינזך (= Ginzak̲); the Venice printing and Vatican 30 and Stuttgart MSS have גינזק של מדי (= Ginzaq of Media) thus supporting the identification of Ginzaq with Ganzaca. See also the notes in the Theodor-Albeck edition.

[4] The Nazir parallel has "Rabbi Isaac."

[5] The Munich MS of Nazir and some of the MSS of Semaḥot have בגנזק של מדי, and see the textual variants in the Higger edition.

[6] The parallel in Nazir has "Rabbi Joshua b. Elisha." The Munich MS of Nazir has "Rabbi Elisha."

Their royal summer palace is situated in a plain at Gazaca, and their winter palace in a fortress called Vera, which was besieged by Antony on his expedition against the Parthians. This fortress is distant from the Araxes, which forms the boundary between Armenia and Atropatene, two thousand four hundred stadia, according to Dellius, the friend of Antony, who wrote an account of Antony's expedition against the Parthians, on which he accompanied Antony and was himself a commander. (trans.: H. L. Jones, LCL)

8. Pliny, *Natural History*, VI 16,42

reliqua vero fronte, qua tendit ad Caspium mare, Atrapatene ab Armeniae Otene regione discreta Araxe; oppidum eius Gazae, ab Artaxatis ccccl p., todidem ab Ecbatanis Medorum, quorum pars sunt Atrapateni.

Adjoining the other front of Greater Armenia, which stretches to the Caspian Sea, is Atrapatene, separated from the district of Otene in Armenia by the Aras; its chief town is Gazae, 450 miles from Artaxata and the same distance from Ecbatana, the city of the Medes, to which the race of the Atrapateni belong. (trans.: H. Rackham, LCL)

9. Ptolemy VI 18,4

Γάζακα ἢ Γάνζακα

Gazaca or Ganzaca

10. Ammianus XXIII 6,39

Per haec loca civitates dispersae sunt plures, quis omnibus praestant Zombis et Patigran et Gazaca . . .

In these lands are many scattered cities; greater than all the others are Zombis, Patigran and Gazaca . . . (trans.: J. C. Rolfe, LCL)

11. Stephanus Byzantius s.v. "Γάζακα"

πόλις μεγίστη τῆς Μηδίας, ὡς Κουάδρατος ἐν ὀγδόῳ Παρθικῶν. Ἀρριανὸς δὲ κώμην μεγάλην αὐτήν φησιν ἐν Παρθικῶν τετάρτῳ καὶ ἑνικῶς "τῆς Γαζάκου" λέγων. τὸ ἐθνικὸν Γαζακηνός, ὡς τοῦ Μάζακα Μαζακηνός.

Gazaca, a very big city in Media as Quadratus says in the eighth book of his *Parthica*. But Arrian calls it a large village in the fourth book of his *Parthica* . . .

12. Georgius Cedrenus I, 721–722, ed. Migne, *Patrologia Graeca* 121, cols. 789–790

Καὶ καταλαβὼν τὴν Γαζακὸν πόλιν, ἐν ᾗ ὑπῆρχεν ὁ ναὸς τοῦ Πυρὸς, καὶ τὰ χρήματα Κροίσου τοῦ Λυδῶν βασιλέως, καὶ ἡ πλάνη τῶν ἀνθράκων, καὶ εἰσελθὼν ἐν αὐτῇ εὗρε τὸ μυσαρὸν εἴδωλον τοῦ Χοσρόου, τό τε ἐκτύπωμα αὐτοῦ ἐν τῇ τοῦ παλατίου σφαιροειδεῖ στέγῃ ὡς ἐν οὐρανῷ καθήμενον, καὶ περὶ τοῦτο ἥλιον, καὶ σελήνην, καὶ ἄστρα, οἷς ὁ δεισιδαίμων ὡς θεοῖς ἐλάτρευε, καὶ ἀγγέλους αὐτῷ σκηπτροφόρους περιέστησεν. Ἐκεῖθέν τε σταγόνας στάζειν ὡς ὑετοὺς καὶ ἤχους ὡς βροντὰς ἐξηχεῖσθαι ὁ θεομάχος ταῖς μηχαναῖς ἐπετεχνάσατο. Ταῦτα γοῦν πάντα πυρὶ ἀναλώσας, καὶ τὸν τοῦ Πυρὸς ναὸν κατακαύσας καὶ πᾶσαν τὴν πόλιν.[7]

The Emperor Heraclius took possession of the city of Gazaca, in which was the temple and the treasures of Croesus, king of Lydia, and the imposture of the burning coals. On entering the city he found the abominable image of Chosru, an effigy of the king seated under the vaulted roof of the palace as though in the heavens, and around it the sun, moon, and stars, to which he did homage with superstitious awe, as if to gods, and he had represented angels bearing sceptres and ministering unto him. And the impious man had arranged by cunning devices to have drops falling from above, like rain, and sounds resembling roaring thunder to peal forth. All these things Heraclius consumed with fire, and burned both the Temple of Fire and the entire city.[7] (cited by Rawlinson *JRGS* 10 [1841]: 52,78)

B. *Already Proposed Location*

Ğaznaq, southeast of Lake Urmiya, east of Marāġa, on the southeastern slopes of the Savalān mountain (on Bab. Env. map).

C. *Identification*

The name occurs more than once, for it is derived from Persian *ganġ* (= treasury).[8] By far the most important town of that name was in a plain in Media Atropatene, and has been identified with the ruins of Persian Taḫt-e Sulaimān, southeast of Marāġa, west of Zenğān.[9] The identification of the Taḫt-e Sulaimān site with Arab Šīz is not in doubt. Schmidt's aerial photographs[10] provide a good view of the ruins of Taḫt-e Sulaimān where a survey was made in the 1930s.[11] The site has been systematically excavated since 1960,[12] and the excavations have made it clear that the site never had a regular

---

[7] Cedrenus wrote in the eleventh century. His text is in fact an abridgement of Theophanes I 474 (of the eighth century). The relevant passage of Theophanes is however corrupt. Cf. Theophanes, *Chronography*, ed. Bonn, vol. 2, p. 147, which gives the parallel text of Anastasius. For these problems see Hoffmann, *Auszüge*, p. 252f.; Herzfeld, *JPK* 41 (1920): 17–18.

[8] See Weissbach, *RE*, vol. 7, col. 886, s.v. "Gazaca."

[9] The site was first explored by Rawlinson, *JRGS* 10 (1841): 1–158. For literature see *RE*, *loc. cit.*

[10] Schmidt, *Flights Over Ancient Cities of Iran*, pp. 72–74, Pls. 87–90.

[11] Pope, Crane & Wilber, *Bull, Am. Inst. Iran. Art & Arch.* (December 1937): 71–105; Wilber, *Antiquity* 12 (1938): 389–410; van den Berghe, *Archéologie de l'Iran Ancien*, p. 118, bibliography no. 293.

[12] von der Osten & Naumann et al., *Takht i Suleiman*, p. 90, plates and maps. For reports on the excavations see *Archäologischer Anzeiger* 1 (1961): 28 to 4 (1964): 619; and the current issues of *Iran*, from 5 (1967) onward.

settlement, only public buildings including a fire temple. Moreover, these all date to the Sassanian period and later, and no Parthian remains have been discovered. Taḫt-e Sulaimān cannot therefore be a Parthian town, and Ganzaca/Phraaspa must be sought elsewhere, despite Rawlinson.[13]
Yāqūt, in his entry on "Ǧaznaq," says "an inhabited town, in Aḏarbaiǧān, near Marāġa, where there are ancient remnants of the Persian kings and a fire temple."[14] Ginzaq also appears in Arabic sources in the form of Ǧanza. According to Ibn Ḫurdāḏbih, Ǧanza is six parasangs from Marāġa.[15] A number of scholars have wished to seek Ganzaca southeast of Lake Urmiya east of Marāġa on the southeastern slopes of the Kūh-e Savalān, but no specific site there has been proposed.[16]

D. *History*

Arab and Persian sources describe the important fire temple, named Adhur-Gušnasp, there, and Persian sources say that Zoroaster came from that city.[17] Strabo in Source 7 mentions Gazaca in connection with Mark Antony's Parthian campaign. In 31 B.C. Mark Antony besieged but failed to take Phraata, "a large city in which were the wives and children of the king of Media."[18] The city is called Φράασπα by Stephanus Byzantius, relying on Asinius Quadratus. It is mentioned also in connection with the campaign of Khusro II against Vahram Chobin in A.D. 589 and that of Heraclius against Khusro II in A.D. 624.

---

13 See Rawlinson's monograph, *op.cit.* The identification was also defended by Williams Jackson, *Persia Past and Present*, pp. 130–143, who allows for the possibility that the city was on the plain and the fortress on the height. See also Pope et al., *op.cit.* (in n. 11); Christensen, *L'Iran*, p. 161; *RE*, *loc.cit.* (in n. 8).

14 See also Yāqūt, s. v. "Kaznā" (= Ginzaq); regarding the dropping of the final *qāf* cf. *ibid.*, s.v. "Narmaq," called Narmah by the inhabitants.

15 P. 121. See Minorsky, *BSOAS* 11 (1943–1946): 252; Muqaddasī (p. 382) reports a similar distance: "Between Marāġa and Ǧanza (as per the reconstruction by Minorsky, *ibid.*, p. 254) one day's distance." An identical distance in parasangs is reported by Yāqūt, s.v. "Kaznā." See Samʿānī, *Ansāb*, s.v. "Ǧanzī"; Abū l-Fidā', p. 215, quoting Ibn al-Aṯīr, *Lubāb*, s.v. "Ǧanzī." Ǧanza-Ginzaq should not be confused with a place in the Arrān district between Širwān and Aḏarbaiǧān also called Ǧanza (q.v. in Yāqūt); Barthold-Boyle, *EI*² s.v. "Gandja." On the problem of the identification of Ginzaq with Šīz (by Yāqūt), cf. Minorsky (*ibid.*, p. 265) who notes there are two other places called Šīz, but their names are doubtful (*ibid.*, p. 253, n. 3; p. 264, n. 2) and cf. Schwarz, *Iran im Mittelalter*, pp. 703, 916–917; Nöldeke, *Perser und Araber*, p. 100, n. 1.

16 Herzfeld, *loc.cit.* (in n. 7); idem., *Arch. Mitt. aus Iran* 2 (1930): 72. Herzfeld notes that Marquart informed him that he had come to the same conclusion; Minorsky, *ibid.*, p. 263.

17 For the Zoroastrian traditions, see Williams Jackson, *op.cit.* (in n. 13), pp. 137–140.

18 Plutarch, *Antony* 38, 2; 39, 6; 50, 1: Φράατα; Cassius Dio XLIX 25, 3; 26, 3; L 27, 5.

There are five bishops of Adarbaiğān attested between 486 and 605. The first is called "Bishop of Ganzak and Adarbaiğān," which means that the former was his place of residence.[19]

E. *Sages and Ginzaq*

Sources 1–3 testify to a visit by Rabbi ʿAqiva in the course of which he preaches a public sermon and is asked questions on halakhic points. Source 1 tells how he permitted the consumption of a certain fish whose fitness seemed in doubt, while Source 2 tells of his inability to answer certain halakhic questions.[20] There is considerable testimony on Rabbi ʿAqiva's journeys abroad, among others to Nəhardəʿa (q.v.), Arabia, Phoenicia, Rome, places in Asia Minor, etc.[21] Other sages of the Yavneh period (A.D. 70–132) likewise undertook such journeys, in order to maintain the contact between Eretz Israel and the Diaspora, and to reinforce the hegemony Eretz Israel then exercised on the Diaspora. Source 4, relating to the end of the Yavneh period, reports that Rabbi Ṣadoq's father[22] died at Ginzaq, and since it took three years for the news to reach the son, a question arose regarding how the mourning was to be conducted. Source 5 refers to Benjamin Ginzakya, apparently a native of Ginzaq, citing a halakhah in Rav's name.[23] In Source 6, Rabbi Abba b. Kahana of the third generation of Eretz Israel amoras identifies the Gozan River—mentioned in the Bible as one of the places to which King Shalmaneser of Assyria exiled the Jews (II Kings 18:11)—with Ginzaq. As usual in such identifications, this lacks any historical or geographical basis; there is no connection between Gozan, a city on the Ḫābūr River in northwestern Mesopotamia,[24] and the talmudic Ginzaq.

Berliner *Beiträge* (1883), pp. 17–18
Christensen, *L'Iran* (1944²), p. 161
Eshel, *Yishuvei ha-Yehudim* (1979), pp. 85, 87–88, 90
Funk, *Juden* (1902–1908). vol. 1, p. 12; vol. 2, p. 149
Funk, *Monumenta* (1913), pp. 4, 277
Herzfeld, *JPK* 41 (1920): 17–18
Herzfeld, *Arch. Mitt. aus Iran* 2 (1930): 72
Hirschenson, *Sheva Ḥokhmot* (1883), p. 95
Hoffmann, *Auszüge*, Excurs. 17, pp. 250–253
Jastrow, *Dictionary* (1950³), p. 258
Joël, *MGWJ* 16 (1867): 380–381
Kohut, *Arukh ha-Shalem* (1878–1892), vol. 2, p. 319; *Tosefot* (1937), p. 127

[19] See Sachau, *APAW phil. hist. Klasse* 1 (1919): 61.

[20] According to the Taʿanit parallel, the source concerns Mar ʿUqba, and see n. 2 above.

[21] On Rabbi ʿAqiva's travels see Safrai, *Rabbi ʿAqiva*, pp. 20–22, and the map of the journeys provided there. The designation on that map of Ginzaq as a district is unfounded.

[22] According to the Nazir parallel the person in question was Rabbi Isaac's father, and see Hyman, p. 202, whose proposal is not however necessarily binding.

[23] This is not, of course, proof that Rav ever visited Ginzaq, despite Eshel (p. 85).

[24] The verse "along the Ḥavor [and] the River Gozan" actually means in the region of the Ḫābūr which is the river of the Assyrian province of Gozan, and see Loewenstamm, *Entziqlopedia Miqra'it*, vol. 2, p. 451, s.v. "גוזן."

Levy, *Wörterbuch* (1924²), vol. 1, p. 347
Minorsky, *BSOAS* 11 (1943–1946): 252–254, 262, 263
Neusner, *History* (1965–1970), vol. 2, pp. 98–99, 104, 137, 241–243, 269; vol. 3, pp. 4, 55–56
Obermeyer, *Landschaft* (1929), pp. 10, 80, n. 1
Pope et al., *Bull. Am. Inst. Iran Art & Arch.*, December 1937: 71–105
Rawlinson, *JRGS* 10 (1841): 1–158
Weissbach, *RE*, vol. 7, col. 886f., s.v. "Gazaca"

Gišra də-Be Pərat גישרא דבי פרת

A. *Source*

Qiddushin 71b–72a

עד היכן היא בבל . . . לעיל בפרת עד היכא, רב אמר עד אקרא דתולבקני,[1] ושמואל אמר עד גישרא דבי פרת,[2] ור׳ יוחנן אמר עד מעברת דגיזמא.[3] לייט אביי, ואיתימא רב יוסף, אדרב. אדרב לייט אדשמואל לא לייט, אלא לייט אדרב וכ״ש אדשמואל. ואב״א לעולם אדרב לייט אדשמואל לא לייט, וגישרא דבי פרת לתתאיה הוה קאי והאידנא הוא דליוה פרסאי.

How far does Babylonia extend? ... On the upper Euphrates, how far? Rav said, To Aqra də-Tulbanqe;[1] and Samuel said, To Gišra də-Be Pərat,[2] and Rabbi Yoḥanan said, To the Gizma crossing.[3] Abbaye, others say Rav Joseph, reviled Rav's [view]. He reviled Rav's and did not revile Samuel's. Rather he reviled Rav's and the more so Samuel's. And if you will, I will say he always reviled Rav's and did not revile Samuel's. And Gišra də-Be Pərat was further down, and now it is where the Persians set it higher.

B. *Proposed Location*

A bridge near Bait Fāriṭ near Anbār (see the entry on "Pumbədita") (C 2 on the Tal. Bab. map).

C. *Identification*

The source above deals with the placement of the border of the Babylonia of pure lineage to the north on the Euphrates. In Samuel's view the bridge at Be Pərat was the border point there.
In Obermeyer's opinion, Gišra də-Be Pərat is the same as the Dimimmā bridge just south of Anbār.[4] His identification of the bridge is not based on the

[1] The source has אקרא דתולבקני. The Venice printing has עקרא דתולבקני.
[2] The Vatican 111 MS has גירש דבי פרת, corrected interlinearly to גישרא, with גירשא דפרת next to it.
[3] The Venice printing has מעברת דגידמ׳; the Vatican 111 MS has מעברא דגימא.
[4] Obermeyer, p. 97.

preservation of the name. However there was a place not far from Anbār, called Bait Fāriṭ, apparently identical with Be Pərat.[5] Yāqūt says Bait Fāriṭ is a village on the Euphrates, a parasang from Anbār,[6] but he does not specify whether it is north or south of Anbār.

Berliner, *Beiträge* (1883), p. 20
Eshel, *Yishuvei ha-Yehudim* (1979), pp. 69, 84
Funk, *Monumenta* (1913), pp. 4, 278
Kohut, *Arukh ha-Shalem* (1878–1892), vol. 2, pp. 53, 384 "גשר"; *Tosefot* (1937), p. 346
Neubauer, *Géographie* (1868), p. 330
Obermeyer, *Landschaft* (1929), pp. 94, 97, 105

Gišra də-Šabistana גישרא דשביסתנא

A. *Sources*

1. Yevamot 121a

ההוא גברא דאטבע בדגלת ואסקוהו אגישרא דשביסתנא[1] ואנסבה רבא לדביתהו אפומא דשושביני לבתר חמשה יומי.

The person who drowned in the Tigris and was brought up on Gišra də (= the bridge of)-Šabistana.[1] Rava married his wife on the evidence of his friends [who identified him] after five days.

2. Berakhot 59b

ואמר רמי בר אבא הרואה דגלת אגשרא דשביסתנא[2] אומר ברוך עושה בראשית.

And Rami bar Abba said, Whoever sees the Tigris up to Gišra də-Šabistana[2] says, Blessed is the Maker of Creation.

B. *Proposed Location*

The Maḥoza (Madā'in) bridge over the Tigris (D3 on the Tal. Bab. map).

---

[5] On the prefix "Bet" see Eshel (p. 77, s.v. "Bet Biltin") who believes it is the only Babylonian place name incorporating that element, which he considers a vestige of the Accadian name. Apparently the prefix was not common in place names in the Muslim period either.

[6] Yāqūt, s.v. "Bait Fāriṭ" (the letter *rā'* is not vocalized in either edition, nor in *Marāṣid* which copies Yāqūt word for word); cf. *Ansāb al-ašrāf*, vol. 5, p. 297: "... in a village named Bait Fāriṭ, near Anbār, on the bank of the Euphrates." A Fāriṭ (= Bait Fāriṭ) very close to Anbār is mentioned as well by Ṭabarī, vol. 6, p. 590 (= vol. 2, p. 1395).

[1] The Munich MS has גישרא דישבישתנא.

[2] The Munich MS has גישרא דשברסתנא, the Florence MS has אדיקרא דשביסתנא; see also *Diq. Sof*.

C. *Identification*

Source 1 reports the case of a man who drowned in the Tigris, and whose body was found five days later at Gišra də-Šabistana. On the basis of the identification of the body made by the deceased's friends, Rava permitted the widow to marry. As Rava to whom the case was submitted was a fourth generation Babylonian amora who headed the Maḥoza yeshiva, some scholars have assumed that Gišra də-Šabistana was probably in the vicinity of Maḥoza.[3]

Obermeyer identifies Šabistana with a place called Nahr Sābus near Wāsiṭ in Mesene. He too thinks the man who drowned in the Tigris was from Maḥoza, which was why the problem was submitted to Rava, but as the body was found only five days after the man's disappearance, he presumes it had drifted a considerable distance in that time, so that the place where it was found could be far downstream from Maḥoza.[4] The identification of the other scholars is preferable to that of Obermeyer as it is confirmed by Saadiah Gaon. In a passage in the latter's commentary on Berakhot, relating to Source 2, he states:[5] *ǧisru l-Madā'in, al-lail kāna yuġlaqu fa-lā yaṣʿadu zauraq wa-lā yanḥadiru, šabī laila li-lisān fārisī, stānā miṣrāʿ* (= Gišra də-Šabistana: the al-Madā'in bridge, at night is closed so that no vessel will go up or down. *šabī* in Persian is 'night,' and *stānā* is 'a leaf of a folding door').[6]

In Source 2, Rami bar Abba (of the third generation of Babylonian amoras) states that anyone seeing the Tigris from its source to Gišra də-Šabistana says

[3] Hirschenson, *Sheva Ḥokhmot*, p. 233; Berliner, p. 63; *Arukh ha-Shalem*, vol. 8, p. 14.

[4] See Obermeyer, pp. 62–65. de Goeje, *ZDMG* 39 (1885): 14, preceded him in this identification. See e.g., Yāqūt, s.v. "Sābus" and cf. "Nahr Sābus" there. Geiger, in *Tosefot Arukh ha-Shalem*, pp. 389–390, reports Obermeyer's view, while expressing some doubts about it.

[5] Wertheimer, *Rav Saadiah Gaon's Commentary to Berakhot*, 21b (on Berakhot 59b). See also Beer, *Amora'ei Bavel*, p. 68, n. 127. Wertheimer's translation of the passage (quoted in Beer) is inaccurate.

[6] See also Herzfeld, *Samarra*, p. 25: "Shabistan is the king's cubiculum, place for nocturnal receptions, and harem;" cf. Streck, *Die alte Landschaft*, vol. 2, pp. 269–270; Iṣṭaḫrī (p. 87) and Ibn Ḥauqal (p. 245) mention a bridge of fired brick at Madā'in on the Tigris, of which no trace survived to their time. On a stone and brick bridge at Madā-'in built by King Ǧamšīd and destroyed by Alexander the Great because it was too great a relic of the kings of Persia, see Ḥamza, *Ta'rīḫ*, p. 31; Mustaufī, vol. 2, p. 50. When Ardashir Bābakān rebuilt Madā'in and made it his capital, he sought to reconstruct that bridge, but was unable to, and consequently set up a pontoon bridge with chains. Ḥamza notes that vestiges of the stone bridge remained in the Tigris River bed to the west of the two cities of Madā'in, and sailors kept away from them when the river was low. Re the pontoon bridge, cf. the section on Physical Features in "Maḥoza" and the section on History in "Ctesiphon" (both in "Maḥoza Area"). Cf. also the undocumented statement of Fiey, *Sumer* 23 (1967): 12—"At Sābāṭ near the Tigris, the Nahar Malka was crossed by a bridge which the Talmud mentions under the name of the bridge of Shebisthana." Sābāṭ, which is talmudic Sabata (q.v.) was one of the cities of Madā'in/Maḥoza and thus corresponds to the location proposed above.

"Blessed is the Maker of Creation," which is not true of a person viewing the river past that point. As that blessing is applicable only where the river has not been diverted from its original bed, evidently downstream from Gišra də-Šabistana there were places where the Tigris had been diverted from its natural channel (see p. 195, Source 6, and p. 224, Source 6). Thus this source likewise indicates that Gišra də-Šabistana was the Maḥoza bridge, and not some place far downstream as Obermeyer believes, for it is unlikely that in such a long section there should have been no diversions of the river from its natural channel for one reason or another.

Beer, *Amora'ei Bavel* (1974), p. 68, n. 127
Berliner, *Beiträge* (1883), p. 63
Eshel, *Yishuvei ha-Yehudim* (1979), pp. 89–90, 235
Fiey, *Sumer* 23 (1967): 12
Funk, *Monumenta* (1913), pp. 6, 51–52, 279, 299
de Goeje, *ZDMG* 39 (1885): 14
Hirschenson, *Sheva Ḥokhmot* (1883), pp. 97; 233
Kohut, *Arukh ha-Shalem* (1878–1892), vol. 8, p. 14; *Tosefot* (1937), pp. 389–390
Krauss, *Qadmoniot ha-Talmud* (1923–1945), vol. 1, p. 162
Levy, *Wörterbuch* (1924²), vol. 1, p. 367; vol. 4, p. 687
Neubauer, *Géographie* (1868), p. 337
Obermeyer, *Landschaft* (1929), pp. 53, 62–65, 67, 196

Guvai גובאי

A. *Sources*

1. Qiddushin 70b

אמר רב יהודה גובאי גבעונאי.

Rav Judah said, Guvaites [are] Gibeonites.

2. Berakhot 17b

"שמעו אלי אבירי לב הרחוקים מצדקה" ... דאמר רב יהודה[1] מאן "אבירי לב" גובאי[2] טפשאי. אמר רב יוסף[3] תדע דהא לא איגייר גיורא מינייהו.

"Listen to Me, you stubborn of heart who are far from deliverance" (Is. 46:12) ... as Rav Judah[1] said, Who are the "stubborn of heart," the silly Guvaites.[2] Said Rav Joseph,[3] Know [it is so] for not one of them converted.

---

[1] The Munich MS has "Rav Yehoseph" (corrected over "Judah"; and see *Diq. Sof.*). The Paris MS has "Rav Joseph" as does the parallel in *Yalquṭ Shim'oni* for Isaiah § 464. "Rav Joseph" may have crept in from the latter part of the passage, for Source 1 also contains a critical statement on Guvai by Rav Judah.

[2] *Aggadot ha-Talmud* has גובהי.

[3] The Munich MS has "Abbaye" (corrected over "Rav Joseph"; and see *Diq. Sof.*).

3. T. J. Qiddushin IV 1 – 65c, 26–27[4]

תמן אמרין[5] מישא מתה מדיי חולה, אילם וגבביי[6] גוססות, חביל ימא תכילתא דבבל
שנייא וגבביא וצררייא[7] תכילתא דחביל ימא.

There they say,[5] Meša is dead, Media is sick, Elam and Guvai[6] are dying, Ḥavel Yama is the blue of Babylonia; Šunya and Guvya and Ṣiṣura[7] are the blue of Ḥavel Yama.

B. *Already Proposed Location*

The Ǧubbā area in the Ḫūzistān district (see the entry on "Be Ḥozai").

C. *Identification*

Guvai is referred to in the sources in connection with the doubtful lineage of its residents. In Source 1, Rav Judah, founder of the Pumbədita yeshiva in the second generation of Babylonian amoras, mentions it in a pun—Guvaites [are] Gibeonites—which supports the form "Guvai" (or "Guva")[8] figuring in Source 2 as well, as opposed to the other variants of the name appearing in the T. J. in particular.

Source 3 cites Guvai as being on a par with Elam in regard to lineage, and the latter is apparently an indication of the direction in which the location of Guvai should be sought. Obermeyer rightly identifies Guvai with the Ǧubbā Yāqūt describes as a locality or province between Baṣra and Ahwāz (i.e. Ḫūzistān) and assigns to Ḫūzistān.[9]

A gaonic responsum dealing with the identification of a place called Gunai is understood by Harkavy to explain the identity of Guvai and to refer to Source 2: "Gunai is a place bayond Babylon on the eastern side of the Tigris beyond Nahrawāni which is called Gunai and the Ishmaelites still call them Guḫi."[10] However, it is by no means clear that there is any connection between

---

[4] And likewise in T. J. Yevamot I 6–3b, 10–12; the parallels in Genesis Rabbah and *Yalquṭ Shim'oni* do not mention Guvai at all. See "Ḥavel Yama," Source 3, and n. 8.

[5] T. J. Yevamot has "There they call . . ."

[6] The source has גבביי, T. J. Yevamot has גוובאי.

[7] The source has שנייא וגבביא וצררייא, T. J. Yevamot has שניות עווניא וגווכייא וצוצרייה.

[8] The word "גובאי" in Sources 1 and 2 refers to the residents of the place, so that the place-name itself could be either the same, or גובא (= Guva).

[9] Obermeyer, p. 214; see "Ǧubbā" in Yāqūt, *Muštarik* and *Marāṣid*; "Ǧabbai" in *ar-Rauḍ al-mi'ṭār*; *Ḥudūd al-'ālam*, pp. 74–75, 130.

[10] *Teshuvot ha-Geonim* Harkavy, § 399, p. 213: "גוניי מקום הוא אחורי בבל בצד מזרחי של חדקל מאחורי נהרואני נקראת גונאי ועדאן קוראין אותן ישמעאלים גוכי." See also Gil, *JESHO* 17 (1974): 318.

Guvai[11] and the Gunai mentioned in the gaonic responsum and identified by the gaon with the Ğūẖā east of the Nahrawān canal.[12]

BERLINER, *Beiträge* (1883), p. 17, n. 2
ESHEL, *Yishuvei ha-Yehudim* (1979), pp. 83–84
HIRSCHENSON, *Sheva Ḥokhmot* (1883), p. 157
JASTROW, *Dictionary* (1950³), p. 217
KOHUT, *Arukh ha-Shalem* (1878–1892), vol. 1, pp. 291, 308 "גוביא"; vol. 2, pp. 167–168 "בר 5"; p. 218 "גאובאי";
Tosefot (1937), pp. 111, 112 "גב 14"
OBERMEYER, *Landschaft* (1929), p. 214

Guvya גוביא

A. *Sources*

1. Qiddushin 72a

אמר רמי בר אבא חביל ימא תכילתא דבבל שוניא[1] וגוביא[2] תכילתא דחביל ימא. רבינא אמר אף ציצורא. תניא נמי הכי חנן בן פנחס אומר חביל ימא תכילתא דבבל, שוניא וגוביא וציצורא תכילתא דחביל ימא.[3]

Rami b. Abba said, Ḥavel Yama is the blue of Babylonia, Šunya[1] and Guvya[2] are the blue of Ḥavel Yama. Ravina said, Also Ṣiṣura. It was also taught that Ḥanan b. Pinḥas says, Ḥavel Yama is the blue of Babylonia; Šunya, Guvya and Ṣiṣura are the blue of Ḥavel Yama.[3]

2. T. J. Qiddushin IV 1 – 65c, 26–27[4]

תמן אמרין[5] מישא מתה מדיי חולה, אילם וגבביי גוססות, חביל ימא תכילתא דבבל שנייא וגבביא[6] וצררייא[7] תכילתא דחביל ימא.

[11] Obermeyer (p. 126, n. 2) disagrees with Harkavy's view that the gaon's explanation relates to Source 2, on the grounds that it deals with "the name of a nation" according to Rashi, and not of a region. However, the two are not mutually exclusive, as the name of a region may be applied to its inhabitants as well (see n. 8 above). In any case, Obermeyer's attempt to identify the "Gunai" in the gaonic responsum does not seem at all tenable, and see details on this in the entry on "Guvya."

[12] See the "Ğūẖā" east of the Nahrawān canal in Yāqūt (q.v.); Bakrī, *ar-Rauḍ al-mi'ṭār*, s.v. "Ğauẖā."

[1] The Munich MS has שנייה.

[2] The Vatican 111 MS has גוניא.

[3] The Munich MS has Rami b. Abba's statement and Ravina saying "And Ṣiṣura too is the blue of Ḥavel Yama," and the *baraita* containing the statement by Ḥanan b. Pinḥas does not appear at all. The following *baraita* appears in Seder Eliahu Zuṭa (XVI [Pirqe Derekh Eretz I] Friedmann ed., p. 13): יוחנן בן פנחס אומר הבא ימרו תבליתא דבבל שוניא שרצוניא ואקח סלא ושיצריא תבלותא דהבלא ימא. רבי עקיבא אומר אף אקרוקיא. Obviously the names in that source are garbled, and see Friedmann's remarks on them.

[4] And similarly in T. J. Yevamot I 6–3b, 10–12. The parallels in Genesis Rabbah and *Yalquṭ Shim'oni* do not mention Guvya at all; and see Source 3 and n. 8 in the entry on "Ḥavel Yama."

[5] T. J. Yevamot has "There they call . . ."

[6] The source has גבביא.

[7] The source has שנייא, גבביא, and צרריא. T.J. Yevamot has שניות עווניא וגווכייא וצוצרייה.

There they say,[5] Meša is dead, Media is sick, Elam and Guvai[6] are dying. Ḥavel Yama is the blue of Babylonia; Šunya and Guvya[7] and Ṣiṣura are the blue of Ḥavel Yama.

B. *Location*

None can be proposed due to insufficient data.

C. *Attempts at Identification*

The sources mentioning Guvya make it clear that it was located in Ḥavel Yama, and was among the purest places as regards lineage, even in Ḥavel Yama (q.v.) which was a district renowned for purity of lineage. The location of the district itself is not definite.

Obermeyer suggested a connection between Guvya and the Ǧūẖā river (or canal) east of the Tigris between Ḫāniqīn in the north and Ḫūzistān in the south.[8] He based his identification on a gaonic responsum "Gunai is a place beyond Babylon on the eastern side of the Tigris beyond Nahrawāni which is called Gunai and the Ishmaelites still call them Guẖi"[9]—and proposed correcting "Gunai" to "Guḵai" in the belief that the gaon was asked about גובאי (that is, the residents of Guvya) referred to in connection with Ḥavel Yama. He believed that the Talmud reference too is meant to be "Guḵya" rather than "Guvya."[10]

Obermeyer's identification is geographically untenable for while Ǧūẖā is east of the Tigris, Guvya was a place whose inhabitants were of the purest lineage, and most of the Babylonian "area of pure lineage" was between the two rivers. Obermeyer proposed to identify Nəhar ʿAzeq (q.v.), according to Rav the eastern border of the "area of pure lineage," with the Ǧūẖā canal, but that proposal is not really acceptable (for the reasons, see the entry on "Nəhar ʿAzeq").[11] Furthermore, while the correction to Guḵai in the gaonic responsum seems reasonable enough, it has no relevance to the passage in Qiddushin, and no support in the manuscripts.

BERLINER, *Beiträge* (1883), pp. 34–35
ESHEL, *Yishuvei ha-Yehudim* (1979), p. 84
FUNK, *Monumenta* (1913), p. 4
HIRSCHENSON, *Sheva Ḥokhmot* (1883), p. 89
LEVY, *Wörterbuch* (1924²), vol. 1, p. 308
NEUBAUER, *Géographie* (1868), p. 327
OBERMEYER, *Landschaft* (1929), pp. 80, 126–127

---

[8] Obermeyer, pp. 126–127.

[9] *Teshuvot ha-Geonim*, Harkavy, § 399, p. 213. See n. 10 in the entry on "Guvai."

[10] See Obermeyer, pp. 144–145.

[11] Note also that Obermeyer's identification does not fit in with his own proposals for Šunya and Ṣiṣura, which like Guvya, were in Ḥavel Yama. He locates the latter two places west of the Tigris (see the entries on them) while Ǧūẖā is east of it.

Hadas (Edessa?) הדס

A. *Source*

Genesis Rabbah XXXVII 4, Theodor-Albeck ed., p. 346[1]

"ותהי ראשית ממלכתו בבל וארך ואכד וכלנה" - הדס[2] ונציבין וקטיספון.[3]

"And the mainstays of his kingdom were Babylon, Ere<u>k</u>, Akkad and Kalneh," (Gen. 10:10) Edessa(?)[2] and Nisibis and Ctesiphon.[3]

B. *Already Proposed Location*

Edessa, in the Ben ha-Nəharot region, between Samosata and Ḥarrān (Carrhae), today Urfa in Turkey (on Bab. Env. map).

C. *Identification*

Hadas can reasonably be assumed to be the town of Edessa,[4] both because of the linguistic similarity in the names, and because of the nature of the other cities — Nisibis and Ctesiphon — together with which it is mentioned.[5]

D. *History*

Edessa was the capital of Osrhoëne, the region east of the upper Euphrates and south of the mountains of Armenia. It is not mentioned in the Babylonian Talmud, but there are indications that it had an important Jewish community. The Jewish community of Edessa is attested by a number of tomb inscriptions,[6] but especially in various Christian sources.[7]

Drijvers, *ANRW* II 8 (1977), pp. 863–896, 902–904 (bibliography)
Eshel, *Yishuvei ha-Yehudim* (1979), pp. 11–12
Frey, *CIJ* (1936–1952), vol. 2, Nos. 1415–1418 (Jewish inscriptions)
Funk, *Juden* (1902–1908), vol. 2, p. 149
Funk, *Monumenta* (1913), p. 280

---

1 Similarly in *Midrash ha-Gadol* to Genesis, 10:10, Margulies ed., p. 195; *Yalquṭ Shim'oni* to Genesis, 10, § 62, Mossad Harav Kook ed., p. 226. Cf. also Targum Jonathan and Targum Yerushalmi for Genesis 10:10.

2 The printings and manuscripts of Genesis Rabbah have the forms הדם, הרם, חרס, חרם, חרים, חרן, הרן; see the Theodor-Albeck ed., and *Midrash ha-Gadol*, Margulies ed., p. 195.

3 For alternate versions see n. 9 under "Ctesiphon" in the "Maḥoza Area."

4 Yāqūt, *Marāṣid*, Bakrī, *ar-Rauḍ al-mi'ṭār*, s.v. "Ruhā;" see Yāqūt, *Marāṣid*, s.v. "Aḏāsā;" *BGA*, passim; Mustaufī, vol. 2, p. 104; Idrīsī, vol. 6, p. 663f.; *Ḥudūd al-'ālam*, pp. 37, 141; Honigmann, *EI*[1], s.v. "Orfa," and the bibliography there.

5 See, e.g., Krauss, *Paras we-Romi*, p. 12; Levy, *Wörterbuch*, vol. 1, p. 454.

6 See Frey, *CIJ*, vol. 2, Nos. 1415–1418; Segal, *Edessa*, p. 41f.

7 *Ibid.*, pp. 41–43, 100–104. See also, in the entry on "Be Lapaṭ," the section on History.

Gafni, *Ha-Yeshiva be-Bavel* (1978), pp. 10, 197
Goodblatt, *Rabbinic Instruction* (1975), p. 285, n. 28
Graetz, *Geschichte* (1908⁴), vol. 4, pp. 118, 342
Honigmann, *EI*¹, s.v. "Orfa" and bibliography there
Jastrow, *Dictionary* (1950³), p. 334
Levy, *Wörterbuch* (1924²), vol. 1, p. 454
Neubauer, *Géographie* (1868), p. 391
Neusner, *PAAJR* 31 (1963): 166f.
Neusner, *History* (1965–1970), passim
Obermeyer, *Landschaft* (1929), pp. 133, 261, 280, 299 n. 4
Segal, *Sefer Segal* (1964), pp. 39*–41*, 93*
Segal, *Edessa* (1970)

Ḥadyav חדייב

See the entry on "Adiabene."

Hagrunya הגרוניא

A. *Sources*

1. Yoma 78a

ריש גלותא איקלע להגרוניא[1] לבי רב נתן, רפרם וכולהו רבנן אתו לפירקא, רבינא לא אתא ,למחר בעי רפרם לאפוקי לרבינא מדעתיה דריש גלותא, אמר ליה מאי טעמא לא אתא מר לפירקא, אמר ליה הוה כאיב לי כרעאי. איבעי לך למיסם מסאני, גבא דכרעא הוה. איבעי לך למרמא סנדלא, אמר ליה עורקמא דמיא הוה באורחא. איבעי לך למעבריה דרך מלבוש, אמר ליה לא סבר לה מר להא דאמר רב אשי סנדל לכתחלה לא.

The Exilarch happened to come to Hagrunya[1] to Rav Nathan's house. Rafram and all the rabbis came to the *pirqa* but Ravina did not. The next day Rafram wanted to absolve Ravina from the mind (= anger) of the Exilarch. He said to him, Why didn't you come to the *pirqa*, sir? He said, My foot hurt me. You should have put on shoes; it was the back of the foot. You should have put on a sandal; he said, there was a puddle in the way. You should have crossed it wearing [the sandal]. He said to him, Don't you hold, sir, as Rav Ashi said, not at the outset in sandals [on the Sabbath].

2. Shabbat 11a

... דאמר רב אדא בר אהבה וכן תנו סבי דהגרוניא אמר רבי אלעזר בר צדוק כשהיינו עוסקין בעיבור השנה ביבנה לא היינו מפסיקין לא לקריאת שמע ולא לתפלה.

---

[1] The Munich MS has לאכזתתא and *Diq. Sof.* notes that it could be read לאכדתתא (Hame'iri in *Beit ha-Beḥirah* for Yoma, p. 192, has a similar version: The Exilarch once came to Hagrunya, and some say לאכזותא); the Munich B MS has לזבזונתא; the London MS mentions no place at all; and see *Diq. Sof.* The Oxford MS has לבי הגרוניא.

. . . For Rav Adda b. Ahavah said, and the elders of Hagrunya taught likewise, Rabbi Eleazar b. Ṣadoq said, When we were intercalating the year at Yavneh, we did not stop for either the recitation of the *Shemaʿ* or for the prayer.

3. Bava Qamma 88a–b

אימיה דרב שמואל בר אבא מהגרוניא[2] הות נסיבא ליה לר׳ אבא כתבתינהו לנכסי לרב שמואל בר אבא ברה, בתר דשכיבא אזל רב שמואל בר אבא קמיה דרבי ירמיה בר אבא[3] אוקמיה בנכסי, אזל ר׳ אבא אמרה למילתא קמיה דרב הושעיא.[4] אזל רב הושעיא אמרה קמיה דרב יהודה, אמר ליה הכי אמר שמואל . . .

The mother of Rav Samuel b. Abba of Hagrunya[2] was married to Rabbi Abba and bequeathed her possessions to Rav Samuel b. Abba, her son. After her death, Rav Samuel b. Abba went to Rabbi Jeremiah b. Abba[3] who placed him in possession of her property. Rabbi Abba went to Rav Hoshaʿya.[4] Rav Hoshaʿya went and spoke of the matter with Rav Judah. He said to him, Samuel said as follows . . .

4. Bava Qamma 7b

בעא מיניה רב שמואל בר אבא מאקרוניא[5] מרבי אבא . . .

Rav Samuel b. Abba of Hagrunya[5] asked of Rabbi Abba . . .

5. ʿAvodah Zarah 39a

רב הונא בר מניומי זבן תכילתא מאנשי דביתיה דרב עמרם חסידא, אתא לקמיה דרב יוסף, לא הוה בידיה, פגע ביה חנן חייטא, א״ל יוסף עניא מנא ליה, בדידי הוה עובדא דזביני תכילתא מאנשי דביתיה דרבנאה אחוה דר׳ חייא בר אבא ואתאי לקמיה דרב מתנא, לא הוה בידיה, אתאי לקמיה דרב יהודה מהגרוניא,[6] אמר לי נפלת ליד הכי אמר שמואל אשת חבר הרי היא כחבר.

Rav Huna b. Manyomi bought blue [wool for fringes] from the household of Rav ʿAmram the Pious' wife, and came before Rav Joseph. He was unable to answer. Ḥanan the tailor happened to meet him. He replied, How could impecunious Joseph know of this? It once happened to me that I bought blue from the household of the wife of Rabbanna'ah, Rabbi Ḥiyya b. Abba's brother, and I came before Rav Mattenah, he could not answer [either]. I went

---

[2] The Munich, Hamburg and Vatican 116 MSS have מאקרוקניא, the Florence MS has מאקרוקינייא, and see *Diq. Sof.* See the entry for "Qurqunya."

[3] The MSS have "Rav Jeremiah b. Abba" and that is what it should be.

[4] The Munich MS has אמרה לקמיה דרב הושעיא, and see *Diq. Sof.*

[5] The sources has מאקרוניא, the Munich MS has מאקרוקניא, the Hamburg MS has מאקרקוניא and see the entry for "Qurqunya." The version in Rabbenu Ḥananel is בעא מיניה רב שמואל בר אבא מרבא (= Rav Samuel b. Abba from Rava) with no place name at all. מרבא appears to be a garble of מרבי אבא, for according to the sages figuring together with Rav Samuel b. Abba in Source 3, he belonged to the second generation of Babylonian amoras and thus antedated Rava.

[6] The Rabbenu Ḥananel version is: ובאתי לפני רב יהודה ואמר לי מתגרניא נפלת ליד.

to Rav Judah of Hagrunya,[6] he said to me, So you depend on me. Thus said Samuel: The wife of a Fellow (= *ḥaver*) is like a Fellow.

6. Taʿanit 24b

רבא[7] איקלע להגרוניא[8] גזר תעניתא ולא אתא מיטרא, אמר להו ביתו כולי עלמא בתעניתייכו, למחר אמר להו מי איכא דחזא חילמא לימא, אמר להו ר׳ אלעזר מהגרוניא לדידי אקריון בחלמי שלם טב לרב טב מריבון טב דמטוביה מטיב לעמיה. אמר שמע מינה עת רצון היא מבעי רחמי, בעי רחמי ואתי מיטרא.

Rava[7] happened to visit Hagrunya[8] and ordained a fast but no rain fell. He said to them, Continue with your fasting overnight. Next morning he said to them, Anyone of you who had a dream, let him tell it. Rabbi Eleazar of Hagrunya said to them, In my dream they said to me, Good greetings to the good teacher from the good Lord who in his goodness is good to his people. He (Rava) said, Deduce from this that this is a favorable time to ask for mercy. He asked for mercy and rain fell.

7. Bava Metziʿa 69a

ר׳ אלעזר מהגרוניא[9] זבין בהמה ויהיב ליה לאריסיה מפטים ליה ויהיב ליה רישא באגריה ויהיב פלגא רווחא . . .

Rabbi Eleazar of Hagrunya[9] bought an animal and gave it to his tenant farmer. He fattened it, and he gave him the head as payment and also half the profit ...

8. ʿEruvin 63a

רבי אלעזר מהגרוניא ורב אבא בר תחליפא[10] איקלעו לבי רב אחא בריה דרב איקא באתריה דרב אחא בר יעקב, בעי רב אחא בריה דרב איקא למיעבד להו עיגלא תילתא, אייתי סכינא וקא מחוי להו, אמר להו רב אחא בר תחליפא לא ליחוש ליה לסבא, אמר להו ר״א מהגרוניא הכי אמר רבא צורבא מרבנן חזי לנפשיה. חזי ואיעניש רבי אלעזר מהגרוניא.[11] והאמר רבא צורבא מרבנן חזי לנפשיה, שאני התם דאתחילו בכבודו. ואי בעית אימא שאני רב אחא בר יעקב דמופלג.

Rabbi Eleazar of Hagrunya and Rav Abba b. Taḥlifa[10] happened to visit the house of Rav Iqa's son Rav Aḥa in Rav Aḥa b. Jacob's place. Rav Iqa's son Rav Aḥa wanted to make them a three-year old calf, and brought them the [slaughtering] knife to show [for examination]. Rav Aḥa b. Taḥlifa said to them, Should we not consider the old man? Rabbi Eleazar of Hagrunya said

---

[7] The Munich MS has Rav, and see *Diq. Sof*. The correct form is undoubtedly Rava, for Source 8 has Rabbi Eleazar of Hagrunya speaking in the name of Rava.

[8] The Munich MS has להרוגנא.

[9] The Munich MS has "Rabbi Eliezer of Agrunya."

[10] The Oxford and Munich MSS and old printings have "Rav Aḥa b. Taḥlifa," which is what it should be, and see *Diq. Sof*.

[11] The Munich MS does not have the words "Rabbi Eleazar of Hagrunya."

to them: Rava said thus, A young scholar may look for himself. Rabbi Eleazar of Hagrunya[11] looked and was punished. But Rava said a young scholar may look for himself. The case is different there since they began [to discuss] his dignity. And if you like, say Rav Aḥa b. Jacob is different as he is distinguished.

9. Ketubot 109b; Bava Metziʿa 77b and 97a (2); Bava Batra 174b; Makkot 13b

אמר ליה רב מרדכי לרב אשי הכי אמר אבימי מהגרוניא[12] משמיה דרבא.[13]

Rav Mordecai said to Rav Ashi, Thus said Avimi of Hagrunya[12] in the name of Rava.[13]

10. Yevamot 64b

א"ל רב מרדכי לרב אשי הכי אמר אבימי מהגרוניא משמיה דרב הונא.[14]

Rav Mordecai said to Rav Ashi, Thus said Avimi of Hagrunya in the name of Rav Huna.[14]

11. Berakhot 31a; Soṭah 46b

רב מרדכי אלוייה לרב שימי בר אשי[15] מהגרוניא[16] ועד בי כיפי[17] ואמרי לה עד בי דורא.[18]

Rav Mordecai escorted Rav Shimi b. Ashi[15] from Hagrunya[16] to Be Kife,[17] or, as some say, to Be Dura.[18]

12. Yevamot 9a; Horayot 8a

מתקיף לה רב חלקיה מהגרוניא . . .

Rav Ḥilqiyah of Hagrunya demurred . . .

Aqra də-Hagrunya

13. Bava Batra 73b

ואמר רבה בר בר חנה לדידי חזיא לי ההיא אקרוקתא דהויא כי אקרא דהגרוניא, ואקרא דהגרוניא כמה הויא, שתין בתי . . .

---

[12] The Vatican 113 MS for Ketubot has מגרני'; the Pesaro printing of Bava Batra has מאגרוניא.

[13] The Munich MS for Ketubot does not have "in the name of Rava"; the Munich MS of Bava Batra has "in the name of Rav."

[14] The Munich MS and *Ginzei Talmud*, vol. 1, p. 175, have "in the name of Rava"; "in the name of Rav Huna" is missing in the Vatican 111 MS.

[15] The variant in Soṭah is "to Rav Ashi," (but *Ein Yaʿaqov* has "to Rav Shimi b. Ashi"). See also Source 13 under "Babylon" and the notes there.

[16] The Florence MS of Berakhot has מגרוניא, and see Soṭah in the ICIT ed. The parallel in *Midrash ha-Gadol* to Genesis has מגרוניא (18:16, Margulies ed., p. 303, and see the variants there).

[17] For the various versions see the entry for "Be Kife."

[18] For the various versions see the entry for "Be Dura."

And Rabbah b. Bar Ḥana said, I saw a frog that was like the Fort of Hagrunya. And how much is the Fort of Hagrunya? Sixty houses . . .

14. Pliny, *Natural History*, VI 30, 120

(Narmalchan) qua dirivatur oppidum fuit Agranis e maximis quod diruere Persae.

At the point where the channel divides there was once a very large town named Agranis which was destroyed by the Persians. (trans.: H. Rackham, LCL)

B. *Already Proposed Location*

Agranum, which was where the Malka River diverges from the Euphrates (C3 on the Tal. Bab. map).

C. *Identification*

A number of scholars have proposed identifying Hagrunya with the Agranum mentioned in classical literature (e.g. Source 14), which is located where the Malka River flows out of the Euphrates.[19] Source 13 refers to Aqra də-Hagrunya, the fort of Hagrunya, and as Agranum was at a fork in the river, a common site for a fort, the identification of Hagrunya with Agranum is reasonable. According to the same source, there were a total of only sixty houses in Hagrunya.[20] The variation Aqrunya in Source 4 was interpreted by Obermeyer as deriving from the word *aqra*, after the fort, and the same etymology should then be assigned to Hagrunya. Hagrunya was near Nəhardəʿa which may very well explain the rather numerous sages mentioned as living or visiting the place (see below). Obermeyer may be correct in his belief that "ʿAnan b. Ḥiyya of Ḥagra that was in Nəhardəʿa"[21] was from Hagrunya, and Ḥagra is simply an abbreviation of Hagrunya. Thus this source confirms the propinquity of Hagrunya and Nəhardəʿa (q.v.).

D. *The Exilarch and Hagrunya*

The importance of Hagrunya is shown in Source 1 dealing with the Exilarch's visit there, which took place toward the end of the amoraic period. He was the guest of Rav Nathan, a sage there is no other information about, and on the Saturday of his visit, a *pirqa* was arranged in Hagrunya. A *pirqa* is a sermon on a halakhic subject of current interest, usually scheduled for the

---

[19] See Neubauer, p. 347; Berliner, p. 31; Obermeyer, p. 265; Funk, *Monumenta*, p. 289.

[20] See Krauss, *Qadmoniot ha-Talmud*, vol. 1A, p. 74.

[21] Yevamot 116a (the Munich MS has מתיגר'). Obermeyer has *hagra*, but the Talmud has *ḥagra*. According to Krauss, *ḥagra*=*ḥaqra*, i.e. fort, (*Lehnwörter*, vol. 2, pp. 252–253).

Saturdays before festivals,[22] and in this case the Exilarch himself may very well have been the expounder. At any rate the source implies that even the very presence of the Exilarch at the *pirqa* made the participation of the sages obligatory, and in the instance described Rafram sought to appease the Exilarch's anger at Ravina's absence by finding some valid reason. The fact that a *pirqa* was conducted at Hagrunya involving the Exilarch and the presence of many sages points to Hagrunya's having been an important Jewish center.

E. *Sages and Hagrunya*

The talmudic sources mentioning Hagrunya give the names of a relatively large number of sages connected with it. In Obermeyer's opinion this was due to its propinquity to Nəhardəʿa and indicates that after the decline of Nəhardəʿa (q.v.) Hagrunya gradually took the former's place, occupying a position in relation to Nəhardəʿa similar to that of Mata Məḥasya to Sura.[23]
Source 2 refers to a group known as *savei də-Hagrunya* (= the elders of Hagrunya) reporting a *baraita* of Rabbi Eleazar b. Ṣadoq of the Yavneh period, evidently a group of sages active in Hagrunya at the start of the amoraic period.[24] Rav Samuel b. Abba of Hagrunya[25] and Rav Judah of Hagrunya, both of the second generation of Babylonian amoras, figure respectively in Sources 2–3 and 5.
Rava, who headed the Maḥoza yeshiva in the fourth generation of Babylonian amoras, visited Hagrunya and proclaimed a rain fast, according to Source 6 where he is mentioned together with Rabbi Eleazar of Hagrunya. The latter is described in Source 8 as basing himself on Rava's ruling that a scholar may himself examine a knife intended for ritual slaughtering, and need not worry about disrespect for any important sage in the vicinity.[26] Source 7 too deals with Rabbi Eleazar of Hagrunya, and presents a case in which he handed over an animal to his tenant farmer for fattening.[27]
Avimi of Hagrunya, of the fifth generation of Babylonian amoras, figures in several sources (e.g. 9–10) in all of which Rav Mordecai reports to Rav Ashi

[22] On the *pirqa* see Zunz, *Ha-Derashot be-Yisrael*, p. 166, and n. 52 including Albeck's supplement; Gafni, *Ha-Yeshiva be-Bavel*, pp. 108–125. On the *pirqa* in Source 1, see Beer, *Rashut ha-Golah*, pp. 134–135.

[23] Obermeyer, pp. 265–267.

[24] See Goodblatt, *HUCA* 48 (1977): 209.

[25] Source 3 has מאקרוניא, which should apparently be identified with Hagrunya as Obermeyer believes. See however also the entry for "Qurqunya."

[26] On the ordination of the fast see Obermeyer (*loc. cit.*) and Newman, *Agricultural Life*, p. 20. On the hospitality practices noted in Source 6 and the custom of providing guests with a "three-year old calf", see Beer, *Amora'ei Bavel*, p. 229 and n. 32, and see Lieberman, *Hellenism*, p. 186, for the expression.

[27] On the significance of this practice in economic life, see Beer, *Amora'ei Bavel*, pp. 121–122 and Newman, *Agricultural Life*, p. 119.

on things Avimi of Hagrunya said in the name of Rava. Source 11 relates that Rav Ashi himself came to Hagrunya[28] and was escorted to Be Kife and Be Dura (qq.v.) by Rav Mordecai. Another sage residing in the place was Rav Ḥilqiyah of Hagrunya, mentioned in Source 12, who questioned the interpretation of scriptures. His dating is unknown.

Bacher, *Palästinensische Amoräer* (1892), vol. 3, p. 5, n. 6

Beer, *Rashut ha-Golah* (1970), p. 134

Beer, *Amora'ei Bavel* (1974), pp. 121–122, 299

Eshel, *Yishuvei ha-Yehudim* (1979), pp. 30, 102–103

Funk, *Monumenta* (1913), pp. 25, 30–31, 289, 291

Goodblatt, *Rabbinic Instruction* (1975), pp. 180, 244, n. 36

Goodblatt, *HUCA* 48 (1977): 209

Hirschenson, *Sheva Ḥokhmot* (1883), pp. 42, 101

Jastrow, *Dictionary* (1950³), pp. 113, 332, 1344 "קורקוניא"

Kohut, *Arukh ha-Shalem* (1878–1892), vol. 1, pp. 260–261 "אקרוקתא"; vol. 3, p. 182; *Tosefot* (1937), pp. 155, 438

Krauss, *Lehnwörter* (1898–1899), pp. 125, 253

Krauss, *Qadmoniot ha-Talmud* (1923–1945), vol. 1A, p. 74

Neubauer, *Géographie* (1868), pp. 347, 387

Neusner, *History* (1965–1970), vol. 4, p. 347; vol. 5, p. 53

Newman, *Agricultural Life* (1932), pp. 7, 20, 119

Obermeyer, *Landschaft* (1929), pp. 265–267

Rapoport, *Erekh Millin* (1914), vol. 2, p. 9

Ḥamdan (Ecbatana) חמדן

A. *Source*

Qiddushin 72a; Yevamot 16b–17a

דאמר רבי אבא בר כהנא מאי דכתיב "וינחם בחלח ובחבור נהר גוזן וערי מדי" . . . ערי מדי זו חמדן וחברותיה.

For Rabbi Abba b. Kahana said, "And he settled them in Ḥalaḥ and along the Ḥavor [and] the River Gozan and in the towns of Media" (II Kings 18:11) . . . the towns of Media is Ḥamdan and its neighbors.

B. *Location*

A town in Media, situated at 1,900 meters above sea-level, close to the foot of Mount Alvand south of it. Called Aḥməta in the Bible,[1] it is the Ecbatana of Greek and Roman sources, and Hamadan today[2] (on Bab. Env. map).

---

[28] Or Rav Shimi b. Ashi did, and see n. 15 above.

[1] Ezra 6:2. Aḥməta is mentioned also in the Book of Judith (1:1–2, 14–Ecbatana).

[2] On Ḥamdan in Arabic sources see Yāqūt, *ar-Rauḍ al-miʿṭār*, s.v. "Hamadhān"; *BGA*, passim; Mustaufī, vol. 2, pp. 74–75, and index; Qazwīnī, *Bilād*, pp. 483–488 and index; Frye, *EI²*, s.v. "Hamadhān"; Le Strange, pp. 194–195; Schwarz, *Iran im Mittelalter*, p. 513f.

C. *Archaeologicals Finds*

Herzfeld has interesting information on the Jewish communities there in the Sassanian period.[3] There is a well-known tomb in Hamadan, universally called Esther's tomb (Pl. XX), and already mentioned by Benjamin of Tudela (Adler ed. p. 53). Herzfeld offers an explanation, based on the Pahlavi work called *Šahrīhā i Erān*, (*Catalogue*, edited by Markwart), for the remarkable fact that there is a traditional tomb of Esther at Hamadan, instead of at Susa where one would expect it:

a) § 26 states that Hamadan was founded by Yazdagird I, A.D. 399–420 (but is in fact much older).

b) § 47 says that Susa and Šuštar were built by Shōshīn-duẖt (see the entries on "Susa" and „Šuštar").

c) § 53 notes that Gay was built by a Yazdagird at the request of his wife Shōshīn-duẖt who founded a Jewish colony there.

Since the Jewish colony at Isfahan owed its establishment to Queen Shōshīn-duẖt, one might expect her to have been honored by the Jews there. The Jewish community at Isfahan is well documented. Gay, which was later called al-Yahūdīya, the ghetto, is the quarter with the great bazaar. Herzfeld notes that "almost all the Muhammadan sanctuaries of that quarter are converted from Jewish ones." The same is probably true for "Esther's tomb." It is quite possible, as Herzfeld suggests, that this is actually the tomb of Queen Shōshīn-duẖt, for the two personages may well have been confused in later tradition. Since Hamadan was said to have been founded by Yazdagird I, while in fact it was much older, we may assume that here too a Jewish community owed its establishment to his Jewish wife.

In Linğān near Isfahan Herzfeld found other remains of the Jewish community of that period. There is a large Ṣūfī sanctuary there usually called Pīr Bakrān, but still known also as Esther Ḫātūr, as is the tomb in Hamadan. Near the Ṣūfī sanctuary, which usurped the Jewish one, stands a building, part of the original, where Herzfeld found three small chambers, called ziyāretgāh, a place of pilgrimage in reverence to Śeraḥ bat Asher (Genesis 46:17).

Berliner, *Beiträge* (1883), pp. 39, 52
Eshel, *Yishuvei ha-Yehudim* (1979), p. 122
Frye, *EI*², s.v. "Hamadhān"
Funk, *Monumenta* (1913), p. 4
Herzfeld, *Archaeological History of Iran* (1935), pp. 104–107
Jastrow, *Dictionary* (1950³), p. 354
Kohut, *Arukh ha-Shalem* (1878–1892), vol. 3, p. 213
Neubauer, *Géographie* (1868), p. 376
Neusner, *History* (1965–1970), vol. 1, pp. 4, 67, 92; vol. 2, pp. 241–242; vol. 3, p. 353; vol. 5, p. 118
Obermeyer, *Landschaft* (1929), pp. 11, 16, 107f., 112, 119
Schwarz, *Iran im Mittelalter* (1969²), p. 513f.

[3] Herzfeld, *Archaeological History of Iran*, pp. 104–107.

Harpanya הרפניא

See the entry on "Nəharpanya."

Ḥarta də-Argiz חרתא דארגיז

A. *Sources*

1. 'Eruvin 63a

רב המנונא אורי בחרתא דארגז[1] בשני דרב חסדא. רבינא סר סכינא בבבל, א"ל רב אשי מאי טעמא עבד מר הכי, א"ל והא רב המנונא אורי בחרתא דארגז בשני דרב חסדא. אמר ליה לאו אורי אתמר, א"ל אתמר אורי ואתמר לא אורי בשני דרב הונא רביה הוא דלא אורי, ואורי בשני דרב חסדא דתלמיד חבר דיליה הוה, ואנא נמי תלמיד חבר דמר אנא.

Rav Hamnuna ruled in Ḥarta də-Argiz[1] in the days of Rav Ḥisda. Ravina having examined a knife in Babylon, Rav Ashi said to him, Why does the master do this? He said, Did not Rav Hamnuna rule at Ḥarta də-Argiz in the days of Rav Ḥisda? He said to him, It was stated that he did not rule. He (Ravina) said to him, It was said that he ruled and that he did not rule. During the time of Rav Huna, his master, he did not rule, and he ruled during the time of Rav Ḥisda who was a disciple and colleague of his, and I too am a disciple and colleague of the master's.

2. Shabbat 19b

ההוא תלמידא דאורי בחרתא דארגיז[2] כרבי שמעון, שמתיה רב המנונא. והא כר' שמעון סבירא לן, באתריה דרב הוה, לא איבעי ליה למיעבד הכי.

That disciple that made a decision in Ḥarta də-Argiz[2] like Rabbi Simeon, and Rav Hamnuna banned him. But we hold with Rabbi Simeon. It was in Rav's place, and he should not have done that.

B. *Already Proposed Location*

Near Sura (q.v., D4 on the Tal. Bab. map) one parasang (about four and a half kilometers) from it.

C. *Identification*

Obermeyer sought to identify Ḥarta də-Argiz with Ḥīra, which is southwest of Kūfa.[3] However, a responsum of Rav Naṭronai, a Sura gaon, says ex-

[1] The Munich and Oxford MSS have בחדתא דארגיז, further on as well. For additional variants see *Diq. Sof.*, and the entry for "Kafri."

[2] The Munich MS and the Venice and Constantinople printings have חדתא דארגיז.

[3] Obermeyer, pp. 234, 318.

plicitly: "Ḥarta də-Argiz a city near our city, one parasang away . . . and Rav Hamnuna used to [live there] and is still buried there."[4] It is thus clear that Ḥarta də-Argiz was in fact some four and a half kilometers from Sura (q.v.).[5]
The propinquity of the two is indicated in Source 1, for Rav Hamnuna, of the third generation of Babylonian amoras, was a colleague and disciple of Rav Ḥisda, head of the Sura yeshiva in that generation. The source deals with the question of whether a disciple may rule on halakhic matters in his master's sphere of influence (see the section on Sages and Babylon in the entry on "Babylon"). That the two places were near each other is shown as well in Source 2, which stresses that rulings contrary to Rav's should not be issued in Ḥarta də-Argiz which was in the "jurisdiction" of Rav, founder of the Sura yeshiva in the first generation of Babylonian amoras.

Beer, *Amora'ei Bavel* (1974), p. 235, n. 43
Berliner, *Beiträge* (1883), p. 37
Eshel, *Yishuvei ha-Yehudim* (1979), p. 124
Funk, *Juden* (1902–1908), vol. 2, p. 154f.
Funk, *Monumenta* (1913), pp. 34, 35, 293
Hirschenson, *Sheva Ḥokhmot* (1883), pp. 116–117
Jastrow, *Dictionary* (1950³), p. 115 "ארגיז"
Kohut, *Arukh ha-Shalem* (1878–1892), vol. 1, p. 271; vol. 3, p. 509
Levy, *Wörterbuch* (1924²), vol. 2, p. 120
Neubauer, *Géographie* (1868), p. 348
Obermeyer, *Landschaft* (1929), pp. 234, 318

Haṣalpuni הצלפוני

A. *Source*

Mo'ed Qaṭan 22a

כי הא דאמר להו רב לבני הצלפוני[1] דאתו בגו תלתא לימנו בהדייכו, דלא אתו בגו תלתא לימנו לנפשיהו.

[4] Assaf, *Teshuvot ha-Geonim mi-tokh ha-Geniza*, p. 155. It was Assaf who proposed locating Ḥarta də-Argiz in the Sura area (see his criticism of Obermeyer's *Landschaft* in *Kiryat Sefer* 7 [1930]: 61–62; see also Beer, *Amora'ei Bavel*, p. 235 n. 43).

[5] The *Arukh* version of the Rav Naṭronai responsum says "a town near Baghdad, a parasang away" (see *Arukh ha-Shalem*, vol. 3, p. 509, s.v. "חדתא") but that version was evidently copied at a time when the geonim already resided in Baghdad by a copyist who thought Rav Naṭronai Gaon was referring to Baghdad when he said "our city." The geonim moved to Baghdad only in the time of Rav Hai Gaon (see Assaf, *ibid.*). The sources given here also indicate that Ḥarta də-Argiz was near Sura, and see below.

There are references in several places in the Talmud (Giṭṭin 7a; Zevaḥim 18b) to Argiza (or Be Argiza); that may be Ḥarta də-Argiz, or it may be a different place, perhaps the Aragiza mentioned by Ptolemy (V 15, 14) which was located on the Euphrates southeast of Ḥilla. On it see *Arukh ha-Shalem*, vol. 1, p. 271; Obermeyer, p. 144; Neubauer, p. 388; Berliner, p. 23; Funk, *Monumenta*, pp. 24, 289; Eshel, pp. 35–36.

[1] The Munich and Munich B MSS have הצלבוני.

As what Rav said to the people of Ḥasalpuni,[1] Those who came within three days will count [the days of mourning] with you, those who did not come within three days will count for themselves.

B. *Location*

None can be proposed due to insufficient data.

C. *Attempts at Identification*

Obermeyer suggests that Ṣalfīyūn, which Yāqūt refers to as a "place mentioned by al-Ǧāḥiẓ",[2] should be identified with Haṣalpuni. While that identification is quite possible, the actual location cannot be determined due to the absence of adequate data in Yāqūt.[3]

BERLINER, *Beiträge* (1883), p. 33
ESHEL, *Yishuvei ha-Yehudim* (1979), p. 110
FUNK, *Monumenta* (1913), pp. 33, 292
HIRSCHENSON, *Sheva Ḥokhmot* (1883), p. 104
JASTROW, *Dictionary* (1950³), pp. 363–364
KOHUT, *Arukh ha-Shalem* (1878–1892), vol. 3, p. 235
LEVY, *Wörterbuch* (1924²), vol. 1, p. 488
OBERMEYER, *Landschaft* (1929), p. 298

Ḥavel Yama חביל ימא

A. *Sources*

1. Qiddushin 72a

אמר רמי בר אבא חביל ימא תכילתא דבבל שוניא[1] וגוביא[2] תכילתא דחביל ימא. רבינא אמר אף ציצורא. תניא נמי הכי חנן בן פנחס אומר חביל ימא תכילתא דבבל, שוניא וגוביא וציצורא תכילתא דחביל ימא.[3] אמר רב פפא והאידנא איערבי בהו כותאי. ולא היא, איתתא הוא דבעא מינייהו ולא יהבו ליה. מאי חביל ימא, אמר רב פפא זו פרת דבורסי.[4]

Rami b. Abba said, Ḥavel Yama is the blue of Babylonia, Šunya[1] and Guvya[2] are the blue of Ḥavel Yama. Ravina said, Also Ṣiṣura. It was also taught that Ḥanan b. Pinḥas says, Ḥavel Yama is the blue of Babylonia; Šunya, Guvya and Ṣiṣura are the blue of Ḥavel Yama.[3] Rav Papa said, And now Cutheans

---

[2] Obermeyer, p. 298. See also Yāqūt's entry. al-Ǧāḥiẓ was a well-known writer from Baṣra who died in 868 (255 A.H.).

[3] *Marāṣid* provides no help either, and see the entry there.

[1] The Munich MS has שנייה.

[2] The Vatican 111 MS has גוניא.

[3] The Munich MS has Rami b. Abba's statement and Ravina saying "And Ṣiṣura too is the blue of Ḥavel Yama," and the *baraita* containing the statement by Ḥanan b. Pinḥas does not appear at all. The following *baraita* appears in Seder Eliahu Zuṭa (XVI

are mixed up with them. That is not so, A wife he wanted from them, but they didn't give [her to] him. What is Ḥavel Yama? Rav Papa said it is Pərat də-Borsif.[4]

2. T. J. Qiddushin IV 1 – 65c, 26–27[5]

תמן אמרין[6] מישא מתה מדיי חולה, אילם וגבביי גוססות, חביל ימא תכילתא דבבל שנייא וגבביא וצררייא[7] תכילתא דחביל ימא.

There they say[6] Meša is dead, Media is sick, Elam and Guvai are dying, Ḥavel Yama is the blue of Babylonia; Šunya and Guvya and Ṣiṣura[7] are the blue of Ḥavel Yama.

3. Genesis Rabbah XXXVII, 8 (Theodor-Albeck ed., p. 350)[8]

ר׳ לעזר בן פפוס[9] אמר מישא[10] מיתה מדי חולה, עילם גוססת, חבל[11] ימא תכילתא דבבל, צוצירה[12] תכילתא דחבל ימא.

Rabbi Leazar b. Papos[9] said, Meša[10] is dead, Media is sick, Elam is dying; Ḥavel[11] Yama is the blue of Babylonia, Ṣiṣura[12] the blue of Ḥavel Yama.

B. *Location*

None can be proposed because of insufficient data.

C. *Attempts at Identification*

The contents of the sources dealing with Ḥavel Yama as well as the name itself indicate clearly that the place was a district (= *ḥevel*) in Babylonia. As Babylonia was not actually on the seacoast, the element *yama* (= sea) in the place name probably implies a site in western Babylonia, or relates to some body of water such as a lake, or river. The "blue of Babylonia" in the de-

---

[Pirqe Derekh Eretz I] Friedmann ed., p. 13): יוחנן בן פנחס אומר הבא ימרו תבליתא דבבל שוניא שרצוניא ואקח סלא ושיצריא תבלותא דהבלא ימא. רבי עקיבא אומר אף אקרוקיא. Obviously the names in that source are garbled, and see Friedmann's remarks on them.

[4] The source has פרת דבורסי, the Munich MS has פרת דבורסיף (which seems the correct version), the Vatican 111 MS has דבורציף, and דבורסיף interlinearly.

[5] T. J. Yevamot I 6–3b, 10–12 has a similar passage.

[6] T. J. Yevamot has תמן קריין (= there they call).

[7] The source has שנייא וגבביא וצררייא; the T. J. Yevamot passage has שניות עווניא וגווכייא וצוצרייה.

[8] Cf. *Yalquṭ Shim'oni* for Genesis (see § 62), Mossad Harav Kook ed., p. 229.

[9] In most versions the speaker is Rabbi Eleazar b. Pinḥas.

[10] On the various versions see n. 10 in the entry for "Mesene."

[11] Here and further on as well the MSS have variously חביל, הבל, הובל; see also the Theodor-Albeck edition.

[12] On the various forms see n. 11 in the entry on "Ṣiṣura."

scription of the district refers to the pure lineage of its inhabitants.[13] Šunya, Guvya and Ṣiṣura[14] are places within the district.
In Obermeyer's view, Ḥavel Yama included the entire region of rivers and canals in Babylonia.[15] Such an extensive area, however, does not fit in with the implication in the sources that the area was rather limited. Furthermore, Obermeyer's proposal does not accord with Rav Papa's suggestion that Ḥavel Yama is Pərat də-Borsif (see note 4)[16] which Obermeyer believes to be the channel of the Euphrates near Borsif (q.v.), now called the Hindīya.[17] Thus, the location of Ḥavel Yama is unclear and dependent on the identification of the places known to be in the district, namely Šunya, Guvya and Ṣiṣura (qq.v.).

BERLINER, *Beiträge* (1883), pp. 34–35
ESHEL, *Yishuvei ha-Yehudim* (1979), p. 117
FUNK, *Juden* (1902–1908), vol. 2, pp. 152, 157
FUNK, *Monumenta* (1913), pp. 4, 278
GRAETZ, *Das Königreich Mesene* (1879), pp. 39–41
HIRSCHENSON, *Sheva Ḥokhmot* (1883), p. 110
JASTROW, *Dictionary* (1950³), p. 419
KOHUT, *Arukh ha-Shalem* (1878–1892), vol. 3, p. 334; vol. 8, pp. 226–227, "תכלית"
LEVY, *Wörterbuch* (1924²), vol. 2, p. 6
NEUBAUER, *Géographie* (1868), pp. 326–328
OBERMEYER, *Landschaft* (1929), pp. 118–122, 125, 145

Ḥelwan (Ḥelzon) חלוון (חלזון)

A. *Sources*

1. Qiddushin 72a

אמר רב איקא בר אבין אמר רב חננאל אמר רב חלזון[1] ניהוונד[2] הרי היא כגולה ליוחסין.
א"ל אביי לא תציתו ליה, יבמה היא דנפלה ליה התם, א"ל אטו דידי היא, דרב חננאל

[13] Cerulean blue is considered the finest color, a thread of that shade being inserted in the "fringes of the garment" (Numbers 15:38); and see also what Rabbi Meir says in the *baraita* in T. B. Soṭah 17a. Here the word is applied to Ḥavel Yama, the finest region of Babylonia as regards purity ol lineage. The *Arukh* provides an additional interpretation, construing תכילתא as deriving from תכלית meaning "end," so that תכילתא דבבל could mean "the end of Babylonia." While geographically suitable, that interpretation does not fit the context, as the passage as a whole deals with purity of lineage (as indicated by Berliner, p. 34, n. 7).

[14] According to the parallels and their various versions, it is possible that other places in the district are mentioned as well.

[15] See Obermeyer, p. 118.

[16] Obermeyer claims that the "Cutheans" referred to in Source 1 were the Christians who had begun to move into Babylonia from Syria and Mesopotamia in the middle of the third century (the term as used in the T.B. does not necessarily denote Samaritans in particular, but any Gentiles or Christians, the specific designation for them being deliberately avoided).

[17] See Obermeyer, p. 135. Obermeyer mistakenly notes that Rav Papa says Pərat də-Borsif is the "blue" of Babylonia (pp. 119, 121); what Rav Papa actually says is that Pərat də-Borsif is Ḥavel Yama.

[1] The source has חלזון here and below, but the Oxford MS has חלוון and below as well.

[2] The Munich MS does not have ניהוונד here, nor further on either.

היא. אזיל שיילוה לרב חננאל, אמר להו הכי אמר רב חלזון ניהוונד הרי היא כגולה ליוחסין. ופליגא דר׳ אבא בר כהנא, דאמר רבי אבא בר כהנא מאי דכתיב "וינחם בחלח ובחבור נהר גוזן וערי מדי," חלח זו חלזון,[3] חבור זו הדייב[4] ... "ותלת עלעין בפומה בין שיניה," אמר רבי יוחנן זו חלזון הדייב ונציבין, שפעמים בולעתן ופעמים פולטתן.

Rav Iqa b. Avin said Rav Ḥananel said citing Rav, Ḥelwan[1] Nihawand[2] is like the Exile (= Babylonia) as to genealogy. Abbaye said to them, Do not obey him. A *yevamah* has fallen to him there. Is it my ruling? He replied, It is Rav Ḥananel's. So they went and asked Rav Ḥananel. He said to them, Rav said thus: Ḥelwan Nihawand is like the Exile as to genealogy. And he differs from Rabbi Abba b. Kahana. For Rabbi Abba b. Kahana said, What is meant by "And he settled them in Ḥalaḥ along the Ḥavor and the River Gozan, and in the towns of Media" (II Kings 18:11). Ḥalaḥ is Ḥelwan,[3] Ḥavor is Adiabene[4] ... "It had three ribs in its mouth between its teeth" (Dan. 7:5), said Rabbi Yoḥanan, That is Ḥelwan, Adiabene and Nisibis which she (Rome) sometimes swallows and sometimes spits out.

2. Yevamot 16b–17a

... דאמר רבי אבא בר כהנא "וינחם בחלח ובחבור נהר גוזן וערי מדי," חלח זה חלזון,[5] וחבור זו חדייב.[6]

... For Rabbi Abba b. Kahana said, "And he settled them in Ḥalaḥ along the Ḥavor and the River Gozan and in the towns of Media" (II Kings 18:11); Ḥalaḥ is Ḥelwan[5] and Ḥavor is Adiabene.[6]

3. Shabbat 139b

אמרו ליה רבנן לרב אשי חזי מר האי צורבא מרבנן ורב הונא ב"ר חיון[7] שמיה, ואמרי לה רב הונא בר׳ חלוון[8] שמיה ...

Sages said to him to Rav Ashi, See this scholar, and his name is Rav Huna the son of Rabbi Ḥeyon,[7] and some say his name is Rav Huna son of Rabbi Ḥelwan[8] ...

B. *Already Proposed Location*

Ḥulwān, two hundred kilometers northeast of Baghdad (on Bab. Env. map).

---

[3] The source has חלזון here and further on; the Venice printing has חלזיון here and further on.

[4] The source has הדייב; the Munich MS has חדייב.

[5] The source has חלזון, the Munich MS and *Ginzei Talmud* have חלזיון, the Venice printing has חלוא׳, and the Vatican 111 MS has חלוון.

[6] The source has חדייב, the Munich MS has הדייב, and the Vatican 111 MS has חדיאב.

[7] The Munich MS has חזיון (= Ḥezyon), and see *Diq. Sof.*

[8] The Munich MS has חילון, the Oxford MS has חיליון, the Rabbenu Asher version has חלזון (XX, 5).

C. *Identification*

The accepted view among scholars is that Ḥelzon should be identified with Ḥelwan, based on the fact that some manuscripts have "Ḥelwan" (see notes 1 and 5).[9]

Ṭabarī says[10] that Ḥulwān was built by Qubād b. Fīrūz who died in 531, but in fact the place is much older.[11] Muqaddasī notes a gate there called "the Gate of the Jews" among the eight gates of Ḥulwān.[12] Another possible indication of a Jewish community there appears in a vision ascribed to Kaʿb (the Jewish convert, Kaʿb al-Aḥbār),[13] according to which in the end of days Ḥulwān and Zaurāʾ (= Baghdad) will be destroyed and its inhabitants will turn into monkeys and pigs.[14]

D. *Purity of Lineage*

Source 1 reports a dispute regarding the purity of lineage of the Ḥelwan people. In Rav's opinion the status of Ḥelwan is as good as that of Babylonia, while Rabbi Abba b. Kahana finds the lineages of the former unsatisfactory, for he identifies Ḥelwan with Ḥalaḥ, one of the places to which the "lost" ten tribes were exiled, and where, according to tradition, Gentiles cohabited with the young Israelite women.

E. *Sages and Ḥelwan*

Source 3 mentions a scholar contemporary with Rav Ashi, of the sixth generation of Babylonian amoras. The Talmud itself is uncertain of his name,

---

[9] Neubauer, p. 373; Funk, *Monumenta*, p. 276; Obermeyer, p. 10; Eshel, p. 121, and others.

[10] Ṭabarī, vol. 2, p. 92 (= vol. 1, p. 885); Nöldeke, *Perser und Araber*, p. 138; and see Ibn al-Faqīh, p. 199; Mustaufī, vol. 2, p. 47.

[11] Nöldeke, *ibid.*, n. 3; Lockhart, *EI*² s.v. "Ḥulwān"; Ḥulwān is at the eastern border of the Sawād (e.g. Yāqūt, s.vv. "Ḥulwān" and "Sawād", p. 272–273); see also Bakrī, *ar-Rauḍ al-miʿṭār*, s.v. "Ḥulwān." The misstatement in *ar-Rauḍ al-miʿṭār* that Ḥulwān is between Fārs and Ahwāz is the result of a deletion in Ṭabarī's text: "He built between Ahwāz and Fārs the town of Arraǧān, and he built also the town of Ḥulwān" (*ibid.*). And see also *Ḥudūd al-ʿālam*, p. 139; *BGA*, passim; Zuhrī, p. 252; Qazwīnī, *Bilād*, pp. 357–358; Idrīsī, vol. 6, pp. 666, 669–670. See also Herzfeld, *Samarra*, pp. 47–48, and the bibliography there.

[12] Muqaddasī, p. 123, also mentions another known as the "Yahūdīya gate," that is, the gate facing the direction of Yahūdīya, the ancient capital of Isfahan, see Yāqūt, s.v. "Iṣbahān," pp. 208–209. Muqaddasī also reports on a synagogue outside of town, which was greatly revered. See also the section on Archaeological Finds in the entry on "Ḥamdan."

[13] See on him *GAS*, vol. 1, pp. 304–305.

[14] Ibn al-Faqīh, p. 258; cf. Qurʾān, 2, 65; 5, 60; 7, 166.

and the manuscripts have numerous variants (see nn. 7 and 8), among them Rav Huna b. Ḥelwan and Rav Huna b. Ḥelzon. The scholar may well have come from Ḥelwan.[15]

BERLINER, *Beiträge* (1883), p. 53
ESHEL, *Yishuvei ha-Yehudim* (1979), pp. 121–122; 170
FUNK, *Monumenta* (1913), pp. 4, 276
HERZFELD, *Samarra* (1948), pp. 47–48
HIRSCHENSON, *Sheva Ḥokhmot* (1883), pp. 168–170 ("ניהוונד")
JASTROW, *Dictionary* (1950³), p. 465
KOHUT, *Arukh ha-Shalem* (1878–1892), vol. 3, pp. 400, 483 ("חדייב")
LEVY, *Wörterbuch* (1924²), vol. 2, pp. 52–54
LOCKHART, *EI²*, s.v. "Ḥulwān"
NEUBAUER, *Géographie* (1868), pp. 373–374
NEWMAN, *Agricultural Life* (1932), p. 12
NÖLDEKE, *Perser und Araber* (1879), p. 138
OBERMEYER, *Landschaft* (1929), pp. 10, 107–110, 147
STRECK, *Die alte Landschaft* (1900), vol. 1, pp. 2f., 8, 15, 36

Hine and Šile היני ושילי

A. *Sources*

1. Betzah 25b

תנו רבנן אין הסומא יוצא במקלו ולא הרועה בתרמילו ואין יוצאין בכסא, אחד האיש ואחד האשה, איני, והא שלח רבי יעקב בר אידי זקן אחד היה בשכונתינו והיה יוצא בגלודקי שלו, באו ושאלו את רבי יהושע בן לוי, ואמר אם רבים צריכין לו מותר, וסמכו רבותינו על דברי אחי שקיא דאמר אנא אפיקתיה לרב הונא מהיני לשילי ומשילי להיני, ואמר רב נחמן בר יצחק אנא אפיקתיה למר שמואל משמשא לטולא ומטולא לשמשא . . .

Our rabbis taught, A blind man may not go out [on a festival] with his cane, nor a shepherd with his bag, and neither a man nor a woman may go out in a sedan-chair. But it is not so. For Rabbi Jacob b. Idi sent [word], In our neighborhood there was an old man who was carried in his litter, and when they came and asked Rabbi Joshua b. Levi he said, When many people need him it is permitted. And our teachers relied on the words of Aḥi Shaqya who said, I brought Rav Huna from Hine to Šile and from Šile to Hine. And Rav Naḥman b. Isaac said, I carried Mar Samuel from the sun into the shade and from the shade into the sun . . .

2. Giṭṭin 80a (= Yevamot 116a; Bava Batra 172a)

כדאמר להו רב[1] לספריה וכן אמר להו רב הונא לספריה כי יתביתו בשילי[2] כתובו בשילי ואע"ג דמימסרן לכו מילי בהיני, וכי יתביתו בהיני כתובו בהיני ואע"ג דמימסרן לכו מילי בשילי.

[15] On the context in which he appears, see Beer, *Amora'ei Bavel*, pp. 84–85.

[1] The Munich and Vatican 115 MSS of the Bava Batra parallel have "Rav Safra (רב ספרא)" which can reasonably be assumed to have been an error arising because of the next word "לספריה" (= to his scribes).

[2] The Hamburg MS and Pesaro printing of the Bava Batra parallel have בשילו and בהינו; the Munich MS has בחינו; and see *Diq. Sof.*

As Rav[1] said to his scribes, and Rav Huna also said to his scribes, When you are in Šile[2] write 'at Šile' even though you were commissioned in Hine, and when you are in Hine write 'at Hine' even though you were commissioned in Šile.

3. Bava Metziʿa 63b

רבה ורב יוסף דאמרי תרוייהו מאי טעמא אמרו רבנן פוסקין על שער שבשוק ואע"פ שאין לו, דאמר ליה שקילא טיבותיך ושדייא אחיזרי, מאי אהנית לי אי הוו לי זוזי בידי הוה מזבנינא בהיני ובשילי[3] בזולא.

Rabbah and Rav Joseph both say, Why did the sages say the current market price can be agreed on even if he (the seller) does not have any [provisions]? Because he (the buyer) can say to him, You have taken your favors and thrown over the hedge, How do you benefit me? If I had money, I could have bought cheaply in Hine and Šile.[3]

4. Bava Metziʿa 72b

אמר רב ששת אמר רב הונא אין לוין על שער שבשוק. אמר ליה רב יוסף בר חמא לרב ששת, ואמרי לה רב יוסי בר אבא לרב ששת, ומי אמר רב הונא הכי, והא בעי מיניה מרב הונא הני בני בי רב דיזפי בתשרי ופרעי בטבת שרי או אסיר, אמר להו הא חיטי בהיני[4] והא חיטי בשילי אי בעי זבני ופרעי ליה.

Rav Sheshet said in Rav Huna's name, One may not borrow upon the market price. Thereupon Rav Joseph b. Ḥama said to Rav Sheshet—others say Rav Yose b. Abba said to Rav Sheshet—Did Rav Huna actually say this? But a question was asked of Rav Huna, The yeshiva students who borrow in Tishri and repay in Ṭevet, is it permitted or forbidden? He replied, There is wheat in Hine[4] and wheat in Šile; if they wish, they can buy [in Tishri] and repay.

B. *Location*

None can be proposed due to insufficient data.

C. *Attempts at Identification*

All the sources mentioning Hine and Šile clearly imply that the two places were very close to each other. Source 1 indicates that the distance between them did not exceed the Sabbath limits—2000 cubits, or about one kilometer (or twice that if the amalgamation of limits is taken as the basis in the present case). See the section on The Exilarch and Hine and Šile.

---

[3] The Munich MS has "הא חיטי בחיני הא חיטי בשלו" and see *Diq. Sof.*

[4] The Munich MS has בחיני.

Obermeyer sought to identify Hine - Šile, together, with Sailaḥīna[5] in the Kūfa region, as in his view the Arabic name derived from the two in reverse order. But the possibility of a merger of two earlier place-names must be considered unlikely.[6]

D. *The Exilarch and Hine and Šile*

Source 1 describes the case of Rav Huna being carried in a chair from Hine to Šile and from Šile to Hine on a holiday. From the contents and context of the passage, the reference seems to be to Rav Huna who was the Exilarch.[7] Generally transportation by chair outside the house was forbidden on the Sabbath and festivals, but permissible for the Exilarch who was allowed greater privileges in matters connected with his dignity and public duties.[8] The Exilarch and his retinue were accorded the courtesies of royalty, among them that of being carried by slaves in a golden carruca covered with a blue cloak.[9] The status and functions of the Exilarch were particularly stressed in his public appearances on holidays and festivals,[10] and that is undoubtedly the basis for allowing him to be carried abroad then as was the custom on ordinary days.

The presence of the Exilarch in Hine and Šile on a holiday provides no help in locating those places, but does indicate that they were probably within an area of dense Jewish settlement, and possibly of some importance.

E. *Sages and Hine and Šile*

Hine and Šile appear in a number of contexts with sages of various generations of Babylonian amoras, such as Rav of the first generation of Babylonian amoras and Rav Huna of the second (both mentioned in Source 2).

A sage named Issi, or Assi b. Hine, of the first generation of Babylonian amoras, is mentioned twice in the T. B. and described as having moved to Eretz Israel.[11] His name may thus indicate that he came from Hine.

---

[5] Obermeyer, pp. 319–321, and see the entry for "Sailaḥūna" in Yāqūt.

[6] For other unsupported attempts at identifying Hine and Šile see Berliner, p. 63; Funk, *Monumenta*, p. 292, and Obermeyer's criticism, p. 190, n. 1.

[7] See Beer, *Rashut ha-Golah*, pp. 172–173.

[8] For the prohibition against transport in a chair on festivals, see Tosefta, Yom Ṭov III, 17; T. J. *ibid.* I 6–60c, 55–58, and see also the entire passage in Betzah 25b. It is interesting to note that according to the T. J. the permission given "to the Exilarch to go forth in a chair" on a holiday is a legal error.

[9] Giṭṭin 31b, and see also Ta'anit 20b; for the Exilarchs in the gaonic period, cf. Neubauer, *Seder ha-Ḥakhamim we-Korot ha-Yamim*, vol. 2, p. 84–85.

[10] See, e.g., the section on The Exilarch and Hagrunya under "Hagrunya."

[11] Ḥullin 137b; Shabbat 147a.

Source 2 utilizes the nearness of the two places to illustrate the halakhah stipulating that the writer of a promissory note must indicate accurately the place where it was written.[12]

Sources 3 and 4 dealing with financial matters suggest that there were grain markets in both Hine and Šile, and that moreover, the grain was so abundant there that the markets were celebrated for their low prices.

BEER, *Rashut ha-Golah* (1970), p. 172
BERLINER, *Beiträge* (1883), pp. 33, 63
ESHEL, *Yishuvei ha-Yehudim* (1979), pp. 108, 240
FUNK, *Juden* (1902–1908), vol. 1, p. 84; vol. 2, pp. 155, 160
FUNK, *Monumenta* (1913), pp. 32, 52, 292, 298
HIRSCHENSON, *Sheva Ḥokhmot* (1883), pp. 103, 135
JASTROW, *Dictionary* (1950³), pp. 348, 1563, 1713
KOHUT, *Arukh ha-Shalem* (1878–1892), vol. 3, p. 223; vol. 8, p. 68
LEVY, *Wörterbuch* (1924²), vol. 1, p. 466; vol. 4, p. 546
NEUBAUER, *Géographie* (1868), p. 362
NEUSNER, *History* (1965–1970), vol. 2, p. 273; vol. 3, p. 281
OBERMEYER, *Landschaft* (1929), pp. 190, n. 1, 319–321

Ḥosqe חוסקי

See the entry on "Nihawand."

Humaniya הומניא

A. *Sources*

1. Yevamot 16b; Qiddushin 72b

״צוה ה׳ ליעקב סביביו צריו,״ אמר רב [1] כגון הומניא [2] לפום נהרא.

"The Lord has commanded against Jacob that his neighbors should be his foes" (Lam. 1:17). Rav[1] said, Like Humaniya[2] to Pum Nahara.

2. Qiddushin 72a

כי הוה ניחא נפשיה דרבי אמר הומניא [3] איכא בבבל כולה עמונאי היא.

When Rabbi was dying he said, There is Humaniya[3] in Babylonia, all Ammonites.

---

[12] On the supervision of court scribes by sages implied by this source see Neusner, *History*, vol. 2, p. 273; vol. 3, p. 281.

[1] The parallel in Qiddushin has "Rav Judah said"; the Munich and Vatican 111 MSS of Yevamot and Qiddushin, as well as *Ginzei Talmud* for Yevamot have "Rav Judah said Rav said."

[2] The Munich MS of Qiddushin has כגון הרפני׳ והרמני׳ לפום נהר׳; the Oxford MS of Qiddushin has כגון הפרניא והימניא לפום נהרא. The Vatican 111 MS of Qiddushin, the Munich MS of Yevamot, and *Ginzei Talmud* for Yevamot have המוניא, the Venice printing of Yevamot has הומנאי.

[3] The Munich MS has הימניא.

B. *Proposed Location*

Near Pum Nahara and Nəharpanya (q.v., C5 on the Tal. Bab. map).

C. *Identification*

There is a place with this name exactly on the current map of Iraq, and it was known to the early Arab geographers as well.[4] It is on the Tigris between Nuʿmānīya and Ctesiphon, slightly south of the point where Nahr Kūṯā flows into the Tigris. Obermeyer proposed identifying talmudic Humaniya with that place.[5] However, Source 1 indicates that Humaniya was close to Pum Nahara (q.v.), and Pum Nahara was close to Nəharpanya.[6] A manuscript version (see note 2) reflects and confirms the propinquity of Humaniya, Pum Nahara and Nəharpanya. The identification of Nəharpanya with Nahr Abān west of the Euphrates in the Kūfa region points to the location of Humaniya in the same region in southwestern Babylonia. It thus appears that there were two places called Humaniya—one on the Tigris between Nuʿmānīya and Ctesiphon (see map), and another, the talmudic one, that was probably in western or southwestern Babylonia.

D. *The Inhabitants*

The two talmudic references to Humaniya both derogate its inhabitants and indicate they were Gentiles. In Source 1 Rav of the first generation of Babylonian amoras (or Rav Judah of the second, see note 1) stresses the hostility of Humaniya's residents to the Jewish inhabitants of Pum Nahara. In Source 2 Rav's teacher, Rabbi Judah ha-Nasi lists faults in a number of Babylonian communities including Humaniya, which he describes as a place whose entire population is Ammonite. This should not be taken as evidence of the actual nationality of the Humaniya people.[7] Calling them Ammonites

---

[4] See Yāqūt, s.v. "Humānīya" (ending in *tā' marbūṭa*; see also Le Strange, "Ibn Serapion," p. 9) and "Humainīyā" (which is the form elsewhere as well); Ṭabarī, vol. 1, p. 568 (= vol. 1, p. 687); Masʿūdī, *Tanbīh*, p. 200; Ḥamza, *Ta'rīḫ*, p. 37; Le Strange, *ibid.*, pp. 9, 42; Suhrāb, p. 118; *Takmilat ta'rīḫ aṭ-Ṭabarī*, p. 195; and see also Yāqūt, s.v. "Nahr Mārī;" Ṣābī, *Wuzarā'*, p. 260; Ṭabarī, vol. 8, p. 496 (= vol. 3, p. 934). On Humaniya see also Nöldeke, *ZDMG* 28 (1874): 94, n. 1; Scoville, *Gazetteer*, vol. 1, p. 383; Herzfeld, *Samarra*, p. 18; Adams, *Land Behind Baghdad*, pp. 74, 91, 107; Ellis, *Mesopotamian Archaeological Sites*, p. 36; Kiepert, *ZGEB* 18 (1883), map; Jones, *SRBG* (n.s.) 43 (1857): 71–74, 100, 147 with note. But cf. Schmidt, *Baghdader Mitteilungen* 9 (1978): 39–47, Fig. 1–3; Barnett (*JHS* 83 [1963]: 23) identifies Humaniya with Sittace (Xenophon, *Anabasis*, II 4,13).

[5] Obermeyer, pp. 192–193. See also Neubauer, p. 367; Berliner, p. 32; Funk, *Monumenta*, p. 292; Streck, *Die alte Landschaft*, vol. 2, pp. 295–296.

[6] That is implied by the T. B. Yevamot 17a, and see the entry on "Pum Nahara."

[7] Thus, e.g., it has been suggested that עמונאי (= Ammonite) is derived from עומאנים (= Omanites), i.e., that the residents of Humaniya originally came from Oman in the southern part of the Persian Gulf (Blau, *ZDMG*, 27 [1873]: 325).

may be a simple play on words—"Humaniya-ʿAmmonai" like "Guvai-Givʿonai"[8]—or a reference to the fact that the prestige of Babylonian Jewish communities depended on the pure lineage of its inhabitants for purposes of marriage, for even if Ammonites converted, "No Ammonite or Moabite shall be admitted into the congregation of the Lord; none of his descendants, even in the tenth generation, shall be admitted into the congregation of the Lord" (Deut. 23:4).

Beer, *Amora'ei Bavel* (1974), p. 92;
Berliner, *Beiträge* (1883), p. 32
Eshel, *Yishuvei ha-Yehudim* (1979), pp. 103–105
Funk, *Monumenta* (1913), pp. 31, 292
Graetz, *Das Königreich Mesene* (1879), p. 26
Hirschenson, *Sheva Ḥokhmot* (1883), pp. 101–102
Jastrow, *Dictionary* (1950³), p. 339
Joël, *MGWJ* 16 (1867): 377
Klein, *MGWJ* 59 (1915): 158
Kohut, *Arukh ha-Shalem* (1878–1892), vol. 3, pp. 215–216; *Tosefot* (1937), p. 159
Krauss, *Paras we-Romi* (1948), p. 21
Levy, *Wörterbuch* (1924²), vol. 1, p. 477
Neubauer, *Géographie* (1868). p. 367
Neusner, *History* (1965–1970), vol. 2, pp. 241, 244, 248
Nöldeke, *ZDMG* 28 (1874): 94, n. 1
Obermeyer, *Landschaft* (1929), pp. 192–194, 196, 200
Streck, *Die alte Landschaft* (1901), vol. 2, pp. 294–296

Hurmiz Ardəšir הורמיז ארדשיר

A. *Source*

Bava Batra 52a

אמר רב נחמן בר יצחק אישתעי לי רב חייא[1] מהורמיז ארדשיד[2] דאישתעי ליה רב אחא בר יעקב משמיה דרב נחמן בר יעקב חלקו לא.

Rav Naḥman b. Isaac said, Rav Ḥiyya[1] of Hurmiz Ardəšir[2] told me that Rav Aḥa b. Jacob told him citing Rav Naḥman b. Jacob—if they divided, it does not.

B. *Location*

Hurmuz Ardašīr in Ahwāz (= Ḫūzistān; s.v. "Be Ḥozai") (on Bab. Env. map).

---

[8] T. B. Qiddushin 70b, and see the entry on "Guvai."

[1] The Vatican 115 MS has just "Ḥiyya" (without "Rav").

[2] The source has **מהורמיז ארדשיד**; the Oxford MS has **מהורמיז דארדשיר**; the Florence, and Hamburg MSS have **מהורמיז דארדשיד**; the Munich MS has **מהורמין דארדשיד**.

C. *History*

The city of Hurmuz Ardašīr was built by the Sassanian king Ardashīr I (A.D. 226–240) the son of Bābak.[3] According to Ḥamza al-Iṣfahānī,[4] the king gave the name, composed of his own and that of a god, to two cities he established. In one he settled ordinary people, and in the other notables and nobles. Eventually the former came to be called Hūǧistān Wāǧār (i.e., the Ḫūzistān market)[5] which was arabized to "Sūq al-Ahwāz," while the name of the latter was arabized to Hurmušīr. When the Muslims conquered Ḫūzistān, they destroyed the latter, but left the former alone.[6]
In the fourth century, Hurmuz Ardašīr became the seat of a bishop.[7] In the fifth century, the monk Hashū, with his bishop's permission, destroyed the local temple of the sun.[8]

D. *Sages and Hurmiz Ardəšir*

The source mentions a sage named Rav Ḥiyya of Hurmiz Ardəšir. Rav Naḥman b. Isaac of the fourth generation of Babylonian amoras, testifies to things in regard to rules of *ḥazaqah* told to him by Rav Ḥiyya of Hurmiz Ardəšir, who had heard them from Rav Aḥa b. Jacob of the third generation of Babylonian amoras.

Berliner, *Beiträge* (1883), p. 24
Christensen, *L'Iran* (1944²), pp. 226–227, 267, 272
Eshel, *Yishuvei ha-Yehudim* (1979), pp. 107–108
Funk, *Monumenta* (1913), pp. 32, 292

---

3 Ṭabarī, vol. 2, p. 41 (= vol. 1, pp. 818–820); Nöldeke, *Perser und Araber*, pp. 13, 19. According to Ṭabarī, Hurmuz Ardašīr is Sūq al-Ahwāz, and see below. See also Ibn al-Faqīh, p. 198; *Kitāb al-maʿārif*, p. 654; Mustaufī, vol. 2, p. 108; *Ḥudūd al-ʿālam*, pp. 74f., 130. See also Christensen, *L'Iran*, pp. 226–227, and cf. Markwart, *Catalogue*, § 46; Herzfeld, *Der Islam* 11 (1921): 148.

4 Ḥamza, *Ta'rīḫ*, pp. 46–47.

5 Nöldeke, *ibid.*, p. 13, n. 3; see also Herzfeld, *The Persian Empire*, p. 303.

6 Cf. Yāqūt, s.v. "Ahwāz" and "Ḫūz"; Muqaddasī, p. 406; Yāqūt, s.v. "Hurmušīr" (quoting Ḥamza, i.e. Ḥamza al-Iṣfahānī); Ibn Rusta, p. 188. The name "Hurmušīr" also figures in a Judaeo-Persian legal document; see Margoliouth, *JQR* 11 (1898–1899): 671; Dinur, *Israel ba-Golah*, vol. A, Part 1, p. 293. On the elimination of a medial syllable see the entry on "Šum Ṭəmaya," n. 2, and see also Eshel, pp. 107–108 (who however includes information, irrelevant here, on Rāmahurmuz, another city of Ḫūzistān). See also Streck, *EI*¹, s.v. "Ahwāz" and Lockhart, *EI*², s.v. "Ahwāz."

7 Christensen, *L'Iran*, p. 267; Labourt, *Le Christianisme*, pp. 20 n. 6, 60. See also Nöldeke, *SAWW phil.-hist. Klasse* 128, 9 (1893) p. 44. According to the Arbela chronicle, Hurmuz Ardašīr was a bishopric as early as 224 (Sachau, *APAW phil.-hist. Klasse* [1915] No. 6, pp. 17, 61–62). This would mean that Ardashir I did not found the city but only rebuilt it. However, the chronicle is now known to be a falsification. Cf. Fiey, *L'Orient Syrien* 12 (1967): 265–302.

8 Christensen, *L'Iran*, p. 272; Labourt, *Le Christianisme*, pp. 105f., 160f., 172, 174; and see also Hoffmann, *Auszüge*, p. 34.

HERZFELD, *The Persian Empire* (1968), p. 303
HOFFMANN, *Auszüge* (1880), p. 34
JASTROW, *Dictionary* (1950³), p. 341
KOHUT, *Arukh ha-Shalem* (1878–1892), vol. 1, p. 276; *Tosefot* (1937), p. 66
LABOURT, *Le Christianisme* (1904²), pp. 20 n. 6, 60, 105f., 160f., 172, 174
LEVY, *Wörterbuch* (1924²), vol. 1, p. 495
NEUBAUER, *Géographie* (1868), p. 359
NEUSNER, *History* (1965–1970), vol. 2, p. 11
NÖLDEKE, *Perser und Araber* (1879), pp. 13, 19

Huṣal הוצל

A. *Sources*

1. Megillah 29a

תניא ר״ש בן יוחי אומר בוא וראה כמה חביבין ישראל לפני הקב״ה שבכל מקום שגלו שכינה עמהן, גלו למצרים שכינה עמהן . . . גלו לבבל שכינה עמהן . . . בבבל היכא, אמר אביי בבי כנישתא דהוצל ובבי כנישתא דשף ויתיב בנהרדעא, ולא תימא הכא והכא אלא זמנין הכא וזמנין הכא. אמר אביי תיתי לי דכי מרחיקנא פרסה עיילנא ומצלינא התם.

It has been taught that Rabbi Simeon b. Yoḥai said, Come and see how beloved is Israel in the sight of God, in that to every place they were exiled the Divine Presence went with them. They were exiled to Egypt and the Divine Presence was with them . . . They were exiled to Babylonia and the Divine Presence was with them . . . Where in Babylonia? Abbaye said, In the synagogue of Huṣal and in the synagogue of Šaf we-Yativ in Nəhardəʿa. Do not, however, say that it is [both] here and there, but sometimes here and sometimes there. Said Abbaye, May evil befall me if whenever I am within a parasang I do not go in and pray there.

2. Ketubot 111a[1]

אמר רב יהודה[2] כל הדר בבבל כאילו דר בארץ ישראל, שנאמר ״הוי ציון המלטי יושבת בת בבל״ אמר אביי נקטינן בבל לא חזיא חבלי דמשיח, תרגמה אהוצל דבנימין[3] וקרו ליה קרנא דשיזבתא.

Rav Judah[2] said, Whoever lives in Babylonia is as though he lived in Eretz Israel, for it is said, "Away, escape, O Zion, you who dwell in Fair Babylon"

[1] Similarly *Midrash ha-Gadol* to Leviticus 25: 38, Steinsalz ed., p. 714; *Yalquṭ ha-Makhiri*, Zechariah 2:11; cf. also *Kaftor wa-Feraḥ*, Ch. 10, Luncz ed., p. 171.

[2] The Munich MS has "Rav Judah said Rav said"; the Vatican 130 MS has "Rav Joseph said" (a Geniza fragment has "Rabbi Eleazar said" and see Ketubot in the ICIT ed., p. 542).

[3] The Munich and Vatican 113 MSS do not have "of Benjamin" (nor do the *Midrash ha-Gadol*: "תרגומה הוציל ומקריא קרנא דשיזבתא" [= applying to Huṣel and called the Corner and Safety] and the *Yalquṭ ha-Makhiri*, see note 1), and see Ketubot in the ICIT ed., p. 542, n. 64.

(Zech. 2:11). Abbaye said, We have a tradition that Babylonia will not see the sufferings [before the coming] of the Messiah, applying this to Huṣal of Benjamin[3] which they call the Corner of Safety.

3. Sanhedrin 19a

אמר רב מנשיא בר עות[4] שאילית את רבי יאשיה רבה בבית עלמין דהוצל ואמר לי אין שורה פחותה מעשרה בני אדם, ואין אבלים מן המנין . . .

Rav Menashya b. ʿAwat[4] said, I asked Rabbi Josiah the Great, in the graveyard of Huṣal and he told me that a [condolence] row must consist of not less than ten people and the mourners are not included ...

4. Giṭṭin 61a

רב כהנא הוה קאזיל להוצל[5] חזייה לההוא גברא דהוה שדי אופיי וקא נתרן תמרי אזל קא מנקיט ואכיל א"ל חזי מר דבידאי שדיתינהו א"ל מאתריה דר׳ יאשיה אתה קרי עליה "וצדיק יסוד עולם."

Rav Kahana was once going to Huṣal[5] when he saw a man throwing twigs [at a tree] and dates dropped down, so he went and picked up some and ate them. He said to him, See, sir, [that] I threw them down with my own hands. He said to him, You are from the same place as Rabbi Josiah, and he applied to him [the verse] "The righteous man is the foundation of the world" (Prov. 10:25).

5. Shabbat 92a–b

אמר רב משום רבי חייא המוציא משאוי בשבת על ראשו חייב חטאת, שכן אנשי הוצל עושין כן. ואנשי הוצל רובא דעלמא, אלא אי איתמר הכי איתמר אמר רב משום רבי חייא אחד מבני הוצל שהוציא משוי על ראשו בשבת חייב, שכן בני עירו עושין כן. ותיבטל דעתו אצל כל אדם, אלא אי איתמר הכי איתמר המוציא משוי על ראשו פטור, ואם תימצא לומר אנשי הוצל עושין כן, בטלה דעתן אצל כל אדם.

Rav said on Rabbi Ḥiyya's authority, One who carries out a burden on his head on the Sabbath is subject to a sin-offering because the people of Huṣal do thus. Are then the people of Huṣal the world's majority? If stated, it was rather thus stated: Rav said on Rabbi Ḥiyya's authority, If a Huṣalite carries out a burden on his head on the Sabbath, he is subject [to a sin-offering], because his fellow townsmen do so. But should his practice not be considered null by comparison with that of all men? If stated, it was rather thus stated, If one carried out a burden on his head, he is exempt. And should you object that the people of Huṣal do thus—their practice is null by comparison with that of all men.

---

[4] The Munich MS has "Rav Menashya b. Eilat (אילת)"; the Florence MS has "Rabbi Menashya b. ʿAzah (עזה)"; the Karlsruhe MS has "Rabbi Menashya b. ʿAza (עזא)."

[5] The Vatican 140 MS has להוציא.

6. Megillah 5b

רב אסי[6] קרי מגילה בהוצל בארביסר ובחמיסר, מספקא ליה אי מוקפת חומה מימות יהושע בן נון היא אי לא. איכא דאמר אמר רב אסי האי הוצל דבית בנימין[7] מוקפת חומה מימות יהושע היא.

Rav Assi[6] read the Megillah in Huṣal on the fourteenth and on the fifteenth, being in doubt whether it was walled in the days of Joshua son of Nun or not. According to another report, Rav Assi said, That Huṣal of the house of Benjamin[7] was walled in the days of Joshua.

7. Ḥullin 26b

היכי תוקע, אמר רב יהודה תוקע ומריע מתוך תקיעה, ורב אסי[8] אמר תוקע ומריע בנשימה אחת. אתקין רב אסי בהוצל כשמעתיה.

How does he blow the shofar then? Rav Judah said, He blows a *teqiʿah* (glissando blast) which in the end he converts into a *teruʿah* (broken tremolo). Rav Assi[8] said, He blows a *teqiʿah* and then a *teruʿah* all in one breath. Rav Assi instituted [the custom] in Huṣal in accordance with his view.

8. Ḥullin 107a

אתקין רב אשי[9] בהוצל כווא בת רביעתא.

Rav Ashi[9] instituted a jug in Huṣal of a quarter [*log* capacity].

9. Qiddushin 58b

. . . א"ל הכי קאמינא רב אסי דהוצל קאי כותיך.

. . . He said to him, (Rav Huna to Rav Ḥiyya b. Avin) I say this, Rav Assi of Huṣal agrees with you.

10. Pesaḥim 113b

אמר רבה בר בר חנה אמר רבי שמואל בר מרתא אמר רב משום רבי יוסי[10] איש הוצל מניין שאין שואלין בכלדיים, שנאמר "תמים תהיה עם ה' אלהיך" . . . תנא הוא יוסף איש הוצל, הוא יוסף הבבלי, הוא איסי בן גור אריה, הוא איסי בן יהודה, הוא איסי בן גמליאל, הוא איסי בן מהללאל, ומה שמו, איסי בן עקביה[11] שמו.

Rabba b. Bar Ḥana said Rabbi Samuel b. Martha said Rav said on the authority of Rabbi Yose[10] man of Huṣal, How do we know that you must not consult astrologers? Because it is said, "You must be wholehearted with the

---

[6] The London MS has רבסי.

[7] The Munich, Munich B and London MSS have ". . . Rav Assi said Huṣal is surrounded by a wall . . ."; the Oxford MS has "הוצל דבי מנימין" (Huṣal of Be Miniamin) as does the Munich B MS margin.

[8] The Munich MS has "רבסי" and thereafter as well.

[9] The Munich MS has "Rabbi Abba"; the Vatican 122 MS has "Ravabba" (רבבא); the Vatican 121 MS has "Rava"; the Hamburg MS has "Rav Assi"; and see *Diq. Sof.*

[10] The Munich, Munich B and Oxford MSS and *Aggadot ha-Talmud* have "on the authority of Joseph man of Huṣal"; and see *Diq. Sof.*

[11] On variants of the names in this source see *Diq. Sof.* in the relevant place.

Lord your God . . ." (Deut. 18:13). It is taught, Joseph man of Huṣal is Joseph the Babylonian, who is Issi b. Gur Aryeh, who is Issi b. Judah, who is Issi b. Gamaliel, who is Issi b. Mahalalel, and what is his [real] name? His name is Issi b. ʿAqavyah.[11]

11. Yoma 52a–b

והיינו דאמר רבי יוחנן בעי יוסף איש הוצל "ודביר בתוך הבית מפנימה הכין לתתן שם את ארון ברית ה'," איבעיא להו היכי קאמר קרא . . . ומי מספקא ליה, והתניא איסי בן יהודה אומר . . . והתניא הוא יוסף איש הוצל, הוא יוסף הבבלי, הוא איסי בן יהודה, הוא איסי בן גור אריה, הוא איסי בן גמליאל, הוא איסי בן מהללאל, ומה שמו איסי בן עקיבא[12] שמו . . . לרב חסדא מספקא ליה לאיסי בן יהודה[13] פשיטא ליה.

And this is as Rabbi Yoḥanan said, Joseph man of Huṣal asked about "In the innermost part of the House he fixed a Shrine in which to place the Ark of the Lord's Covenant" (I Kings 6:19). The question was asked by them, What does the verse say? . . . But could he have any doubt? Surely it was taught that Issi b. Judah said . . . It is also taught Joseph man of Huṣal is Joseph the Babylonian, who is Issi b. Judah, who is Issi b. Gur Aryeh, who is Issi b. Gamaliel, who is Issi b. Mahalalel. And what is his [real] name? His name is Issi b. ʿAqiva[12] . . . Rav Ḥisda has his doubts about it, but to Issi b. Judah[13] it is obvious.

12. T. J. Nedarim XI (XII) 1–42c, 33–34 (= T. J. Sheviʿit VIII 5–38b, 7–8).

יהוד' איש הוצא[14] עביד טמיר במערתא תלתא יומין מיקו' על הדין טעמ' מנין שחיי העיר הזאת קודמין לחיי עיר אחרת.

Judah man of Huṣal[14] concealed himself in a cave for three days to ascertain why the life of this city is preferred to that of another city.

13. Nedarim 49b

א"ר חסדא דמשאיל להון להלין נקדני דהוצל, הדין דייסא היכין מעלי למיכלה, דחיטי בלחמא דחיטי ודשערי בלחמא דשערי, או דלמא דחיטי בדשערי ודשערי בדחיטי.

Rav Ḥisda said, They should ask those epicureans of Huṣal how that porridge is best eaten, whether a wheat [porridge] with wheat bread and a barley with barley bread, or perhaps wheat with barley and barley with wheat.

14. Ḥullin 132b

אמר רב חסדא האי כהנא דלא מפריש מתנתא ליהוי בשמתא דאלהי ישראל. אמר רבה בר רב שילא הני טבחי דהוצל קיימי בשמתא דרב חסדא הא עשרים ותרתין שנין.

---

[12] On variants of the names in this source see *Diq. Sof.* in the relevant place.

[13] The manuscripts have "to Joseph man of Huṣal" and see *Diq. Sof.*

[14] The source has הוצא; the parallel in the T. J. Sheviʿit has "Judah man of Ḥuṣi" (חוצי); the Vatican 133 MS of T. J. Sheviʿit has "Yoḥanan of Ḥuṣar" (חוצר).

Rav Ḥisda said, A priest who does not set apart priestly gifts [due to another priest] is to be put under the ban of the Lord God of Israel. Rabbah son of Rav Shela said, Those butchers of Huṣal have been under Rav Ḥisda's ban for the last twenty-two years.

15. Keritot 13b

רב אחא דהוצל הוה נידרא עלה דביתהו אתא לקמיה דרב אשי . . .

Rav Aḥa of Huṣal had a vow in regard to his wife. He came before Rav Ashi . . .

16. Betzah 32b

א"ל רבינא לרב אשי אמר לן רב אחא[15] מהוצל דמר שרקין ליה תנורא ביומא טבא, אמר ליה אנן ארקתא דפרת סמכינן.

Ravina said to Rav Ashi, Rav Aḥa[15] of Huṣal told us that they plastered up the oven for him on the festival. He replied to him, We rely on [the clay from] the bank of the Euphrates.

B. *Already Proposed Location*

Near Nəhardəʿa (q.v., C3 on the Tal. Bab. map) toward the south.

C. *Identification*

Obermeyer locates Huṣal south of Nəhardəʿa in the direction of Sura, and within its jurisdiction.[16] The location is based on what Rav Sherira Gaon said, expanding on Source 1: "'Rav said in the synagogue of Huṣal and Samuel said in the synagogue of Šaf we-Yativ in Nəhardəʿa' . . . and that synagogue of Huṣal is close to the study house of Ezra the Scribe, down from Nəhardəʿa."[17] It appears from what Rav Sherira Gaon says that Rav, the founder of the Sura yeshiva, located the Divine Presence in the ancient synagogue of Huṣal while Samuel found it in the synagogue of Šaf we-Yativ in his hometown of Nəhardəʿa. The connection between Huṣal and the Sura yeshiva and sages is indicated in Source 14 as well, in which Rav Ḥisda, head of the Sura yeshiva in the third generation of Babylonian amoras, banned the butchers of Huṣal (and see below). In Source 15 Rav Aḥa of Huṣal requests a halakhic decision of Rav Ashi, of the sixth generation of Babylonian amoras, head of the Sura yeshiva which was then in neighboring Mata Məḥasya.

---

[15] The Munich MS has Rava of Huṣal which may have been the acronym רב"א (= Rav Aḥa) garbled to Rava and see *Diq. Sof.*

[16] Obermeyer, pp. 299–300.

[17] *Iggeret Rav Sherira Gaon*, Lewin ed., p. 73: רב אמר בכנישתא דהוצל ושמואל אמר בכנישתא דשף ויתיב בנהרדעא . . . והדא כנישתא דהוצל קרובה היא לבית מדרשו של עזרא הסופר למטה מנהרדעא היא.

Sources 2 and 6 mention "Huṣal of Benjamin", which led a number of scholars to posit the existence of two places, a Babylonian Huṣal and one in Eretz Israel probably in the area assigned to Benjamin.[18] But Source 2 clearly refers to Babylonia, and applies to Huṣal Abbaye's statement that Babylonia would not have to experience pre-messianic suffering. The choice of that place seems to be based on popular etymology deriving the name "Huṣal" from *haṣalah* (= rescue). It should be noted that some of the manuscripts for Sources 2 and 6 have "Huṣal" alone, Source 6 has "Huṣal of the house of Benjamin" and other versions are "Huṣal of the children of Benjamin," "Huṣal of Miniamin" etc.[19] Presumably then, Sources 2 and 6 likewise refer to the Babylonian place, and the name "Huṣal of Benjamin" if authentic derives from traditions regarding the first settlers there at the time of the Babylonian exile, one of which was that they were Jews of the tribe of Benjamin.[20]

D. *Sages and Huṣal*

The considerable activity in Huṣal by sages reported by the sources, especially at the start of the amoraic period, gives the impression that there was an independent study house there. Some scholars seeking to push back the dating of the Huṣal center of learning to the tannaitic period have considered Rabbi Josiah, mentioned in Sources 3 and 4 as residing and teaching in Huṣal, to be the tanna who was Rabbi Ishmael's disciple. They have evolved a theory about a group of Rabbi Ishmael's disciples who moved to Babylonia after the Bar Kokhva revolt, and set up a study house in Huṣal headed by Rabbi Josiah, a counterpart of the one in Nisibis (q.v.) in the same period. These scholars believe that the Huṣal study house was involved in the literary work of the tannas, and that parts of the Mekhilta and Sifre Numbers were redacted there.[21] That theory was questioned by other scholars among other reasons, on account of the basic argument that Rabbi Josiah, the disciple of Rabbi Ishmael who was active in the Ušah period, cannot be identified with Rabbi Josiah of Huṣal. Rav Sherira Gaon's *Iggeret* says: "And after Rabbi there were tannas from there [Eretz Israel] ... and from here [Babylonia] like Rabbi Josiah of Huṣal."[22] In other words, Rabbi Josiah

[18] Neubauer, p. 152; Schwartz, *Tevuot ha-Aretz*, pp. 163–167; Horowitz, *Eretz Israel u-Shekhenoteha*, pp. 73–74.

[19] See n. 3 and n. 7 above.

[20] If the form Miniamin (see n. 7) is accepted, the tradition may be that the early Huṣal residents were from the family of Miniamin, a Levite listed in Hezekiah's census (II Chron. 31:15, and see Obermeyer, p. 300, n. 6); or were of the Mijamin priestly course (I Chron. 24:9; Büchler, *'Am ha-'Areṣ*, p. 322, n. 2).

[21] On the redaction in Huṣal of tannaitic *midrashim* at Rabbi Ishmael's study house see Halevy, *Dorot ha-Rishonim*, vol. 4, pp. 679–681; Neusner, *History*, vol. 1, pp. 128–135, 179–187; Eshel, pp. 106–107.

[22] *Iggeret Rav Sherira Gaon*, Lewin ed., p. 59: ובתר רבי הוו תנאי מן התם ... ומן הכא כגון ר' יאשיה דמן הוצל.

was active after the time of Rabbi Judah ha-Nasi, which was the first generation of Babylonian amoras.[23] This does not eliminate the possibility of there having already been a study house in Huṣal in the tannaitic period, and in fact it is logical to assume that there were study houses in Babylonia before Rav arrived in A. D. 219, and the evidence of the antiquity of the Huṣal Jewish community in Source 1 supports that possibility. But that is a far cry from stipulating exactly which parts of tannaitic literature were compiled in Huṣal.

Another Huṣal sage of the first generation of Babylonian amoras was Rav Assi many of whose doings and ordinances are reported in the Talmud. According to Source 6, he read the Book of Esther in Huṣal on both the fourteenth and fifteenth of Adar, because it was one of the cities about which there was doubt as to whether it had been surrounded by a wall in Joshua's time. That source thus shows that there was a tradition regarding the antiquity of Huṣal, and also that the injunction to read the scroll on the fifteenth of Adar in cities that had walls in Joshua's time applied to places outside of Eretz Israel as well. Source 7 deals with a disagreement between Rav Assi and Rav Judah regarding the manner in which the shofar should be blown to usher in the Sabbath when Friday coincides with a festival, and Rav Assi asserts that in Huṣal his opinion should be followed. The Hamburg MS version of Source 8 naming Rav Assi seems the correct one (see note 9) and there Rav Assi is reported as issuing another ordinance in his place, this time regarding a clay vessel called a *kuz*, of a quarter *log* capacity, used for washing the hands.[24] Source 9 has Rav Huna referring to Rav Assi of Huṣal, telling Rav Ḥiyya b. Avin that the former agrees with him. Rav Kahana, also of the first generation of Babylonian amoras, is often mentioned together with Rav Assi.[25] Source 4 reports Rav Kahana as going to Huṣal, and his purpose was most likely to call on Rav Assi of Huṣal.[26]

Sources 10 and 11 deal with Joseph man of Huṣal, who is identified with Issi b. Judah of the end of the tannaitic period, and whose numerous aliases are listed.[27] It is doubtful whether there is any connection or identity between

---

[23] See Epstein, *Mevo'ot le-Sifrut ha-Tana'im*, p. 570, n. 179; Gafni, *Ha-Yeshiva be-Bavel*, pp. 15–17. See also Gafni and the literature he cites for the refutation of the view that the literature of the tannaitic interpretations was redacted in Huṣal.

[24] On *kuz*, see Brand, *Kelei ha-Ḥeres*, pp. 207–210.

[25] E.g., Sanhedrin 36b; Shabbat 146b, and see Albeck, *Mavo la-Talmudim*, pp. 174–175.

[26] Some scholars claim that *sidra de-Assi* (T. J. Betzah I 6–60c, 51) is a study house headed by Rav Assi that operated in Huṣal and attracted sages (see e.g. Halevy, *Dorot ha-Rishonim*, vol. 5, pp. 234–235). This was rightly refuted by Goodblatt (*Rabbinic Instruction*, p. 137) who claims among other things that the reference is not to Rav Assi of the first generation of Babylonian amoras, that the name Huṣal itself is not mentioned in the source, and that there is therefore no reason to discuss the matter further.

[27] Cf. also Niddah 36b.

Joseph man of Huṣal and Rav Assi of Huṣal. The multiplicity of names of the former led to a proliferation of theories, not all of them well founded, on the reasons for it, but this is not the place to discuss them.[28]
Source 12 describes a man named Judah from a place called Huṣa or Ḥuṣi, which sounds like Huṣal, who spent three days alone in a cave seeking the sense of a particular halakhah. The continuation of the passage states that since he did not find the answer, he applied to Rabbi Yose b. Ḥalafta, which shows the episode took place in Eretz Israel in the Ušah period. A parallel source in the Babylonian Talmud has a variation: "Issi b. Judah did not come to Rabbi Yose's study house for three days."[29] As according to Sources 10 and 11, Issi b. Judah is Joseph of Huṣal, it is reasonable to assume that Judah of Huṣa is also to be identified with him.[30]
Sources 15 and 16 mention an additional Huṣal sage, of the end of the amoraic period. Rav Aḥa of Huṣal, who was in touch with Rav Ashi, head of the Mata Məḥasya yeshiva (see "Sura"), in the sixth generation of Babylonian amoras.

E. *The Inhabitants*

The sources provide various details on the manners and customs of the Huṣalites. The Babylonians used to eat porridge with bread, a culinary custom the people from Eretz Israel ridiculed, and in the context of Source 13, stated, "And Rabbi Zera said, The Babylonians are foolish people who eat bread with bread."[31] It is perhaps typical that the statement was made by Rabbi Zera, a sage who came to Eretz Israel from Babylonia. In Source 13, Rav Ḥisda, head of the Sura yeshiva in the third generation of Babylonian amoras, asks the Huṣalites who apparently have the reputation of being gourmets, which is the better choice, wheat porridge with wheat bread and barley porridge with barley bread, or the opposite.[32]
Source 14 refers to the Huṣal butchers who were priests but did not comply with the halakhah stipulating that they should set the shoulder, cheeks and stomach apart as priestly gifts to other priests.[33] Rabbah b. Rav Shela, of

---

[28] See Hyman, pp. 151–153; Hacohen, *Sinai* 33 (1953): 355–364; 34 (1954): 231–240, 325–334, 407, 423; Neusner, *History*, vol. 1, passim.

[29] Nedarim 81a (איסי בר יהודה לא אתא למתיבתא דר' יוסי תלתא יומי).

[30] See Bacher, *Tannaiten*, vol. 2, p. 417; Hyman, *loc. cit.* (n. 28) and pp. 552–553; Gafni, *Ha-Yeshiva be-Bavel*, p. 124, n. 54.

[31] Nedarim 49b, and cf. also Rabbi Zera's statement in Betzah 16a. See Krauss, *Qadmoniot ha-Talmud*, vol. 1B, pp. 194–195; Newman, *Agricultural Life*, pp. 91–92.

[32] Zadok notes that eating bread with porridge was already customary in Babylonia in the second millennium B.C., and that today too in Iraq wheat porridge (*burġul*) is commonly eaten with bread (Zadok, *JQR* 68 [1977/8]: 255).

[33] The allocation of gifts of unconsecrated meat to priests was the practice outside of Eretz Israel as well, cf. Ḥullin X 1, and see Newman, *Agricultural Life*, pp. 155–156; Beer, *Amora'ei Bavel*, p. 245, and see also Büchler, n. 20 above.

the fourth generation of Babylonian amoras and Rav Ḥisda's disciple, reports that the ban against the Huṣal butchers that Rav Ḥisda had issued for that reason twenty-two years earlier was still in effect.
Source 5 refers to the Huṣalite custom of carrying loads on the head without using the hands. It is mentioned by Rav in the name of his uncle Rabbi Ḥiyya who was of Babylonian origin. The custom does not seem to have had any particular significance, except in the context of the Sabbath laws in connection with which it is mentioned.

BACHER, *Tannaiten* (1884–1890), vol. 2, p. 417
BEER, *Amora'ei Bavel* (1974), p. 245
BERLINER, *Beiträge* (1883), p. 32
BÜCHLER, *'Am ha-'Areṣ* (1906), p. 222, n. 2
ESHEL, *Yishuvei ha-Yehudim* (1979), pp. 105–107
FUNK, *Juden* (1902–1908), vol. 1, p. 100
FUNK, *Monumenta* (1913), pp. 31, 32, 44, 292
GAFNI, *Ha-Yeshiva be-Bavel* (1978), pp. 16, 124
GETZOW, *Al Neharot Bavel* (1887), p. 105
GOODBLATT, *Rabbinic Instruction* (1975), pp. 20, 137
HALEVY, *Dorot ha-Rishonim* (1897–1939), vol. 4, pp. 679–681; vol. 5, passim
HIRSCHENSON, *Sheva Ḥokhmot* (1883), p. 102
JASTROW, *Dictionary* (1950³), p. 340: "הוצל", "הוצא II"
KOHUT, *Arukh ha-Shalem* (1878–1892), vol. 3, p. 194; *Tosefot* (1937), p. 157
KRAUSS, *Qadmoniot ha-Talmud* (1923–1945), vol. 1A, p. 220; vol. 2A, p. 194
LEVY, *Wörterbuch* (1924²), vol. 1, p. 460
NEUBAUER, *Géographie* (1868), pp. 152, 350
NEUSNER, *History* (1965–1970), vol. 1–5, passim
NEWMAN, *Agricultural Life* (1932), pp. 22, 29, 39, 91, 155
OBERMEYER, *Landschaft* (1929), pp. 299–300
RAPOPORT, *Erekh Millin* (1914), vol. 2, p. 177
RAPOPORT, *Hamagid* 17 (1873): 401

Ihi də-Qira (Hīt) איהי דקירא

A. *Sources*

1. Qiddushin 72a

אמר אביי[1] אמר ר' חמא בר עוקבא אמר רבי יוסי בר' חנינא בין הנהרות הרי היא כגולה ליוחסין. והיכא קיימא, אמר רבי יוחנן מאיהי דקירא[2] ולעיל. והא אמר רבי יוחנן עד מעברתא דגיזמא,[3] אמר אביי רצועה נפקא.

Abbaye[1] said that Rabbi Ḥama b. ʿUqba said, Rabbi Yose son of Rabbi Ḥanina said, Between the rivers is like the Exile (= Babylonia) in respect of genealogy. And where is it? Rabbi Yoḥanan said, From Ihi də-Qira[2] up. But Rabbi Yoḥanan said, To the ford of Gizma.[3] Abbaye said, A strip extends.

---

[1] The Munich MS has "Rabbi Abbahu."
[2] The Munich and Vatican 111 MSS have האי דקירא.
[3] The Vatican 111 MS has מעברתא דאגמא.

2. Berakhot 59b

ואמר רמי בר אבא א״ר יצחק הרואה פרת אגשרא דבבל אומר ברוך עושה בראשית,
והאידנא דשניוה פרסאי מבי שבור ולעיל,[4] רב יוסף אמר מאיהי דקירא[5] ולעיל.

Rami b. Abba said, Rabbi Isaac said, A person who sees the Euphrates at the bridge of Babylon says, Blessed is the Doer of the work of creation. And now that the Persians have changed it (the course of the river), from Be Šabur up.[4] Rav Joseph said, From Ihi də-Qira[5] up.

3. Bava Batra 24a

איתמר חבית שצפה בנהר אמר רב נמצאת כנגד עיר שרובה ישראל מותר כנגד עיר שרובה
נכרים אסירא, ושמואל אמר אפילו נמצאת כנגד עיר שרובה ישראל אסירא, אימור מהאי
דקרא[6] אתאי . . . והכא בהא קמיפלגי, דמר סבר אם איתא דמהאי דקרא[7] אתאי עקולי ופשורי
הוה מטבעי לה, ומר סבר חריפא דנהרא נקט ואתאי.

It is said, A barrel floating in the river. Rav said, Found opposite a city mostly Jewish, [it is] allowed; opposite a city mostly Gentile, forbidden. And Samuel said, Even if found opposite a city mostly Jewish, forbidden. Say it came from Ihi də-Qira[6] . . . and here in this they are divided, for this one is of the opinion, If it comes from Ihi də-Qira,[7] bays and thaws would have sunk it. And this one is of the opinion, The current of the river caught it and it came.

4. Ammianus XXIV 2,3

Unde amne transito miliario septimo disparata, Diacira invaditur civitas, habitatoribus vacua, frumento et salibus nitidis plena, in qua templum alti culminis arci vidimus superpositum, qua incensa caesisque mulieribus paucis, quae repertae sunt, traiecto fonte scatenti bitumine, Ozogardana occupavimus oppidum, quod formidine advenientis exercitus itidem deseruere cultores. In quo principis Traiani tribunal ostendebatur.

From there (i.e. Paraxmalcha) we crossed the river and entered the city of Diacira, seven miles distant. This place was without inhabitants, but rich in grain and fine white salt; there we saw a temple, standing on a lofty citadel. After burning the city, and killing a few women whom we found, we passed over a spring bubbling with bitumen and took possession of the town of Ozogardana, which the inhabitants had likewise deserted through fear of the approaching army. Here a tribunal of the emperor Trajan was to be seen. (trans.: J. C. Rolfe, LCL)

---

[4] The sentence ״האידנא . . . מבי שבור ולעיל״ is missing in the Munich MS.

[5] The Munich MS has מהאיקר׳.

[6] The source has האי דקרא; the Munich and Hamburg MSS have מהאי דקירא, the Vatican 111 MS and Lublin printing have מאיהי דקירא, the Oxford MS has מההוא דקירה and the Florence MS has מאיהא דקרירא.

[7] The Oxford MS has דמההיא דקירא; the other versions as in n. 6.

5. Zosimus III 15,2–3

. . . εἰς Δάκιρα παρεγένετο, πόλιν ἐν δεξιᾷ πλέοντι τὸν Εὐφράτην κειμένην· ἥν τινα τῶν οἰκούντων ἔρημον εὑρόντες οἱ στρατιῶται σῖτόν τε πολὺν ἐναποκείμενον ἥρπασαν καὶ ἁλῶν πλῆθος οὐ μέτριον, γυναῖκάς τε τὰς ἐγκαταλειφθείσας ἀποσφάξαντες οὕτω κατέσκαψαν ὥστε οἴεσθαι τοὺς ὁρῶντας μηδὲ γεγονέναι πόλιν αὐτόθι. 3 Ἐπὶ δὲ τῆς ἀντικρὺ ἠόνος, δι' ἧς ὁ στρατὸς ἐποιεῖτο τὴν πορείαν, πηγή τις ἦν ἄσφαλτον ἀνιεῖσα· μεθ' ἣν εἰς Σίθα, εἶτα εἰς Μηγίαν ἀφικόμενος, μετ' ἐκείνην εἰς Ζαραγαρδίαν πόλιν ἦλθεν, ἐν ᾗ βῆμα ἦν ὑψηλὸν ἐκ λίθου πεποιημένον, ὃ Τραϊανοῦ καλεῖν εἰώθασιν οἱ ἐγχώριοι.

. . . he arrived at Dakira, a town on the right bank of the Euphrates. The soldiers found it deserted by its inhabitants but they seized much grain which was stored there and a considerable quantity of salt. They killed a few women who had been left behind and destroyed the town in such a manner that one who saw the place would not have believed there was a town there. On the opposite bank, where the army marched, there was a spring bubbling with bitumen. Thereafter it arrived at Sitha, next at Megia — then to the town of Zaragardia, where there was a high tribunal built of stone, which the local inhabitants were wont to call after Trajan.

B. *Already Proposed Location*

Hīt, on the Euphrates, a hundred kilometers northwest of al-Fallūğa near Anbār (A 1 on the Tal. Bab. map).

C. *Identification*

The linguistic similarity between the talmudic name—Ihi də-Qira—and the ancient name of Hīt as it appears in Sources 4 and 5—Diacira/Dakira—and other sources from classical literature (see below) leaves no room for doubt as to the identity of Ihi də-Qira and Hīt, as many scholars have proposed.[8]

D. *History*

The name Īdu first appears in inscriptions of the early Babylonian period.[9] It appears to be derived from the Accadian *ittû* which means "asphalt." Herodotus (I 179) mentions the name Ἴς. Isidorus of Charax refers to the city as Ἀείπολις, ἔνθα ἀσφαλτίτιδες πηγαί (= Aeipolis, a place where there are asphalt springs).[10] According to Musil (see note 9), Ispolis is the right spelling. Trajan passed

---

[8] Thus Neubauer, p. 353; Berliner, p. 62; Funk, *Monumenta*, p. 288; Obermeyer, p. 51; Eshel, p. 17; etc.

[9] For references see Weissbach, *RE*, vol. 9, col. 2047, s.v. "Is;" Musil, *The Middle Euphrates*, p. 350; Postgate, *Reallex. d. Assyriologie*, vol. 5, p. 33.

[10] *Mansiones Parthicae* 1 (late first century).

through the place in A.D. 116, though only the asphalt, not the town, is mentioned in connection with his campaign.[11] Ptolemy refers to the town of ʼΙδικάρα;[12] that name is certainly taken from the form of the name Ihi də-Qira that figures in the Talmud.[13] Zosimus, in Source 5, mentions a place near Dakira called Sitha, but it is not clear whether there is any connection between the latter and the ancient towns of Id or Ἴς.[14] The Syriac form Hīt was later adopted by the Arabs.[15]

Hīt was strategically important because it controlled the caravan route from Palmyra to Ctesiphon (later from Aleppo to Baghdad). An inscription found southeast of Palmyra[16] indicates that there was a road directly from Palmyra to Hīt that bypassed Dura.

The town of Hīt is on a low hill near the Euphrates. The local asphalt springs are very productive, and a small stream carries lumps of asphalt down to the Euphrates. Asphalt was used to caulk ships with, and was burned in kilns to produce cement. Hīt exported various bituminous products as well. The salt springs mentioned in Sources 4 and 5 also provided income for the town.

Below Hīt the Euphrates begins to be divided into irrigation channels,[17] and perhaps that is what is suggested in Source 2 where Rav Joseph says that only a person who has seen the Euphrates from Ihi də-Qira and up must say "Blessed is the Doer of the work of creation."

E. *The Boundary of "Between the Rivers"*

Source 1 implies that "between the rivers" extends north from Ihi də-Qira (see the entry on "Šuṭ Mišuṭ"), and Arabic sources too sometimes refer to Hīt as a border point of the region that included mainly the area between the rivers known as al-Ǧazīra (= "the island"). Hīt is also referred to as at the border of Iraq, which amounts to the same thing.[18]

---

11 Cassius Dio LXVIII 27, 1. 12 V 19, 6.

13 Herzfeld, *Samarra*, p. 11, n. 4, and cf. the forms of the name in Sources 4 and 5.

14 For comments on the topography reported by Ammianus and Zosimus (Sources 4 and 5) see Herzfeld, *ibid.*, p. 12.

15 On Hīt see *BGA*, passim; Yāqūt, *ar-Rauḍ al-miʿṭār*, Bakrī, s.v. "Hīt" (on the destruction of Hīt and the reason for it see e.g. Bakrī, s.v. "ʿĀnāt"); Abū l-Fidā', p. 169; Idrīsī, vol. 6, p. 656; Mustaufī, vol. 2, p. 53; *Ḥudūd al-ʿālam*, p. 141; Qazwīnī, *Bilād*, p. 281; Ibn Saʿīd, *Geography*, p. 156; Musil, *The Middle Euphrates*, pp. 26–31, appendix 17, pp. 350–353; Streck, *Die alte Landschaft*, vol. 1, p. 19; Streck, *EI*^{1,2}, s.v. "Hīt"; Fransīs & ʿAwwād, *Sumer* 8 (1952): 279–280.

16 The inscription was set up in honor of a man whose statue was erected at Charax and Vologesias and elsewhere (Mouterde & Poidebard, *Syria* 12 [1931]: 107ff.).

17 Yāqūt, s.v. "Furāt"; Qazwīnī, *Bilād*, p. 421. Cf. Le Strange, "Ibn Serapion," p. 10; Suhrāb, p. 119.

18 See Ibn Saʿīd, *Geography*, p. 156; and cf. Ibn al-Faqīh, pp. 161–162; *ʿUyūn al-aḫbār*, vol. 1, p. 214; Yāqūt, s.v. "ʿIrāq," pp. 94–95; Bakrī, *ar-Rauḍ al-miʿṭār*, s.v. "ʿIrāq." See also Yāqūt, s.v. "Manāẓir"; Qudāma, *Ḫarāǧ*, p. 252; Masʿūdī, *Tanbīh*, p. 39; Ibn

F. *The Inhabitants*

Source 3 indicates that the inhabitants of Ihi də-Qira were all, or at any rate, mostly, Gentiles. The problem there is whether a barrel of wine found floating in the river should be considered libation wine (and therefore unusable) or not. The decision depends on the origin of the wine, and Ihi də-Qira is cited as an example of a place whose wine would automatically be considered libation wine.[19]

BERLINER, *Beiträge* (1883). p. 62
ESHEL, *Yishuvei ha-Yehudim* (1979), pp. 17–18. 112
FRANSĪS & ʿAWWĀD, *Sumer* 8 (1952): 279–280
FUNK, *Juden* (1902–1908), vol. 1, pp. 12–13
FUNK, *Monumenta* (1913), pp. 22, 288
GRAETZ, *MGWJ* 2 (1853): 194–195
GRAETZ, *Geschichte* (1908⁴), vol. 4, p. 248
HERZFELD, *Samarra* (1948), pp. 11–12
HIRSCHENSON, *Sheva Ḥokhmot* (1883), pp. 32–33
JASTROW, *Dictionary* (1950³), p. 46
KOHUT, *Arukh ha-Shalem* (1878–1892), vol. 1, pp. 66–67; *Tosefot* (1937), p. 19
KRAUSS, *Qadmoniot ha-Talmud* (1923–1945), vol. 1A, p. 207
LEVY, *Wörterbuch* (1924²), vol. 1, p. 62
MOUTERDE & POIDEBARD, *Syria* 12 (1931): 107ff.
MUSIL, *The Middle Euphrates* (1927), pp. 26ff., 350ff.
NEUBAUER, *Géographie* (1868), pp. 353–354
NEWMAN, *Agricultural Life* (1932), pp. 3–6
OBERMEYER, *Landschaft* (1929), pp. 26, 49–53, 59–60, 67–68, 72–73, 78, 100–105
RAPOPORT, *Erekh Millin* (1914), vol. 1, pp. 63–68
STRECK, *EI*¹˒², s.v. "Hīt"
STRECK, *RE*, vol. 5, col. 317, s.v. "Diakira"
STRECK, *Die alte Landschaft* (1900), vol. 1, p. 19
WEISSBACH, *RE*, vol. 9, col. 2047f., s.v. "Is"
WIESNER. *Scholien* (1859–1867), vol. 1, pp. 147–148

Kafri כפרי

A. *Sources*

1. ʿEruvin 62b

רב חסדא אורי בכפרי בשני דרב הונא.

Rav Ḥisda ruled at Kafri in the time of Rav Huna.

2. Bava Metziʿa 6a–b

ת"ש דההיא מסותא דהוו מנצו עלה בי תרי, האי אמר דידי הוא והאי אמר דידי הוא, קם חד מינייהו אקדשה, פרשי מינה רב חנניה ורב אושעיא וכולהו רבנן, וא"ל רב אושעיא

Ḫurdāḏbih, p. 173; Streck, *EI*¹˒², s.v. "Hīt." Other sources mention Anbār as the border of Iraq; cf. the entry on "Aqra də-Tulbanqe." See e.g. Yāqūt, *ar-Rauḍ al-miʿṭār*, s.v. "Anbār" ("the border of Babylonia"); cf. Yāqūt, s.v. "Fīrūzasābūr"; Bakrī, s.v. "Anbār" ("and it is the border of Persia"). Ibn Ḥauqal, pp. 208–209; Iṣṭaḫrī, pp. 71–72, set the border of al-Ǧazīra at Anbār.

[19] On the Hīt wine, celebrated for its excellence, see the sources in Streck, *EI*¹˒², s.v. "Hīt."

לרבה כי אזלת קמיה דרב חסדא לכפרי[1] בעי מיניה, כי אתא לסורא א"ל רב המנונא מתניתין היא . . .

Come and hear, the case of a bathhouse about which two people quarreled. This one said, It is mine, and that one said, It is mine. One rose and dedicated it. Rav Hananiah and Rav Oshaʿya and all the sages kept away from it. And Rav Oshaʿya said to Rabbah, When you go before Rav Ḥisda to Kafri[1], ask him. When he came to Sura, Rav Hamnuna said to him, This is [made clear in] a Mishnah . . .

3. Qiddushin 44b

איתמר קטנה שנתקדשה שלא לדעת אביה אמר שמואל צריכה גט וצריכה מיאון. אמר קרנא דברים בגו אם גט למה מיאון אם מיאון למה גט, אמרו ליה הא מר עוקבא[2] ובי דיניה בכפרי. אפכוה שדרוה לקמיה דרב . . .

It has been stated, If a minor is betrothed without her father's knowledge, Samuel said, She requires both a bill of divorcement and an annulment. Qarna said, This is inherently open to objection. If *geṭ*, why *mi'un*, and if *mi'un*, why *geṭ*? They said to him, But there is Mar ʿUqba[2] and his Bet Din at Kafri. They reversed, and they sent the question to Rav . . .

4. Bava Batra 153a

אמר להו רב חסדא כי אתא רב הונא מכופרי[3] פירשה . . .

Rav Ḥisda said to them, When Rav Huna came from Kafri[3] he explained it . . .

5. Sanhedrin 5a

והאמר מר איבו וחנה ושילא ומרתא ורבי חייא כולהו בני אבא בר אחא כרסלא[4] מכפרי הוו.

But a master said that Aibu and Ḥana and Shela and Marta and Rabbi Ḥiyya were all sons of Abba b. Aḥa Karsela[4] of Kafri.

6. Bava Metziʿa 73a

בסורא אזלי ארבעה, בכפרי אזלן שיתא.

In Sura they go four, in Kafri they go six [for a *zuz*].

B. *Already Proposed Location*

In the vicinity (south) of Sura (q.v., D4 on the Tal. Bab. map).

---

[1] The Vatican 114 MS does not have כפרי at all.

[2] Rav Sherira Gaon, in his responsum to the people of Fez, has "Rabbi ʿAqiva and his Bet Din at Kafri;" see *Otzar ha-Geonim* for Qiddushin, *ha-Teshuvot*, p. 120, § 273 and p. 119, § 268; see also below.

[3] The source has מכופרי; the Munich and Vatican 115 MSS have מבי כפרי'; the Hamburg MS has מכפרי and the Florence MS has מכפריה.

[4] The Munich MS has "bar Sela," the Florence MS has "Sela," and see *Diq. Sof.*

C. *Identification*

The sources above indicate the propinquity of Kafri to Sura. Source 1, for instance, testifies that Rav Ḥisda ruled at Kafri in the time of his master, Rav Huna, head of the Sura yeshiva in the second generation of Babylonian amoras. The passage deals with the question of whether a disciple may rule in his master's town in the latter's lifetime, and cites a number of examples of disciples who ruled not in their master's own town, but in a nearby place.[5] Source 4 describes a case in which Rav Huna himself came to Kafri. Obermeyer claims that Source 2 indicates that Kafri was south of Sura; Rabbah, head of the yeshiva at Pumbədita (q.v.) in the third generation of Babylonian amoras, is asked to submit the question to Rav Ḥisda in Kafri, but is said to have reached Sura before arriving in Kafri.[6] Source 6 compares the prices of fruit in two places, Kafri and Sura; most likely the lower prices in the former reflect the usual differential between prices in a city and those in a smaller place in the vicinity.

D. *The Exilarch and Kafri*

Source 3 notes that "there is Mar ʿUqba and his Bet Din at Kafri." Mar ʿUqba was the Exilarch in the first generation of Babylonian amoras, and in Beer's opinion the source means that the Exilarch had his seat at Kafri for a time.[7] If so, Kafri must have been an important place then.

Beer, *Rashut ha-Golah* (1970), pp. 21, 66, 71
Beer, *Amora'ei Bavel* (1974), pp. 92, 191
Berliner, *Beiträge* (1883), pp. 37, 67
Eshel, *Yishuvei ha-Yehudim* (1979), pp. 133–134
Funk, *Juden* (1902–1908), vol. 1, p. 8
Funk, *Monumenta* (1913), pp. 35, 293
Halevy, *Dorot ha-Rishonim* (1897–1939), vol. 5, p. 595
Jastrow, *Dictionary* (1950^3), p. 662
Kohut, *Arukh ha-Shalem* (1878–1892), vol. 4, p. 300 "כפר"
Levy, *Wörterbuch* (1924^2), vol. 2, p. 389
Neubauer, *Géographie* (1868), p. 361
Neusner, *PAAJR* 31 (1963): 183f.
Neusner, *History* (1965–1970), vols. 2 & 3, passim
Newman, *Agricultural Life* (1932), pp. 7, 25, 100, 109, 171
Obermeyer, *Landschaft* (1929), pp. 39, 315–318

[5] Thus Rav Hamnuna ruled in Ḥarta də-Argiz (q.v.) that was only one parasang (ca. 4½ kilometers) from Sura, when Rav Ḥisda had already been appointed head of the Sura yeshiva following Rav Huna's death (see the entry on "Sura"); Ravina examined a knife in Babylon (q.v.) in the lifetime of Rav Ashi, head of the Sura yeshiva in Mata Məḥasya (see the entry on Sura and Mata Məḥasya) in the sixth generation of Babylonian amoras. All these are cases of a disciple ruling in a place close to Sura while his master was still active in Sura itself.

[6] Obermeyer, p. 316.

[7] See Beer's detailed discussion of this question (*Rashut ha-Golah*, pp. 70–73).

Kaškar כשכר

A. *Sources*

1. Yoma 10a

תני רב יוסף . . . "ותהי ראשית ממלכתו בבל וארך ואכד וכלנה," בבל כמשמעה, ארך זה אוריכות,[1] ואכד זה בשכר,[2] כלנה זה נופר נינפי.[3]

Rav Joseph taught ... "And the mainstays of his kingdom were Babylon, Ereḵ, Akkad and Kalneh" (Gen. 10:10); Babylon is what it says, Ereḵ is Oriḵut,[1] Akkad is Kaškar,[2] and Kalneh is Nufar Ninəfe.[3]

2. Giṭṭin 80b

ההוא גיטא דהוה כתיב ביה לשם איסטנדרא[4] דבשכר, שלחה רב נחמן בר רב חסדא לקמיה דרבה[6] כי האי גוונא מאי.

A certain *geṭ* that had written in it the name of the *isṭāndār*[4] (= governor) of Kaškar,[5] Rav Naḥman b. Rav Ḥisda, sent to Rabbah[6] [to ask], Such a one, what is it.

3. Shabbat 139a–b

שלחו ליה בני בשכר ללוי כילה מהו, כשותא בכרמא מהו, מת בי"ט מהי, אדאזיל נח נפשיה דלוי. אמר שמואל לרב מנשיא אי חכימת שלח להו. שלח להו כילה חזרנו על כל צידי כילה ולא מצינו לה צד היתר. ולישלח להו כדרמי בר יחזקאל, לפי שאינן בני תורה. כשותא בכרמא עירבובא. ולישלח להו כדר"ט . . . לפי שאינן בני תורה . . . מת, שלח להו מת לא יתעסקו ביה לא יהודאין ולא ארמאין לא ביום טוב ראשון ולא ביום טוב שני. איני . . . לפי שאינן בני תורה.

The people of Kaškar[7] applied to Levi [asking] what about a canopy, what about cuscuta in a vineyard, what about a corpse on a festival, but till he (the messenger) went, Levi died. Samuel said to Rav Menashya, If you are a sage, send them [answers]. He sent them, Canopy, we went over all aspects and did not find one permitted. And to send them as Rami b. Ezekiel [said that there is a permit, he did not] because they are not learned in the Law. Cuscuta in

---

[1] For variants see the entry on "Orchoi."

[2] The source has בשכר (= Baškar), but the Munich B and London MSS, the Warsaw printing and *Aggadot ha-Talmud* have כשכר (= Kaškar). That form appears preferable also in view of the Arabic name of the place. Cf., e.g., *Arukh ha-Shalem*, s.v. "Baškar": "A scribal error instead of Kaškar, q.v." (although no such entry occurs in *Arukh ha-Shalem* at all; and see *ibid.*, vol. 1, p. 206; *ibid.*, *Tosefot*, s.v. "Baškar;" cf. also Ginzberg, *Geonica*, vol. 2, p. 156). See below as well.

[3] For variants see the entry on "Nippur."

[4] A Geniza fragment has אוסתן דרא (or רדא, and interlinearly אומנדנא), and see *Diq. Sof.* (Feldblum).

[5] The source has בשכר (= Baškar).

[6] The Munich and Vatican 130 MSS have "Rava," and see *Diq. Sof.* (Feldblum).

[7] The source has בשכר (= Baškar).

the vineyard is a mixture, and to send them as Rabbi Ṭarfon . . . [he did not] because they are not learned in the Law . . . A corpse, he sent them [word] that neither Jews nor Arameans (= Gentiles) should deal with a corpse neither on the first festival day nor the second. Is that really so? . . . [he sent them] as they are not learned in the Law.

B. *Location*

Kaskar in the Mesene region, near Wāsiṭ (on Bab. Env. map).

C. *History*

Kaskar is located on a straight line from Kūt al-Imāra to Imām ʿAlī Šarqī and Imāra, 48 kilometers east and 40 degrees south of Kūt al-Imāra, and 20 kilometers east and 10 degrees north of Kūt al-Hai. The official name of the Sassanian province was Isṭān Šād Ḫusro Šāpur, Kaškar in the local language and Kaskar in Arabic. The capital, also Kaskar, was on the east bank of the Tigris. During the Umayyad period, the governor of Iraq, al-Ḥaǧǧāǧ, reportedly established Wāsiṭ on the west bank, and connected the two places by means of a pontoon bridge. It was, however, in existence before al-Ḥaǧǧāǧ's time.[8] It has been said that Wāsiṭ means "Middletown" and was so named because it was situated midway between Baṣra, Ahwāz, Kūfa and Madā'in. Kaskar was a bishopric at the start of the fourth century. After 410, the bishop of Kaskar would assume the duties of the partriarch of Ctesiphon when there was no incumbent. Church council acts covering the period between 410 and 790 indicate that Kaskar bishops participated in the deliberations.[9]

Muslim traditions connect Kaskar and Wāsiṭ with biblical personages and events, such as the establishment of Wāsiṭ on a piece of earth carried from the Holy Land by the flood;[10] the construction of the Wāsiṭ mosque on the basis of an echo of Kaskar's great lamentation over the destruction of *bait al-maqdis*

---

[8] See Herzfeld, *Samarra*, pp. 16–17, idem, *Der Islam* 11 (1921): 150. On Wāsiṭ see also Yāqūt; Bakrī; *ar-Rauḍ al-miʿṭār*, s.v. "Kaskar"; *BGA*, passim; Mustaufī, vol. 2, p. 159; *Ḥudūd al-ʿālam*, index ("Wāsiṭ"); Šābuštī, *Diyārāt*², p. 274; Morony, *Iran* 14 (1976): 44ff.; Streck, *Die alte Landschaft*, vol. 1, pp. 15, 18; vol. 2, p. 321f.; Le Strange, pp. 39ff., 80; Streck, *EI*¹, s.v. "Kaskar"; Streck-Lassner, *EI*², s.v. "Kaskar," and see the entry on "Mesene," and the discussion on the Kaskar district in the entry on "Apamea."

[9] See Sachau, *APAW*, *phil.-hist. Klasse*, 1 (1919): 30–31; Lantschoot, *Dictionnaire*, p. 1266f., s.v. "Cascar"; Fiey, *Assyrie Chrétienne*, vol. 3, pp. 151–187, and references, p. 151, n. 2.

[10] *Ta'rīḫ Wāsiṭ* , p. 36; cf. *ar-Rauḍ al-miʿṭār*, s.v. "Wāsiṭ"; Ṭabarī, vol. 6, p. 384 (= vol. 2, p. 1126); Streck, *Die alte Landschaft*, vol. 2, p. 324. This tradition has parallels in regard to other places too.

(= the Temple) by Nebuchadnezzar;[11] a visit to Kaskar by King Solomon.[12]
Yāqūt reports a quarter called Ḥazzāmūna in east Wāsiṭ (i.e. Kaskar) where a descendant of ʿAlī b. Abī Ṭālib is buried,[13] and there a tomb purported to be that of ʿAzra b. Hārūn b. ʿImrān (= Ezra b. Aaron b. ʿAmram) to which both Muslims and Jews made pilgrimages.[14]
Arabic literature contains various details on the residents and economy of Kaskar, such as the people being among the cleverest in the Persian Empire,[15] their wealth as reflected in the amount of tax levied on them,[16] their celebrated fine poultry,[17] the superior rice grown there, and the custom in the nearby rural districts of eating rice bread.[18] Muqaddasī notes that the *baṭāʾiḥ*, the swampy region of southern Iraq, produces flour.[19] Cf. one of the etymologies proffered for Kaskar, namely that in the language of the Harāt people it means "land of barley."[20]

D. *Sages and Kaškar*

No testimony is available on sages residing in Kaškar, but a number of sages refer to the place. Rav Joseph (b. Ḥiyya) of the third generation of Babylonian amoras cites a *baraita* in Source 1 that identifies Kaškar with Akkad mentioned in Genesis 10:10, an identification which of course has no historical or geographical basis. In Source 2, Rav Naḥman b. Rav Ḥisda, of the fourth generation of Babylonian amoras, refers a question to Rabbah (or Rava, see note 6 above) about the validity of a letter of divorcement dated according to the year in office of the governor of Kaškar (cf. *isṭandra* də-Mešan, and see the entries on "Mesene" and "Apamea"). Source 3 contains questions that the Kaškar people themselves addressed to Levi (b. Sisi) of the first generation of amoras who left Eretz Israel for Babylonia and settled in Nəhardəʿa. As

---

11 *Taʾrīḫ Wāsiṭ*, p. 35; *bait al-maqdis* in Arabic also means "Jerusalem." This tradition too has parallels applying to other places.

12 Dīnawarī, *Aḫbār ṭiwāl*, vol. 1, p. 23. Cf. the tradition about a place in the Kaskar area called Zandaward (q.v. in Yāqūt), holding that it was built by King Solomon, etc. (Ṭabarī, vol. 7, p. 651 [= vol. 3, p. 321]; Yāqūt, *ibid.*).

13 This was Muḥammad b. Ibrāhīm b. al-Ḥasan b. al-Ḥasan b. ʿAlī b. Abī Ṭālib (who was executed on the orders of the Abbasid caliph al-Manṣūr; Ṭabarī, vol. 7, p. 546 [= vol. 3, p. 182]; Ibn Ḥazm, *Ansāb*, p. 43).

14 Yāqūt, s.v. "Ḥazzāmūna," and see, Streck, *ibid.*, p. 327.

15 Ibn al-Faqīh, p. 210.

16 Idem, p. 262–263; Yāqūt, s.v. "Kaskar"; cf. Streck, *ibid.*, p. 332.

17 *Ṯimār al-qulūb*, p. 536; Ibn Ṭaifūr, *Baġdad*, p. 122; Ǧāḥiẓ, *Ḥayawān*, vcl. 3, p. 295

18 Yāqūt, s.v. "Baṭīḥa"; Qazwīnī, *Bilād*, p. 446; Ibn Saʿīd, *Geography*, p. 158; and see the section on Economy in the entry on "Be Ḥozai."

19 Muqaddasī, p. 119.

20 Yāqūt; Bakrī, s.v. "Kaskar"; Streck, *ibid.*, p. 321.

Levi had died before the messenger from Kaškar arrived, Samuel, then head of the Nəhardəʿa yeshiva, assigned Rav Menashya to reply to the Kaškar people (see below).

E. *The Inhabitants*

The talmudic passage in Source 3 deals with replies the Kaškar people were sent to the halakhic problems they had posed. The question arises as to why the replies all embodied prohibitions, while it is possible to find some allowances in regard to the subjects under discussion. The answer given in the source to that question is that the Kaškar people were not learned in the Law, so that there was a danger that they would not know how to remain within the confines of partial allowances. Such an answer cannot be construed as implying limited intelligence or ignorance of the Law on the part of the Kaškar people, first of all because they themselves brought up such particular halakhic problems, and secondly because the talmudic text is in fact aimed at justifying the prohibitions sent to the Kaškar people and harmonizing them with other cases relating to the same subjects where allowances were made.

Adams, *Land Behind Baghdad* (1965), pp. 86, 91, 97
ʿAwwad, ed., *Taʾrīḫ Wāsiṭ* (1967), Intro. pp. 21–28
al-Dīn, *Sumer* 13 (1957): 119–147
Ellis, *Mesopotamian Archaeological Sites* (1972), p. 90
Eshel, *Yishuvei ha-Yehudim* (1979), pp. 81–82, 138
Feuchtwang, *MGWJ* 42 (1898): 152–153
Funk, *Monumenta* (1913), pp. 20, 294
Graetz, *Das Königreich Mesene* (1879), p. 25, n. 1
al-Haik, *Key Lists* (1968), No. 113
Herzfeld, *Samarra* (1948), pp. 16–17
Hirschenson, *Sheva Ḥokhmot* (1883), p. 84
Jastrow, *Dictionary* (1950³), p. 676
Kohut, *Arukh ha-Shalem* (1878–1892), vol. 2, p. 206; *Tosefot* (1937), p. 109
Krauss, *MGWJ* 39 (1895): 58
Krauss, *Paras we-Romi* (1948), p. 147
Le Strange, *The Lands* (1905), pp. 39ff., 80
Levy, *Wörterbuch* (1924²), vol. 1, p. 273
Maricq, *Syria* 35 (1958): 349 = *Classica et Orientalia* (1965), p. 91
Neubauer, *Géographie* (1868), pp. 346, 383–384
Neusner, *History* (1965–1970), vol. 1, pp. 145–146; vol. 5, p. 7
Obermeyer, *Landschaft* (1929), pp. 91–93, 196–197, 199, 310–311; index "Wāsiṭ"
Safar, *Wāsiṭ* (1945)
Schaeder, *Der Islam* 14 (1924): 17–18
Streck, *Die alte Landschaft* (1900–1901), vol. 1, pp. 15–18; vol. 2, p. 321ff.
Streck, *EI*¹, s.v. "Wāsiṭ"
Streck-Lassner, *EI*² s.v. "Kaskar"
Zuri, *Shilton* (1938), p. 225

Kəfar Panya כפר פניא

See the entry on "Nəharpanya."

Kəraḵ כרך

See the entry on "Nihawand."

Kuta כותא

A. *Source*

Bava Batra 91a

ואמר רב חנן בר רבא אמר רב עשר שנים נחבש אברהם אבינו, שלש בכותא[1] ושבע בקרדו, ורב דימי מנהרדעא מתני איפכא. אמר רב חסדא עיברא זעירא דכותא[2] זהו אור כשדים.

And Rav Ḥanan b. Rava said Rav said, Our forefather Abraham was imprisoned for ten years, three in Kuta[1] and seven in Qardu, and Rav Dimi of Nəhardəʿa taught the opposite. Said Rav Ḥisda, ʿIvra Zəʿira (= small crossing) də-Kuta,[2] that is Ur of the Chaldeans.

B. *Location*

Kūṯā Rabbā, presentday Tall Ibrāhīm, on the Ḥabl Ibrāhīm canal, thirty kilometers northeast of Babylon (D3 on the Tal. Bab. map).

C. *Identification*

The tradition cited in the source above relates that the patriarch Abraham was imprisoned for three (or seven) years in Kuta. Arab sources too connect Kūṯā with Abraham (cf. section B above).[3] Arabic sources also mention Ūr and Ūr Kašd (= Ur of the Chaldeans). It was to a village called Ūr situated between Kūfa and Baṣra that Abraham's father dispatched his wife when fleeing from Nimrod.[4] In another account Ūr Kašd which Abraham left to go

---

[1] The Munich MS has שלש בבית האיסורין ושבע באור כשדים (= three in prison and seven in Ur of the Chaldeans). The Hamburg MS has בכותי and see *Diq. Sof.* On the various versions of "Qardu" see the relevant entry. There is a parallel to this statement in Pirqe de-Rabbi Eliezer: נסיון השני נתנוהו בבית האסורים עשר שנים ג׳ בכותה וז׳ בקרדי, ויש אומרים ג׳ בקרדי וז׳ בכותה. (= The second trial they put him in prison for ten years, three in Kuta and seven in Qardu, and some say, three in Qardu and seven in Kuta; Ch. XXVI). Cf. also *Yalquṭ Shimʿoni* for Genesis, § 68, Mossad Harav Kook ed., pp. 257–258 and the note to l. 67 there: הנס השני, נחבש בבית האסורין עשר שנים, שלש בכותי ושבע בכרדו, ויש אומרים שבע בכותי ושלש בכרדו. (= The second miracle, he was imprisoned for ten years, three in Kuti and seven in Kardu, and some say, seven in Kuti and three in Kardu); see also p. 303, and the note to l. 79 there.

[2] The Munich MS has דכותי; the Hamburg MS has עיבדא זעירא דכותי.

[3] See Le Strange, "Ibn Serapion," p. 75; cf. also Nöldeke, *Perser und Araber*, p. 17, n. 4. On Kūṯā see Yāqūt, Bakrī, *ar-Rauḍ al-miʿṭār*, s.v. "Kūṯā"; *ar-Rauḍ al-miʿṭār*, s.v. "Bābil"; Qazwīnī, *Bilād*, p. 449; *Ḥudūd al-ʿālam*, p. 139; *BGA*, passim; ʿAwwād, *Sumer* 5 (1949): 246–247.

[4] Ṭabarī, vol. 1, p. 236 (= vol. 1, p. 257). The location noted fits the site of Ur of the Chaldeans according to the usual identification with Tall al-Muqayyar.

to Eretz Israel is in the neighborhood of Kūṯā.[5] One of the traditions on Abraham's birth sets it in Kūṯā.[6]

Two towns and districts bore the name Kūṯā. One was called Kūṯā Rabbā and the other Kūṯā aṭ-Ṭarīq (= of the road), the former being the one associated with Abraham.[7] Kūṯā Rabbā was on the route the Muslim conquerers followed from Babylon to Be Ardəšir. The testimony on the conquest of Iraq includes an interesting tradition regarding a visit of a Muslim commander, Sa'd b. Abī Waqqāṣ, to the house where Abraham was imprisoned in Kūṯā.[8]

D. *History*

Kuta already existed in the Sumerian period, in the third millennium B.C., and was a cult-center of Nergal, the god of the netherworld. The Bible mentions Kuta[9] as one of the cities from which the king of Assyria brought settlers to Samaria to replace the Israelites that were deported, and states that those settlers brought their ceremonials with them and continued to worship Nergal.

In 275/274 B.C. land was taken over from Babylon, Kuta and Borsippa, apparently due to the exigencies of the first Syrian war. In 238/237 B.C. those lands were restored to the cities.[10]

Kuta is one of the sites dealt with in Gibson's book,[11] which includes sections by Adams. The two scholars do not agree in their descriptions of Kuta[12] and give different accounts of the history of the region. Gibson believes that the population of the region was stable or even increased in the Parthian period (there were then at least four important cities in the region),[13] and that the

---

[5] Mas'ūdī, *Tanbīh*, p. 79 (literally, "from the countries of Kūṯā").

[6] Ta'labī, *Qiṣaṣ al-anbiyā'*, p. 63. According to another version (see *ibid.*) he was born in Warkā' (see the entry on "Orchoi") and then his father moved him to Kūṯā where Nimrod was. Cf. e.g. Ibn Sa'd, vol. 1, p. 46.

[7] See e.g. Ibn Ḥauqal, p. 245; Iṣṭaḫrī, p. 86; Idrīsī, vol. 6, p. 671; Muqaddasī, pp. 26, 121–122, 130. See also Le Strange, "Ibn Serapion," p. 75.

[8] Ṭabarī, vol. 3, p. 622 (= vol. 1, p. 2424); *ar-Rauḍ al-mi'ṭār*, s.v. "Kūṯā" (*ǧalasa fīhi*, in Ṭabarī, and cf. also Ibn al-Aṯīr, *Kāmil*, vol. 2, p. 507, should read *ḥubisa fīhi*, as in *ar-Rauḍ al-mi'ṭār*; Ibn Kaṯīr, Bidāya, vol. 7, p. 61. According to Ibn Sa'd, *loc.cit.*, he was imprisoned for seven years). In connection with this tradition, *ar-Rauḍ al-mi'ṭār* notes that there are mounds of hardened ash in Kūṯā, said to be the remains of the fire Nimrod b. Canaan lit to throw Abraham into.

[9] "The king of Assyria brought from Babylon, Kuta . . . and he settled them in the towns of Samaria in place of the Israelites" (II Kings 17:24); ". . . and the men of Kut made Nergal . . ." (*ibid.* 17:30).

[10] See the entry on "Babylon," especially Inscriptions 2 and 3 there. See also the section on History in the entry on "Seleucia" under the "Maḥoza Area."

[11] Gibson, *The City and Area of Kish.*

[12] Cf. Adams (in Gibson, *op.cit.*), p. 196, No. 140, with Gibson (*ibid.*), p. 127, No. 48.

[13] *Ibid.*, pp. 51–52.

transition from Parthian to Sassanian rule was quite smooth. This conclusion is based on his surface survey of the settlements concentrated around the Kūṯā canal. In Gibson's view, after the dense settlement that reached a peak in the Sassanian period, a gap in habitation is discernible in the early Muslim period. The courses of the canals changed completely and 68% of the settlements were abandoned, their population once again moving to the banks of the Babylon (Ḥilla) canal. Gibson suggests that the cause may have been the massive flooding of both the Tigris and the Euphrates late in the Sassanian period during the reign of Khusro II (590/1–628). Adams believes that the Parthian period saw the densest inhabitation of the region. It subsequently became sparser due at least in part to repeated Roman incursions that caused the population to flee and seek more secure locations.[14] For the Sassanian period Adams observes a considerable decline in the overall number of inhabited sites, while the number of those of urban proportions increased.

E. *ʿIvra Zəʿira də-Kuta*

Southwest of Tall Ibrāhīm flows a canal, known today as the Kūṯā river, mentioned also by Josephus.[15] Rav Ḥisda's "ʿIvra Zəʿira də-Kuta" apparently refers to a bridge across that river, or perhaps to a settlement by that name near the crossing.[16] His designation of the bridge as "small crossing" is evidently intended to distinguish between this and another more central bridge spanning the Kūṯā river.[17] The identification of ʿIvra Zəʿira də-Kuta with Ur of the Chaldeans proposed by Rav Ḥisda in the source above has no basis in fact.[18] Remains of Ur were excavated at Tall al-Muqayyar about half way between Baghdad and the Persian Gulf, that is, some 250 kilometers southeast of the ruins of Babylon.

Berliner, *Beiträge* (1883), p. 57
Eshel, *Yishuvei ha-Yehudim* (1979), pp. 14, 130, 173, 203–204
Funk, *Monumenta* (1913), pp. 21, 287, 293, 302, 305
Gibson, *The City and Area of Kish* (1972)

---

[14] *Ibid.*, p. 187.

[15] Josephus, *Antiquities*, IX, 279.

[16] Alternatively, *ʿIvra* may come from עבר meaning "side" or "bank" rather than from מעבר meaning "crossing" but then it would be difficult to explain זעירא (= small).

[17] The Nahr Kūṯā branches off from the Euphrates three parasangs below the place where the Nahr al-Malik branches off from it, then passes near Kūṯā Rabbā and flows into the Tigris ten parasangs below Madā'in. See Le Strange, "Ibn Serapion", p. 15–16; Suhrāb, p. 124; Ibn Saʿd, vol. 1, p. 64; Masʿūdi, *Murūǧ*, vol. 1, p. 254 (= vol. 2, p. 96); cf. Ibn Ḥauqal's maps, pp. 206, 232. See also Streck, *Die alte Landschaft*, vol. 1, p. 28; vol. 2, p. 293f.; Plessner, *EI*[1] s.v. "Kūthā." A pontoon bridge on Nahr Kūṯā is mentioned by Ibn Rusta, p. 174, and see also p. 182.

[18] There may be some connection between Rav Ḥisda's statement and the Munich MS version reporting that Abraham was imprisoned in Ur of the Chaldeans (see n. 1 above).

Hirschenson, *Sheva Ḥokhmot* (1883), p. 139
Jastrow, *Dictionary* (1950³), pp. 627, 1066
Levy, *Wörterbuch* (1924²), vol. 2, p. 311; vol. 3, p. 613
Kohut, *Arukh ha-Shalem* (1878–1892), vol. 4, pp. 211, 317 "כרדו", 360; vol. 6, pp. 161–162 "עבר"
Neubauer, *Géographie* (1868), pp. 379–380
Neusner, *History* (1965–1970), vol. 2, p. 248
Obermeyer, *Landschaft* (1929), pp. 8, 10, 132, 273, 278–283

Ləvai לבאי

A. *Source*

Moʿed Qaṭan 11a

בדיתא לבאי[1] כוורי אזיל כולי עלמא צוד אייתו כוורא, שרא להו רבא למימלח מינייהו.

Levai[ans][1] fished in the Badita [canal or river]; they all went to catch and brought fish. Rava allowed them to salt some of them [on the intermediate days of a festival].

B. *Location*

None is proposed due to insufficient data.

C. *Attempts at Identification*

Obermeyer proposes identifying Ləvai with Lauba which was located between Wāsiṭ and the swamps (*baṭāʾiḥ*) on the Badāt canal.[2] This would place it in Mesene far from the important Jewish communities in Babylonia. While that locale is not impossible, the absence of any supporting evidence makes it doubtful. Eshel argues that Ləvai is within the Maḥoza jurisdictional area because it was Rava, the head of the Maḥoza yeshiva, who ruled on the question relating to it.[3] Such grounds for identifications, quite common in Eshel's book, are unacceptable, certainly in this case, since Rava issued halakhic rulings for many places in Babylonia.[4]

---

[1] The R-i-f has Pumbədita Ləvai, which would mean that the reference is to Pumbədita and Ləvai is not a place name at all. The *Arukh* has Pum Bəditai Ləvai, which may mean that Ləvai was at the mouth (= *pum*) of the Badita. The name of the waterway is sometimes rendered as בריתה (= Bərita). The *Arukh* offers a version in which Ləvai appears in a similar description involving fishing in Qiddushin 72a: דאקפו פירא דכוורי לבאי בשבתא (see *Arukh ha-Shalem*, vol. 2, p. 17, under "בדיתא"; vol. 5, p. 6 under "2 לבא"; *Tosefot*, p. 240 under "2 לבא"; and see also *Diq. Sof.*, note ש).

[2] Obermeyer, pp. 310–312. See "Lauba" in Yāqūt. For the Badāt canal, see Le Strange, "Ibn Serapion," p. 16, 259–260; Suhrāb, p. 125; and cf. Ṭabarī, vol. 6, p. 130 (= vol. 2, p. 769) and Yāqūt, s.v. "Bihqubāḏ."

[3] Eshel, p. 138.

[4] See e.g., the entry for "Nəharpanya."

D. *Economy*

Babylonia was celebrated for an abundance of fish, and fishing provided added income for people of various professions.[5] The source above concerns Ləvai people who during the intermediate days of a festival caught more fish in the Badita canal than they could consume. Rava then allowed the surplus to be salted for use after the festival. The method yielding such large catches apparently involved digging an opening to allow the water to flow out of the canal and then removing the fish that remained in its bed.[6]

Beer, *Amora'ei Bavel* (1974), pp. 150–153
Berliner, *Beiträge* (1883), pp. 38, 67
Eshel, *Yishuvei ha-Yehudim* (1979), p. 138
Funk, *Juden* (1902–1908), vol. 2, p. 156
Funk, *Monumenta* (1913). pp. 7, 280, "בדיתא"
Hirschenson, *Sheva Ḥokhmot* (1883), pp. 65–66
Jastrow, *Dictionary* (1950³), pp. 140, 687
Kohut, *Arukh ha-Shalem* (1878–1892), vol. 1, p. 17; vol. 5, p. 6; *Tosefot* (1937), pp. 77, 240
Levy, *Wörterbuch* (1924²), vol. 1, p. 193; vol. 2, p. 464
Newman, *Agricultural Life* (1932), p. 137
Obermeyer, *Landschaft* (1929), pp. 310–312

The Maḥoza Area

I. Maḥoza מחוזא

A. *Sources* (*a selection*)

1. Yoma 11a

א"ל אביי לרב ספרא הני אבולי דמחוזא מ"ט לא עבדו להו רבנן מזוזה, אמר ליה הנהו חזוק לאקרא דכובי[1] הוא דעבידי. א"ל ואקרא דכובי גופה תבעי מזוזה, דהא אית בה דירה לשומר בית האסורין, דהא תניא בית הכנסת שיש בו בית דירה לחזן הכנסת חיבת במזוזה, אלא אמר אביי[2] משום סכנה.

Abbaye said to Rav Safra, Those gates of Maḥoza, why did not the sages make a *mezuzah* for them? He said to him, They are supports for Aqra də-Kube.[1] He said to him, But Aqra də-Kube itself requires a *mezuzah*, for it contains a dwelling for the prison guard. For it has been taught, a synagogue that contains a dwelling for the attendant of the congregation must have a *mezuzah*. Rather, said Abbaye,[2] it is for fear of danger.

---

[5] See Beer, *Amora'ei Bavel*, pp. 150–153.

[6] For the various interpretations of the source in question, see Beer, *ibid.* p. 152, n. 136.

[1] The Munich B MS has דכוכי, further on as well (and see below), the Oxford MS has דבובי, and the London MS has ליוקרא דכובי.

[2] The Munich B, Oxford and London MSS have "Rava" as does the parallel in *Yalquṭ Shim'oni* for Deuteronomy 6, § 844.

2. ʿEruvin 6b

ואמר עולא הני אבולי דמחוזא אילמלא דלתותיהן ננעלות חייבין עליהן משום רשות הרבים.

And ʿUlla said, Those gates of Maḥoza, if their doors were not locked, they would be subjected, because of the public domain.

3. Moʿed Qaṭan 22a

אמר להו רבא לבני מחוזא אתון דלא אזליתו בתר ערסא מכי מהדריתו אפייכו מבבא דאבולא אתחילו מנו.

Rava said to the people of Maḥoza, You who do not follow the litter, when you return from the [city] gate, begin counting [the days of mourning].

4. Niddah 67b

אתקין רב אידי[3] בנרש למטבל ביומא דתמניא משום אריותא. רב אחא בר יעקב בפפוניא[4] משום גנבי. רב יהודה בפומבדיתא משום צנה. רבא במחוזא משום אבולאי.

Rav Idi[3] ordained in Nareš to immerse [for purification] on the eighth day because of the lions; Rav Aḥa b. Jacob in Papuniya,[4] because of the thieves; Rav Judah in Pumbədita, because of the cold; Rava in Maḥoza, because of the gate guards.

5. Bava Batra 73a–b

אמר רבה[5] לדידי חזי לי הורמין בר לילית כי קא רהיט אקופיא דשורא דמחוזא ורהיט פרשא כי רכיב חיותא מתתאיה ולא יכיל ליה. זמנא חדא הוה מסרגאן ליה תרתי כודנייתי וקיימן אתרי גישרי דרוגנג[6] ושואר מהאי להאי ומהאי להאי ונקיט תרי מזגי דחמרא בידיה ומוריק מהאי להאי ומהאי להאי ולא נטפא ניטופתא לארעא, ואותו היום "יעלו שמים ירדו תהומות" הוה, עד דשמעו בי מלכותא וקטלוהו.

Rabbah[5] said, I saw Hormin bar Lilith running on the parapet of the Maḥoza wall, and a rider on an animal galloping below could not [overtake] him. Once they saddled two mules for him, and they stood on two bridges of the Rognag,[6] and he jumped back and forth from one to the other, and held two glasses of wine in his hands, and emptied one into the other and the latter into the former, and not a drop fell to the ground. And that day was "They mount up to the heaven, they go down again to the depth" (Ps. 107:26) till the government heard and put him to death.

6. ʿEruvin 26a; 60a

דהא רבה בר אבוה מערב לה לכולא מחוזא ערסייתא משום פירא דבי תורי.

---

[3] The Munich and Vatican 111 MSS have "Rav Idi b. Avin."

[4] The Vatican 111 MS does not have בפפוניא.

[5] The Munich, Hamburg and Oxford MSS and *Aggadot ha-Talmud* have "Rava."

[6] The Munich MS has דרונג, the Hamburg MS has דאגנג, the Vatican 115 MS, *Ein Yaʿaqov* and *Aggadot ha-Talmud* have דדונג; see also *Diq. Sof.*

For Rabbah b. Avuha made an ʿ*eruv* for all of Maḥoza, neighborhoods by neighborhoods, because of the cattle ditches.

7. Shabbat 95a

אמימר שרא זילחא במחוזא, אמר טעמא מאי אמור רבנן דילמא אתי לאשויי גומות, הכא ליכא גומות.

Ameimar allowed sprinking water in Maḥoza. He said, What is the reason the sages said [it is forbidden]? In case someone comes to level the ruts. Here there are no ruts.

8. ʿEruvin 104a–b

אמימר שרא למימלא בגילגלא במחוזא, אמר מאי טעמא גזרו רבנן, שמא ימלא לגינתו ולחורבתו, הכא לא גינה איכא ולא חורבה איכא, כיון דקא חזא דקא תרו בה כיתנא אסר להו.

Ameimar allowed filling with a wheel in Maḥoza. He said, Why did the sages forbid it? In case he fills for his garden or ruin. Here there is no garden and no ruin. Since he saw they soaked flax in it, he forbade them.

9. Bava Metziʿa 83a

ההוא גברא דהוה קא מעבר חביתא דחמרא[7] בריסתקא דמחוזא[8] ותברה בזיזא דמחוזא, אתא לקמיה דרבא, א"ל ריסתקא דמחוזא שכיחי בה אינשי זיל אייתי ראיה ואיפטר.

The man who moved a barrel of wine[7] in the Maḥoza market[8] and broke it on a projection of Maḥoza, came before Rava. He said to him, The Maḥoza market, people are numerous there, bring proof and you will be free [from liability].

10. Bava Batra 36a

אמר רב יוסף אכלה שחת לא הוי חזקה. אמר רבא[9] ואי בצואר[10] מחוזא קיימא הוי חזקה.

Rav Joseph said, If he eats (i.e. reaps) low growth it does not grant *ḥazaqah*. Said Rava,[9] And if it stands in the "neck[10] of Maḥoza" it is *ḥazaqah*.

11. Giṭṭin 6a; Qiddushin 72a (as per manuscripts and versions)

עד היכן היא בבל אמר רב פפא כמחלוקת ליוחסין כך מחלוקת לגיטין ורב יוסף אמר מחלוקת ליוחסין אבל לגיטין דברי הכל עד ארבא תניינא דגישרא דמחוזא.[11]

---

[7] The Munich, Vatican 117 and Florence MSS have "to his friend" added.

[8] The word *ristaq* means "market," and see *Arukh ha-Shalem*, vol. 7, p. 287, s.v. "רסתק" and *Tosefot*, p. 386. Other places too (Berakhot 54a, ʿEruvin 44b, Bava Batra 12b) have *ristaqa də-Maḥoza*.

[9] The Florence MS has "Rabbah."

[10] The Florence MS has **אצוור**, *Halakhot Gedolot* has **בצוור**, and see below.

[11] The word **דמחוזא** does not appear in the printing; it appears in the Vatican 127 MS of Giṭṭin, in *Otzar ha-Geonim* for Giṭṭin, *ha-Teshuvot*, p. 1, and also in Rav Sherira Gaon's version of Qiddushin cited in *Teshuvot ha-Geonim Shaʿarei Tzedeq*, 15b, and see below.

How far does Babylonia extend, Rav Papa said, Like the disagreement regarding lineage, so the disagreement for bills of divorcement. And Rav Joseph said, A disagreement exists regarding lineage, but for bills of divorcement all say to the second boat of the Maḥoza bridge.[11]

12. Qiddushin 73a

דרש רבי זירא[12] במחוזא גר מותר בממזרת, רגמוהו כולי עלמא באתרוגייהו. אמר רבא מי איכא דדריש מילתא כי האי בדוכתא דשכיחי גיורי. דרש רבא במחוזא[13] גר מותר בכהנת, טענוהו בשיראי, הדר דרש להו גר מותר בממזרת, אמרו ליה אפסידתא לקמייתא . . .

Rabbi Zera[12] preached in Maḥoza, A convert is allowed [to marry] a *mamzeret*, and all pelted him with their citrons. Rava said, Is there anyone who preaches thus in a place abounding with converts. Rava preached in Maḥoza,[13] A convert is permitted a priest's daughter. They loaded him with silks; he again preached to them, A convert is allowed a *mamzeret*. They said to him, You have lost the first [present] . . .

13. Qiddushin 70b

מכריז רבא במחוזא בלאי דנאי טלאי מלאי זגאי[14] כולם לפסול.

Rava announces in Maḥoza, the Belans, Denans, Ṭelans, Melans and Zegans[14] are all unfit.

14. Giṭṭin 6a

ורבא מצריך באותה שכונה . . . שאני בני מחוזא דניידי.

And Rava requires in the same neighborhood [that the messenger testify before whom the bill of divorcement was written and signed] . . . because the people of Maḥoza are different, for they move about.

15. Berakhot 59b

ואמר רבא האי דחריפי בני מחוזא משום דשתו מיא דדגלת.

And Rava said, The Maḥozans are sharp because they drink the water of the Tigris.

16. ʿAvodah Zarah 58a

אמר רבא כי אתאי לפומבדיתא אקפן נחמני שמעתתא ומתניתא דאסיר, שמעתתא, דההוא עובדא דהוה בנהרדעא ואסר שמואל, בטבריא ואסר רבי יוחנן, ואמרי ליה לפי שאינן בני תורה, ואמר לי טבריא ונהרדעא אינן בני תורה, דמחוזא[15] בני תורה . . .

Rava said, When I came to Pumbədita Naḥmani surrounded me with precedents and teachings that it (wine a heathen dabbled in) is forbidden. There

---

[12] The Munich MS has "Rava"; the Vatican 111 MS has "Rav Judah."

[13] The Venice printing does not have במחוזא.

[14] The manuscripts and versions contain many variations of these names, and see below.

[15] The Munich MS has ומחוזא, the Spanish MS of ʿAvodah Zarah edited by Abramson has מחוזא.

was that case in Nəhardəʿa, and Samuel forbade, in Tiberias and Rabbi Yoḥanan forbade, and I said to him, [They were strict] because they are not familiar with the Torah. He said to me, Tiberias and Nəhardəʿa are not familiar with the Torah, of Maḥoza[15] they are . . .

17. Taʿanit 26a

... והא רב פפא איקלע לבי כנישתא דאבי גובר[16] וגזר תענית וירדו להם גשמים עד חצות ואמר הלל ואחר כך אכלו ושתו, שאני בני מחוזא דשכיחי בהו שכרות.

. . . For Rav Papa happened to be in the synagogue of Be Govar,[16] and ordained a fast, and rains fell before noon, and he said *Hallel* and afterwards they ate and drank. The Maḥoza people are different, for drunkenness is common among them.

18. Ketubot 65a

דביתהו דרב יוסף בריה דרבא אתאי לקמיה דרב נחמיה בריה דרב יוסף[17] אמרה ליה פסוק לי מזוני, פסק לה. פסוק לי חמרא, פסק לה, אמר לה ידענא בהו בבני מחוזא דשתו חמרא.

The wife of Rav Joseph b. Rava came before Rav Nehemiah b. Rav Joseph[17] and said to him, Grant me my food (allowance), and he did. Grant me wine, and he did. He said to her, I know the Maḥozans, that they drink wine.

19. Shabbat 109a

ואמר מר עוקבא מי שנגפה ידו או רגלו צומתה ביין ואינו חושש ... אמר רבא והני בני מחוזא כיון דמפנקי אפילו חמרא נמי מסי להו.

And Mar ʿUqba said, Whoever knocks his hand or foot soaks it [on the Sabbath] in wine without fear . . . Rava said, Those Maḥozans, because they are delicate, even wine heals them.

20. Rosh ha-Shanah 17a

ואמר רבא ואינהו משפירי שפירי[18] בני מחוזא ומקריין בני גיהנם.

And Rava said, The Maḥozans are the handsomest of the handsome[18] and called "sons of Gehinnom."

21. Bava Qamma 119a

רבינא איקלע לבי מחוזא[19] אתו נשי דבי מחוזא[20] רמו קמיה כבלי ושירי קביל מינייהו, א"ל רבה תוספאה[21] לרבינא והתניא גבאי צדקה מקבלין מהן דבר מועט אבל לא דבר מרובה, א"ל הני לבני מחוזא דבר מועט נינהו.

---

16 The Munich B MS has דאבי גבר; Rashi in the Pesaro printing has דאבר גובר.

17 The Leningrad MS has לקמיה דרב יוסף לפום בדיתא.

18 All the manuscripts have שפירי משפירי, which seems correct; see also *Diq. Sof.*

19 The Munich, Hamburg and Florence MSS have למחוזא.

20 The Munich, Hamburg and Florence MSS have נשי בני מחוזא.

21 The Munich, Florence and Vatican 115 MSS have "Rava Tosəfa'a." See also the section on Sages and Ctesiphon in the entry on "Ctesiphon" under the "Maḥoza Area."

Ravina happened to come to Be Maḥoza.[19] The wives of Be Maḥoza[20] came and threw chains and bracelets before him, and he accepted. Rabbah Tosəfa'a[21] said to Ravina, But it is taught that charity collectors accept small things but not big ones. He said to him, For the Maḥozans, these are small things.

22. Shabbat 12a

אמר רבא לא אמרן אלא דבני מחוזא אבל דבני חקליתא מידע ידעי, ודבני מחוזא נמי לא אמרן אלא דזקנות אבל דילדות מידע ידיעי.

Rava said, We spoke only [of the clothing] of the Maḥozans, but those of the villagers are distinctive, and of the Maḥozans' too we spoke only [of the clothing] of the old women, but those of the girls are distinctive.

23. Shabbat 112a

איתמר התיר רצועות מנעל וסנדל תני חדא חייב חטאת, ותניא אידך פטור אבל אסור, ותניא אידך מותר לכתחילה . . . מותר לכתחלה בדבני מחוזא.

It is said, If someone untied laces from a shoe and sandal, one [*baraita*] taught, He is liable to a sin offering. Another taught, He is exempt, but it is forbidden. And another taught, It is permitted in the first place . . . It is permitted in the first place to the Maḥozans.

24. Sukkah 20b

אמר עולא הני בודיתא[22] דבני מחוזא אלמלא קיר שלהן מסככין בהו.

ʿUlla said, Those mats[22] of the Maḥozans, if not for the border in them, they could be used as a *sukkah* ceiling.

25. Bava Metziʿa 68a

אמר רבא לית הלכתא לא כטרשי פפונאי ולא כשטרי מחוזנאי ולא כחכירי נרשאי. כטרשי פפונאי, כטרשי דרב פפא.

Rava said, The halakhah is not like the credit interests of the Papuniyans, or the bonds of the Maḥozans, or the leases of the Narešans. The credit interests of the Papuniyans are like the credit interests of Rav Papa.

26. Bava Qamma 115a

נרשאה גנב ספרא, זבניה לפפונאה[23] בתמנן זוזי, אזל פפונאה זבניה לבר מחוזאה במאה ועשרין זוזי, לסוף הוכר הגנב, אמר אביי ליזיל מרי דספרא ויהב ליה לבר מחוזא תמנן זוזי ושקיל ספריה ואזיל בר מחוזנאה ושקיל ארבעין מפפונאה . . . אלא אמר רבא ליזיל מריה דספרא ויהיב ליה לבר מחוזאה מאה ועשרין זוזי ושקיל ספריה וליזיל מרי דספרא ולישקול ארבעין מפפונאה ותמנן מנרשאה.

A Narešan stole a book, sold it to a Papuniyan[23] for eighty *zuz*. The Papuniyan went and sold it to a Maḥozan for a hundred and twenty *zuz*. In the end

---

[22] The Munich MS has ביריתא, and see *Diq. Sof.*

[23] For variants, see the entry on "Papuniya," n. 7.

the thief was recognized. Abbaye said, The owner of the book should go and give the Maḥozan eighty *zuz* and take his book, the Maḥozan should go and take forty from the Papuniyan ... Rava said, The owner of the book should go and pay the Maḥozan a hundred and twenty *zuz* and take his book, and the owner of the book should [then] go and recover forty *zuz* from the Papuniyan, and eighty *zuz* from the Narešan.

27. Ḥullin 94b

כי הא דמר זוטרא בריה דרב נחמן הוה קאזיל מסיכרא לבי מחוזא,[24] ורבא ורב ספרא הוו קא אתו לסיכרא,[25] פגעו אהדדי, הוא סבר לאפיה הוא דקאתו, אמר להו למה להו לרבנן דטרוח ואתו כולי האי ...

... Mar Zuṭra son of Rav Naḥman was going from Sik̲ra to Be Maḥoza[24] and Rava and Rav Safra were going to Sik̲ra,[25] and they met. He thought they were coming to meet him and said, Why did the sages trouble to come all this [way] ...

28. ʿEruvin 47b

הנהו דכרי דאתו למברכתא שרא להו רבא לבני מחוזא למיזבן מינייהו ... הדר אמר רבא ליזדבנו לבני מברכתא,[26] דכולה מברכתא לדידהו כד׳ אמות דמיא.

Some rams that arrived in Mavrak̲ta [on the Sabbath] Rava allowed the Maḥozans to buy them ... Rava repeated, Let them be sold to the Mavrak̲ta[26] people, as for them all Mavrak̲ta is considered only four cubits.

29. Ketubot 54a

ההיא בת מחוזא דהות נסיבא לנהרדעא,[27] אתו לקמיה דרב נחמן שמעה לקלה דבת מחוזא היא, אמר להו בבל וכל פרוודהא נהוג כרב, אמרו ליה והא לנהרדעא נסיבא, אמר להו אי הכי נהרדעא וכל פרוודהא נהוג כשמואל. ועד היכא נהרדעא, עד היכא דסגי קבא דנהרדעא.

That woman of Maḥoza who was married to [a man of] Nəhardəʿa,[27] they came before Rav Naḥman, who heard from her voice that she was a Maḥozan and said to them, Babylon and all its surroundings acted according to Rav. They said to him, But she is married to Nəhardəʿa. He said to them, If so, Nəhardəʿa and all its surroundings acted according to Samuel. And how far is Nəhardəʿa? As far as the *qav* of Nəhardəʿa extends.

---

[24] The Munich MS has מסיכרא למחוזא, and see *Diq. Sof.*

[25] The Munich MS has ממחוזא לסיכרא, and see *Diq. Sof.*

[26] The Munich MS has "אמר רבא לבני מחוזא לזבנינהו לבני מברכתא"; the Salonika printing has "אמר רבא בני מחוזא לא ליזבנו מינייהו אבל לזבונינהו בני מברכתא" (see the entry on "Mavrak̲ta").

[27] The Vatican 113 and Vatican 487 MSS have לבר נהרדעא; the Vatican 130 and Leningrad MSS have בנהרדעא; a Geniza fragment (Oxford 2835 MS) has לנהרדעאה, further on as well, see also the ICIT edition.

30. Ammianus XXIV 4,2

Cumque Maiozamalcha venisset, urbem magnam et validis circumdatam moenibus, tentoriis fixis, providit sollicite ne castra repentino equitatus Persici turbarentur adcursu, cuius fortitudo in locis patentibus, inmane quantum gentibus est formidata.

And when he (Julian) had come to Maiozamalcha, a great city surrounded by strong walls, he pitched his tents and took anxious precautions that the camp might not be disturbed by a sudden onset of the Persian cavalry, whose valour in the open field was enormously feared by all peoples. (trans.: J. C. Rolfe, LCL)

B. *Location*

The site of one of the Babylonian yeshivas, in the city whose Persian name is Veh Ardašir (see "Be Ardəšir-Koke" below; and on the Maḥoza Area plan).

C. *History*

Maḥoza was one of the chief yeshiva towns of talmudic Babylonia. The name comes from the Accadian word *maḫāzu* meaning "city." The Hebrew word *maḥoz* also means "port,"[28] and fits Babylonian Maḥoza which had a port. In Kutscher's opinion, the word *maḥoz* came to denote a port through its similarity to the biblical *maʿoz* which means both "fort" and "port."[29] Kutscher thus explains Ammianus' reference (Source 30) to Maḥoza as Maiozamalcha,[30] as well as the connection between *maioza* and Maḥoza.[31]

The Maḥoza yeshiva was in existence for centuries. Its initial flowering was connected with the destruction of Nəhardəʿa (q.v.) in 261, and the departure of some of the latter's sages to Maḥoza.[32] It was especially important during the period when its head was Rava (d. 352) in particular when Abbaye's disciples moved there from Pumbədita after their master's death in 338.[33] The selection of sources cited above reflects Rava's preeminance in Maḥoza, and it is clear that many sources in which Rava figures in fact deal with Maḥoza, even if the town is not actually mentioned.

---

[28] Thus in the Bible and its translations; see Kutscher, *Milim we-Toledotehen*, pp. 41–45.

[29] E.g., Isaiah 23:4 and 14; and see Kutscher, *ibid.*

[30] See "Be Ardəšir-Koke" below and n. 28 there; see also the section on The Center in Nəhardəʿa in the entry on "Nəhardəʿa."

[31] For the Syriac form Maḥozē and the Arabic name al-Madāʾin, see below.

[32] See *Iggeret Rav Sherira Gaon*, Lewin ed., p. 82.

[33] See *ibid.*, p. 83f.

D. *Physical Features*

Sources 1 and 2 refer to the gates of Maḥoza, and Source 1 indicates that Aqra də-Koḵe was a fort at the entrance to the town.[34] The Aqra də-Koḵe prison mentioned in Source 1 is referred to in a Syriac source (see "Be Ardəšir-Koḵe"). The Maḥoza wall is mentioned in Sources 5 and 30, and Source 4 testifies that the Maḥoza gatekeepers frightened the women who wished to immerse for purification in the evening.

A number of *halakhot* dealing with Sabbath rules provide information on the physical features of Maḥoza: Source 6 mentions ditches dug between the various neighborhoods of Maḥoza for fodder which the oxen of Maḥoza used to eat.[35] Source 7 indicates that the Maḥoza homes had stone floors which could be watered on the Sabbath since there was no danger of any temptation to smooth out ruts developing. Source 8 deals with Ameimar's permission to draw water in Maḥoza on the Sabbath by means of a wheel, since in an urban place like Maḥoza there were no gardens and consequently no danger that anyone would use the water for irrigation.

Source 9 mentions the Maḥoza market (see note 8 above) and Source 10 the valley of Maḥoza.[36] That was where the Maḥozans who owned numerous animals had their fields, where they used to reap low growth to feed their livestock with.

Another source that can reasonably be construed to refer to Maḥoza reports a case in which it rained so hard that the water "of the Sepphoris gutters flowed into the Tigris" (Taʿanit 24b). Of course there is no connection between Sepphoris and the Tigris, and the reference is undoubtedly to Maḥoza as the Pesaro printing and *Ein Yaʿaqov* have it.

Source 11 mentions the Maḥoza bridge (according to the manuscripts and versions, see note 11 above) in connection with the question of the borders of Babylonia in respect to genealogy and divorce (see the Introduction).[37] Source 5 mentions the Rognag river, and the bridges over it, indicating the existence of that waterway in the vicinity of Maḥoza.

---

34 The Munich MS version, אקרא דכוכי, is preferable (see n. 1 above). The version in the printing, אקרא דכובי, apparently comes from the name "Be Kube" (q.v.).

35 The *Arukh* interpretation is that the ditches were the boundary of Maḥoza on one side, while its wall was the boundary on the other three sides, rather than that the ditches separated various neighborhoods (and see *Arukh ha-Shalem*, vol. 6, p. 407, s.v. "פרא 2").

36 Epstein (*Mevo'ot le-Sifrut ha-Amora'im*, p. 262) interprets the word *ṣawar* (צואר = צוור) to mean "neighborhood" but this makes little difference for our purposes.

37 On the preference of the form Gišra də-Maḥoza see Ginzberg, *Geonica*, vol. 2, pp. 167f., 174. For the interpretation of the concept of ארבא תניינא, see Krauss, *Qadmoniot ha-Talmud*, vol. 1A, p. 163. See the section on Identification in the entry on "Gišra də-Šabistana," and note 6 there.

E. *The Inhabitants*

The cumulative testimony on the inhabitants of Maḥoza presents a picture of city life, and of the major trade center represented by Maḥoza and its neighboring towns. Source 22 dealing with a particular halakhic problem contrasts the urban Maḥozans with villagers.[38] Source 14 defines the Maḥozans as "mobile," that is, engaged in trade and consequently often away from home.

The sources note many traits of the Maḥozans which suggest their urban nature: their fondness for drink and their frequent inebriation (Sources 17 and 18, and also see the section on History in the entry on "Ctesiphon" [in the "Maḥoza Area"]); their wealth (e.g. Source 21); their delicacy and self-indulgence (Sources 14 and 19). Some more admirable Maḥozan traits are indicated as well: their cleverness (Source 15), their knowledge of the Torah (Source 16) and their generosity (Source 21).

Source 12 notes the many converts to Judaism in Maḥoza, and this aspect of the population is no doubt attributable as well to its urban nature and the relations between Jews and Gentiles that evolved in the wake of commercial contacts and residential proximity.

F. *Connections with Other Places*

Maḥoza maintained contacts on various planes with other localities. Sources 17 and 28 mention Be Govar and Mavrak̲ta (qq.v.) which were adjacent to Maḥoza. Source 29 notes, in regard to conditions in a marriage contract, that "Babylon and all its surroundings acted according to Rav" although Maḥoza was closer to Nəhardəʿa, and the latter "and all its surroundings" acted according to Samuel's differing opinion (see the entry on "Babylon"). Yet relations between Maḥoza and Nəhardəʿa were close, at least so far as trade was concerned. Bava Batra reports a case of a Nəhardəʿan who brought dried figs to Maḥoza in a boat, and the Exilarch assigns Rava to ascertain whether the man is really a scholar and thus entitled to preferential treatment in the market.[39] Evidently the Nəhardəʿan sailed to Maḥoza with his dried figs on the Nəhar Malka that flowed into the Tigris south of Maḥoza; as it connected the two towns (see the entry on "Nəhardəʿa"), that waterway was the channel for much of the trade between them.

Just as the Maḥozans used to go out of town on business (Source 14), people from other places used to visit Maḥoza. That is most likely the reason for dis-

---

[38] There is no reason to assume that Maḥoza here means any city, especially since it is Rava who is cited.

[39] Bava Batra 22a; the version in the Florence MS says explicitly that the figs were brought to Maḥoza. See also Beer, *Rashut ha-Golah*, p. 126; idem., *Amora'ei Bavel*, pp. 221–224. At that time the Exilarch resided in Maḥoza (see Beer, *ibid.*, p. 103, n. 31).

cussions on marriage (Sources 12 and 13).[40] In Source 13 Rava at Maḥoza announces several names associated with unfitness for marriage. There is no way of knowing whether they are names of places whose residents are considered unmarriageable, or of families whose members are so deemed.

Source 3 deals with the rules on mourning in cases of Maḥozans whose deceased relative is to be buried elsewhere, since the exact time of the burial, usually marking the start of the mourning period is unknown in such cases. Rava's ruling is that their mourning should begin the moment the funeral procession passes through the Maḥoza city gates. The problem arises, of course, because the burial is to take place far from Maḥoza, perhaps in Eretz Israel, perhaps across the Euphrates (see the entries on "Tarbiqna," "Šum Ṭəmaya" and "Nəhar Anaq").

G. *The Yehudai Romai Synagogue* בי כנישתא דיהודאי רומאי

The tractate Megillah contains a passage referring to the *yehudai romai* synagogue (26b), and since Rava was asked to rule on an urgent, practical, halakhic matter that cropped up there, probably the synagogue was in or near Maḥoza. The question arises whether the adjective *romai* denotes the name of a place or the provenance of the Jews who attended the synagogue. Possibly the second alternative is preferable, for there is testimony that in Eretz Israel Jews from various parts of the Diaspora had their own synagogues.[41] Thus it would be reasonable for Jews originating in Rome to have a synagogue in so central a place as Maḥoza.

If *romai* is the name of a place, its identity is by no means certain. A place called Rūmīya (sometimes Rūmīyat al-Madā'in)[42] was located on the east bank of the Tigris south of Ctesiphon. It was built in mid-sixth century by captives from Antioch who made it an exact copy of their native city. When Be Ardəšir (q.v.) was founded by Ardashīr I, the new city was made the chief town of a large region thenceforth known as Ardašīr Bābakān,[43] one of whose

---

[40] It is reasonable to suppose that Ameimar's permission for Rav Huna b. Nathan to marry a מחוזייתא woman refers to a woman from Maḥoza, particularly since Ameimar is described as ruling for the Maḥozans (cf. Sources 7 and 8). At the same time the reason for hesitation in regard to marriage with a Maḥoza woman is not clear, and that led various scholars to assume that the reference is to another city outside the borders of the Babylonia of pure lineage (that was Rashi's interpretation and see e.g., Eshel, pp. 144–145).

[41] Cf., e.g., כנישתא דבבלאי בציפורי (= the synagogue of the Babylonians in Sepphoris) in Genesis Rabbah XXXIII, 3, Theodor-Albeck ed., p. 305 [cf. ibid., LII, 4; ibid., p. 543]: בית הכנסת של טרסיים (= the synagogue of the Tarsians) in Nazir 52a.

[42] See Streck, *Die alte Landschaft*, vol. 2, p. 266f.; Fiey, *Sumer* 23 (1967): 25f.; al-ʻAlī, *Sumer* 23 (1967): 51f.; Mustaufī, vol. 2, p. 48; Ṯaʻālibī, *Ġurar*, pp. 612–613, 636.

[43] Ṭabarī, vol. 2, p. 41 (= vol. 1, p. 819); Nöldeke, *Perser und Araber*, pp. 16 n. 4, 165 n. 4; Streck, *op.cit.*, vol. 1, pp. 16; 19; vol. 2, pp. 264, 267.

districts was Rūmaqān. In Nöldeke's opinion Rūmaqān is identical with Rūmīya, and as the latter was built in the reign of Khusro I Anūširwān (531–579), the administrative division would have had to be instituted at the end of the Sassanian period rather than the beginning. In any case the identification does not seem correct,[44] for the region apparently included only districts west of the Tigris, and the chief city, Be Ardəšir, was also west of it.[45] So long as no evidence points to the Rūmīyat al-Madā'in east of the Tigris antedating the sixth century, it cannot be connected with *yehudai romai* (if their name suggests a place in Babylonia at all).

At the same time it is difficult to decide whether or not those Jews were so named after the district of Rūmaqān in the Ardašīr Bābakān region.[46] Evidently the district was not in the immediate vicinity of Maḥoza and that makes it even more unlikely that it was the place where those Jews lived. There seems to be some support for the proximity of Rūmaqān and Bahurasīr in the name Bahurasīr ar-Rūmaqān which Yāqūt (s.v. "Bahurasīr") cites as an alternative name for Bahurasīr, and in fact Bahurasīr and Rūmaqān are connected in other places as well. But the Ardašīr region included most of the territory of Iraq, and each of its districts was rather large (see the districts of Nahr Durqaiṭ and Kūṯā in the entries on "Dəruqart" and "Kuta" respectively; on Nahr Ǧaubar cf. the entry on "Be Govar"). The Maḥoza area was included in the Bahurasīr district. While the Rūmaqān district may have been contiguous, it could not have been in the immediate vicinity of Maḥoza. Another indication that the Rūmaqān and Bahurasīr districts were not identical is the testimony that the former was more productive than Bahurasīr (or any other district in the Ardašīr Bābakān region).[47] Whether there was

---

[44] Cf. also Obermeyer, p. 180.

[45] Cf., e.g., *Futūḥ al-buldān*, p. 271. Obermeyer believes (*ibid.*) that the *yehudai romai* did not live in Rūmīya as it was founded only in the sixth century. Another version, certainly unhistorical, has Alexander the Great as the founder of Rūmīyat al-Madā'in east of the Tigris. See *ar-Rauḍ al-mi'ṭār*, s.v. "Rūmīyat al-Madā'in"; *Ta'rīḫ Baġdād*, vol. 1, p. 128. Cf. Yāqūt, s.v. "*Madā'in*," p. 74; Streck, *op.cit.*, vol. 2, p. 250f.; Mas'ūdī, *Murūǧ*, vol. 1, pp. 306–307 (= vol. 2, pp. 198–200). What al-'Alī (*op.cit.* in n. 42) says, pp. 52–53, 59, has not been verified. Cf. an unusual tradition whereby Anūširwān was the first Persian king to live in Madā'in, and he built it. Ya'qūbī, *Buldān*, p. 321; Qazwīnī, *Bilād*, p. 453; cf. also Streck, *op.cit.*, vol. 2, pp. 252, 266. There is a very strange tradition cited on the authority of aš-Ša'bī (d. 721; see *GAS*, vol. 1, p. 277 on him) connecting the construction of Rūmīya with the Byzantine victory over the Persians in 628; al-Qurṭubī, *Tafsīr*, vol. 14, p. 3; see also Ya'qūbī, *ibid.*; Streck, *ibid.*, vol. 2, p. 278 and n. 4; al-'Alī, *ibid.*, p. 52.

[46] Up to now there is no evidence of a town called Rūmaqān, only of a district. But it may be assumed that there was a place by the same name that was the center of the district.

[47] See Ibn Ḫurdāḏbih, p. 9, cf. *ibid.*, p. 7; Qudāma, *Ḫarāǧ*, p. 236; *Futūḥ al-Buldān*, p. 271; Yāqūt, s.v. "Rūmaqān," and cf. *ibid.*, s.v. "Abrūqā." Some impression of the territory included in the Bahurasīr district can be gleaned from what Ibn Ḥauqal says,

another Rūmīya near Maḥoza west of the Tigris is a question that requires further study.[48]

H. *The Jews and Insurrections*

The seder Olam Zuṭa chronicle contains testimony on an independent Jewish realm led by the Exilarch, Mar Zuṭra, that existed in the Maḥoza region in A.D. 495–502: "A pillar of fire appeared to him (to Mar Zuṭra) and four hundred men went forth with him and did battle with the Persians. And he inherited the kingdom. He collected taxes for seven years. At the end of seven years those with him sinned, and he found them drinking wine versed for pagan libations and eating in the palace of the kings of Persia, and the pillar of fire which had moved before him disappeared, and the Persians took him and killed him and crucified the Exilarch Mar Zuṭra and the head of the yeshiva on the Maḥoza bridge."[49]

Scholars have labored to determine the historical nucleus of the story, which appears to be a mixture of fact and legend.[50] In any case, the general outline of the event is understandable against the background of the confusion that reigned in Persia at the time of the riots that developed in the course of the growth of the Mazdaic movement during the reign of Kavād I (488–531) who was actually imprisoned at the time. Scholars do not agree on the role of the Jews in the events, but the existence for a number of years of a Jewish autonomous region where, according to our source, the Exilarch collected taxes, seems to be a fact.[51] The remarks on the sins of the Exilarch's soldiers

---

p. 245, about the jurisdiction of Madā'in. According to him, al-Ǧāmiʿān (= al-Ǧāmiʿain; later Ḥilla; see the entries on "Sura" and "Dəruqart") has a very fertile rural area contiguous with the environs of Madā'in (*al-Ǧāmiʿān . . . ḥawālaihā rustāq ʿāmir ḫaṣib ǧiddan yuḥāddu nawāḥiya l-Madā'in*).

[48] *Futūḥ al-buldān* (p. 263) reports on the conquest of Sābāṭ (see the entry on "Sabata"), afterwards the conquest of Rūmīya (following a siege) and then the crossing of the Tigris, thus suggesting that Sābāṭ and Rūmīya were on the same side of the Tigris, that is, the western side (see "Be Ardəšir-Koke" on the course of the Tigris). Cf. also *ibid.*, p. 275: A contract was signed with the inhabitants of Rūmīya and Bahurasīr, and then Madā'in (i.e. the cities east of the Tigris) was conquered. In Obermeyer's view, the author of *Futūḥ al-buldān* confused Rūmaqān and Rūmīya, and Rūmaqān was meant here (cf. above). Cf. also al-ʿAlī, *ibid*,. p. 59f.; ʿAwwād, *Sumer* 5 (1949): 248. The existence of another Rūmīya west of the Tigris would have to be confirmed by other sources. Or perhaps the information in *Futūḥ al-buldān* regarding the conquest of Madā'in is garbled. For a similar case, see Ṭabarī, vol. 3, p. 578 (= vol. 1, pp. 2358–2359), and below, regarding the course of the Tigris; cf. also Mustaufī, vol. 2, p. 50.

[49] Seder Olam Zuṭa, Grossberg ed., pp. 52–53 (Neubauer ed., p. 76). See also Graetz, *Geschichte*, vol. 5, pp. 394–397.

[50] See Lazarus, *Die Häupter*, pp. 119ff., 168–169; Funk, *Juden*, vol. 2, pp. 143–145; Klíma, *Archiv Orientální* 24 (1956): 420–431; Widengren, *Iranica Antiqua* 1 (1961): 143–145; Neusner, *History*, vol. 5, pp. 95–105.

[51] See Beer, *Rashut ha-Golah*, pp. 121–122.

fit in with the sages' censure of the licentiousness of the Exilarch's slaves,[52] although it is clear that they figure in the Mar Zuṭra episode as a justification for the collapse of his realm. Seder Olam Zuṭa goes on to report that Mar Zuṭra's son, also called Mar Zuṭra, moved to Eretz Israel.[53]

About a century after the Mar Zuṭra revolt Jews were involved in Vahram VI Chobin's rebellion against King Hormizd IV and his son Khusro II, in 589–591. This is clearly indicated by the report of the Byzantine historian Theophylactus on the capture of the Jews in Vēh Antioch when the rebellion was suppressed.[54]

In the course of the rebellion, Vahram managed to take Ctesiphon and crown himself king of Persia (on 9 March 590). Khusro II, who had also been crowned a few days earlier, after his father's murder in the palace, was forced to flee. He sought the help of his former enemy, the Byzantine emperor Mauricius, and together with him managed to defeat Vahram and reinstate himself.

Theophylactus describes the military expedition commanded by Mahbod which Khusro II despatched to conquer Ctesiphon and the neighboring cities. After taking Be Ardəšir and Ctesiphon, and proclaiming Khusro II king in the latter, Mahbod set out to conquer Vēh Antioch, a town founded by Khusro I on the east bank of the Tigris south of Ctesiphon. (See the Maḥoza Area plan.) At Mahbod's insistence the inhabitants handed over Vahram's supporters who were slain by the sword. Among the rebels taken Theophylactus mentions the Jews: "On the sixth day he also condemned to death and executed many Jews who had actively taken part in the rebellion of Vahram. For the Jews had given Vahram considerable support for his usurpation. For great numbers of this people lived at that time prosperously in Persia."[55]

Presumably Jewish supporters of Vahram were taken not only in Vēh Antioch but also in Maḥoza (Be Ardəšir), although it is also possible that only the Jews in Vēh Antioch are meant, since they included Vahram supporters from the already conquered neighboring towns who had taken refuge in it.

Theophylactus goes on to stress the special contribution of the Jews to the Vahram rebellion, as a result of their economic status: "They traded in the most expensive items, and by crossing the Red sea earned great profits in their commerce. Thus they readily joined the civil wars and uprisings of the

---

[52] See Beer, *ibid.*, pp. 152–159.

[53] See Hirschberg, *Kol Eretz Naftali*, pp. 139–146.

[54] Theophylactus V 7,4–9, de Boor ed., pp. 201–202. See also Graetz, *ibid.*, pp. 13–16; Baron, *Social and Religious History*, vol. 3, pp. 58–59; Widengren, *Iranica Antiqua* 1 (1961): 146; Neusner, *History*, vol. 5, pp. 107–108; Dan, *Meḥqarim*, vol. 5 (1980), pp. 147–153. See the section on History in the entry on "Ctesiphon" and nn. 37, 38 in the entry on "Be Ardəšir-Koḵe."

[55] Theophylactus V7, 5–6: ἕκτη δὲ ἡμέρα, καὶ πολλοὺς τοῦ Ἰουδαϊκοῦ ἱκανῶς μετεσχηκότας τῶν ὑπὸ τοῦ Βαρὰμ νεωτερισθέντων τῷ ἀκινάκῃ διώλεσε θάνατον ἐπιθεὶς ζημίαν αὐτοῖς. οὐκ ἀναξιόλογος γὰρ ἡ ὑπὸ τῶν Ἰουδαίων τῷ Βαρὰμ γεγονυῖα πρὸς τὴν τυραννίδα ῥοπή. πλῆθος γὰρ τοῦ τοιούτου ἔθνους πλούτῳ κατάκομον τὸ τηνικαῦτα καιροῦ τὴν Περσίδα κατῴκει.

Babylonian peoples."[56] So Theophylactus ascribed the great wealth he attributes to the Jews to their engaging in maritime trade.[57] No doubt included was trade in spices and raw silk with India and the Far East. Although Theophylactus is an early seventh century historian writing of the end of the sixth century, it may reasonably be inferred from his report that Jews were involved in commercial expeditions from Babylonia in the Indian Ocean throughout the entire Sassanian period (see also the entries on "Mesene" and "Mašmahig").[58]

Theophylactus then adds a series of derogatory comments on the Jews, such as "a most wicked and disloyal people" and "fond of uproar and tyranny." Presumably his anti-Semitic remarks may be attributed in part to his Egyptian origin, and to his originating among the Byzantine elite in Heraclius' time when the Persians with Jewish help conquered Eretz Israel and Jerusalem. The background for such remarks, however, must be sought not only in the Byzantine world but also in sources Theophylactus may have used which stemmed from the Persian and Babylonian environments. Underlying the anti-Semitism in such sources was certainly the loyalty to Khusro II of groups who supported him against Vahram, but also the reaction to events that preceded the Vahram rebellion, in particular the Mar Zuṭra revolt (see above).

The Maḥoza Area

II. **Opis** (Akšak)

A. *Sources*

1. Herodotus I 189

ἐπείτε δὲ ὁ Κῦρος πορευόμενος ἐπὶ τὴν Βαβυλῶνα ἐγίνετο ἐπὶ Γύνδῃ ποταμῷ, τοῦ αἱ μὲν πηγαὶ ἐν Ματιηνοῖσι εἰσί, ῥέει δὲ διὰ Δαρδανέων, ἐκδιδοῖ δὲ ἐς ἕτερον ποταμὸν Τίγρην, ὁ δὲ παρὰ Ὦπιν πόλιν ῥέων ἐς τὴν Ἐρυθρὴν θάλασσαν ἐκδιδοῖ, τοῦτον δὴ τὸν Γύνδην ποταμὸν ὡς διαβαίνειν ἐπειρᾶτο ὁ Κῦρος ἐόντα νηυσιπέρητον.

---

[56] Theophylactus V 7, 8: τὰ τιμιώτατα τοίνυν οὗτοι ἐμπορευσάμενοι καὶ τὴν Ἐρυθρὰν διαπεραιούμενοι θάλατταν, περιουσίας χρηματισθέντες μεγάλας περιεβάλοντο. ἐντεῦθεν καὶ πρὸς τὰς στάσεις καὶ τὰς Βαβυλωνίας τῶν δήμων ἐκκαύσεις ἑτοιμότατα διωλίσθαινον.

[57] The "Red sea" that the Jews sail is the Indian Ocean, and in Greek and Latin literature may include the two extensions of that ocean, the Persian Gulf and the Red Sea (see Dan, *op.cit.* [in n. 54], p. 152, n. 19, and the bibliography there). Cf. n. 10 in the entry on "Tarbiqna."

[58] Dan, *ibid.* On the place of the Jews in international trade see also Jacobs, *Melilah* 5 (1954): 84f.; Beer, *Amora'ei Bavel*, p. 156f.; Neusner, *PAAJR* 31 (1963): 165ff.; Ghirshman, *Iran*, p. 342; Pigulevskaja, *Byzanz*, p. 218ff.; Gil, *JESHO* 17 (1974): 229ff.

When Cyrus on his way to Babylon came to the river Gyndes, which rises in the mountains of the Matieni and flows through the Dardanean country into another river, the Tigris, which again passes the city of Opis and issues into the Red Sea . . . (trans.: A. D. Godley, LCL)

2. Xenophon, *Anabasis* II 4,25

Ἀπὸ δὲ τοῦ Τίγρητος ἐπορεύθησαν σταθμοὺς τέτταρας παρασάγγας εἴκοσιν ἐπὶ τὸν Φύσκον ποταμόν, τὸ εὖρος πλέθρου· ἐπῆν δὲ γέφυρα. καὶ ἐνταῦθα ᾠκεῖτο πόλις μεγάλη ὄνομα Ὦπις· πρὸς ἣν ἀπήντησε τοῖς Ἕλλησιν ὁ Κύρου καὶ Ἀρταξέρξου νόθος ἀδελφὸς ἀπὸ Σούσων καὶ Ἐκβατάνων στρατιὰν πολλὴν ἄγων ὡς βοηθήσων βασιλεῖ·

From the Tigris they marched four stages, twenty parasangs, to the Physcus river, which was a plethrum in width and had a bridge over it. There was situated a large city named Opis, near which the Greeks met the bastard brother of Cyrus and Artaxerxes, who was leading a large army from Susa and Ecbatana to the support, as he said, of the King. (trans.: C. L. Brownson, LCL)

3. Arrian, *The Anabasis of Alexander*, VII 6,6–7

ἐκεῖθεν δ' αὖθις ἔπλει ἐς Ὦπιν, πόλιν ἐπὶ τοῦ Τίγρητος ᾠκισμένην. ἐν δὲ τῷ ἀνάπλῳ τοὺς καταρράκτας τοὺς κατὰ τὸν ποταμὸν ἀφανίζων ὁμαλὸν πάντῃ ἐποίει τὸν ῥοῦν, οἳ δὴ ἐκ Περσῶν πεποιημένοι ἦσαν τοῦ μή τινα ἀπὸ θαλάσσης ἀναπλεῦσαι εἰς τὴν χώραν αὐτῶν νηΐτῃ στόλῳ κρατήσαντα.

Thence he (Alexander) sailed again to Opis, a city situated on that river. In his voyage up he destroyed the weir which existed in the river and thus he made the stream quite level. These weirs had been constructed by the Persians, to prevent any enemy having a superior naval force from sailing up from the sea into their country. (trans.: E. J. Chinnock, London, 1893)

4. Strabo II 1,26(80)

. . . ἐπειδὰν παραμείψωνται τὰ τῶν Γορδυαίων ὄρη, κύκλον μέγαν περιβαλομένους καὶ ἐμπεριλαβόντας χώραν πολλὴν τὴν Μεσοποταμίαν ἐπιστρέφειν πρὸς χειμερινὴν ἀνατολὴν καὶ τὴν μεσημβρίαν, πλέον δὲ τὸν Εὐφράτην· γενόμενον δὲ τοῦτον ἔγγιον ἀεὶ τοῦ Τίγριδος κατὰ τὸ Σεμιράμιδος διατείχισμα καὶ κώμην καλουμένην Ὦπιν, διασχόντα ταύτης ὅσον διακοσίους σταδίους καὶ ῥυέντα διὰ Βαβυλῶνος ἐκπίπτειν εἰς τὸν Περσικὸν κόλπον.

. . . and then, as soon as they (the rivers) pass the mountains of Gordyene, they describe a great circle and enclose a considerable territory, Mesopotamia; and then they turn toward the winter rising of the sun and the south, but more so the Euphrates; and the Euphrates, after becoming ever nearer to the Tigris in the neighbourhood of the Wall of Semiramis and a village called Opis (from which village the Euphrates was distant only about two hundred stadia), and, after flowing through Babylon, empties into the Persian Gulf. (trans.: H. L. Jones, LCL)

5. Strabo XI 14,8(529)

ἐκεῖθεν δ' ἤδη πρὸς τὴν Ὦπιν καὶ τὸ τῆς Σεμιράμιδος καλούμενον διατείχισμα ἐκεῖνός τε καταφέρεται τοὺς Γορδυαίους ἐν δεξιᾷ ἀφεὶς καὶ τὴν Μεσοποταμίαν ὅλην, καὶ ὁ Εὐφράτης τοὐναντίον ἐν ἀριστερᾷ ἔχων τὴν αὐτὴν χώραν.

Thence the river begins to flow down towards Opis and the wall of Semiramis, as it is called, leaving the Gordiaeans and the whole of Mesopotamia on the right, while the Euphrates, on the contrary, has the same country on the left. (trans.: H. L. Jones, LCL)

6. Strabo XVI 1,9(739–740)

ἔχουσι δ' ἀνάπλους, ὁ μὲν ἐπὶ τὴν Ὦπιν καὶ τὴν νῦν Σελεύκειαν (ἡ δὲ Ὦπις κώμη ἐμπόριον τῶν κύκλῳ τόπων), ὁ δ' ἐπὶ Βαβυλῶνα, πλειόνων ἢ τρισχιλίων σταδίων, οἱ μὲν οὖν Πέρσαι τοὺς ἀνάπλους ἐπίτηδες κωλύειν θέλοντες, φόβῳ τῶν ἔξωθεν ἐφόδων, καταράκτας χειροποιήτους κατεσκευάκεισαν· ὁ δὲ Ἀλέξανδρος ἐπιών, ὅσους οἷός τε ἦν, ἀνεσκεύασε, καὶ μάλιστα τοὺς ἐπὶ τὴν Ὦπιν.

And they are navigable inland; the Tigris to Opis and the present Seleuceia (the village Opis is an emporium of the places situated round it) and the Euphrates to Babylon, a distance of more than three thousand stadia. Now the Persians, wishing on purpose to prevent voyaging up these rivers, for fear of attacks from without, had constructed artificial cataracts, but Alexander, when he went against them, destroyed as many of them as he could, and in particular those to Opis. (trans.: H. L. Jones, LCL)

B. *General Location*

In the Maḥoza area; the precise location cannot be determined due to insufficient data.

C. *Attempts at Identification*

Because of its obvious importance and the references in classical authors, the site of Opis is a subject of much debate.[1] Winckler was the first to observe that all good sources point to a site on the east bank of the Tigris, not far from the Diyāla.[2] The inscriptions of Nebuchadnezzar II have decided the matter by showing that Opis must be sought opposite the eastern end of the "Median Wall" and the Royal Canal. Herzfeld suggested that Opis may have been in the area opposite Seleucia which formerly lay on the east bank, but is now

---

[1] See the references in Herzfeld, *Samarra*, pp. 4–7; idem, *The Persian Empire*, pp. 35–36; Barnett, *JHS* 83 (1963): 19; see also Grayson, *Assyrian and Babylonian Chronicles*, pp. 261, 294. Cuneiform texts found at Tall 'Umar were reported to have fixed the site of Opis on the west bank, but the readings have been withdrawn (Barnett, *loc.cit.*, n. 19, referring to a personal communication from Prof. Leroy Waterman).

[2] *Altorientalische Forschungen*, II vol. 1, pp. 514–528.

on the west bank of the Tigris. This would mean that part or most of Opis may have been where the present bed of the river is. The old mouth of the Royal Canal can be seen immediately south of Tall ʿUmar (which was part of Seleucia).

D. *History*

An important town is reported to have existed in the region of Maḥoza as early as the Sumerian period, and indeed stray finds of that period and of the second millennium B.C. have been discovered in the vicinity.[3] Old Babylonian lists mention the dynasty of Akshak as the twelfth after the flood.[4] In the second millennium Akšak became Opis. When Seleucia was founded, Opis and Ctesiphon (see below) already existed. A succession of towns can be traced there from the beginning of history up to the foundation of Sāmarrā further north in A.D. 834. The very nature of Mesopotamian geography led to the growth of a major population center in that particular region. The great eastern trunk road, later called the Khurasan road, reached the Tigris at that spot.[5] It was therefore the border station in Mesopotamia for those traveling to and from Susa and Ecbatana. From Opis-Ctesiphon roads led to both Babylonia and Assyria.[6] Again at this point the Nār Šarri (later Nəhar Malka = Royal Canal) discharged into the Tigris providing a connection with the Euphrates in the line of the nearest approximation of the two rivers.[7] In antiquity the Tigris was navigable from Opis down, as noted by Strabo in Source 6 and Arrian in Source 3.[8]

---

[3] Herzfeld, *Samarra*, p. 6; idem, *The Persian Empire*, p. 38; Hopkins, *Topography*, p. 9; Barnett (*op.cit.* [in n. 1 above], pp. 23–24) like Winckler, prefers a site nearer to the Diyāla, since Xenophon says that Opis was beside a river named Physcus that was crossed by a bridge. Barnett notes that this sounds like no name at all but rather like a version of an Aramaic word for "crossing," from the Aramaic-Semitic root *psḥ* also found in Thapsacus. He concludes that the Physcus was the Diyāla. Herzfeld is of the same opinion but suggests that Physcus derives from Assyrian *hubuskia*, a common name for the region of the Diyāla. Gullini, *Mesopotamia* 1 (1966): 19f., notes that a *plethrum*, i.e. 30 meters, cannot refer to the Diyāla, and suggests that a canal may be meant.

[4] For references see Meier, *RE*, vol. 18, cols. 683–685, s.v. "Opis"; Herzfeld, *The Persian Empire*, p. 35ff.; Barnett, *op.cit.* (in n. 1), p. 18f.

[5] For the Khurasan road, see Sarre & Herzfeld, *Archäologische Reise*, vol. 2, pp. 77–89.

[6] For a brief and lucid discussion of these matters, see Herzfeld, *The Persian Empire*, pp. 35–38; idem, *Samarra*, pp. 22–25. The road to Assyria went by Arbela (q.v.).

[7] The canal is first mentioned in middle-Babylonian times, see Nashef, *Répertoire Géographique des Textes Cunéiformes* 5 (1982): 310f. with references. For Opis in the region of the nearest approximation of the rivers see Strabo, Source 4.

[8] On the navigability of the Tigris see Herzfeld, *loc.cit.* Later in the second millennium there are references to sailors from Opis.

The Akkade-king Sharkalisharri, in the twenty-third century B.C., advanced as far as Opis.[9] Again in about 1170 B.C. Shutruk Naḫunte of Elam, in attacking Babylon, followed the main road to Opis.[10] The town is mentioned in Assyrian, Neo-Babylonian and Persian documents.[11] Tiglath Pileser I calls Upē a "*maḫāzu*" on the other (east) bank of the Tigris, with a fort.[12] Opis lay opposite the eastern end of the great defensive wall constructed by Nebuchadnezzar II (604–561 B.C.) to keep out the Medes: "To strengthen the fortification of Babylon, I continued, and from Opis upstream to the middle of Sippar, from Tigris bank to Euphrates bank, 6(?) *bēru*, I heaped up a mighty earthwall . . ."[13] Land north of this wall was flooded. Not very long afterwards, in 539, Cyrus marched down the river Gyndes (Diyāla) and decisively defeated the Babylonian forces near Upē (Opis).[14] In 401 Xenophon marched to the north along the east bank of the Tigris, to Opis, "a great city," which lay beside the Physcus river, a *plethrum* wide, crossed by a bridge.[15] There the Greeks met enemy forces coming from Susa and Ecbatana. Alexander crossed the Tigris at Opis on his way to Babylonia. As noted by Herzfeld, "It is geography that enforces the repetition of historical events."[16] Strabo was the last author to mention Opis, noting in Source 6 that the Tigris was navigable "to Opis and the present Seleucia (the village Opis is an emporium of the places situated round it.")[17] Thereafter, as Ctesiphon grew, Opis declined.

---

[9] Cameron, *History of Early Iran*, p. 39f.

[10] Herzfeld, *loc. cit.*

[11] Note in particular the letter to Sargon II in which a governor of Assyria refers to a ferry boat at Upē (Waterman, *Royal Correspondence of the Assyrian Empire*, No. 89, p. 61).

[12] The other "*maḫāzī rabūti*" (= major cities) mentioned are Dūr Kurigalzu (modern ʿAqr Qūf), the two Sippars and Babylon (in the description of the campaign against Karduniaš [Kassite Babylon]), references in Herzfeld, *loc. cit.* and *RE*, *loc. cit.* (in n. 4 above). See in particular Winckler (*op. cit.* in n. 2 above), p. 520.

[13] Citing Barnett, *op. cit.* (in n. 1 above), p. 18. For the texts see Weissbach, *Die Inschriften Nebukadnezars II in Wadi Brisa*, p. 27; Levy, *Sumer* 3 (1947): 4ff. This is the Median Wall mentioned by Herodotus, I 185–186 (defences built by "Nitocris") and Strabo in Source 4 (the Wall of Semiramis). It was seen, further to the west, by Xenophon, *Anabasis* II 4, 12. For the location of that wall see Herzfeld, *Samarra*, pp. 4–7; Barnett, *op. cit.*, pp. 18–20.

[14] Herodotus in Source 1 and V 52; the *Nabunaid Chronicle* col. 3, lines 12–14, see A. K. Grayson, *Assyrian and Babylonian Chronicles*, p. 109.

[15] Source 2.

[16] *Loc. cit.*, Herzfeld also points out that as a result Opis became a main point on the Tigris (like Thapsacus on the Euphrates) in the surveying carried out by Alexander's staff.

[17] Meissner, *Klio* 19 (1925): 103, understands Strabo to mean that Opis and Seleucia are identical. Meissner wanted to show that Opis is to be sought near the mouth of the Diyāla, not at Tall Manǧūr near the mouth of the ʿAẓaim further north. That is in order (see below), but Meissner's interpretation would also place Opis on the west bank of the Tigris, which is untenable. Moreover, it would entail the conclusion that Strabo calls Seleucia a village.

To sum up, the Maḥoza region was one of the crossroads of the ancient world. Long before the foundation of Seleucia, there was an important town there, first named Akšak, then Opis. The very same geographical factors which long afterwards led to the development of the urban conglomeration of Seleucia-Ctesiphon contributed to its earlier eminence, though the varying political configurations affected its prosperity differently in each period.

The Maḥoza Area

III. Ctesiphon קטיספון(א)

A. *Sources*

1. ʿEruvin 57b

א״ל רב ספרא לרבא[1] הרי בני אקיסטפון[2] דמשחינן להו תחומא מהאי גיסא דארדשיר[3] ובני דארדשיר משחינן להו תחומא מהאי גיסא דאקיסטפון, הא איכא דגלת דמפסקא יתר ממאה וארבעים ואחת ושליש, נפק אחוי ליה הנך אטמהתא דשורא דמבלעי בדגלת בע׳ אמה ושיריים.

Rav Safra said to Rava,[1] The people of Ctesiphon[2] whose Sabbath limits we measure for them from this side of Ardəšir,[3] and the people of Ardəšir whose limits we measure for them from this side of Ctesiphon, there is the Tigris that separates them more than $141^1/_3$ (cubits). He went out and showed him those foundations of the wall swallowed by the Tigris 70 cubits and a bit.

2. Giṭṭin 6a

רב חסדא מצריך מאקטיספון[4] לבי ארדשיר, ומבי ארדשיר לאקטיסְפון[5] לא מצריך.

Rav Ḥisda requires [a person bringing a bill of divorcement] from Ctesiphon[4] to Be Ardəšir [to say in whose presence it was written and signed] and from Be Ardəšir to Ctesiphon[5] he does not so require.

3. Yoma 10a

... ״ואת רסן בין נינוה ובין כלח היא העיר הגדולה,״ רסן זה אקטיספון.[6]

... "and Resen between Nineveh and Kalaḥ, that is the great city" (Gen. 10:12) Resen is Ctesiphon.[6]

---

[1] The Munich MS has "Rabbah," and see *Diq. Sof.*

[2] The source has אקיסטפון, the Munich MS has קטיספון and the same further on; see also *Diq. Sof.*

[3] The Munich and Oxford MSS have אדרשיר, and the same further on; see also *Diq. Sof.*

[4] The source has אקטיספון, the Munich MS has מקטיספון.

[5] The source has אקטיספון, the Munich MS has לקטיספון.

[6] The source has אקטיספון, the Munich B and Oxford MSS have קטיספון; the Munich MS has אקטספון.

4. Genesis Rabbah XXXVII 4 (Theodor-Albeck ed., p. 346)[7]

״ותהי ראשית ממלכתו בבל וארך ואכד וכלנה,״ הדס[8] ונציבין וקטיספון.[9]

"And the mainstays of his kingdom were Babylon, Ere<u>k</u>, Akkad and Kalneh," (Gen. 10:10), Edessa(?),[8] and Nisibis and Ctesiphon.[9]

5. Leviticus Rabbah V 3 (Margulies ed., p. 104)[10]

״עברו כלנה וראו,״ זו קטיספון.[11]

"Cross over to Kalneh and see" (Amos 6:2), it is Ctesiphon.[11]

6. Bava Batra 93b–94a; Betzah 38b

והאמר רבה בר חייא[12] קטוספאה[13] משמיה דרבה[14] בורר צרור מגרנו של חברו נותן לו דמי חטין.

But Rabbah b. Ḥiyya[12] Qəṭosəfa'a[13] said in Rabbah's[14] name, If a man picks out a pebble from his neighbor's threshing floor, he must pay him the price of wheat.

7. Yevamot 104a

רבה בר חייא[15] קטוספאה[16] עבד עובדא במוק וביחידי ובלילה.

Rabbah b. Ḥiyya[15] Qəṭosəfa'a[16] carried out the act [of *ḥalitzah*] with a felt sock, alone and at night.

8. Polybius V 45

διὸ τὸ μὲν πρῶτον ἐπεβάλετο διαβὰς τὸν Τίγριν πολιορκεῖν τὴν Σελεύκειαν· κωλυθείσης δὲ τῆς διαβάσεως ὑπὸ Ζεύξιδος διὰ τὸ καταλαβέσθαι τὰ ποτάμια πλοῖα,

[7] And similarly *Midrash ha-Gadol* to Genesis, 10:10, Margulies ed., p. 195; *Yalquṭ Shim'oni* to Genesis, 10, § 62, Mossad Harav Kook ed., p. 226; and cf. *Targum Jonathan* and *Targum Yerushalmi* for Genesis 10:10.

[8] The source has הדס. For variants see the entry on "Hadas."

[9] The source has קטיספון; the printings and the MS of Genesis Rabbah have the forms וקטיספין, וקטספו, וקטוספא, ואיקיטוספון, וקטיפון, and see the Theodor-Albeck ed. *Midrash ha-Gadol* has וקטספין.

[10] And the same in Numbers Rabbah, X 3; *Yalquṭ Shim'oni* for Amos, 6 § 545.

[11] The source has קטיספון; the MSS have the form קטיספו as well, and see the Margulies ed. *Yalquṭ Shim'oni* has קטספון.

[12] In Betzah, the father of Rabbah b. Ḥiyya Qəṭosəfa'a is credited with the statement. The printing there has "Rabbi Ḥiyya Qəṭosəfa'a." The Munich MS has "Rav Ḥiyya Qəṭosəfa'a" which seems preferable as he was a Babylonian sage. But it appears that Betzah too should be "Rabbah (or Rava) b. Ḥiyya Qəṭosəfa'a," and see *Diq. Sof.*

[13] The Hamburg MS of Bava Batra has כטיספאה (and obviously corrected to קטיפסאה).

[14] The Munich, Vatican 115 and Hamburg MSS of Bava Batra and the Betzah parallel have משמיה דרב, which seems correct. The form משמיה דרבה בורר צרור is a garble resulting from the shifting of the letter *heh*; it should be משמיה דרב הבורר צרור, and see *Diq. Sof.*

[15] The R-i-f and the R-o-sh have "Rava b. Ḥiyya."

[16] The Vatican 111 MS has קטיספאה.

τοῦτον τὸν τρόπον ἀναχωρήσας εἰς τὴν ἐν τῇ Κτησιφῶντι λεγομένη στρατοπεδείαν παρεσκεύαζε ταῖς δυνάμεσι τὰ πρὸς τὴν παραχειμασίαν.

... he (namely Molon) first of all resolved to cross the Tigris and lay siege to Seleucia; but when his passage across the river was stopped by Zeuxis seizing the river boats, he retired to the camp at Ctesiphon and set about preparing winter quarters for his army. (trans.: W. R. Paton, LCL)

9. Strabo XVI 1,16 (743)

Πάλαι μὲν οὖν ἡ Βαβυλὼν ἦν μητρόπολις τῆς Ἀσσυρίας, νῦν δὲ Σελεύκεια, ἡ ἐπὶ τῷ Τίγρει λεγομένη. πλησίον δ' ἐστὶ κώμη, Κτησιφῶν λεγομένη, μεγάλη· ταύτην δ' ἐποιοῦντο χειμάδιον οἱ τῶν Παρθυαίων βασιλεῖς, φειδόμενοι τῶν Σελευκέων, ἵνα μὴ κατασταθμεύοιντο ὑπὸ τοῦ Σκυθικοῦ φύλου καὶ στρατιωτικοῦ. δυνάμει οὖν Παρθικῇ πόλις ἀντὶ κώμης ἐστί, καὶ τὸ μέγεθος τοσοῦτόν γε πλῆθος δεχομένη καὶ τὴν κατασκευὴν ὑπ' ἐκείνων αὐτῶν κατεσκευασμένη καὶ τὰ ὤνια καὶ τὰς τέχνας προσφόρους ἐκείνοις πεπορισμένη. εἰώθασι γὰρ ἐνταῦθα τοῦ χειμῶνος διάγειν οἱ βασιλεῖς διὰ τὸ εὐάερον· θέρους δὲ ἐν Ἐκβατάνοις καὶ τῇ Ὑρκανίᾳ διὰ τὴν ἐπικράτειαν τῆς παλαιᾶς δόξης. ὥσπερ δὲ Βαβυλωνίαν τὴν χώραν καλοῦμεν, οὕτω καὶ τοὺς ἄνδρας τοὺς ἐκεῖθεν Βαβυλωνίους καλοῦμεν, οὐκ ἀπὸ τῆς πόλεως, ἀλλ' ἀπὸ τῆς χώρας· ἀπὸ δὲ τῆς Σελευκείας ἧττον, κἂν ἐκεῖθεν ὦσι, καθάπερ Διογένη τὸν Στωικὸν φιλόσοφον.

And in ancient times Babylon was the metropolis of Assyria; but now Seleuceia is the metropolis, I mean the Seleuceia on the Tigris, as it is called. Near by is situated a village called Ctesiphon, a large village. This village the kings of the Parthians were wont to make their winter residence, thus sparing the Seleuceians, in order that the Seleuceians might not be oppressed by having the Scythian folk or soldiery quartered amongst them. Because of the Parthian power, therefore, Ctesiphon is a city rather than a village; its size is such that it lodges a great number of people, and it has been equipped with buildings by the Parthians themselves; and it has been provided by the Parthians with wares for sale and with the arts that are pleasing to the Parthians; for the Parthian kings are accustomed to spend the winter there because of the salubrity of the air, but the summer at Ecbatana and in Hyrcania because of the prevalence of their ancient renown. And as we call the country Babylonia, so also we call the men from there Babylonians, that is, not after the city, but after the country; but we do not call men after Seleuceia, if they are from there, as for example, Diogenes the Stoic philosopher. (trans.: H. L. Jones, LCL)

10. Pliny, *Natural History*, VI 30,122

invicem ad hanc exhauriendam Ctesiphontem iuxta tertium ab ea lapidem in Chalonitide condidere Parthi, quod nunc est caput regnorum.

For the purpose of drawing away the population of Seleucia in its turn, the Parthians founded Ctesiphon, which is about three miles from Seleucia in the

Chalonitis district and is now the capital of the kingdoms of Parthia. (trans.: H. Rackham, LCL)
(See further Source 3 in "Walašpaṭ" for this passage.)

11. Pliny, *Natural History*, VI 31,131

Proxima Tigri regio Parapotamia appellatur. in ea dictum est de Mesene—oppidum eius Dabitha; iungitur Chalonitis cum Ctesiphonte, non palmetis modo verum et olea pomisque arbusta.

The country adjacent to the Tigris is called Parapotamia. It contains the district of Mesene, mentioned above; a town in this is Dabitha, and adjoining it is Chalonitis, with the town of Ctesiphon, a wooded district containing not only palm groves but also olives and orchards. (trans.: H. Rackham, LCL)

B. *Location*

On the east bank of the Tigris, across from Seleucia, about 25 kilometers southeast of Baghdad (on the Maḥoza Area plan).

C. *History*

Before the Parthians

The earliest mention of Ctesiphon, by Polybius (Source 8) refers to 221 B.C., the year in which Molon, satrap of Media, revolted against Antiochus III. Molon first planned to lay siege to Seleucia but was prevented from crossing the Tigris, and consequently "retired to the camp at Ctesiphon" which thus appears to have been the site of a fort opposite Seleucia. This was a natural site for a military stronghold, for the Khurasan road crossed the Tigris there, and there was a fort at nearby Opis (see above) already in the time of Tiglath Pileser I. There is evidence that Ctesiphon was a garrison town of some importance in the Persian period as well. For the Achaemenids it was clearly more centrally located than the old capital Babylon, which lost all of its prerogatives under Xerxes I.[17]
Winckler connected Ctesiphon with *Kasifya ha-maqom* in Ezra 8:17, a place in Babylonia from which Ezra got the priests needed for the Temple in Jerusalem.[18] He noted that it must have been an important Jewish center, and since it is not the name of any old Babylonian city, was presumably the suburb of one, most likely Opis. Winckler accepted the etymology of the

[17] Winckler, *Altorientalische Forschungen*, II, vol. 1, p. 528f.; see also the entry on "Babylon".

[18] *Ibid.*, pp. 509–530; see also *RE* Suppl. 4, cols. 1102–1119, s.v. "Ktesiphon." Streck, who wrote the first part of the entry (on the name Ctesiphon), agrees that the name is not Greek, but does not accept Winckler's suggestion. Honigmann, author of the second part (on the history of Ctesiphon), still believed that the name was Greek.

Septuagint which translates כספיא המקום as ἀργύριος τόπος = Silvertown, which would then be the original meaning of Ctesiphon. Herzfeld accepted Winckler's identification of Ezra's Kasifya with Ctesiphon, but suggested the name derived from the Caspians who had composed the garrison there as far back as Cyrus.[19]

The Parthian and Sassanian Period

The earliest reference to Ctesiphon in the Parthian period is by Strabo who calls it a large village (κώμη μεγάλη).[20] Strabo tells us that the Parthians made it their winter residence, "thus sparing the Seleuceians ..." The Seleucids had made Seleucia a royal residence, although eventually Antioch on the Orontes became their capital, and it is quite conceivable that the Parthians would prefer their winter residence not in a city, and especially not in a turbulent Hellenistic city of doubtful loyalty.

The site of a garrison long before the Parthians, Ctesiphon controlled the crossing of the old Royal Road till the foundation of Baghdad diverted traffic to a crossing further north. The Royal Road led to Ecbatana where the Parthians had their summer residence, so that geographically a site on the east bank of the Tigris made sense for their winter residence. Strabo describes Ctesiphon as "urbanized" but not yet officially a city, and clearly suggests that its growth was a natural consequence of the establishment of the court there during part of the year. At the time, however, Opis was still the emporium of the area on the east bank.

Strabo wrote around the turn of the millennium, but we do not know the date of his source. Ctesiphon was certainly a royal residence in 53 B.C. at the time of the Crassus campaign.[21] Ammianus states that it was founded by Vardanes (ca. A.D. 39–47/48) and later expanded, provided with walls and "a Greek name" by Pacorus (II apparently, 78–115/6?).[22] That, obviously, does not help.[23] Pliny combines contemporary information with unhistorical conjecture: Ctesiphon is in Chalonitis, three miles from Seleucia, *now* the capital of the Parthian empire.[24] His assertion that Ctesiphon was founded in order to ruin Seleucia, widely believed, is discussed in the entries on "Seleucia" and "Walašpaṭ." Pliny knows Chalonitis, with Ctesiphon, as "a wooded district containing not only palm groves but also olives and orchards." Chalonitis was

---

[19] See Herzfeld, *Samarra*, pp. 29–32; idem, *The Persian Empire*, p. 198f.

[20] Strabo, (Source 9).

[21] Cassius Dio XL 20 (see Source 17 in "Seleucia"). Other sources mentioning the royal residence include Josephus, *Antiquities*, XVIII 377; Pliny (Source 10); Tacitus, *Annals* VI 42 (see Source 13 in "Seleucia").

[22] XXIII 6, 23 (see Source 21 in "Seleucia").

[23] Ammianus' information is unhistorical.

[24] Pliny, Source 10.

especially famous for its wine, even more so than the other bank of the Tigris.[25] Referring to the time of the revolt of Seleucia (the thirties), Josephus calls Ctesiphon "a Greek city (πόλιν Ἑλληνίδα), i.e. a Hellenized town and Parthian winter residence, where most of the baggage is stored."[26]

In the second century, Ctesiphon was taken three times by Roman troops—by Trajan (116), Avidius Cassius (165) and Septimius Severus (198).[27] Avidius Cassius razed the palace of Vologaeses there to the ground.[28] By the time of Severus' campaign both Babylon and Seleucia had been abandoned, says Cassius Dio, but not Ctesiphon which was captured and plundered by the Romans. Severus "slew a vast number of people, besides taking as many as a hundred thousand captives."[29] Under the Sassanians Ctesiphon retained its status as a royal residence. Caracalla, Severus Alexander and Gordian III did not reach the Ctesiphon area in their Persian campaigns. Odaenathus of Palmyra in 262 and Julian in 363 came as far as the walls of the city. Only Carus, in 283, is said to have taken both Koḵe and Ctesiphon in a campaign about which nothing else is known.[30] In 591 Byzantine troops entered all parts of Ctesiphon to restore Khusro II to the throne.[31]

Apart from the basic facts mentioned here, Ctesiphon has remained an unknown city. Now that it has been discovered that the "round city" was Be Ardəšir-Koḵe, even the exact site of the town center and the outlines of the plan are a matter of speculation.[32] Pliny says that Ctesiphon was three miles from Seleucia. Gregory of Nazianzus says that Koḵe and Ctesiphon "are united in such a manner that they look a single town, being separated only by the river."[33] Procopius too says that Seleucia (i.e. Koḵe) and Ctesiphon "are separated by the Tigris river only, for they have nothing between them."[34] Theophanes

---

[25] See Herzfeld, *Samarra*, p. 33. For the Sassanian period Herzfeld cites *Khusrau u rētak* § 55; "Aber mit dem *Asūrīk* (von Asūristān, Ktesiphon) Wein und dem Most *bāzrangīk* (von Bāzrang in Fārs) kann sich keiner messen." See Sources 17, 18, 19 in "Maḥoza."

[26] Josephus, *Antiquities* XVIII 377.

[27] See sources cited by Honigmann, *RE*, Suppl. 4, s.v. "Ktesiphon," col. 1111f. For Trajan's campaign, see Lepper, *Trajan's Parthian War*; for those of Avidius Cassius and Severus, see "Seleucia," nn. 40 and 42.

[28] Cassius Dio, LXXI 2, 3 (see Source 19 in Seleucia").

[29] See "Seleucia" and Source 20 there (Cassius Dio, LXXVI 9, 4).

[30] For Odaenathus see Eutropius 9, 10; Zonaras, *Epitome* 12, 24; Zosimus I 39; Orosius 7, 22, 12; *SHA*, *Life of Valerian* 4, 2–4; *Life of Gallienus* 10; 12. For Carus and Julian see "Be Ardəšir-Koḵe" (n. 5). That Koḵe and Ctesiphon were really taken by Carus may not be absolutely certain, since all references clearly go back to a single source, which is, however, generally considered reliable.

[31] See "Be Ardəšir-Koḵe," nn. 37 and 38.

[32] In regard to the identification of the "round city" with Be Ardəšir-Koḵe and the reliability of that identification, see "Be Ardəšir-Koḵe."

[33] *Oration* V 10 (see Source 8 in "Be Ardəšir-Koḵe").

[34] Procopius, *The Persian War*, II 28, 4 (see Source 9 in "Be Ardəšir-Koḵe").

states that the two were linked by a pontoon bridge.[35] (Source 11 in the entry on "Maḥoza" also refers to a pontoon bridge—"the second boat of the Maḥoza bridge"—which may well be the same bridge, for both sources speak of *the* bridge.) The apparent discrepancy between Pliny, Procopius and later sources presents no problem, for it is recognized that the former measures the distance between old Seleucia and Ctesiphon, while the later writers describe the relative position of Ctesiphon and Koke, east of Seleucia (see also Section D below). For the site of Ctesiphon see further the discussion in the entry on Be Ardəšir-Koke.

So far only one expedition has carried out excavations in the area east of the "round city."[36] There is no agreement on the exact location of Ṭāq-e Kisrā (= Īwān Kisrā), the most famous structure in Seleucia-Ctesiphon. Theophilactus Simocatta seems to indicate that it was near, but not in, Ctesiphon.[37] Nothing

---

[35] *Chronography* 323 (see Source 10 in "Be Ardəšir-Koke").

[36] A German expedition excavated remains of a Sassanian settlement at Tall aḏ-Ḏahab, south of Salmān Pāk, Sassanian villas at Umm az-Zaʿatir east of Salmān Pāk and at al-Maʿarid north of it. Cf. Kühnel, *Die Ausgrabungen 1931/2*; Schmidt, *Syria* 15 (1934): 1–23.

[37] Theophylactus V 6, 10. The Īwān was not actually in Ctesiphon but in Asbānbur which was likewise on the east bank of the Tigris, south of Ctesiphon (see the plan of the Maḥoza Area). According to one version, the Īwān was "in the other city (Asbānbur) which the kings used to live in," and which was contiguous with the eastern part of Madā'in, al-ʿAtīqa (= "the ancient," i.e. Ctesiphon) (*ar-Rauḍ al-miʿṭār*, s.v. "Rūmīyat al-Madā'in" and "Abyaḍ al-Madā'in"; *Ta'rīḫ Baġdād*, vol. 1, p. 128; al-ʿAlī, *Sumer* 23 [1967]: 52ff. Cf. *ar-Rauḍ al-miʿṭār*, s.v. "Īwān"). According to another version, Asbānbur was a mile away from "al-ʿĀtīqa" (*ar-Rauḍ al-miʿṭār*, s.v. "Madā'in" [the beginning of the entry is completely garbled]; Yaʿqūbī, *Buldān*, p. 321; cf. Yāqūt, s.v. "Ṭaisafūn"; Streck, *Die alte Landschaft*, vol. 2, pp. 253f., 265, 270, and esp. 278, nn. 2 and 5; al-ʿAlī, *ibid.*, pp. 52, esp. 54, 56; Fiey, *Sumer* 23 [1967]: 28f.) Syriac sources report Christians in Asbānbur. A church is mentioned in connection with events in 524, and see Fiey, *L'Orient Syrien*, 12 (1967): 416f. The date of the construction of the Īwān is not clear. According to one version (see below) it was built by Shapur I (240–272), according to another by Shapur II (309–379) (*Kitāb al-maʿārif*, p. 659; *Ṯimār al-qulūb*, p. 180 [quoting *Kitāb al-maʿārif*]; *ar-Rauḍ al-miʿṭār*, s.v. "Rūmīyat al-Madā'in and "Abyaḍ al-Madā'in"). According to a third version, it was built by Khusro I Anūširwān (531–579) (*Ṯimār al-qulūb*, *loc.cit.*; cf. Yāqūt, s.v. "Īwān," pp. 294–295; Mustaufī, vol. 2, pp. 50–51; Qazwīnī, *Bilād*, pp. 453–454; Streck, *ibid.*, p. 257; cf. also Theophylactus, *ibid.* According to still another version, it was Khusro II Parwez (590/1–628) who built it in the course of twenty some years (*Ṯimār al-qulūb*, *loc.cit.*, and cf. *Ṯaʿālibī*, *Ġurar*, p. 614, 698). There is also a version saying that the Īwān was built by Shapur II and completed in a number of places by Parwez (Masʿūdī, *Murūǧ*, vol. 1, p. 301 [= vol. 2, p. 186]; Dimašqī, *Nuḫbat ad-dahr*, p. 38); and in another version it was established by Shapur, the son of Ardashir (i.e. Shapur I), destroyed by the Abbasid caliph al-Manṣūr (754–775) and the Īwān that was left was built by Parwez (Yāqūt, s.v. "Īwān"; cf. Streck, *ibid.*, p. 259; al-ʿAlī, *ibid.*, p. 56ff., and cf. al-Ibšaihī, *al-Mustaṭraf*, vol. 2, pp. 142–143). On the problem of the dating of the Īwān, see also Herzfeld, *Archäologische Reise*, vol. 2, pp. 74–76; Kurtz, *JRAS* (1941): 37–41. For the plan of the Ṭāq, see the preliminary excavation reports by Reuther, *Die Ausgrabungen 1928/29*; idem, *Antiquity* 3 (1929): 440–448, Pls. I–IV and plan.

is known about Ctesiphon, its layout or population, in the Sassanian period. The Jewish and Christian center was on the other side of the river.[38] Between 604 and 627, Khusro II had his residence in Dastagerd.[39]
Adams, in his survey of the Diyāla plains, has shown that the Sassanian period witnessed a spectacular growth in settlement beyond the level already attained in the Parthian period. He calculated that there are slightly more than twice the number of individual Sassanian sites and proportionately the same increase in the total built-up area—that is, a thirty-five-fold increase as compared with the Achaemenid period.[40] As regards Ctesiphon, Adams notes that the city "embraced a larger area within its walls than the total area of the 130 known sites in the entire basin during the Isin-Larsa period, the apogee of earlier antiquity," and concludes that in the Sassanian period, territorial expansion reached the maximum allowed by ancient technology. The entire cultivable area was made productive, an achievement made possible only thanks to the dredging of a vast network of new canals. Both the construction and upkeep of the canals demanded forms of central organization previously unknown, and when the centralized administration broke down, the network could not be maintained.
As Adams pointed out, this expansion in the Sassanian period took place on the east bank of the river rather than on the west bank, as in previous periods. An important reason for this might be that the east bank would suffer far less from the passing of Roman troops than the west bank.[41] The advance of Julian's army, as described by Ammianus, is an illustration of the destruction of towns and agricultural facilities both by the attacking army and by the defending Persians. On the other hand, in the Sassanian period, the founding of cities was a policy often linked with the conclusion of a successful military campaign (Buzurğ-Sābūr/ʿUkbarā, Vēh Antioch).[42]
An isolated piece of information in Masʿūdī[43] says Ctesiphon was west of the Tigris. According to him, the Sassanian kings before Shapur II, and many of

[38] For the Christians at Ctesiphon see Fiey, *L'Orient Syrien* 12 (1967): 412f. Syriac sources mention Christian individuals born there in the sixth and seventh centuries. There were several churches.

[39] Theophanes, *Chronography*, p. 320f., de Boor ed. (= Bonn ed., p. 494); cf. Sarre & Herzfeld, *Archäologische Reise*, vol. 2, pp. 78, 87–89. Khusro II Parwez "could not bear to see Ctesiphon" and returned to the city only when fleeing the Byzantine forces under Heraclius.

[40] Adams, *Land Behind Baghdad*, pp. 71–73, Table 19.

[41] *Ibid.*, p. 70. Only Julian in 363 and Heraclius in 627/8 marched through territory east of Ctesiphon.

[42] The consolidation of royal power at the expense of the nobility was one of the purposes of forced transfer of populations and the foundations of new cities, according to Adams, *ibid.*, pp. 69–70.

[43] *Murūğ*, vol. 1, p. 301 (= vol. 2, p. 186). On Ctesiphon in Arabic sources see Yāqūt, s.v. "Ṭaisafūn," "Madā'in," "Niffar," "'Irāq" (p. 94); *ar-Rauḍ al-miʿṭār*, s.v. "Bahurasīr," "Abyaḍ al-Madā'in," "Īwān," "Madā'in;" Masʿūdī, *ibid.*; and cf. Mustaufī, vol. 2,

the ancient Persians, had their residence in Ṭaisafūn (= Ctesiphon), which was in the wets of Madā'in (or, west of Madā'in).[44] This statement seems insufficient backing for the choice of a different location for Ctesiphon contrary to all other sources, and can be ignored.

D. *Ctesiphon and Be Ardəšir in Talmudic Sources*

Sources 1 and 2 testify to connections between the Jewish residents of Ctesiphon and Be Ardəšir. Source 1 states that in respect to "Sabbath limits" Ctesiphon and Be Ardəšir are considered one town. While they were on opposite banks of the Tigris, they were adjacent and joined by vestiges of a wall between them. (On the contribution of Source 1 to the location of Ctesiphon, see "Be Ardəšir-Koḵe.") Source 2 indicates that the Be Ardəšir people often went to Ctesiphon on business, so that their signatures were known there, and a messenger bringing a bill of divorcement from Be Ardəšir to Ctesiphon did not need to declare that it had been written and signed in his presence. Sources 3–5 identify biblical sites with Ctesiphon. The identifications have no historical or geographical basis, and are merely examples of the talmudic sages' method of connecting places mentioned in the Bible with familiar sites in their vicinity (cf. the entries on "Borsif," "Nippur," etc.).[45]

E. *Sages and Ctesiphon*

Sources 6 and 7 refer to Rabbah b. Ḥiyya Qəṭosəfa'a,[46] of the second generation of Babylonian amoras, the Qəṭosəfa'a added to his name evidently meant to indicate that he was from Ctesiphon. He cites a halakhah of Rav's[47] in connection with a person who removed foreign matter from his friend's threshing floor, and must compensate him because the latter could have sold his wheat

---

p. 50. See also Streck, *Die alte Landschaft*, vol. 2, pp. 248f.; idem, *EI*[1], s.v. "Madā'in," pp. 75–76; Fiey, *Sumer* 23 (1967): 9f.; ʿAwwād, *Sumer* 5 (1949): 248; Fransīs & ʿAwwād, *Sumer* 8 (1952): 266–267; al-ʿAlī, *Sumer* 23 (1967): 51f.

[44] *wa-qad kāna man qablahū min mulūki s-sāsānīya wa-kaṯīrun mimman salafa mina l-fursi l-ūlā yaskunu bi-Ṭaisafūn wa-ḏālika ġarbīya l-Madā'in min arḍi l-ʿIrāq.*

[45] Source 3 identifies Ctesiphon with Resen which is "between Nineveh and Kalaḥ" (Genesis 10: 12) Resen itself is not known—but the location, between Nineveh and Kalaḥ (= Kalḫu, today Nimrūd, Assyria's second capital, 35 kilometers south of Nineveh) makes it clear that it had no connection with Ctesiphon. Source 5 identifies Ctesiphon with Kalneh), mentioned in Amos 6:2, which was in northern Syria (and see Artzi, *Entziqlopedia Miqra'it*, vol. 4, pp. 185–186, s.v. "2 כלנה"), while Source 4 identifies it with "Kalneh in the land of Šinʿar" (Genesis 10:10) whose location is unclear, but cannot be shown to have any connection with Ctesiphon (and see *Entziqlopedia Miqra'it*, ibid., s.v. "1 כלנה." Similar identifications of biblical places with contemporary ones figure in the Syriac chronicles as well (Nöldeke, *SAWW phil.-hist. Klasse* 128, 9 (1893) p. 41 and n. 3).

[46] For variants see n. 12 above.

[47] The version משמיה דרב is preferable to משמיה דרבה, and see n. 14 above.

with the foreign matter mixed in with it.[48] A *ḥalitzah* he conducted is also reported.
Rabbah (or Rava) Tosəfa'a is mentioned in several places in the Talmud. Mostly he is reported in discussions with Ravina, of the seventh generation of Babylonian amoras.[49] The appellation may very well indicate the sage's provenance from Ctesiphon (= Ṭaisafūn, also Ṭausafūn in Arabic sources, although the substitution of *taw* for *ṭet* is not common).[50]

The Maḥoza Area

IV. Seleucia

A. *Sources*

1. Makkot 10a

אמר רב יוסף תרתי קדש הואי, אמר רב אשי כגון סליקום ואקרא דסליקום.

Rav Joseph said, There were two places called Qedeš, Rav Ashi said, Like Səliqum and Aqra di-Səliqum.

2. Yoma 10a; Ketubot 10b[1]

תני רב יוסף "אשור" זה סילק.[2]

Rav Joseph taught, "Aššur" (Gen. 10:11) is Sileq.[2]

3. Midrash Tehillim IX 8 (Buber ed., p. 85)[3]

סלייקוס בנה סליקיא,[4] סקילוס בנה סקילייא.

Selequs built Səliqia,[4] Seqilus built Səqilia.

4. Strabo XVI 1,5 (738), see Source 14 in the entry on "Babylon."

---

48 See Newman, *Agricultural Life*, p. 80.

49 A ruling of his is cited in Berakhot 50a, a deed of his in Yevamot 80b, discussions with Ravina in Shabbat 95a, Sukkah 32a, Mo'ed Qaṭan 4a (twice), Yevamot 75b, Bava Qamma 119a, Bava Batra 64a and Zevaḥim 81b. For variants see *Diq. Sof.* for the sources mentioned (mostly Rabbah Tosəfa'a alternating with Rava Tosəfa'a).

50 See Eshel, p. 245.

1 And also *Yalquṭ Shim'oni*, Genesis 38, § 145, Mossad Harav Kook ed., p. 737; *Midrash ha-Gadol* to Leviticus 21:14, Steinsalz ed., p. 603.

2 In the Ketubot and *Midrashim* parallels, the reference is to Gen. 2:14. The Munich, Munich B and Oxford MSS of Yoma have סליק; the London MS of Yoma has אשור זה נח; the Ketubot parallel has סליקא; the Munich, Vatican 112, Vatican 130 and Vatican 487 MSS of Ketubot have סליק; *Yalquṭ Shim'oni* and *Midrash ha-Gadol* have סליק.

3 Cf. *Yalquṭ Shim'oni* for Psalms 9, § 643.

4 This first sentence is missing in most of the versions, which have only "סקילוס בנה סקילייא". The latter is actually identical with the first sentence, except that the letters *quf* and *lamed* are interchanged. See Buber's note 68.

5. Strabo XVI 2,5 (750)

(Ἀντιοχεία) οὐ πολύ τε λείπεται καὶ δυνάμει καὶ μεγέθει Σελευκείας τῆς ἐπὶ τῷ Τίγρει καὶ Ἀλεξανδρείας τῆς πρὸς Αἰγύπτῳ.

(Antioch in Syria) does not fall much short, either in power or in size, of Seleuceia on the Tigris or Alexandria in Egypt. (trans.: H. L. Jones, LCL)

6. Strabo XVI 1,16 (743), see Source 9 under "Ctesiphon."

7. Strabo XVI 1,9 (739), see Source 6 under "Opis."

8. Livy XXXVIII 17,11

Macedones, qui Alexandriam in Aegypto, qui Seleuciam ac Babyloniam, quique alias sparsas per orbem terrarum colonias habent, in Syros Parthos Aegyptios degenerarunt;

The Macedonians, who hold Alexandria in Egypt, who hold Seleucia and Babylonia and other colonies scattered throughout the world, have degenerated into Syrians, Parthians, Egyptians. (trans.: E. T. Sage, LCL)

9. Isidore of Charax, *Parthian Stations* 1–2

Εἶτα Ἀείπολις, ἔνθα ἀσφαλτίτιδες πηγαί, σχοῖνοι ις'. Ἔνθεν Βεσήχανα πόλις, ἐν ᾗ ἱερὸν Ἀτάργατι, σχοῖνοι ιβ'. Εἶτα Νεάπολις παρὰ τὸν Εὐφράτην, σχοῖνοι κβ'. Ἔνθεν διαβάντων τὸν Εὐφράτην καὶ Ναρμάλχαν ἐπὶ Σελεύκειαν τὴν πρὸς τῷ Τίγριδι, σχοῖνοι θ'. Ἄχρι τούτου Μεσοποταμία καὶ Βαβυλωνία· καὶ εἰσὶν ἀπὸ Ζεύγματος ἄχρι Σελευκείας σχοῖνοι ροα'.
Ἐντεῦθεν ἄρχεται ἡ Ἀπολλωνιᾶτις, ἥτις κατέχει σχοίνους λγ'. Ἔχει δὲ κώμας, ἐν αἷς σταθμός, πόλιν δὲ Ἑλληνίδα Ἀρτέμιτα· διὰ μέσης δὲ ταύτης ῥεῖ ποταμὸς Σίλλα. Εἰσὶ δὲ εἰς αὐτὴν ἀπὸ Σελευκείας σχοῖνοι ιε'. Νῦν μέντοι ἡ πόλις καλεῖται Χαλάσαρ.

Then Aipolis [the city of Is], where there are bituminous springs, 16 schoeni. Beyond is the city of Besechana, in which is a temple of Atargatis, 12 schoeni. Then Neapolis by the Euphrates, 22 schoeni. From that place those leaving the Euphrates and passing through Narmalchan come to Seleucia on the Tigris, 9 schoeni. To this place [extend] Mesopotamia and Babylonia; and from Zeugma to Seleucia there are 171 schoeni. From that place begins Apolloniatis, which extends 33 schoeni. It has villages, in which there are stations; and a Greek city, Artemita; through the midst of which flows the river Silla. To that place from Seleucia is 15 schoeni. But now the city is called Chalasar. (trans.: W. H. Schoff, Philadelphia, 1914)

10. Pliny, *Natural History* VI 30,122, see Source 3 in the entry on "Walašpaṭ."

11. Josephus, *Antiquities* XII 119

Ἔτυχον δὲ καὶ τῆς παρὰ τῶν βασιλέων τῆς Ἀσίας τιμῆς, ἐπειδὴ συνεστράτευσαν αὐτοῖς· καὶ γὰρ Σέλευκος ὁ Νικάτωρ ἐν αἷς ἔκτισεν πόλεσιν ἐν τῇ Ἀσίᾳ καὶ τῇ κάτω

Συρίᾳ καὶ ἐν αὐτῇ τῇ μητροπόλει Ἀντιοχείᾳ πολιτείας αὐτοὺς ἠξίωσεν καὶ τοῖς ἐνοικισθεῖσιν ἰσοτίμους ἀπέφηνεν Μακεδόσιν καὶ Ἕλλησιν, ὡς τὴν πολιτείαν ταύτην ἔτι καὶ νῦν διαμένειν· τεκμήριον δὲ τοῦτο· τοὺς Ἰουδαίους μὴ βουλομένους ἀλλοφύλῳ ἐλαίῳ χρῆσθαι λαμβάνειν ὡρισμένον τι παρὰ τῶν γυμνασιάρχων εἰς ἐλαίου τιμὴν ἀργύριον ἐκέλευσεν.

They also received honour from the kings of Asia when they served with them in war. For example, Seleucus Nicator granted them citizenship in the cities which he founded in Asia and Lower Syria and in his capital, Antioch, itself, and declared them to have equal privileges with the Macedonians and Greeks who were settled in these cities, so that this citizenship of theirs remains to this very day; and the proof of this is the fact that he gave orders that those Jews who were unwilling to use foreign oil should receive a fixed sum of money from the gymnasiarchs to pay for their own kind of oil. (trans.: R. Marcus, LCL)

12. Josephus, *Antiquities* XVIII 372–379

οἱ δ' ἐν δεινῷ τιθέμενοι τὴν ὕβριν τὴν ἐκ τῶν Βαβυλωνίων καὶ μήτε ἀντιτάξασθαι μάχῃ δυνάμενοι μήτε ἀνεκτὸν ἡγούμενοι τὴν συνοικίαν ᾤχοντο εἰς Σελεύκειαν τῶν ἐκείνῃ πόλιν ἀξιολογωτάτην Σελεύκου κτίσαντος αὐτὴν τοῦ Νικάτορος. οἰκοῦσιν δ' αὐτὴν πολλοὶ μὲν Μακεδόνων, πλεῖστοι δὲ Ἕλληνες, ἔστιν δὲ καὶ Σύρων οὐχ ὀλίγον τὸ ἐμπολιτευόμενον. εἰς μὲν δὴ ταύτην καταφεύγουσιν οἱ Ἰουδαῖοι καὶ ἐπὶ μὲν πέντε ἔτη ἀπαθεῖς κακῶν ἦσαν, τῷ δὲ ἕκτῳ ἔτει μετὰ τὸ πρῶτον φθορὰ ἐν Βαβυλῶνι ἐγένετο αὐτῶν καὶ καιναὶ κτίσεις ἐκ τῆς πόλεως καὶ δι' αὐτὴν ἄφιξις εἰς τὴν Σελεύκειαν ἐκδέχεται μείζων αὐτοὺς συμφορὰ δι' αἰτίαν, ἣν ἀφηγήσομαι.
Σελευκέων τοῖς Ἕλλησι πρὸς τοὺς Σύρους ὡς ἐπὶ πολὺ ἐν στάσει καὶ διχονοίᾳ ἐστὶν ὁ βίος καὶ κρατοῦσιν οἱ Ἕλληνες. τότε οὖν συνοικούντων αὐτοῖς Ἰουδαίων γενομένων ἐστασίαζον, καὶ οἱ Σύροι καθυπέρτεροι ἦσαν ὁμολογίᾳ τῇ Ἰουδαίων πρὸς αὐτοὺς φιλοκινδύνων τε ἀνδρῶν καὶ πολεμεῖν προθύμως ἐντεταγμένων. καὶ οἱ Ἕλληνες περιωθούμενοι τῇ στάσει καὶ μίαν ὁρῶντες αὐτοῖς ἀφορμὴν τοῦ ἀνασώσασθαι τὸ πρότερον ἀξίωμα, εἰ δυνηθεῖεν παῦσαι ταὐτὸν λέγοντας Ἰουδαίους καὶ Σύρους, διελέγοντο ἕκαστοι πρὸς τῶν Σύρων τοὺς αὐτοῖς συνήθεις πρὸ τοῦ γεγονότας εἰρήνην τε καὶ φιλίαν ὑπισχνούμενοι. οἱ δὲ ἐπείθοντο ἄσμενοι. ἐγίνοντο οὖν ἀφ' ἑκατέρων λόγοι καὶ τῶν πρώτων παρ' ἑκατέροις ἀνδρῶν πρασσόντων ἐπιδιαλλαγὰς τάχιστα ἡ σύμβασις ἐγένετο, ὁμονοήσαντές τε μέγα τεκμήριον ἑκάτεροι εὐνοίας [παρ'] ἀλλήλοις ἠξίουν παρασχεῖν τὸ πρὸς τοὺς Ἰουδαίους ἔχθος, ἐπιπεσόντες τε αἰφνίδιον αὐτοῖς κτείνουσι μυριάδας ὑπὲρ πέντε ἀνδρῶν, ἀπώλοντό τε πάντες πλὴν εἴ τινες ἐλέῳ φίλων ἢ γειτόνων ἐπιχωρηθὲν αὐτοῖς ἔφυγον. τούτοις δὲ ἦν εἰς Κτησιφῶντα ἀποχώρησις πόλιν Ἑλληνίδα καὶ τῆς Σελευκείας πλησίον κειμένην, ἔνθα χειμάζει τε ὁ βασιλεὺς κατὰ πᾶν ἔτος καὶ πλείστη τῆς ἀποσκευῆς αὐτοῦ τῇδε ἀποκειμένη τυγχάνει. ἀσύνετα δὲ ἦν αὐτοῖς τὴν ἵδρυσιν πεποιημένοις τιμῇ τῆς βασιλείας Σελευκέων πεφροντικότων. ἐφοβήθη δὲ καὶ πᾶν τὸ τῇδε Ἰουδαίων ἔθνος τούς τε Βαβυλωνίους καὶ τοὺς Σελευκεῖς,

ἐπειδὴ καὶ ὁπόσον ἦν Σύρων ἐμπολιτεῦον τοῖς τόποις ταὐτὸν ἔλεγον τοῖς Σελευκεῦσιν ἐπὶ πολέμῳ τῷ πρὸς τοὺς Ἰουδαίους. καὶ συνελέγησαν ὥστε πολὺ εἴς τε τὰ Νέαρδα καὶ τὴν Νίσιβιν ὀχυρότητι τῶν πόλεων κτώμενοι τὴν ἀσφάλειαν, καὶ ἄλλως πληθὺς ἅπασα μαχίμων ἀνδρῶν κατοικεῖται. καὶ τὰ μὲν κατὰ Ἰουδαίους τοὺς ἐν τῇ Βαβυλωνίᾳ κατῳκημένους τοιαῦτα ἦν.

The latter [the Jews] were indignant at the insolent conduct of the Babylonians, but neither were able to face them in battle nor considered it tolerable to live together with them. So off they went to Seleucia, the most notable city of the region, which Seleucus Nicator had founded, whose inhabitants consisted of many Macedonians, a majority of Greeks, and not a few Syrians holding civic rights. Here then the Jews took refuge. For five years they lived there unmolested, but in the sixth year after they were first despoiled in Babylon and formed new settlements upon leaving that city, and in consequence came to Seleucia, there ensued a greater misfortune, the cause of which I shall relate. At Seleucia life is marked by general strife and discord between the Greeks and the Syrians, in which the Greeks have the upper hand. Now when the Jews came to live in the city there was continued strife, and the Syrians got the upper hand by coming to terms with the Jews, who were adventurous and joined the ranks in battle with gusto. Now the Greeks, harried by this civil conflict, saw that there was only one possibility of regaining their former prestige, namely, by breaking up the alliance between Jews and Syrians. To this end various groups among the Greeks parleyed with any of the Syrians with whom they had formerly been on intimate terms, offering a promise of peace and friendship. The Syrians on their part gladly assented. Proposals were put forward by the two parties. The leading men on both sides effected a reconciliation and an agreement was very speedily reached. Once they were on good terms, both parties agreed, as a great proof of mutual loyalty, to show enmity to the Jews. They fell upon them suddenly and slew more than 50,000 men. Indeed all were slain except for some who were mercifully granted the chance to flee by friends or neighbours. Those who escaped retreated to Ctesiphon, a Greek city situated near Seleucia, where the king spends the winter each year and where most of his baggage is stored, as it happens. But it was without prudence that they settled there, since the Seleucians had no respect for the authority of the crown. All the Jewish people in this region now became terrified of both the Babylonians and the Seleucians since all the Syrians who were citizens of these places fell in line with the Seleucians and made war against the Jews their policy. Most of the Jews flocked to Nearda and Nisibis,* where they were safe because these cities were fortified and were furthermore populated by men who were valiant fighters every one. Such is the story of the Jewish inhabitants of Babylonia. (trans.: L. H. Feldman, LCL)
(* See the entries on "Nəhardəʿa" and "Nisibis".)

13. Tacitus, *Annals*, VI 42

Plurimum adulationis Seleucenses induere, civitas potens, saepta muris neque in barbarum corrupta, sed conditoris Seleuci retinens, trecenti opibus aut sapientia delecti ut senatus, sua populo vis. et quoties concordes agunt, spernitur Parthus; ubi dissensere, dum sibi quisque contra aemulos subsidium vocant, accitus in partem adversum omnes valescit. id nuper acciderat Artabano regnante, qui plebem primoribus tradidit ex suo usu: nam populi imperium iuxta libertatem, paucorum dominatio regiae libidini propior est. tum adventantem Tiridaten extollunt veterum regum honoribus et quos recens aetas largius invenit; simul probra in Artabanum fundebant, materna origine Arsaciden, cetera degenerem. Tiridates rem Seleucensem populo permittit.

The extreme of adulation was shown by the powerful community of Seleucia, a walled town, which, faithful to the memory of its founder Seleucus, has not degenerated into barbarism. Three hundred members, chosen for wealth or wisdom, form a senate: the people has its own prerogatives. So long as the two orders are in unison, the Parthian is ignored: if they clash, each calls in aid against its rival; and the alien, summoned to rescue a part, overpowers the whole. This had happened lately in the reign of Artabanus, who consulted his own ends by sacrificing the populace to the aristocrats: for supremacy of the people is akin to freedom; between the domination of a minority and the whim of a monarch the distance is small. They now celebrated the arrival of Tiridates with the honours paid to the ancient kings, along with the innovations of which a later age has been more lavish; at the same time, they poured abuse on Artabanus as an Arsacid on the mother's side, but otherwise of ignoble blood. Tiridates handed over the government of Seleucia to the democracy. (trans.: J. Jackson, LCL)

14. Plutarch, *Lucullus* XXII 5

ἐτελεύτησε δὲ παρὰ τῷ Τιγράνῃ καὶ Ἀμφικράτης ὁ ῥήτωρ, εἰ δεῖ καὶ τούτου μνήμην τινὰ γενέσθαι διὰ τὰς Ἀθήνας. λέγεται γὰρ φυγεῖν μὲν αὐτὸν εἰς Σελεύκειαν τὴν ἐπὶ Τίγριδι, δεομένων δ' αὐτόθι σοφιστεύειν ὑπεριδεῖν καταλαζονευσάμενον, ὡς οὐδὲ λεκάνη δελφῖνα χωροίη.

Amphicrates, the rhetorician, also lost his life at the court of Tigranes, if, for the sake of Athens, we may make some mention of him too. It is said that when he was exiled from his native city, he went to Seleucia on the Tigris, and that when the citizens asked him to give lectures there, he treated their invitation with contempt, arrogantly remarking that a stewpan could not hold a dolphin. (trans.: B. Perrin, LCL)

15. Pausanias I 16, 3

Σέλευκον δὲ βασιλέων ἐν τοῖς μάλιστα πείθομαι καὶ ἄλλως γενέσθαι δίκαιον καὶ πρὸς τὸ θεῖον εὐσεβῆ. τοῦτο μὲν γὰρ Σέλευκός ἐστιν ὁ Μιλησίοις τὸν χαλκοῦν καταπέμψας

Ἀπόλλωνα ἐς Βραγχίδας, ἀνακομισθέντα ἐς Ἐκβάτανα τὰ Μηδικὰ ὑπὸ Ξέρξου· τοῦτο δὲ Σελεύκειαν οἰκίσας ἐπὶ Τίγρητι ποταμῷ καὶ Βαβυλωνίους οὗτος ἐπαγόμενος ἐς αὐτὴν συνοίκους ὑπελίπετο μὲν τὸ τεῖχος Βαβυλῶνος, ὑπελίπετο δὲ τοῦ Βὴλ τὸ ἱερὸν καὶ περὶ αὐτὸ τοὺς Χαλδαίους οἰκεῖν.

Seleucus I believe to have been one of the justest and most pious of kings; for he sent back to the Milesians at Branchidae the bronze Apollo . . .; and when he founded Seleucia on the river Tigris, and brought Babylonian colonists to it, he left standing both the walls of Babylon and the sanctuary of Bel, and allowed the Chaldaeans to dwell round about the sanctuary as before.[5] (trans.: J. G. Frazer, London, 1898)

16. Cassius Dio XL 16

ὁ οὖν Κράσσος ἐκείνῳ τε ἐν Σελευκείᾳ (ἔστι δὲ πόλις ἐν τῇ Μεσοποταμίᾳ, πλεῖστον τὸ Ἑλληνικὸν καὶ νῦν ἔχουσα) τὰς αἰτίας τοῦ πολέμου ἐρεῖν ἔφη. καὶ αὐτῷ τῶν Πάρθων τις ἐς τὴν χεῖρα τὴν ἀριστερὰν τοῖς τῆς ἑτέρας δακτύλοις κρούσας εἶπεν ὅτι "θᾶσσον ἐντεῦθεν τρίχες ἀναφύσουσιν ἢ σὺ ἐν Σελευκείᾳ γενήσῃ."

Now Crassus said that he would tell him (Orodes) in Seleucia the causes of the war; this is a city in Mesopotamia which even at the present day has a very large Greek population. And one of the Parthians, striking the palm of his left hand with the fingers of the other, exclaimed: "Sooner will hair grow here than you shall reach Seleucia." (trans.: E. Cary, LCL)

17. Cassius Dio XL 20

τοῦ γὰρ Κράσσου πρὸς Σελεύκειαν ὁρμῆσαι διανοουμένου, ὥστε ἐκεῖσέ τε ἀσφαλῶς παρά τε τὸν Εὐφράτην καὶ δι' αὐτοῦ τῷ τε στρατῷ καὶ τοῖς ἐπιτηδείοις κομισθῆναι, καὶ μετ' αὐτῶν (προσποιήσεσθαι γάρ σφας ἅτε καὶ Ἕλληνας ῥᾳδίως ἤλπιζεν) ἐπὶ Κτησιφῶντα μὴ χαλεπῶς περαιωθῆναι.

Crassus was intending to advance to Seleucia so as to reach there safely with his army and provisions by proceeding along the banks of the Euphrates and on its stream; accompanied then by the people of that city, whom he hoped to win over easily, because they were Greeks, he would cross without difficulty to Ctesiphon. (trans.: E. Cary, LCL)

18. Cassius Dio LXVIII 30

ἑάλω δὲ καὶ ἡ Σελεύκεια πρός τε Ἐρυκίου Κλάρου καὶ πρὸς Ἰουλίου Ἀλεξάνδρου ὑποστρατήγων, καὶ ἐκαύθη. Τραϊανὸς δὲ φοβηθεὶς μὴ καὶ οἱ Πάρθοι τι νεοχμώσωσι. βασιλέα αὐτοῖς ἴδιον δοῦναι ἠθέλησε, καὶ ἐς Κτησιφῶντα ἐλθὼν συνεκάλεσεν ἐς πεδίον τι μέγα πάντας μὲν τοὺς Ῥωμαίους πάντας δὲ τοὺς Πάρθους τοὺς ἐκεῖ τότε

[5] This passage is usually considered proof that after the foundation of Seleucia citizens of Babylon were evacuated and forced to settle in Seleucia. Pausanias in fact states the opposite: While Babylonians, i.e. residents of the country, were resettled in Seleucia, there was no forced evacuation of the old capital.

ὄντας, καὶ ἐπὶ βῆμα ὑψηλὸν ἀναβάς, καὶ μεγαληγορήσας ὑπὲρ ὧν καὶ κατειργάσατο, Παρθαμασπάτην τοῖς Πάρθοις βασιλέα ἀπέδειξε, τὸ διάδημα αὐτῷ ἐπιθείς.

Seleucia was also captured by Erucius Clarus and Julius Alexander, lieutenants, and was burned. Trajan, fearing that the Parthians, too, might begin a revolt, desired to give them a king of their own. Accordingly, when he came to Ctesiphon, he called together in a great plain all the Romans and likewise all the Parthians that were there at the time; then he mounted a lofty platform, and after describing in grandiloquent language what he had accomplished, he appointed Parthamaspates king over the Parthians and set the diadem upon his head. (trans.: E. Cary, LCL)

19. Cassius Dio LXXI 2

καὶ ὃς ἐπιόντα τε τὸν Οὐολόγαισον γενναίως ὑπέμεινε, καὶ τέλος ἐγκαταλειφθέντα ὑπὸ τῶν συμμάχων καὶ ὀπίσω ἀναχωρήσαντα ἐπεδίωξε, μέχρι τε Σελευκείας καὶ Κτησιφῶντος ἤλασε, καὶ τήν τε Σελεύκειαν διέφθειρεν ἐμπρήσας, καὶ τὰ τοῦ Οὐολογαίσου βασίλεια τὰ ἐν τῇ Κτησιφῶντι κατέσκαψεν.

The latter made a noble stand against the attack of Vologaesus, and finally, when the king was deserted by his allies and began to retire, he pursued him as far as Seleucia and Ctesiphon, destroying Seleucia by fire and razing to the ground the palace of Vologaesus at Ctesiphon. (trans.: E. Cary, LCL)

20. Cassius Dio LXXVI 9

τὰ κατασκευασθέντα, ταχέως τήν τε Σελεύκειαν καὶ τὴν Βαβυλῶνα ἐκλειφθείσας ἔλαβε. καὶ μετὰ τοῦτο καὶ τὴν Κτησιφῶντα ἑλὼν ἐκείνην τε πᾶσαν διαρπάσαι τοῖς στρατιώταις ἐφῆκε, φόνον τε ἀνθρώπων πλεῖστον εἰργάσατο, καὶ ζῶντας ἐς δέκα μυριάδας εἷλεν. οὐ μέντοι οὔτε τὸν Οὐολόγαισον ἐπεδίωξεν οὔτε τὴν Κτησιφῶντα κατέσχεν, ἀλλ' ὥσπερ ἐπὶ τοῦτο μόνον ἐστρατευκὼς ἵν' αὐτὴν διαρπάσῃ ᾤχετο, τὸ μὲν ἀγνωσίᾳ τῶν χωρίων τὸ δ' ἀπορίᾳ τῶν ἐπιτηδείων.

Thus he soon had seized Seleucia and Babylon, both of which had been abandoned. Later, upon capturing Ctesiphon, he permitted the soldiers to plunder the entire city, and he slew a vast number of people, besides taking as many as a hundred thousand captives. He did not, however, pursue Vologaesus, nor even occupy Ctesiphon, but, just as if the sole purpose of his campaign had been to plunder this place, he was off again, owing partly to the lack of acquaintance with the country and partly to the dearth of provisions. (trans.: E. Cary, LCL)

21. Ammianus XXIII 6,23–24

In omni autem Assyria, multae sunt urbes. inter quas Apamia eminet, Mesene cognominata, et Teredon et Apollonia et Vologessia, hisque similes multae. splendidissimae uero et peruulgatae hae solae sunt tres: Babylon cuius moenia bitumine Samiramis struxit—arcem enim antiquissimus rex condidit

Belus—, et Ctesiphon, quam Vardanes temporibus priscis instituit, posteaque rex Pacorus, incolarum uiribus amplificatam et moenibus, Graeco indito nomine, Persidis effecit specimen summum. post hanc Seleucia, ambitiosum opus Nicatoris Seleuci. qua per duces Veri Caesaris (ut ante rettulimus), expugnata, auulsum sedibus simulacrum Comaei Apollinis, perlatumque Romam, in aede Apollinis Palatini deorum antistites collocarunt.

But in all Assyria there are many cities, among which Apamia, formerly called Mesene, and Teredon, Apollonia and Vologessia, and many similar ones are conspicuous. But there three are especially magnificent and widely known: Babylon, whose walls Semiramis built with bitumen (for the ancient king Belus built the citadel), and Ctesiphon, which Vardanes founded long ago; and later king Pacorus strengthened it with additional inhabitants and with walls, gave it a Greek name, and made it the crowning ornament of Persia. And finally there is Seleucia, the splendid work of Seleucus Nicator. When this city was stormed by the generals of Verus Caesar (as I have related before), the statue of Apollo Comaeus was torn from its place and taken to Rome, where the priests of the gods set it up in the temple of the Palatine Apollo. (trans.: J. C. Rolfe, LCL)

B. *Location*

On the west bank of the Tigris, across from Ctesiphon, about 25 kilometers southeast of Baghdad (on the Maḥoza Area plan).

C. *History*

Seleucia was by far the most important town in Babylonia and the most successful of the Seleucid towns founded throughout the Hellenistic and Parthian period. It was not, however the first town established at or near that site. Ctesiphon and Opis already existed when Seleucia was founded, and in fact a succession of important towns can be traced there earlier, as noted under "Opis."[6]

---

[6] Pre-Hellenistic towns in the vicinity were ignored by German scholars whose prejudices persuaded them that only Hellenes were capable of choosing the right site for a city (e.g., Beloch, *Griechische Geschichte*, vol. 3, 1 p. 140). Typical of Beloch are such phrases as "Semitischer Schmutz" and "Chaldäische Pfaffen," which are rather astonishingly cited with approval by an orientalist, in a German standard work of reference, as early as 1921 (Streck, *RE*, vol. 2A, col. 1151, s.v. "Seleukeia [am Tigris])." For crude racial prejudice formulated independently in that article see col. 1165: "Die von den Römern gegeisselte und gewiss auch vorhandene Entartung der Stadtbevölkerung hatte vielleicht mehr die spezifisch orientalischen Elemente derselben ergriffen." And the learned author of these lines is here discussing the speech of a Roman consul before his troops in 189 B.C., as invented by Livy in the reign of Augustus (Livy XXXVIII 17, 11). Equally reprehensible are the concluding lines of McDowell's *Coins from Seleucia*, p. 236.

Seleucia was established by Seleucus I. The date is not mentioned in any source, and various years before 299 have been suggested.[7] Pliny says that Babylon was "drained of its population by the proximity of Seleucia, founded for that purpose by Nicator not quite 90 miles away, at the point where the canalised Euphrates joins the Tigris."[8] This statement has been taken seriously by many scholars, even though Pliny's information on the foundation of Ctesiphon and Vologesias is demonstrably false.[9] Winckler,[10] on the other hand, argued that the Seleucids had no reason at all to ruin Babylon. Alexander had gone to great trouble to restore that city to its former eminence and there is no evidence of an anti-Babylon policy on the part of his successors.[11] Babylon's decline no doubt followed a pattern familiar in Mesopotamian history: the drying up or shifting of an essential waterway. Alexander inspected the major rivers and canals of Babylonia, regulated the flow of many

---

[7] Strabo, Source 4, informs us that Seleucus I was the founder. See the discussion in *RE, loc.cit.*; Hopkins, *Topography*, p. 5; McDowell in *Topography*, p. 150; most recently Hadley, *Historia* 22 (1978): 228–230, who supports 300 B.C. as proposed by Bouché-Leclercq, *Histoire des Séleucides*, vol. 2, p. 524.

[8] Pliny, *Natural History*, VI 30, 122 (Source 3 in the entry on "Walašpaṭ"). Strabo, *loc.cit.*, says that Seleucia superseded Babylon, not that it was founded for that express purpose.

[9] *RE, op.cit.*, col. 1151; Hopkins, *loc.cit.*; McDowell, *ibid.* (in n. 7), p. 152. Pliny in the same passage claims that the Parthians founded Ctesiphon, which they did not, and that Vologesias was founded to supersede Seleucia, which it was not. Appian, *Syriaca* 58, tells a well-known story which shows that the *magi* did not approve of the foundation of Seleucia. If historical, the story shows that there was opposition to the establishment of Seleucia, not that it was meant to replace Babylon. Forty-nine stamped tiles from the neo-Babylonian period have been found at Seleucia (Pettinato, *Mesopotamia* 5/6 [1970–71]: 49–66). These may come from Babylon or, as suggested by Pettinato, from a structure nearby (Opis? Nebuchadnezzar's wall?). On the other hand, the wall of the Round City was built on three layers of neo-Babylonian bricks (Sarre & Herzfeld, *Archäologische Reise*, vol. 2, pp. 53–56, figs. 161–165). Herzfeld calculated that some 1.5 million bricks were used. He thought it was the wall of Hellenistic Seleucia. We now know that it was that of Be Ardəšir, and it must have been Ardashīr I who robbed the bricks. For this wall see further Reuther, *Ausgrabungen 1928–1929*, pp. 6–9; idem, *Antiquity* 3 (1929): 451.

[10] Winckler, *Altorientalische Forschungen*, II, vol. 1, pp. 513–515; supported by Herzfeld, *Samarra*, p. 23.

[11] Antiochus II built the sanctuary of Ezida at Borsippa (Inscription 1 in the entry on "Babylon"). Orchoi built an entirely traditional temple under Epiphanes. Cuneiform texts indicate that in 275/4 B.C. land was taken over from Babylon, Borsippa, and Kuta and population transferred from Babylon to Seleucia, but this was apparently due to the first Syrian war (Inscription 2 in the entry on "Babylon"). Thirty-seven years later under Antiochus II, land was allocated to Kuta, Borsippa and Babylon (Inscription 3 in the entry on "Babylon"). See Timothy Doty, *Mesopotamia* 13/14 (1978–1979): 96–97 and nn. 13–15; Smith, *BHT*, pp. 150–159; Sarkisian, *Ancient Mesopotamia*, ed., Diakonoff, pp. 315–319, 321–327. See also the entry on "Orchoi" for references to cuneiform documents of the Hellenistic period.

of them and cleared some for shipping.[12] The Euphrates, however, was no longer navigable below Babylon, where the Pallacottas had become marshy. Thus the Tigris became the main waterway, and Seleucia the heir to Babylon's prosperity.

Seleucia flourished for various reasons. First there was the great fertility of the region.[13] Secondly, it was one of the most important way stations of the Near East.[14] That had been true of Opis as well, but urbanization, traffic and commerce were of a different scale in the Hellenistic period. Seleucia was greater than any of the Mesopotamian cities of the previous periods. Its population numbered 600,000 according to Pliny, writing in the seventies of the first century but using older sources. Orosius gives the number of 400,000 for the time of Avidius Cassius' campaign, in 165.[15] Archaeological exploration suggests a far smaller figure. Yeivin estimated that Seleucia could have had only 20,000 inhabitants. Adams, who paid a good deal of attention to the problems of calculating the population of ancient sites, suggests that the surface area of the site, about 4 sq. kms, could have had a population of about 80,000.[16] Analyzing the results of his survey of the Diyāla region, Adams concludes that the Seleucid and Parthian periods saw an immense and unprecedented expansion in the built-up area of settlement, with many new towns and settlements established. This expansion was coupled with an extension of the cultivated zone, based on the gradual transformation of the irrigation system, which Adams sees as the result of Seleucid and Parthian imperial control, combining centrally organized urbanization with the improvement of communications and commerce.[17]

We know little about the political institutions of Seleucia, and most of what we do know refers to the Parthian period.[18] Seleucia was a royal capital,[19] so that a strong link developed between the dynasty and the city. Describing events in the last quarter of the third century, Polybius mentions an *epistates*

---

[12] Strabo XVI 1, 11 (741); Arrian, *Anabasis* VII 7, 6; VII 27 and Curtius Rufus X 4, 3 clearly state that the Pallacottas below Babylon had become marshy when Alexander explored the region.

[13] Herodotus I 193; Pliny, *Natural History* VI 30, 122; XVIII 47, 170; Theophrastus, *An Inquiry into Plants* VIII, 7, 4; Strabo XVI 1, 14 (742); Ammianus XXIII 6, 25; XXIV 5, 1; Theophylactus Simocatta V 6, 5; cf. McDowell in Hopkins, *Topography*, p. 154, with contemporary observations on the fertility of the region.

[14] For trade routes leading to and from Seleucia, see *RE*, *op. cit.* (in n. 6), cols. 1155–1157; McDowell, in Hopkins, *Topography*, p. 155.

[15] Pliny, *Natural History* VI 30, 122; Orosius VII 15; cf. *RE*, *op. cit.*, col. 1158, for parallel sources.

[16] Yeivin in Waterman et al., *Second Preliminary Report*, p. 39; Adams, *Land Behind Baghdad*, Appendix A, esp. p. 123f., and n. 7 to chapter 6.

[17] Adams, *op. cit.*, chapter 6, pp. 61–68, Table 18.

[18] *RE*, *op. cit.* (in n. 6 above), cols. 1163–1164; McDowell, in Hopkins, *Topography*, pp. 152–154.

[19] Strabo, Source 4: Seleucus τὸ transferred βασίλειον to the new city.

(commander?) of the city,[20] and tells us that after the collapse of the Molon revolt, "those called the *adeiganes* were driven out."[21] Seleucia had the usual institutions of a polis, and there is mention of a council.[22] Tacitus states that there was a senate representing the aristocracy that was made up of three hundred members chosen for their wealth or wisdom, and that "the people has its own prerogatives," but does not say how those prerogatives were exercised.[23] The senate and people evidently clashed regularly. After the Seleucian revolt, from A.D. 43/4 to 45/6, the senate publicly emphasized its status by coins which show on the reverse a personification of the Boule, accompanied by the legend βουλή.[24] Tacitus and Josephus both describe civil strife in Seleucia in the same period. We may therefore assume they are referring to the same groups, namely the Hellenized citizens on the one hand, and the non-Hellenized Babylonians organized in a *politeuma* ("*sua populo vis*") on the other. It is not known whether the same pattern existed in the Seleucid period.

The seals and bullae found in the excavations are instructive on the administration and fiscal organization of Seleucid Babylonia.[25] They appear to have been fully developed early in the third century. Comparing the stamps of tax collectors from Orchoi with those found at Seleucia,[26] McDowell concluded that Seleucia's autonomy was more restricted than Orchoi's. The Seleucid coins found in the excavations at Seleucia have been published and tentative historical conclusions drawn.[27]

---

[20] Polybius V 48.

[21] Polybius V 54. It has been suggested that the reading should be [πελ]ιγᾶνας since *peliganes* are attested among other places in Laodicea in Syria, cf. Jalabert & Mouterde, *Inscriptions Grecques et Latines de la Syrie*, vol. 4, No. 1261, pp. 23–24. There is no support in the MSS for such a correction.

[22] Plutarch, *Crassus* 32, 3.

[23] Tacitus, Source 13.

[24] See McDowell, *op.cit.* (in n. 6), p. 71, no. 89, on coins. On civil strife, see McDowell, *loc.cit.* (in n. 18 above). Furneaux, *The Annals of Tacitus*, vol. 1, p. 645, understands "sua populo vis" as a further reference to the senate of Seleucia: "the senate may have been chosen by popular election." Koestermann, *Cornelius Tacitus, Annalen*, vol. 2, books 4–6, pp. 340–341, implicitly accepts this interpretation: "Die Verfassung war also im Prinzip leidlich ausgewogen. Die Wahl des Senates erfolgte anscheinend durch das Volk, wobei nicht nur der Vermögensstand berücksichtigt wurde, . . ." See also *RE*, *op.cit.*, (in n. 6), cols. 1162–1163. This is almost certainly wrong since the point of Tacitus' story is that the two groups were at odds with each other.

[25] McDowell, *Stamped and Inscribed Objects*. The information concerns the functions of the *bibliophylax* and *chreophylax*, the registration of slaves, *katagraphe* (registration in connection with the levy of sales tax), officials responsible for weights and measures, taxes on the sale of slaves and salt. Additional bullae discovered by the Italian expedition have been published by Invernizzi, *Mesopotamia* 3/4 (1968–1969): 69–124; idem, *Sumer* 32 (1976): 167–175.

[26] McDowell, *ibid.*, pp. 165–173.

[27] McDowell, *op.cit.* (in n. 6), Part I with conclusions in Chapter 3.

The transition from Seleucid to Parthian rule seems not to have been accompanied by very drastic changes at least until the revolt in the first century. As indicated by Tacitus, as long as the Seleucians were united, they had little to fear from the Great King, who had no standing army and no artillery. The Parthians could make incursions but not conquests.[28] Actually the sources indicate that Seleucia was treated with tolerance.[29] In McDowell's view, it was the only Parthian city which had its own coinage. All Parthian tetradrachms were struck there, the drachms elsewhere.[30] That may have been the result of natural economic demand, but it is noteworthy that the motifs employed on the tetradrachms are Hellenistic Greek rather than Oriental in concept.[31]

A gymnasiarch is mentioned in inscriptions dating from 72/1;[32] a *hieromnemon*, an *agonothetes* and a *tamias* appear on an inscription of the third century B.C.[33]

Although the Parthians set their winter residence at Ctesiphon and maintained a garrison there, there is no real evidence that they did much to foster the growth of Ctesiphon as a city, and indeed the greatest expansion of town life east of the Tigris occurred in the Sassanian period (see "Ctesiphon"). A survey west of the Tigris in the area of ancient Akkad shows that the most extensive settlement there took place in Parthian times, and was followed by a substantial contraction.[34] Evidently the decline of Seleucia was a gradual process.

The history of Seleucia as far as it is known has been treated in various easily accessible works against the background of Seleucid and Parthian history.[35] Following is a brief survey of some of the major events. First was the revolt of Seleucia, A.D. 36–42 described by Tacitus and reflected in the coinage.[36]

---

[28] As observed by Syme, *Tacitus*, vol. 1, p. 236.

[29] See the remarks of McDowell, in Hopkins, *Topography*, p. 154, on the events described by Diodorus Siculus XXXIV 19 (the murder of a Parthian official during the campaign of Antiochus VII); Plutarch, *Crassus* 32 (Surena's mock triumph following the defeat of Crassus in 53 B.C.).

[30] McDowell, *op.cit.* (in n. 6), p. 158.

[31] *Ibid.*, p. 163; Mithridates I called himself Philhellenos and from 66 B.C. onwards the Parthian king appears together with the city goddess on Seleucian coins (218–220). Le Rider, *Suse*, pp. 455–457, proposes dates for the coins different from those of McDowell, *ibid.*, pp. 94–111; 183–192. He prefers the Macedonian era of the Seleucids to the Babylonian.

[32] McDowell, *op.cit.* (in n. 25), p. 354f.

[33] *Ibid.*, p. 258; most recently, Hopkins, *Topography*, p. 24.

[34] Adams, *Land Behind Baghdad*, p. 70.

[35] Streck, *RE*, vol. 2A, cols 1171–1184; McDowell, in Hopkins, *Topography*, pp. 149–163; idem., *op.cit.* (in n. 6), pp. 44–60, 201–240.

[36] *Annals*, VI 41–42; XI 8–9; for the coinage see McDowell, *op.cit.* (in n. 6), pp. 141–142; 225–226; cf. *RE*, *op.cit.* (in n. 6), cols. 1178–1181; Debevoise, *A Political History of Parthia*, pp. 157–169; von Gutschmid, *Geschichte Irans und seiner Nachbarländer*,

The revolt took place during a civil war in Parthia, and it has been plausibly suggested that Josephus' story about Anilaeus and Asinaeus from Nəhardəʿa, the later mass immigration of Jews to Seleucia and their subsequent extermination belongs to the period of anarchy before the revolt. It is, however, questionable whether we can gain a clear picture of the events in Seleucia by combining the account of Tacitus and Josephus.

Coinage confirms the description of the general state of affairs as described in our sources. Before the revolt broke out no coinage had been struck in Seleucia for several years. During the years of the revolt, an extensive series of bronze coins was struck, which for the first time in thirty years bore the name of the city. It was "of a very inferior execution and had on the reverse the characteristic Oriental motif of the humped bull."[37] This series was replaced by a regular series in 40/41. Similar autonomous series were struck in 59/60, 60/61 and 69/70.

During the following years the Tigris moved away from Seleucia, and Vologesias was founded (see the entry on "Walašpaṭ"). In 115/116 Trajan occupied Seleucia and Ctesiphon.[38] Following its participation in the general revolt against Rome, Seleucia was captured and burned. A layer of desctruction in the excavated block G6 marks the burning of the city at that time.[39]

No such break marks the burning of the city by Avidius Cassius in 165, mentioned in Latin and Greek sources.[40] Moreover, coins were struck at Seleucia about December 165, and again about November 166 and thereafter, with no apparent decrease in the rate of issue.[41] The archaeological evidence thus shows that the damage inflicted by the Romans was less extensive than the literary sources suggest.

Severus, in 198, again captured Babylon, Seleucia and Ctesiphon.[42] Cassius Dio states that Babylon and Seleucia were both abandoned. (Ctesiphon was

---

pp. 121–125. On the calendar in Seleucia see Simonetta, *Schweizer Münzblätter* 28 (1978): 2–8, who argues for two calendars valid at the same time, the Seleucid on official Parthian coinage, and the Babylonian for local issues of the polis.

[37] McDowell, *ibid.*, pp. 188, 225.

[38] Festus, *Breviarium* 20, Eutropius VII 3; Orosius VII 12, 2; cf. Cassius Dio, LXVIII 17, 3 and 28, 3. A considerable number of Roman coins connected with that campaign (the latest dated 115/6) have been found at Seleucia; cf. McDowell, *ibid.*, pp. 194, 232.

[39] Cassius Dio, Source 18, says Seleucia was captured and burned, but does not specify which Seleucia. Some scholars therefore argued that another Seleucia is meant; cf. *RE*, vol. 2A, col. 1182f. The archaeological evidence has decided this point.

[40] Cassius Dio, Source 19; Ammianus, Source 21; *SHA*, *Life of Verus* 8, 3–4, which, as it so frequently does, adds details not found elsewhere but of questionable reliability. Cf. *RE*, *op.cit.*, cols. 1183–1184 for further references. For the campaign of Avidius Cassius see Debevoise, *op.cit.* (in n. 36), pp. 246–253; for the chronology see Birley, *Marcus Aurelius*, p. 161.

[41] McDowell, *op.cit.* (in n. 6), p. 234.

[42] For the expedition see Debevoise, *op.cit.* (in n. 36), pp. 259–262. For the chronology of the campaign, see Millar, *A Study of Cassius Dio*, p. 143; Hasebroek, *Untersuchungen*

plundered, a vast number of its people slain, and "a hundred thousand" of them taken captive. Severus did not occupy Ctesiphon but left after plundering it.) Babylon and Seleucia were undoubtedly evacuated both because these cities were by that time less important and less populous than Ctesiphon, and because the Parthians hoped to defend the left bank of the Tigris. Archaeological evidence from Seleucia consists of a cache of coins, the latest of which is dated 198/9.[43] The city block excavated by an American expedition was inhabited until at least the end of the Parthian period.[44]

The topography of the city is the subject of recent readily available literature. Italian excavations have confirmed that a branch of the Royal Canal flowed through the city, and have proved the existence of a Sassanian tower at Tall ʿUmar.[45] It must be noted that the references to Seleucia in literature of the Sassanian period really refer to Be Ardəšir. The last author to refer to old Seleucia as a living city is Cassius Dio.[46] Seleucia naturally rarely appears in talmudic literature. It is mentioned in Source 2 as identical with Aššur and in Obermeyer's opinion another Seleucia, presentday Kirkūk, is meant, since the counterpart is Aššur.[47] However, in the same *baraita* Rav Joseph identifies various biblical locations outside of Babylonia with Babylonian places. The identification of sites mentioned in the Bible with places in their own immediate vicinity was a common practice for talmudic sages (see the section on Ctesiphon and Be Ardəšir in Talmudic Sources, and note 45, in "Ctesiphon"). In any case, in Obermeyer's view too, Seleucia (near Ctesiphon) is meant in Source 1, although the Aqra di-Səlequm in the same source refers to the northern Seleucia (now Kirkūk). In Syriac, Seleucia is referred to as Sliq Ḥaravta (see "Be Ardəšir-Koḵe").[48]

D. *The Inhabitants*

The nature of Seleucian society is misunderstood in modern literature because crucial information from Josephus—who all agree is authoritative—is misinterpreted.[49] Josephus says that Seleucia's inhabitants "consisted of many Macedonians, a majority of 'Hellenes' and not a few Syrians holding civic rights."[50] He also says that Seleucian life was "marked by general strife and

---

zur Geschichte des Kaisers Septimius Severus, pp. 119–120. The sources are Cassius Dio, Source 20; *SHA*, *Life of Severus* 16, 1; Herodian III 9, 9–12.

[43] McDowell, *op.cit.* (in n. 6), pp. 91–92, 130, 235.

[44] *Ibid.*, pp. 93–94, 199–200, 235–236.

[45] Invernizzi, *Mesopotamia* 3/4 (1968–1969): 15–16; Gullini, *ibid.*, pp. 39–41.

[46] Cassius Dio, Source 16, writing between 212 and 225.

[47] Obermeyer, p. 141, and others in his wake.

[48] See Hoffmann, *Auszüge*, p. 37f.

[49] *RE*, *op.cit.* (in n. 6), col. 1161f.; McDowell, in Hopkins, *Topography*, p. 151. See also below.

[50] *Antiquities* (Source 12 [XVIII 372]).

discord between 'Hellenes' and Syrians in which the 'Hellenes' have the upper hand."[51] This has been understood as meaning that Seleucia was populated by a majority of Greek settlers, a smaller group of settlers from Macedonia, and somewhat fewer "native elements," i.e. Arameans. The term "Hellenes," however, has another meaning as Josephus uses it. "Hellenes" in Near Eastern cities are Hellenized natives, i.e. Syrians, Arameans or others.[52] Josephus thus means to tell us that in Seleucia there was a substantial group of descendants of the original settlers from Greece and Macedonia, whom he calls "Macedonians."[53] The major part of the population were Hellenized Babylonians (called "Hellenes" by Josephus), but there was also a considerable group of non-Hellenized Babylonians (Josephus' "Syrians") who had their own civic organization. There may have been Jews as well.[54] The strife and discord mentioned by Josephus represent conflicts between the Hellenized majority and a non-Hellenized Aramaic-speaking minority, not between Greeks and Orientals, as is usually thought. In antiquity people cared more about language and culture and less about race than modern historians give them credit for. Political power and economic advantage were shared by members of a group with a common language and way of life. Whatever the differences between "Macedonians" and "Hellenes," the two groups were united against the Babylonians who had not accepted Hellenism. Pliny too refers to the culture of Seleucia, not to the ethnic origins of its population when he calls Seleucia *Macedonum moris* (= city of Macedonian culture), and so does Tacitus in Source 13 when he states that the city "has never lapsed into barbarism and is loyal to its founder Seleucus."

---

[51] *Ibid.* XVIII 3–4.

[52] See Josephus on Caesarea. The non-Jewish inhabitants of that city are sometimes called "Syrians," but more often "Hellenes" (*Antiquities*, XX 183–184 has "Syrians"; *Jewish War* II, 266–268 has "Syrians" once, "Hellenes" twice, and "Hellene" once; *ibid.*, II 284–285 has "Hellenes"). No one ever claimed that Caesarea was inhabited by settlers from Greece. Note also the "Hellene" cities (Ἑλληνίδας) of Gaza, Gadara, Hippos in *Jewish War*, II 97. "Syrians" usually refers either to people living in Syria or to speakers of Aramaic (*Antiquities*, I 144. For Macedonians and "Hellenes" in cities founded by Seleucus I, see n. 54 below.

[53] The term "Macedonians" is ambiguous; cf. Cohen, *The Seleucid Colonies* (*Historia Einzelschriften* No. 30, 1978), pp. 31–32.

[54] Pausanias, Source 15, says that Seleucus I brought in Babylonians upon completion of the city (see n. 11 above). This means that the city, right from the start, was inhabited by Greco-Macedonian settlers as well as Babylonians (i.e. from Babylonia). Josephus says that the Jews were given πολιτεία and equal rights with the "Macedonians and Hellenes" in the cities which Seleucus I founded, but does not mention Seleucia explicitly. He mentions Jews in connection with the city only when they migrated there *en masse* during the troubles in the thirties. Georgius Cedrenus, *Historiarum Compendium*, P 166 D (Bekker, *Corpus Scr. Hist. Byz.*, 34, 292) lists cities founded by Seleucus I including Seleucia and adds that Jews were settled there together with Greeks.

E. *Archaeological Finds*

Archaeological evidence, fully published, has contributed to a better understanding of Seleucian culture. To the third century and first half of the second B.C. belongs a collection of private seals used in wholesale transactions by merchants and bankers.[55] The motifs of the impressions are almost exclusively derived from Greek religion, mythology and legends.[56] Comparable material from Orchoi (bullae) shows a majority of Oriental motifs, while at Nippur both Greek and Oriental motifs are found (see the entries on these towns). The quality of the execution of the seals is rather inferior compared with similar objects from Hellenistic Asia Minor and Greece.[57]

A group of "token sealings" of the first and second centuries A.D. is interesting material for comparison.[58] The group is rather small, however, comprising twenty-four different seals with twenty different motifs. Greek motifs are still the majority, but there is a larger proportion of Oriental motifs than is found in the attached sealings of the Seleucid period.[59]

In the block excavated by the American expedition, in about the middle of the first century the character of the residences changed: "Columns disappear and open rooms or occasionally the liwan of the Parthians replace the columned porches or chief rooms on the side of the court."[60] More evidence is needed before the reason for this change can be suggested. Was it a matter of taste, and hence of culture, or perhaps a cheaper way of building at a time of declining prosperity? In any event, the fact itself that such a change took place at this time may well be significant, even though the excavators emphasize that the evidence derives from one block only.

Another category of finds which has been studied thoroughly are the terracotta and bone figurines.[61] Both Greek and Oriental types of terracotta figurines persist throughout the four levels excavated. There is no gradual or sudden change at any stage from Hellenistic to Oriental types and styles.[62] There are, however, more Greek types than at other Mesopotamian sites (e.g., Nippur and Warka). The execution is slightly better, and the figurines seem

[55] McDowell, *op.cit.* (in n. 25), ch. 8.

[56] See *ibid.*, table on p. 225.

[57] *Ibid.*, p. 229.

[58] McDowell, *ibid.*, pp. 231–250. The function of these sealings is uncertain: "It must be assumed that these objects had not been associated with documents or containers . . . They had no intrinsic or aesthetic value, and they were not durable" (p. 231).

[59] *Ibid.*, p. 232f. The Oriental motifs are mainly representations of animal life (Catalogue, pp. 239–241). While McDowell's presentation of all this material is admirable, his conclusions about the "race" of the owners serve merely to confirm his own prejudices and would be better forgotten (pp. 225–230; 232–233; 265).

[60] Hopkins, *Topography*, p. 6.

[61] van Ingen, *Figurines from Seleucia on the Tigris*; Invernizzi, *Mesopotamia* 3/4 (1968–1969): 227–292; Ahmed, *Annales Archéologiques de la Syrie* 17 (1967): 85ff.

[62] van Ingen, *ibid.*, p. 8.

to show more Greek influences.[63] Greek types often encountered are: Aphrodite unveiling, Heracles resting, Erotes, little boys playing, nude and draped men and women, dwarfs, etc. Oriental types well represented are the goddess of fecundity and love ("mother goddess") and certain figures of children which may depict her son Tammuz. Certain men are thought to be priests. The costumes are varied and cosmopolitan.[64] The bone figurines are all from Parthian levels and include nude female figures ("mother goddess") and squatting boys.

Thus Seleucia was inhabited by a majority of Hellenized citizens, both descendants of settlers and Babylonians. A minority consisted of non-Hellenized Babylonians. There is no firm evidence of the presence of Jews, although it is very likely that some were there. Evidence of material culture shows Hellenistic and Oriental elements side by side and intermingled. The seals are said to have become "more Oriental" in the first and second century than in the Seleucid period, but no such development can be observed in the case of the figurines, which are far greater in number. The architecture changed around the middle of the first century. It is suggested (under "Be Ardəšir-Koke" [q.v.]) that in the same period the bed of the Tigris moved to the east, effecting a decided change for the worse in the position of Seleucia. This was no doubt the reason for the foundation of Vologesias, emporium of Seleucia and Ctesiphon.

The Maḥoza Area

V. Be Ardəšir-Koke (בי ארדשיר (אקרא דכוכי

A. *Sources*

1. ʿEruvin 57b

See Source 1 in "Ctesiphon."

2. Giṭṭin 6a

See Source 2 in "Ctesiphon."

3. Yoma 11a

See Source 1 in "Maḥoza."

4. Stephanus Byzantius, s.v. Χωχή

κώμη πρὸς τῷ Τίγριδι ποταμῷ. Ἀρριανὸς δεκάτῳ "καὶ βασιλεὺς δ' ἐξελαύνει ἐκ Σελευκείας οὐ πρόσω τοῦ Τίγριδος ἐς κώμην ᾗ τινι Χωχὴ ὄνομα."

---

[63] *Ibid.*, pp. 18, 47.

[64] *Ibid.*, p. 34.

A village near the Tigris. Arrian in the tenth book (i.e. of his *Parthica*): and the emperor (Trajan) marched from Seleucia not far from the river Tigris to a village named Choche.

5. Ammianus XXIV 5,3

quo loco pingui satis et cultu, qui . . . bus Coche (quam Seleuciam nominant) haud longius disparatur . . .
(text uncertain)

Not far from this place, which is fertile and cultivated, is Coche, which they call Seleucia. (text uncertain) (trans.: R. C. Rolfe, LCL)

6. Ammianus XXIV 6,1–3

Ventum est hinc ad fossile flumen, Naarmalcha nomine (quod amnis regum interpretatur), tunc aridum. id antehac Traianus, posteaque, Seuerus egesto solo fodiri in modum canalis amplissimi, studio curauerat summo, ut aquis illuc ab Eufrate transfusis, naues ad Tigridem conmigrarent. tutissimumque ad omnia uisum est, eadem loca purgari, quae quondam similia Persae timentes, mole saxorum obruere multorum. hacque ualle purgata, auulsis cataractis undarum magnitudine classis secura, stadiis triginta decursis, in alueum eiecta est Tigridis, et contextis ilico pontibus, transgressus exercitus iter Cochen uersus promouit. utque lassitudini succederet quies oportuna, in agro consedimus opulento, arbustis et uitibus et cupressorum uiriditate laetissimo, cuius in medio diuersorium opacum est et amoenum, gentiles picturas per omnes aedium partes ostendens, regis bestias uenatione multiplici trucidantis; nec enim apud eos pingitur uel fingitur aliud, praeter uarias caedes et bella.

Then we came to an artificial river, by name Naarmalcha, meaning "the king's river," which at that time was dried up. Here in days gone by Trajan, and after him Severus, had with immense effort caused the accumulated earth to be dug out, and had made a great canal, in order to let in the water from the Euphrates and give boats and ships access to the Tigris. It seemed to Julian in all respects safest to clean out that same canal, which formerly the Persians, when in fear of a similar invasion, had blocked with a huge dam of stones. As soon as the canal was cleared, the dams were swept away by the great flow of water, and the fleet in safety covered a distance of thirty stadia and came into the channel of the Tigris. Thereupon bridges were at once made, and the army crossed and pushed on towards Coche. Then, so that a timely rest might follow the wearisome toil, we encamped in a rich territory, abounding in orchards, vineyards, and green cypress groves. In its midst was a pleasant and shady dwelling, displaying in every part of the house, after the custom of the nation, paintings representing the king killing wild beasts in various ways; for nothing in their country is painted or sculptured except slaughter in divers forms and scenes of war. (trans.: J. C. Rolfe, LCL)

7. Libanius, *Oration* XVIII 245, 247

... λαβὼν γὰρ αἰχμαλώτους τῶν αὐτοῦ που πλησίον οἰκούντων ἐζήτει διώρυχα ναυσίπορον καὶ ταύτην ἐκ βίβλων, ἔργον μὲν παλαιοῦ βασιλέως, ἄγουσαν δὲ τὸν Εὐφράτην ἐπὶ τὸν Τίγρητα ταῖν δυοῖν ἀνωτέρω πόλεων ... νεύσαντος δὲ τοῦ κρατοῦντος ἅπαν τὸ κώλυμα ἐξῄρητο καὶ τοῖν ῥείθροιν τὸ μὲν ξηρὸν ἑωρᾶτο, τὸ δὲ ἦγεν ἐπὶ τὸν Τίγρητα πλοῖα παραπλέοντα τῷ στρατῷ, καὶ τοῖς ἐν ταῖς πόλεσι μείζων ἐπελθὼν ὁ Τίγρης ἅτε προσλαβὼν τὸν Εὐφράτην φόβον ἐπήνεγκε μέγαν ὡς οὐ φεισόμενος τῶν τειχῶν.

... Having taken some captives from the inhabitants of the surrounding area, Julian began to enquire about a navigable channel, his information here also derived from his books. This, the work of a king of days gone by, led from the Euphrates to the Tigris upstream of the cities ... The old fellow, then, told where it was situated and revealed that the channel had been closed and that the blockage at its mouth was under cultivation. At the emperor's command the whole obstruction was removed, and of the channels the old one was seen to dry up, while this other conveyed the boats parallel with the army to the Tigris. The Tigris, descending with greater volume upon the inhabitants of the cities since it had also been swollen by the water of the Euphrates, caused great panic among them, for it seemed that it would not spare their walls. (trans.: A. F. Norman, LCL)

8. Gregory of Nazianzus, *Oration* V 10 (Migne, *Patrologia Graeca*, vol. 35, col. 676 BC)

Ἡ γὰρ Κτησιφῶν φρούριόν ἐστι καρτερὸν καὶ δυσάλωτον, τείχει τε (65) ὀπτῆς πλίνθου, καὶ τάφρῳ βαθείᾳ, καὶ τοῖς ἐκ τοῦ ποταμοῦ τενάγεσιν ὠχυρωμένη. Ποιεῖ δὲ αὐτὴν ὀχυροτέραν (66) καὶ φρούριον ἕτερον, ᾧ προσηγορία (67) Κωχὴ, μετὰ τῆς ἴσης ἀσφαλείας συγκείμενον ὅση τε φυσικὴ καὶ ὅση χειροποίητος, τοσοῦτον ἑνούμενον, ὡς (68) μίαν πόλιν δοκεῖν ἀμφοτέρας, τῷ ποταμῷ μέσῳ διειργομένας ταύτας·

Ctesiphon is a strong fortress and hard to be taken with walls made of baked bricks and a deep moat, deriving additional strength from a marsh which is fed by the river. Another fortress named Koke makes Ctesiphon even stronger. Its security is the work both of nature and of man and the two are united in such a manner that they look a single town, being separated only by the river.

9. Procopius, *The Persian War* II 28, 4

... οἱ δὲ αὐτὸν καταλαμβάνουσιν ἐν Ἀσσυρίοις, οὗ δὴ πολίσματα δύο Σελεύκειά τε καὶ Κτησιφῶν ἐστι, Μακεδόνων αὐτὰ δειμαμένων, οἳ μετὰ τὸν Φιλίππου Ἀλέξανδρον Περσῶν τε ἦρξαν καὶ τῶν ταύτῃ ἐθνῶν. ἄμφω δὲ ταῦτα Τίγρης ποταμὸς διορίζει· οὐ γὰρ ἄλλην χώραν μεταξὺ ἔχουσιν.

... Seleucia and Ctesiphon, built by the Macedonians who after Alexander, the son of Philip, ruled over the Persians and the other nations there. These two towns are separated by the Tigris river only, for they have nothing between them. (trans.: H. B. Dewing, LCL)

10. Theophanes, *Chronography* 323

καὶ οὐδὲ ἐν ταύτῃ ἐθάρρησε στῆναι, ἀλλὰ περάσας τὴν ποντογέφυραν τοῦ Τίγριδος ποταμοῦ εἰς τὴν ἐκεῖθεν πόλιν, τὴν λεγομένην Σελεύκειαν παρ' ἡμῖν, παρὰ δὲ Πέρσαις Γουεδεσήρ...[1]

Even there he did not dare to stay, but he crossed over the pontoon bridge to the city there, called Seleucia by us and Gouedesir by the Persians...[1]

B. *Location*

On the west bank of the Tigris, across from Ctesiphon, some 25 kilometers southeast of Baghdad (on the Maḥoza Area plan).

C. *History*

Koḵe, the site of which is discussed below, was refounded around 230 by Ardashīr as Vēh-Ardašīr, "the good city of Ardashīr,"[2] but as the name Koḵe is still used in many later sources, the two settlements can be discussed together.

Koḵe is first mentioned in classical literature by Arrian in connection with Trajan's Parthian campaign.[3] That passage makes it clear that at that time Koḵe was a village near the Tigris that could be reached from Seleucia without crossing any river. In the reign of Ardashīr, as noted, Vēh-Ardašīr (= Be Ardəšir, in the Talmud and in Syriac sources) was founded on the site.[4]

[1] Khusro II then fled to Ctesiphon pursued by Heraclius who approached from Dastagerd.

[2] For the name see Christensen, *L'Iran*, p. 387–388.

[3] Arrian, *Parthica*, X, quoted by Stephanus Byzantius. Pliny, *Natural History* VI 31, 129, "campos cauchas," could be the earliest reference to Koḵe, but this is uncertain. Cf. Herzfeld, *Samarra*, p. 56f.

[4] Information on the foundation of Be Ardəšir is provided in Ṭabarī (vol. 2, p. 41 [= vol. 1, pp. 819–820] and see also Markwart, *Catalogue* § 52 with commentary on pp. 102–103; Nöldeke, *Perser und Araber*, pp. 15–16, and see also the section on "Yehudai Romai" above). Ṭabarī distinguishes between the city with its Persian name Bih Ardašīr, and the district it was in. The district was in the Ardašīr Bābakān region which was subordinated to the city when the latter was established. The district is referred to only by its Arabized name, Bahurasīr, and bore that name for many years after the name of the city had been forgotten. (See Ṭabarī, vol. 2, p. 215 [= vol. 1, p. 1041]; Streck, *Die alte Landschaft*, vol. 1, pp. 16, 19; vol. 2, p. 264; Morony, *Iran* 14 (1976): 43 [on the Sassanian period]; and see Ibn Ḥazm, *Ansāb*, p. 325, [who refers to the governor of Bahurasīr appointed by ʿAlī b. Abī Ṭālib]; Ṭabarī, vol. 5, pp. 203–204 [= vol. 2, p. 57]; Nöldeke [*ibid.*, p. 16, n. 3] has the Arabized name as Behrasīr, and see Streck, *op. cit.*, vol. 2, p. 262, n. 5; idem, *EI*[1], s. v. "Madā'in," p. 75; however, Yāqūt, s. v. "Bahurasīr," specifies that vocalization, and cf. Ḥamza, *Ta'rīḫ*, p. 46; Herzfeld, *Der Islam* 11 [1921]: 148).

Several sources mention that the Emperor Carus, in 283 took "Koḵe and Ctesiphon, most noble cities."[5] In these sources, therefore, Koḵe rather than Seleucia appears on the west bank as counterpart of Ctesiphon on the east bank. In 363 Julian's army operated in the area. Ammianus twice mentions Koḵe. The first passage is corrupt, but it is clear that Ammianus identifies Koḵe with Seleucia (q.v.).[6] Near Koḵe Julian visited a deserted city destroyed by an emperor whose name has been restored as Carus. The deserted city certainly was old Seleucia (with which Ammianus identifies Koḵe).[7] Following the Royal Canal, the army arrived at a branch of it which was dried up. According to Zosimus and Ammianus, it was a very large canal said to have been dug by Trajan and Severus at the time of their Parthian expeditions.[8] Julian ordered the clearing of "Trajan's canal" which the Persians had blocked, the army crossed it and pushed on toward Koḵe,[9] "formerly Zochase, now called Seleucia,"[10] where it encamped. Next Julian crossed back to the other side, fought a battle near Ctesiphon (q.v.) and decided not to besiege that city. In connection with the same event, Gregory of Nazianzus too, describes Koḵe and Ctesiphon as twin fortified towns on opposite banks of the river.[11] The sources are thus very consistent in their descriptions of Koḵe as a fortified town across from Ctesiphon and north of the Royal Canal.

While the site of Seleucia was established without doubt by an American expedition of 1930–1932 through inscriptions found *in situ*, no such evidence exists for the other settlements in the area. The German expedition to Ctesiphon discovered that in antiquity the Tigris followed a course west of the modern bed, past the old city of Seleucia. East of that old river bed lies a round

---

[5] Festus, *Breviarium*, 24: *"Cochen et Ctesiphontem urbes Persarum nobilissimas cepit."* Eutropius, *Breviarium*, 9, 18, 1; Orosius 7, 24, 4; Jerome, *Annals*, 284; cf. Eadie, *The Breviarium of Festus*, p. 94f. Zonaras 12, 30 III, p. 156 (Dindorf ed., p. 14), however, says that Carus took Seleucia and Ctesiphon. These Latin sources derive from a common source (probably Enmann's *Kaisergeschichte*) from the period of Constantine and are generally considered reliable, cf. Eadie, *loc.cit.* Zonaras derives from a Greek source.

[6] Source 5. Gullini, *Mesopotamia* 1 (1966): 30, understands this passage as indicating that Koḵe was on the east bank of the Tigris. Ammianus says no such thing.

[7] There is no good reason to think of Meinas Sabatha (Zosimus III 23, 4; see the entry on "Sabata") as argued by Brok, *De Perzische Expeditie van Keizer Julianus volgens Ammianus Marcellinus*, p. 146. The town existed throughout antiquity and Seleucia by 363 was obviously the major deserted site in the region.

[8] Ammianus, Source 6; Zosimus III 24, 2, but cf. Cassius Dio LXVIII 28.

[9] Source 6.

[10] Described by Zosimus as being 30 stadia (about 5.5 kilometers) from Meinas Sabatha. Ammianus (Source 6) gives the length of Trajan's canal as 30 stadia. We may therefore assume that both refer to the same points, i.e., Trajan's canal ran from Meinas Sabatha ("Sabata") to Koḵe. This is an important confirmation of the reliability of these two sources.

[11] Source 8; cf. Libanius, *Oration* XVIII 245 (Förster, vol. 2, p. 343).

city thought to be Ctesiphon.[12] (Although this did not help identify Be Ardəšir-Koḵe, it kept Seleucia and Ctesiphon on opposite banks of the river as required by our sources.) The present river bed runs through the round city.

Be Ardəšīr-Koḵe was assumed to have lain in part of the old town of Seleucia. The discoveries made by the Italian expedition which started excavating in 1964, however, proved this reconstruction to be impossible. Soundings in the round city demonstrated that it was a Sassanian town founded in the reign of Ardashīr, around 230 (which Herzfeld had concluded on the basis of surface finds at Tall Baruda[13]), and was thus Be Ardəšir-Koḵe.

Consequently Ctesiphon had to be sought elsewhere. The ruins further north, also intersected by the present river bed, were suggested. This raised problems regarding the interpretation of the literary sources, for the Tigris was thought not to have moved to its present course until the fifth century. Gullini attempted to show that Koḵe was on the east bank of the Tigris, but that is clearly impossible.

Herzfeld had proposed a solution long before the recent discoveries. The description of Julian's campaign in literary sources shows that in 363 the Royal Canal no longer joined the Tigris near Seleucia. Following the Royal Canal, Julian's army arrived at a branch of it which was dried up at the time, and a link with the Tigris was provided by a canal said to have been dug by Trajan. Herzfeld suggested that this canal followed the old Tigris bed which was dried up when the river moved eastwards.[14] However, descriptions by Ammianus and Libanius of the movements of Julian's fleet clearly indicate that Trajan's canal joined the Tigris north of Koḵe and Ctesiphon. If Trajan's canal did indeed exist at the time of Trajan's campaign, then obviously by the early second century the Tigris had already moved away from Seleucia to the later

---

[12] See Bachmann's map in Reuther, *Die Ausgrabungen 1928–1929*. The course of the Tigris as indicated there has been accepted by all subsequent publications; e.g., Hopkins, *Topography*, Pl. 1.

[13] Gullini, *op.cit.* in n. 6, pp. 7–38. For preliminary reports on the excavations in this and subsequent seasons, see the current volumes of *Mesopotamia*. Note the coin hoards which Schinaja published in *Mesopotamia* 2 (1967): 105–133 and Göbl in 8/8 (1973–1974): 229–258. On surface finds at Tall Baruda see Sarre & Herzfeld, *Archäologische Reise*, vol. 2, p. 52.

[14] For the Royal Canal, see Herzfeld, *Samarra*, pp. 7–16, and for "Trajan's canal," *ibid.* p. 9. The Arabic sources are discussed, with full references by Streck, *Die alte Landschaft*, vol. 1, pp. 27–30; idem, *RE*, suppl. 4, s.v. "Ktesiphon," cols. 113–115, and by Musil, *The Middle Euphrates*, pp. 272–274. Totally wrong are Paschoud, *Syria* 55 (1978): 345–359; id., *Zosime*, *Histoire nouvelle*, vol. 2A, n. 68, pp. 167–173 and Appendix B, pp. 246–250. These studies were written in ignorance of the cuneiform and Arabic sources, of research on them, and of recent archaeological exploration. For the probable course of Trajan's canal, see below. For the confused treatment by Dillemann, *Syria* 38 (1961): 153, see the entry on "Walašpaṭ" (n. 8). Dillemann too ignores the consensus of all good sources, preferring instead the distortions of Ptolemy.

bed. Fiey reached the same conclusion independently, and found support for it in an aerial photograph exhibited in the Sassanian gallery, Hall 17, of the new Iraqi Museum in Baghdad, but apparently unpublished. In Fiey's opinion, the river originally circled the ruins north of the round city, flowing along the west side of the site which Gullini and Fiey think is Ctesiphon. The German map shows a dike encircling an area marked "Busch" ("jungle" in the English version). It then moved to its present bed in two stages:

a. "(It) came down round the eastern wall of Veh Ardashir, where a short stretch of its dry bed can still be seen on the photographs, North West of Salman Pak. It then joined the present course of the river south of the Round City."[15]

b. Later it moved its bed eastwards through the ruins now thought to be Ctesiphon and westwards through the round city.

So far there is no solid evidence for the identification of any ancient site with Ctesiphon. However, Source 1 in the entry on "Ctesiphon" may give an indication. There a wall is mentioned, swallowed by the Tigris, which linked Maḥoza with Ctesiphon. This can best be explained by assuming that by that time the Tigris had moved to its present course through the "round city." If this is true, then the eastern part of Koḵe became part of Ctesiphon because of its new position on the left bank of the river. On the right bank Gullini saw signs of ancient repairs, where the north wall of Koḵe was swept away by the Tigris.[16] Source 1 (under "Ctesiphon") and this observation combined may well confirm that Ctesiphon was east of Koḵe rather than northeast, as thought by Gullini and Fiey.

The site of Seleucia was initially at the confluence of the Royal Canal and the Tigris. When the course of the Tigris first moved, Seleucia was cut off from the river. As Herzfeld and Fiey suggested, this rather than the alleged destruction by Avidius Cassius in 165 was the cause of Seleucia's decline,[17] for the city was now situated only on the Royal Canal, not the Tigris, and another branch of the Canal further south bypassed it (as the aerial photograph confirms). Exactly when the first change occurred is not clear. It was certainly before 116, as the existence of "Trajan's canal" indicates. Moreover, Arrian sets Koḵe on the west bank, which gives us a *terminus ante*. Do we have a *terminus post quem*? Strabo seems to be describing the original situation, and Tacitus,

---

[15] Fiey, *Sumer* 23 (1967): 3–38, with two plans.

[16] Gullini, *Mesopotamia* 1 (1966): 27f.

[17] Herzfeld, *Samarra*, p. 9; Fiey, *ibid.*, p. 5. Pliny says that Vologesocerta was founded to draw away the population of Seleucia; although classical sources were wont to attribute the foundation of cities to a ruler's eagerness to ruin existing towns (Babylon-Seleucia, Seleucia-Ctesiphon) a better insight into the history of these cities usually shows that there were other factors at work.

Josephus and Pliny are of no help.[18] Although the Seleucia port became useless when the Tigris moved away, trading went on, and a new port was constructed, the emporium called Vologesias (see "Walašpaṭ") after Vologaeses I (51–80).[19] It is very likely that the southern branch of the Royal Canal was dug at the time Vologesias was founded.[20]

The American and Italian excavations at Seleucia have shown that it was inhabited until the Sassanian period, so that presumably the city suffered a gradual decline rather than sudden ruin at the hands of Roman armies (although it is natural for classical sources to attribute the misfortune of such a city to the action of Romans rather than to geographical developments unknown or misunderstood).

Vologesias replaced Seleucia as a port, but the latter was inhabited until about 230. The suburb of Ko̱ke had been developing since the first century A.D., but the foundation on its site of Be Ardəšir meant the official transfer of the urban center to a place near the Tigris.[21] The town's official name was now Vēh Ardašīr, but it was still called Ko̱ke (its former name), or Seleucia (out of a

[18] Strabo XVI 1, 5 (738); 1, 16 (743); 2, 5 (750); Tacitus, *Annals* VI 36ff.; Josephus, *Antiquities*, XVIII 373. Pliny VI 30, 122 says that Seleucia "was founded at the point where the canalised Euphrates joins the Tigris." This tells us nothing about the first century A.D., contrary to the suggestion made by Fiey, (*op.cit.* in n. 15), p. 5.

[19] For the dates of Vologaeses I see McDowell, *Coins from Seleucia*, pp. 227–230.

[20] As pointed out by Adams, *Land Behind Baghdad*, p. 77, the construction of canals was conceived as an integral part of the foundation of cities in Sassanian times. Here we have a parallel case in the Parthian period.

[21] Bihardašīr figures in Ṭabarī, vol. 2, p. 59 (= vol. 1, p. 842) in connection with Julian's expedition. Ṭabarī, vol. 2, p. 72 (= vol. 1, p. 858) mentions "Ṭaisabūn (= Ctesiphon) and Bihardašīr, the two royal cities" (*madīnatai l-malik*); cf. Fiey, *Sumer* 23 (1967): 16. Ṭabarī, vol. 2, p. 86 (= vol. 1, p. 878) mentions Madīnat Ṭaisabūn and Madīnat Bahurasīr and says "both were residences of the kings (*wa-kānatā maḥallatā l-mulūk*)." In manuscript versions the name is given as Bih.r.dāšīr. The garble Nahr Sīr of Nahr Šīr is common for the city, and see Streck, *Die alte Landschaft*, vol. 2, p. 262, n. 5; Fiey, *ibid.*, p. 16, n. 107. Cf. perhaps *Ġāyatu l-iḫtiṣār*, p. 151, who refers to an estate in Madā'in called al-Bandašīr. The form Madīnat Bahurasīr appears also e.g. in Ṭabarī, vol. 6, p. 260 (= vol. 2, p. 946); *Ansāb al-ašrāf*, vol. 4a, p. 144. Once Ṭabarī mentions Madīnat Bahurasīr with the addition of "the nearest" (*ad-dunyā*). Cf. on this Ṭabarī, vol. 4, p. 8 (= vol. 1, pp. 2431–2432); *ar-Rauḍ al-mi'ṭār*, s.v. "Madā'in," p. 528; Bahurasīr is *al-madīna d-dunyā*, while the city or cities on the east bank of the Tigris is/are "the further" (*al-madīna/al-madā'in al-quṣwā*). In the location accepted today, Ctesiphon was north of Be Ardəšir. The adjectives cited thus refer to the direction of the Muslim advance or relate to the place the Muslims came from in the Arabian peninsula. See already al-'Alī, *Sumer* 23 (1967): 60, and cf. Fiey, *ibid.*, p. 6. On the conquest of Be Ardəšir by the Muslims, see Macler, *Histoire d'Heraclius par l'évèque Sebeos traduite de l'Arménien et annotée*, p. 2, which states that "all the cities of Syrian Mesopotamia, Tizbon, Veh Artašir, Marand, Hamatan, as far as the city of Gindzak and the great city of Hrat" were occupied by the Muslims.

sense of continuity), or Maḥoza (q.v.).[22] Contrary to what has been suggested in the past, it is doubtful whether much of the old Seleucia remained inhabited after 230, but this is a matter to be decided by archaeological exploration. So far only a tower of Sassanian date has been found (at Tall ʿUmar),[23] possibly the Sassanian site of execution mentioned frequently in our sources.[24]

Far less is known about Be Ardəšir than about its predecessor, Seleucia. Adams has observed that in the Sassanian period the main emphasis of urban development and settlement was on the east bank.[25] The new town certainly lacked the advantage which Seleucia had enjoyed of being located at the confluence of the Royal Canal and the Tigris, even though we know that the authority of the bureau of the *magi* at Be Ardəšir extended as far as Vologesias on the Royal Canal.[26]

Apart from what is said above, classical sources are not informative about Be Ardəšir. They never use the official Persian name, but always Koke or Seleucia. Maḥoza, common in the Talmud and in Syriac (see "Opis"), had a long tradition.[27] Ammianus must have heard the name, for Maiozamalcha is undoubtedly *maḥōzā malkā* "the royal capital."[28] This is confirmed by Malalas who mentions the χώρα Μαυζανιτῶν which obviously also refers to Maḥoza (q.v.).[29]

---

[22] See e.g. Procopius, Source 9: "Seleucia and Ctesiphon"; Theophanes, Source 10: "called Seleucia by us and Gouedesir by the Persians."

[23] Invernizzi, *Mesopotamia* 5/5 (1970–1971): 18–19.

[24] Ammianus, Source 5; for Christians executed there see the references in Fiey, *Sumer* 23 (1967): 9. In the story of Narsai both Seleucia (Koke) and Ctesiphon appear as living cities, while Sliq Ḥaravta is mentioned as the site of executions (Hoffman, *Auszüge*, p. 37f.).

[25] See the section on History under "Ctesiphon."

[26] This appears from the seals published by Maricq, *Syria* 36 (1959): 267f. = *Classica et Orientalia*, p. 116f. (see Source 7 in the entry on "Walašpaṭ").

[27] For Maḥoza in Syriac, see Streck, *Die alte Landschaft*, vol. 2, p. 275; Hoffmann, *Auszüge*, pp. 83. Fiey, *Sumer* 23 (1967): n. 127.

[28] Ammianus XXIV 4,2. Herzfeld, *Samarra*, pp. 14f., 25, notes that Maiozamalcha is mentioned where Sippar must be meant. Ammianus has transferred Maiozamalcha to the other end of the Royal Canal (see the entry on "Maḥoza"). Here Zosimus mentions Βησοῦχις—Pliny (V 21,90) Massicen near Sippar, deriving from *māsōkhā* (= weir). Herzfeld suggests that Ammianus may have confused "*mahoza malkha*" with "*māsōkhā de (nehar) malkhā.*"

[29] Malalas, *Chronography* (Dindorf ed., p. 330), based on Magnus of Carrhae. Herzfeld, *Samarra*, p. 63, suggests that Zosimus, III 26,1 Ἀβουζαθα = Βαουζα(θα) = Maḥoza. Note as a matter of curiosity, Hoffmann, *Auszüge*, p. 23 (Mar Sabha): "zu der Zeit da Julianos in Māḥōzē, der Stadt des Königs Šābhōr residierte und sich dort einige Tage lang an den Festen seiner Götter mästete, erhielt Jobinian auf seinen Vortrag und Besuch von ihm die Erlaubnis diese Länder zu colonisieren. Und es sandte Jobinianos Menschen nach diesen Provinzen von Arabh, von Arzōn und von Bet Zabdai. Und es stiegen herauf diese Menschen von Māḥōzē und wurden Bewohner dieser Provinz."

Papa, the first recorded bishop of Seleucia-Ctesiphon, was ordained at the end of the third century.[30] At the council of Seleucia in 410, the primacy of the bishop of Seleucia-Ctesiphon was established.[31] The see of the Catholicos was based at the great church of Koḵe. The sources call it "the elevated See of the church of Kokhe in the territory of Seleucia," the "church of the throne at al-Madā'in" or the "great church of Kokhe, which is in the cities of Seleucia and Ctesiphon."[32] The Catholicoi or Grand Metropolitans were ordained in that church, and many of them were buried there. The German expedition partially excavated a church at Qaṣr bint al-qāḍī, in the round city,[33] but there are no indications so far that this was the great church. An important theological seminary was established at Koḵe in the fifth century, the "School of Seleucia."[34] A fort is mentioned in the Acts of Gīwargīs. Bishop Georgios of Īzalā (Ṭūr ʿAbdīn) was accused of deserting the Mazdaean religion in the reign of Khusro Parwez and Shīrīn. He was sent "to Maḥoza and kept prisoner in a castle named Aqra də-Koḵe."[35] After his execution on the hay market, he was buried in the church of St. Sergios in nearby Mavraḵta (q.v.).[36]

Be Ardəšir was apparently taken by Carus in 283 (see above). Julian's army passed by but did not take it. In 591 Byzantine troops entered all parts of the capital to restore Khusro Parwez to the throne.[37] Apart from the usurper himself, the Jews more than any other group were held responsible for the revolt, and many of them were punished, to the satisfaction of our source, Theophylactus Simocatta.[38] Archaeological evidence of the presence of Jews in the town—five incantation bowls of the kind found previously at Nippur and Babylon—has recently been published.[39] On Jews in Be Ardəšir see the section

---

[30] Labourt, *Le Christianisme*, p. 20. Christian tradition held that there were Christians at Koḵe in the late first century; see references in Fiey, *Sumer* 23 (1967): 16f., and discussion in Labourt, Chapter 1.

[31] Labourt, *ibid.*, p. 98. A century before, Papa had attempted to unite Persian Christianity under the hegemony of the bishop of Seleucia-Ctesiphon; see Labourt, Chapter 2.

[32] Labourt, *ibid.*, passim; Fiey, *Sumer* 23 (1967): 17, with references in nn. 121–126; Hoffmann, *Auszüge*, p. 114; Sachau, *APAW phil.-hist. Klasse*, 1 (1919), pp. 26–28.

[33] Reuther, *Die Ausgrabungen 1928–1929*, p. 11ff., plan 1, pl. 5; idem, *Antiquity* 3 (1929): 449–451; Fiey, *op.cit.*, p. 18.

[34] Fiey, *op.cit.*, p. 19f.

[35] Cf. Source 1 in "Maḥoza" and the section on Physical Features there. On the Sassanian prisons in Be Ardəšir, see Ṭabarī, vol. 2, p. 217 (= vol. 1, p. 1043).

[36] Hoffmann *Auszüge*, p. 110; Nöldeke, *SAWW phil.-hist. Klasse* 128,9 (1893), p. 21f.

[37] Theophylactus Simocatta V 6, 7–7, 3. The palace and garden of Parwez which are mentioned in Ṭabarī do not appear to have been in Be Ardəšir; on his hiding from his son Šīrūyah, see Ṭabarī, *ibid.*; Ṯaʿālibī, *Ġurar*, p. 716; cf. al-ʿAlī, *Sumer* 23 (1967): 61; Nöldeke, *Perser und Araber*, p. 357 n. 2, p. 362 n. 1; Christensen, *L'Iran*, p. 494.

[38] V 7, 5–10. The author explains that great numbers of Jews fled to Persia after the destruction of the Second Temple, taking their riches with them across the Red Sea.

[39] Franco, *Mesopotamia* 13/14 (1978–1979): 233–249. They are said to date to the end of the sixth or the beginning of the seventh century.

THE MAḤOZA AREA

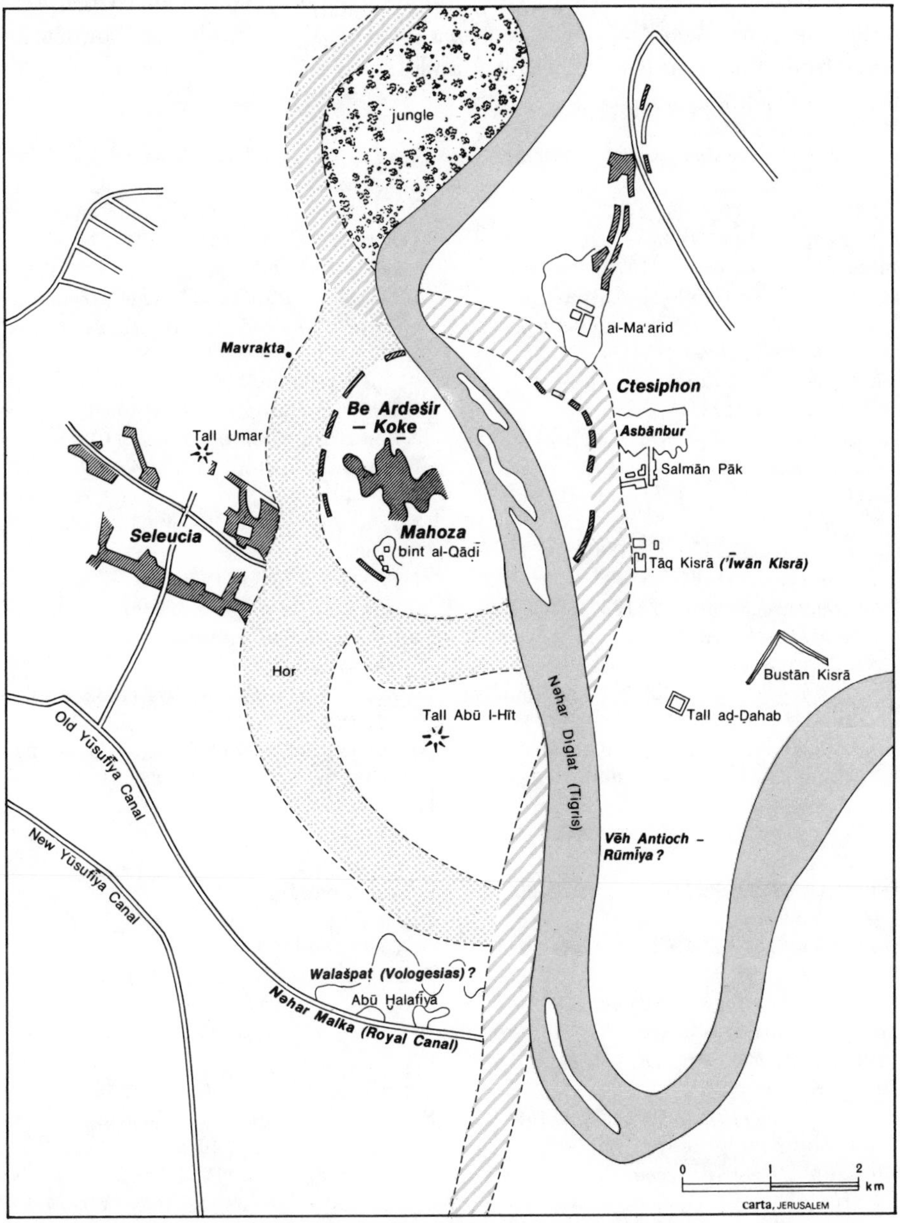

Old river bed till mid-first century

Later river bed till third–fourth century

Current river bed

Mavrakta Ancient place name

Salmān Pāk Modern place name

on Ctesiphon and Be Ardəšir in Talmudic Sources in the entry on "Ctesiphon" under "Maḥoza Area" and the sections on The Inhabitants, on Connections with Other Places and on The Jews and Insurrections in the entry on "Maḥoza" under "Maḥoza Area."

ADAMS, *Land Behind Baghdad* (1965), passim

AL-ʿALĪ, *Sumer* 23 (1967): 47–67

BARNETT, *JHS* 83 (1963): 1–26

BEER, *Rashut ha-Golah* (1970), passim

BEER, *Amora'ei Bavel* (1947), passim

BERLINER, *Beiträge* (1883), relevant entries

CHRISTENSEN, *L'Iran* (1944²), pp. 383–393

DEBEVOISE, *Parthian Pottery from Seleucia on the Tigris* (1934)

DEBEVOISE, *The Political History of Parthia* (1938), passim

ESHEL, *Yishuvei ha-Yehudim* (1979), relevant entries

FEUCHTWANG, *MGWJ* 42 (1898): 153

FIEY, *Sumer* 23 (1967): 3–38

FIEY, *L'Orient Syrien* 12 (1967): 397–420

FUNK, *Juden* (1902–1908), vol. 1, p. 103; vol. 2, pp. 3, 20

FUNK, *Monumenta* (1913), relevant entries

GULLINI, *Mesopotamia* 1 (1966): 7–38

GRAETZ, *MGWJ* 2 (1853): 193, 196–197

GRAETZ, *Geschichte* (1908–1909⁴), vols. 4 & 5, passim

HALEVY, *Dorot ha-Rishonim* (1897–1939), vol. 5, passim

HERZFELD, *Samarra* (1948), pp. 22–25, 29–34 and passim

HERZFELD, *The Persian Empire* (1968), pp. 35–38; 197–199

HIRSCHENSON, *Sheva Ḥokhmot* (1883), relevant entries

HONIGMANN, *RE* Suppl. 4, col. 1109–1119, s.v. "Ktesiphon"

HOPKINS, *Topography* (1972), pp. 149–163 and bibliography on pp. viii–x

VAN INGEN, *Figurines from Seleucia on the Tigris* (1939)

JASTROW, *Dictionary* (1950³), relevant entries

KOHUT, *Arukh ha-Shalem* (1878–1892), relevant entries; *Tosefot* (1937), pp. 66, 85, 295

KRAUSS, *Qadmoniot ha-Talmud* (1923–1945), vol. 1A, pp. 36, 50, 75, 159, 202

KÜHNEL, *Die Ausgrabungen 1931/2* (1933)

KURTZ, *JRAS* (1941): 37–41

LACOSTE, *Sumer* 10 (1954): 3–22

LEVY, *Wörterbuch* (1924²), relevant entries

MARICQ, *Syria* 36 (1959): 264–276 = *Classica et Orientalia* (1965), pp. 113–126

McDOWELL, *Papers Michigan Academy of Science, Arts & Letters* 18 (1932): 101–119

McDOWELL, *Coins from Seleucia on the Tigris* (1935)

McDOWELL, *Stamped and Inscribed Objects from Seleucia on the Tigris* (1935)

McDOWELL, in Hopkin, *Topography* (1972), pp. 149–163

MEIER, *RE* vol. 18, cols. 683–685, s.v. "Opis"

Mesopotamia (from 1966 on)

NEUBAUER, *Géographie* (1868), passim

NEUSNER, *History* (1965–1970), vols. 1–5, passim

NEWMAN, *Agricultural Life* (1932), pp. 80, 111, 123, 185, 192

NÖLDEKE, *SAWW phil. hist. Klasse* 128, 9 (1893), pp. 7–8, 16, 21, 28, 31–33, 40–41

OBERMEYER, *Landschaft* (1929), pp. 165–186 and passim

POPE (ed.), *A Survey of Persian Art* (1938), vol. 2, passim

PUTRICH-REIGNARD, *Die Glasfunde von Ktesiphon* (1939)

RAPOPORT, *Erekh Millin* (1914), vol. 2, pp. 4, 9, 11, 241–242

REUTHER, *Die Ausgrabungen 1928/9* (1930), passim

REUTHER, *Antiquity* 3 (1929): 434–452

SARRE & HERZFELD, *Archäologische Reise* (1920), vol. 2, pp. 46–93

SCHMIDT, *Syria* 15 (1934): 1–23

SMALLWOOD, *The Jews Under Roman Rule* (1975), pp. 415, 418, 420

STERN, *Greek and Latin Authors* (1980), vol. 2, pp. 609–611

STRECK, *EI*¹, s.v. "Madā'in"

STRECK, *RE*, vol. 2A, cols. 1149–1183, s.v. "Seleukeia (am Tigris)"

STRECK, *RE*, Suppl. 4, cols. 1102–1109, s.v. "Ktesiphon"

Streck, *Die alte Landschaft* (1901), vol. 2, pp. 246–279
Streck, *Der alte Orient* 16, 3/4 (1917): 1–64
Tarn, *The Greeks* (1951²), passim
Waterman (ed.), *Preliminary Report at Tel Umar, Iraq* (1931)
Waterman (ed.), *Second Preliminary Report at Tel Umar* (1933)
Weiss, *Dor Dor we-Doreshaw* (1904⁴), vol. 3, passim
Weissbach, *RE*, vol. 11, cols. 943–944, s.v. "Koche"
Winckler, *Altorientalische Forschungen*, II, vol. 1 (1898): 514–518
Yudelevitz, *Maḥoza* (1947)

Maloga מלוגא

A. *Source*

Pesaḥim 48a–b

אמר רב[1] קבא מלוגנאה[2] לפיסחא, וכן לחלה. והתניא חמשת רבעים קמח ועוד חייבין בחלה, הכי קאמר קבא מלוגנאי נמי אהאי שיעורא קאי.

Rav[1] said, The *qav* of Maloga[2] is for Passover, and also for *ḥallah*. But we were taught five fourths [of a *qav*] and more is subject to the *ḥallah*. So he says, the Malogan *qav* too is based on that quantity.

B. *Location*

None can be proposed due to insufficient data.

C. *Attempt at Identification*

Various scholars have proposed identifications for Maloga,[3] but none is well founded.

D. *Material Culture*

The source above indicates that there was a measure named after Maloga.[4] Rav states that it is the measure to be used for making dough for Passover, and also indicates the quantity which is subject to the *ḥallah* law.

Berliner, *Beiträge* (1883), p. 45
Eshel, *Yishuvei ha-Yehudim* (1979), p. 147
Funk, *Monumenta* (1913), pp. 40, 295
Getzow, *Al Neharot Bavel* (1887), p. 87
Hirschenson, *Sheva Ḥokhmot* (1883), p. 159
Jastrow, *Dictionary* (1950³), p. 787
Kohut, *Arukh ha-Shalem* (1878–1892), vol. 5, p. 76 "מגלון"
Levy, *Wörterbuch* (1924²), vol. 3, p. 17

---

[1] The Munich MS has "Rava," and the Munich B MS has "Rav Papa." See also *Diq. Sof.*

[2] The Munich B MS has מגלונאה, further on as well; see also *Diq. Sof.*

[3] See Hirschenson, p. 159; Funk, *Monumenta*, p. 295; Eshel, p. 147. Note Rav Tsemaḥ Gaon's comment: "... a city whose name is Maglo (מגלו) which is the one where Ḥoni ha-Me'aggel is" (Lewin, *Otzar ha-Geonim* for Pesaḥim, *ha-Perushim*, p. 147).

[4] Similarly, there is also (Ketubot 54a) a Nəhardəʿa *qav* (see the entries on "Nəhardəʿa," "Maḥoza" and "Babylon").

Mašmahig משמהיג

A. *Sources*

1. Rosh ha-Shanah 23a

תלת פרוותא הויין, תרתי בי ארמאי[1] וחדא דבי פרסאי, דבי ארמאי[1] מסקן כסיתא, דבי פרסאי מסקן מרגנייתא, ומקרייא פרוותא דמשמהיג.

They are three ports, two Roman[1] and one Persian. From that of the Romans,[1] they bring up corals, from that of the Persians, pearls, and it is called the port of Mašmahig.

2. Yoma 77a[2]

יהבו ליה עשרין וחד מלכי ופרוותא דמשהיג,[3] אמר כתיבו לי לישראל באכרגא, כתבו ליה. כתיבו לי רבנן באכרגא, כתבו ליה. בעידנא דבעו למיחתם עמד גבריאל מאחורי הפרגוד ואמר . . .

They gave him [the Persian official] twenty-one kings (= provinces) and the port of Mašmahig.[3] He said, Write to me that Israel [has to pay] the *karga* (= poll tax). They wrote to him. Write down the sages to me in [the list of payers of] poll tax. They wrote to him. When they wanted to sign, Gabriel stood behind the curtain and said . . .

B. *Already Proposed Location*

Samāhīǧ, a port on Muḥarraq, a small island northeast of the island of Baḥrain.

C. *Identification*

Mašmahig figures in the talmudic sources in connection with its port, and from the linguistic point of view it may reasonably be identified with the Samāhīǧ mentioned in Arabic sources. In Fleischer's view, the name is of Persian origin, and the last part of it recalls the Persian word *mahīk* (= fish).[4] According to Yāqūt, Samāhīǧ (q.v. there) is an island in the middle of the sea between

---

[1] The source has בי ארמאי; the Munich MS and most of the versions have רומאי (= Roman), and see *Diq. Sof.*

[2] Similarly in *Midrash ha-Gadol* to Numbers 17:2, Rabinowitz ed., p. 282; *Yalquṭ Shim'oni* to Ezekiel 8 § 347.

[3] The source has משהיג, the Munich MS does not have the clause ending here at all (and see n. 15 below); the London MS and the parallels in *Midrash ha-Gadol* to Numbers and in *Yalquṭ Shim'oni* to Ezekiel have דמשמהיג; the Oxford MS has דמשנהיג; and see *Diq. Sof.*

[4] See Fleischer, in Levy, *Wörterbuch*, vol. 3, p. 320; and see *Arukh ha-Shalem*, vol. 5, p 276, and *Tosefot* to *Arukh ha-Shalem*, p. 272; cf. Sachau, *APAW phil.-hist. Klasse*, (1915), No. 6, p. 25.

ʿOmān and Baḥrain.[5] Sachau identified Samāhīǧ with a still inhabited place of that name[6] at the northeastern corner of Muḥarraq,[7] an island very close to Baḥrain.

Ancient Tylos can definitely be identified with Baḥrain.[8] Tylos is first mentioned as a landing place for the expeditions that Alexander sent out to circumnavigate Arabia.[9] In 206/5 B.C. Antiochus III visited Gerrha and, on his way back, Tylos.[10]

Baḥrain belonged to Persia from the time of Shapur II (309–379). The Persian king was represented there by a high official with the title of *marzbān*.[11]

D. *Economy*

Source 1 mentions the port of Mašmahig,[12] which was known as a place where pearls are fished. That testimony fits those of Theophrastus and Pliny who note that pearls were the basis of the Baḥrain economy.[13] In general, Baḥrain has a very hot, humid climate, with plenty of water provided by springs and rainfall. Theophrastus describes its rich vegetation as including palm trees, mangroves, figs and other fruit, and cotton. Another factor of importance was

[5] Further on he cites a source stating that in Persian the island is called Māš Māhī, and another stating that Samāhīǧ is a village near Baḥrain in the vicinity of Ǧuwāṯā (*hiya qarya ʿalā ǧānibi l-Baḥraini wa-min Ǧuwāṯā*). That description is related to a poem quoted there; see e.g. Kuṯayyir ʿAzza, *Dīwān*, p. 211. Cf. Yāqūt, s.v. "Buʿāṯ" Wüstenfeld ed. (Masāhīǧ, instead of Samāhīǧ; and cf. the variants). See also Sachau, *loc.cit.* (in n. 4 above), who suggests that "Haiǧ" in Ṭabarī, vol. 2, p. 57 (= vol. 1, p. 839), is a remnant of the name Samāhīǧ. There Ṭabarī says that Shapur II moved members of the Banū Taġlib from the western border of Persia to Baḥrain and settled them in two places: Dārīn, "and it is called Haiǧ" and al-Ḫaṭṭ (q.v. in Yāqūt). Cf. Bakrī, s.v. "Mīṯab" ("Samāhīǧ: in Baḥrain, belongs to the ʿAbd al-Qais [tribe]"); Nöldeke, *Perser und Araber*, p 57, n. 2; Sachau, *ibid.* A place called Haiǧ is mentioned in the poetry of ʿAbīd b. al-Abraṣ, see Lyall (ed.), *The Dīwāns*, p. 17; see also Bakrī, s.v. "Faiḥān," but it is not relevant here; and see al-Ǧawālīqī, *al-Muʿarrab*, pp. 202–203.

[6] See *Official Standard Names Gazetteer*, U.S. Board on Geographic Names, 1976 (Baḥrain), s.v. "Samāhīǧ"; see also ʿUmar Riḍā Kaḥḥāla, *Ǧuġrāfīyat šibh ǧazīrati l-ʿarab*, p. 405. According to him, Samāhīǧ on the island of Muḥarraq is a fifteen-minute walk east of ad-Dair. The inhabitants get their water from the springs on the sea coast; cf. Rentz-Mulligan, *EI*², s.v. "Bahrayn," and the map there.

[7] Sachau, *ibid.*, pp. 26–27, and map 3.

[8] See Stein, *RE* vol. 7A, s.v. "Tylos (2)," cols. 1732–1733.

[9] Cf., *RE*, *loc.cit.*

[10] Polybius XIII 9. This expedition has been interpreted as an effort to attract trade through Gerrha to southern Mesopotamia and to draw it away from Petra and Egypt. Cf. Rostovtzeff, *Social and Economic History of the Hellenistic World*, vol. 1, p. 458, and most recently Le Rider, *Suse*, p. 304. Walbank, *A Commentary on Polybius*, vol. 2, p. 422, notes that Polybius' journey probably implies the presence of a Seleucid fleet in those waters.

[11] Rothstein, *Die Dynastie*, pp. 131–133.

[12] *Parwata* means both "port" and "market;" see Herzfeld, *Samarra*, p. 33f.

[13] Theophrastus, *Historia Plantarum*, IV 7, 7; *De Causis Plantarum*, II 5, 5; cf. Pliny, *Natural History*, VI 32, 148; XII 38, 40.

its position as a port of call on major sea routes from Šaṭṭ al-ʿArab (Mesene) to southern Arabia and India, and from Gerrha to southern Mesopotamia.[14] Mentioning the twenty-one provinces and the port of Mašmahig under the Persian official incidentally, Source 2 deals with the *karga* (= poll tax) on Jews that included scholars. In the legendary context of the source, the angel Gabriel, Israel's protector, appears in order to persuade the Persian official to exempt scholars from payment of the tax.[15] Beer believes the event took place in mid-fourth century,[16] during the reign of Shapur II, who was known to have levied heavy taxes to pay the expenses of his wars. There is testimony that Rava, then head of the Maḥoza yeshiva, made great efforts to have the scholars exempted from paying the poll tax. That chronology fits in nicely with the fact that Baḥrain belonged to Persia from the reign of Shapur II on (see above), and explains the mention of Mašmahig in Source 2.

Eshel, *Yishuvei ha-Yehudim* (1979), pp. 148–149
Funk, *Monumenta* (1913), pp. 40, 295
Jastrow, *Dictionary* (1950³), p. 856
Kohut, *Arukh ha-Shalem* (1878–1892), vol. 5, p. 276; *Tosefot* (1937), p. 272
Le Rider, *Suse* (1965), p. 304
Levy, *Wörterbuch* (1924²), vol. 3, pp. 283, 320; vol. 4, p. 228
Markwart, *Catalogue* (1931), pp. 52, 103
Nöldeke, *Perser und Araber* (1879), pp. 18, 20, 53–57, 259f.
Nöldeke, *SAWW phil,-hist. Klasse* 128, 9 (1893), pp. 25, 47
Rentz-Mulligan, *EI²*, s.v. "Bahreyn"
Rothstein, *Die Dynastie* (1899), pp. 131–133
Rostovtzeff, *Social and Economic History of the Hellenistic World* (1941), vol. 1, p. 458
Sachau, *APAW phil.-hist. Klasse* (1915), No. 6, pp. 25–27
Stein, *RE* vol. 7A, s.v. "Tylos (2)", cols. 1732–1733
Tkač, *RE* vol. 7, s.v. "Gerrha (2)" cols. 1270–1272
Widengren, *Iranica Antiqua* 1 (1961): 143, n. 4

Mata Məḥasya מתא מחסיא

See the entry on "Sura and Mata Məḥasya."

---

14 Gerrha was on the western shore of the Persian Gulf in the southern part of the modern province of Ḥasā. For Gerrha see Strabo XVI 3, 3 (766); 4, 19 (778); Diodorus III 42, 5; Pliny, *Natural History* VI 32, 147; XXXI 39, 78; Ptolemy VI 7, 16; VIII 22, 10. The town of Gerrha is mentioned as al-Ǧarʿāʾ by the Arab geographer Hamdānī, Müller ed., *al-Hamdānī's Geographie der Arabischen Halbinsel*, Vol. 1, p. 137; cf. Tkač,, *RE*, vol. 7 s.v. "Gerrha (2)," cols. 1270–1272. The site of the town is uncertain. The Gerrhaei were very wealthy because they served as important middlemen in the trade from India and southern Arabia to southern Mesopotamia on the one hand, and Petra on the other.

15 On this and the poll tax in general, see Beer, *Amora'ei Bavel*, pp. 230–241. The case figures in some of the versions in fragmented form due to deletions by the censorship, and see *Diq. Sof.* on the passage, note ג; Beer, *ibid.*, p. 236. See also Goodblatt, *JESHO* 22 (1979): 238.

16 According to the time of the sages mentioned, and the way the source was compiled; and see Beer, *ibid.*, p. 238; cf. Goodblatt, *ibid.*

Mavrak̲ta מברכתא

A. *Sources*

1. ʿEruvin 61b

מר יהודה אשכחינהו לבני מברכתא דקא מותבי עירובייהו בבי כנישתא דבי אגובר,[1] אמר להו גוו ביה טפי כי היכי דלישתרי לכו טפי, אמר ליה רבא פלגאה בעירובין לית דחש להא דרבי עקיבא.

Mar Judah found the people of Mavrak̲ta putting their *ʿeruv* in the Be Govar[1] synagogue. He said to them, Put it further in, so that you will be allowed [to walk] further. Rava said to him, Disputer, in regard to *ʿeruv*, no one bothers about Rabbi ʿAqiva's ruling.

2. ʿEruvin 47b

הנהו דכרי דאתו למברכתא שרא להו רבא לבני מחוזא למיזבן מינייהו . . . הדר אמר רבא ליזדבנו לבני מברכתא,[2] דכולה מברכתא לדידהו כד׳ אמות דמיא.

Some rams that arrived in Mavrak̲ta [on the Sabbath] Rava allowed the Maḥozans to buy them . . . Rava repeated, Let them be sold to the Mavrak̲ta[2] people, as for them all Mavrak̲ta is considered only four cubits.

3. Ketubot 10a

ההוא דאתא לקמיה דרב נחמן, אמר ליה פתח פתוח מצאתי, אמר ליה רב נחמן אסבוהו כופרי, מברכתא חביטא ליה.

The one who came before Rav Naḥman said to him, I found an open door. Rav Naḥman said to him, Lash him with palm switches. Mavrak̲ta [harlotry] is prostrate before him.

B. *Location*

West of the Tigris in the vicinity of Maḥoza (see on the Maḥoza Area plan).

C. *Identification*

Source 1 and 2 testify to the propinquity of Mavrak̲ta to Maḥoza and to the close relations between the two places. Source 2 deals with the question of whether the Maḥozans were allowed to buy on the Sabbath (without using money, of course) rams brought to Mavrak̲ta; this shows that it was permissible to walk from Maḥoza to Mavrak̲ta on the Sabbath (see also below). Source 1 indicates that a person wishing to go from Mavrak̲ta to Maḥoza on the Sabbath could do so on condition that before then he arranged an *ʿeruv teḥumim.*

---

[1] The source has בי אגובר; the Munich MS and Venice printing have דאבי גובר, and see *Diq. Sof*. The *She'iltot* has דאבי גוברי (*be-shalaḥ*, *She'ilta*, 48).

[2] The Munich MS has אמר רבא לבני מחוזא לזבנינהו לבני מברכתא; the Salonika printing has אמר רבא בני מחוזא לא ליזבנו מינייהו אבל ליזבונינהו בני מברכתא.

Thus the distance between the two places was more than two thousand cubits (about a kilometer), the permitted Sabbath walking distance in the absence of an *'eruv*. It was less than four thousand cubits, and between the two places was Be Govar (q.v.) where the *'eruv* could be placed.[3]
The Syriac Chronicle published by Guidi contains testimony on Bishop Georgios of Īzalā (Ṭūr 'Abdīn) who in the reign of Khusro II Parwez (590/1–628) was accused of abandoning the Mazdaic faith, was imprisoned in Aqra də-Koke (a fort in Maḥoza; see the entry on "Be Ardəšir-Koke"). After a while he was crucified in the hay market and eventually buried in the St. Sergios Church in nearby Mavrakta.[4]
Ammianus mentions Macepracta,[5] and locates it north of Anbār (see the entry on "Pumbədita"). According to Herzfeld, this is a mistake, and Mavrakta near Maḥoza is really meant.[6]
The word *mavrakta* means "caravan" (perhaps of camels) and was probably applied to the place because it was a way station for camels and merchants.[7] Source 2 may be an illustration of the role of Mavrakta as a caravan and trade center (see also below). A number of scholars have sought to deny the existence of a place called Mavrakta in Babylonia, and interpreted all the talmudic instances as referring to *mavrakta* meaning "caravan."[8] Perhaps Source 3 can be explained that way (see below) but extra-talmudic testimony definitely proves the existence of Mavrakta, and there is thus no reason to take Sources 1 and 2 other than literally.

D. *Sages and Mavrakta*

In Sources 1 and 2 which deal with rules on *'eruv*, Rava, head of the Maḥoza yeshiva in the fourth generation of Babylonian amoras, issued rulings to the residents of neighboring Mavrakta. In Source 3, Rav Naḥman, of the third generation of Babylonian amoras, speaks disparagingly of the women of Mavrakta in discussing the case of a person claiming that he had found his bride was not a virgin. Some have sought to interpret Mavrakta in that

---

[3] See Obermeyer, pp. 177–178.

[4] Hoffmann, *Auszüge*, p. 110; Nöldeke, *SAWW phil.-hist. Klasse*, 128, 9 (1893), p 21f. Fiey, *Sumer* 23 (1967): 32–35, identified the church and placed Mavrakta on the map accordingly.

[5] Ammianus XXIV 2, 6–7.

[6] Herzfeld, *Samarra*, pp. 15–16. The identification of Macepracta with Mavrakta was already proposed by Berliner (p. 38) following Mannert, but some have objected to it. Among them was Obermeyer (p. 178, n. 6) who argues on the basis of the context that Ammianus is speaking of a place in the neighborhood of Fīrūz Šāpūr (= Anbār).

[7] See e.g., "a caravan (*mavrakta*) passed (T. J. Ketubot XIII 1–35d, 4; T. J. Soṭah I 4–17a, 1; "a caravan (*mavrakta*) passed in Bə'er Ševa'" (Genesis Rabbah LXXXV 12, Theodor-Albeck ed., p. 1047).

[8] E.g., Pineles, *Darkah shel Torah*, pp. 27–28; cf. Levy, *Wörterbuch*, vol. 3, p. 11; *Arukh ha-Shalem*, vol. 5, p. 70, Kohut's comment, but see *Tosefot Arukh ha-Shalem*, p. 245.

source as meaning "caravan," in which case the reference would be to prostitutes accompanying a caravan, and not to those native to Mavrak̲ta.[9] Those scholars have based their contention in part on the fact that Rav Naḥman was from Nəhardəʿa, which was quite far from Mavrak̲ta. However, aside from the fact that there is no reason why a sage from Nəhardəʿa could not cite an example from a relatively distant place, Rav Sherira Gaon reported that in Rav Naḥman's time, Nəhardəʿa was destroyed and its sages moved to Šək̲anṣiv, Šilḥe and Maḥoza.[10]

E. *Economy*

Source 2, telling of rams that were brought to Mavrak̲ta on the Sabbath, implies that the Maḥozans used to buy sheep from Gentiles. A similar case appears in Ḥullin, regarding Ishmaelites that brought rams to Jewish butchers from Ṣiqonya[11] (q.v. in the appendix). Beer views these cases as related to the reports indicating that the Jews were unable to raise sufficient sheep for their needs, and that there were economic ties between Jews and non-Jews.[12]

Beer, *Amora'ei Bavel* (1974), pp. 141, 209–210
Berliner, *Beiträge* (1883), p. 38
Eshel, *Yishuvei ha-Yehudim* (1979), p. 139
Fiey, *Sumer* 23 (1967): 32–35
Funk, *Monumenta* (1913), pp. 36, 288, 294
Herzfeld, *Samarra* (1948), pp. 15–16
Hirschenson, *Sheva Ḥokhmot* (1883), pp. 151–152
Jastrow, *Dictionary* (1950³), p. 725
Kohut, *Arukh ha-Shalem* (1878–1892), vol. 5, p. 70; *Tosefot* (1937), p. 245
Levy, *Wörterbuch* (1924²), vol. 3, p. 11
Neubauer, *Géographie* (1868), pp. 169, 357–358
Neusner, *History* (1965–1970), vol. 3, p. 275; vol. 4, pp. 169, 172
Nöldeke, *SAWW phil. hist. Klasse* 128, 9 (1893), pp. 21–22, 36
Obermeyer, *Landschaft* (1929), pp. 177–178, 232, 290
Pineles, *Darkah shel Torah* (1861), pp. 27–28

Mesene (Mešan) מישן

A. *Sources*

1. Qiddushin 71b

א״ר פפא סבא[1] משמיה דרב בבל בריאה, מישון[2] מיתה, מדי חולה, עילם גוססת. ומה בין חולין לגוססין, רוב חולין לחיים רוב גוססים למיתה. עד היכן היא בבל . . . לתחתית

[9] See the previous note; cf. also Hirschenson, pp. 151–152.

[10] *Iggeret Rav Sherira Gaon*, Lewin ed., p. 82. See also the section on Sages and Šək̲anṣiv in the entry on "Šək̲anṣiv."

[11] Ḥullin 39b.

[12] Beer, *Amora'ei Bavel*, pp. 141, 209–210.

[1] The Vatican 111 MS has just "Rav Papa."

[2] The Munich and Vatican 111 MSS have מישן.

בדיגלת עד היכא, אמר רב שמואל[3] עד אפמייא[4] תתאה. תרתי אפמייא[4] הויין, חדא עיליתא וחדא תתייתא, חדא כשירה וחדא פסולה, ובין חדא לחדא פרסה וקא קפדי אהדדי ואפילו נורא לא מושלי אהדדי. וסימניך דפסולתא הא דמישתעיא מישנית.[5]

Rav Papa the Elder[1] in Rav's name said, Babylonia is healthy, Mešon[2] is dead, Media is sick, ʻElam is dying. And what is [the difference] between sick and dying, most sick are for life, most dying for death.

How far does Babylonia extend . . . on the lower Tigris how far? Said Rav Samuel,[3] To Lower Apamea.[4] There are two Apameas,[4] the Upper and the Lower, one fit and one unfit, and between one and the other one parasang, and they are particular with each other and do not even lend each other fire. And your sign of the unfit, the one that speaks Mesenean.[5]

2. T. J. Qiddushin IV 1–65c, 26–27[6]

תמן אמרין[7] מישא מתה מדיי חולה, אילם וגבביי[8] גוססות . . .

There they say[7] Meša is dead, Media is sick, Elam and Guvai[8] are dying . . .

3. Genesis Rabbah XXXVII 8, Theodor-Albeck ed., p. 350[9]

ר׳ לעזר בן פפוס אמר מישא[10] מיתה, מדי חולה, עילם גוססת . . .

Rabbi Leazar b. Papos said Meša[10] is dead, Media sick, Elam is dying . . .

4. Qiddushin 72b

מישון[11] לא חשו לה לא משום עבדות ולא משום ממזרות אלא כהנים שהיו בה לא הקפידו על הגרושות.

Mešon[11] was not a concern because of slavery or bastardy, but because the priests there were not scrupulous about divorcees.

5. T. J. Yevamot I 6–3b, 9–10

רבי חנינה ברוקא בשם רבי יהודה בני מישא לא חשו להו אלא משם ספק חללות, וכהנים ששם לא הקפידו על הגרושות.

Rabbi Ḥanina Beroqa in the name of Rabbi Judah [said], the Meša people are a concern only because of doubt about the priests' illegal spouses, and because the priests there were not scrupulous about divorcees.

---

[3] The Munich and Vatican 111 MSS have "Rav Papa b. Samuel," which seems correct for Samuel did not have the title of "Rav."

[4] For variants see the entry on "Apamea."

[5] The source has מישנית, the Vatican 111 MS has משונית.

[6] Also in T. J. Yevamot I 6–3b, 10–12.

[7] The T. J. Yevamot version is תמן קריין (= there they call).

[8] The source has גבביי, and see the entry on "Guvai."

[9] Cf. *Yalquṭ Shimʻoni* (for Genesis § 62, Mossad Harav Kook ed., p. 229): מישא מתה מדי חולה עילם וגונבי גוססת.

[10] Most of the versions have "Rabbi Eleazar b. Pinḥas." Various MSS have the forms מישה; משא; מישן; משן.

[11] The Munich MS has מישן.

6. Yevamot 17a

פסולי דהרפניא משום פסולי דמישון,[12] ופסולי דמישון משום פסולי דתרמוד[13] ... והיינו דאמרי אינשי קבא רבא וקבא זוטא מיגנדר ואזיל לשאול ומשאול לתרמוד ומתרמוד למישן וממישן להרפניא.

The unfit of Harpanya on account of the unfit of Mešon,[12] the unfit of Mešon on account of the unfit of Tarmod[13] . . . Thus it is that people say, the small *qav* and the big *qav* roll down to the nether-world, from the nether-world to Tarmod, from Tarmod to Mešan, from Mešan to Harpanya.

7. Qiddushin 49b

עשרה קבים עזות ירדו לעולם תשעה נטלה מישן.

Ten *qabim* of impudence descended to the world, Mešan took nine.

8. Qiddushin 72b

כי הא דאיסתנדרא דמישן חתניה דנבוכדנצר הוה.

For the *istāndār* (governor) of Mešan was Nebuchadnezzar's son-in-law.

9. Bava Batra 73a

רבי נתן בבלאה הוה קארי לה בוצית, כדאמרי אינשי בוציאתא דמיאשן.[14]

Rabbi Nathan the Babylonian called it (the *dugit* boat) *boṣit*, as people say *boṣiata də-Mešan*.[14]

10. Shabbat 101a

אמר רב הונא הני ביצאתא דמישן[15] אין מטלטלין בהן אלא בארבעה.

Rav Huna said, Those *biṣata də-Mešan*,[15] we may carry in them only within four [cubits].

11. Bava Qamma 97a–b

איתמר המלוה את חבירו על המטבע ונפסלה המטבע רב אמר נותן לו מטבע היוצא באותה שעה, ושמואל אמר יכול לומר לו לך הוציאו במישן. אמר רב נחמן מסתברא מילתיה דשמואל דאית ליה אורחא למיזל למישן אבל לית ליה אורחא[16] לא.

It was stated, If a man lends his fellow on [the basis of] a [particular] coin and the coin became unusable, Rav said, He gives him a coin having currency, and Samuel said, He can tell him, Go spend it in Mešan. Rav Naḥman said, Samuel's words would be reasonable if he is accustomed to going to Mešan, but not if he is not.[16]

---

[12] The Vatican 111 MS, the Venice printing and *Ginzei Talmud* have פסולי דמישן.

[13] For variants see the entry on "Tadmor."

[14] The source has בוציאתא דמיאשן, the Munich MS has ביציא' דמישן, the Florence and Vatican 115 MSS have בוצייתא דמישן, and the Oxford MS has דמיישן.

[15] The source has ביצאתא דמישן, the Munich MS has ביציאתא דמישני (corrected to דמייאשן), the Oxford MS has ביצייתא, and see *Diq. Sof.*

[16] The source has אבל לית ליה אורחא לא but the Munich, Vatican 116 and Hamburg MSS have אבל לית ליה אורחא למישן.

12. Shabbat 37b

אמר ליה רב עוקבא ממישן לרב אשי[17] אתון דמקרביתו לרב ושמואל עבידו כרב ושמואל, אנן נעביד כרבי יוחנן.

Rav ʿUqba of Mešan said to Rav Ashi,[17] You who are close to Rav and Samuel, do as Rav and Samuel, we will do as Rabbi Yoḥanan.

13. Shabbat 43a–b (= Betzah 36a)

ת"ש פורסין מחצלת על גבי כוורת דבורים בשבת... א"ל רב עוקבא ממישן[18] לרב אשי תינח בימות החמה דאיכא דבש, בימות הגשמים דליכא דבש מאי איכא למימר...

Come and hear, One may spread mats over a beehive on the Sabbath . . . Said Rav ʿUqba of Mešan,[18] to Rav Ashi, That would be acceptable on sunny (summer) days when there is honey, on rainy days when there is no honey, what can be said?

14. Josephus, *Antiquities*, I 145

Μησαναίους, Σπασίνου Χάραξ ἐν τοῖς νῦν καλεῖται.

. . . the Mesaneans in the region today called Spasinou Charax.

15. Josephus, *Antiquities*, XX 22–23

τὸν δὲ νεανίαν, σφόδρα γὰρ ἐδεδοίκει περὶ αὐτοῦ, μὴ μισούμενος ὑπὸ τῶν ἀδελφῶν πάθοι τι, πολλὰ δωρησάμενος πρὸς Ἀβεννήριγον ἐκπέμπει τὸν Σπασίνου χάρακος βασιλέα, παρακατατιθέμενος ἐκείνῳ τὴν τοῦ παιδὸς σωτηρίαν. ὁ δὲ Ἀβεννήριγος ἄσμενός τε δέχεται τὸν νεανίαν καὶ διὰ πολλῆς εὐνοίας ἄγων γυναῖκα μὲν αὐτῷ τὴν θυγατέρα, Σαμαχὼς δ' ἦν ὄνομα ταύτῃ, δίδωσι· δωρεῖται δὲ χώραν, ἐξ ἧς μεγάλας λήψοιτο προσόδους.

(King Monobazus of Adiabene) as he was greatly alarmed for the young Izates (his son) lest the hatred of his brothers should bring him to some harm, he gave him an abundance of presents and sent him off to Abennerigus, the king of Charax Spasini, to whom he entrusted the safety of the boy. Abennerigus welcomed the lad and viewed him with such goodwill that he gave him his daughter, named Symmacho, as a wife and conferred on him a territory that would insure him a large income. (trans.: L. H. Feldman, LCL)

16. Josephus, *Antiquities*, XX 34–35

Καθ' ὃν δὲ χρόνον ὁ Ἰζάτης ἐν τῷ Σπασίνου χάρακι διέτριβεν Ἰουδαῖός τις ἔμπορος Ἀνανίας ὄνομα πρὸς τὰς γυναῖκας εἰσιὼν τοῦ βασιλέως ἐδίδασκεν αὐτὰς τὸν θεὸν σέβειν, ὡς Ἰουδαίοις πάτριον ἦν, καὶ δὴ δι' αὐτῶν εἰς γνῶσιν ἀφικόμενος τῷ Ἰζάτῃ κἀκεῖνον ὁμοίως συνανέπεισεν μετακληθέντι τε ὑπὸ τοῦ πατρὸς εἰς τὴν Ἀδιαβηνὴν

---

[17] The Munich MS has "Rav Assi," apparently a scribal error, and see *Diq. Sof.*

[18] The Betzah parallel in the Munich MS has "Rav ʿAqiva," evidently a scribal error. The old printings of Betzah have the spelling ממיישן and see *Diq. Sof.*

συνεξῆλθεν κατὰ πολλὴν ὑπακούσας δέησιν· συνεβεβήκει δὲ καὶ τὴν Ἑλένην ὁμοίως ὑφ' ἑτέρου τινὸς Ἰουδαίου διδαχθεῖσαν εἰς τοὺς ἐκείνων μετακεκομίσθαι νόμους.

Now during the time when Izates resided at Charax Spasinus, a certain Jewish merchant named Ananias visited the king's wives and taught them to worship God after the manner of the Jewish tradition. It was through their agency that he was brought to the notice of Izates, whom he similarly won over with the co-operation of the women. When Izates was summoned by his father to Adiabene, Ananias accompanied him in obedience to his urgent request. It so happened, moreover, that Helena had likewise been instructed by another Jew and had been brought over to their laws. (trans.: L. H. Feldman, LCL)

17. Pliny, *Natural History*, VI 31,129–132

Tigris autem, ex Armenia acceptis fluminibus claris Parthenia ac Nicephorione, Arabas Orroeos Adiabenosque disterminans et quam diximus Mesopotamiam faciens, lustratis montibus Gordyaeorum circa Apameam Mesenes oppidum, citra Seleuciam Babyloniam CXXV p. divisus in alveos duos, altero meridiem ac Seleuciam petit Mesenen perfundens, altero ad septentrionem flexus eiusdem gentis tergo campos Cauchas secat, ubi remeavere aquae, Pasitigris appellatur, postea recipit ex Media Choaspen atque, ut diximus, inter Seleuciam et Ctesiphontem vectus in lacus Chaldaicos se fundit eosque LXII p. amplitudine implet; mox vasto alveo profusus dextra Characis oppidi infertur mari Persico X p. ore. inter duorum amnium ostia XXV p. fuere, ut alii tradunt, VII, utroque navigabili. sed longo tempore Euphraten praeclusere Orcheni et accolae agros rigantes, nec nisi per Tigrim defertur in mare.
Proxima Tigri regio Parapotamia appellatur. in ea dictum est de Mesene; oppidum eius Dabitha. cui iungitur Chalonitis cum Ctesiphonte, non palmetis modo, verum et olea pomisque arbusta. ad eam pervenit Zagrus mons, ex Armenia inter Medos Adiabenosque veniens supra Paraetacenen et Persida. Chalonitis abest a Perside CCCLXXX p.; tantum a Caspio mari et a Syria abesse conpendio itineris aliqui tradunt. inter has gentes atque Mesenen Sittacene est, eadem Arbelitis et Palaestine dicta. oppidum eius Sittace Graecorum, ab ortu et Sabdata, ab occasu autem Antiochia inter duo flumina Tigrim et Tornadotum, item Apamea, cui nomen Antiochus matris suae inposuit; Tigri circumfunditur haec, dividitur Archoo.

The Tigris, however, after receiving as tributaries from Armenia those notable rivers the Parthenias and Nicephorion, makes a frontier between the Arab tribes of the Orroei and Adiabeni and forms the region of Mesopotamia mentioned above; it then traverses the mountains of the Gurdiaei, flowing round Apamea, a town belonging to Mesene, and 125 miles short of Babylonian Seleucia splits into two channels, one of which flows south and reaches Seleucia, watering Mesene on the way, while the other bends northward and passing behind the same people cuts through the plains of Cauchae; when the two streams have reunited, the river is called Pasitigris. Afterwards it is joined by the Kerkhah from Media, and, as we have said, after flowing between Seleucia and Ctesiphon, empties itself into the Chaldaean Lakes, and broadens them out to a width of 62 miles. Then it flows out of the Lakes in a vast channel and passing on the right-hand side of the town of Charax discharges into the Persian Sea, the mouth of the river being 10 miles wide. The mouths of the two rivers used to be 25 miles apart, or as others record, 7 miles, and both were navigable; but a long time ago the Euphrates was dammed by the Orcheni and other neighbouring tribes in order to irrigate their lands, and its water is only discharged into the sea by way of the Tigris.

The country adjacent to the Tigris is called Parapotamia. It contains the district of Mesene, mentioned above; a town in this is Dabitha, and adjoining it is Chalonitis, with the town of Ctesiphon, a wooded district containing not only palm groves but also olives and orchards. Mount Zagrus extends as far as Chalonitis from Armenia, coming between the Medes and the Adiabeni above Paraetacene and Farsistan. The distance of Chalonitis from Farsistan is 380 miles, and some persons say that by the shortest route it is the same distance from the Caspian Sea and from Syria. Between these races and Mesene is Sittacene, which is also called Arbelitis and Palaestine. Its town of Sittace is of Greek origin, and also to the east of this is Sabdata and to the west Antiochia, which lies between the two rivers, Tigris and Tornadotus, and also Apamea, which Antiochus named after his mother; this town is surrounded by the Tigris, and the Archous intersects it. (trans.: H. Rackham, LCL)

18. Pliny, *Natural History*, VI 31,138–141

Charax, oppidum Persici sinus intimum, a quo Arabia Eudaemon cognominata excurrit, habitatur in colle manu facto inter confluentes dextra Tigrim, laeva Eulaeum, II p. laxitate. conditum est primum ab Alexandro Magno, colonis ex urbe regia Durine, quae tum interiit, deductis, militum inutilibus ibi relictis; Alexandriam appellari iusserat pagumque Pellaeum a patria sua, quem proprie Macedonum fecerat. flumina id oppidum expugnavere; postea restituit Antiochus quintus regum et suo nomine appellavit, iterumque infestatum Spaosines Sagdodonaci filius, rex finitimorum Arabum, quem Iuba satrapen Antiochi fuisse falso tradit, oppositis molibus restituit nomenque suum dedit, emunito situ iuxta in longitudinem VI p., in latitudinem paulo minus. prius fuit a litore stadiis X—maritimum etiam Vipsania porticus habet—Iuba vero prodente L p.; nunc abesse a litore CXX legati Arabum nostrique negotiatores, qui inde venere, adfirmant. nec ulla in parte plus aut celerius profecere terrae fluminibus invectae. magis id mirum est, aestu longe ultra id accedente non repercussas, hoc in loco genitum esse Dionysium, terrarum orbis situs recentissimum auctorem, quem ad commentanda omnia in orientem praemiserit Divus Augustus ituro in Armeniam ad Parthicas Arabicasque res maiore filio, non me praeterit nec sum oblitus sui quemque situs diligentissimum auctorem visum nobis introitu operis: in hac tamen parte arma Romana sequi placet nobis Iubamque regem, ad eundem Gaium Caesarem scriptis voluminibus de eadem expeditione Arabica.

The town of Charax is situated in the innermost recess of the Persian Gulf, from which projects the country called Arabia Felix. It stands on an artificial elevation between the Tigris on the right and the Karun on the left, at the point where these two rivers unite, and the site measures two miles in breadth. The original town was founded by Alexander the Great with settlers brought from the royal city of Durine, which was then destroyed and with the invalided soldiers from his army who were left there. He had given orders that it was to be called Alexandria, and a borough which he had assigned specially to the Macedonians was to be named Pellaeum, after the place where he was born. The original town was destroyed by the rivers, but it was afterwards restored by Antiochus, the fifth king of Syria, who gave it his own name; and when it had been again damaged it was restored and named after himself by Spaosines son of Sagdodonacus, king of the neighbouring Arabs, who is wrongly stated by Juba to have been a satrap of Antiochus; he constructed embankments for the protection of the town and raised the level of the adjacent ground over a space of six miles in length and a little less in breadth. It was originally at a distance of $1^1/_4$ miles from the coast, and had a harbour of its own, but when Juba published his work it was 50 miles inland; its present distance from the coast is stated by Arab envoys and our own traders who have come from the place to be 120 miles. There is no part of the world where earth carried down by rivers has encroached on the sea further or more rapidly; and what is more surprising is that the deposits have not been driven back by the tide, as it approaches far beyond this point.
It has not escaped my notice that Charax was the birthplace of Dionysius, the most recent writer dealing with the geography of the world, who was sent in advance to the East by his late majesty Augustus to write a full account of it when the emperor's elder son was about to proceed to Armenia to take command against the Parthians and Arabians; nor have I forgotten the view stated at the beginning of my work that each author appears to be most accurate in describing his own country; in this section however my intention is to be guided by the Roman armies and by King Juba, in his volumes dedicated to the above mentioned Gaius Caesar describing the same expedition to Arabia. (trans.: H. Rackham, LCL)

19. Pliny, *Natural History*, VI, 32,145–146

a Petra incoluere Omani ad Characen usque oppidis quondam claris ab Samiramide conditis Abaesamide et Soractia; nunc sunt solitudines. deinde est oppidum quod Characenorum regi paret in Pasitigris ripa, Forat nomine, in quod a Petra conveniunt, Characenque inde XII p. secundo sestu navigant.

e Parthico autem regno navigantibus vicus Teredon infra confluentem Euphratis et Tigris; laeva fluminis Chaldaei optinent, dextra nomades Scenitae. quidam et alia duo oppida longis intervallis Tigri praenavigari tradunt, Barbatiam, mox Dumatham, quod abesse a Petra dierum X navigatione, nostri negotiatores dicunt Characenorum regi parere et Apameam, sitam ubi restagnatio Euphratis cum Tigri confluat, itaque molientes incursionem Parthos operibus obiectis inundatione arceri.

After Petra the country as far as Charax was inhabited by the Omani, with the once famous towns of Abaesamis and Soractia, founded by Samiramis; but now it is a desert. Then there is a town on the bank of the Pasitigris named Forat, subject to the king of the Characeni; this is resorted to by people from Petra, who make the journey from there to Charax, a distance of 12 miles by water, using the tide. But those travelling by water from the kingdom of Parthia come to the village of Teredon below the confluence of the Euphrates and the Tigris; the left bank of the river is occupied by the Chaldaeans and the right bank by the Scenitae tribe of nomads. Some report that two other towns at long distances apart are also passed on the voyage down the Tigris, Barbatia and then Dumatha, the latter said to be ten days' voyage from Petra. Our merchants say that the king of the Characeni also rules over Apamea, a town situated at the confluence of the overflow of the Euphrates with the Tigris; and that consequently when the Parthians threaten an invasion they are prevented by the construction of dams across the river, which cause the country to be flooded. (trans.: H. Rackham, LCL)

20. Cassius Dio LXVIII 28,4

καὶ τὴν μὲν νῆσον τὴν ἐν τῷ Τίγριδι τὴν Μεσήνην, ἧς Ἀθάμβηλος ἐβασίλευεν, ἀπόνως ᾠκειώσατο, ὑπὸ δὲ δὴ χειμῶνος τῆς τε τοῦ Τίγριδος ὀξύτητος καὶ τῆς τοῦ ὠκεανοῦ ἀναρροίας ἐκινδύνευσε.

ὅτι ὁ Ἀθάμβηλος ὁ τῆς νήσου ἄρχων τῆς ἐν τῷ Τίγριδι οὔσης πιστὸς διέμεινεν τῷ Τραϊανῷ, καίπερ ὑποτελεῖν προσταχθείς, καὶ οἱ τὸν Χάρακα τὸν Σπασίνου καλούμενον οἰκοῦντες (ἐν δὲ δὴ τῇ τοῦ Ἀθαμβήλου ἐπικρατείᾳ ἦσαν) καὶ φιλικῶς αὐτὸν ὑπεδέξαντο.

He (Trajan, A.D. 116) easily won over Mesene, the island in the Tigris of which Athambelus was king, but as a result of a storm, combined with the strong current of the Tigris and the tide coming in over the ocean, he found himself in serious danger. Athambelus, the ruler of the island in the Tigris, remained loyal to Trajan, even though ordered to pay tribute and the inhabitants of Charax Spasinu, as it is called, received him kindly; they were subject to the dominion of Athambelus. (trans.: E. Cary, LCL)

21. Ammianus XXIII 6,23

In omni autem Assyria, multae sunt urbes. inter quas Apamia eminet, Mesene cognominata, et Teredon et Apollonia et Vologessia, hisque similes multae.

But in all Assyria there are many cities, among which Apamia, also named Mesene, and Teredon, Apollonia and Vologessia, and many similar ones are conspicuous. (trans.: C. Rolfe, LCL)

22. Ammianus XXIII 6,43

His propinquant Parthyaei sub aquilone ... et haec potiora residuis sunt oppida: Oenunia, Moesia, Charax, Apamia, Artacana et Hecatompylos ...

Near these (namely the Persians) to the north are the Parthians . . . and the following cities are more important than the others: Oenunia, Moesia, Charax, Apamia, Artacana and Hecatompylos . . . (trans.: J. C. Rolfe, LCL)

23. Ammianus XXIV 3,12

In his regionibus agri sunt plures, constiti vineis varioque pomorum genere ubi oriri arbores assuetae palmarum, per spatia ampla ad usque Mesenen et mare pertinent magnum, instar ingentium nemorum.

In these regions there are many fields, planted with vineyards and various kinds of fruits. Here too palm trees are wont to grow, extending over a wide area as far as Mesene and the great sea, in mighty groves. (trans.: J. C. Rolfe, LCL)

24. Tomb Inscription, M. Schwabe & B. Lifshitz, *Beth She'arim*, vol. 2, No. 101; *CIJ*, vol. 2, No. 1124

Μισηνὴ	[From] Mesene
Σάρα	Sara
ἡ Μαξίμ[α]	[also named] Maxima

B. *Location*

A region stretching from the Persian Gulf to Kūt al-Imāra, the southern part of presentday Iraq (on Bab. Env. map).

C. *History*

Mesene was a country at the head of the Persian Gulf and the confluence of the Euphrates and Tigris. Its chief city was first founded by Alexander as Alexandria in 324 B.C. and was a real *polis*, as appears from its name and from the existence of a *deme* (quarter) with a Macedonian name.[19] The region was of vital interest because it controlled communications between Mesopotamia and the Persian Gulf. In the Hellenistic, Parthian and Sassanian periods, that meant control of the trade with India, the Far East and South Arabia, which exported aromatics and spices. In the third century B.C. the Arab city of

[19] See Source 18: *pagus Pellaeum*. See also the inscription, Dittenberger, *OGIS* No. 233, line 100.

Gerrha (see the entry on Mašmahig) also occupied a key position on the trade routes through the Persian Gulf and across the Arabian peninsula to Mesene. It has been argued that the expedition to Gerrha of Antiochus III (206/205 B.C.) aimed at diverting trade away from Petra and Egypt through Gerrha to Mesene and thence to Seleucia. Another trade route of importance ran from Mesene to Petra.[20] For the first century A.D. a maritime route round the Arabian peninsula to Egypt is attested through a description in *Periplus Maris Erythraei*, a nautical handbook composed in that century.

The city of Alexandria in Mesene was destroyed by a flood and refounded by Antiochus III or IV,[21] under Hyspaosines as eparch.[22] Trade policy may have played a role in the appointment. After the death of Antiochus VII in 129 B.C. Hyspaosines perhaps made himself an independent king,[23] evidently profiting from the weakening of the Seleucid Empire before the Parthians were well established.[24] At that time the city came to be called Charax Spasinu, that is, the *karka*[25] of Hyspaosines, and the kingdom was known also as Characene.

A cuneiform tablet attests that by 128 B.C. Hyspaosines was recognized as king in Babylon.[26] He is recorded as having been active even in Elymais and Media.[27] On their coins he and his successors appear in the guise of Seleucid kings. (The names of thirteen kings are given in Greek and dated by the Seleucid era up to A.D. 112.) Bronze coins of Hyspaosines overstruck with a Mithridates II type dated 121/120 B.C. show that by that time Characene had become a vassal state of the Parthians.[28] From then on Characene was for the most part under varying degrees of Parthian political control. The only evidence for the following period is the coins issued by Hyspaosines and his successors, which have been interpreted in the light of major historical events by Nodelman.

---

20 Cf. Musil, *Arabia Deserta* (1927), p. 82.

21 See Source 18: *postea restituit Antiochus quintus regum*. The identity of this Antiochus is in doubt. Cf. Bellinger, *YCS* 8 (1942): 55; Le Rider, *Suse*, p. 304, n. 2.

22 For Hyspaosines in particular see Bellinger, *op.cit.*, p. 53–67; cf. Le Rider, *Suse*, p. 370, n. 3. For the extent of the region see Weissbach, *RE*, vol. 15, cols. 1082–1083 and the entry on "Apamea."

23 Hyspaosines issued coins from 125/124 B.C. onwards; see Le Rider, *Suse*, p. 40.

24 See Nodelman, *Berytus* 13 (1959–1960): 87ff.

25 The element *karka* appears in the names of several cities (see Fleisher's addenda to Levy's *Wörterbuch*, vol. 2, p. 456). A city of that name in Media is mentioned by Samuel in the T. B. (Qiddushin 72b, Yevamot 17a) but cannot be identified with the Mesenean town as Neubauer wished (p. 337).

26 Cf. Bellinger, *op.cit.* (in n. 21), p. 58, who cites Pinches, *The Babylonian and Oriental Record* 4 (1889–1890): 131–144.

27 Cf. Pinches, *The Old Testament*, p. 483f.; cited by Debevoise, *A Political History of Parthia*, p. 39f.; Bellinger, *op.cit.* (in n. 21), p. 60.

28 Newell, *NNM*, 26 (1925); Bellinger, *op.cit.* (in n. 21), pp. 60–62; Le Rider, *Suse*, pp. 387–388.

Charax produced two famous geographers, both representing Hellenistic culture in the period of Augustus:[29] Dionysius, of whose writings nothing has been preserved; and Isidore, the author of *Mansiones Parthicae*, who probably wrote later in the first century A. D.[30]

In the first and second centuries, Mesene was an important center for the trade between Rome and the East, via Palmyra (see the entry on "Tadmor"). This has been shown by inscriptions found at Palmyra.[31] The earliest of the series seems to show that in A. D. 18/19 a Palmyran undertook a mission to Mesene at Germanicus' behest.[32] In either 50/1 or A. D. 70/1 mention is made of a statue set up by Palmyrans at Charax (Palmyrans at Babylon are mentioned in one or two earlier inscriptions).[33] Several inscriptions mention leaders of caravans traveling from Charax and Vologesias (see the entry on "Walašpaṭ") to Palmyra from A. D. 81 on.[34] In 116 Trajan visited Charax and drew up fresh tariffs for the Eastern trade passing through Mesene.[35] Trajan's Mesopotamian conquest was shortlived, however, and the region reverted to the status of a Parthian vassal. An undated inscription honors a man of a prominent Palmyran family who served as archon in Charax.[36] An inscription of 131 records a Palmyran satrap "of the king" in Charax, whom the Characenians honored with a statue in Palmyra.[37] Another Palmyran inscription of 140 honors an unknown man who served in an unknown capacity at Forat near Charax and led a caravan from Charax to Palmyra and Vologesias.[38] The city of Forat appears as a starting point of caravans in 142.[39] There are indications that in the preceding decade the mint shifted from Charax to Forat,[40] and it has been suggested that the latter became the capital of Mesene in that period. The

[29] See Source 18.

[30] For the *Parthian Stations* by Isidore of Charax, see e.g. the Greek text with translation and comments by W. H. Schoff. For the date see references in Nodelman, *op.cit.* (in n. 24), p. 107, n. 160.

[31] On these inscriptions see Rostovtzeff's article in *Mélanges Gustave Glotz*, vol. 2 (1932), pp. 793–811. The inscriptions can be found in Cantineau, *Inventaire des inscriptions de Palmyre*, vols. 3 and 9, and Starcky, *Inventaire*, vol. 10, and most recently, Dunant, *Museum Helveticum*, 13 (1956): 216–225, with references in n. 2 (cf. J. & L. Robert, *Bulletin Épigraphique*, [1958]: 506); Rostovtzeff, *op.cit.*, pp. 800–803; *Berytus* 2 (1935): 143–148; cf. Schlumberger, *Syria* 38 (1961): 256-260; Seyrig, *Syria* 22 (1941): 252–263 = *Antiquités Syriennes*, vol. 3 (1946), pp. 196–199. See also Will, *Syria* 34 (1957): 262–277.

[32] Cantineau, *Syria* 12 (1931): 139f.; cf. Seyrig, *Syria* 13 (1932): 266f.; Le Rider, *Syria* 36 (1952): 252; Nodelman, *op.cit.* (in n. 24), p. 99f.

[33] For Babylon, see Rostovtzeff, *Mélanges Glotz*, vol. 2 (in n. 31), pp. 796–798.

[34] *Ibid.*, p. 801f.

[35] See Source 20; Fronto, *Principia Historiae* 16 (Haines, vol. 2, p. 214).

[36] See Schlumberger, *op.cit.* (n. 31 above).

[37] Seyrig, *Syria* 22 (1941): 197f.

[38] Seyrig, *loc.cit.*

[39] Rostovtzeff, *Mélanges Glotz*, vol. 2, p. 802.

[40] Seyrig, *Syria* 22 (1941): 198f.; Nodelman, *op.cit.* (in n. 24), p. 113f.

Palmyran inscriptions are informative solely about the activities of Palmyra in both cities.

The role of Meseneans in the caravan trade remains obscure. However, it is clear that Palmyra played a leading role in the organization of the caravan trade from Mesene and far beyond Mesopotamia. Two inscriptions of the period mention Palmyran merchants sailing from northwestern India to Characene.[41] There are no Palmyran inscriptions mentioning Mesene between 161 and 193. Charax is mentioned for the last time in A.D. 193.[42] As pointed out by Rostovtzeff, the two caravan inscriptions dating to the third century mention a voyage from Palmyra to Vologesias, apparently the alternative replaced the previous Characene-to-Palmyra route. The start of the interruption following 161 coincides with the Parthian campaign of Lucius Verus (162–165) and the conquest of Dura, and the one after 193 with Severus' conquest of northern Mesopotamia. As concluded by Rostovtzeff, caravans were apparently organized by Parthian merchants and the Palmyrans were permitted only to carry western goods to Vologesias, the Parthian trade center near Ctesiphon (q.v.). Another city which controlled a caravan route, the one linking Singara with the Tigris, was Hatra.[43]

Nodelman has attempted to sketch the relationship of the kings of Characene to the Parthians and Romans through the analysis of numismatic material in the light of historical events known from literary sources.

The wealth of Mesene in this period emerges also from the *Hymn of the Soul* in the *Acts of Thomas* composed originally in Syriac in the first or second century A.D.[44] The prince there declares, "I quitted the East and went down . . . I passed through the borders of Mešan, the meeting place of the merchants of the East and I reached the land of Babylonia," and on his way back, "I left Babylon on my left hand and came to the great Mešan, the haven of merchants, which sits on the shore of the Sea."

In 221/2 Ardashīr conquered Mesene and made it a Sassanian province (*istān*) under an *istāndār* (the "istāndār of Mešan" is mentioned in Source 8[45]), and Charax and Forat were refounded as Astārābāḏ Ardašīr and Bahman Ardašīr.[46]

---

[41] Seyrig, *op.cit.*, pp. 202–207.

[42] Cantineau, *Inventaire*, vol. 3, No. 28; Rostovtzeff, *Mélanges Glotz*, vol. 2., p. 803.

[43] On Hatra see Treidler, *KP*, vol. 2, col. 957; Drijvers, *ANRW*, vol. II 8, pp. 803–837, and bibl. on pp. 877–879. See also the entry on "Ḥuṭra" in the appendix.

[44] The attribution of the *Hymn of the Sun* to Bardaiṣan is no longer accepted, cf. Drijvers, *Bardaiṣan of Edessa*, pp. 209–211; Segal, *Edessa*, pp. 31, 68; For a full translation, see Bevan, *The Hymn of the Soul*, Texts and Studies, vol. 3.

[45] Cf. *istandara də-Baškar* (Giṭṭin 80b) and see the entry on "Kaškar." See also Schaeder, *Der Islam* 14 (1924): 34.

[46] Ardašīr b. Bābak built Astarābāḏ Ardašīr, which is Karḫ Maisān. See (Astābāḏ Ardašīr) in Ṭabarī, vol. 2, pp. 40, 41 (= vol. 1, pp. 818, 820); Nöldeke, *Perser und Araber*, pp. 13, 20; Schaeder, *op.cit.*, p. 29f.

In about 224 Forat had a bishop.[47] Mesene was a metropolitanate as early as 310, but evangelization still went on in the fourth and even the sixth century. The see of the metropolitan was first Pərat də-Mešan, later Baṣra. Bishops had their sees at Karẖ (Charax), Rīma and Nahrgūz. Al-Ubulla never was a bishopric in its own right, but is said to have been visited by Māri (the legendary apostle) to whom the foundation of a church was attributed.[48] By mid-fourth century there were bishops in both Forat and Charax.[49] After the council of Seleucia (410) Forat became a metropolitanate,[50] and it is clear that even earlier, by the third century, it had superseded Charax as the provincial capital.

With the cessation of Characenean coinage and Palmyran caravan inscriptions, information on the region is practically nil. It is generally assumed that the Parthian-Sassanian measures to curb the Palmyran caravan trade and the foundation of Ḥīra in the third century led to a steady decline in the prosperity and importance of the region.[51] The third century crisis must indeed have made itself felt at Mesene, but all assumptions for this period are based on the absence of any evidence.

In the early Islamic period Charax is called Karẖ Maisān (from Karak Mešan) and Forat is called Furāt al-Baṣra or Furāt Maisān or just Furāt. In Syriac it was Pərat də-Mešan[52] which is how it is referred to in the T. B. (see "Pərat də-Mešan"). Both Karẖ and Furāt later appear as Umayyad mint cities.

Archaeological exploration has so far been limited to attempts to identify the towns of Mesene. For Charax various sites have been suggested.[53] Most recently Hansman has proposed a site which he has investigated both on the ground and with the help of aerial photographs.[54] Sarre and Herzfeld tentatively place Forat on the site of modern Baṣra, and Apologos (Ubulla) men-

---

[47] Sachau, *APAW phil.-hist. Klasse* (1915) No. 6, pp. 6, 17, 62, but see above, p. 155.

[48] Fiey, *Assyrie chrétienne*, vol. 3, pp. 263–282.

[49] Labourt, *Le Christianisme*, p. 20, n. 6; p. 66.

[50] *Ibid.*, p. 98.

[51] See e.g. Nodelman, *op.cit.* (in n. 24); Nissen, *Baghdader Mitteilungen* 6 (1973): 79–86.

[52] Yāqūt, s.v. "Karẖ Maisān"; *Muštarik*, s.v. "Karẖ," p. 370; Ibn al-Faqīh, p. 198; *Kitāb al-maʿārif*, p. 654 (Astarābāḏ Ardašīr); Ibn Biṭrīq, vol. 1, p. 108 (Astād[!] Abād, and in another version Astarābāḏ). Cf. Ḥamza, *Ta'rīẖ*, pp. 46, 47 (Ašā Ardašīr/Anšā Ardašīr, "on the banks of the Duǧail, and it is also called Karẖ Maisān"; cf. Streck, *EI*^{1}, s.v. "Maisān"). And see Herzfeld, *Der Islam* 11 (1921): 150. On the meaning of the word cf. Streck, *Die alte Landschaft*, vol. 1, p. 92, n. 1; vol. 2, p. 186, n. 4; Streck-Lassner, *EI*^{2}, *karẖ* s.v. "Karkh"; cf. Hansman, *Iranica Antiqua* 7 (1967): 26. Stephanus, referring to Arrian, *Parthica* (2nd century) mentions Ὄραθα πόλις τῆς ἐν Τίγρητι Μεσήνης.

[53] See the bibliography in Le Rider, *Suse*, p. 259, n. 3; see also Rawlinson, *JRGS* 27 (1857): 185–190, whose opinion is based on a personal visit.

[54] Hansman provides aerial photographs, maps and an extensive discussion of ancient authors and modern literature. He places Charax at a site officially called Ǧabal Ḫayābir, but termed Naisān by the local villagers.

tioned in the *Periphus Maris Erythraei* as a harbor on or near the site of ʿAššār, the modern harbor of Baṣra, on an island between Šaṭṭ al-ʿArab and two canals.[55] Here too Hansman has new suggestions. For Apamea, sometimes referred to as a town of Mesene, see the entry for "Apamea."

D. *The Borders of Babylonia*

Talmudic literature too distinguishes between Babylonia and Mesene, and locates the latter outside the borders of the "Babylonia of pure lineage" (see Introduction). Sources 1–3, in comparing the lineage of natives of various places with that of Babylonians, rank Mesene lowest, contrasting "healthy Babylonia" with "dead Mesene" whose inhabitants are unfit for marriage.
Source 1 notes that the border of Babylonia passes between Upper Apamea and Lower Apamea so that the residents of those neighboring towns refrained from all contact with each other. The same source indicates that a particular dialect known as Mesenean was spoken in Lower Apamea.
Sources 4 and 5 seek to pinpoint the reasons the Meseneans were reputedly unfit, attempting to mitigate matters by stating that it was not because of slavery or bastardy, but because the priests there did not comply with the prohibition against their marrying divorcees. Probably the "impudence" in Source 7 is also related to the dubious lineage of the Meseneans.[56]

E. *Sages and Mesene*

The one sage mentioned in the sources (12 and 13) as originating in Mesene is Rav ʿUqba of Mesene, of the sixth generation of Babylonian amoras. In Source 12 he argues with Rav Ashi, separating Rav Ashi's domain where he may act as Rav and Samuel did, from his own domain, where he may act as Rabbi Yoḥanan did. Evidently in Rav ʿUqba's opinion certain matters in Mesene were decided according to the Eretz Israel halakhah, contrary to that of the Babylonian sages. A further indication of the rift between Mesene and Babylonia, this source suggests close ties between Mesene and Eretz Israel, probably fostered by the international commercial traffic that passed through Mesene.

[55] Sarre & Herzfeld, *Archäologische Reise*, vol. 1, p. 250f. Rawlinson, *op.cit.* (in n. 53), p. 188, notes that the name Furāt still applies to the ruins close to the modern site of Muḥammara. Muḥammara is now called Ḫurramšahr. Muḥammara according to Rawlinson, is built on the island usually called ʿAbbadān. "Ubulla" (Apologos) he locates on the left bank of the Tigris, 12 miles below Baṣra, without identifying the site. Regarding the place-name "Furāt" see Herzfeld, *Samarra*, pp. 33–34. Hansman, *op.cit.* (in n. 52), pp. 46–53, fig. 2, has come up with new proposal for the site of Furāt, 17.4 kilometers southeast of Ǧabal Ḫayābir, 4.2 kilometers east of the old Tigris, a site now called Maġlūb.

[56] Cf. Rav Judah's statement citing Samuel: "Four hundred slaves, and some say four thousand slaves, had Pashḥur b. Immer, and all became interbred in the priesthood, and any priest that is impudent is only of them" (Qiddushin 70b).

F. *Economy*

Mesene was a well known commercial center traversed by international trade routes, and the Jews had a share in the commerce. That this was true as early as the Parthian period is indicated in Source 16 where Josephus reports that a Jew named Ananias (Hananiah) visited the court of Abennerigus, king of Charax Spasinu.

Source 11 deals with a loan that was to be repaid in a certain currency which was no longer legal tender in Babylonia. Samuel believes the debtor can repay in the currency originally agreed on, telling the creditor it can be used in Mesene. The fact that Mesene was a center of international trade made it possible to use many types of coins there.

Some scholars have connected Mesene with a tradition cited in the T. J. as reported by Rabbi Abba, testifying that "the people of Meša agreed not to sail in the great sea" and even when they asked Rabbi Judah ha-Nasi to be released from their vow, they were not allowed to.[57] The scholars concluded from this that the Mesenean Jews refrained from engaging in international commerce despite its profitability. If so their compliance represents additional evidence of the ties between Mesene and Eretz Israel.[58] There is also a possibility that the problem dealt with is whether one is permitted to leave Eretz Israel to go abroad, so that the reference could be to a place within Eretz Israel called Meša.[59]

G. *Material Culture*

The lower Tigris was obstructed long before the end of the Sassanian period, and gradually developed into swamps (*baṭā'iḥ*),[60] which were crossed in boats of a particular construction, the "*biṣata*" (Hebrew *biṣa* = swamp) of Mesene that are mentioned in Sources 9 and 10.

Andreas, *RE*, vol. 1, col. 1390ff., s.v. "Alexandria (13)"
Beer, *Amora'ei Bavel* (1974), pp. 156–157
Bellinger, *YCS* 8 (1942): 51–67
Berliner, *Beiträge* (1883), pp. 17, 43–44
Eshel, *Yishuvei ha-Yehudim* (1979), pp. 135–137, 146, 174–175
Funk, *Monumenta* (1913), pp. 39, 294–295

57 T. J. Pesaḥim IV 1–30d, 22–24; and see Berliner, p. 44, and Krauss, *Qadmoniot ha-Talmud*, vol. 1 A, p. 116.

58 It seems reasonable to link the time of the appeal of the Mesenean Jews to Rabbi Judah ha-Nasi with Mesenean acquisition of control, replacing Palmyra, of the trade between India and the west routed through Mesene (see the section on History above); see Oppenheimer, *Zion* 47 (1982): 335–341, esp. p. 339 and n. 17. The ties between Mesene and Eretz Israel are reflected also by the burial of Meseneans in Eretz Israel, as shown in Source 24.

59 See T. J. Mo'ed Qaṭan III 1–81c, 40–41, and see Lieberman, *Yerushalmi ki-Fshuto*, vol. 1, p. 434, and Beer, *Amora'ei Bavel*, pp. 156–157. Klein places Meša in the Tyre region (see *Sefer ha-Yishuv*, vol. 1, pp. 106–107) which does not seem tenable.

60 On the formation of the "straight" course of the Tigris, see the entry on "Apamea"; see also Obermeyer, pp. 201–202.

GRAETZ, *Das Königreich Mesene* (1879)
HANSMAN, *Iranica Antiqua* 7 (1967): 21–58 (= Mélanges Ghirshman, vol. 2)
HILL, *BMC Arabia* (1922): 194f.
HIRSCHENSON, *Sheva Ḥokhmot* (1883), pp. 157–158
JASTROW, *Dictionary* (1950[3]), p. 779
JOËL, *MGWJ* 16 (1867): 330–342, 375–387
KOHUT, *Arukh ha-Shalem* (1878–1892), vol. 5, p. 265; *Tosefot* (1937), p. 271
KRAUSS, *HUCA* 1 (1924): 182–183
KRAUSS, *Qadmoniot ha-Talmud* (1923–1945), vol. 1 A, pp. 22, 116, 189
KRAUSS, *Paras we-Romi* (1948), p. 29
LE RIDER, *Syria* 36 (1959): 229–253
LE RIDER, *Suse* (1965), pp. 40f., 370, n. 2, 387f., 461
LEVY, *Wörterbuch* (1924[2]), vol. 2, p. 456 "כרך", vol. 3, p. 107
MØRKHOLM, *Coin Hoards* 4 (1978): 25–27
NEUBAUER, *Géographie* (1868), pp. 324–326, 377, 382
NEUSNER, *History* (1965–1970), vols. 1–5, passim
NEWMAN, *Agricultural Life* (1932), p. 22
NISSEN, *Baghdader Mitteilungen* 6 (1973): 79–86
NODELMAN, *Berytus* 13 (1959–1960): 83–121 (bibliography, p. 120)
OBERMEYER, *Landschaft* (1929), passim
OPPENHEIMER, *Zion* 47 (1982): 335–341
RAPOPORT, *Erekh Millin* (1914), vol. 2, p. 210
SAINT-MARTIN, *Recherches* (1838)
WEISSBACH, *RE*, vol. 3, cols. 2116–2119, s.v. "Charakene"; col. 2122, s.v. "Charax"; vol. 15, cols. 1082–1095, s.v. "Mesene"
WIDENGREN, *Iranica Antiqua* 1 (1961): 117, n. 2

Moškani מושכני

A. *Sources*

1. Qiddushin 71b

עד היכן היא בבל . . . לעיל בדיגלת עד היכא, רב[1] אמר עד בגדא (כ"י ואטיקאן 111: עכברא) ואוונא,[2] ושמואל אמר עד מושכני.[3] ולא מושכני בכלל, והאמר רבי חייא בר אבא[4] אמר שמואל מושכני הרי היא כגולה ליוחסין, אלא עד מושכני ומושכני בכלל.

How far does Babylonia extend? ... Upstream, how far on the Tigris? Rav[1] said, To Bagda (the Vatican 111 MS has ʿUḵbara) and Awana.[2] And Samuel said, To Moškani.[3] And is not Moškani included? For Rabbi Ḥiyya b. Abba[4] said that Samuel said, Moškani is like the Exile as to lineage. But as far as and including Moškani.

---

[1] The Vatican 111 MS has "Rava," but as the difference of opinion is with Samuel, the correct version is most likely "Rav," the former being a scribal error produced by the addition of the letter *alef* to "Rav" under the influence of the initial *alef* in the next word (רב[א] אמר).

[2] The Munich MS has **עד נגד' וחוונא**; the Vatican 111 MS has **עד עכברא ואוינא** as does the *Arukh* (see *Arukh ha-Shalem*, vol. 1, p. 45, s.v. "**אונא**", and *Tosefot*, p. 13 of the entry.

[3] The Vatican 111 MS and the Venice printing have **משכני**, further on as well.

[4] The Munich and Vatican 111 MSS have "Rav Ḥiyya b. Avin."

2. Qiddushin 72a

... קסלקא דעתא מושכי היינו מושכני, והאמר ר' חייא בר אבין⁵ אמר שמואל מושכני
הרי היא כגולה ליוחסין, אלא מושכי לחוד ומושכני לחוד.

Does it enter the mind that Moške is Moškani? For Rabbi Ḥiyya b. Avin[5] said
that Samuel said, Moškani is like the Exile as to lineage. But Moške separately
and Moškani separately.

B. *Location*

Maskin[6] adjacent to Awana (q.v.) on the west bank of the Tigris (D 1 on the
Tal. Bab. map).

C. *The Borders of Babylonia*

Source 1 is part of the section dealing with the borders of Babylonia in regard
to genealogy, and cites Samuel's view that Moškani is the northeastern extremity of that border on the Tigris. The propinquity of Moškani to 'Uḳbara
and Awana, which in Rav's opinion mark that border, shows that the
difference between the views of the two sages was a minor one. In any case
Rav cites places on both sides of the Tigris while Samuel cites only one, west
of it. As to the region involved, Obermeyer pointed out the connection between
the administrative borders of Babylonia in the Sassanian period and its
"genealogical" borders (see the entry on "'Uḳbara").[7]
Source 2 distinguishes between Moške and Moškani which bear similar names.
Moške, however, was in the region of Nihawand (q.v.) which was deemed one
of "impure" lineage, while Moškani was within the region of pure lineage (and
see the Introduction).

BERLINER, *Beiträge* (1883), pp. 19, 38
ESHEL, *Yishuvei ha-Yehudim* (1979),
   pp. 140–141
FUNK, *Juden* (1902–1908), vol. 2, p. 150
FUNK, *Monumenta* (1913), pp. 4, 36, 277
JASTROW, *Dictionary* (1950³), p. 751
KOHUT, *Arukh ha-Shalem* (1878–1892),
   vol. 5, p. 273

LEVY, *Wörterbuch* (1924²), vol. 3, p. 280
NEUBAUER, *Géographie* (1868), p. 331
OBERMEYER, *Landschaft* (1929), pp. 81, 85,
   144
STRECK, *Die alte Landschaft* (1901). vol. 2,
   p. 235f.

---

[5] The Vatican 111 MS has "Rabbi Ḥiyya b. Abba" here and in Source 1 as well.

[6] On which see Yāqūt, Bakrī, *Marāṣid, ar-Rauḍ al-mi"ṭār*, s.v. "Maskin"; *Ansāb al-
ašrāf*, vol. 5, p. 350; *Aġānī*, vol. 17, p. 162; Yāqūt, Bakrī, s.v. "Dair al-ġāṯalīq"; Bakrī,
s.v. "Buṭnān"; Ibn Rusta, p. 104; cf. Ibn al-Faqīh, pp. 198, 199 (the text is garbled in
both places); *BGA*, vols. 6, 8, index; *Masālik al-abṣār*, p. 308 (and the references there);
Streck, *Die alte Landschaft*, vol. 1, pp. 16, 19, vol. 2, p. 235f.; Le Strange, pp. 51, 80.
Presentday Tall Miskīn is on the west bank of Nahr ad-Duġail, about three kilometers
south of ad-Duġail (formerly Sumaika).

[7] Obermeyer, p. 85.

Moške מושכי

See the entry on "Nihawand."

Nareš נרש

A. *Sources*

1. Soṭah 10a

כתיב "וירד שמשון תמנתה," וכתיב "הנה חמיך עולה תמנתה," . . . ר' שמואל בר נחמני אמר שתי תמנאות היו, חדא בירידה וחדא בעליה. רב פפא אמר חדא תמנה הואי, דאתי מהאי גיסא ירידה ודאתי מהאי גיסא עליה כגון ורדוניא[1] ובי בארי[2] ושוקא דנרש.[3]

It is written "Samson went down to Timnah" (Jud. 14:1) and it is written "Your father-in-law is coming up to Timnah" (Gen. 38:13) . . . Rabbi Samuel b. Naḥmani said, There were two Timnahs, one down and one up. Rav Papa said, There is one Timnah. Whoever came from one direction went down, and whoever came from another direction went up, such as Wardunya,[1] Be Bire[2] and the market of Nareš.[3]

2. ʿEruvin 56a

אמר רב יהודה אמר רב כל עיר שיש בה מעלות ומורדות אדם ובהמה שבה מתים בחצי ימיהן, מתים ס"ד, אלא אימא מזקינין בחצי ימיהן. אמר רב הונא בריה דרב יהושע הני מולייתא דבי בירי ודבי נרש[4] אזקנון.

Rav Judah said Rav said, Every town that has ascents and descents, man and beast die in the prime of life. Die would you say? Rather say, they age in the prime of life. Rav Huna the son of Rav Joshua said, Those ascents at Be Bire and Be Nareš[4] have made us old.

3. Bava Metziʿa 93b

בר אדא[5] סבולאה הוי קא מעבר חיותא אגמלא דנרש דחפה חדא לחברתה ושדיתה במיא, אתא לקמיה דרב פפא, חייביה. אמר ליה מאי הוה לי למעבד, א"ל אבעי לך לעבורי חדא חדא. א"ל ידעת ביה בבר אחתיך דמצי למעבר חדא חדא, א"ל כבר צווחו קמאי דקמך ולא איכא דאשגח בהו.

---

[1] For variants, see the entry on "Wardina."

[2] The source has ובי בארי. For variants, see the entry on "Be Bire."

[3] The Oxford MS has ושוקא דנריש, the Vatican 110 MS has ונרש. The parallels in *Yalquṭ Shimʿoni* (Genesis § 145, Mossad Harav Kook ed., p. 737; Judges § 69) do not have the sentence "כגון ורדוניא ובי בארי ושוקא דנרש" at all, nor does the British Museum 406 MS of *Aggadot ha-Talmud*. See also Soṭah, ICIT edition.

[4] The Munich MS has דבי בארי דנרש, the Oxford MS has דבי בירי ונרש, the Salonika printing has דבי בירי דנרש, and see the entry on "Be Bire."

[5] The Florence and Vatican 117 MS as well as the R-i-f have "Rav Adda."

Bar Adda,[5] the porter, was leading animals across the Nareš bridge, and one pushed another and threw it into the water. He came before Rav Papa who inculpated him. He said to him, What should I have done? He said, You should have taken them across one by one. He said to him, Do you know of your sister's son, that he can lead them across one by one? He said to him, Your predecessors before you already complained, and nobody listened to them.

4. Ketubot 27b; Ḅava Metziʿa 81b; Bekhorot 36a

... דההוא גברא דאגר ליה חמרא לחבריה א״ל לא תיזיל באורחא דנהר פקוד דאיכא מיא זיל באורחא דנרש דליכא מיא, ואזל איהו באורחא דנהר פקוד ומית חמרא, אתא לקמיה דרבא א״ל אין באורחא דנהר פקוד אזלי מיהו לא הוו מיא, אמר רבא מה לי לשקר אי בעי א״ל באורחא דנרש אזלי ...

... A man hired out an ass to a fellow and said to him, Don't go by the Nəhar Pəqod road where there is water, go by the Nareš road where there is no water. But he went by the Nəhar Pəqod road and the ass died. He came before Rava and said to him, Yes, I went by the Nəhar Pəqod road, but there was no water. Rava said, "Why should I lie?" If he wanted he could have said, I went by the Nareš road ...

5. Ḥullin 127a

אמר רב הונא בריה דרב יהושע ביברי דנרש[6] אינן מן הישוב. אמר רב פפא בשמתא נרש, תרביה משכיה ואליתיה. ״ארץ ארץ ארץ שמעי דבר ה׳״, אמר רב פפא לא אבה נרש שמוע דבר ה׳. אמר רב גידל אמר רב[7] נרשאה נשקיך מני ככיך, נהר פקודאה לוייך מגלימא שפירא דחזי עלך, פומבדיתאה לוייך אשני אושפיזך.

Rav Huna the son of Rav Joshua said, The beavers of Nareš[6] are not of the land. Rav Papa said, The ban of Nareš [includes] its fat, its hide and its tail. "Oh land, land, land, hear the word of the Lord" (Jer. 22:29) Rav Papa said, [The people of] Nareš did not wish to hear the word of the lord. Rav Giddal said Rav[7] said, If a Narešan kisses you, count your teeth, if a Nəhar Pəqodan accompanies you, it is because of the fine cloak he saw on you, if a Pumbəditan accompanies you, change your accommodations.

6. Bava Qamma 115a

נרשאה גנב ספרא, זבניה לפפונאה[8] בתמנן זוזי, אזל פפונאה זבניה לבר מחוזאה במאה ועשרין זוזי, לסוף הוכר הגנב, אמר אביי ליזיל מרי דספרא ויהב ליה לבר מחוזא תמנן זוזי ושקיל ספריה ואזיל בר מחוזאה ושקיל ארבעין מפפונאה ... אלא אמר רבא ליזיל מריה דספרא ויהיב ליה לבר מחוזאה מאה ועשרין זוזי ושקיל ספריה וליזיל מרי דספרא ולישקול ארבעין מפפונאה ותמנן מנרשאה.

---

[6] The parallel in the *Yalquṭ Shimʿoni* manuscript has ובי בארי דנרש (Psalms § 862 according to the MS); the version in Rabbenu Tam in the *Tosafot* is ביברי ונרש.

[7] The Vatican 121 MS has "Rav Papa," and see *Diq. Sof.*, nn. ד and ו.

[8] The source has לפפונאה. For variants, see the entry on "Papuniya."

A Narešan stole a book, sold it to a Papuniyan[8] for eighty *zuz*. The Papuniyan went and sold it to a Maḥozan for a hundred and twenty *zuz*. In the end the thief was recognized. Abbaye said, The owner of the book should go and give the Maḥozan eighty *zuz* and take his book, the Maḥozan should go and take forty from the Papuniyan ... Rava said, The owner of the book should go and pay the Maḥozan a hundred and twenty *zuz* and take his book, and the owner of the book should [then] go and recover forty *zuz* from the Papuniyan and eighty *zuz* from the Narešan.

7. Bava Metziʿa 68a

אמר רבא לית הלכתא לא כטרשי פפונאי ולא כשטרי מחוזנאי ולא כחכירי נרשאי ... חכירי נרשאי, דכתבי הכי משכן ליה פלניא ארעיה לפלניא והדר חכרה מיניה, אימת קנאה דאקנייה נהליה.

Rava said, The halakhah is not like the credit interests of the Papuniyans, or the bonds of the Maḥozans or the leases of the Narešans ... The leases of the Narešans are written thus: A mortgaged his field to B and then rented it from him. But when did he acquire it to transfer it to the debtor?

8. Yoma 69a; Betzah 15a; Tamid 27b

... כי הא דאמר רב הונא בריה דרב יהושע האי נמטא גמדא דנרש שריא.

... As Rav Huna the son of Rav Joshua said, The hard felt of Nareš is permitted [although a mixture (= *kilayim*), for it is not for wearing].

9. Betzah 28b–29a

היכי עביד, כי הא דבסורא[9] אמרי תרטא ופלגו תרטא, בנרש אמרי חלקא ופלגו חלקא, בפומבדיתא אמרי אוזיא ופלגו אוזיא, בנהר פקוד ובמתא מחסיא אמרי רבעא ופלגו רבעא.

What should he do [on holidays]? In Sura[9] they say, [Give me] a third and half a third; in Nareš they say, A half and half a half; in Pumbədita they say, A sixth and half a sixth; in Nəhar Pəqod and Mata Məḥasya they say, A quarter and half a quarter.

10. Yevamot 110a

... והא ההיא עובדא דהוה בנרש ואיקדישה כשהיא קטנה וגדלה ואותביה אבי כורסייא ואתא אחרינא וחטפה מיניה, ורב ברונא ורב חננאל תלמידי דרב הוו התם ולא הצריכוה גיטא מבתרא, אמר רב פפא בנרש מינסב נסיבי והדר מותבי אבי כורסייא.

... That case in Nareš where a fellow betrothed [a girl] when she was young, and she grew up and he sat her on the [bridal] chair, another came and snatched her away from him, and Rav's disciples, Rav Beruna and Rav Ḥananel, were there and did not make her get a bill of divorcement from the latter. Rav Papa said, At Nareš they marry [first] and then place [the bride on the bridal] chair.

---

[9] The Munich MS has דבנהרדעא.

11. Niddah 67b

אתקין רב אידי[10] בנרש למטבל ביומא דתמניא משום אריותא. רב אחא בר יעקב בפפוניא[11] משום גנבי. רב יהודה בפומבדיתא משום צנה. רבא במחוזא משום אבולאי.

Rav Idi[10] ordained in Nareš to immerse on the eighth day because of the lions, Rav Aḥa b. Jacob in Papuniya,[11] because of the thieves, Rav Judah in Pumbədita, because of the cold, Rava in Maḥoza because of the gate guards.

12. Shabbat 140a

איבעיא להו שרה מאי, תרגמא רב אדא[12] נרשאה קמיה דרב יוסף[13] שרה חייב חטאת.

They were asked, If [laserwort] is dissolved [in tepid water], what [is the law]? Rav Adda[12] Narša'a explained before Rav Joseph,[13] If one dissolves it, he is liable to a sin offering.

13. Shabbat 60a

... אלא תרגמא רב אדא נרשאה[14] קמיה דרב יוסף הואיל ואשה חולקת בה שערה. בשבת למאי חזיא, אמר רבא טס של זהב יש לה על ראשה, בחול חולקת בה שערה, בשבת מניחתה כנגד פדחתה.

... But Rav Adda Narša'a[14] explained before Rav Joseph: Since a woman parts her hair with it, what is it fit for on the Sabbath? Rava said, She has a golden plate on her head. On weekdays she parts her hair with it, on the Sabbath she rests it against her forehead.

14. Pesaḥim 107a

אמר רב הונא אמר רב[15] וכן תני רב גידל[16] דמן נרש המקדש וטעם מלא לוגמא יצא, ואם לאו לא יצא. אמר רב נחמן בר יצחק[17] אנא תנינא לה לא גידול בר מנשיא[18] ולא גידול בר מניומי[19] אלא גידול סתמא. למאי נפקא מינה, למירמא דידיה אדידיה.

Rav Huna said that Rav[15] said, and Rav Giddal[16] of Nareš also taught, He who recites *Qiddush* and drinks a mouthful has complied, and if he does not, he has not complied. Rav Naḥman b. Isaac[17] said, I taught it [and I mention] not Giddol b. Menashya[18] and not Giddol b. Manyomi[19] but just Giddol. What is the difference in practice? One can be set against the other.

---

[10] The Munich and Vatican 111 MS have "Rav Idi b. Avin."

[11] The Vatican 111 MS does not have "in Papuniya."

[12] The Oxford MS has "Adda" (without "Rav").

[13] The Munich MS has "Rav Huna."

[14] The Munich MS has "Rav Aḥa b. Shesha," the R-i-f has "Rav Aḥa Narša'a," the R-i-f MS is like the source.

[15] The Munich MS has only "Rav Huna" (without "Rav said"), and see *Diq. Sof.*

[16] The Munich B MS has Giddal (without "Rav").

[17] The Munich MS has "Rav Naḥman" (without "b. Isaac"), and see *Diq. Sof.*

[18] The Munich B MS has גידול בר מנשי, the Oxford MS has גידול בר מנשה, and see *Diq. Sof.*

[19] The Oxford MS has in addition ולא גידול דמן נרש (= and not Giddol of Nareš).

15. Yoma 81b

דתניא רבי אומר חומץ משיב את הנפש. דרש רב גידל בר מנשה[20] מבירי דנרש[21] אין הלכה כרבי.

It was taught Rabbi says, Vinegar refreshes the soul. Rav Giddal b. Manasseh[20] of Bire də-Nareš[21] expounded, The halakhah is not like Rabbi.

16. Giṭṭin 69b

רבין[22] דמן נרש עבד לה לברתיה דרב אשי[23] מאה וחמשין מהני דידן ואתסיא.

Ravin[22] of Nareš made a hundred and fifty of those of ours for the daughter of Rav Ashi[23] and cured her.

B. *Proposed Location*

At the bank of the Nars canal. The name Nareš may be preserved in that of the village of Narsā near Ḥilla (D4 on the Tal. Bab. map).

C. *Identification*

The name Nars which scholars have proposed as the identity of Nareš[24] is frequently mentioned in Arabic sources, but only some instances seem to actually be Nars, while others are apparently Burs (= Borsif, q.v.) since only the placement of the diacritical dot differentiates between *nūn* and *bā'* in Arabic. Moreover, Nars was quite close to Burs which further contributed to the confusion of the two.

As Le Strange pointed out, the course of the Nahr Nars which diverges from Nahr Sūrā (the eastern branch of the Euphrates) can be determined through the location of Niffar at its bank;[25] Yāqūt describes Niffar (q.v.) as being a place on Nahr Nars. Since the identification of Niffar with Nippur (q.v.) seems certain, Nahr Nars obviously flowed in a generally southeastern direction, toward the *baṭā'iḥ* (= swamps).[26]

Only part of the information that Yāqūt provides in his entry on Nars appears to relate to Nars (= Nareš), while the rest seems to apply to Burs.

---

[20] The Munich MS has רב גידל בר מניו׳, the Oxford and London MSS have רב גידל בר מנשיא, the Munich B MS has גדול בר מנשי.

[21] The Munich B MS has בביברי דנרש, the London MS has מבירא דגרש, the Oxford MS does not have מבירי דנרש at all, and see *Diq. Sof.*

[22] The Arras MS has "Rami," the Vatican 140 does not name a sage at all.

[23] The Paris MS of *Aggadot ha-Talmud* does not have "of Rav Ashi."

[24] See, e.g., Obermeyer, pp. 306–310.

[25] Le Strange, "Ibn Serapion," p. 260. He does not comment on the difficulty raised below.

[26] The Nars canal is also mentioned by Sam'ānī, *Ansāb*, s.v. "Narsī": "One of the Kūfa canals with a number of villages at its banks; after it a number of the celebrated traditionists in Kūfa are named." See Streck, *Die alte Landschaft*, vol. 1, pp. 30, 32; Nöldeke, *ZDMG* 28 (1874): 93 n. 2.

Yāqūt says that Nars is a canal dug by the Sassanian ruler Narse (A. D. 293–303), the son of Vahram (the Third), in the Kūfa area (it should be noted that the reference is not to its immediate vicinity), which flows out of the Euphrates, and has a number of villages at its banks (cf. note 26 below).[27] He goes on to state that Nars is a village where Ḍaḥḥāk[28] lived in Babylonia, and that the canal was named after the village. This seems to be an instance of "Burs" being garbled to "Nars." For according to one version, Ḍaḥḥāk is the Nimrod who wanted to burn up the Patriarch Abraham,[29] and it is Birs (= Burs) known also as Birs Nimrūd,[30] that is connected with Nimrod.[31]

Obermeyer's decision regarding the location of Nareš is likewise based on a dubious text. Following Ibn Serapion, Obermeyer assumed that Nareš was not far from the start of Nahr Nars which flows out of the Euphrates near

[27] Yāqūt, under "Nars," reports further that a certain type of garment is called "Narsīya clothing." However, Masʿūdī states that Abū Muslim al-Ḫurāsānī was an inhabitant of the Burs and Ğāmiʿain area, of a village called Ḫuṭarnīya, which gave its name to the Bursīya clothes known as Ḫuṭarnīya, and that the village is a "daughter" of Kūfa and located in its Sawād (Murūǧ, vol. 4, p. 78 [= vol. 6, p. 59]). Thus in Yāqūt too the correction should be made to "Bursīya clothes," after Burs (= Borsif) near Ğāmiʿain (Ḥilla). See also Source 8 in the entry on "Borsif." Cf. Hoffmann, Auszüge, p. 26, n. 206. Hoffmann also indicates textile manufacture there, beginning in very ancient times and continuing up through the Sassanian period to the Muslim era. Cf. similarly Herzfeld, EI¹ ², s.v. "Birs."

[28] On him see Masʿūdī, Murūǧ, vol. 1, p. 264 (= vol. 2, pp. 113–114).

[29] See, e.g., Ṭabarī, vol. 1, pp. 196–197 (= vol. 1, p. 205).

[30] See the entry on "Borsif," and Herzfeld, ibid. (n. 27 above).

[31] See also Ṭabarī, vol. 1, p. 196 (= vol. 1, p. 204) who reports that Ḍaḥḥāk lived in the Sawād, in a village called Nars, beside the road to Kūfa (= fī nāḥiyati ṭarīqi l-Kūfa). The textual variations (see the Leiden ed.) include B.r.š.; Nūs; and a variant identical to the latter without the diacritical dot on the nūn. Here too Burs is preferable (see Hoffmann, n. 27 above) and see also Murūǧ, vol. 1, p. 265 (= vol. 2, p. 115) who says the village of Bābil which gave its name to the entire region is on the banks of one of the Euphrates canals, an hour's distance from the town of Ğisr Bābil and Nahr Nars; and "Narsīya clothes" are named after it (read "Nahr Burs" and "Bursīya clothes"). Under "Yamāma" Yāqūt has Ḍaḥḥāk's village corrupted to T.r.s. instead of "Burs." Mustaufī (vol. 2, p. 202) mentions Nahr Nars as one of the canals flowing out of the Euphrates. He also mentions (vol. 2, p. 162) the village of Nars, and the text is difficult because here too he refers to Nimrod and Abraham. In describing the road from Baghdad to Naǧaf he says that there are seven parasangs between Farāšā (see the entry on "Pərišna") and the Nīl canal through the village of Nars where Nimrod threw Abraham into the fire. The village is one parasang to the left of the road, and there are two parasangs from Nīl to Ḥilla. In this case it is impossible to correct to "Burs" because of the location specified, between Farāšā and the Nīl canal, north of the canal. For it is definite that Burs is south of the canal, in fact west of the eastern branch of the Euphrates. On the other hand Kūṭā Rabba which is likewise connected with Abraham and Nimrod (see the entry on "Kuta") fits the location of the village of Nars indicated in this source, and is possibly the place meant (cf. variations in the place-name Nars in Mustaufī, vol. 1, p. 166; cf. also Ibn Ǧubair, pp. 214–215).

Ǧāmiʿain (Ḥilla).[32] The Ibn Serapion MS, however, in the first place where the canal is mentioned, has no diacritical marks, these having been inserted by the editor (in the same place Suhrāb has a *šadda* rather than a dot) so that here too possibly Burs was meant. The course of the Nahr Nars flowing out of the lower Sūrā river, is identical in its initial sector with that of "the ancient al-Ǧāmiʿ,"[33] that is, the old al-Ǧāmiʿ canal. The name Ǧāmiʿ is certainly connected with Ǧāmiʿain which is Ḥilla (and see the entry on "Dəruqart"), and Burs and Ǧāmiʿain are near each other (and mentioned together above). Furthermore the course of the Nahr Nars described by Ibn Serapion[34] ran between the two branches of the Euphrates and for at least part of the way in a generally southwesterly direction from the Ḥilla area toward Kūfa. This direction does not fit in with the location of Nippur on Nahr Nars (see above) so that here too apparently "Burs" is intended.[35] As noted above, Nareš can probably be identified with the Arab village of Narsā in the countryside of Ḥilla.[36]

In Sources 1 and 2, Rav Papa and Rav Huna b. Rav Joshua, both of Nareš (see below) indicate that Nareš is in a hilly district, testimony that must be considered in the light of the level topography of most of Babylonia. Source 1 names Be Bari (= Be Bire) and Wardina (qq.v.) as places near Nareš.

D. *Sages and Nareš*

A number of sages of various generations of Babylonian amoras were active in Nareš, the outstanding figure undoubtedly being Rav Papa of the fifth generation. He describes the topographical conditions of Nareš (see above), reports a local wedding custom (Source 10), acts as a judge in a case in which due to a shepherd's negligence an animal pushed another over the Nareš bridge (Source 3), criticizes the Narešans and issues a ban against them (Source 5). The variety of matters dealt with indicates Rav Papa's position in Nareš and his involvement in what happened there. In addition, Rav Sherira Gaon n his *Iggeret* reports that Rav Papa headed a yeshiva in Nareš. After the death in 352 of Rava, head of the Maḥoza yeshiva, Rav Papa

---

[32] Le Strange, "Ibn Serapion," pp. 16–17 and the notes there, p. 260; and see also Suhrāb, p. 125.

[33] *awwaluhū maʿā l-Ǧāmiʿi l-qadīm.*

[34] It passed between Ḥammām ʿUmar which was halfway between Qaṣr Ibn Hubaira and Kūfa (*Futūḥ al-buldān*, p. 281), and was apparently identical with Ḥammām Ibn ʿUmar, on which see Muqaddasī, pp. 53, 114, 134.

[35] The bank of the Nars canal, between "the place of the Ḥammām of Abū Burda" (that is, the place where Abū Burda's bath was later) and Ḥammām ʿUmar, is mentioned in the description of a journey from Kūfa to Babylon (*Šarḥ nahǧ al-balāġa*, vol. 1, p. 277; Naṣr b. Muzāḥim, *Kitāb Ṣiffīn*, p. 134) where Burs seems preferable as well.

[36] See *Taʾrīḫ al-Ḥilla*, vol. 1, p. 12, where either Narsā or Narsī can be read; and cf. perhaps Ṭabarī, vol. 6, p. 132 (= vol. 1, p. 773).

founded a yeshiva in Nareš directing it until his own death in 371.[37] Thus in Rav Papa's time the Nareš yeshiva had a status equal to that of the leading yeshivas of Babylonia.

Another amora active in the same generation was Rav Huna b. Rav Joshua. He too refers to the topography of Nareš and the physical difficulties it presents (see above); reports on the beavers of Nareš (see below), mentions the density of the Nareš felt (see below). According to the following testimony in T. B. Berakhot, he was *rosh li-venei kallah* (= chief speaker at the conference) along with Rav Papa: "A person entering a lake in a dream becomes a yeshiva head, a forest becomes a conference head. Rav Papa and Rav Huna b. Joshua saw a dream. Rav Papa went into a lake, became a yeshiva head; Rav Huna b. Rav Joshua entered a wood, became a conference head. Some say both entered a lake, but Rav Papa [who dreamed] that a drum hung [from his neck] became a yeshiva head, Rav Huna b. Rav Joshua who had no drum hanging became a conference head."[38] However, this function is not ascribed to Rav Huna b. Rav Joshua in every manuscript, and in any case the matter is doubtful.[39]

Another sage active in Nareš was Rav Idi, who according to Source 11 ordained that a woman could immerse for purification by day, so as to avoid the lions that inhabited the region. This was Rav Idi b. Avin (the Second) who was Rav Papa's disciple (see note 10 above).

Source 14 mentions Rav Giddal of Nareš and Source 15 Rav Giddal b. Manasseh of Bire də-Nareš, both apparently the sage who was active in the second generation of Babylonian amoras and was Rav's disciple, appearing also in Source 5 in which he stigmatizes the Narešans.[40]

Also referred to are Rav Adda Narša'a (Sources 12 and 13) who was a disciple of Rav Joseph's of the third generation of Babylonian amoras, and Ravin of Nareš, reported in Source 16 as having compounded some medicine for the daughter of Rav Ashi who headed the Mata Məḥasya yeshiva in the sixth generation of Babylonian amoras.

E. *Nareš and Its Environs*

The sources mention the Nareš market (Source 1) and the bridge over the river or canal of Nareš (Source 3). The presence of lions in the neighborhood is indicated by the ordinance of Rav Idi in Source 11 which determines that the

---

[37] *Iggeret Rav Sherira Gaon*, Lewin ed., p. 89, and see the variants there and the notes.

[38] Berakhot 57a. On the *kallah* see Gafni, *Ha-Yeshiva be-Bavel*, pp. 131–148; Goodblatt, *Rabbinic Instruction*, pp. 155–170.

[39] The Munich MS for instance has "Rav Huna b. Rav Joshua said, Whoever enters a forest in a dream becomes head of all the exiles," and see *Diq. Sof.* and n. פ there.

[40] Source 14 mentions another sage named Rav Giddal, Rav Giddol b. Manyomi, who was Rav's disciple as well. On the difficulty of identifying the amoras named Rav Giddal see them in Hyman; Albeck, *Mavo la-Talmudim*, p. 194; and see also nn. 16, 18–20 above.

women of Nareš should not immerse for purification at night (and see the entry on "Parziqiya"). Another reference to fauna in the area appears in Source 5, in connection with problems involving various animals, among them the beavers which abounded around the banks of the Nareš river.[41]

F. *Economy*

A product peculiar to Nareš was the hard felt mentioned in Source 8.

G. *The Inhabitants*

Source 5 contains criticism of the Narešans, whom Rav Papa accuses of godlessness, calling for their excommunication, while Rav Giddal characterizes them as thieves ("If a Narešan kisses you, count your teeth"). However, as they are made by sages themselves residents of Nareš, these judgements are probably to be taken with a grain of salt.

Beer, *Amora'ei Bavel* (1974), pp. 175, 178
Berliner, *Beiträge* (1883), p. 54
Eshel, *Yishuvei ha-Yehudim* (1979), pp. 177–178, 191–193
Funk, *Juden* (1902–1908), vol. 2, pp. 152, 156–157
Funk, *Monumenta* (1913), pp. 19, 46, 278, 297
Halevy, *Dorot ha-Rishonim* (1897–1939), vol. 5, pp. 222, 506–507
Hirschenson, *Sheva Ḥokhmot* (1883), p. 172
Jastrow, *Dictionary* (1950³), p. 937
Kohut, *Arukh ha-Shalem* (1878–1892), vol. 2, p. 9 "ביברי"; vol. 5, p. 390; *Tosefot* (1937), p. 285
Krauss, *Qadmoniot ha-Talmud* (1923–1945), vol. 1A, pp. 37, 52
Levy, *Wörterbuch* (1924²), vol. 3, p. 445
Neubauer, *Géographie* (1868), p. 365
Newman, *Agricultural Life* (1932), passim
Obermeyer, *Landschaft* (1929), pp. 171, 208, 275, 277, 306–310
Yudelevitz, *Sinai* 14 (1943/4): 94–98; 15 (1944/5): 93–98, 226–229
Zadok, *JQR* 68 (1977/8): 255–256
Zuri, *Shilton* (1938), pp. 5–6

Na'usa נאוסא

A. *Source*

'Eruvin 83a

כי אתא רב דימי אמר שיגר בוניוס[1] לרבי מודיא דקונדיס דמן נאוסא[2] ושיער רבי מאתן ושבע עשרה ביעין.

[41] According to the versions in n. 6 above, the reference is not to beavers (= ביברים) but to residents of Be Bire (= בי בירי) near Nareš, who are disparagingly described as "not of the land."

[1] The Munich MS has Ben Bonyas; and see *Diq. Sof.*

[2] The Oxford MS has נאונסא, the Salonika printing has ניסא, Rashi there has נאסא; and see *Diq. Sof.*

When Rav Dimi came he said, Bonyos[1] sent Rabbi a measure of artichokes from Na'usa,[2] and Rabbi estimated [that it contained] two hundred and seventeen eggs.

B. *Already Proposed Location*

On an island in the Euphrates between Ihi də-Qira and Aluš, about 32 kilometers northwest of Hīt[3] (A1 on the Tal. Bab. map).

C. *Identification*

Na'usa is mentioned in many Arabic sources.[4] According to an Arab tradition, Aluš, Talbuš and Na'usa are named after three brothers of the ʿĀd tribe who fled for their lives and settled there.[5] Na'usa is listed among the Euphrates fortresses along the route of the Muslim conquest of Mesopotamia.[6]
In the talmudic source above, Na'usa figures in a statement by Rav Dimi—one of the *naḥote* sages who brought the law of Eretz Israel to Babylonia—dealing with a shipment of artichokes Rabbi Judah ha-Nasi received. At first glance it appears that Na'usa could be located in Eretz Israel, but the existence on the Euphrates of a place with exactly the same name tips the scales in favor of a Babylonian location.[7]

Eshel, *Yishuvei ha-Yehudim* (1979), p. 151
Hirschenson, *Sheva Ḥokhmot* (1883), p. 163
Jastrow, *Dictionary* (1950³), p. 866
Kohut, *Arukh ha-Shalem* (1878–1892), vol. 5, p. 296
Levy, *Wörterbuch* (1924²), vol. 3, p. 322
Musil, *The Middle Euphrates* (1927), pp. 26, 253–256
Neubauer, *Géographie* (1868), p. 395
Obermeyer, *Landschaft* (1929), p. 102

Nəhar Abba נהר אבא

A. *Source*

Shabbat 140b

ואמר רב חסדא בר בי רב דזבין כיתוניתא ליזבן מדנהר אבא וניחוורה כל תלתין יומין, דמפטיא ליה תריסר ירתי שתא, ואנא ערבא.

---

[3] Musil, *The Middle Euphrates*, pp. 26, 253–256 and map.

[4] E.g. Yāqūt, s.v. "Nawūsa"; *ar-Rauḍ al-miʿṭār*, s.v. "ʿĀnāt"; *BGA*, passim; Idrīsī, vol. 6, p. 656; *Futūḥ al-buldān*, p. 179; and see Le Strange, "Ibn Serapion," pp. 10, 52; Suhrāb, p. 119.

[5] See the entry on "ʿAnat" and nn. 11, 12 there.

[6] See the entry on "Talbuš."

[7] The identifica ion was proposed by Obermeyer (p. 102) and Eshel (p. 151) in his train. Hirschensontthinks Na'usa was in Eretz Israel and judges it to have been in the Bet Šə'an valley (p. 103). Neubauer too mentions Na'usa (p. 395) but does not propose any location. He believes the source refers to Rabbi Modia, but the reference is certainly to Rabbi Judah ha-Nasi as a person named Bonyos or Ben Bonyas is mentioned in connection with him in other sources too (cf. ʿEruvin 85b, Giṭṭin 59a). The word *modia* means "measure," and is probably derived from Latin *modius* (or Greek μόδιος).

And Rav Ḥisda said, A pupil who buys a garment should buy one of Nəhar Abba's, and wash it every thirty days, and I guarantee it will do him for twelve months of the year.

B. *Proposed Location*

Tall Aba (= Abbā) in the Sura area, a little north of the latitude of Sura, between the Euphrates and Sura rivers (D4 on the Tal. Bab. map).

C. *Identification*

Yāqūt, in his entry on "Abbā" reports that the Nahr Abbā was a place between Kūfa and Qaṣr Ibn Hubaira that was named after Abbā b. aṣ-Ṣāmiġān, "a king of the Nabateans," i.e. the Arameans.[1] Qaṣr Ibn Hubaira was built near the Sura bridge at the end of the Umayyad period.[2] It appears that the name of Nəhar Abba has survived in that of Tall Aba,[3] which is close to Sura.

In another work, Yāqūt places Nahr Abbā between Kūfa and Qaṣr Banī Muqātil west of the Euphrates,[4] which means that Nahr Abbā would be west of the Euphrates. The version with Qaṣr Ibn Hubaira seems preferable, however, not only because of the possibility of identifying Nəhar Abba with Tall Aba, but also because of Masʿūdī's testimony. He says[5] that the Aramean kings controlled the Qaṣr Ibn Hubaira area (and lists some more places in the vicinity). The Aramean king, Bābā (= Papa) b. Bardīnā, was the ruler of Qaṣr Ibn Hubaira (that is, of the place that bore that name later, in the Muslim period).[6]

---

[1] See Nöldeke, *Perser und Araber*, p. 22, n. 2; idem, *ZDMG*, 25 (1871): 122ff. While Obermeyer cited Yāqūt, he referred only to "Nahr Abbā" where the information is incomplete. That entry states that Nahr Abbā was *min nawāḥī Baġdād* and that it was dug by Abbā b. aṣ-Ṣamġān (*sic*) the Nabatean (= Aramean). Obermeyer (p. 239) renders the definition as "Nahr Abā(!) gehört zum Kreise Baghdad," notes that the area on the Euphrates around Anbār was also part of the Baghdad region in Yāqūt's time, and suggests a connection with Anbār (identified by him with Pumbədita, q.v.) which like Nəhar Abba was noted for its flax (see below). It would seem, however, that in Yāqūt's usage Baghdad means simply Iraq.

[2] See, e.g., Yāqūt's entry on "Qaṣr Ibn Hubaira."

[3] See Kiepert's map, *ZGEB* 18 (1883).

[4] See the entry on "Abbā" in *Muštarik* and in *Marāṣid* (which is mostly an abridgement of Yāqūt's geographical dictionary). The latter states "a river between Kūfa and Qaṣr Banī Muqātil, named after Abbā b. aṣ-Ṣamigān, one of the kings of the Nabateans." See also Yāqūt's entry on "Qaṣr Banī Muqātil."

[5] Masʿūdī, *Murūǧ*, vol. 1, pp. 275–276 (= vol. 2, p. 134).

[6] Masʿūdī, *ibid.*, p. 289 (= vol. 2, p. 161). And see Nöldeke, *loc.cit.*, in n. 1.

D. *Sages and Nəhar Abba*

Rav Ḥisda, head of the Sura yeshiva in the third generation of Babylonian amoras advises the students of the study house to acquire linen garments made at Nəhar Abba as those wore very well.[7]

E. *Economy*

The source indicates that flax was raised in the area of Nəhar Abba which was noted for its linen and linen products. Flax was a common crop in great demand,[8] playing an important role in the economy of Babylonia.

Beer, *Amora'ei Bavel* (1974), pp. 187–188, 191
Berliner, *Beiträge* (1883), p. 47
Eshel, *Yishuvei ha-Yehudim* (1979), pp. 152, 159
Funk, *Monumenta* (1913), p. 16
Hirschenson, *Sheva Ḥokhmot* (1883), p. 164
Jastrow, *Dictionary* (1950³), p. 883
Kohut, *Arukh ha-Shalem* (1878–1892), vol. 5, p. 320
Krauss, *Qadmoniot ha-Talmud* (1923–1945), vol. 2B, p. 58
Levy, *Wörterbuch* (1924²), vol. 3, p. 352
Neubauer, *Géographie* (1868), pp. 341–342
Newman, *Agricultural Life* (1932), p. 104
Obermeyer, *Landschaft* (1929), pp. 239–240
Wiesner, *Scholien* (1859–1867), vol. 2, p. 255

Nəhar Anaq נהר אנק

A. *Source*

Berakhot 42b (as per the Munich MS)

כי נח נפשיה דרב אזלי תלמידיה בתריה כי הדור אמרי ניזול ניכול נהמא בנהר אנק.[1]

When Rav died, his disciples followed after him. When they returned, they said, Let us go and eat bread in Nəhar Anaq.[1]

B. *Proposed Location*

Nəhar Anaq is a channel of the Euphrates River near the village of Dimimmā (see the entry on "Damim") beyond Anbār.

[7] Because of the reference to Rav Ḥisda, Eshel assumed that Nəhar Abba was not far from Sura (Eshel, p. 152). In this case it appears that there was a connection between Rav Ḥisda's recommendation to his pupils, and the propinquity of Sura to Nəhar Abba.

[8] For flax growing at Nəhar Abba in particular and in Babylonia in general, see Newman, *Agricultural Life*, pp. 104–105; Beer, *Amora'ei Bavel*, pp. 187–191, and the bibliography there (Beer's puzzlement, p. 191, n. 108, is dispelled if the proposed location of Nəhar Abba in the vicinity of Sura is accepted).

[1] This is the form in the Munich and Paris MSS as well as the *Arukh*; on the other hand the form in the printing is נהר דנק (see below), and see *Diq. Sof.*

C. *Identification*

Various speculations on the site of Nəhar Anaq appear in the literature. Funk mentions a river by that name in northern Mesopotamia near Samosata[2]; Berliner deduces from the connotation in the source above that the river was in the vicinity of the place where Rav died[3]; Obermeyer, on the basis of gaonic literature (below) concludes that Nəhar Anaq is a channel of the Euphrates, and since it is mentioned in connection with Rav's death, must be near Sura which was where he had resided.[4]

Nəhar Anaq can be located quite accurately by means of information in Ṭabarī: "... until he camped at Dimimmā and wished to span Nahr Anaq[5] with a bridge; ... near Nahr Anaq and Nahr Rufail, above the village of Dimimmā."[6]

Dimimmā itself is a large village on the east bank of the Euphrates, near Fallūğa, not far from Anbār.[7]

Ṭabarī's information fits in well with evidence found in gaonic responsa. Someone from Qairawān submitted a question on the meaning of the word *anəharnaq*[8] in Tractate Berakhot, and the Gaon replies: "Nəhar Naq are two words. And it is a well-known river in Babylonia, Nəhar ʿAnaq,[9] and it starts off from the Euphrates River."[10] It is reasonable to assume that the real name of the river was Anaq, which gave rise to the various versions in the sources: Danaq (= də-Anaq)[11] in the Talmud and Naq (dropping the initial *alef*) and ʿAnaq (substituting *ʿayin* for *alef*)[12] in the gaonic literature.

---

[2] Funk, *Monumenta*, p. 280, and see also his article in *Jahrbuch* 6 (1908/9): 338.

[3] Berliner, p. 30. His designation, on the basis of Petaḥyah of Regensburg, of the neighborhood of Kūfa as the place where Rav was buried is unfounded (see Eisenstein, *Otzar Masaʿot*, p. 52). Eshel's reiteration (p. 160) of Hyman's view p. 41 that Rav was buried in Kafri is groundless as well.

[4] Obermeyer, pp. 300–301.

[5] Ṭabarī, vol. 9, p. 321 (= vol. 3, pp. 1605–1606).

[6] *Ibid.*, vol. 9, p. 325 (= vol. 3, p. 1612). Nahr Rufail flows out of the Nahr ʿĪsā and into the Tigris near Baghdad (see Yāqūt, s.v. "Rufail"); the ʿĪsā flows out of the Euphrates near the bridge (= *qanṭara*) of Dimimmā (see Yāqūt, s.v. "ʿĪsā").

[7] See Yāqūt, s.v. "Dimimmā"; and see the preceding note.

[8] The inquirer had the form אנהרנק written as one word, and cf. *Halakhot Gedolot*, Hildesheimer ed., vol. I, p. 116, and the variants there.

[9] Harkavy asserted that Nəhar ʿAnaq is mentioned in Qiddushin 71b, but as many have previously noted, the reference there is to Nəhar ʿAzeq.

[10] "נהר נק שתי מילין הן. ונהר ידוע הוא בבבל והוא נהר ענק, ומנהר פרת הוא נושא." *Teshuvot ha-Geonim*, Harkavy, vol. 1, Section 4, p. 141 (§ 280), and see *Otzar ha-Geonim* on Berakhot 42b, and note 1 there.

[11] This has already been noted by Neubauer (p. 341, n. 4) and Funk (*Monumenta*, p. 7 and his article cited in n. 2 above, p. 335).

[12] On the permutation of *alef* and *ʿayin* in Babylonian Aramaic, see Epstein, *Diqduq Aramit Bavlit*, pp. 17–18.

D. *Burial Across the Euphrates*

According to the identification made for Nəhar Anaq, the source above deals with disciples of Rav's who escorted their late master on his last journey, and on the way back from the cemetery stopped at Nəhar Anaq east of the Euphrates in the neighborhood of Pumbədita. The logical inference is that Rav was buried in the Pumbədita area; on the one hand it is obvious that he was not buried near Sura (where he had lived) and on the other the context makes it clear that his corpse was not carried all the way to Eretz Israel. The talmudic statement seems to fit in with other evidence on the burial of Babylonian Jews in places west of the Euphrates in the region which the sages considered to be within the boundaries of Eretz Israel (see the entries for "Tarbiqna" and "Šum Ṭəmaya"). That is to say, Rav's disciples took his corpse west of the Euphrates near Pumbədita for burial.

The remains of Jewish gravestones were found in the Anbār district at a place called Ǧūḫā which later became an Arab cemetery.[13] The following responsum of Rav Hai Gaon throws light on the practice of interment in that district: "And Rav Hai said, It is not our custom to move the deceased from the grave in his place [of residence], but it does happen that the deceased is buried in *Bagd* (read: Baghdad[14]) and some time later taken several parasangs to the west of the *Pəras* (read: *Pərat* = Euphrates[15]) to the desert near the wasteland . . . and in the matter of moving a woman's bones from one place to another we would hear from the elders saying, How nice not to do so . . . and yet when an important woman dies, her corpse is sent from Baghdad to Firi Šabur to the desert wasteland, certainly there is no prohibition in the matter, etc."[16] Thus this responsum not only makes reference to the custom of burying the dead west of the Euphrates, but actually mentions the place, the district of Firi (= Fīrūz) Sābūr, which is Anbār.[17]

Berliner, *Beiträge* (1883), p. 30
Eshel, *Yishuvei ha-Yehudim* (1979), pp. 160–161
Funk, *Jahrbuch* 6 (1908–1909): 338
Funk, *Juden* (1902–1908), vol. 2, p. 148
Funk, *Monumenta* (1913), pp. 7, 280

---

[13] Peters, *Nippur*, vol. 1, pp. 171–172, 179.

[14] As properly corrected by Mann (see n. 16).

[15] As properly corrected by Obermeyer (see n. 16).

[16] The responsum was cited in Mann, *JQR* 11 (1921): 436 (= Mann, *Collected Articles* vol. 2, p. 208). Obermeyer referred to this responsum (p. 323) but being familiar only with the Jewish cemetery in Bāniqyā (see entry for "Tarbiqna") he thought that Piri (= Piruz) Šabur was mentioned here only to indicate the direction in which the corpse was carried. There are no grounds for Mann's proposal (see n. 16) to identify Fīrūz Sābūr with Nəhardəʿa and his consequent conclusion that burial in Nəhardəʿa was a supreme virtue.

[17] See Yāqūt, "Fīrūzasābūr" (referring to a district of that name of which Anbār is the center).

HIRSCHENSON, *Sheva Ḥokhmot* (1883), p. 98
KOHUT, *Arukh ha-Shalem* (1878–1892), vol. 3, pp. 98–99
LEVY, *Wörterbuch* (1924²), vol. 1, p. 415
NEUBAUER, *Géographie* (1868), p. 341
OBERMEYER, *Landschaft* (1929), pp. 300–301

Nəhar ʿAzeq נהר עזק

A. *Sources*

1. Qiddushin 71b

עד היכן היא בבל, רב אמר[1] עד נהר עזק, ושמואל אמר עד נהר יואני.[2]

How far does Babylonia extend, Rav said,[1] To Nəhar ʿAzeq, and Samuel said, To Nəhar Yo'ani.[2]

2. T. J. Qiddushin IV 1 – 65c, 22–23[3]

רבי יוסה בי רבי בון בשם רב נחמן[4] בבל ליוחסין עד נהר יזק.[5] ר' יוסי בי רבי בון אמר רב ושמואל חד אמר עד נהר יזק, וחד אמר עד נהר יואני.[6]

Rabbi Yose b. Rabbi Bun in the name of Rav Naḥman,[4] Babylonia in respect to lineage, to Nəhar Yazeq.[5] Rabbi Yose b. Rabbi Bun said, Rav and Samuel, one said to Nəhar Yazeq, and one said to Nəhar Yo'ani.[6]

B. *Location*

None can be proposed due to insufficient data.

C. *Attempts at Identification*

The sources above both present the difference of opinion between Samuel and Rav concerning the eastern border of Babylonia in regard to purity of lineage (see the Introduction). Obermeyer proposed identifying Nəhar ʿAzeq, which Rav posited as the eastern boundary of "genealogical" Babylonia, with Nahr Ǧūẖā, a canal east of the Nahrawān canal (see the entry on "Nəhar Yo'ani").[7] Obermeyer's reason was that, aside from the Nahrawān which he identified with Nəhar Yo'ani, the Ǧūẖā was the only canal that could serve as the eastern boundary of Babylonia.

However, that identification is unsatisfactory for several reasons:

a. As it is based on geographical features only, and not the preservation of the name Nəhar ʿAzeq, it is not sufficiently well founded.

---

[1] The Vatican 111 MS does not have "Rav said."
[2] The Munich MS has נהר גאני, and the Vatican 111 MS has נהר ינאי.
[3] Similarly in T. J. Yevamot I 6–3b, 6–8.
[4] T. J. Yevamot has "Rabbi Naḥman b. Jacob."
[5] T. J. Yevamot has נהר זרוק, further on as well.
[6] T. J. Yevamot has נהר וואניי.
[7] Obermeyer, pp. 79–80.

b. There is no need to assume (cf. the entry on "Nəhar Yo'ani") that the eastern boundary of Babylonia is marked by a canal. The name Nəhar ʿAzeq may well designate a settlement, like other names marking the border which are cited in the continuation of Source 1.

c. This identification of Nəhar ʿAzeq would mean that Rav was considerably expanding "genealogical" Babylonia on the east. The Ǧūḫā canal flowed between Ḫāniqīn and Ḫūzistān (see the entry on "Be Ḥozai"). Ḫāniqīn is forty kilometers southwest of Ḥelwan on the way to Khurasan.[8] It is not reasonable to suppose that the area of Jewish settlement noted for the pure lineage of its inhabitants would extend so far.

Berliner, *Beiträge* (1883), p. 17
Eshel, *Yishuvei ha-Yehudim* (1979), p. 171
Funk, *Monumenta* (1913), pp. 4, 277
Jastrow, *Dictionary* (1950³), p. 572
Kohut, *Arukh ha-Shalem* (1878–1892), vol. 4, pp. 121, 183–184
Levy, *Wörterbuch* (1924²), vol. 2, p. 232
Neubauer, *Géographie* (1868), p. 324
Obermeyer, *Landschaft* (1929), pp. 78–80, 108

Nəharbil נהרביל

A. *Sources*

1. Berakhot 50a

תניא רבי אומר בטובו חיינו הרי זה תלמיד חכם, חיים הרי זה בור. נהרבלאי[1] מתני[2] איפכא, ולית הלכתא כנהרבלאי.

It was taught, Rabbi says that if someone says "By his goodness we lived" he is a scholar, and "we live" he is an ignoramus. The Nəharbilans[1] teach[2] the opposite, and the halakhah is not as the Nəharbilans.

2. Betzah 8b

נהרבלאי[3] אמרי אפילו הכניס עפר לכסות בו דם צפור מותר לכסות בו צואה.

Nəharbilans[3] say, Even if one brought in earth [before a holiday] to cover the blood of a bird, he may cover excrement with it.

---

[8] See Yāqūt, s.v. "Ǧuḫā," and see Bab.Env. map.

[1] The source has נהרבלאי; the Munich MS has נהרבילאי, later in the passage as well.

[2] The Munich MS has אמרי (= say). See also *Diq. Sof.*

[3] The source has נהרבלאי, the Munich MS has ונהרבלי אמרי, *Ginzei Talmud* has ונהר בלאי אמרי.

3. Bava Metziʿa 104b

... דתניא רבי יוסי[4] אומר מקום שנהגו לעשות כתובה מלוה גובה מלוה, לכפול גובה מחצה. נהרבלאי[5] גבו תילתא. מרימר מגבי נמי שבחא.

... It has been taught that Rabbi Yose[4] says, In a place where the *ketubah* is customarily a debt, he [the husband] can collect it as a debt, where it is doubled, he can collect half. The Nəharbilans[5] collect a third. Maremar collected even the accretion.

4. Sanhedrin 17b

... דייני דפומבדיתא רב פפא בר שמואל. דייני דנהרדעא רב אדא בר מניומי. סבי דסורא רב הונא ורב חסדא. סבי דפומבדיתא רב יהודה ורב עינא. חריפי דפומבדיתא עיפה ואבימי בני רחבה. אמוראי דפומבדיתא רבה ורב יוסף. אמוראי דנהרדעי רב חמא נהרבלאי[6] מתנו רמי בר ברבי.[7]

... The judges of Pumbədita Rav Papa b. Samuel; the judges of Nəhardəʿa Rav Adda b. Manyomi; the elders of Sura Rav Huna and Rav Ḥisda; the elders of Pumbədita Rav Judah and Rav ʿEina. The keen minds of Pumbədita ʿEfah and Avimi sons of Raḥavah; the amoras of Pumbədita Rabbah and Rav Joseph; the amoras of Nəhardəʿa Rav Ḥama; The Nəharbilans[6] claim [the reference is to] Rami b. Berabbi.[7]

5. Ḥullin 87b

ר׳ אסי[8] מנהרביל[9] אומר בצללתא דדמא.

Rabbi Assi[8] of Nəharbil[9] says, The thin [part of the] blood.

6. Ḥullin 136a

אי מה תרומה בארץ אין בחוצה לארץ לא אף מתנות[10] בארץ אין בחוצה לארץ לא, אמר רבי יוסי[11] מנהרביל[12] אין.

---

[4] The *baraita* appears in the Tosefta Ketubot IV 13 attributed to Rabbi Yose ha-Gelili but the parallels in T. J. Ketubot IV 8–29a, 9–10 and Yevamot XV 3–14d, 48–49 have "Rabbi Yose" alone. For the intrepretation of the *baraita* see Lieberman, *Tosefta ki-Fshutah*, vol. 6, pp. 250–251.

[5] The source has נהרבלאי, the Munich and Hamburg MSS have נהרבילאי, the Vatican 117 MS has נהר בלאי, the R-i-f MS has נהר בולאי.

[6] The source has נהרבלאי, the Munich and Florence MSS have נהרבילאי.

[7] The Munich and Florence MSS have "Rami b. Barukhi as do R-a-ḥ and the *Arukh* (under "נהר"). The Karlsruhe MS has "Rami b. Avimi" and a correction to "Rami b. Ḥama"; and see *Diq. Sof.* See also Hyman, p. 1101.

[8] The Vatican 122 MS has "Rabbi Yose"; and see *Diq. Sof.* The Rabbi Gershom commentary has "Rav Joseph."

[9] The Munich MS has מנהרבל, the Soncino printing has מנהר ביל, the Vatican 121 MS has מהונהמל.

[10] The Munich MS has ראשית הגז (= the first shearing); and see *Diq. Sof.*

[11] The Munich MS has "Rav Joseph"; and see *Diq. Sof.*

[12] The Munich and Vatican 121 MSS do not have the place at all; the Vatican 122 MS has מנהרבל; and see *Diq. Sof.*

The *terumah* if in Eretz Israel yes, if abroad no. Also presents[10] [other priestly gifts] in Eretz Israel yes, abroad no. Rabbi Yose[11] of Nəharbil[12] said, Right.

B. *Already Proposed Location*

In the Baghdad area, southeast of the city (D2 on the Tal. Bab. map).

C. *Identification*

Obermeyer proposed locating Nəharbil near Baghdad where there is a river or region by that name mentioned by Yāqūt.[13] This location seems well-grounded. Nahr Bīn, called also Nahr Bīl, was east of the Tigris in the southeast corner of greater Baghdad which encompassed both banks of the river.[14]

D. *Sages and Nəharbil*

Sources 1–3 cite the "Nəharbilans"[15] which was evidently the term used to designate the sages at the local study house in Nəharbil. In Source 1 they have an independent tradition in regard to a *baraita* of Rabbi's, although the halakhah is not determined by that tradition. In Source 2 they deal with holiday laws, and in Source 3 with ways of collecting a *ketubah*.[16]
Source 4 establishes that the term "the Nəharbilans taught" refers to Rami b. Barukhi (see note 7) who, incidentally, appears nowhere else in the Talmud. The interpretation of "Nəharbilans" as referring to a single sage does not eliminate the possibility of its usual application to a group of sages representing the local study house. The term in Source 4 appears in the context of similar forms (based on the names of the most celebrated yeshivas of Babylonia)[17] referring in some cases to one amora, in some to two.
Another relevant sage is Rabbi Assi (or Yose) of Nəharbil, mentioned in Sources 5 and 6. Apparently the same sage is meant, as shown by the simi-

---

13 Obermeyer, p. 269. See also Streck, *Die alte Landschaft*, vol. 1, p. 15 (on the region), p. 38 (on the river), vol. 2, p. 243 (on the canal).

14 See "Nahr Bīl" in Yāqūt, who says it is an alternate version of "Nahr Bīn" (q.v.); *Muštarik*, s.v. "Nahr," p. 425. On Nahr Bīn east of the Tigris, see Suhrāb, p. 129; Le Strange, "Ibn Serapion," p. 21, who writes that it starts at the Nahrawān canal, a little above the bridge (see the entry on "Nəhar Yo'ani"), and flows into the Tigris less than two parasangs south of Baghdad. On Nahr Bīn see also *BGA*, passim: Le Strange, *Baghdad* (see index); Lassner, (see index). On Nahrabīn in Ǧazīra see *Naqā'iḍ*, vol. 2, p. 829, and cf. the Bīn near Kūfa.

15 נהרבלאי, which seems to be the correct version, and see nn. 1, 5 and 6 above.

16 The disagreement with Maremar indicates that it was not a local custom for Nəharbil but the expression of an halakhic opinion by the Nəharbil sages. See Goodblatt, *HUCA* 48 (1977), pp. 207–208.

17 But see Goodblatt's view in the article referred to in n. 16.

larity of the names (אסי vs יוסי) and by the variant forms (see notes 8 and 11). The context of the sources does not provide any information making it possible to date this sage, however.

Bacher, *Tradition* (1914), p. 587
Berliner, *Beiträge* (1883), p. 47
Eshel, *Yishuvei ha-Yehudim* (1979), pp. 153, 163
Funk, *Monumenta* (1913), pp. 41, 295
Goodblatt, *HUCA* 48 (1977), pp. 207–208
Hirschenson, *Sheva Ḥokhmot* (1883), p. 164
Jastrow, *Dictionary* (1950³), p. 883
Kohut, *Arukh ha-Shalem* (1878–1892), vol. 1, p. xvii, vol. 5, pp. 320–321
Neubauer, *Géographie* (1868), p. 395
Obermeyer, *Landschaft* (1929), p. 269

Nəhardəʿa נהרדעא

A. *Sources* (*a selection*)

1. Ketubot 54a

אתמר רב אמר הלכה כאנשי יהודה ושמואל אמר הלכה כאנשי גליל. בבל וכל פרוודהא[1] נהוג כרב, נהרדעא וכל פרוודהא נהוג כשמואל. ההיא בת מחוזא דהות נסיבא לנהרדעא,[2] אתו לקמיה דרב נחמן שמעה לקלה דבת מחוזא היא, אמר להו בבל וכל פרוודהא נהוג כרב, אמרו ליה והא לנהרדעא נסיבא, אמר להו אי הכי נהרדעא וכל פרוודהא נהוג כשמואל. ועד היכא נהרדעא, עד היכא דסגי קבא דנהרדעא.

It was stated Rav said, The halakhah is like the men of Judaea and Samuel said, The halakhah is like the men of Galilee. Babylon and all its surroundings[1] acted according to Rav, Nəhardəʿa and all its surroundings acted according to Samuel. That woman of Maḥoza who was married to [a man of] Nəhardəʿa,[2] they came before Rav Naḥman, who heard from her voice that she was a Maḥozan and said to them, Babylon and all its surroundings acted according to Rav. They said to him, But she is married to Nəhardəʿa. He said to them, If so, Nəhardəʿa and all its surroundings acted according to Samuel. And how far is Nəhardəʿa? As far as the *qav* of Nəhardəʿa extends.

2. ʿEruvin 6b

בעו מיניה מרב ענן צריך לנעול או אין צריך לנעול, אמר להו תא חזי הני אבולי דנהרדעא דטימן עד פלגייהו בעפרא ועייל ונפיק מר שמואל ולא אמר להו ולא מידי.

---

[1] Derived from **פרוור** (see *Arukh ha-Shalem*, vol. 6, p. 416, s.v. "**פרוור**"). The *dalet* in the printing is not in the root and does not appear in most of the MSS. Thus e.g. the Munich MS has **פרואה**, the Vatican 130 MS has **פרווהא**, the Leningrad MS has **פרוארהא**. The *Arukh* version is **פרוורהא**, and see Ketubot in the ICIT edition, n. 36. See also Gafni, *Ha-Yeshiva be-Bavel*, p. 210.

[2] The Vatican 113 and 487 MSS have **לבר נהרדעא**, further on as well. The Vatican 130 and Leningrad MSS have **בנהרדעא**. A Geniza fragment (Oxford 2835) has **לנהרדעאה**, further on as well.

Rav ʿAnan was asked, Is it necessary to lock [the door of an alley] or not? He replied, Come and see those gateways of Nəhardəʿa which are half buried in the ground, and Mar Samuel goes in and out and did not say anything to them.

3. Taʿanit 20b

כי ההיא אשיתא רעועה דהואי בנהרדעא דלא הוה חליף רב ושמואל תותה אע״ג דקיימא באתרה תליסר שנין.

Like that dilapidated wall that was in Nəhardəʿa that Rav and Samuel would not go past although it had remained standing in the same position for thirteen years.

4. Ḥullin 50b

אמר רבי חייא בר אבא לדידי מפרשא לי מיניה דגניבא אמברא דנהרדעא ...

Rabbi Ḥiyya b. Abba said, Geniva explained it to me on the Nəhardəʿa crossing ...

5. ʿAvodah Zarah 70b

ההוא פולמוסא דסליק לנהרדעא, פתחו חביתא טובא, כי אתא רב דימי אמר עובדא הוה קמיה דרבי אלעזר ושרא, ולא ידענא אי משום דסבר לה כרבי אליעזר דאמר ספק ביאה טהור, אי משום דסבר רובא דאזלי בהדי פולמוסא ישראל נינהו.

That army that came up to Nəhardəʿa opened some casks. When Rav Dimi came he said, There was a similar case before Rabbi Eleazar, and he permitted [the wine], and I do not know whether it was because he believed as did Rabbi Eliezer who said if there is uncertainty it is pure, or he believed that most of those in the army were Jewish.

6. ʿEruvin 34b

ההוא פולמוסא דאתא לנהרדעא, אמר להו רב נחמן פוקו עבידו כבושי כבשי באגמא ולמחר ניזיל וניתיב עלויהו.

That army that once came to Nəhardəʿa, Rav Naḥman told them, Go out and flatten [the reeds] so that tomorrow [on the Sabbath] we can go and sit on them.

7. ʿEruvin 45a

ובעיר הסמוכה לספר אפילו לא באו על עסקי נפשות אלא על עסקי תבן וקש יוצאין עליהן בכלי זיינן ומחללין עליהן את השבת. אמר רב יוסף בר מניומי אמר רב נחמן ובבל כעיר הסמוכה לספר דמיא, ותרגומא נהרדעא.

In the town that was close to the border, they (the Gentiles) did not even come with any intention of taking lives but merely straw and stubble, but the people are permitted to go forth with their weapons and desecrate the Sabbath on their account. Rav Joseph b. Manyomi said in Rav Naḥman's name, Babylon is on a par with a border town, and this was interpreted to refer to Nəhardəʿa.

8. Bava Qamma 83a

תנו רבנן לא יגדל אדם את הכלב אלא אם כן קשור בשלשלת אבל מגדל הוא בעיר הסמוכה לספר וקושרו ביום ומתירו בלילה . . . אמר רב יוסף בר מניומי אמר רב נחמן בבל[3] כעיר הסמוכה לספר דמי, תרגמה נהרדעא.

The rabbis taught that a man should not raise a dog unless it is chained, but if he raises it in a border town, he ties it up by day and releases it by night . . . Rav Joseph b. Manyomi said in Rav Naḥman's name, Babylon[3] is on a par with a border town; this was interpreted to refer to Nəhardəʿa.

9. Rosh ha-Shanah 24b; ʿAvodah Zarah 43b

. . . והא ההיא בי כנישתא דשף ויתיב בנהרדעא דהוה ביה[4] אנדרטא והוו עיילי רב ושמואל[5] ואבוה דשמואל ולוי ומצלו התם.

But that Šaf we-Yativ synagogue in Nəhardəʿa that had in it[4] a statue, Rav and Samuel[5] and Samuel's father and Levi used to go in to pray there.

10. Niddah 13a

רב יהודה ושמואל הוו קיימי אאיגרא דבי כנישתא דשף ויתיב בנהרדעא, אמר ליה רב יהודה לשמואל צריך אני להשתין, א"ל שיננא אחוז באמתך והשתן לחוץ.

Rav Judah and Samuel once stood on the roof of the Šaf we-Yativ synagogue in Nəhardəʿa. Rav Judah said to him, to Samuel, I have to urinate. He said to him, You keen scholar, take hold of your organ and urinate outward.

11. Megillah 29a

תניא ר"ש בן יוחי אומר בוא וראה כמה חביבין ישראל לפני הקב"ה שבכל מקום שגלו שכינה עמהן, גלו למצרים שכינה עמהן . . . גלו לבבל שכינה עמהן . . . בבבל היכא, אמר אביי בבי כנישתא דהוצל ובבי כנישתא דשף ויתיב בנהרדעא, ולא תימא הכא והכא אלא זמנין הכא וזמנין הכא. אמר אביי תיתי לי דכי מרחיקנא פרסה עיילנא ומצלינא התם. אבוה דשמואל ולוי[6] הוו יתבי בכנישתא דשף ויתיב בנהרדעא, אתיא שכינה . . . רב ששת הוה יתיב בבי כנישתא דשף ויתיב בנהרדעא, אתיא שכינה . . .

It has been taught that Rabbi Simeon b. Yoḥai said, Come and see how beloved is Israel in the sight of God, in that to every place they were exiled the Divine Presence went with them. They were exiled to Egypt and the Divine Presence was with them . . . They were exiled to Babylonia and the Divine Presence was with them . . . Where in Babylonia? Abbaye said, in the synagogue of Huṣal and in the synagogue of Šaf we-Yativ in Nəhardəʿa. Do not, however, say that it is [both] here and there, but sometimes here and sometimes there. Said Abbaye, May evil befall me if whenever I am within a parasang I do not go in and pray there. Samuel's father and Levi[6] were sitting in the Saf we-Yativ

[3] The Vatican 116 MS does not have the word "Bavel."
[4] The Munich MS of Rosh ha-Shanah has ואקימו בה.
[5] All the MSS and the parallel in ʿAvodah Zarah have no mention of Rav and Samuel.
[6] The Munich MS does not mention Levi.

synagogue in Nəhardəʿa, the Divine Presence came ... Rav Sheshet sat in the Šaf we-Yativ synagogue in Nəhardəʿa, the Divine Presence came ...

12. Qiddushin 70b

...רב מתנה לא חזייה לנהרדעא תליסר שני ההוא יומא אתא, אמר ליה דכיר מר מאי אמר שמואל כי קאי חדא כרעא אגודא וחדא כרעא במברא, א״ל הכי אמר שמואל כל דאמר מדבית חשמונאי מלכא קאתינא עבדא הוא... אכרוז עליה דעבדא הוא. ההוא יומא אקרען כמה כתובתא בנהרדעא. כי קא נפיק נפקי אבתריה למירגמיה, אמר להו אי שתיקו שתיקו ואי לא מגלינא עלייכו הא דאמר שמואל תרתי זרעייתא איכא בנהרדעא, חדא מיקריא דבי יונה וחדא מיקריא דבי עורבתי, וסימניך טמא טמא טהור טהור. שדיוה להוא ריגמא מידייהו וקם אטמא בנהר מלכא. מכריז רב יהודה בפומבדיתא[7] אדא ויונתן עבדי, יהודה בר פפא ממזירא... אמר רב יהודה אמר שמואל ארבע מאות עבדים, ואמרי לה ארבעת אלפים עבדים היו לו לפשחור בן אימר וכולם נטמעו בכהונה, וכל כהן שיש בו עזות פנים אינו אלא מהם. אמר אביי כולהו יתבן בשורא דבנהרדעא.[8]

... Rav Mattenah had not seen Nəhardəʿa for thirteen years, but on that day [when Rav Judah proclaimed the man who said he was a Hasmonean slave] he came. He said to him, Do you remember what Samuel said when he stood with one foot on the bank and one foot on the ferry? He said to him that Samuel said thus, Whoever says I am descended from the royal house of the Hasmoneans is a slave ... So he was proclaimed a slave. On that day some *ketubot* were torn up in Nəhardəʿa. When he (Rav Judah) went out they came out after him to stone him. He said to them, If you will be silent it is better; if not, I will disclose what Samuel said. There are two families in Nəhardəʿa, one called the House of Yonah (= dove) and the other the House of ʿOrev (= raven) and the sign of it is that the unclean is unclean and the clean clean. They threw the stones out of their hands, and a stoppage was created in the Royal Canal. Rav Judah announced in Pumbədita,[7] Adda and Jonathan are slaves, Judah b. Papa is a *mamzer* ... Rav Judah said in Samuel's name, Pashḥur b. Immer had four hundred slaves—some say four thousand slaves—and all became mixed up in the priesthood, and every priest who displays impudence is from none but them. Said Abbaye, And they all dwell in the wall of Nəhardəʿa.[8]

13. Mishnah, Yevamot XVI 7

אמר רבי עקיבא, כשירדתי לנהרדעא לעבר השנה מצאתי נחמיה איש בית דלי[9] אמר לי...

Rabbi ʿAqiva said, When I went down to Nəhardəʿa to intercalate the year, I met Nehemiah man of Bet Dəli,[9] who said to me ...

---

[7] The Munich MS has בנהרדעא, as does *She'iltot de-Rav Aḥai Gaon, She'ilta* 41.

[8] A letter of Rav Hai Gaon's has בסורא ונהרדעא (*Otzar ha-Geonim* for Qiddushin, *ha-Teshuvot*, p. 187). The Munich and Vatican 111 MSS do not have Abbaye's statement at all.

[9] The Lowe MS has איש בית דְלָא; the T. J. Mishnah has בדלא. Bet Dəli seems to be a place in Eretz Israel, although its location has not been clarified (for attempts at identification see Neubauer, p. 263; Schwarz, *Tevuot ha-Aretz*, p. 139f.; Horowitz, *Eretz Israel u-Shekhenoteha*, p. 131; Segal, *Ha-Geografiah ba-Mishnah*, p. 37.

14. Giṭṭin 36b

ת״ש דאמר שמואל לא כתבינן פרוסבול אלא אי בבי דינא דסורא אי בבי דינא דנהרדעא.

Come and hear, Samuel has said, We do not write a *prosbul* except either in the Bet Din of Sura or in the Bet Din of Nəhardəʿa.

15. Berakhot 58b[10]

ואמר שמואל נהירין לי שבילי דשמיא כשבילי דנהרדעא.

And Samuel said, the paths of heaven are as clear to me as the paths of Nəhardəʿa.

16. Giṭṭin 89b

והא נהרדעא אתריה דשמואל הוא ולא[11] מבטלי קלא.

How is it since Nəhardəʿa is Samuel's place that it is not[11] customary to suppress a report.

17. Shabbat 116b

. . . אמר רב לא שנו אלא במקום בית המדרש אבל שלא במקום בית המדרש קורין, ושמואל אמר בין במקום בית המדרש בין שלא במקום בית המדרש בזמן בית המדרש אין קורין שלא בזמן בית המדרש קורין. ואזדא שמואל לטעמיה, דבנהרדעא פסקי סידרא דכתובים במנחתא דשבתא.

. . . Rav said, They did not teach [it is forbidden to read the Hagiographa on the Sabbath] except in the place of the study house, but not in the place of the study house one reads. And Samuel said, Whether in the place of the study house or not in the place of the study house, at the time of the study house one does not read, and not at the time of the study house one reads. And Samuel went by his system in Nəhardəʿa, and they read an excerpt from the Hagiographa at *Minḥah* on the Sabbath.

18. Sanhedrin 17b

דייני דנהרדעא רב אדא בר מניומי . . . אמוראי דנהרדעא רב חמא.

The judges of Nəhardəʿa Adda b. Manyomi . . . the amoras of Nəhardəʿa Rav Ḥama.

19. Pesaḥim 62b

ר׳ שמלאי אתא לקמיה דרבי יוחנן,[12] א״ל ניתני לי מר ספר יוחסין, א״ל מהיכן את, א״ל מלוד, והיכן מותבך, בנהרדעא. א״ל אין נידונין לא ללודים ולא לנהרדעים וכל שכן דאת מלוד ומותבך בנהרדעא.

---

[10] Parallels in T. J. Berakhot IX 3–13c, 31; Midrash Tehillim XIX 4 (Buber ed., p. 163).

[11] The Munich and other manuscripts and printings have ובנהרדעא לא מבטלי קלא; and see *Diq. Sof.* (Feldblum). The same appears in the parallel in Giṭṭin 81a.

[12] The Munich MS has "Rabbi Nathan."

Rabbi Simlai came before Rabbi Yoḥanan,[12] said to him, Let the Master teach me the Book of Genealogies. He said to him, Where are you from? He said to him, From Lod. And where is your dwelling? In Nəhardəʿa. He said to him, We do not discuss it with either the Lodians or the Nehərdəʿans, and how much more so with you who are from Lod and live in Nəhardəʿa.

20. T. J. Pesaḥim V 3–32a, 61–64

רבי שמלאי אתא גבי רבי יונתן אמר ליה אלפן אגדה, אמר ליה מסורת בידי מאבותי שלא ללמד אגדה לא לבבלי ולא לדרומי שהן גסי רוח ומעוטי תורה, ואת נהרדעאי ודר בדרום.

Rabbi Simlai came to Rabbi Jonathan and said to him, Teach me Aggadah. He said to him, It is a tradition I have from my forefathers not to teach Aggadah to Babylonians or to Daromeans, for they are vulgar and unlearned, and you are a Nəhardəʿan and live in the Darom.

21. ʿAvodah Zarah 58a

... דההוא עובדא דהוה בנהרדעא ואסר שמואל, בטבריא ואסר רבי יוחנן, ואמרי ליה לפי שאינן בני תורה, ואמר לי טבריא ונהרדעא אינן בני תורה, דמחוזא בני תורה ...

There was that case in Nəhardəʿa (that a Gentile dabbled in the wine with his hand) and Samuel forbade, and in Tiberias and Rabbi Yoḥanan forbade, and I said to him (Rava to Abbaye), [They were strict] because they are not familiar with the Torah. He said to me, Tiberias and Nəhardəʿa are not familiar with the Torah, of Maḥoza they are ...

22. Yoma 19b

תניא אבא שאול אמר אף בגבולין היו עושין כן זכר למקדש אלא שהיו חוטאין. אמר אביי ואיתימא רב נחמן בר יצחק, תרגומא נהרדעא, דא"ל אליהו לרב יהודה אחוה דרב סלא חסידא אמריתו אמאי לא אתי משיח והא האידנא יומא דכיפורי הוא ואבעול כמה בעולתא בנהרדעא ...

It is taught, Abba Saul said that even on the borders (outside Jerusalem) they did so [stayed awake the whole night of the Day of Atonement] in memory of the Temple, but they sinned. Abbaye, and some say Rav Naḥman b. Isaac, ascribed this to Nəhardəʿa, for Elijah said to Rav Judah, Rav Sela the Pious's brother, You say why doesn't the Messiah come, now it is the Day of Atonement and a few virgins in Nəhardəʿa were deflowered.

23. Pesaḥim 56a

אמר רבי אבהו התקינו שיהו אומרים אותו בקול רם מפני תרעומת המינן, ובנהרדעא דליכא מינין עד השתא אמרי לה בחשאי.

Rabbi Abbahu said they ordained that this ["Blessed be His glorious kingdom for all eternity" from the *Shemaʿ* recitation] should be said aloud, on account of the resentment of heretics. But in Nəhardəʿa where there are no heretics so far they say it silently.

24. Giṭṭin 14a–b[13]

ר׳ אחי בר׳ יאשיה הוה ליה איספקא דכספא בנהרדעא, אמר להו לר׳ דוסתאי ב״ר ינאי ולר׳ יוסי בר כיפר בהדי דאתיתו אתיוה ניהלי, אזול, יהביה ניהליה, אמרי להו נקני מינייכו, אמרי להו לא, אמרי להו אהדריה ניהלן, ר׳ דוסתאי ברבי ינאי אמר להו אין, ר׳ יוסי בר כיפר אמר להו לא, הוו קא מצערו ליה, א״ל חזי מר היכי קא עביד, אמר להו טב רמו ליה. כי אתו לגביה א״ל חזי מר לא מיסתייה דלא סייען אלא אמר להו נמי טב רמו ליה. א״ל אמאי תיעבד הכי, א״ל אותן בני אדם הן אמה וכובען אמה ומדברין מחצייהן ושמותיהן מבוהלין ארדא וארטא ופילי בריש, אומרין כפותו כופתין אומרין הרוגו הורגין, אילו הרגו את דוסתאי מי נתן לינאי אבא בר כמותי, א״ל בני אדם הללו קרובים למלכות הן, א״ל הן, יש להן סוסים ופרדים שרצים אחריהן, א״ל הן, א״ל אי הכי שפיר עבדת.

Rabbi Aḥi son of Rabbi Josiah had a silver cup in Nəhardəʿa. He said to Rabbi Dostai son of Rabbi Yannai and to Rabbi Yose b. Kippar, When you come back from there bring it with you. They went and got it. They said, We'll buy it from you. They said, No. Then give it back, they said. Rabbi Dostai son of Rabbi Yannai said, Yes; Rabbi Yose b. Kippar said, No. They gave him a thrashing. They said to him, See, Master, what your friend is doing. He said, Thrash him well. When they returned to Rabbi Aḥi, Rabbi Yose said, Look sir, not only did he not assist me, but he also said to them, Thrash him well. He said to Rabbi Dostai, Why did you do so? He said, Those people are one cubit [tall] and their hats one cubit. Their voice comes from their middle and their names are outlandish beginning with Arda and Arṭa and Pile. If they say to put him in stocks he is put in stocks, if they say to kill him he is killed. If they had killed Dostai, who would have given Yannai my father a son like me. He said, Have these men influence with the government? He said, Yes. Have they horses and mules running after them? Yes, He said, If so, you acted rightly.

25. Bava Qamma 59a–b

אליעזר[14] זעירא הוה סיים מסאני אוכמי וקאי בשוקא דנהרדעא, אשכחוהו דבי ריש גלותא וא״ל מאי שנא הני מסאני, אמר להו דקא מאבילנא אירושלים, אמרו ליה את חשיבת לאיתאבולי אירושלים. סבור יוהרא הוה, אתיוה וחבשוה. אמר להו גברא רבא אנא, אמרו ליה מנא ידעינן, אמר להו או אתון בעו מינאי מילתא או אנא איבעי מינייכו מילתא, אמרו ליה בעי את ... שדרו קמיה דשמואל, אמר להו שפיר קאמר לכו . . ., ושבקוהו.

Eliezer[14] Zeʿira would put on a pair of black shoes and stand in the market place of Nəhardəʿa. When the stewards of the Exilarch's house met him they said to him, What is different [about] the shoes. He said to them, I am mourning for Jerusalem. They said to him, Are you such a distinguished person as to mourn over Jerusalem. They thought this was arrogance and brought him and

[13] Cf. T. J. Gittin I 6 – 43d, 45seq.; T. J. Qiddushin III 4 – 64a, 28seq.

[14] The Munich MS and others have "Eleazar"; the Vatican 116 MS has "Rabbi Eleazar."

put him in prison. He said to them, I am a great man. They asked him, How can we tell? He said, Either you ask me a point or let me ask you one. They said to him, You ask . . . They sent [the problem] before Samuel. He said to them, The statement he made to you is correct . . . and they released him.

26. Bava Batra 22a

רב דימי מנהרדעא אייתי גרוגרות בספינה,[15] א"ל ריש גלותא לרבא פוק חזי אי צורבא מרבנן הוא נקיט ליה שוקא, א"ל רבא לרב אדא בר אבא[16] פוק תהי ליה בקנקניה. נפק אזל בעא מיניה . . . לא הוה בידיה . . . לא נקטו ליה שוקא, פסיד גרוגרות דידיה.

Rav Dimi from Nəhardəʿa brought a load of figs in a boat.[15] The Exilarch said to Rava, Go and see if he is a scholar, and reserve the market for him. Rava said to Rav Adda b. Abba,[16] Go and smell his jar. He went out and asked him . . . He could not give [an answer] . . . They did not reserve the market for him and he lost his figs.

27. Qiddushin 70a

ההוא גברא דמנהרדעא[17] דעל לבי מטבחיא בפומבדיתא, אמר להו הבי לי בישרא, אמרו ליה נטר עד דשקיל לשמעיה דרב יהודה בר יחזקאל וניתיב לך, אמר מאן יהודה בר שויסקאל דקדים לי דשקל מן קמאי, אזלו אמרו ליה לרב יהודה, שמתיה. אמרו רגיל דקרי אינשי עבדי, אכריז עליה דעבדא הוא. אזל ההוא אזמניה לדינא לקמיה דרב נחמן . . .

That man from Nəhardəʿa[17] who entered the slaughterhouse in Pumbədita said to them, Give me meat. They said to him, Wait until the steward of Rav Judah b. Ezekiel takes and we will give you. He said, Who is Judah b. Sheviskel (= roast gobbler) that has precedence over me, that takes before me. They went and told Rav Judah. He banned him. They said, The man calls people slaves, and he proclaimed him a slave. That man went and summoned him to judgement before Rav Naḥman . . .

28. Bava Batra 36a

הנהו עיזי דאכלו חושלא בנהרדעא, אתא מרי חושלא תפסינהו והוה קא טעין טובא, אמר אבוה דשמואל יכול לטעון עד כדי דמיהן, דאי בעי אמר לקוחות הן בידי. והאמר ריש לקיש הגודרות אין להן חזקה, שאני עיזי דמסירה לרועה. והא איכא צפרא ופניא, בנהרדעא טייעי שכיחי ומידא לידא משלמי.

Those goats that ate peeled barley in Nəhardəʿa, the owner of the barley came and seized them and made a heavy claim. Samuel's father said, He can claim up to their value because if he wishes he can say he holds them. But Resh Laqish said, On livestock there is no *ḥazaqah*. It's different for goats entrusted to a shepherd. But there is morning and evening [when goats are unsupervised].

---

[15] The Florence MS has in addition the word במחוזא.

[16] The Florence and Oxford MSS have "Rav Adda b. Ahavah"; the Hamburg MS has "Rav Aḥa b. Abba"; see also *Diq. Sof*.

[17] The Munich MS and Venice printing do not have דמנהרדעא.

In Nəhardəʿa, however, there are Arabs, and the goats are delivered from hand to hand.

29. Ketubot 97a

ת״ש דההוא בצורתא דהוה בנהרדעא זבנינהו כולי עלמא לאפדנייהו, לסוף אתו חיטי, אמר להו רב נחמן דינא הוא דהדרי אפדני למרייהו, התם נמי זביני בטעות הוו, דאיגלאי מילתא דארבא בעקולי הוה קיימא . . . אמר ליה אטו כל יומא בצורתא שכיחא, אמר ליה אין, בצורתא בנהרדעא משכח שכיחא.

Come and hear. That drought in Nəhardəʿa, everybody sold their houses. In the end wheat came. Rav Naḥman said to them, It is the law that they should return the houses to their owners, there too the sales were by mistake, for it turned out that the barge was present in the bends [of the river] . . . He said to him, Is the drought common every day? He said to him, Yes, a drought in Nəhardəʿa is common.

30. T. J. Shabbat I 11 – 4a, 45–46

אי זהו מקום קרוב ייבא כיי דמר שמואל כגון מן חוטרה לנהרדעא.

What is a nearby place? It corresponds to what Samuel said, As from Ḥuṭra to Nəhardəʿa.

31. Qiddushin 81b

רב חנן מנהרדעא איקלע לרב כהנא לפום נהרא חזייה דיתיב וקא גרס וקיימא בהמה קמיה . . .

Rav Ḥanan of Nəhardəʿa happened to visit Rav Kahana at Pum Nahara, and saw him sitting and studying while an animal stood before him . . .

32. Ḥullin 95b

רב נחמן [18] מנהרדעא איקלע לגבי רב כהנא לפום נהרא [19] במעלי יומא דכפורי, אתו עורבי שדו כבדי וכוליתא, אמר ליה שקול ואכול האידנא דהיתרא שכיח טפי.

Rav Naḥman [18] of Nəhardəʿa happened to visit Rav Kahana at Pum Nahara [19] on the eve of the Day of Atonement, and ravens came and dropped livers and kidneys. He said to him, Take and eat them, now that the permitted is more common.

33. Makkot 5a

ואמר רבא באו שנים ואמרו בסורא בצפרא בחד בשבתא הרג פלוני את הנפש ובאו שנים ואמרו בפניא בחד בשבתא עמנו הייתם בנהרדעא, חזינן אי מצפרא לפניא מצי אזיל מסורא לנהרדעא . . .

---

[18] The Munich and Hamburg MSS and the Soncino printing have "Rav Ḥanan"; see also *Diq. Sof.*

[19] The Vatican 122 MS has לפום בדיתא; the Munich MS has no place named; see also *Diq. Sof.*

And Rava said, If two came and declared in Sura on Sunday morning that someone had killed, and two came and said, You were with us at sunset on Sunday evening at Nəhardəʿa, we have to consider, if one can get from Sura to Nəhardəʿa between the early morning and sunset . . .

34. Yevamot 116a

ובדקו רבנן מסורא ועד נהרדעא ולא הוה ענן בר חייא אחרינא לבר מענן בר חייא מחגרא דהוה בנהרדעא.[20]

Sages checked from Sura to Nəhardəʿa and there was no other ʿAnan b. Ḥiyya besides ʿAnan b. Ḥiyya from Ḥagra who was in Nəhardəʿa[20].

35. Josephus, *Antiquities*, XVIII 311–314

Νέαρδα τῆς Βαβυλωνίας ἐστὶ πόλις ἄλλως τε πολυανδροῦσα καὶ χώραν ἀγαθὴν καὶ πολλὴν ἔχουσα καὶ σὺν ἄλλοις ἀγαθοῖς καὶ ἀνθρώπων ἀνάπλεων. ἔστιν δὲ καὶ πολεμίοις οὐκ εὐέμβολος περιόδῳ τε τοῦ Εὐφράτου πᾶσαν ἐντὸς αὐτὴν ἀπολαμβάνοντος καὶ κατασκευαῖς τειχῶν. ἔστιν δὲ καὶ Νίσιβις πόλις κατὰ τὸν αὐτὸν τοῦ ποταμοῦ περίρρουν, ὅθεν Ἰουδαῖοι τῇ φύσει τῶν χωρίων πεπιστευκότες τό τε δίδραχμον, ὃ τῷ θεῷ καταβάλλειν ἑκάστοις πάτριον, ταύτῃ κατετίθεντο καὶ ὁπόσα δὲ ἄλλα ἀναθήματα, ἐχρῶντό τε ὥσπερ ταμιείῳ ταῖσδε ταῖς πόλεσιν. ἐντεῦθεν δὲ ἐπὶ Ἱεροσολύμων ἀνεπέμπετο ᾗ καιρός, πολλαί τε ἀνθρώπων μυριάδες τὴν κομιδὴν τῶν χρημάτων παρελάμβανον δεδιότες τὰς Παρθυαίων ἁρπαγὰς ὑποτελούσης ἐκείνοις τῆς Βαβυλωνίας. καὶ ἦσαν γὰρ Ἀσιναῖος καὶ Ἀνιλαῖος Νεερδᾶται μὲν τὸ γένος, ἀλλήλων δὲ ἀδελφοί. καὶ αὐτούς, πατρὸς δ' ἦσαν ὀρφανοί, ἡ μήτηρ προσέταξεν ἱστῶν μαθήσει ποιήσεως, οὐκ ὄντος ἀπρεποῦς τοῖς ἐπιχωρίοις ὥστε τοὺς ἄνδρας ταλασιουργεῖν παρ' αὐτοῖς. τούτοις ὁ τοῖς ἔργοις ἐφεστώς, καὶ γὰρ ἐμεμαθήκεσαν παρ' αὐτῷ, βραδυτῆτα ἐπικαλέσας τῆς ἀφίξεως ἐκόλασε πληγαῖς.

Nearda is a city in Babylonia that is not only populous but also possesses a rich and extensive district, which, in addition to its other advantages, is also thickly settled. It is, moreover, not easily exposed to hostile invasion because it is entirely encompassed by a bend of the Euphrates and the construction of walls. There is also a city Nisibis situated on the same bend of the river. The Jews, in consequence, trusting to the natural strength of these places, used to deposit there the two-drachm coins which it is the national custom for all to contribute to the cause of God, as well as any other dedicatory offerings. Thus these cities were their bank of deposit. From there these offerings were sent to Jerusalem at the appropriate time. Many tens of thousands of Jews shared in the convoy of these monies because they feared the raids of the Parthians, to whom Babylonia was subject. Now there were two brothers, Asinaeus and Anilaeus, who were natives of Nearda. Since they had lost their father, their mother apprenticed them to learn the weaving trade, for it is not

[20] The Munich MS has מתיג' בנהרדעא. On *ḥagra* see the section on Identification in the entry on "Hagrunya."

considered undignified by the inhabitants of that country for men to spin wool. The man in charge of their work, from whom they had learnt their trade, called them to task for arriving late and punished them with a whipping. (trans.: L. H. Feldman, LCL)

36. Josephus, *Antiquities*, XVIII 379

καὶ συνελέγησαν ὥστε πολὺ εἴς τε τὰ Νέερδα καὶ τὴν Νίσιβιν ὀχυρότητι τῶν πόλεων κτώμενοι τὴν ἀσφάλειαν, καὶ ἄλλως πληθὺς ἅπασα μαχίμων ἀνδρῶν κατοικεῖται.

The Jews flocked to Nearda and Nisibis, where they were safe because these cities were fortified and were furthermore populated by men who were valiant fighters every one. (trans.: L. H. Feldman, LCL)

37. Stephanus Byzantius, s.v. "Ναρδα"

Ναρδα, πόλις Συρίας πρὸς τῶι Εὐφράτηι ὥς Ἀρριανὸς Παρθικῶν ἑνδεκάτωι.

Naarda, a town of Syria on the Euphrates, according to Arrian in Book XI of his *Parthica*.

(Arrian, *Parthica* XI, dates from Trajan's time.)

38. Ammianus XXV 4, 1

In hoc tractu civitas ob muros humiles ab incolis Iudaeis deserta iratorum manu militum conflagravit. quibus actis pergebat ulterius imperator placida ope numinis, ut arbitrabatur, erectior, cumque Maiozamalcha venisset . . .

In this tract a city which because of its low walls, had been abandoned by its Jewish inhabitants, was burned by the hands of the angry soldiers. This done, the emperor went on farther, still more hopeful because of the gracious aid of the deity, as he interpreted it. And when he had come to Maiozamalcha . . . (trans.: J. C. Rolfe, LCL)

B. *Proposed Location*

Tall Nihar on the left bank of the Euphrates, due west of Maḥoza (C3 on the Tal. Bab. map.).

C. *Identification*

The area where Nəhardəʿa is to be sought is shown in both classical and talmudic literature. Josephus in Source 35 refers to the fortified city of Nəhardəʿa on the Euphrates, where for a number of years there was an independent Jewish realm (see the section below on The Center in Nəhardəʿa). Ptolemy places Nəhardəʿa on the east bank of the Euphrates above Sippar.[21]

---

[21] Ptolemy V 17, 10. Cf. also. Ravenna Cosmography 53, 20 which mentions a place called Narta that may derive from one of the two places called Naharra on the *Tabula Peutingeriana*.

The talmudic sources too point to the location of Nəhardəʿa on the Euphrates, and to its propinquity to Nəhar Malka. A passage in Taʿanit indicates the "superior" location of Nəhardəʿa on the Euphrates compared with Sura (see the section below on Economy). Nəhardəʿa's connection with Nəhar Malka is demonstrated by many sources, among them Source 12 which reports that the Nəhardəʿans got rid of the stones they had meant to throw at Rav Judah by dropping them into Nəhar Malka (and creating an obstruction).[22] Within the area described is a site named Tall Nihar on modern maps—directly across from Maḥoza (q.v.). Linguistic similarity leaves no doubt that this site may be identified with ancient Nəhardəʿa.[23] Source 30 mentions a place near Nəhardəʿa called Ḥuṭra (q.v. in appendix).

D. *The Center in Nəhardəʿa*

Nəhardəʿa is known as the location of one of the largest yeshivas in Babylonia at the start of the amoraic period, but testimony is available on Jewish Nəhardəʿa as early as the Second Temple and mishnaic periods. In Source 35 Josephus refers to Nəhardəʿa and Nisibis near it (distinct from the famous Nisibis; see the section on Nisibis near Nəhardəʿa in the entry on "Nisibis") as places where the Jews deposited their annual contribution of a half *sheqel* each that was to be taken to the Temple.

According to Josephus, Nəhardəʿa was the center of a Jewish realm led by the brothers Asinaeus and Anilaeus that existed from about A.D. 20 to A.D. 35.[24] The brothers founded their "state" after defeating the local Babylonian satrap, and gained the support of the Parthian king, Artabanus III (A.D. 23–38). When the state collapsed, thousands of Jews were slain, and many fled for their lives to the fortresses of Nəhardəʿa and Nisibis.[25] The episode clearly indicates the vitality of the Nəhardəʿa Jewish community, the effectiveness of the city's fortifications at the time, and the special relationship the Jews had with the Parthian sovereign when they had attained a position of strength making it possible to cooperate with them in internal struggles against local feudal lords.

---

22 See additional examples in Obermeyer, pp. 246–249. However. Obermeyer's view that Nəhardəʿa was at the diffluence of the Nəhar Malka and the Euphrates is unacceptable, and see below. On talmudic testimony on the distance between Sura and Nəhardəʿa, see Sources 33 and 34, and see also Obermeyer, *ibid.* See also Assaf's review of Obermeyer's book, *Kiryat Sefer* 7 (1930): 61. On the location of Nəhardəʿa (relative to Sura) see also *Otzar ha-Geonim* for Taʿanit, *ha-Teshuvot*, p. 12 and the notes there.

23 The identification is based on Bewsher, *JRGS* 37 (1867): 160–182 and the map there. See the British one-inch map of 1917 marking Tall Quhr Nahār on the same spot. We are grateful to Dr. J. Matthews for this reference. The site also appears on Kiepert's map (*ZGEB* 18 [1883]: 1–26 and map 5), which is based partly on Bewsher.

24 See Josephus, *Antiquities*, XVIII 310–379.

25 Neusner, *History*, vol. 1, pp. 50–58, and the bibliography on p. 50, n. 1; Schalit, *ASTI* 4 (1965): 163–188.

The Nəhardəʿa fortifications are mentioned also in Sources 2 and 3 which deal with the start of the amoraic period when they were already dilapidated and neglected, to the point where (according to Source 2) the city gates could not be closed as they were sunk halfway into the earth.

Indirect evidence of the importance of the Nəhardəʿa center already in the mishnaic period is provided in Source 13, reporting a visit of Rabbi ʿAqiva for the purpose of intercalating the leap year. The affair is itself astonishing because the determination of the leap year was at the time the exclusive prerogative of the Yavneh leadership. In fact once when the Patriarch Rabban Gamaliel was in Syria, the sages of Yavneh intercalated the leap year provisionally, subject to the Patriarch's subsequent consent.[26] And Rabbi ʿAqiva intercalated the leap year in Babylonia, outside the center in Eretz Israel, in the time of that same Patriarch.[27] In Alon's opinion, the leap year was sometimes intercalated abroad in consideration of economic requirements there and in order to foster closer connections between Eretz Israel and the Diaspora.[28] In the early amoraic period Nəhardəʿa was the seat of the Exilarch, to whom the messages setting the leap year were sent.[29] If the institution of the Exilarchy already existed at the start of the second century, that would mean that Rabbi ʿAqiva intercalated the leap year in Nəhardəʿa where the Exilarch resided, perhaps with the latter's collaboration in the actual process. Source 24 relates an event that took place in Nəhardəʿa at the end of the tannaitic period. Rabbi Aḥi son of Rabbi Josiah, requests two sages leaving Eretz Israel for Nəhardəʿa[30] to bring with them a silver piece that belongs to him. They encounter some menacing, violent people closely associated with the royal house, with the power to arrest and even condemn to death.[31] The reference may be to the court of the Exilarch, which in the Parthian period was empowered to pass death sentences.[32]

---

[26] Mishnah, ʿEduyot VII 7.

[27] The continuation of Source 13 says that upon his return to Eretz Israel Rabbi ʿAqiva reported to Rabban Gamaliel on his journey.

[28] Alon, *Toledot*, vol. 1, pp. 151–156, and the history of the research on the matter. Cf. also the attempt of Hananiah son of Rabbi Joshua's brother to intercalate the leap year in Babylonia, and see on that the section on Sages and Nisibis in the entry on "Nisibis."

[29] See e.g. T.J. Megillah I 7–71a, 5 seq. On the Exilarch's residence in Nəhardəʿa see already Rapoport, *Erekh Millin*, vol. 2, p. 226; see also Beer, *Rashut ha-Golah*, pp. 15–16.

[30] Regarding the view that Rabbi Aḥi son of Rabbi Josiah was from Huṣal, see the section on Sages and Huṣal in the entry on "Huṣal."

[31] On the whole episode, see Neusner, *History*, vol. 1, pp. 94–97.

[32] Cf. Rav's remark to Rav Kahana that up to their time the authorities were not concerned with bloodshed associated with the transfer from Parthian to Sassanian rule which was more centralized (Bava Qamma 117a). On the Exilarch's authority to pass death sentences see Beer, *Rashut ha-Golah*, pp. 58–65.

Source 25 provides more definite testimony on the activity of the Exilarch's court in Nəhardəʿa, in the time of Samuel, of the first generation of Babylonian amoras. The Exilarch's men arrested Eliezer Zeʿira for wearing black shoes in Nəhardəʿa, but released him when he proved he was a scholar.[33] Thus the scholars had considerable prestige with the Exilarch's people. A parallel of a sort is shown in Source 26 which suggests that scholars had priority in selling in the market. That source relates to the fourth generation of Babylonian amoras, when the Exilarch resided in Maḥoza, and issued instructions to check whether Rav Dimi of Nəhardəʿa was indeed a scholar meriting a reserved place in the market. In the case reported Rav Dimi did not come up to standard, was denied priority, and eventually incurred a loss for his goods (see the section on Connections with Other Places in the entry on "Maḥoza").

Testimony on the existence of the central yeshiva in Nəhardəʿa appears in connection with the period of Rav Shela, and thereafter Samuel, under whose direction it was institutionalized, following the arrival in Babylonia in 219 of Rav, who founded the yeshiva at Sura (q.v.). The basis for the Babylonian Talmud was laid at the Nəhardəʿa and Sura yeshivas. Their special importance also emerges from Source 14, which stipulates that a loan registration (*prosbol*) may be effected only at the Bet Din of Nəhardəʿa or of Sura (the Maḥoza and Pumbədita yeshivas had not yet been established). Source 1 indicates that in case of a disagreement between Nəhardəʿa and Sura, each of the yeshivas had its own sphere of influence where its rulings were to be followed. According to this source, the jurisdictional area of Nəhardəʿa was coextensive with the area that used the Nəhardəʿa *qav* as a measure.[34]

Numerous sources reporting that troops arrived at Nəhardəʿa reflect its siting on a strategic road.[35] Sources 7 and 8 define Nəhardəʿa as a border town; its problems were thus typical of all the places along the Euphrates which were subject to raids by Arab nomads from the Syrian desert (see the section on Relations with Gentiles in the entry on "Pumbədita"). The ensuing problems are dealt with in *halakhot* covering fighting on the Sabbath (Source 7), raising dogs and letting them loose at night (Source 8), making a reed embankment on which to sit on the Sabbath (Source 6; perhaps because

---

[33] On the prohibition against wearing black shoes, see Beer, *Rashut ha-Golah*, p. 86, n. 115. Eliezer Zeʿira was caught in the Nəhardəʿa *šuq*—the street or the market; see also Source 15 where the T.B. has "paths" while the parallels have the plural of *šuq* although it is clear that paths or ways are meant (see n. 10).

[34] In contrast to Nəhardəʿa, the source mentions Babylon rather than Sura where the yeshiva headed by Rav was situated (see the section on Sages and Babylon in the entry on "Babylon"). Maḥoza is referred to in the source as a place within the sphere of influence of Babylon (Sura) although it is closer to Nəhardəʿa (see the section on Connections with Other Places in the entry on "Maḥoza").

[35] Possibly the continuation of Source 13 testifying that "the state is disrupted by troops" refers to the same situation.

the study house was occupied by troops), suspecting that wine in a cask opened by the troops might be libation wine (Source 5),[36] and so on.[37]
Rav Sherira Gaon states that in 259 (four years after Samuel's death) the Palmyrans destroyed Nəhardəʿa (see the entry on "Tadmor")[38]: "And in 570 (of the Seleucid calendar) Papa b. Natzer came and destroyed Nəhardəʿa, and Rabbah b. Avuha our ancestor[39] went to Šəkanṣiv and Šilḥe and Maḥoza. And Rav Joseph b. Ḥama, Rava's father, was there. (And the rest of) our sages to Pumbədita, which from the days of the Second Temple was the chief Exile, as we learned from Rosh ha-Shanah,'until he sees the Exile before him like a bonfire' (Mishnah Rosh ha-Shanah II 4) and Abbaye said the Exile is Pumbədita." According to this testimony, the Nəhardəʿa yeshiva was transferred to Pumbədita at that time, and some of the Nəhardəʿa sages also went to Šekanṣiv, Šilḥe and Maḥoza (see the entries on "Šekanṣiv," "Maḥoza" and "Pumbədita").
The Nəhardəʿa yeshiva never regained its former glory, and never again came to rival Pumbədita which superseded it. Some sages did however eventually return to Nəhardəʿa and maintain a yeshiva there.[40]
Source 38 is part of Ammianus' description of Julian's war against the Parthians in 363. In the course of his report, Ammianus tells of Julian's destruction of a Jewish town after conquering Pirisabora (see the entry on "Pumbədita") but before reaching Maiozamalcha. In Herzfeld's opinion that Jewish town was Nəhardəʿa, and Maiozamalcha is Maḥoza-Be Ardəšir. If the latter identification is accepted—and there seems to be no alternative—the former fits what we know of Julian's route.[41]

E. *Be Keništa de-Šaf we-Yativ*

The tradition regarding the establishment of the Šaf we-Yativ synagogue reflects the antiquity of the Jewish community in Nəhardəʿa. That tradition

[36] According to one of the opinions mentioned in the source, the wine could be drunk, because most of the troops were Jewish, but that may have been just a convenient excuse.

[37] E.g., the case in which the congregation did not conduct the *musaf* prayer service because of "the troops that came to Nəhardəʿa" (Berakhot 30a–b), but cf. T. J. Berakhot IV 6-8c, 26–28 where Samuel says the service was not conducted because of the death of the Exilarch's son (see Beer, *Rashut ha-Golah*, p. 178).

[38] *Iggeret Rav Sherira Gaon*, Lewin ed., p. 82. On the identity of the people who destroyed Nəhardəʿa, see Sorek, *Zion* 37 (1972): 117–119.

[39] The French version has "and Rav Naḥman" added.

[40] E.g., Source 26 mentions Rav Dimi of Nəhardəʿa of the fourth generation of Babylonian amoras. Source 18 mentions Rav Ḥama of the fifth generation, known as the "Nəhardəʿan amoras" (Rav Zevid of Nəhardəʿa, also of the fifth generation, was one too). On the restoration of the Nəhardəʿa yeshiva see also Epstein, *Mevo'ot le-Sifrut ha-Amora'im*, p. 129.

[41] See also Stern, *Greek & Latin Authors*, vol. 2, pp. 609–611; Herzfeld, *Samarra*, p. 13f. See also, under "Maḥoza Area," Source 30 in the entry on "Maḥoza," and the entry on "Be Ardəšir," esp. nn. 28, 29.

is cited by Rav Sherira Gaon as follows: "Know that at the outset when Israel was exiled to the exile of Jehoiachin . . . they were brought to Nəhardəʿa, and King Jehoiachin of Judah and his company built a synagogue on a foundation of stones and earth they had brought with them from the Temple ... and they called that synagogue the Šaf we-Yativ synagogue in Nəhardəʿa, that is, that the Temple traveled and settled here."[42] Thus, according to Rav Sherira Gaon, the name Šaf we-Yativ is indicative of the history of that synagogue that was transferred from Jerusalem and established in Babylonia.[43] Sources 9, 10 and 11 show the importance of the synagogue, and its popularity with the Nəhardəʿa amoras, despite the statue in it (see also the section on Identification in the entry on "Huṣal"). Benjamin of Tudela in reporting on his travels in the region says nothing about a Jewish community in Nəhardəʿa but does note that he saw the ruins of the Šaf we-Yativ synagogue.[44] According to Herzfeld (*Samarra*, p. 14), it is marked by the Tall al-Kanīsa, almost halfway between Anbār and Sippar.

Barnett suggests "that it is to be identified with the village of Al Nasiffiyāt or Nuseffiat, about 50 miles north of Babylon, which still in 1861 preserved the remnants of its original name [*ku]neisesafyat[ib]."[45] He further suggests that this was the site of the battle of Kunaxa described by Xenophon.[46] Considering Kunaxa a Greek rendering of the Aramaic *keništa*, he believes "it is clear that the memory of the battle was preserved by the Babylonian Jews until Plutarch's time, or that of his source, Dinon or Ctesias."

F. *The Inhabitants*

The importance of Nəhardəʿa and the great yeshiva there did not prevent the voicing of harsh criticism of its citizens. Source 12 makes various accusations against the Nəhardəʿans pointing to defects in their lineage. Especially noted are the "unfit" in the town's priestly families, which at some phase in their history had intermarried with slaves. The source also shows that the Nəhardəʿans were sensitive about their honor in that respect, and wished to stone Rav Judah for his allegations. The source further reports women whose marriage contracts were invalidated when their defective lineage was discovered.

---

[42] *Iggeret Rav Sherira Gaon*, Lewin ed., pp. 72–73 (see also *ibid.*, Appendix 14). הוו יודעים דמעקרא כד גלו ישראל בגלות יכניה . . . אייתינהו לנהרדעא ובנו יכניה מלך יהודה וסיעתו בי כנישתא ויסדוה באבנים ועפר שהביאו עמהם מבית המקדש . . . וקריוה לההוא בי כנישתא ביה כנישתא דשף ויתיב בנהרדעא, כלומר שנסע בית המקדש וישב כאן.

[43] On the name of the synagogue see *Arukh ha-Shalem*, vol. 8, pp. 124–125, s.v. "שף."

[44] See *Itinerary of Benjamin of Tudela*, Adler ed., p. 46.

[45] Barnett, *JHS* 83 (1963): 16–17; cf. Selby & Bewsher, *Survey of Mesopotamia*; Nasīfijāt on Kiepert's map (see n. 23 above).

[46] The name Kunaxa is mentioned only by Plutarch, *Artaxerxes* 8, 2. Xenophon, *Anabasis* I 7, 14ff. nowhere mentions the name of the place where the battle was fought.

This source is just one of a long series relating to various Babylonian towns and dealing with problems in the sphere of purity of lineage. The fact that the subject is discussed in regard to Nəhardə'a too, as its residents are suspected of dubious lineage, is an indication of the central role the question of pure lineage played for the residents and sages of Babylonia (see also the Introduction).

A number of sources castigate the Nəhardə'ans for their ignorance, noting not only that many of them are unfamiliar with the Torah and halakhah (Source 21) but that all of them, including the sages, are vulgar and unlearned, so that there is no sense in teaching them even if they are interested (Sources 20, 21). Although these sources seem astonishing at first glance, they should be taken not literally but as a reflection of the rivalry between centers of learning. In the same way, after the destruction of the Second Temple, the Yavneh sages used expressions like "foolish Galilean" or "Galilee, Galilee, you hated the Torah." And the sources above, along with disparagement of the Nəhardə'ans, contain vilifications of southerners by sages from Galilee to which the Eretz Israel center was transferred after the Bar Kokhva revolt. To the Babylonians in general the Eretz Israel sages applied the term "foolish Babylonians" (בבלאי טפשאי).[47] Such expressions do not denote stupidity on the part of all Babylonians or Nəhardə'ans in particular, but merely local patriotism and concern on the part of Eretz Israel at the rise of the Babylonian center. In addition some if not all of these expressions represent clichés, rather than exactly what the speakers meant to say.[48] The case of virgins deflowered in Nəhardə'a on the night of the Day of Atonement (Source 22) is an example of attempts to find the reason for the ills besetting the nation, or for the delay in the coming of the Messiah, and questions arise as to how much of the case is fact and how much legend or apologetics.

G. *Economy*

A passage in Ta'anit regarding the timing of a prayer for rain contains a disagreement between Rav and Samuel, with the former specifying a later date.[49] The explanation given for the difference of opinion is that "The upper ones need water, the lower ones do not need water." Thus a distinction is made between Nəhardə'a, Samuel's town, which was upstream on the Euphrates, and Sura, Rav's town, which was far downstream. The current in the upper Euphrates was much stronger than that in the lower Euphrates from which the water spread out, with the result that the Nəhardə'ans were more depen-

---

[47] E.g. Pesaḥim 34b; Betzah 16a; Ketubot 75a; Nedarim 49b.

[48] See Lieberman, *Cathedra* 17 (1980): 3–10.

[49] Ta'anit 10a.

dent on rain than the Surans who could take greater advantage of the Euphrates water.[50]

Source 29 clearly shows the Nəhardəʿans dependence on rain, and the frequency of droughts which in the case cited forced the residents to sell their homes in order to buy food. In the same case it appeared that a barge carrying wheat was stuck in a bend of the river en route to Nəhardəʿa, and the question arose as to whether the sale of the houses had not been an error, so that the houses and money could be returned to their rightful owners.[51]

Source 28 deals with a person whose goats trespassed in a man's field and ate his barley. The discussion reveals that there were Arab shepherds in Nəhardəʿa to whom the animals were turned over for grazing. In these instances, the goats did not proceed to the meadows alone, but were brought to the Arab shepherds in the morning and recovered from them in the evening.[52]

Alon, *Toledot* (1959³), vol. 1, pp. 151–156

Beer, *Rashut ha-Golah* (1970), passim

Beer, *Amora'ei Bavel* (1974), passim

Berliner, *Beiträge* (1883), p. 47

Bewsher, *JRGS* 37 (1867): 160–182

Eshel, *Yishuvei ha-Yehudim* (1979), pp. 153–156

Funk, *Juden* (1902–1908), vol. 1, passim; vol. 2, p. 153

Funk, *Monumenta* (1913), pp. 32, 34, 36, 41, 43, 44, 74, 289, 302, 304

Funk, *Nehardea* (1914)

Gafni, *Ha-Yeshiva be-Bavel* (1978), passim

Goodblatt, *Rabbinic Instruction* (1975), passim

Goodblatt, *HUCA* 48 (1977): 187–217

Graetz, *Geschichte* (1908⁴), vol. 4, pp. 249f., 349

Herzfeld, *Samarra* (1948), pp. 14–16

Hirschenson, *Sheva Ḥokhmot* (1883), pp. 164–166

Jastrow, *Dictionary* (1950³), p. 883

Joël, *MGWJ* 16 (1867): 383

Kohut, *Arukh ha-Shalem* (1878–1892), vol. 6, p. 321; vol. 8, p. 124f., "שף"

Krauss, *Qadmoniot ha-Talmud* (1923–1945), passim

Levy, *Wörterbuch* (1924²), vol. 3, p. 352

Neubauer, *Géographie* (1868), pp. 350–351

Neusner, *History* (1965–1970), 5 vols., passim

Newman, *Agricultural Life* (1932), index

Obermeyer, *Landschaft* (1929), pp. 244–265, index

Smallwood, *The Jews under Roman Rule* (1976), pp. 415f., 420, 531f.

Sorek, *Zion* 37 (1972): 117–119

Yudelevitz, *Nehardea* (1905)

Zuri, *Toledot Darkei ha-Limud* (1914), passim

Zuri, *Shilton* (1938), passim

---

[50] See Beer, *Amora'ei Bavel*, pp. 31–32. See also *Otzar ha-Geonim* for Taʿanit, *ha-Teshuvot*, p. 12.

[51] See Beer, *op.cit.*, pp. 32–35.

[52] The goats were personally turned over to Arab shepherds perhaps because the latter were suspected of an inclination for theft. Whether they were dishonest or not, the differential practices employed for Jewish and Arab shepherds show the ambivalence in the Jews' attitude to the Arab desert nomads who arrived from across the Euphrates (see the section on Relations with Gentiles in the entry on "Pumbədita").

Nəharpanya נהרפניא

A. *Sources*

1. Yevamot 17a

יתיב רב המנונא קמיה דעולא וקא הוי בשמעתא, אמר מה גברא ומה גברא אי לאו דהרפניא מאתיה, איכסיף, א״ל כסף גלגלתא להיכא יהבת, א״ל לפום נהרא, א״ל א״כ מפום נהרא[1] את. מאי הרפניא, אמר ר׳ זירא הר שהכל פונין בו. במתניתא תנא כל שאין מכיר משפחתו ושבטו נפנה לשם. אמר רבא והיא עמוקה משאול, שנאמר ״מיד שאול אפדם ממות אגאלם״ ואילו פסול דידהו לית להו תקנתא. פסולי דהרפניא[2] משום פסולי דמישון, ופסולי דמישון משום פסולי דתרמוד, פסולי דתרמוד משום עבדי שלמה, והיינו דאמרי אינשי קבא רבא וקבא זוטא מיגנדר ואזיל, לשאול ומשאול לתרמוד ומתרמוד למישן וממישן להרפניא.

Rav Hamnuna sat before ʿUlla and was [discussing] tradition when the latter said, What a great man [he would be] if Harpanya were not his town. [As the other] was embarrassed he said to him, Where do you pay poll tax? He said, To Pum Nahara. If so, he (ʿUlla) said, you are from Pum Nahara.[1] What is [the meaning of] Harpanya? Rabbi Zera said, A mountain to which everybody turns. In a *baraita* it was taught, Whosoever did not know his family and his tribe made his way there. Rava said, And it was deeper than the nether-world, for it is said, "I shall ransom them from the power of the nether-world; I shall redeem them from death" (Hos. 13:14), but for the unfitness of these there is no remedy at all; the unfit of Harpanya[2] on account of the unfit of Mešon, and the unfit of Mešon on account of the unfit of Tarmod, and the unfit of Tarmod on account of the slaves of Solomon. Thus it is that people say, the small *qav* and the biq *qav* roll down to the nether-world, from the nether-world to Tarmod, from Tarmod to Mešan, and from Mešan to Harpanya.

2. Shabbat 127a

... והא דמשתקלי תלתא ובדקורי דהרפניא.[3]

... and there, where they can be carried in threes, of the size of the jugs of Harpanya.[3]

---

[1] Qiddushin 72b: "The Lord commanded against Jacob that his neighbors should be his foes (Lam. 1:17). Rav Judah said, Like Humaniya to Pum Nahara." The Munich MS has כגון הרפני׳ והרמני׳ לפום נהר׳ and the Oxford MS has כגון הפרניא והימניא לפום נהרא. As in the parallel Yevamot 16b, Harpanya does not appear in printings, and it is identified with Pum Nahara in manuscripts, but there Rav rather than Rav Judah is credited with the statement. See the entries on "Pum Nahara" and "Humaniya."

[2] The Venice printing has פסולי דנה׳ פניא and וממישן לנה׳ פני׳ at the end of the passage. In the question answered by Rabbi Zera, the version in the Venice printing is מאי הרדפני.

[3] The Munich MS has דהרדפנאי; the Oxford MS has דהדפנאי.

3. Bava Metziʿa 84a

א״ר יוחנן איבריה דרבי ישמעאל ברבי יוסי כחמת בת תשע קבין. אמר רב פפא איבריה דרבי יוחנן כחמת בת חמשת קבין, ואמרי לה בת שלשת קבין. דרב פפא גופיה כי דקורי דהרפנאי.[4]

Rabbi Yoḥanan said, Rabbi Ishmael b. Rabbi Yose's organ is like a skinbottle of nine *qabin*. Said Rav Papa, the organ of Rabbi Yoḥanan is like a skinbottle of five *qabin* and others say of three *qabin*. That of Rav Papa himself is like the jugs of Harpanya.[4]

4. ʿAvodah Zarah 74b

רבא כי הוה משדר גולפי להרפניא סחיף להו אפומייהו וחתים להו אבירצייהו, קסבר כל דבר שמכניסו לקיום אפילו לפי שעה גזרו ביה רבנן.

When Rava sent jars to Harpanya he placed them mouth downwards and sealed their rims, being of the opinion that the rabbis decreed against every utensil into which [wine] is put for keeping [by a heathen] even temporarily.

5. Giṭṭin 65b

גניבא יוצא בקולר הוה, כי הוה קא נפיק אמר הבו ארבע מאה זוזי לרבי אבינא מחמרא דנהר פניא.[5]

Geniva was being led out to execution. On his way he said, Give four hundred *zuz* to Rabbi Avina of the wine [which I have] of Nəhar Panya.[5]

6. T. J. Giṭṭin VI 7–48a, 48–49 (parallel to Source 5)

כהדא גניבא אתאפק למקטלא, אמר יבון לר׳ אבונא זוז מן חמרא דכפר פנייא ...

Similarly, Geniva departed to be killed, saying, Let them give Rabbi Avuna a *zuz* for the wine of Kəfar Panya ...

7. Nedarim 55a

בר מר שמואל פקיד דליתנון תליסר אלפי זוזי לרבא מן עללתא דנהר פניא.

Bar Mar Samuel ordered [in his will] that thirteen thousand *zuze* [worth] of grain from Nəhar Panya should be given to Rava.

8. ʿEruvin 19a

גן עדן, אמר ריש לקיש אם בא״י הוא בית שאן פתחו, ואם בערביא בית גרם פתחו, ואם בין הנהרות הוא דומסקנין פתחו, בבבל אביי משתבח בפירי דמעבר ימינא, רבא משתבח בפירי דהרפניא.

Paradise, Resh Laqish said, If it is in the Land of Israel its gate is Bet Šəʾan; if it is in ʿArabia its gate is Bet Gerem, and if it is between the rivers its gate

[4] The source has דקורי דהרפנאי. The Munich MS has כדקוראי דהרפניא, the Vatican 117 MS has דנהר פניא, and see "3 רקד" in *Arukh ha-Shalem*.

[5] The Munich MS for the chapter *ha-omer* has דנהר פקוד and see *Diq. Sof.* (Feldblum). Before the *Tosafot* to Ketubot 54b under "ארבע" the form was דהרפניא.

is Dumasqanin. In Babylonia Abbaye praised the fruit of ʿEver Yamina and Rava praised the fruit of Harpanya.

9. Sanhedrin 48b

אמר ליה רבינא לרבא, מי איכא דוכתא דרמו ביה מת וארגי בגד למת, א"ל אין, כגון שכבי דהרפניא.[6]

Ravina said to Rava, Is there any place where the dead lie [about] while the shroud is being woven? Yes, he answered, it is so with the dead of Harpanya.[6]

10. ʿEruvin 59b

בעי מיניה רב אמי בר אדא הרפנאה[7] מרבה, סולם מכאן ופתח מכאן מהו, א"ל הכי אמר רב, סולם תורת פתח עליו.

Rav Ammi b. Adda Harpəna'a[7] inquired of Rabbah, What is the ruling [where a town has] a ladder on one side and a gate on the other? Thus said Rav, the other replied, A ladder has the legal status of a door.

B. *Proposed Location*

Nahr Abān in the neighborhood of Kūfa[8] (C5 on the Tal. Bab. map).

C. *Identification*

Talmudic literature has the form Harpanya, and it appears that Harpanya and Nəharpanya were equally acceptable.[9] The proposal to identify Nəharpanya with Nahr Abān was already made by Obermeyer, but he referred to a place of that name situated south of Wāsiṭ on the Tigris. While there are no objections on linguistic grounds, that location must be rejected for two reasons:

a. The Nahr Abān indicated by Obermeyer is in Mesene which is outside the Babylonian area of pure lineage.[10] Although Source 1 casts doubt on the purity of the Nəharpanya residents' lineage, the passage explicitly indicates that Nəharpanya is not in Mesene: "the unfit of Harpanya on account of the unfit of Mešon . . . and from Tarmod to Mešan and from Mešan to Harpanya."

---

[6] The Munich MS has דנהר פניא.

[7] The source has הרפנאה, the Salonika printing has הרסנאה, and the Oxford MS has both קרפניא and הרפנא (evidently drawn from two different versions). In the Munich MS the question is addressed to Rabbah bar Avuha rather than Rabbah. See also *Diq. Sof.*

[8] Linguistically the identification seems correct: the syllable *ya* would fall, being final (see Nöldeke, *ZDMG* 28 [1874]: 94); cf., e.g., ʿAwwād, *Sumer* 17 (1961): 51, where Bāṣaḥ-rāyā in the Mosul area is also called Bāṣaḥrā. The analogy with Abānān and Abān which were well-known to the Arabs may have been operative here. See these entries in Yāqūt; cf. the etymology he proposes under "Nağrān." See also below.

[9] There is a general scholarly agreement on this. See, e.g., Berliner, p. 33; Obermeyer, p. 197; Eshel, pp. 110–111; and especially Zadok, *JQR* 48 (1977/78): 255.

[10] See Introduction.

b. Talmudic passages mention the fertile soil of Nəharpanya, frequently praising its excellent produce, and the wine in particular. Although the Wāsiṭ region too is known for its fine soil, grapevines did not grow there.[11]

Among the sources for Nahr Abān, Obermeyer mentions Yāqūt, s.v. "Nağrān," but a careful perusal of that entry makes it clear that the reference is not to the Nahr Abān south of Wāsiṭ down the Tigris, as Obermeyer thought and before him Le Strange, but to the place with the identical name in the Kūfa region.[12] Yāqūt states: "And Nağrān also, a place two days' distance from Kūfa, between it and Wāsiṭ at the road; and it is said that the Christians of Nağrān when they were exiled settled there and it is therefore named for their place ... And when ʿUmar came to power he exiled them and bought their property from them; Abū Ḥasan az-Ziyādī said: The inhabitants of Nağrān moved to a village called Nahr Abān in the region of the "reverted sea" (*al-baḥr al-munqaṭiʿ*) in the district (*kūra*) of Bihqubād, of the districts (= *ṭasāsīğ*) of Kūfa. That village was a border settlement (*min aḍ-ḍawāḥī*)[13] and the king of Persia granted it to a woman named Abān whose husband, named Bānī, was one of the kingdom's heroes. He excavated the canal of the estate for his wife and called it Nahr Abān (= Abān's canal) ... And when ʿUmar, may God be pleased with him, expelled the people of Nağrān ... the Nağrānīs moved to Nahr Abān and settled there."[14] Thus Nahr Abān where the Nağrān exiles settled and which was named for their original place of residence was apparently west or southwest of Ḥīra.[15]

---

[11] This is indicated by a conversation between Ğāḥiẓ and the people of Kaskar (across from Wāsiṭ on the east bank of the Tigris), in *Kitāb al-ḥayawān*, vol. 4, p. 15: "I asked the residents of Kaskar: Your barley is a wonder of wonders, your rice is a wonder of wonders ... if you only had grapevines! They said: Any soil that has lots of ants is not good for raising grapevines."

[12] Le Strange, "Ibn Serapion," p. 45. Cf. Massignon, *Mélanges Maspero*, vol. 3, p. 356.

[13] *Ḍawāḥī*, and also the singular *Ḍāḥiya*, was the name applied to the border region of Iraq that included all the territory west of the Euphrates between Ḥīra and Anbār. See Ṭabarī, vol. 1, p. 612 (= vol. 1, pp. 749–750) where the members of the Tanūḫ tribe who inhabited that region in antiquity are called "the Beduins of the border" (*ʿarab aḍ-ḍāḥiya*); see also Yāqūt, s.v. "Ḥīra," p. 330.

[14] On Bihqubād, see Yāqūt, s.v. The *ṭassūğ* of Kūfa was in the "lower Bihqubād." On the expression "the reverted sea" meaning the sea that receded, see n. 13 in the entry on "Tarbiqna."

[15] In specifying the boundaries of the Arabian peninsula, al-Qurṭubī, *al-Masālik wa-l-mamālik*, Nūr Osmaniya MS, f. 66b, mentions Nağrān as-Sawād, left (*ʿalā yasār*) of Kūfa. The places listed are Kūfa, Nağaf, Qādisīya, al-Ḥīra and Nağrān as-Sawād. The Nağrānī exiles erected a church called al-Ukairāḥ in their new place. See Yāqūt, s.v. "Nağrān." According to Ḥāzimī, *Kitāb al-amākin*, fol. 185a–b of the Laleli MS, Nağrān is the name of a place two days' distance from Kūfa. Evidently it was on the edge of the cultivated part of Iraq; see also Zuhrī, No. 127: "And in western Iraq is the mountain called Ğabal ar-Rayyān and it is opposite the city of Ḥīra, and close to this mountain is the city(!) of Nağrān." Under "Ukairāḥ" Yāqūt says it was seven parasangs from Ḥīra, to the west.

Along with Nəharpanya, Source 8 mentions ʿEver Yamina, evidently a region in the southern Euphrates area (see ʿEver Yamina in the appendix).

D. *Sages and Nəharpanya*

Rav Hamnuna, of the third generation of Babylonian amoras, is mentioned together with ʿUlla[16] in Source 1, where he appears as a resident of Nəharpanya.[17] Rav Hamnuna figures in other sources as a colleague and disciple of ʿUlla's, citing opinions of the latter's and even disagreeing with him.[18] Rav Hamnuna is also mentioned in connection with other places in Babylonia. He is reported present at the Sura yeshiva,[19] and ruling in Ḥarta də-Argiz (qq. v.).[20] Five different sources (1, 4, 7, 8, 9) report Rava's connection with Nəharpanya, indicating that this sage of the fourth generation of Babylonian amoras, head of the Maḥoza yeshiva, had a particular relationship with that place. The references Rava makes to the place fall into two categories: those in which he is critical of its residents (Sources 1 and 9; and see below), and others showing that he had business dealings with them, and in which he praises the fruit they grow (Sources 4, 7 and 8, and see below). Rav Ammi b. Adda Harpəna'a (= of Harpanya) is mentioned just once in the Talmud, in Source 10, as addressing a question to Rabbah, who replies citing Rav. Here the more logical version is that of the Munich MS — "Ammi b. Adda Harpəna'a asked Rabbah b. Avuha"—because here the former does not have the title of *rav*, and if he was not ordained, the absence of other talmudic references to him is understandable, and also because Rabbah b. Avuha was Rav's disciple so that it would be natural for him to cite his master.[21]

E. *The Inhabitants*

The references to Nəharpanya reflect an attitude of suspicion and scorn to its Jewish population. Source 1 stresses the dubious lineage of Nəharpanya residents, comparing it to that of the Jews of Mesene and other regions outside the Babylonian area of pure lineage. This defective lineage is shown in the shame that overcame Rav Hamnuna when he was reminded that he stemmed from Nəharpanya, and in Rabbi Zera's remark that anyone who is himself

---

[16] ʿUlla, of the second generation of Eretz Israel amoras, was one of those *naḥote* who wandered between Eretz Israel and Babylonia (see Albeck, *Mavo la-Talmudim*, pp. 302–304).

[17] For the identification of Rav Hamnuna and the possibility that there were several sages by that name in the third generation of Babylonian amoras, see Hyman, pp. 376–379; *Yiḥusei Tana'im we-Amora'im*, Maimon ed., p. 62; *Sefer Yuḥasin*, pp. 130–131; Beer, *Rashut ha-Golah*, p. 127; Albeck, *Mavo la-Talmudim*, pp. 281–283.

[18] See, e.g., Shabbat 10b, Giṭṭin 5b, Qiddushin 78b, Nedarim 28b–29a.

[19] Bava Metziʿa 6b; Bava Batra 31b.

[20] ʿEruvin 63a.

[21] On Rabbah b. Avuha see Albeck, *Mavo la-Talmudim*, p. 207.

unfit and has difficulty finding a wife looks to Nəharpanya, and in Rava's comment implying that there is no remedy in the next world for the unfit of Nəharpanya.

Criticism is leveled also at various practices of the Nəharpanya people. In Source 9 Rava accuses them of disrespect for the dead, in that they begin weaving a shroud only when the corpse is laid out. Rava's critical view did not however prevent him from doing business with them. He was a man of property and engaged in the wine trade.[22] Source 4 reports that he dispatched *gulfe*—wine jugs—to Nəharpanya, apparently in order to have them returned filled with local wine.[23] Source 7 notes that Bar Mar Samuel bequeathed money from grain he had in Nəharpanya to Rava.[24] Source 5 and its parallel in the T. J. (Source 6) tell of the amora Geniva, obviously a wine merchant, who before the end of his trial, or just before his execution, asked to have the money he had invested in Nəharpanya wines transferred to Rabbi Avina.[25]

F. *Economy*

All references to the inhabitants of Nəharpanya indicate that they were prosperous. The local soil was fertile, and in the context of locating "the gate of Paradise" (Source 8) "Rava praised the fruits of Harpanya." In the economy of the place, vineyards and wines were first and foremost. Babylonia in general was celebrated for its flourishing agriculture, but vineyards were rare, accounting for the high cost of wine,[26] and for the preoccupation with wine in the sources on Nəharpanya.

G. *Material Culture*

In the wake of its viniculture, Nəharpanya also developed an industry producing wine jars, which became known as the *dequre* (= perforated, i.e. wicker-covered) of Harpanya. Source 3, likening Rav Papa's penis to a Nəhar-

---

[22] On Rava's activity in the wine trade, see also Berakhot 56a; on his wealth in general, see, e.g., Bava Metziʿa 73a.

[23] On the *gulfe*, see Brand, *Kelei ha-Ḥeres*, pp. 81–83. His suggestion, cited elsewhere (p. 110), that Rava sealed the vessels hermetically because the Nəharpanya people were suspected of making libations, is unfounded, because clearly wine was acquired from the Nəharpanya Jews. Probably Rava was afraid of the Gentiles that came in contact with the jars on the way from Maḥoza to Nəharpanya, and in fact Gentiles may very well have served as jar carriers.

[24] On the custom of bequeathing property to scholars, see Beer, *Amora'ei Bavel*, pp. 263–264. On the identification of Bar Mar Samuel and the possibility that he was a member of the Exilarch's family, see Beer, *PAAJR* 35 (1967): 71–73.

[25] On Geniva, see Beer, *Tarbiẓ* 31 (1962): 281–286. On the identity of Rabbi Avina, see Albeck, *Sinai, Sefer Yovel*, pp. 57–73; Albeck, *Mavo la-Talmudim*, pp. 274–275.

[26] On the absence of vineyards everywhere in Babylonia, see Beer, *Amora'ei Bavel*, pp. 83–94. See also, Mann, *JQR* 10 (1920): 314, 317. See also n. 11 above.

panya wine jar, and Source 2, noting that three Nəharpanya wine jars would fit into a crate while only one or two differently shaped jars did, indicate that the Nəharpanya type was relatively small and narrow.[27]
An Arabic source testifies to the production of clay jugs near Kūfa. The wine jug made in the village of Ḫuṣūṣ in the Kūfa region was called a *dann ḫuṣṣī*.[28]
It is interesting to note that the gaonic commentary on Ṭohorot (ascribed to Rav Hai Gaon) says of the containers (*piṭasin*) mentioned in Mishnah Kelim III 6 "that they are '*dequre*' and '*dani*'."[29]

ALBECK, *Mavo la-Talmudim* (1969), pp. 274–275, 281–283
ALBECK, *Sinai Sefer Yovel* (1958), pp. 57, 73
BEER, *Amora'ei Bavel* (1974), pp. 83–94, 166 n. 30, 263–264, 325 n. 42
BEER, *PAAJR* 35 (1967): 71–73
BEER, *Rashut ha-Golah* (1970), pp. 127, 217, n. 27
BEER, *Tarbiẓ* 31 (1962): 281–286
BERLINER, *Beiträge* (1883), pp. 33–34, 47, 66
BRAND, *Kelei ha-Ḥeres* (1953), pp. 103, 109–110
ESHEL, *Yishuvei ha-Yehudim* (1979), pp. 110–111
FRAENKEL, *Fremdwörter* (1886), p. 73
FUNK, *Jahrbuch* 6 (1908): 336
FUNK, *Monumenta* (1913), pp. 32–33, 292
GETZOW, *Al Neharot Bavel* (1887), p. 112
DE GOEJE, *ZDMG* 39 (1885): 2
GRAETZ, *Geschichte* (1908⁴), vol. 4, p. 272
HIRSCHENSON, *Sheva Ḥokhmot* (1883), pp. 108, 156
HYMAN, *Toledot Tana'im we-Amora'im* (1964), vol. 1, pp. 376–378
JASTROW, *Dictionary* (1950³), p. 368
JOËL, *MGWJ* 16 (1867): 375–378
KOHUT, *Arukh ha-Shalem* (1878–1892), vol. 3, p. 247; vol. 8, pp. 301–302; *Tosefot* (1937), p. 164
KRAUSS, *Qadmoniot ha-Talmud* (1923–1945), vol. 1, pp. 18, 20
LEVY, *Wörterbuch* (1924²), vol. 1, p. 572; vol. 4, p. 62
NEUBAUER, *Géographie* (1868), pp. 328, 352, 395
NEUSNER, *History* (1965–1970), vol. 2, p. 248; vol. 3, pp. 76–77; vol. 4, pp. 60, 388–389
NEWMAN, *Agricultural Life* (1932), pp. 7, 21, 38, 96–97, 169–170
OBERMEYER, *Landschaft* (1929), pp. 197–201
WIESNER, *Scholien* (1867), vol. 3, p. 16
ZADOK, *JQR* 48 (1977–78): 255
ZURI, *Shilton* (1938), pp. 123, 225

Nəhar Pəqod נהר פקוד

A. *Sources*

1. T. J. Sanhedrin I 2–19a, 7–14 (T. J. Nedarim VII 13–40a, 30–37)

חנניה בן אחי רבי יהושע עיבר בחוצה לארץ ... קם רבי יצחק וקרא באוריתא אלה מועדי (ה') חנניה בן אחי רבי יהושע, אמרין ליה (אמר) אלה הם מועדי ה', אמר לון גבן, קם רבי נתן ואשלים כי מבבל תצא תורה ודבר ה' מנהר פקוד, אמרין ליה "כי מציון תצא תורה ודבר ה' מירושלים," אמר לון גבן.

---

[27] See Brand, *Kelei ha-Ḥeres*, pp. 109–110.
[28] See Yāqūt, s.v. "al-Ḫuṣūṣ."
[29] See Brand, *Kelei ha-Ḥeres*, p. 103; cf. also Fraenkel, *Fremdwörter*, p. 73.

Hananiah the son of Rabbi Joshua's brother intercalated abroad; . . . Rabbi Isaac rose and read in the Torah, These are the fixed times of Hananiah the son of Rabbi Joshua's brother. They said to him, These are the fixed times of the Lord. He said to them, With us [they are]! Rabbi Nathan rose and concluded, For instruction shall come forth from Babylonia and the word of the Lord from Nəhar Pəqod. They said to him, "For instruction shall come forth from Zion and the word of the Lord from Jerusalem" (Is. 2:3) He said to them, With us [they will]!

2. Ḥullin 127a

אמר רב גידל אמר רב[1] נרשאה נשקיך מני ככיך, נהר פקודאה לוייך מגלימא שפירא דחזי עלך, פומבדיתאה לוייך אשני אושפיזך.

Rav Giddal said Rav[1] said, If a Narešan kisses you, count your teeth, if a Nəhar Pəqodan accompanies you, it is because of the fine cloak he saw on you, if a Pumbəditan accompanies you, change your accommodations.

3. Ketubot 27b; Bava Metziʿa 81b; Bekhorot 36a

. . . ההוא גברא דאגר ליה חמרא לחבריה א"ל לא תיזיל באורחא דנהר פקוד דאיכא מיא זיל באורחא דנרש דליכא מיא, ואזל איהו באורחא דנהר פקוד ומית חמרא, אתא לקמיה דרבא א"ל אין באורחא דנהר פקוד אזלי מיהו לא הוו מיא, אמר רבא מה לי לשקר אי בעי א"ל באורחא דנרש אזלי . . .

. . . A man hired out an ass to a fellow and said to him, Don't go by the Nəhar Pəqod road where there is water, go by the Nareš road where there is no water. But he went by the Nəhar Pəqod road and the ass died. He came before Rava and said to him, Yes, I went by the Nəhar Pəqod road, but there was no water. Rava said, "Why should I lie?" If he wanted he could have said, I went by the Nareš road . . .

4. Betzah 28b–29a

היכי עביד, כי הא דבסורא[2] אמרי תרטא ופלגו תרטא, בנרש אמרי חלקא ופלגו חלקא, בפומבדיתא אמרי אוזיא ופלגו אוזיא, בנהר פקוד ובמתא מחסיא אמרי רבעא ופלגו רבעא.

What should he do [on holidays]? In Sura[2] they say, [Give me] a third and half a third; in Nareš they say, A half and half a half; in Pumbədita they say, A sixth and half a sixth; in Nəhar Pəqod and Mata Məḥasya they say, A quarter and half a quarter.

5. Ḥullin 107a

אתקין רב יעקב[3] מנהר פקוד נטלא בת רביעתא.

Rav Jacob[3] of Nəhar Pəqod ruled that a *naṭla* (a vessel for washing hands) must contain one-fourth [of a *log*].

---

[1] The Vatican 121 MS has "Rav Papa"; and see *Diq. Sof.* under ד and ו.

[2] The Munich MS has דבנהרדעא.

[3] The Vatican 121 MS has "Rav Joseph," which does not seem correct.

6. ʿAvodah Zarah 72a

ההוא גברא דאמר ליה לחבריה אי מזביננא לה להא ארעא מזביננא לך במאה זוזי, אזל זבנה לאיניש אחרינא במאה ועשרין, אמר רב כהנא קנה קמא, מתקיף לה רב יעקב מנהר פקוד האי זוזי אנסוהו. והלכתא כרב יעקב מנהר פקוד.

The man who said to his fellow, if I sell this land I'll sell it to you for a hundred *zuze*, went and sold it to another for a hundred and twenty. Rav Kahana said, The first one bought it. Rav Jacob of Nəhar Pəqod objected. It was those *zuze* that compelled him. And the halakhah is like Rav Jacob of Nəhar Pəqod.

7. ʿAvodah Zarah 60a

הוה עובדא בכח כוחו ואסר רב יעקב מנהר פקוד.

There was a case once of such indirect action, and Rav Jacob of Nəhar Pəqod prohibited it.

8. Zevaḥim 6a; 8b

. . . מתקיף לה רב יעקב מנהר פקוד . . .

. . . Rav Jacob of Nəhar Pəqod objected to that . . .

9. Ketubot 33b

. . . מתקיף לה רב יעקב מנהר פקוד . . . אלא אמר רב יעקב מנהר פקוד משמיה דרבא[4] . . .

. . . Rav Jacob of Nəhar Pəqod objected to that . . . Rav Jacob of Nəhar Pəqod said in the name of Rava[4] . . .

10. Sanhedrin 69a

יתיב רבי יעקב[5] מנהר פקוד קמיה דרבינא ויתיב וקאמר משמיה דרב הונא בריה דרב יהושע.

Rabbi Jacob[5] of Nəhar Pəqod sat before Ravina and sat and said thus in the name of Rav Huna b. Rav Joshua.

11. Ketubot 93a; 98b; Bava Batra 157b

אמר רב יעקב מנהר פקוד משמיה דרבינא . . .

Rav Jacob of Nəhar Pəqod said in Ravina's name . . .

(12. Giṭṭin 65b)[6]

B. *Location*

None can be proposed due to insufficient data.

---

[4] The Munich, Vatican 112 and Vatican 130 MSS, the Venice printing and a Geniza fragment all have "Ravina" and see Ketubot in the ICIT edition, and see below.

[5] The Munich MS and other versions have "Rav Jacob."

[6] See Source 5 and n. 5 in the entry on "Nəharpanya."

C. *Attempts at Identification*

Obermeyer (pp. 271–273) identifies Nəhar Pəqod with Nahr al-Malik, a place near Sura which at the beginning of the tenth century was still populated mainly by Jews. Thinking it unreasonable that a settlement like Nahr al-Malik should not be mentioned in talmudic and gaonic literature, Obermeyer concludes that the Jews had a different name for it. He believes the original name was Nəhar Pəqod, which was changed to Nahr al-Malik after the canal it was situated on, while the original name was retained in the Jewish sources. This proposal of Obermeyer's is not adequately supported, however. The fact that Nahr al-Malik does not appear in Jewish sources does not necessarily mean that the Jews had another name for it, and in any case there are no grounds for identifying Nahr al-Malik with Nəhar Pəqod. Generally speaking, it is preferable for the identification of Babylonian places to be based on the retention of the place name by the Arabs, and different criteria may be adopted only where other convincing evidence is available.

Some cuneiform documents suggest that Nəhar Pəqod was in southern Babylonia near Nippur (q.v.),[7] but that is not necessarily proof of the location of the talmudic Nəhar Pəqod.

Source 3 gives some indication of the location of Nəhar Pəqod as it mentions two roads together, those of Nəhar Pəqod and Nareš, but not enough for a definite identification.

D. *Sages and Nəhar Pəqod*

Some scholars have sought on the basis of Source 1 to establish that Nəhar Pəqod in the tannaitic period was a teaching center headed by Hananiah the son of Rabbi Joshua's brother.[8] Hananiah came from Eretz Israel to Babylonia where he had a study house.[9] As it was doubtful after the Bar Kokhva revolt whether the Eretz Israel institutions could function, Hananiah attempted to calculate the leap year independently. A delegation from Eretz Israel was despatched in response, and Source 1 contains their ironic remarks, among them Rabbi Nathan's comment that "instruction shall come forth from

---

[7] See Obermeyer, p. 271; Eshel, pp. 181, 215; Zadok, *IOS* 8 (1978): 263–264.

[8] See, e.g., Bacher, *Tannaiten*, vol. 1, p. 385, n. 3; Obermeyer, pp. 273–274; Eshel, p. 157 (Eshel's statement that Rabbi ʿAqiva visited Nəhar Pəqod is unfounded. Apparently his error is based on the claim of Hananiah the son of Rabbi Joshua's brother, that Rabbi ʿAqiva too intercalated leap year while abroad. But the Mishnah says explicitly that he did so in Nəhardəʿa [see T.B. Berakhot 63a; Mishnah Yevamot XVI 7]).

[9] The rabbis taught "Justice, only justice, you shall follow" (Deut. 16:20) [means] follow the scholars to the yeshiva . . . Rabbi Hananiah the son of Rabbi Joshua's brother, to the Exile (Sanhedrin 32b, according to the Munich, Florence and Karlsruhe MSS; cf. *Yalquṭ Shimʿoni*, Leviticus, § 611). Here the word "Exile" (= גולה) is apparently intended to refer to Babylonia as a whole and not a particular community there.

Babylonia and the word of the Lord from Nəhar Pəqod."[10] That comment, however, does not seem to constitute convincing proof that Hananiah's study house was in Nəhar Pəqod, and Rabbi Nathan may have used the place name because it was known from the Prophets[11] or for some other reason.

Rav Jacob of Nəhar Pəqod was active in the sixth generation of Babylonian amoras, and Sources 10 and 11 show that he was Ravina's disciple. In Source 9 he cites Rava, but the versions in the manuscripts cite Ravina in this case too (note 4 above). Source 6 describes a disagreement between him and Rav Kahana regarding the sale of land, and the halakhah accords with his opinion. Source 5 refers to a vessel used for washing the hands, of a capacity determined by Rav Jacob of Nəhar Pəqod.[12]

E. *The Inhabitants*

Rav, the founder of the Sura yeshiva in the first generation of Babylonian amoras, characterizes the Nəhar Pəqod people as likely to be thieves. In Source 2 he warns that if one of them accompanies someone on a journey, it is only because of interest in the other person's cloak.

Testimony of this sort is not to be taken literally or considered to apply to all the residents.[13] In the same source Rav describes the people of Nareš and Pumbədita as thieves as well. At the same time, the very mention of Nəhar Pəqod together with definitely Jewish places like Nareš and Pumbədita in Source 2, and Sura (or Nəhardəʿa, see n. 2 above), Nareš, Pumbədita and Mata Məḥasya in Source 4, shows that Nəhar Pəqod was an important Jewish community.

Nəhar Pəqod apparently continued to be a leading Jewish center after the talmudic period as well, for Rav Sherira Gaon lists four eighth-century geonim at Sura who came from there.[14]

Bacher, *Tannaiten* (1884–1890), vol. 1, p. 385, n. 3
Berliner, *Beiträge* (1883), p. 52
Eshel, *Yishuvei ha-Yehudim* (1979), pp. 157–158, 181–182, 215
Funk, *Monumenta* (1913), pp. 44–45, 296
Hirschenson, *Sheva Ḥokhmot* (1883), pp. 166–167
Kohut, *Arukh ha-Shalem* (1878–1892), vol. 5, p. 320

---

[10] On the whole see Source 8 and the section on Sages and Nisibis in the entry on "Nisibis." Cf. also Berakhot 63a–b.

[11] The name "Pəqod" appears in Jeremiah, as a synonym for Babylonia (Jer. 50:21; cf. Ezek. 23:23). Rabbi Nathan's statement is a kind of "*hafṭarah*," after Rabbi Isaac's "Torah reading," and the original verse too comes from the Prophets (Is. 2:3).

[12] On this vessel see Brand, *Kelei ha-Ḥeres*, pp. 38–41.

[13] Cf., e.g., Source 3 and the sections on Sages and Papuniya and The Inhabitants in the entry on "Papuniya."

[14] See *Iggeret Rav Sherira Gaon*, Lewin ed., pp. 106–108.

Neubauer, *Géographie* (1868), pp. 363–365
Neusner, *History*, 5 vols. (1965–1970), passim
Newman, *Agricultural Life* (1932), p. 158
Obermeyer, *Landschaft* (1929), pp. 73, n. 2, 270–276
Zadok, *IOS* 8 (1978): 293–294
Zuri, *Shilton* (1938), p. 240

Nəhar Yo'ani נהר יואני

A. *Sources*

1. Qiddushin 71b

עד היכן היא בבל, רב אמר[1] עד נהר עזק, ושמואל אמר עד נהר יואני.[2]

How far does Babylonia extend? Rav said,[1] To Nəhar ʿAzeq, and Samuel said, To Nəhar Yo'ani.[2]

2. T. J. Qiddushin IV 1–65c, 22–24[3]

רבי יוסה בי רבי בון בשם רב נחמן[4] בבל ליוחסין עד נהר יזק.[5] ר׳ יוסי בי רבי בון אמר רב ושמואל חד אמר עד נהר יזק, וחד אמר עד נהר יואני.[6]

Rabbi Yose b. Rabbi Bun in the name of Rav Naḥman,[4] Babylonia in respect to lineage, to Nəhar Yazeq.[5] Rabbi Yose b. Rabbi Bun said, Rav and Samuel, one said to Nəhar Yazeq, and one said to Nəhar Yo'ani.[6]

B. *Proposed Location*

The town of Nahrawān, on the banks of the Diyāla river and the Nahrawān canal, some twenty kilometers northeast of Baghdad (D 2 on the Tal. Bab. map).

C. *Identification*

The sources above indicate a difference of opinion between Rav and Samuel in regard to the eastern boundary of Babylonia so far as purity of lineage is concerned (see the Introduction).
Obermeyer and others have proposed identifying Nəhar Yo'ani, according to Samuel the eastern boundary of Babylonia as regards purity of lineage, with a canal called the Nahrawān.[7] While that identification is acceptable from the linguistic point of view, geographically it leaves something to be desired.

---

[1] The Vatican 111 MS does not have "Rav said."
[2] The Munich MS has נהר גאני, the Vatican 111 MS has נהר ינאי.
[3] Similarly in T. J. Yevamot I 6–3b, 6–8.
[4] T. J. Yevamot has "Rabbi Naḥman b. Jacob."
[5] T. J. Yevamot has נהר זרוק, further on as well.
[6] T. J. Yevamot has נהר וואניי.
[7] Obermeyer, p. 79; and see already Neubauer, p. 324.

Most of the places designated as having pure lineage were in the region between the Euphrates and the Tigris, and it is not reasonable without further evidence to extend the region to include territory between the Tigris and the Nahrawān canal which flows east of it and into the Tigris in the neighborhood of Kūt al-Imāra. However, the proposal is not entirely unfounded, as the area bounded by the Nahrawān on the east and the Tigris on the west parallels the area of the Babylonia of pure lineage between the Tigris and the Euphrates. Furthermore, the confluence of the Nahrawān and the Tigris at Kūt al-Imāra near Apamea (q.v.) is in the neighborhood of the border of Mesene (q.v.) and Babylonia, and according to the continuation of Source 1, the location of the southern border on the Tigris of the Babylonia of pure lineage.

As to the northernmost point at which the canal east of the Tigris was called the Nahrawān, there are two versions, both demarcating an area paralleling the Babylonia of pure lineage that was between the Tigris and the Euphrates. According to one, the canal was called Nahrawān only from the town of Nahrawān down to its confluence with the Euphrates,[8] while according to the second, the canal was already called Nahrawān from Bāğisrā (also called Bāb Kisrā) on.[9] In regard to the second version it should be noted that the distance of ten parasangs from Baghdad to Bāğisrā to the northeast[10] is equivalent to that from Baghdad to ʿUkbara (q.v.) on the Tigris to the northwest. One of the border points of the Babylonia of pure lineage, ʿUkbara was situated at about the same longitude as Bāğisrā, the northern extremity of the Nahrawān canal. Thus the second version would establish a parallel to the northern border on the Tigris of the Babylonia of pure lineage. At the same time, it must again be stressed that it is not reasonable to suppose, in the absence of additional evidence, that such a large area east of the Tigris was included in the Babylonia of pure lineage. Moreover, the names cited in the continuation of Source 1 as demarcating the border of "genealogical Babylonia" are names of settlements and not waterways, so that they are border points, not lines (see the entry on "Nəhar ʿAzeq").[11] All in all, the identification of Nəhar Yo'ani with Nahrawān is definitely acceptable, but it is more reasonable to suppose that Nahrawān refers to the town rather than to the canal. The town of Nahrawān was situated on both banks of the Nahrawān canal, about four parasangs (nearly twenty kilometers) northeast of Baghdad (see the Tal. Bab. map). Thus the border east of the Tigris is at the end of a "strip of settlements" that extend-

---

[8] See Le Strange, "Ibn Serapion," p. 19; Suhrāb, pp. 127–128; Mustaufī, vol. 2, pp. 52–53; Cf. also Yāqūt, s.v. "Nahrawān," pp. 324–325.

[9] See *ar-Rauḍ al-miʿṭār*, s.v. "Nahrawān"; Ibn Rusta, p. 90; Masʿūdī, *Tanbīh*, p. 53; Ibn Ḫurdāḏbih, p. 175; Yāqūt, s.v. "Bāğisrā."

[10] See Yāqūt, s.v. "Bāğisrā."

[11] The Papi Yona'a mentioned in the Talmud as a pauper who got rich (Bava Batra 25b) may have come from Nəhar Yo'ani if it is in fact a settlement.

ed eastward from the Tigris to Nahrawān (cf. a similar "strip" in the entry on "Ihi də-Qira"), and in Samuel's view were still included in the Babylonia of pure lineage.[12]

Berliner, *Beiträge* (1883), pp. 17–18, 34
Eshel, *Yishuvei ha-Yehudim* (1979), p. 156
Funk, *Monumenta* (1913), pp. 4, 277
Graetz, *Geschichte* (1908⁴), vol. 4, p. 249
Jastrow, *Dictionary* (1950³), p. 372
Kohut, *Arukh ha-Shalem* (1878–1892), vol. 3, p. 253; vol. 4, p. 115; *Tosefot* (1937), p. 165
Levy, *Wörterbuch* (1924²), vol. 1, p. 500; vol. 2, p. 225
Neubauer, *Géographie* (1868), p. 324
Obermeyer, *Landschaft* (1929), pp. 64, 79–81, 92f., 126f., 143–146, 196, 269

Nəṣivin נציבין

See the entry on "Nisibis."

Nihawand ניהוונד

A. *Sources*

1. Qiddushin 72a

אמר רב איקא בר אבין אמר רב חננאל אמר רב חלזון[1] ניהוונד[2] הרי היא כגולה ליוחסין. א״ל אביי לא תציתו ליה, יבמה היא דנפלה ליה התם, א״ל אטו דידי היא, דרב חננאל היא.

---

[12] On the town of Nahrawān see *Marāṣid*, Bakrī, *ar-Rauḍ al-mi'ṭār*, s.v. "Nahrawān." On the interpretation of the name, Yāqūt cites at-Tanūḫī, see also Abū 'Alī at-Tanūḫī, *Nišwār al-muḥāḍara*, vol. 8, pp. 80–83; *BGA*, passim. Mas'ūdī, *Murūǧ*, vol. 1, p. 123 (= vol. 1, p. 228) mistakenly has Nahr Ruwān (the canal), see Mas'ūdī, *Tanbīh*, p. 53, and see already Pellat's French translation of Mas'ūdī, vol. 1, p. 92; Le Strange, pp. 59, 61; Mustaufī, vol. 2, pp. 52–53; Idrīsī, vol. 6, p. 668. *Ḥudūd al-'ālam*, p. 139, notes that there are various places in Nahrawān that were built by the kings of Persia. Ya'qūbī, *Buldān*, p. 269, says that Nahrawān (or Ǧisr Nahrawān) was an ancient settlement.

It should be noted that there is further information, not sufficiently clear, on a canal called the Nahrawān which was evidently a branch of the main one, and flowed into the Tigris south of Baghdad. Mustaufī, vol. 2, p. 41, reports that the Nahrawān flowed into the Tigris two parasangs below Baghdad. That location fits what is known about a branch of the Nahrawān called Nahr Bīn (see the entry on "Nəharbil"). See Le Strange, "Ibn Serapion," p. 21; Suhrāb, p. 129; Ibn Rusta, p. 163; Le Strange, p. 59. In any case, cf. Iṣṭaḫrī, p. 86; Ibn Ḥauqal, p. 244; Muqaddasī, p. 20. Ibn Rusta, p. 186, mentions a canal called the Nahrawān, which in view of its route must have been near Madā'in on the north (Madā'in was six or seven parasangs from Baghdad, Yāqūt s.v. "Madā'in," p. 75; Ya'qūbī, *Buldān*, pp. 320–321).

[1] The Source has חלזון. The Oxford MS has חלוון, further on as well.

[2] The Munich MS does not have ניהוונד here, nor further on either.

אזיל שיילוה לרב חננאל, אמר להו הכי אמר רב חלזון ניהוונד הרי היא כגולה ליוחסין. ופליגא דר׳ אבא בר כהנא, דאמר ר׳ אבא בר כהנא מאי דכתיב "וינחם בחלח ובחבור נהר גוזן וערי מדי"... ערי מדי זו חמדן וחברותיה, ואמרי לה זו נהוונד וחברותיה[3] מאי חברותיה, אמר שמואל כרך מושכי חוסקי ורומקי.[4] אמר רבי יוחנן וכולם לפסול. קסלקא דעתא מושכי היינו מושכני, והאמר ר׳ חייא בר אבין[5] אמר שמואל מושכני הרי היא כגולה ליוחסין, אלא מושכי לחוד ומושכני לחוד.

Rav Iqa b. Avin said Rav Ḥananel said citing Rav, Ḥelwan[1] Nihawand[2] is like the Exile (= Babylonia) as to genealogy. Abbaye said to them, Do not obey him, A *yevamah* has fallen to him there. Is it my ruling? He replied, It is Rav Ḥananel's. So they went and asked Rav Ḥananel. He said to them, Rav said thus: Ḥelwan Nihawand is like the Exile as to genealogy. And he differs from Rabbi Abba b. Kahana. For Rabbi Abba b. Kahana said, What is meant by "And he settled them in Ḥalaḥ along the Ḥavor and the River Gozan, and in the towns of Media" (II Kings 18:11) . . . The cities of Media is Ḥamdan and its neighbors, and others say, Nihawand and its neighbors.[3] What are its neighbors? Samuel said, Kərak̠, Moškani, Ḥosqe and Romqe.[4] Rabbi Yoḥanan said, And all of them unfit. Does it enter the mind that Moške is Moškani? For Rabbi Ḥiyya b. Avin[5] said that Samuel said, Moškani is like the Exile as to lineage, but Moške is separate and Moškani is separate.

2. Yevamot 16b–17a

... דאמר רבי אבא בר כהנא "וינחם בחלח ובחבור נהר גוזן וערי מדי"... וערי מדי זו חמדן וחברותיה, ואמרי לה זו ניהר[6] וחברותיה, חברותיה מאן, אמר שמואל כרך מושכי חידקי ודומקיא,[7] אמר רבי יוחנן וכולן לפסול.

. . . And Rabbi Abba b. Kahana said, "And he settled them in Ḥalaḥ along the Ḥavor and the River Gozan and in the towns of Media" (II Kings 18:11); . . . and the cities of Media is Ḥamdan and its neighbors; others say it is Nihar[6] and its neighbors. Who are its neighbors? Samuel said, Kərak̠, Moške Ḥidqe and Domqiya.[7] Rabbi Yoḥanan said, And all of them unfit.

---

[3] The Vatican 111 MS has א"ל זו ניהוונד, the Munich MS does not have the sentence ואמרי לה זו ניהוונד וחברותיה at all.

[4] The place names mentioned by Samuel figure in sundry forms in Source 2, and in the various versions of both the sources. Obviously they designate places in Media near Nihawand, but no reference to them occurs anywhere else in talmudic literature (except for Moške which is noted as being distinct from Moškani). On these places, including attempts at identifying them, see Neubauer, pp. 377–378; Berliner, pp. 18, 38–39; Funk, *Monumenta*, pp. 4, 277; Obermeyer, p. 11; Eshel, the various entries. (In regard to "Domqiya" in Source 2 which parallels the "Romqe" in Source 1, the letter *alef* may have been shifted from the following word, of which it is the initial letter.)

[5] The Vatican 111 MS has "Rabbi Ḥiyya b. Abba."

[6] The Munich MS has נהרואי, the Vatican 111 MS has נהווינר, and *Ginzei Talmud* has נהיאר.

[7] See n. 4.

B. *Location*

A city in Media, presentday Nehāvend, seventy-five kilometers south of presentday Hamadan (see the entry on "Ḥamdan," q.v., Bab. Env. map).

C. *Purity of Lineage*

Source 1 contains two views of the purity of lineage of the inhabitants of Nihawand. The first, attributed to Rav, considers the status of Nihawand equal to that of Babylonia. The second, expressed by Rabbi Yoḥanan on the basis of Rabbi Abba b. Kahana's interpretation, finds their lineage impure, as Samuel did that of the residents of the places in the vicinity of Nihawand that he lists. Rabbi Yoḥanan's position fits in with the general attitude to Media—"Media is sick"[8]—and seems to reflect the situation also of the considerable distance between Nihawand and the Babylonia between the rivers.[9]

It should be noted that the Munich MS of Source 1 does not have "Nihawand" at all (see notes 2 and 3 above). Perhaps the Munich MS version should be preferred, for the combination "Ḥelzon-Nihawand" is difficult or even impossible, taking into account the distance between Ḥelwan (q.v.) and Nihawand. It is unreasonable to suppose even that Nihawand is like the Exile as to lineage, because of the great distance between it and the centers of Jewish population in Babylonia. In regard to Ḥelwan that is possible, for it is referred to in Arabic sources as the border of the Sawād of Iraq.

BERLINER, *Beiträge* (1883), pp. 39, 52
ESHEL, *Yishuvei ha-Yehudim* (1979), pp. 151f., 187f. "ניהר"
FUNK, *Juden* (1902–1908), vol. 1, Appendix I
FUNK, *Monumenta* (1913), pp. 4, 277
JASTROW, *Dictionary* (1950³), p. 881
KOHUT, *Arukh ha-Shalem* (1878–1892), vol. 5, p. 320 "נהר"
MINORSKY, *EI*¹, s.v. "Nihāwand"
NEUBAUER, *Géographie* (1868), p. 377
NEUSNER, *History* (1965–1970), vol. 2, pp. 241–242, 256; vol. 5, p. 118
OBERMEYER, *Landschaft* (1929), pp. 11, 107f.
SCHWARZ, *Iran im Mittelalter* (1969²), p. 498f.

---

[8] Qiddushin 71b; T. J. ibid., IV 1 – 65c, 26; T. J. Yevamot I 6 – 3b, 11; Genesis Rabbah XXXVII 8 (Theodor-Albeck ed., p. 350).

[9] On Nihawand in Arabic literature see Yāqūt, *ar-Rauḍ al-miʿṭār*, s.v.; *BGA*, passim; Qazwīnī, *Bilād*, pp. 471–472; Mustaufī, vol. 2, p. 76; *Ḥudūd al-ʿālam*, p. 132; Le Strange, pp. 196–197; Minorsky, *EI*¹, s.v. "Nihāwand"; Schwarz, *Iran im Mittelalter*ʻ p. 498f.

Nineveh נינוה

A. *Sources*[1]

1. Yoma 10a[2]

"מן הארץ ההיא יצא אשור," תני רב יוסף אשור זה סילק.[3] "ויבן את נינוה ואת רחובות עיר ואת כלח", נינוה כמשמעו, רחובות עיר זו פרת דמישן, כלח זו פרת דבורסיף. "ואת רסן בין נינוה ובין כלח היא העיר הגדולה," רסן זה אקטיספון,[4] היא העיר הגדולה איני יודע אם נינוה העיר הגדולה אם רסן העיר הגדולה, כשהוא אומר, "ונינוה היתה עיר גדולה לאלהים[5] מהלך שלשת ימים," הוי אומר נינוה היא העיר הגדולה.

"From that land Aššur went forth," (Gen. 10:11) Rav Joseph taught, Aššur is Sileq.[3] "and built Nineveh, Rəḥovot-ʿir, Kalaḥ" Nineveh is what it says, Rəḥovot-ʿir is Pərat də-Mešan, Kalaḥ is Pərat də-Borsif. "and Resen between Nineveh and Kalaḥ, that is the great city" (Gen. 10:12) Resen is Ctesiphon.[4] "that is the great city" I don't know if Nineveh is the great city or if Resen is the great city, when Scripture says, "Nineveh was a large city of God,[5] a three days' walk across" (Jonah 3:3) that means Nineveh is the great city.

2. Shabbat 121b[6]

מתיב רב יוסף חמשה נהרגין בשבת, ואלו הן זבוב שבארץ מצרים וצירעה שבנינוה ועקרב שבחדייב ונחש שבא"י וכלב שוטה בכל מקום.

Rav Joseph argued, Five may be killed on the Sabbath, and they are the fly that is in the land of Egypt, the hornet that is in Nineveh, the scorpion that is in Ḥadyav, the snake that is in Eretz Israel and a mad dog anywhere.

3. Genesis Rabbah XVI 4 (Theodor-Albeck ed., p. 148)[7]

אמר ר' יוסי בר' יהודה[8] כל המלכיות נקראו לשם נינוה על שם שהן מתנאות מישראל.

---

[1] In addition to the following sources there are many with aphorisms and interpretations connected with the story of Jonah and biblical (= Assyrian) Nineveh. See the T.B. for Taʿanit 16a, Megillah 11b, Yevamot 98a, Sanhedrin 89b, ʿArakhin 12a, Keritot 6b, and T.J. Taʿanit II 1–65b, 28 seq. and many *midrashim* besides.

For talmudic instances of Nineveh apparently referring to Transjordanian Nawe see the section on Inhabitants.

[2] Partial parallels to this source appear in Genesis Rabbah XXXVII 4 (Theodor-Albeck ed., p. 347); *Yalquṭ Shimʿoni* for Genesis, § 62 (Mossad Harav Kook ed., p. 227); *Yalquṭ Shimʿoni* for Jonah, § 550. See also *Diq. Sof.* for Yoma 10a, n. מ.

[3] See the entry on "Seleucia," under "Maḥoza Area."

[4] See the entry on "Ctesiphon" (under "Maḥoza Area") where the interpretation of this source is discussed.

[5] The standard non-literal translation of this verse (Jonah 3:3) is "an enormously large city" or "an exceeding great city."

[6] Similarly in T.J. Shabbat XIV 1–14b, 60–61.

[7] Similarly in Leviticus Rabbah XIII 5 (Margulies ed., p. 283). For the meaning of the interpretation, see the commentary in the Theodor-Albeck edition. In any case the Nineveh mentioned here seems to be the scriptural city and the interpretation as a whole,

Rabbi Yose b. Rabbi Judah[8] said, All the kingdoms were called Nineveh because they adorned themselves [with what they take] from Israel.

4. Strabo XVI 1,2–3 (737)

οἱ δ' ἱστοροῦντες τὴν Σύρων ἀρχὴν ὅταν φῶσι Μήδους μὲν ὑπὸ Περσῶν καταλυθῆναι Σύρους δὲ ὑπὸ Μήδων, οὐκ ἄλλους τινὰς τοὺς Σύρους λέγουσιν ἀλλὰ τοὺς ἐν Βαβυλῶνι καὶ Νίνῳ κατεσκευασμένους τὸ βασίλειον· ...
Ἡ μὲν οὖν Νίνος πόλις ἠφανίσθη παραχρῆμα μετὰ τὴν τῶν Σύρων κατάλυσιν. πολὺ δὲ μείζων ἦν τῆς Βαβυλῶνος, ἐν πεδίῳ κειμένη τῆς Ἀτουρίας·

When those who have written histories of the Syrian empire say that the Medes were overthrown by the Persians and the Syrians by the Medes, they mean by the Syrians no other people than those who built the royal palaces in Babylon and Ninus; ... Now the city of Ninus was wiped out immediately after the overthrow of the Syrians (608 B.C.). It was much greater than Babylon, and was situated in the plain of Aturia. (trans.: H. L. Jones, LCL)

5. Strabo, XVI 1,1 (736)

ἧς ἐν μέρει καὶ ἡ Ἀτουρία ἐστίν, ἐν ἧπερ ἡ Νίνος καὶ ἡ Ἀπολλωνιᾶτις καὶ Ἐλυμαῖοι καὶ Παραιτάκαι καὶ ἡ περὶ τὸ Ζάγρον ὄρος Χαλωνῖτις καὶ τὰ περὶ τὴν Νίνον πεδία.

Aturia, in which are Ninus, Apolloniatis, the Elymaei, the Paraetacae, the Chalonitis in the neighbourhood of Mt. Zagrus, the plains in the neighbourhood of Ninus. (trans.: H. L. Jones, LCL)

6. Strabo XI 14, 15 (532)[9]

... αὐξηθεὶς δὲ καὶ ταῦτα ἀπέλαβε τὰ χωρία καὶ τὴν ἐκείνων ἐπόρθησε τήν τε περὶ Νίνον καὶ τὴν περὶ Ἄρβηλα·

... but when he had grown in power he not only took these places back but also devastated their country, both that about Ninus and that about Arbela. (trans.: H. L. Jones, LCL)

7. Pliny, *Natural History* VI 16, 42

fuit et Ninos inposita Tigri ad solis occasum spectans, quondam clarissima.

There was also once the town of Ninos, which was on the Tigris facing west, and was formerly very famous. (trans.: H. Rackham, LCL)

---

based on the phonetic similarity between "Nineveh" and Hebrew "adorn" (נאה ;נוה), seems to refer to Rome.

[8] In some of the manuscripts the speaker is Rabbi Yose b. Rabbi Ḥanina, as in some of the Leviticus Rabbah MSS (others have Rabbi Yose b. Rabbi Ḥalafta).

[9] Referring to Tigranes of Armenia (ca. 95–55 B.C.) in his war against the Parthians.

8. Tacitus, *Annals* XII 13,2 (A.D. 49)

sed capta in transitu urbs Ninos, vetustissima sedes Assyriae et castellum insigne fama, quod postremo inter Darium atque Alexandrum proelio Persarum illic opes conciderant.

In passing the city of Ninos was captured, the old capital of Assyria and a widely celebrated fort, because there, in the last battle between Darius and Alexander, the Persian empire was destroyed. (trans.: J. Jackson, LCL)

9. Ammianus XXIII 7,1

. . . Ninive Adiabenae ingenti civitate . . .

Ninive, a great city of Adiabene . . . (trans.: J. C. Rolfe, LCL)

10. Ammianus XIV 8,7[10]

. . . Commagena (nunc Euphratensis) clementer assurgit, Hierapoli, vetere Nino et Samosata civitatibus amplis illustris.

Commagene, now called Euphratensis, is gradually rising to eminence; it is famous for the great cities of Hierapolis, the ancient Ninus, and Samosata. (trans.: J. C. Rolfe, LCL)

B. *Location*

On the east bank of the Tigris, across from presentday Mosul (on Bab. Env. map).

C. *History*

Ancient Nineveh, the capital of the Assyrian kingdom, was destroyed in 612 B.C.[11] While literary and epigraphic sources indicate that it was rebuilt in the first century B.C. at the latest, a hoard of coins found at the site shows that from the time of Mithridates II (123–87 B.C.) on, the place was important enough to have its own mint and a municipal status.[12] Thus, it was probably resettled as early as the second century B.C.

Nineveh controlled the most important crossing of the Tigris, giving access to Adiabene (q.v.) and the plain north of Ğabal Sinğār which formed the

[10] Strabo in Source 4 and Lucian, *Contemplantes* 23, represent Nineveh as a city of the past, as does Pliny in Source 7 in describing its greatness. Strabo, Tacitus, Ptolemy and Ammianus—in Sources 5, 8, 9 and 10 respectively—deal with it as an existing city, as does Philostratus, *The Life of Apollonius* I 19. Besides the sources above see also Ptolemy VI 2, 3.

[11] See Thompson & Hutchinson, *Exploration at Nineveh*. For Assyrian Nineveh see Honigmann, *RE*, vol. 17, s.v. "Ninos," col. 641.

[12] Le Rider, *Iranica Antiqua* 7 (1970): 4–20.

eastern part of the Roman province of Mesopotamia.[13] Hellenistic and post-Hellenistic Nineveh must be identified with modern Nebi Yūnis rather than Tall Quyunǧuq, the site of Assyrian Nineveh. Excavations at Nebi Yūnis have yielded, Assyrian remains, following a hiatus in settlement, and also Parthian, Sassanian and Arab remains. Two Greek inscriptions were found there as well. The first, of unknown date, is a dedication to the *theoi epekooi* (= the gods who listen) by the *strategos* and *epistates* of the city.[14] The offices mentioned in it, though characteristic of Greek cities in the Parthian period, indicate a Seleucid origin for the municipal organization.[15] The second inscription, dating from the first century A. D.,[16] contains a list of the months of the Macedonian calendar. A small shrine reminiscent of Assyrian prototypes was also found there; the statue of Hermes in it, however, is of the Seleucid or Parthian period. Philostratus reports that a first-century Greek-writing native, Damis of Nineveh, accompanied Apollonius of Tyana on his travels in the east.[17] Three bishops of Nineveh are mentioned, for 554, 576 and 585.[18] Nineveh is well known to the Arab authors, who associated it and other nearby places with the prophet Jonah b. Amittai (Arabic, Yūnus b. Mattā).[19]

D. *The Inhabitants*

Nineveh appears in talmudic literature as a well-known place, and also in references to biblical Nineveh. There was presumably a Jewish community there in mishnaic and talmudic times, but the talmudic sources provide no information on it. Some scholars[20] have considered the following tradition as referring to the residents of Nineveh: "שלחו ליה בני נינוה לרבי כגון אנן דאפילו

---

[13] Oates, *Northern Iraq*, p. 77.

[14] Thompson & Hutchinson, *Archaeologia* 79 (1929): 140–142 = *SEG*, vol. 7, No. 37; cf. Rostovtzeff, *JHS* 55 (1935): 57. A combination *strategos* and *epistates* is also known from Dura and Babylon. See Holleaux, *Études d'épigraphie et d'histoire grecques*, vol. 3, p. 217, n. 4; Bengtson, *Die Strategie*, pp. 297–307, 416–417.

[15] Oates, *loc.cit.* in n. 13. [16] *CIG* 4672. [17] *The Life of Apollonius* I 19.

[18] Sachau, *APAW phil.-hist. Klasse* 1 (1919): 53.

[19] On Nineveh see Yāqūt, *ar-Rauḍ al-miʿṭār*, s.v. "Nīnawā"; the latter source says it is also the city of Ayyūb (Job) where he bathed in the spring and purified himself. Thereafter *ar-Rauḍ al-miʿṭār* mentions Yūnus' spring. See also *BGA*, passim. In Muqaddasī it appears also as "Naunawā"; Mustaufī, vol. 2, p. 105; Idrīsī, vol. 6, p. 659; Masʿūdī, *Murūǧ*, vol. 1, pp. 252–253 (= vol. 2, pp. 92–95), and see Pellat's translation into French, vol. 1, pp. 191–192; Qazwīnī, *Bilād*, p. 477; Ibn Saʿīd, p. 157; Ibn Ǧubair, p. 236; Ibn Baṭṭūṭa, vol. 2, pp. 136–138; Šābuštī, *Diyārāt*, p. 115; *Masālik al-abṣār*, p. 299; Harawī, *Ziyārāt*, pp. 68, 70; see Ṭabarī, vol. 2, p. 183 (= vol. 1, p. 1004) regarding Heraclius' expedition in 628. There was another Nineveh near Karbalā (C4 on Tal. Bab. map). See Yāqūt ibid and *ar-Rauḍ al-miʿṭār*, ibid. Le Strange, pp. 87–89; ʿAwwād, *Sumer* 5 (1949): 77–78 (Tall at-Tauba), 250–251.

[20] See e.g. Funk, *Monumenta*, pp. 45, 279; Obermeyer, p. 139; Eshel, p. 188; Segal, *Sefer Segal*, p. 37* (English section).

בתקופת תמוז בעינן מיטרא היכי נעביד"[21] (= The people of Nineveh sent to Rabbi, [People] like us, that even in the period of Tammuz need rain, what shall we do?).[21] But Klein already suggested that it is not Nineveh that is meant but Nawe in the Bashan region of Transjordan, also sometimes called Nineveh.[22] Klein's suggestion seems logical because the above question is addressed to Rabbi Judah ha-Nasi who headed the Sanhedrin in Bet Šəʿarim and later in Sepphoris.[23] However, some evidence is available on Rabbi Judah ha-Nasi's concern for the residents of Babylonia and its environs.[24] Nawe seems to be meant also by the Nineveh that is mentioned in the following passage: "אמר רבה בר בר חנה אני ראיתי את רבי אלעזר דמן ננוה שיצא בסנדל של שעם בתענית צבור, ואמינא ליה ביום הכפורים מאי, א"ל לא שנא."[25] (= Rabbah b. Bar Ḥana said, I saw Rabbi Eleazar of Nineveh going out in bamboo sandals on a public [rain] fast, and I asked him, What about the Day of Atonement, and he said, There is no difference.)[25] Rabbi Eleazar of Nineveh, a sage of Eretz Israel according to his title, probably belonged to Nawe. It should be noted that some of the manuscripts do not mention Nineveh in this source, and the Munich B manuscript has נוי. Another sage the references to whom show a similar alternation in the place name is Rabbi Tanḥum, mentioned in the T. B. Shabbat 30a. The printing has "Rabbi Tanḥum of נוי" while the Munich manuscript has "Rabbi Tanḥum of Nineveh." Evidently Rabbi Eleazar and Rabbi Tanḥum both belong to the "scholars of Nawe" (*rabbanan də-Nawe*) group who constituted the celebrated study house that functioned at Nawe at the time of the amoras.[26]

Berliner, *Beiträge* (1883), p. 53
Ellis, *Mesopotamian Archaeological Sites* (1972), pp. 56, 59–61
Eshel, *Yishuvei ha-Yehudim* (1979), p. 188
Funk, *Monumenta* (1913), pp. 45, 297
al-Haik, *Key Lists* (1968), No. 18

---

[21] Taʿanit 14b. Similarly T. J. Berakhot V 2 – 9b, 32–33; Taʿanit I 1 – 63d, 29–31.

[22] Klein, *JQR* 2 (1911–12): 545–556. Thus e.g. Eusebius' *Onomasticon* p. 136, 2–3 (Klostermann ed.) lists Nawe as Nineveh:

Ἔστι δὲ καὶ Ἰουδαίων εἰς ἔτι νῦν πόλις Νινευῆ καλουμένη περὶ τὴν Γωνίαν τῆς Ἀραβίας.

"And there is to the present day a[nother] city (besides Assyrian Nineveh) of the Jews called Nineveh in the corner of Arabia." For the inscriptions attesting the existence of a Jewish colony at Nawe cf. Schürer (revised edition), vol. 1, p. 338, n. 3; vol. 2, p. 14, n. 46.

[23] Klein proffers a third argument to prove that the place in question is Nawe, namely, that there could not be a Jewish community in Nineveh which had been devastated long before, but that argument obviously does not hold water.

[24] See the section on Economy in the entry on "Mesene," the sections on Inhabitants in the entries on "Birta" and "Humaniya," and the section on Sages and Šəḵanṣiv in the entry on "Šəḵanṣiv."

[25] Yoma 78b. The Oxford MS and the margin of the Munich MS have just "Rabbi Eleazar"; the Munich B MS has "Rabbi Eleazar of נוי" and the London MS has "Rabbi Eleazar of ניניה."

[26] On the *rabbanan də-Nawe* see Oppenheimer, *Cathedra* 8 (1978): 80–89.

Hirschenson, *Sheva Ḥokhmot* (1883), p. 170
Honigmann, *RE*, vol. 17, cols. 634–643, s.v. "Ninos"
Jastrow, *Dictionary* (1950³), p. 905
Kohut, *Arukh ha-Shalem* (1878–1892), vol. 5, p. 338
Levy, *Wörterbuch* (1924²), vol. 3, p. 388
Neubauer, *Géographie* (1868), pp. 360–361
Neusner, *History* (1965–1970), vol. 5, p. 116
Oates, *Northern Iraq* (1968), pp. 30, 61, 77
Obermeyer, *Landschaft* (1929), pp. 13, 136–139
Sarre & Herzfeld, *Archäologische Reise* (1920), vol. 2, p. 205ff.
Segal, *Sefer Segal* (1964), p. 37*
Thompson & Hutchinson, *Exploration at Nineveh* (1929)

Nippur (Nufar) **נופר**

A. *Source*

Yoma 10a

תני רב יוסף ... "ותהי ראשית ממלכתו בבל וארך ואכד וכלנה", בבל כמשמעה, ארך זה אוריכות,[1] ואכד זה בשכר,[2] כלנה זה נופר[3] נינפי.[4]

Rav Joseph taught ... "And the mainstays of his kingdom were Babylon, Ereḵ, Akkad and Kalneh" (Gen. 10:10); Babylon is what it says, Ereḵ is Oriḵut,[1] Akkad is Kaškar,[2] and Kalneh is Nufar[3] Ninəfe.[4]

B. *Location*

The Nufar mentioned in the source above (see note 3) is Nippur, which is ninety kilometers southeast of Babylon (E5 on the Tal. Bab. map).

C. *History*

One of the great Babylonian cult centers before the Hellenistic period,[5] Nippur under the Seleucids and thereafter was a small provincial settlement. It does

---

[1] For other versions see the entry on "Orchoi."

[2] The source has **בשכר**. For other versions see the entry on "Kaškar."

[3] The Munich MS has **נפגר**; the Munich B MS, *Aggadot ha-Talmud*, and the *Arukh* have **ניפר**; and see *Diq. Sof.*

[4] The supplement "Ninəfe" which does not appear in other versions (see *Diq. Sof.*) may be intended to explain the name "Kalneh" in the passage as νύμφη (= nymph) meaning "bride" in Greek. Underlying that explanation is the double resemblance between Kalneh and *kallah* ("bride" in Hebrew) and Nufar or Nifar (see n. 3) and Ninəfe (see *Arukh ha-Shalem*, s.v. "**נפר**," "**נמפה**" and Krauss, *Lehnwörter*, vol. 2, pp. 361–362). In regard to the identification with Kalneh, see also n. 45 under "Ctesiphon," under "Maḥoza Area."

[5] For reference see al-Haik, *Key Lists*, No. 111; Ellis, *Mesopotamian Archaeological Sites*, pp. 61–62. For the nineteenth century excavations see Fisher, *Excavations at Nippur*; Hilprecht, *Exploration in Bible Lands*; Peters, *Nippur*, 2 vols. For the recent excavations see Crawford, *Archaeology* 12 (1959): 74–83; Knutstad, *Sumer* 22 (1966): 111–114;

not appear in Greek or Latin literature, nor did it have its own coinage,[6] or the status of a polis. The present knowledge about Nippur comes exclusively from Arabic sources and archaeological findings.

Al-Ḫaṭīb al-Baġdādī mentions a person of the fourth/tenth century who is from Niffar, "which is a place on the Nars (i.e. the Nars canal, see the entry on "Nareš") of the places belonging to the Persians."[7] Yāqūt quotes this and is concerned with the meaning. "If he means that it was of the Persian places in ancient times—all right, but now it is in Iraq, in the Kūfa region."[8] Samʿānī, who likewise quotes al-Ḫaṭīb al-Baġdādī, believes it is a place in the Baṣra district.[9] Yāqūt also quotes Ibn al-Faqīh, according to whom Niffar was first a town of the Kaskar district, and later included among those of the Baṣra district, but says that it actually belonged to Kūfa.[10] Evidently the apparent discrepancy reflects the successive administrative pertinence of Niffar.[11] Niffar is recorded as a bishopric from 900 on.[12]

Nippur was excavated in the last two decades of the nineteenth century and again in the 1960s and 1970s. The remains of the Seleucid and later periods have never been described systematically. Evidence of Hellenization is furnished by bullae found at Nippur,[13] three of which, bearing impressions of private seals, show among others Nike, probably Athene, and perhaps Apollo.[14]

McCown & Haines, *Nippur*, vol. 1; McCown et. al., *Nippur*, vol. 2. For the eleventh and twelfth season see Gibson, *Oriental Institute Communications*, 22 (1975); 23 (1977); *Sumer* 31 (1975): 33–39; *Expedition* 16/1 (1973): 9–14; 16/4 (1974): 23–32; *Iraq* 35 (1973): 194f.; 37 (1975): 60f.; 39 (1977): 310.

[6] For coins found at Nippur see Legrain, *U. of P. Mus. Jour.* 15 (1924): 70–76. They cover the period from about 400 B.C. to A.D. 744. Peters and Hilprecht, however, mention ninth century coins (see below and n. 23).

[7] "*aṣluhū min Niffar wa-hiya balad ʿalā n-Nars min bilādi l-furs*" (al-Ḫaṭīb al-Baġdādī, *Taʾrīḫ Baġdād*, vol. 12, p. 17).

[8] "*min nawāḥī Bābil, bi-arḍi l-Kūfa*" (Yāqūt, s.v. "Niffar"); and see below.

[9] Samʿānī, *Ansāb*, s.v. "Niffarī."

[10] Yāqūt, *loc. cit.*, and see also Yāqūt, s. v. "Kaskar." It should be noted that according to Ibn al-Faqīh (p. 210), the inhabitants of Niffar were among the most intelligent in the Persian Empire.

[11] See also "Niffar" in Bakrī: "A village in the Kūfa countryside (*sawād*), between Mosul and Ubulla." This definition seems to be a garble of information derived from Ibn al-Kalbī on a war between the Armānīyūn and the Ardawānīyūn—the former inhabiting the region around Babylon up to the Mosul area, and the latter the region between Niffar, a village in the Iraq Sawād, down to Ubulla and the edge of the desert (see Ṭabarī, vol. 1, p. 611 [= vol. 1, pp. 747–748] and Nöldeke, *Perser und Araber*, pp. 22–23). On Niffar see also Ṭabarī, vol. 5, pp. 117–118 (= vol. 1, pp. 3423–3424): Morony, *Iran* 14 (1976): 55; Scoville, *Gazetteer*, vol. 2, p. 125, s.v. "Afaj"; Streck, *EI*¹, s.v. "Niffar"; ʿAwwād, *Sumer* 5 (1949): 249–250.

[12] See Fiey, *L'Orient Syrien* 12 (1967): 250–253; Sachau, *APAW phil.-hist. Klasse* 1 (1919): 32–33.

[13] For bullae see also the entries on "Orchoi" and "Seleucia," under "Maḥoza Area."

[14] Published by Legrain, *Seals*, Nos. 1001–1012; 1014–1021.

Many of the terracottas found are of the Hellenistic period. They are provincial copies of Greek models, among them Greek mythological figures such as Eros, Nike, Apollo Kythareidos, Heracles, etc., mortals in Greek dress, as well as horsemen wearing flat Macedonian hats. Greek influence is evident in some architectural ornaments, published by Legrain in his volume on the terracottas. However, as pointed out by Legrain, many objects produced by the local industry belong to an Oriental tradition which maintained itself uninterruptedly throughout the Achaemenid, Seleucid and Parthian periods.[15]

Among the data available is the plan of a small palace (or villa) ascribed to the third/second century B.C.; in the Parthian period the old ziggurat was incorporated into a fortress or fortified palace, the plan of which has been published.[16] This Parthian structure was preceded by buildings in the same area dating from the Seleucid period. Other remains of Seleucid and Parthian buildings are briefly mentioned in preliminary reports but nowhere described.[17]

More than 2,500 tombs of the Parthian and Sassanian period are reported to have been found.[18] A rich one of the first century A.D. has been described in some detail.[19] The slipper- and bathtub-shaped terracotta coffins found there are distinctive; others are brick boxes and urns of various shapes.

The literature on the excavations carried out in the last century makes repeated reference to a settlement occupying the most prominent parts of Nippur in the Parthian and later periods,[20] but does not describe it in detail (since the excavators were primarily interested in the early town and in the massive remains of the Parthian and Seleucid palace). However, this settlement is of special interest because of its inhabitation by Jews. The nature of its population is evidenced by the discovery in the houses of incantation bowls (over a hundred), some written in Syriac or Arabic but most in Hebrew.[21] What follows is the translation of one of these texts:

> A remedy from heaven for Darbah, son of Asasarieh, and for Shadkoi daughter of Dada his wife, for their sons and daughters, their houses and possessions; that they may have children, and that these live and be

---

[15] *Terra-cottas*, p. 11.

[16] Hilprecht, *ibid.*, pp. 563–568. For the ziggurat see *ibid.*, pp. 558–563; Fisher, *ibid.*, Pl. 14; Knutstad, *op.cit.* (in n. 5), p. 111.

[17] Crawford, *op.cit.* (in n. 5); Gibson on the eleventh season (see n. 5).

[18] Hilprecht, *ibid.*, p. 337f., 422f., 448f.

[19] *Ibid.*, pp. 504–508.

[20] *Ibid.*, pp. 447–448, 555–556; Peters, *op.cit.* (in n. 5), pp. 182–187; Fisher, *op.cit.* (in n. 5), p. 17f.

[21] More have been found in recent excavations; cf. *Nippur*, vol. 1 (*op.cit.* in n. 5), p. 153, Pls. 163:3; 166A–B; 167B. Pognon, *Inscriptions Mandaïtes des Coupes de Khouabir*, reports having acquired some Hebrew bowls but has not published any Hebrew texts. For the incantation bowls from Nippur see Montgomery, *Aramaic Incantation Texts from Nippur*.

preserved from Shedim and Daevas, from Shubhte and Satans, from curses, night-demons and destruction which may have been prepared for them. I adjure you, O angel who has come down from heaven, whose horn is welted in blood . . . O angel; who hath command in the East over the secrets of the Almighty . . . may these live and be preserved from this day on. May the spells (of the evil spirits) never be seen hovering over his food; but may they remain in their own place, biting at the chain . . .

May be banned and excommunicated all Kisi, woundings, trouble, cursing, laceration, calamity, ban, curse; all Shedim, Daevas, Shubhte, Lilith, Spirits—all destruction and anything else of evil—that they depart from out of Darbah son of Asasarieh, from Shadkoi daughter of Dada his wife; from Honik, from Yasmon, Ku Kithi, Mahduch, Abraham, Panui, Shiluch (?), Shadkoi, from their houses and possessions, and from everything which may be theirs. By means of this we loosen their hold from this day and forever. In the name of Yahweh of Hosts! Amen! Amen! Selah! May Yahweh, by this, preserve him from every Ashmodai of his soul![22]

The houses containing such bowls are, according to the excavators, dated by coins from the Parthian to the early Arab periods (the latter indicated by Kufic coins of the seventh century). The latest coins found at Nippur are of ninth century caliphs.[23] Most of the incantation bowls were found upside down in the ground.[24] According to Hilprecht, "it is very evident that they had been placed thus intentionally, in order to prevent the demons adjured by the spiral inscription on the inner face of most of the vases from doing any harm to the people living in that neighborhood. Sometimes two bowls facing one another had been cemented together with bitumen. In one case an inscribed hen's egg was concealed under the bowl."[25] Other bowls contained inscribed skulls in pieces.[26]

Two discoveries are specifically mentioned in connection with houses where such bowls were found. One is a "curious pottery object . . . supposed to have belonged to a Jewish doctor or apothecary, and to have been intended rather for ornament or advertisement than for use. We concluded that it belonged to an apothecary or doctor from the fact that there were in the same place several clay bottles sealed with bitumen, containing a mixture which we judged to be intended as medicine, although no chemical analysis has yet been made."[27]

---

[22] Translated by Gottheil for Peters, *Nippur*, vol. 2, pp. 182–183.

[23] Peters, *op.cit.* (in n. 5), p. 186; Hilprecht, *op.cit.* (in n. 5), p. 556.

[24] Hilprecht, *ibid.*, p. 447f. Many of the bowls published by Pognon, *op.cit.* (in n. 21), p. 2f., were found upside down.

[25] Hilprecht, *ibid.*, p. 448.

[26] *Ibid.*, pp. 440, 448. Hilprecht observes that skulls and an egg were also found in the mortar of the Parthian fortress which incorporated the old ziggurat at Nippur. See also Pognon, *op.cit.* (in n. 21).

[27] Peters, *ibid.*, p. 183.

The other find is the wooden box of a Jewish scribe containing his pen-holder and inkstand and a scrap of parchment inscribed with a few Hebrew characters.[28]
No photograph or drawing of these finds seems to have been made, nor has any plan of the houses of this settlement been published. The latter are described as follows: "These houses are in all cases of unburned brick, and resemble or, in fact, seem to be identical with the houses of ordinary town Arabs of the present day in Hillah, Shatra, Diwaniah, and similar towns in that region." The excavator actually found it impossible to distinguish between the ordinary houses of various periods.[29] Peters reports seeing "ancient Jewish tombstones on the mound called Juha near Anbar," and similar ones at Nippur, but no details are given.[30]

Beer, *Amora'ei Bavel* (1974), pp. 17–18
Crawford, *Archaeology* 12 (1959): 74–83
Ellis, *Mesopotamian Archaeological Sites* (1972), pp. 61–62
Eshel, *Yishuvei ha-Yehudim* (1979), pp. 186–187, 131, 132 "כלנה"
Feuchtwang, *MGWJ* 42 (1898): 152–153
Fischer, *Excavations at Nippur* (1905)
Funk, *Monumenta* (1913) pp. 20, 279
al-Haik, *Key Lists* (1968), No. 111
Hilprecht, *Exploration in Bible Lands* (1903), passim
Jastrow, *Dictionary* (1950³), p. 907
Knutstad, *Sumer* 22 (1966): 111–114
Kohut, *Arukh ha-Shalem* (1878–1892), vol. 5, p. 367
Krauss, *MGWJ* 39 (1895): 58–59
Krauss, *Lehnwörter* (1898–1899), vol. 1, p. 425
Legrain, *U. of P. Mus. Jour.* 15 (1924): 70–76
Legrain, *Seals* (1925), Nos. 1001–1012; 1014–1021
Legrain, *Terra-cottas* (1930), p. 11
Neubauer, *Géographie* (1868), p. 346
Obermeyer, *Landschaft* (1929), pp. 57, 328, 335–336
Peters, *Nippur*, 2 vols. (1897)

Nisibis (Nəṣivin) נציבין

A. *Sources*

1. Qiddushin 72a

"ותלת עלעין בפומה בין שיניה", אמר רבי יוחנן זו חלזון[1] הדייב ונציבין, שפעמים בולעתן ופעמים פולטתן.

"It had three ribs in its mouth between its teeth," (Dan. 7:5) said Rabbi Yoḥanan, That is Ḥelwan,[1] Hadyav and Nisibis, which she [Rome] sometimes swallows and sometimes spits out.

---

[28] Hilprecht, *ibid.*, pp. 555–556, no illustration.
[29] Peters, *ibid.*, p. 185.
[30] *Nippur*, vol. 1, p. 171f.

[1] The source has חלזון; the Pirqoi Ben Baboi version is זו חרן חדייב ונציבין (*Ginzei Schechter*, vol. 2, p. 563), and see below.

2. Genesis Rabbah XXXVII, 4, Theodor-Albeck ed. p. 346

"ותהי ראשית ממלכתו בבל וארך ואכד וכלנה" — הדס ונציבין וקטיספון[2].

"And the mainstays of his kingdom were Babylon, Erek, Akkad and Kalneh," (Gen. 10:10) Edessa (?) and Nisibis and Ctesiphon.[2]

3. Pesaḥim 3b

ההוא ארמאה[3] דהוה סליק ואכיל פסחים בירושלים, אמר כתיב "כל בן נכר לא יאכל בו", "כל ערל לא יאכל בו", ואנא הא קאכילנא משופרי שופרי, אמר ליה רבי יהודה בן בתירא מי קא ספו לך מאליה, אמר ליה לא, כי סלקת להתם אימא להו ספו לי מאליה, כי סליק אמר להו מאליה ספו לי, אמרו ליה אליה לגבוה סלקא. אמרו ליה מאן אמר לך הכי, אמר להו רבי יהודה בן בתירא. אמרו מאי היא דקמן, בדקו בתריה ואשכחוהו דארמאה הוא וקטלוהו. שלחו ליה לרבי יהודה בן בתירא שלם לך רבי יהודה בן בתירא דאת בנציבין ומצודתך פרוסה בירושלים.

That Aramite[3] who used to go up and eat of the Passover sacrifice in Jerusalem said, It is written "No foreigner shall eat of it," (Ex. 12:43) "no uncircumcised person may eat of it," (12:48) and I eat of the finest [part]. Rabbi Judah b. Bathyra said to him, Did they feed you from the fat-tail? He said, No. When you go up there, tell them, Feed me from the fat-tail. When he went up there he said to them, Feed me from the fat-tail. They said to him, The fat-tail goes to Most High. They said to him, Who told you that? He said to them, Rabbi Judah b. Bathyra. They said, What is this before us? They investigated and found he was an Aramite and killed him. Then they sent to Rabbi Judah b. Bathyra, Peace be with you, you are in Nisibis and your net is spread in Jerusalem.

4. Sanhedrin 32b[4]

ת"ר "צדק צדק תרדף" הלך אחר חכמים לִישיבה, אחר ר' אליעזר ללוד, אחר רבן יוחנן בן זכאי לברור חיל, אחר רבי יהושע לפקיעין, אחר רבן גמליאל ליבנא, אחר רבי עקיבא לבני ברק, אחר רבי מתיא לרומי, אחר רבי חנניא בן תרדיון לסיכני, אחר ר' יוסי לציפורי, אחר רבי יהודה בן בתירה לנציבין, אחר רבי יהושע לגולה,[5] אחר רבי לבית שערים, אחר חכמים ללשכת הגזית.

The rabbis taught, "Justice, only justice, you shall follow" (Deut. 16:20) [means] follow the scholars to the yeshiva, Rabbi Eliezer to Lod, Rabban

---

[2] The source has הדס ונציבין וקטיספון. See the entries for "Hadas" and "Ctesiphon," under "Maḥoza Area."

[3] The source has ארמאה; the Munich and Oxford MSS and old printings have גוי (= Gentile), in the rest of the passage as well, and see *Diq. Sof.*

[4] Cf. *Yalquṭ Shim'oni*, Leviticus § 611.

[5] The Munich MS has "Rabbi Hananiah the son of Rabbi Joshua's brother" as do the Florence and Karlsruhe MSS, as well as *Yalquṭ Shim'oni, loc. cit.* and see *Diq. Sof.* The word "*golah*" by itself means "Babylonia"; on the activity of Rabbi Joshua b. Hananiah there see Source 8.

Yoḥanan b. Zakkai to Bəror Ḥayil, Rabbi Joshua to Pəqi'in, Rabban Gamaliel to Yavneh, Rabbi 'Aqiva to Bəne Bəraq, Rabbi Mattia to Rome, Rabbi Hananiah b. Teradyon to Sikhnin, Rabbi Yose to Sepphoris, Rabbi Judah b. Bathyra to Nisibis, Rabbi Joshua to the Exile,[5] Rabbi to Bet Šə'arim, the sages to the Chamber of Hewn Stones.

5. Lamentations Rabbah III, 6

רבי יהודה בן בתירה אזל לנציבין בערבי צומא רבא אכל ופסק, שמע ריש גלותא[6] ואתא לגביה, אמר ליה ישגח עלי רבי, א"ל אכלית ופסקית, א"ל ישגח עלי רבי דלא יהון אמרין לא חשביה כלום מטרח עלוי אזל עימיה . . .

Rabbi Judah b. Bathyra went to Nisibis on the eve of the great fast, ate and stopped. The Exilarch[6] heard and came to him and asked him, Will the Rabbi do me the courtesy? He said to him, I have already eaten and stopped. He said to him, Would the Rabbi do me the courtesy, so they do not say he was not considered at all. He took the trouble and went with him . . .

6. Yevamot 108b

מאן תנא, אמר רב יהודה אמר רב מאי דכתיב "מימינו בכסף שתינו עצינו במחיר יבאו," בשעת הסכנה נתבקשה הלכה זו הרי שיצאה מראשון בגט ומשני במיאון מהו שתחזור לראשון, שכרו אדם אחד בארבע מאות זוז ושאלו את ר' עקיבא בבית האסורין ואסר, את רבי יהודה בן בתירה בנציבין ואסר, אמר רבי ישמעאל בר' יוסי לזו לא הוצרכנו . . . שכרו שני בני אדם בארבע מאות זוז ובאו ושאלו את רבי עקיבא בבית האסורין ואסר, את רבי יהודה בן בתירה בנציבין ואסר.

Who taught? Rav Judah said that Rav said, What is the meaning of "We must pay for the water we drink, the wood we get must be bought." (Lam. 5:4) In the time of danger this halakhah was requested: If she (a minor) left her first [husband] with a divorce paper and her second through annulment, may she return to the first? They hired a man for four hundred *zuz* and addressed a query to Rabbi 'Aqiva in prison who forbade, and Rabbi Judah b. Bathyra in Nisibis who forbade. Rabbi Ishmael the son of Rabbi Yose said, We didn't need that . . . They hired two man for four hundred *zuz* and they came and asked Rabbi 'Aqiva in prison who forbade, and Rabbi Judah b. Bathyra in Nisibis who forbade.

7. Sifre Deuteronomy LXXX, Finkelstein ed. p. 146

מעשה ברבי אלעזר בן שמוע ורבי יוחנן הסנדלר שהיו הולכים לנציבים אצל רבי יהודה בן בתירה ללמוד ממנו תורה והגיעו לציידן[7] וזכרו את ארץ ישראל . . . אמרו ישיבת ארץ ישראל שקולה כנגד כל המצוות שבתורה, חזרו ובאו להם לארץ ישראל.

---

[6] The source has *resh galuta*. Most of the *Rishonim* versions have *resh kenishta* (= synagogue head); and see the Buber edition of Lamentations Rabbah, p. 130, n. 75. (See also Beer, *Rashut ha-Golah*, p. 21, n. 25, and see below.)

[7] The source has ציידן and the place name appears in several forms in the MSS, all evidently referring to Sidon.

It happened that Rabbi Eleazar b. Shammua and Rabbi Yoḥanan ha-Sandelar were going to Nisibis to Rabbi Judah b. Bathyra to learn the Torah from him and they arrived in Sidon[7] and remembered Eretz Israel... They said, Residing in Eretz Israel outweighs all the precepts in the Torah, and returned and came to Eretz Israel.

8. T. J. Sanhedrin I, 2–19a, 7–18 (= T. J. Nedarim VII, 13–40a, 30–41)[8]

חנניה בן אחי רבי יהושע עיבר בחוצה לארץ, שלח ליה רבי ג׳ איגרן גבי ר׳ יצחק ורבי נתן, בחדא כתב לקדושת חנניה, וחדא כתב גדיים שהנחת נעשו תיישים, ובחדא כתב אם אין את מקבל עליך צא לך למדבר האטד ותהי שוחט ונחוניון זורק, קרא קדמייתא ואוקרון, תנייתא ואוקרון, תליתא בעא מבסרתהון, אמרין ליה לית את יכיל דכבר אוקרתנין, קם רבי יצחק וקרא באוריתא אלה מועדי (ה׳) חנניה בן אחי רבי יהושע, אמרין ליה (אמר) אלה הם מועדי ה׳, אמר לון גבן, קם רבי נתן ואשלים כי מבבל תצא תורה ודבר ה׳ מנהר פקוד, אמרין ליה ״כי מציון תצא תורה ודבר ה׳ מירושלים״, אמר לון גבן, אזל קבל עליהן קמי רבי יהודה בן בתירה לנציבין, א״ל אחריהם אחריהם, א״ל לי נא ידע מה תמן מה מודע לי דאינון חכמין מחשבה דכוותי, מכיון דלא ידעי מחשבה דכוותיה ישמעון ליה, ומכיון דאינון חכמין מחשבה דכוותיה ישמע לון, קם ורכב סוסיא הן דמטא מטא והן דלא מטא נהגין בקילקול.

Hananiah the son of Rabbi Joshua's brother intercalated abroad; Rabbi sent him three letters by Rabbi Isaac and Rabbi Nathan. In one he wrote, To his holiness Hananiah, and in one he wrote, Kids that you left became goats, and in one he wrote, If you do not accept [the authority of Eretz Israel] go out to the desert of thorns and be a slaughterer, and Neḥonyon will dash the blood. He read the first and honored them, the second and honored them, the third and wished to disparage them. They said to him, You cannot, for you already honored us. Rabbi Isaac rose and read in the Torah, These are the fixed times of Hananiah the son of Rabbi Joshua's brother. They said to him, These are the fixed times of the Lord. He said to them, With us [they are]! Rabbi Nathan rose and concluded, For instruction shall come forth from Babylonia and the word of the Lord from Nəhar Pəqod. They said to him, "For instruction shall come forth from Zion and the word of the Lord from Jerusalem." (Is. 2:3) He said to them, With us [they will]! He (Hananiah) went and complained about them before Rabbi Judah b. Bathyra in Nisibis. He said, After them, after them. He said to him, I don't know what there is there, who will tell me they are wise enough to calculate [leap year] like me. Because if they don't know how to calculate like you, should they listen to you? [The more so] because they are wise enough to calculate like you, you should listen to them. He rose and rode on the horse and wherever he got to he got to, and where he did not get to, they perverted the Law.

---

[8] Cf. T. B. Berakhot 63a–b, which does not, however, have Hananiah the son of Rabbi Joshua's brother going to Rabbi Judah b. Bathyra in Nisibis.

9. T. J. Berakhot III 4–6c, 39–41

מעשה באחד שעמד לקרות בתורה בנציבין כיון שהגיע להזכרה התחיל מגמגם בה אמר לו רבי יהודה בן בתירה פתח פיך ויאירו דבריך שאין דברי תורה מקבלין טומאה.

There was a case of one who rose to read the Torah at Nisibis and when he came to the mention (of the Lord) began to stammer. Rabbi Judah b. Bathyra said to him, Open your mouth and say your words, for words of the Law do not become unclean.

10. Sanhedrin 96a

אמר רבי זירא אע"ג דשלח רבי יהודה בן בתירא[9] מנציבין הזהרו בזקן ששכח תלמודו מחמת אונסו . . .

Rabbi Zera said, Though Rabbi Judah b. Bathyra[9] of Nisibis sent (a message saying], Be respectful of an elder who has lost his learning through misfortune . . .

11. Qiddushin 10b[10]

תא שמע וכבר שלח יוחנן בן בג בג אצל רבי יהודה בן בתירה לנציבין שמעתי עליך שאתה אומר ארוסה בת ישראל אוכלת בתרומה.

Come hear, Yoḥanan b. Bag Bag already sent to Rabbi Judah b. Bathyra of Nisibis [noting] I've heard you claim that an Israelite [girl] betrothed [to a priest] eats of the *terumah*.

12. Yevamot 102a[11]

דתניא א"ר יוסי[12] פעם אחת הלכתי לנציבין מצאתי זקן אחד, אמרתי לו כלום אתה בקי בר' יהודה בן בתירא, אמר לי הן ועל שולחני הוא תדיר, כלום ראית שחלץ ביבמה, אמר לי ראיתי שחלץ הרבה פעמים, במנעל או בסנדל, אמר לי וכי חולצין במנעל . . .[13]

For it was taught, Rabbi Yose[12] related, Once I went to Nisibis, found an elder, asked him, Are you acquainted with Rabbi Judah b. Bathyra? He said, Yes, and he is generally at my table. Have you ever seen him conducting a *ḥalitzah* ceremony for a *yevamah*? He told me, I saw him do so many times. With a shoe or a sandal? He said to me, Is it done with a shoe . . .[13]

---

[9] The Florence and Karlsruhe MSS have "Judah" alone. But this should be construed as "Rabbi Judah b. Bathyra" because of the mention of Nisibis. The term שלח (= sent) suggests that the reference is not to a place within Babylonia, and see *Diq. Sof.*

[10] Parallels to this source occur in Tosefta Ketubot V, 1; Sifre Numbers, CXVII, Horovitz ed., p. 137; T. J. Ketubot V 4–29d, 54–56.

[11] Parallels to this source occur in Tosefta Yevamot XII, 11; T. J. Yevamot XII 1–12c, 11–14. On the differences between the parallels and their significance see Lieberman, *Tosefta ki-Fshutah*, Seder Nashim, pp. 134–136.

[12] The Tosefta parallel in both the printing and the Vienna MS has "Rabbi Simeon."

[13] The T. J. parallel has וכי יש סנדל במקומינו (= and is there a sandal in our place?), and see Lieberman, *loc.cit.* On the question of whether the elder mentioned was a *shulḥani* (= banker) and the various relevant versions, see Beer, *Amora'ei Bavel*, p. 218.

13. T. J. Sanhedrin VIII, 6–26b, 29–38

אמר רבי יאשיה סח לי זעירה משם אנשי ירושלם שלשה הן שאם ביקשו למחול מוחלין, ואילו הן סוטה, ובן סורר ומורה, וזקן ממרא על פי בית דין . . . וכשבאתי אצל ר׳ יהודה בן בתירה לנציבין[14] על שנים הודה לי ועל אחד לא הודה לי . . .

Rabbi Josiah said, Zeʿira told me in the name of the Jerusalemites, There are three if asking forgiveness are forgiven, and they are an adulteress and a disloyal and defiant son, and an elder disregarding the decision of the court . . . and when I came to Rabbi Judah b. Bathyra to Nisibis[14] on two he agreed with me and on one he did not . . .

14. Midrash Samuel X, 3 (Buber ed., p. 77)[15]

אבא אבוי דשמואל בר אבא הוה מתעסק במטכסא ושלח גבי׳ רבי יודה בן בתירה לנציבין, בתר זמן קם עמו, אמר ליה לית רבי בעי האי מילתא, אמר ליה ולא מילין הוון, אמר ליה לית מלתך הימנה עלי סגי מן ממונה, אמר ליה את היימנת במילתי עלך, תזכה למקמא בר כשמואל נביאה . . .

Abba, the father of Samuel b. Abba, dealt in silk and sent to Rabbi Judah b. Bathyra to Nisibis. Some time later, he (Abba) met him. He said to him, Doesn't the Rabbi want this? He said, And weren't there [just] words? He said to him, Is your word not more trustworthy for me than money? He said, You, for whom my word was trustworthy, will have the merit of having a son like the prophet Samuel.

15. ʿAvodah Zarah 36a

. . . דכי אתא רב יצחק בר שמואל בר מרתא ואמר דריש רבי שמלאי בנציבין שמן ר׳ יהודה[16] ובית דינו נמנו עליו והתירוהו.

. . . when Rav Isaac b. Samuel b. Marta came, he related that Rabbi Simlai preached in Nisibis that Rabbi Judah[16] and his court took a vote and permitted the oil [of Gentiles].

16. T. J. ʿAvodah Zarah, II, 9 – 41d, 46–47 (= T. J. Shabbat, I, 7 – 3d, 24–25)

יצחק בר שמואל בר מרתא נחת לנציבין, אשכח שמלאי הדרומי יתיב דרש רבי ובית דינו התירו בשמן.

Isaac b. Samuel b. Marta came down to Nisibis, found Simlai the Daromean sitting and preaching that Rabbi and his court permitted the oil.

---

[14] The parallels do not mention Nisibis, the T. B. (in Soṭah 25a and Sanhedrin 88b) having וכשבאתי אצל חבירי שבדרום (= and when I came to my friends in the Darom); cf. also Sifre Deuteronomy, CCXVIII, Finkelstein ed., p. 251, and T. J. Soṭah IV 3 – 19c, 46–48.

[15] Cf. *Yalquṭ Shimʿoni* for I Samuel, § 100.

[16] The Munich MS and the ʿAvodah Zarah MS edited by Abramson have "Rabbi Judah ha-Nasi," and see below.

17. Pliny, *Natural History* VI 16, 42

totam eam Macedones Mygdoniam cognominaverunt a similitudine. oppida Alexandria, item Antiochia quam Nesebin vocant; abest ab Artaxatis DCCL mp.

The Macedonians have given to the whole of Adiabene the name of Mygdonia from its likeness to Mygdonia in Macedon. Its towns are Alexandria and Antiochia, the native name for which is Nesebis; it is 750 miles from Artaxata. (trans.: H. Rackham, LCL)

18. Cassius Dio XXXVI 6[17]

ὁ οὖν Λούκουλλος, ἐπειδή τε πολλοὶ ἐτραυματίζοντο, καὶ οἱ μὲν ἔθνησκον οἱ δ' ανάπηροι γοῦν ἐγίγνοντο, καὶ ἅμα καὶ τὰ ἐπιτήδεια αὐτοὺς ἐπέλιπεν, ἐκεῖθέν τε ἀπεχώρησε καὶ ἐπὶ Νίσιβιν ὥρμησεν. ἡ δὲ δὴ πόλις αὕτη ἐν τῇ Μεσοποταμίᾳ καλουμένῃ πεπόλισται (οὕτω γὰρ πᾶν τὸ μεταξὺ τοῦ τε Τίγριδος καὶ τοῦ Εὐφράτου ὀνομάζεται) καὶ νῦν μὲν ἡμετέρα ἐστὶ καὶ ἄποικος ἡμῶν νομίζεται, τότε δὲ ὁ Τιγράνης τῶν Πάρθων αὐτὴν ἀφελόμενος τούς τε θησαυροὺς ἐν αὐτῇ καὶ τὰ ἄλλα τὰ πλεῖστα τῶν λοιπῶν ἀπετέθειτο, φύλακά οἱ τὸν ἀδελφὸν προστάξας. πρὸς οὖν ταύτην ὁ Λούκουλλος ἐλθὼν ἐν μὲν τῷ θέρει, καίπερ μὴ παρέργως τὰς προσβολὰς ποιησάμενος, οὐδὲν ἐπέρανε· τὰ γὰρ τείχη καὶ διπλᾶ καὶ πλίνθινα ὄντα, τήν τε παχύτητα πολλὴν ἔχοντα καὶ τάφρῳ βαθείᾳ διειλημμένα, οὔτε κατασεισθῆναί πῃ οὔτε διορυχθῆναι ἠδυνήθη.

Since many, then, were getting wounded, of whom some died, and the others were in any case maimed, and since provisions at the same time were failing them, Lucullus retired from that place (i.e. Armenia) and marched against Nisibis. This city is built in the region called Mesopotamia (the name given to all the country between the Tigris and the Euphrates) and now belongs to us, being considered a colony of ours. But at that time Tigranes who had seized it from the Parthians had deposited in it his treasures and most of his other possessions, and had stationed his brother as guard over it. Lucullus reached this city in the summer time and although he directed his attacks upon it in no half-hearted fashion, he effected nothing. For the walls, being of brick, double, and of great thickness, with a deep moat intervening, could be neither battered down anywhere, nor undermined . . . (In the end Lucullus captured Nisibis all the same.) (trans.: E. Cary, LCL)

19. Ammianus XXV 7, 11[18]

. . . difficile hoc adeptus, ut Nisibis et Singara sine incolis transirent in iura Persarum, a munimentis vero alienandis reverti ad nostra praesidia Romana permitterentur.

. . . with difficulty he (i.e. Jovian) succeded in bringing it about that Nisibis and Singara should pass into control of the Persians without their inhabitants, and

[17] Lucullus, 68 B.C.

[18] On the peace treaty between Jovian and the Persians, A.D. 364.

that the Romans in the fortresses that were to be taken from us should be allowed to return to our protection. (trans.: J. C. Rolfe, LCL)

20. Ammianus XXV 8, 13–9, 2

Hos tabellarios fama praegrediens index tristiorum casuum uelocissima per prouincias uolitabat et gentes maximeque omnium Nisibenos acerbo dolore perculsit, cum urbem Sapori deditam comperissent, cuius iram metuebant et simultates, recolentes, quae assidue pertulerit funera eam saepius oppugnare conatus. constabat enim orbem eorum in dicionem potuisse transire Persidis, ni illi haec ciuitas habili situ et moenium magnitudine restitisset. miseri tamen, licet maiore uenturi pauore constringerentur, spe tamen sustentari potuerunt exigua, hac scilicet uelut suopte motu uel exoratus eorum precibus imperator eodem statu retinebit urbem, orientis firmissimum claustrum . . .
. . . post quae itinere festinato Nisibi cupide uisa extra urbem statiua castra posuit princeps rogatusque enixe precante multiplici plebe, ut ingressus palatio more succederet principum, pertinaciter reluctatus est erubescens agente se intra muros urbem inexpugnabilem iratis hostibus tradi . . .
Postridie Bineses, unus ex Persis, quem inter alios excellere diximus, mandata regis complere festinans promissa flagitabat instanter et principe permittente Romano ciuitatem ingressus gentis suae signum ab arce extulit summa migrationem e patria ciuibus nuntians luctuosam. et uertere solum extemplo omnes praecepti manus tendentes flentesque orabant, ne imponeretur sibi necessitas abscendendi, ad defendendos penates se solos sufficere sine alimentis publicis affirmantes et milite satis confisi affuturam iustitiam pro genitali sede dimicaturis, ut experti sunt saepe. et haec quidem suppliciter ordo et populos precabatur, sed uentis loquebantur in cassum imperatore, ut fingebat alia metuens, periurii piacula declinante.

Meanwhile rumour, the swiftest messenger of sad events, outstripping these messengers, flew through provinces and nations, and most of all struck the people of Nisibis with bitter grief; when they learned that their city had been surrendered to Sapor, whose anger and hostility they feared, recalling as they did what constant losses he had suffered in his frequent attempts to take their city. For it was clear that the entire Orient might have passed into the control of Persia, had not this city with its advantageous situation and mighty walls resisted him, Nevertheless, however much the unhappy people were tormented with great fear of the future, yet they could sustain themselves with one slight hope, namely, that the emperor would, of his own accord or prevailed upon by their entreaties, keep the city in its present condition, as the strongest bulwark of the Orient . . .
. . . After this we went on more speedily, and looking eagerly at Nisibis, the emperor made a permanent camp outside of the city; but in spite of the earnest request of many of the populace to enter and take up his residence in the palace

as was usual with the emperors, he obstinately refused, from shame that during his own stay within its walls the impregnable city should be handed over to the enemy . . .
On the following day Bineses, one of the Persians, who (as I have said) was eminent beyond all others, hastening to fulfil the orders of his king, urgently demanded what had been promised. Therefore, with the permission of the Roman emperor, he entered the city and raised the flag of his nation on the top of the citadel, announcing to the citizens their sorrowful departure from their native place. And when all were commanded to leave their homes at once, with tears and outstretched hands they begged that they might not be compelled to depart, declaring that they alone, without aid from the empire in provisions and men, were able to defend their hearths, trusting that Justice herself would, as they had often found, aid them in fighting for their ancestral dwelling-place. But suppliantly as the magistrates and people entreated, all was spoken vainly to the winds, since the emperor (as he pretended, while moved by other fears) did not wish to incur the guilt of perjury.

21. *Justinian Code* (ed. Krueger) IV 63, 4

Impp. Honorius et Theodosius AA. Theodoro pp.
Mercatores tam imperio nostro quam Persarum regi subiectos ultra ea loca, in quibus foederis tempore cum memorata natione nobis convenit, nundinas exercere minime oportet, ne alieni regni, quod non convenit, scrutentur arcana. Nullius igitur posthac imperio nostro subiectus ultra Nisibin Callinicum et Artaxata emendi sive vendendi species causa proficisci audeat nec praeter memorates civitates cum Persa merces existimet commutandas.

The august emperors Honorius and Theodosius to the praetorian prefect Theodorus.
Not only merchants who owe allegiance to our government, but also those who are subject to the King of the Persians, must not hold markets beyond the places agreed upon at the time of the treaty concluded with the above-mentioned nation, in order to prevent the secrets of either kingdom from being disclosed (which is improper). Therefore no subject of our Empire shall hereafter presume to travel for the purpose of selling merchandise beyond Nisibis, Callinicum and Artaxata, nor think that he can exchange merchandise anywhere beyond the above-mentioned cities. (trans.: S. P. Scott, *Corpus Iuris Civilis, The Civil Law* [Cincinnati 1932])

Nisibis near Nəhardəʿa

22. Josephus, *Antiquities* XVIII, 312

ἔστιν δὲ καὶ Νίσιβις πόλις κατὰ τὸν αὐτὸν τοῦ ποταμοῦ περίρρουν, ὅθεν Ἰουδαῖοι τῇ φύσει τῶν χωρίων πεπιστευκότες τό τε δίδραχμον, ὃ τῷ θεῷ καταβάλλειν ἑκάστοις πάτριον, ταύτῃ κατετίθεντο καὶ ὁπόσα δὲ ἄλλα ἀναθήματα, ἐχρῶντό τε ὥσπερ ταμιείῳ ταῖσδε ταῖς πόλεσιν.

There is also a city Nisibis situated on the same bend of the river (namely the Euphrates near Nəhardəʿa). The Jews, in consequence, trusting to the natural strength of these places, used to deposit there the two-drachm coins which it is the national custom for all to contribute to the cause of God, as well as any other dedicatory offerings. Thus these cities were their bank of deposit. (trans.: L. H. Feldman, LCL)

23. Josephus, *Antiquities* XVIII, 379

καὶ συνελέγησαν ὥστε πολὺ εἴς τε τὰ Νέερδα καὶ τὴν Νίσιβιν ὀχυρότητι τῶν πόλεων κτώμενοι τὴν ἀσφάλειαν, καὶ ἄλλως πληθὺς ἅπασα μαχίμων ἀνδρῶν κατοικεῖται.

The Jews flocked to Nearda and Nisibis, where they were safe because these cities were fortified and were furthermore populated by men who were valiant fighters every one. (trans.: L. H. Feldman, LCL)

B. *Location*

In northern Mesopotamia, on the river Ǧaǧǧag (Mygdonios, in Greek), one of the tributaries of the Ḫābūr; today it is Nusaybin in Turkey, near the Syrian border (on Bab. Env. map).

C. *History*

Nisibis is one of the main cities of Mesopotamia, its importance stemming from its location on a crossroads from which the road from southern Mesopotamia branches out to the Euphrates crossings at Sura, Hierapolis, Zeugma and Melitene. The town lies in a fertile plain suitable for growing grapevines and vegetables.

Nisibis is mentioned in Assyrian sources from the ninth century B.C. It was founded as a Hellenistic town called Antiochia Mygdonia (i.e. Antioch on the Mygdonios) apparently by Antiochus IV[19]; presumably a group of Macedonian settlers was then installed there, and the town came to have a mixed population.

In 129 B.C. the Parthians conquered all of Mesopotamia. In 80 B.C. the town was captured by Tigranes of Armenia and flourished under Armenian rule. It was held briefly by the Romans (under Lucullus, in 68 B.C.) and then reverted

[19] For its establishment as a Hellenistic city, see Tscherikower, *Städtegründungen*, pp. 89–90. For Nisibis in general see the comprehensive entry by Sturm in *RE*, vol. 17, cols. 714–757, and see also Dillemann, *Haute Mésopotamie*, passim; Pigulevskaja, *Les Villes*, pp. 49–59; Oates, *Northern Iraq*, pp. 70–75, 78–79 (for the roads). On the name Nisibis on coins and in inscriptions see Robert, *Hellenica* 2 (1946): 79–80; *BMC Arabia*, pp. cviii–cix. For a coin-hoard buried after 32/31 B.C. see Seyrig, *Revue Numismatique* 17 (1955): 82–122.

to Armenia which held it until Artabanus III handed it over to Izates of Adiabene. Nisibis was briefly under Roman rule again during Trajan's Parthian campaigns, which coincided with the revolt of Diaspora Jews against Rome (A. D. 115–117); together with the Jews of Mesopotamia and the other dispersions, the Nisibis Jews most probably fought Trajan's legions at the same time as the Parthians fought them.

Nisibis was once again captured, by Lucius Verus in A. D. 162–165, but no information is available on what arrangements he instituted in northern Mesopotamia. At the time of Septimius Severus, the town was called Colonia Septimia Nisibis and was the capital of the province of Mesopotamia. The Sassanians tried repeatedly to capture the town and finally succeeded in the reign of Maximus, but soon lost it to Gordian III in 243. The struggle of the Sassanians and the Romans over control of Nisibis is reflected in Source 1, where Rabbi Yoḥanan lists it among the towns "which she [Rome] sometimes swallows and sometimes spits out."[20] Shapur I managed to take the town after an eleven-year siege which is mentioned in the Seder Olam Zuṭa ("And in his day [in the days of Huna Mar the Exilarch] Shapur ascended to Nisibis and conquered it"[21]) but in 262 had to surrender it to Odaenathus of Palmyra. After its recapture by Diocletian and Galerius, Nisibis became the seat of the Roman commander (*dux Mesopotamiae*), an important stronghold in Diocletian's *limes*, and the only point where trade between Rome and Persia was permitted.[22]

The Persians did not relax their efforts to gain permanent control of Nisibis, and finally captured it from Jovian in 363, at which time most of the residents are thought to have left for Amida.[23] Shapur II moved settlers in from other

---

[20] See n. 1. That sermon was explicated in Pirqoi Ben Baboi as follows: שפעמים פלטתן [צ״ל בולעתן] רומי הרשעה שהן מולכין במדינות הללו, ופעמים פולטתן שהן באין פרסיים וטורדין אותן ושולטין מלכי פרסיים על אדום . . . (= Sometimes evil Rome swallows them that ruled those countries and sometimes spits them out, when the Persians come and annoy them and the Persian kings rule Edom [= Rome] . . .; *Ginzei Schechter*, vol. 2, p. 563; *Otzar ha-Geonim* on Qiddushin, *ha-Teshuvot*, p. 178, and see note א there).

[21] Seder Olam Zuṭa, Neubauer ed., p. 72. The Grossberg ed., p. 47, has נציבא; and see Krauss, *Paras we-Romi*, pp. 95–96; Neusner, *History*, vol. 4, pp. 45–46, 82.

[22] *RE*, vol. 17, col. 740 quoting Petrus Patricius (= *FHG* vol. 4, p. 189 no. 14) which states that after the reconquest of Nisibis by Diocletian, it was stipulated that the town would be the point of trade between the two empires.

[23] Source 20 vividly describes the inhabitants' sorrow at the surrender (see also Zosimus III 34). Arabic sources say the inhabitants left the city out of fear of the Persians. Subsequently Nisibis was populated by 12,000 Persians of the nobility from Isfahan and other places (see Ṭabarī, vol. 2, p. 60 [= vol. 1, p. 843]; Nöldeke, *Perser und Araber*, p. 63; Morony, *Iran* 14 [1976]: 41, n. 3). On Nisibis in Arabic sources see Dīnawarī, *Aḫbār ṭiwāl*, p. 52; Yāqūt, Bakrī and *ar-Rauḍ al-miʿṭār*, s.v. "Naṣībīn"; *BGA*, passim; Ibn Saʿīd, *Geography*, pp. 156–157; Idrīsī, vol. 6, pp. 661–662; *Ḥudūd al-ʿālam*, p. 140; Le Strange, "Ibn Serapion," p. 60; Honigmann, *EI*[1], s.v. "Naṣībīn." On its conquest by Shapur I, see Ṯaʿālibī, *Ġurar*, pp. 488–489.

places and Nisibis became the seat of the district governor (*istāndār*).[24] Being a border town Nisibis was then a base for operations against Byzantine Mesopotamia.[25] The Romans tried in vain time and again to recapture the town, but it remained in Persian hands till the Muslim conquest in 640.

Nisibis was one of three trading stations between Rome and Persia stipulated by the Justinian Code, the other two being Circesium and Artaxata.[26] From a late fifth-century source, it appears that both travelers and inhabitants there suffered from nomad raids.[27]

Nisibis became Christian in the second and third centuries, the earliest document attesting to the presence of a bishop there dating from around 300,[28] and remained so under Persian rule despite periodic persecution.[29]

Nisibis was one of the important centers of Christianity in the Persian empire. Aside from being the seat of a bishop, it was the site of a well-known Christian school and hospital.[30]

Nisibis with its considerable Jewish community, was a notable center of Jewish learning not only in the amoraic period, but also in the tannaitic period, and perhaps even in the days of the Second Temple (see below on Sages and Nisibis). Nisibis is thus of interest in connection with the question of the antiquity of Torah study outside Eretz Israel, which perhaps antedated Rav's move to Babylonia in A. D. 219.

Thus Nisibis, was both a center of Jewish learning and the site of a celebrated Christian school. While most of the testimony on the Jewish instructional center refers to a relatively early period and the Nestorian school was founded at the end of the talmudic era, nonetheless, the fact that Jewish and Christian institutions of learning were located in the same town is interesting. Even if there was no Jewish center of learning in Nisibis later, there were yeshivas elsewhere in Babylonia, and it would be illuminating to compare the Jewish and Christian

---

[24] *RE* vol. 17, col. 751.

[25] Procopius, *Persian Wars*, I 10, 14; 17, 25; cf. Oates (*loc.cit.* n. 19 above).

[26] Source 21, A. D. 408/9; see also *RE*, vol. 17, col. 754.

[27] See Oates (*op.cit.* n. 19 above), p. 96, who refers to a letter Barsauma, bishop of Nisibis, wrote in A. D. 484 to the Nestorian patriarch Acacius (quoted by Nau, *Les Arabes chrétiens*, pp. 13–15).

[28] Cf. *RE*, vol. 17, col. 741, for the sources. Nisibis may have been influenced by Christians from Edessa. The earliest church extant in Nisibis, the Jacob's church, is dated by an inscription to A. D. 359. Cf. Sarre & Herzfeld, *Archäologische Reise*, vol. 2, p. 336ff. For Nisibis within the Persian realm see Segal, *Proceedings of the British Academy* (1955): 109–139, esp. 129–136.

[29] *RE*, vol. 17, col. 755; also above, n. 27. In the fifth century the Christians of Nisibis became Nestorians.

[30] Ephraem, the first writer of Christian prose and poetry in Syriac, founded the school in the fourth century. It became even more important later, when the emperor Zenon closed the Edessa school in the fifth century. See *RE*, vol. 17, col. 755; Segal, *Edessa*, p. 71; for Ephraem see bibliography in *KP*, vol. 2, col. 301. See also n. 6 in the entry on "Pərat də-Mešan."

institutions as to their organization, the purpose and content of their curricula, the relationship of the heads of the institutions to the surrounding community, and the like.[31]

D. *Sages and Nisibis*

Most of the talmudic sources mentioning Nisibis deal with Rabbi Judah b. Bathyra, who headed the study house in the town. It appears that there were two sages by that name, perhaps grandfather and grandson.[32] Source 3 describes an incident that occurred while the Temple still stood, when Rabbi Judah b. Bathyra caught a non-Jew who habitually went to Jerusalem at Passover and ate of the pascal lamb, although "no foreigner shall eat of it." On the other hand, most of the other sources on Rabbi Judah b. Bathyra apply to the period of the Bar Kokhva revolt and later.

Source 4 lists academies in Eretz Israel and the sages that headed them,[33] and mentions as well the study house of Rabbi Judah b. Bathyra in Nisibis, and that of Hananiah the son of Rabbi Joshua's brother in Exile (= Babylonia). Evidently this was the second Rabbi Judah b. Bathyra. That study house, and especially Rabbi Judah b. Bathyra who headed it, were considered important not only in Nisibis and Babylonia, but in Eretz Israel as well. Source 6 testifies that during the political persecutions in the wake of the Bar Kokhva revolt, halakhic queries on matrimonial matters were addressed simultaneously to Rabbi ʿAqiva who was then in the Caesarea prison, and Rabbi Judah b. Bathyra in Nisibis.

One of the results of the Bar Kokhva revolt was a considerable emigration from Eretz Israel, in particular to Babylonia where there was a well-established Jewish community and which was outside the borders of the Roman Empire. In that connection Source 7 tells of a group of sages who sought to leave Eretz Israel and join Rabbi Judah b. Bathyra's study house.[34] Another sage of the Ušah period who, according to Source 13, arrived in Nisibis was Rabbi Josiah, although the parallels to this source do not mention Nisibis.[35] The

[31] See Gafni, *Ha-Yeshiva be-Bavel*, pp. 196–203, and the bibliography there.

[32] According to Rav Sherira Gaon's letter, there was only one Rabbi Judah b. Bathyra (Lewin ed., p. 12) but that is not tenable given the length of time between the final days of the Second Temple and the Ušah period. See Frankel, *Darkei ha-Mishnah*, pp. 99–102; Hyman, vol. 2, pp. 555–558.

[33] Most of the sages in the list belong to the Yavneh period, but Rabbi Judah b. Bathyra is listed between Rabbi Yose b. Ḥalafta and Hananiah the son of Rabbi Joshua's brother, both of whom were of the Ušah period, and Rabbi Judah ha-Nasi is listed next.

[34] A previous passage in the same section of the Sifre contains a tradition on the departure from Eretz Israel of Rabbi Judah b. Bathyra and Rabbi Hananiah the son of Rabbi Joshua's brother themselves. Possibly Source 5 refers to Rabbi Judah b. Bathyra's first arrival in Nisibis; see also below the section on the Exilarch and Nisibis.

[35] In Halevy's view "my friends in the Darom" mentioned in the T.B. version of the episode (see n. 14 above) were pupils of Rabbi ʿAqiva's who fled to Nisibis following the

city was then held by the Parthians, to whom it was returned after Trajan's campaigns, and there is no doubt that Parthian control contributed a great deal to the development of the Nisibis study house, at a time when Jewish life was still overcast by the shadow of the Bar Kokhva revolt and the subsequent persecution.

Source 8 provides evidence of the special status of Rabbi Judah b. Bathyra. It deals with the attempts of Hananiah the son of Rabbi Joshua's brother, to intercalate leap year independently in Babylonia,[36] and seems to be related on the one hand to the decline of Eretz Israel in the aftermath of the Bar Kokhva revolt, and on the other to the waxing strength of the Babylonian Jewish community as more and more emigrants from Eretz Israel joined it. However, messengers proceeded from Eretz Israel with a note for Hananiah[37] informing him that "kids you left became goats," meaning that since he had departed from Eretz Israel, the strength of the sages had revived and the Sanhedrin had been restored. The messengers then made it clear to Hananiah and the Babylonian notables that a separate calculation of the leap year was tantamount to withdrawing from the Jewish people and founding a new religion. According to the tradition in Source 8, which does not appear in the Babylonian Talmud,[38] Hananiah submitted the matter in Nisibis to Rabbi Judah b. Bathyra, who ruled that the right to calculate the leap year belonged exclusively to Eretz Israel. The fact that Hananiah took the trouble to travel to Nisibis and then accepted Rabbi Judah b. Bathyra's decision although it was in favor of the messengers from Eretz Israel is ample proof of Rabbi Judah b. Bathyra's authority.

In connection with Rabbi Judah b. Bathyra, Source 14 mentions Avuha di-Shemuel (Samuel's father), a merchant from whom he bought some silk. Abba's business trips are mentioned in a number of sources.[39] Presumably he went to Nisibis not merely to fill Rabbi Judah b. Bathyra's order, but also because the

---

Bar Kokhva revolt and Rabbi Josiah met them at Rabbi Judah b. Bathyra's study house when he came there (Halevy, *Dorot ha-Rishonim*, Part One, vol. 5, p. 674). But it seems more reasonable to suppose that the Jerusalem and Babylonian Talmuds had different traditions as to where Rabbi Josiah went. See also Epstein, *Mevo'ot le-Sifrut ha-Tanna'im* p. 570, n. 179, who considers the Babylonian version a garble, and see Gafni, *Ha-Yeshiva be-Bavel*, p. 15.

[36] See Alon, *Toledot*, vol. 2, pp. 75–76; Beer, *Rashut ha-Golah*, p. 17, and the bibliography there.

[37] The sender is designated "Rabbi" in the source. While in Eretz Israel sources several patriarchs are called just "Rabbi," evidently the reference here is to Rabban Simeon ben Gamaliel, patriarch of the Sanhedrin at Ušah.

[38] See n. 8. Source 11 too may involve Eretz Israel intervention to impose its rulings, this time on Rabbi Judah b. Bathyra himself. Naturally the importance of calculating the leap year cannot be compared with the clarification of the halakhah, important as it may be, on the right to eat of the *terumah* (and see Alon, *Toledot*, vol. 1, pp. 352–353).

[39] Cf. the story on Avuha di-Shemuel in 'Eruvin 65a, Berakhot 30a, and see n. 40.

city was an important commercial center. The end of the source explains that Abba's son was named Samuel because of Rabbi Judah b. Bathyra's prediction that Abba would have a son as fine as the prophet Samuel. Another tradition dealing with Abba's travels connects Samuel's birth and wisdom with his father's ability to withstand the attempts of a Median woman to induce him to sin.[40] Sources 15 and 16 refer to Rabbi Simlai of the second generation of Eretz Israel amoras during a visit to Nisibis where he reported on Rabbi Judah Nesiah's ordinance allowing the use of Gentile oil.[41] This permission is connected on the one hand with the diminished fear of alien religions, and on the other with the severe economic crisis in Eretz Israel during the anarchy that reigned there in the third century.

E. *The Exilarch and Nisibis*

Source 5 indicates that when Rabbi Judah b. Bathyra moved from Eretz Israel to Babylonia and settled in Nisibis, he found the Exilarch living there, and insistent on being accorded the proper respect.[42] If the source is to be interpreted literally, it would mean that the position of Exilarch was already in existence shortly after the Bar Kokhva revolt, and that the seat of the Exilarch was then in Nisibis. These assumptions raise certain difficulties, among them that most of the *Rishonim* versions have *resh kenishta* (= head of the synagogue) rather than *resh galuta* (= head of the Exile = Exilarch)[43] although perhaps the solution is provided by Beer's proposal that *resh kenishta*, a common title in Eretz Israel, is in this case used to explain the less familiar *resh galuta* which originated in Babylonia. The main difficulty, however, is the Exilarch's residence at Nisibis which was far from the main Jewish community in Babylonia.[44] The Nisibis mentioned in this connection may well be the one near Nəhardəʿa (q.v.), one of the places where the Exilarch used to live.

F. *Nisibis near Nəhardəʿa*

Sources 22 and 23 deal with the Nisibis near Nəhardəʿa,[45] which is of course distinct from the celebrated Nisibis located between the Tigris and the Euphrates. There are no other sources having clear reference to the Nisibis near

---

[40] *Iggeret Rav Sherira Gaon, Toledot ha-Iggeret ha-Shenit*, Lewin ed., p. 130; and see Beer, *Amora'ei Bavel*, pp. 183–185, and n. 87 there in particular.

[41] On the ordinance allowing the oil, see Alon, *Toledot*, vol. 2, pp. 157–158; idem, *Studies*, vol. 1, pp. 146–189.

[42] See Beer, *Rashut ha-Golah*, pp. 20–23.

[43] See n. 6 above, and see Beer, *ibid.*, p. 21, n. 25.

[44] Beer's argument that Nisibis was generally in Roman hands so that the Exilarch would not have his seat there does not apply to the period under discussion. Hadrian returned Nisibis to the Parthians after Trajan's campaigns and they held it till it was retaken by Lucius Verus (A. D. 162–165); and see the section on History.

[45] Cf. Sturm, *RE*, vol. 17, col. 757, s.v. "Nisibis (3)" and Honigmann, s.v. "Nisibyn."

Nəhardəʿa, though some of the talmudic ones could apply to that place.[46] According to Sturm (see note 19), some of the classical sources refer to still a third Nisibis. An epitaph from Korykos refers to one of the lesser places by that name.[47]

ALON, *Toledot* (1958), vol. 2, pp. 75f.
BEER, *Rashut ha-Golah* (1970), pp. 1, 17, 20–23, 28
BEER, *Amora'ei Bavel* (1974), pp. 182–185, 218
BERLINER, *Beiträge* (1883), p. 53
DILLEMANN, *Haute Mésopotamie* (1962), passim
ESHEL, *Yishuvei ha-Yehudim* (1979), pp. 189–191
FIEY, *Nisibe* (1977)
FUNK, *Juden* (1902–1908), vol. 1, pp. 4, n. 6, 59; vol. 2, pp. 8, 78
FUNK, *Monumenta* (1913), pp. 87, 297
GAFNI, *Ha-Yeshiva be-Bavel* (1978): 196–203
GETZOW, *Al Neharot Bavel* (1887), pp. 14–18, 22, 86
GOODBLATT, *Rabbinic Instruction* (1975), passim
GRAETZ, *Geschichte* (1908⁴), vol. 4, passim
HALEVY, *Dorot ha-Rishonim* (1897–1939), passim
HILL, *BMC Arabia*, pp. cviii–cix.
HIRSCHENSON, *Sheva Ḥokhmot* (1883), p. 171
HONIGMANN, *EI*¹, s.v. "Naṣībīn"
HONIGMANN, *RE*, vol. 17, col. 757, s.v. "Nisibyn"
JASTROW, *Dictionary* (1950³), pp. 1719, 1720
KOHUT, *Arukh ha-Shalem* (1878–1892), vol. 5, p. 372
KRAUSS, *Qadmoniot ha-Talmud* (1923–1945), vol. 2B, p. 231
KRAUSS, *Paras we-Romi* (1948), pp. 10, n. 24, 12, 96, 254
LEVY, *Wörterbuch* (1924²), vol. 3, "נציב", pp. 428, 1719
NEUBAUER, *Géographie* (1868), p. 370
NEUSNER, *History* (1965–1970), 5 vols., passim
NEUSNER, *Talmudic Judaism* (1976), passim
NEWMAN, *Agricultural Life* (1932), pp. 12, 141
OATES, *Northern Iraq* (1968), pp. 70–75, 78–79
OBERMEYER, *Landschaft* (1929), pp. 35, 128–130
PIGULEVSKAJA, *Les Villes* (1963), chap. IV, pp. 49–59
ROBERT, *Hellenica* 2 (1946): 79–80
SCHÜRER, *Geschichte des jüdischen Volkes* (1909⁴), vol. 3, p. 9, n. 18
SEGAL, *Proceedings of the British Academy* (1955): 109–139
SEGAL, *Sefer Segal* (1964), pp. 38*–42*
SMALLWOOD, *The Jews Under Roman Rule* (1976), pp. 416, 420, 510
STURM, *RE*, vol. 17, cols. 714–757 s.v. "Nisibis"
TSCHERIKOWER, *Städtegründungen* (1927), pp. 89–90

Orchoi (Ori<u>k</u>ut) אוריכות

A. *Sources*

1. Yoma 10a

תני רב יוסף . . . "ותהי ראשית ממלכתו בבל וארך ואכד וכלנה", בבל כמשמעה, ארך זה אוריכות,[1] ואכד זה בשכר, כלנה זה נופר ניפר.[2]

---

[46] As noted in Oppenheimer, "Ha-Merkaz bi-Nəṣivin bi-Tequfat ha-Mishnah," *Umah we-Toledoteha*, vol. 1, Jerusalem 1983, pp. 141–150.

[47] *MAMA* 3 (1931) p. 160 no. 408; cf. also Honigmann's note.

[1] The Munich MS has ארכת, the Munich B MS has אורך and the London MS has ארכית. *Aggadot ha-Talmud* has ארחבת, and see *Diq. Sof.* Cf. Ephraem, *Comment. in Gen.*

Rav Joseph taught ... "And the mainstays of his kingdom were Babylon, Ere*k*, Akkad and Kalneh" (Gen. 10:10); Babylon is what it says, Ere*k* is Ori*k*ut,[1] Akkad is Kaškar, and Kalneh is Nufar Ninəfe.[2]

2. Strabo XVI 1, 6 (739)

ἔστι δὲ καὶ τῶν Χαλδαίων τῶν ἀστρονομικῶν γένη πλείω· καὶ γὰρ Ὀρχηνοί τινες προσαγορεύονται καὶ Βορσιππηνοὶ καὶ ἄλλοι πλείους ὡς ἂν κατὰ αἱρέσεις ἄλλα καὶ ἄλλα νέμοντες περὶ τῶν αὐτῶν δόγματα.

There are also several tribes of the Chaldaean astronomers. For example, some are called Orcheni, others Borsippeni, and several others by different names, as though divided into different sects which hold to various dogmas about the same subjects. (trans.: H. L. Jones, LCL)

3. Pliny, *Natural History* VI 31, 130

Sed longo tempore Euphraten praeclusere Orcheni et accolae agros rigantes, nec nisi per Tigrim defertur in mare.

But a long time ago the Euphrates was dammed by the Orcheni and those who live near by in order to irrigate their lands and its water is only discharged into the sea by way of the Tigris. (trans.: H. Rackham, LCL)

4. Inscription found at Orchoi (near a small Parthian temple)[3]

Ἔτους βκυʹ, μηνὸς Δείου,
Ἀρτεμίδωρος Διογένους ὁ
ἐπικαλούμενος Μινναναιος
Τουφαιου στοιχῶν τῆι τῶν προ-
γόνων αὑτοῦ ἀγαθῆι προαιρέσει
ἀνέθηκεν Γαροι θεῶι χωρίον Δα-
ιαμεινα· τὸ δὲ κοινὸν τῶν
Δολλαμηνων ὃν εὐχά-
ριστον ἔκρ⟨ι⟩εινεν ἀμεί-
ψεσθαι ἀντὶ ἀναθέματος, ἀν-
δριάντα αὐτῶι στῆσαι ἐν ναῶι Γαρειο̣ς̣,
στεφανοῦν τε αὐτὸν ἐν ἑκάστηι γε-

10:10; "Nimrod built three towns: Arak, Ur and Kala, that is Orhay, Nisibis and Seleucia" (cited by J. Markwart, *Catalogue*, § 65, also Michael the Syrian, *Chronicle*, p. 9a 43–37 – I 20a Gs p. 639, 26–27 – III 278). On the form of the name see also Rosenthal in *Sefer Hanoch Yalon*, p. 335, and Eshel, pp. 14–15.

[2] The source has בשכר, נופר נינפי. See the entries on "Kaškar" and "Nippur" for variants in the manuscripts and their meanings.

[3] Meier, *Baghdader Mitteilungen* 1 (1960): 104–114 = *SEG*, vol. 18, No. 596ff.; cf. Robert, *Hellenica* 11–12 (1960): 130; J. & L. Robert, *Bulletin Épigraphique* (1962): 322; Le Rider, *Suse*, pp. 41–43; *Nouveau Choix d'Inscriptions Grecques*, par l'Institut Fernand-Courby (Paris 1971), pp. 168–170, no. 33.

νεθλιακῆι αὐτοῦ τὸν σύνπαντα χρόνον
οὔσηι ἕκτηι 'Απελλαίου, παρειστᾶν αὐτῶι
ἱερόθυτον καὶ ἀπὸ τοῦ αὐτοῦ ἱερο-
θύτου πέμπειν αὐτῶι 'Αρτεμι-
δώρωι ὀσφὺν εὐσεβείας
καὶ εὐνοίας ἕνεκεν.

In the year 422, in the month of Dios, Artemidoros son of Diogenes, also called Minnanaios, son of Touphaios, who lives in accordance with the good principles of his ancestors, has dedicated to the god Gareus the place of Daiameina. The association of the Dollamenians has decided, out of gratitude, to respond to the dedication with the erection of a statue in the temple of Gareus and to crown it on each birthday of his, in perpetuity, on the eighth of the month of Apellaios, and to provide him with an animal for sacrifice and to send the loin of that animal to Artemidoros, because of his piety and benevolence.

B. *Location*

Warka[4] (biblical Ereḵ), east of the Euphrates, 193 kilometers southeast of Babylon (on Bab. Env. map).

C. *History*

Situated south of Seleucia on the Tigris, on the right bank of the Euphrates, Orchoi was a natural port of call on the river route from Seleucia to the Gulf. In the Seleucid period, Orchoi (Sumerian Uruk, modern Warka) was a town with perhaps a polis-type organization, under a governor with the title of

---

[4] On Warka see 'Awwād, *Sumer* 5 (1949): 252; Fransīs & 'Awwād, *Sumer* 8 (1952): 240; Streck, *EI*[1], s.v. "al-Warkā'." It is in connection with the conquest of Iraq that Yāqūt mentions Warka (q.v. there): "a place in the neighborhood of az-Zawābī where our forefather Abraham, may he rest in peace, was born, and it is on the border of the district of Kaskar." See n. 6 in the entry on "Kuta." See also in Yāqūt the end of the entry on "al-Ǧiʿrāna" and the entry on "Naʿmān," and see Ṭabarī, vol. 1, p. 233 (= vol. 1, p. 252). On az-Zawābī, cf. Yāqūt and see there "az-Zāb." See also "az-Zābiyān" in Bakrī and "az-Zāb" in *Muštarik*. Cf. also "az-Zābān" in *ar-Rauḍ al-miʿṭār*.

The location of Warka that emerges from Yāqūt's tradition on the conquest does not fit in very well with the actual one, (see Bab. Env. map). In the wake of the victory achieved by forces from the Tamīm and ar-Ribāb tribes, Warka as well as Hurmuzǧird up to Furāt Bādaqlā were captured. Hurmuzǧird was far north of the place usually assigned to Warka, for according to Yāqūt it can be located in the Kūfa region (see Yāqūt, at the end of the entry on "Bihqubāḏ," which lists for the lower part of that region (al-Bihqubāḏ al-Asfal) among others the districts (*ṭasāsīǧ*) of Kūfa, Furāt Bādaqlā, Ḥīra and Hurmuzǧird. See in Yāqūt also "Naʿmān" (although it is not a really independent source): "In the vicinity of Kūfa, on the desert side." Cf. Bakrī, the end of the entry on "Naʿmān."

It is interesting that in his translation of the Genesis verse mentioned, Rav Saadia Gaon identified Ereḵ with al-Burs, that is, Borsif (q.v.).

epistates.[5] An archaeological survey has led to the conclusion that there was a hiatus in the occupation of the town of about 130 years between the last years of the Seleucid era and the late first century B.C.[6] This lack of continuity has been observed also at other sites in southern Iraq such as Nippur. On the other hand, a coin hoard found at Warka contains coins from the early part of those "missing years," the earliest belonging to Antiochus IV (?), the latest to the Parthian kings, probably including Mithridates II (123–87 B.C.).[7] Among the coins found were small bronze ones, struck at Orchoi for local use in the Seleucid and Parthian period, comparable to the coins issued at Nineveh (q.v.) in the Parthian period. Lists of scribes at Orchoi show an uninterrupted sequence from 302 to 138 B.C., three years after the Parthians entered Seleucia.[8] The region was again densely populated in the later Parthian period. Adams and Nissen note that the first and second centuries A.D. seem to have constituted the culminating epoch in the entire settlement record. They concluded that the extensive debris including imposing public buildings indicates a Parthian city at that time not appreciably smaller than any previously known. In the final years of the Parthian period, the entire southern half of the region, including Orchoi, was abandoned almost totally.[9] The reasons for both the decline at the end of Seleucid and Parthian rule and the prosperity in the first and second centuries are a matter of speculation. Adams and Nissen assume that the final abandonment was due to swamps which had begun to engulf the region. They also note that the evidence of dense and flourishing settlement stands in remarkable contrast to the absence of historical and textual references to the region (notably in the Talmud).[10] Obermeyer thought that there were no settlements at all south of modern Ḥilla, because of the swamps.[11] Since this has proved to be untrue, the explanation suggested by Adams and Nissen is that Jews did not settle in the southern districts, which were under the control of the Arab vassal dynasty of the Lakhmids. From A.D. 115 to 117 the region was briefly attached to Trajan's Roman province of Assyria.[12] A recent survey of the immediate surroundings of Warka has shown substantial remains of the Sassanian period. While the city of Orchoi itself ceased to exist in the third century, southeast of it, outside the old walls along the Šaṭṭ an-Nīl, there was a city in the Sassanian period. Elsewhere too outside Orchoi between the walls and Nufaiǧi two kilometers north, small settlements existed

[5] Tarn, *The Greeks*, pp. 25–26, 140; Rostovtzeff, *YCS* 3 (1932): 73; idem, *Social and Economic History of the Hellenistic World*, vol. 3, pp. 513–516. Aymard has pointed out that there is no proof that Orchoi was refounded as a polis. The fact that it did not receive a Greek name points to the contrary (*Études d'histoire ancienne*, pp. 203–204 = *RÉA*, pp. 33–35).

[6] Adams & Nissen, *The Uruk Countryside*, pp. 57–58.

[7] Cf. Le Rider, *Suse*, pp. 458–459.

[8] Cf. Aymard, *Études*, p. 188 = *RÉA*, p. 16.

[9] Le Rider, *Suse*, p. 59.

[10] *Ibid.*, pp. 62–63.

[11] Obermeyer, p. 97.

[12] Maricq, *Classica et Orientalia*, pp. 103–111.

in this period, and further north small tells have been noted along the river. A place named Tine eight kilometers north of Orchoi was occupied until the early Islamic period. Around Orchoi in fact, most of the Parthian settlements were still occupied in the Sassanian period.[13] In A.D. 775 Orchoi (*VRK*) appears together with Kaškar as a bishopric.[14]

D. *The Inscription* (*Source* 4) *and Its Implications*

The year 422 mentioned in the inscription may refer to the Arsacid era beginning in 247 B.C. (which would make it A.D. 175) or what is more probable, to the Seleucid era counting from either 311 or 312 B.C. (which would date it to the beginning of the second century A.D.).[15]
The first editor of the inscription notes that it is an indication of Greek influence in a region where one would not have expected it in that period, for evidence of Greek culture then is mostly related to the great trade centers such as Seleucia, Babylon and Ctesiphon (qq.v.). The question is whether the Greek-speaking inhabitants of Orchoi were the remnants of the Graeco-Macedonian colonists of the Seleucid period, or a few Hellenized merchants.[16] The archaeological evidence of a break in the occupation of Orchoi and other sites in the region seems to exclude the possibility of a continuous Hellenistic tradition. Adams and Nissen think that the inscription is perhaps at best a doubtful indication of the possible survival of a Greek *politeuma* there.[17] It must be kept in mind, however, that the inscription was a dedication by a local cult association[18] on behalf of a man owning real estate in Orchoi. Both the form of the inscription and the honors described are completely Hellenistic and have parallels in Greek countries.[19] Thus the inscription is evidence of a genuine Hellenistic tradition among the Semitic citizens of Orchoi. Aymard has pointed out that cuneiform texts of the third and second centuries B.C. reflect the importance of the Hellenized Babylonians in that period as well.[20]

E. *Archaeological Finds*

In the second half of the third century B.C., the temples at Orchoi were entirely rebuilt, the last major building project there. The chief god in this period was

[13] Finster & Schmidt, *Baghdader Mitteilungen* 8 (1976): 166–167.

[14] Le Rider, *Suse*, p. 310, n. 1; Appendix 3, p. 458ff.

[15] On the dating see Le Rider, *Suse*, p. 33f.; *Nouveau Choix*, pp. 169–170.

[16] See Meier, (*op.cit.* in n. 3), p. 114.

[17] See Adams & Nissen (*op.cit.* in n. 6), p. 58.

[18] The Dollomenians were probably natives of the Dollomene region north of Nineveh mentioned by Strabo XVI 1, 1 (736).

[19] *Nouveau Choix*, p. 170; Robert, *Hellenica* 11–12 (1960): 126–131.

[20] Aymard, *Études*, p. 206 = *RÉA*, p. 36. Aymard's study has shown the importance of the Hellenistic cuneiform documents for the social and economic history of Orchoi in that period. Other relevant Greek inscriptions can be found in *SEG*, vol. 7, No. 12–13.

Anu, replacing Inanna. In the Parthian period, primitive dwellings are found in the temples.[21] According to brick stamps, the temple complex of Anu was rebuilt in 243 B.C. by Anu-uballit, also named Nicarchos, and in 201 B.C. by Anu-uballit, also called Kephalon. The latter, presumably a relative of the former, was "the great, the city-lord of Uruk." These men were Hellenized Babylonians. The sanctuary, however, was purely Babylonian with no sign of Hellenization. Found scattered all over the rooms of the temple were a great many clay seals and so-called bullae, clay objects bearing private and official seal impressions. According to Rostovtzeff, who published the Orchoi bullae, they served as sealed containers for documents. They all belong to the Seleucid period, and bear inscriptions of private individuals and officials: χρεοφυλακικὸς (χαρακτὴρ) Ὄρχων, βυβλιοφυλακικὸς (χαρακτὴρ) Ὄρχων. (= the seal of the keeper of contracts of Orchoi; the seal of the keeper of documents of Orchoi). Rostovtzeff's analysis has shown that the seals contribute a great deal to our knowledge of the Seleucid Empire and of the society of Orchoi in that period, furnishing striking information on the mixed Hellenistic-Babylonian character of religion and business life in that town.[22]

The publication of terracotta figurines found at Warka allows a number of interesting observations.[23] Great numbers of them dating to the Parthian period display a great variety of forms and motifs. As at Seleucia, there is no development from purely Hellenistic patterns to a stage dominated by Babylonian types. Throughout the Seleucid and Parthian period Hellenistic and Babylonian forms and types are found side by side. Many are believed to have been used for cultic purposes. Heracles, Erotes and a Mithras relief fragment figure among the Hellenistic types, and the "mother goddess," horses and other animals, and horsemen among the Oriental. Relevant in this connection are the observations made regarding the architecture of the temple of Gareus (first century A. D.), in which the Babylonian conception of religious architecture is reflected by the traditional plan, but is combined with Graeco-Roman architectural elements such as Ionic column bases. Coin finds interestingly seem to be limited to the period between the late first century B.C. and the early years of Ardashīr I's reign.[24]

---

[21] Falkenstein, *Topographie von Uruk*, Part 1. For recent excavations see Schmidt, *Baghdader Mitteilungen* 5 (1970): 51–96; *UVB* 6 (1935):33; 7 (1937):32 and passim; Rostovtzeff, *Social and Economic History of the Hellenistic World*, vol. 3, pp. 436f. and n. 235; 514 and n. 292.

[22] For the bullae from Orchoi see also McDowell, *Stamped and Inscribed Objects from Seleucia*, pp. 165–173. For the Hellenistic character of seals at Orchoi see Naster, *Greek Numismatics*, pp. 215–219.

[23] Ziegler, *Die Terrakotten von Warka*, pp. 175–188. Cf. Heinrich, *UVB* 5 (1934): 33–36, Pls. 12, 13, 23–26.

[24] Cf. Nissen, *Baghdader Mitteilungen*, 6 (1973): 82.

ADAMS & NISSEN, *The Uruk Countryside* (1972), p. 57ff.
AYMARD, *RÉA* 40 (1938): 5ff. = *Études d'histoire ancienne* (1967), pp. 178–211
ELLIS, *Mesopotamian Archaeological Sites* (1922), pp. 87–89
ESHEL, *Yishuvei ha-Yehudim* (1979), p. 14
FUNK, *Monumenta* (1913), pp. 23, 87
AL-HAIK, *Key Lists* (1968), No. 119
HEINRICH, *UVB* 5 (1934); 6 (1935); 7 (1937)
HIRSCHENSON, *Sheva Ḥokhmot* (1883), p. 30
JASTROW, *Dictionary* (1950³), p. 122
JORDAN & PREUSSER, *Uruk-Warka* (1928)
JORDAN et al., *AAB* 7 (1929): 1–67
KOHUT, *Arukh ha-Shalem* (1878–1892), vol. 1, p. 284
KRAUSS, *MGWJ* 39 (1895): 58
KRAUSS, *Paras we-Romi* (1948), p. 12
KRAUSS, *Lehnwörter* (1898–1899), vol. 2, p. 601
LENZEN, *AFO* 17 (1954–1955): 198–201
LENZEN, *Sumer* 10 (1954): 86–88, 195–196; 11 (1955): 73–75
LE RIDER, *Suse* (1965), passim
LEVY, *Wörterbuch* (1924²), p. 167
LOFTUS, *JRGS* 26 (1856): 131–153
NASTER, in *Greek Numismatics* (1979), pp. 215–219
NEUBAUER, *Géographie* (1868), p. 346
NEUSNER, *History* (1965–1970), vol. 1, pp. 3–4
OBERMEYER, *Landschaft* (1929), pp. 77, 97, 329 n. 1
RAPOPORT, *Erekh Millin* (1914), vol. 2, p. 36
ROSENTHAL, *Sefer Hanoch Yalon* (1963), p. 335
ROSTOVTZEFF, *YCS* 3 (1932): 73
ROSTOVTZEFF, *Social and Economic History of the Hellenistic World* (1941), vol. 3, pp. 436f., 513–516

Papuniya פפוניא

A. *Sources*

1. Pesaḥim 42a

אמר רב יהודה אשה לא תלוש אלא במים שלנו. דרשה רב מתנה בפפוניא, למחר אייתו כולי עלמא חצבייהו ואתו לגביה ואמרו ליה הב לן מיא, אמר להו אנא במיא דביתו אמרי.

Rav Judah said, A woman may not knead [unleavened bread] except with water *shelanu*. Rav Mattenah preached this in Papuniya. The next day everybody brought their barrels and came to him and said to him, Give us water. He said to them, I said water kept overnight (= *she-lanu*, and not *shelanu* = "ours").

2. Ḥullin 139b

אמרי ליה פפונאי לרב מתנה [1] מצא קן בראשו של אדם מהו, אמר "ואדמה על ראשו" . . .

The Papuniyans said to Rav Mattenah,[1] If a nest is found on a man's head, what is it? He said, "And earth on his head" (II Sam. 15:32). . . .

[1] The Soncino printing has "אמרו ליה בפפונאי", the Venice and Salonika printings have "אמר ליה פפונא." See *Diq. Sof.* in whose view the sage is Rav Aḥa b. Jacob (on the basis of Source 5 below). The Munich MS has "to Rav Papa," the Vatican 121 and Vatican 122 MSS have "to Rav Mattena," the Vatican 123 MS has "to Rav Judah" and the Benveniste printing has "to Rav Kahana."

3. Niddah 67b

אתקין רב אידי[2] בנרש למטבל ביומא דתמניא משום אריותא. רב אחא בר יעקב בפפוניא[3] משום גנבי. רב יהודה בפומבדיתא משום צנה. רבא במחוזא משום אבולאי.

Rav Idi[2] ordained in Nareš to immerse on the eighth day because of the lions. Rav Aḥa b. Jacob in Papuniya,[3] because of the thieves, Rav Judah in Pumbədita, because of the cold, Rava in Maḥoza because of the gate guards.

4. Bava Batra 16a

א״ר לוי שטן ופנינה לשם שמים נתכוונו. שטן, כיון דחזיא להקדוש ברוך הוא דנטיה דעתיה בתר איוב אמר חס ושלום מינשי ליה לרחמנותיה דאברהם. פנינה, דכתיב ״וכעסתה צרתה גם כעס בעבור הרעימה.״ דרשה רב אחא בר יעקב[4] בפפוניא, אתא שטן נשקיה לכרעיה.

Rabbi Levi said, Satan and Penina had a pious purpose: Satan, because of seeing the Holy One Blessed Be He inclining toward Job, said, Far be it that God should forget the love of Abraham; Penina because it is written "Her rival to make her miserable would taunt her" (I Sam. 1:6). Rav Aḥa b. Jacob[4] expounded this in Papuniya, Satan came and kissed his foot.

5. Bava Qamma 54b

... אי הכי אפילו אדם ליתסר, אלמה תנן אדם מותר עם כולן לחרוש ולמשוך, אמר רב פפא[5] פפונאי ידעי טעמא דהא מילתא, ומנו, רב אחא בר יעקב, אמר קרא ״למען ינוח עבדך ואמתך כמוך,״ להנחה הקשתיו ולא לדבר אחר.

... If so [that we learn about *kilayim* from the Sabbath] then a person is even forbidden [to pull a wagon with a beast] so why did we learn that a human being is allowed to plough and pull with all of them, Rav Papa[5] said, Papuniyans know the reason for this. And who is it? Rav Aḥa b. Jacob. In the verse, "so that your male or female slave may rest as you do" (Deut. 5:14), the analogy is for rest, and not for anything else.

6. Qiddushin 35a

... הניחא למ״ד שני כתובים הבאים כאחד אין מלמדין אלא למ״ד מלמדין מאי איכא למימר, אמר רבא[6] פפונאי ידעי לה לטעמא דהא מילתא, ומנו, רב אחא בר יעקב, אמר קרא ״והיה לך לאות על ידך ולזכרון בין עיניך למען תהיה תורת ה׳ בפיך,״ הוקשה כל התורה כולה לתפילין, מה תפילין מצות עשה שהזמן גרמא ונשים פטורות, אף כל מצות עשה שהזמן גרמא נשים פטורות.

---

[2] The Munich and Vatican 111 MSS have "Rav Idi b. Avin."

[3] "In Papuniya" is missing in the Vatican 111 MS.

[4] The Oxford MS has "Rav Jacob." The parallels in *Yalquṭ Shimʿoni* for I Sam. § 76 and Job § 893 have "Rav Aḥa."

[5] The Munich and Hamburg MS have "Rava said" as does Qiddushin 35a (Source 6 below) and that appears to be correct. "Rav Papa" may be a garble resulting from the similar place name (see also above, Source 2 and n. 1).

[6] The Vatican 111 MS has "Rav said."

. . . that is convenient to whoever says that two verses coming together teach nothing, but to others who say they do what can be said, Rava[6] said the Papuniyans know the reason for it. And who is it? Rav Aḥa b. Jacob. In the verse "this shall serve you as a sign on your hand and as a reminder on your forehead, in order that the teachings of the Lord may be in your mouth" (Ex. 13:9) the whole Torah is equated with phylacteries. Just as phylacteries are a positive precept limited to time and women are exempt, so women are exempt from any positive precept limited to time.

7. Bava Metziʿa 68a

אמר רבא לית הלכתא לא כטרשי פפונאי ולא כשטרי מחוזנאי ולא כחכירי נרשאי. כטרשי פפונאי, כטרשי דרב פפא.

Rava said, The halakhah is not like the credit interests of the Papuniyans, or the bonds of the Maḥozans or the leases of the Narešans. The credit interests of Papuniyans are like the credit interests of Rav Papa.

8. Bava Qamma 115a

נרשאה גנב ספרא, זבניה לפפונאה[7] בתמנן זוזי, אזל פפונאה זבניה לבר מחוזאה במאה ועשרין זוזי, לסוף הוכר הגנב, אמר אביי ליזיל מרי דספרא ויהב ליה לבר מחווא תמנן זוזי ושקיל ספריה ואזיל בר מחוזנאה ושקיל ארבעין מפפונאה . . . אלא אמר רבא ליזיל מריה דספרא ויהיב ליה לבר מחוזאה מאה ועשרין זוזי ושקיל ספריה וליזיל מרי דספרא ולישקול ארבעין מפפונאה ותמנן מנרשאה.

A Narešan stole a book, sold it to a Papuniyan[7] for eighty *zuz*. The Papuniyan went and sold it to a Maḥozan for a hundred and twenty *zuz*. In the end the thief was recognized. Abbaye said, The owner of the book should go and give the Maḥozan eighty *zuz* and take his book, the Maḥozan should go and take forty from the Papuniyan . . . Rava said, The owner of the book should go and pay the Maḥozan a hundred and twenty *zuz* and take his book, and the owner of the book should [then] go and recover forty *zuz* from the Papuniyan and eighty *zuz* from the Narešan.

9. Bava Batra 90b

רב פפא בר שמואל תקין כיילא בר תלתא קפיזי, אמרו ליה והא אמר שמואל אין מוסיפין על המדות יותר משתות, אמר להן אנא כיילא חדתא תקיני. שדריה לפומבדיתא ולא קבלוה, שדריה לפאפוניא[8] וקבלוה, וקרו ליה רוז פפא.

Rav Papa b. Samuel introduced a measure of three *qefize*. They said to him, But Samuel said a measure cannot be increased by more than a sixth. He said to them, I introduced a new measure. He sent it to Pumbədita and they didn't accept it. He sent it to Papuniya[8] and they did, and called it *roz-Papa*.

---

[7] The source has לפפונאה, the Munich MS has 'לפפונ here and later in the passage; the Vatican 116 MS has לפפוניא here and later in the passage; and see *Diq. Sof.*

[8] The source has פאפוניא, the Munich, Hamburg and Vatican 115 MSS have לפפוניא.

B. *Already Proposed Location*

Bābūniyā in the vicinity of Baghdad (q.v., D2 on the Tal. Bab. map).

C. *Identification*

Obermeyer already pointed out the identity of Papuniya and Bābūniyā to which Yāqūt devoted an entry in his dictionary.[9] The substitution of /b/ for /p/ is normal, and the identification is perfectly reasonable.
Bābūniyā, it transpires, was close to Baghdad. Yāqūt makes two points concerning it. He notes first that Bābūniyā was one of the "Baghdad villages" and secondly that a certain scholar from Bābūniyā was active in Baghdad. This information is not, however, entirely unambiguous, and cannot serve to pinpoint the location of Bābūniyā.[10] Obermeyer believes it was between Baghdad and Pumbədita, "perhaps on Nəhar Papa which flows through Pumbədita, accounting for the name Papuniya," and the matter still requires study.

D. *Sages and Papuniya*

Two amoras active in Papuniya were Rav Mattenah and Rav Aḥa b. Jacob. Rav Mattenah of the second generation of Babylonian amoras, preaches in public (Source 1) and answers questions put by Papuniyans (Source 2). Rav Aḥa b. Jacob, of the third generation of Babylonian amoras, likewise preaches in public in Papuniya (Source 4) and introduces an ordinance allowing a woman to immerse for purification by day, so as not to fall into the hands of thieves present in Papuniya at night (Source 3). In two sources Rava (see n. 5) represents Rav Aḥa b. Jacob as a Papuniyan capable of clarifying a problem through a scriptural verse (Sources 5 and 6). Rava himself refers indirectly to Papuniya in Sources 7 and 8.

E. *The Inhabitants*

The Papuniyans are cited in Source 1 as people who did not grasp Rav Mattenah's sermon, in which he quoted a ruling by Rav Judah that "a woman may not knead except with water *shelanu*, which they understood to mean "that belongs to us." As a result they applied to the sage the next day for water "that belonged to him." What Rav Judah meant, however, was *she-lanu*, "that stood overnight" (to cool). The episode cannot be construed as proof of the intelligence of the Papuniyans, but it does present a characteristic picture

---

[9] Obermeyer, p. 242.

[10] Cf. e.g. Yāqūt's description of Nahr Abbā (see the entry on "Nəhar Abba"), although it is near Sura, as "*min nawāḥī Baġdād*" (= among the "daughters" of Baghdad). There, and perhaps also here, Baghdad seems to denote "Iraq."

of public lectures where mistaken interpretation could easily occur.[11] The many sources reporting sages preaching in Papuniya, questions the citizens addressed to those sages, and the references to Papuniya as one of the chief towns of Jewish Babylonia (see Sources 7, 8, 9) indicate that it had a population of considerable size that followed a Jewish way of life guided by sages. The fact of the Papuniyan amoras, and Rava's remark that "the Papuniyans know the reason" also show that the place was not inhabited exclusively by fools and thieves.

BERLINER, *Beiträge* (1883), p. 58
ESHEL, *Yishuvei ha-Yehudim* (1979), pp. 214–215
FUNK, *Monumenta* (1913), pp. 49, 298
HIRSCHENSON, *Sheva Ḥokhmot* (1883), p. 196
JASTROW, *Dictionary* (1950^{3}), p. 1203
KOHUT, *Arukh ha-Shalem* (1878–1892), vol. 6, p. 391
LEVY, *Wörterbuch* (1924^{2}), vol. 4, p. 85
NEUBAUER, *Géographie* (1868), pp. 304, 360
NEUSNER, *History* (1965–1970), vol. 3, pp. 221, 242, 255, 320; vol. 4, p. 189
OBERMEYER, *Landschaft* (1929), pp. 242–243, 266, 277, 309–310

Parzina פרזינא

A. *Source*

Ta'anit 24b

אמר רב מרי ברה דבת שמואל אנא הוה קאימנא אגודא דנהר פפא חזאי למלאכי דאידמו למלחי דקא מייתי חלא ומלונהו לארבי והוה קמחא דסמידא, אתו כולי עלמא למיזבן, אמר להו מהא לא תיזבנון דמעשה נסים הוא. למחר אתיין ארבי דחיטי דפרזינא.[1]

Rav Mari son of Samuel's daughter said, I stood on the bank of the Papa River [during a famine] and saw angels resembling sailors bringing sand and loading it on barges, and it turned into choice flour, everyone came to buy it; and he (Rav Judah) said to them, Do not buy of that for it is a miraculous deed; the next day barges of wheat of Parzina came.[1]

B. *Proposed Location*

Fizrāniyā, a village on Nahr al-Malik (D3 on the Tal. Bab. map).

---

[11] In this connection it is worth recalling the comment of Rabbi Zera: "**אגרא דפרקא רהטא**" (= The reward of the sermon is the running; Berakhot 6b), meaning that most of the listeners do not fully understand what the sage is explaining, and they gain merit primarily for hastening to hear words of the Law.

[1] The Munich MS has **חיטין דפרזינאי**, and see *Diq. Sof.*; *Ein Ya'aqov* has **חיטי מפרזוניא** – the *Arukh* has **ארבי דארזנאי** (= barges of rice), which appears to be a garble (*Arukh ha-Shalem*, vol. 1, p. 278, s. v. "ארזן" and see also *Tosefot Arukh ha-Shalem*, p. 66), and see n. 4 below.

C. *Identification*

Very few scholars have dealt with the identification of Parzina. Obermeyer proposed identifying it with Parziqiya (q.v.)[2] but his proposal does not seem acceptable. It appears that Parzina should be identified with Fizrāniyā (derived by metathesis). Yāqūt, under "Fizrāniyā," says: "A village among the villages of Nahr al-Malik[3] in the vicinity of Baghdad, and generally its inhabitants pronounce the name without *alif* and say Fizrīniyā, as though "deflecting" the *alif*, and it changes into a *yā'*." It is possible to entertain the notion that the original form was Parzīniyā,[4] which through metathesis became Fizrīniyā/ Fizrāniyā (perhaps by popular etymology from the name of a celebrated Bedouin tribe, the Fazāra).

Eshel, *Yishuvei ha-Yehudim* (1979), p. 216
Hirschenson, *Sheva Ḥokhmot* (1883), pp. 191, 198
Kohut, *Arukh ha-Shalem* (1878–1892), vol. 1, p. 278, "ארזן"; *Tosefot* (1937), p. 66
Newman, *Agricultural Life* (1932), p. 19
Obermeyer, *Landschaft* (1929), p. 227, n. 2

Parziqiya פרזיקיא

A. *Sources*

1. Pesaḥim 76b

היא ביניתא דאיטווא בהדי בישרא אסרה רבא[1] מפרזיקיא[2] למיכליה בכותחא.

A *binita* (fish) that was roasted together with meat Rava[1] of Parziqiya[2] forbade eating it with *kutaḥ* (porridge made with milk).

2. Yevamot 59b

א"ל רבא מפרקין[3] לרב אשי...

Rava of Parziqiya[3] said to Rav Ashi...

3. Soṭah 26b; Temurah 30a

אמר ליה רבא מפרזקיא[4] לרב אשי...

Rava of Parziqiya[4] said to Rav Ashi...

---

[2] Obermeyer, p. 227, n. 2.

[3] On Nahr al-Malik see the entries on "Sikra," "Disqarta," etc.

[4] Cf. the entries on "Parziqiya" and "Šaliniya". This is implied in the *Ein Ya'aqov* version—פרזניא—and possibly also in the Munich MS—פרזינאי.

[1] The Munich MS has "Rabbah," and see *Diq. Sof.*

[2] "Parziqiya" seems to reflect the proper pronunciation (although the name is sometimes spelled without the first *yod*); cf. below, the Arabic pronunciation.

[3] The source has מפרקין, the Munich, Oxford and Vatican 111 MSS have מפרזקיא, the Hamburg MS has מפרזיקיא, and the Florence MS has מפרזקי.

[4] The source has מפרזקיא; some of the manuscripts have מפרזיקיא. These two sources are parallels to Yevamot 59b.

4. Ketubot 39b; Bava Qamma 36a; Bava Batra 4b; Zevaḥim 10b, 108a

אמר ליה רבא מפרזקיא[5] לרב אשי...

Rava of Parziqiya[5] said to Rav Ashi...

5. Nazir 38b

א"ל רבינא[6] מפרזקיא לרב אשי...

Ravina[6] of Parziqiya said to Rav Ashi...

6. Ketubot 10a

אמר ליה הונא מר בריה דרבא מפרזקיא לרב אשי...

Huna Mar the son of Rava of Parziqiya said to Rav Ashi...

7. Qiddushin 81a (as per the Munich MS)

א"ל רב רחומי מפרזקיא[7] לרב אשי...

Rav Reḥumei of Parziqiya[7] said to Rav Ashi...

B. *Proposed Location*

Bazīqiyā in the neighborhood of Sura (D4 on the Tal. Bab. map).

C. *Identification*

The literature contains a number of attempts to identify Parziqiya with similarly named places. Neubauer, Berliner and Funk proposed identifying it with Porsica on the upper Euphrates.[8] That proposal was rightly rejected by Obermeyer because of the great distance between that place and the Jewish centers in Babylonia. He suggested identifying Parziqiya with Farausiağ in west Baghdad,[9] and believed it to be identical with the Parzina mentioned in Ta'anit 24b.[10] However, in addition to the linguistic consideration (the usual substitution of *b* for *p* and the dropping of the *r*),[11] the constant contact between Rava of Parziqiya and his son with Rav Ashi, head of the Mata Məḥasya yeshiva near Sura, supports the view that the place should be identified with the Bazīqiyā adjacent to Sura.

---

[5] The source has מפרזקיא, some versions have מפרזיקיא others מפרזיקא, the Vatican 112 MS of Ketubot 39b has מפרוקיא, and the Leningrad MS has מפרזקא there.

[6] The source has מפרזקיא, the Munich MS has "And Rava of Parziqiya said to Rav Ashi" which on the basis of the other sources seems to be the correct version.

[7] In the printing and other manuscripts the text reads "Rav Naḥman of Parhaṭya said to Rav Ashi." See "Parhaṭya" in the appendix.

[8] For the references see the bibliography for this entry.

[9] See this entry in Yāqūt, and see Obermeyer, pp. 227, 269.

[10] See the entry for "Parzina," and Obermeyer, p. 227.

[11] The *r* may have been dropped by analogy with Aramaic names beginning with *b*. Cf. the *br-b'* alternation in the names Bardarāyā-Bādarāyā, apparently referring to the same place. See these entries in Yāqūt.

Arabic literature makes possible quite an exact location of Bazīqiyā. Yāqūt notes under that entry: "A village adjacent to Ḥillat Banī Mazyad of the Kūfa subordinates." Ibn Rusta says: "Between Nahr Kūṯā (see the entry on "Kuta") and Bazīqiyā there were six miles, between Bazīqiyā and Qaṣr Ibn Hubaira nine miles; and from Qaṣr [Ibn Hubaira] to the Sura bridge (see the entry for "Dəruqart") two miles."[12] A place called ad-Dair al-Ḫaṣīb (= the monastery of the fertile soil), which was a fort, was in the vicinity of Babylon (q.v.), near Bazīqiyā.[13]

D. *Sages and Parziqiya*

All passages citing Parziqiya do so in order to identify Rava, a member of the sixth generation of Babylonian amoras. Source 1 has him ruling on a halakhic question; the others refer to him in connection with yeshiva head Rav Ashi whom he consults and sometimes contradicts. Source 6 mentions the son of Rava of Parziqiya, Huna Mar, who likewise applies to Rav Ashi.

BERLINER, *Beiträge* (1883), p. 58
ESHEL, *Yishuvei ha-Yehudim* (1979), pp. 216–217
FUNK, *Monumenta* (1913), pp. 50, 298
HIRSCHENSON, *Sheva Ḥokhmot* (1883), p. 198
KOHUT, *Arukh ha-Shalem* (1878–1892), vol. 6, p. 419; vol. 7, p. 244, "רבינא"; *Tosefot* (1937), p. 339
LEVY, *Wörterbuch* (1924²), vol. 4, p. 683
NEUBAUER, *Géographie* (1868), p. 396
OBERMEYER, *Landschaft* (1929), p. 227, n. 2; p. 269
ZURI, *Shilton* (1938), p. 228, n. 9

Pərat də-Borsif פרת דבורסיף

See the entry on "Borsif."

Pərat də-Mešan פרת דמישן

A. *Source*

Yoma 10a

"מן הארץ ההיא יצא אשור," תני רב יוסף אשור זה סילק.[1] "ויבן את נינוה ואת רחובות עיר ואת כלח," נינוה כמשמעו, רחובות עיר זו פרת דמישן, כלח זו פרת דבורסיף.

---

[12] Ibn Rusta, p. 182. On Bazīqīya cf. al-ʿAlī, *Sumer* 21 (1965): 235; Streck, *Die alte Landschaft*, vol. 1, p. 11.

[13] See Yāqūt, s.v. "ad-Dair al-Ḫaṣīb." Lake Abzīqiyā (with the prosthetic *alif*, was a place where lions lurked (Ǧāḥiẓ, *Ḥayawān*, vol. 7, p. 139, and see *Ansāb al-ašrāf*, vol. 5, p. 297). On the danger of lions, cf. also, in the entry on "Nareš," Source 11 and the sections on Sages and Nareš and Nareš and Its Environs.

[1] See the entry on "Seleucia" under the "Maḥoza Area."

"From that land Aššur went forth" Rav Joseph taught, Aššur is Sileq,[1] "and built Nineveh, Rəḥovot-ʿir, Kalaḥ," (Gen. 10:11) Nineveh is what it says, Rəḥovot-ʿir is Pərat də-Mešan, Kalaḥ is Pərat də-Borsif.

B. *General Location*

A town on the lower Tigris in the district of Mesene[2] (on Bab. Env. map)

C. *Identification*

The town of Pərat də-Mešan, like Pərat də-Borsif (see the entry on "Borsif") also mentioned in the source above, was named after one of the Parthian kings, Phraates. By the third century A.D. it was the capital of Mesene.
Called Pərat də-Mešan in Syriac just as in the talmudic source,[3] it was known to the Arabs variously as Furāt al-Baṣra, Furāt Maisān, or just Furāt. It was built by Ardašīr b. Bābak, and sometimes called Bahman Ardašīr as well.[4]
A number of scholars have proposed identifying it with presentday Baṣra or even ancient Baṣra, but that proposal was rejected by Streck who located it across from ʿAššār on the east bank of the Šaṭṭ al-ʿArab, at or near the site of the small town of at-Tanūma.[5] Rav Joseph's proposal for identifying the town of Rəḥovot-ʿir mentioned in Genesis (10:11) is untenable; the biblical context makes it clear that Rəḥovot-ʿir, Nineveh and Kalaḥ were ancient towns in Assyria.[6]
For details on the history of the place, see the entry on "Mesene."

---

[2] See the entry on "Mesene" and especially n. 55 there.

[3] Cf. Hansman, *Iranica Antiqua* 7 (1967): 26.

[4] See *Kitāb al-maʿārif* p. 654; Ibn Biṭrīq, vol. 1, p. 108. According to Ibn al-Faqīh, p. 198, Bahman Ardašīr Ḫurra was its name. Cf. Ḥamza, *Taʾrīḫ*, pp. 37–38, who ascribes its construction to Bahman b. Isfandiyār. See also Muṣtaufī, vol. 2, p. 46, who asserts that Maisān—the place where Satan (= Iblīs) appeared on earth (when he was ejected from the Garden of Eden)—was founded by Bahman b. Isfandiyār and restored by Alexander the Great. Ḥamza (p. 46) reports that Ardašīr b. Bābak built Bahman Ardašīr on the banks of the "blind Tigris" (actually, the "one-eyed Tigris") in the Mesene region (*arḍ*), and the Baṣrans have two names for it, Bahmanšīr and Furāt Maisān. On the name Bahmanšīr see also Yāqūt, s.v. "Bahman Ardašīr," who quotes Ḥamza al-Iṣfahānī. See also Schaeder, *Der Islam* 14 (1924): 29f. Yāqūt also says that the city was on the banks of the "blind Tigris" (the Tigris in its lower reaches, near al-Maftaḥ, Ubulla and ʿAbbadān; Masʿūdī, *Tanbīh*, p. 52) opposite Ubulla; it was in ruins, and no traces remained, but the name survived. According to Yāqūt, Furāt al-Baṣra (= Bahman Ardašīr) was also the name of an extensive district between Wāsiṭ and Baṣra.

[5] See Streck, *EI*[1], s.v. "Maisān," p. 152, and see already Schaeder, *ibid*,. p. 31. See also Obermeyer, p. 91; Herzfeld, *Der Islam* 11 (1921): 149.

[6] See Artzi in *Entziqlopedia Miqraʾit*, vol. 7, p. 352. "Rəḥovot-ʿir" may not be the name of a particular town at all, but a term meaning "town squares" or "town neighborhoods." To the source above, cf. Ephraem, *Commentary on Genesis* 10:10: "Nimrod built three towns: Arak, Ur and Kala, that is Orhāy, Nisibis and Seleucia" (cited by J. Markwart, *Catalogue*, § 65, also: Michael the Syrian, *Chronicle*, p. 9a 43–47 = I 20a Gs p. 639, 26–27 = III 278).

Berliner, *Beiträge* (1883), p. 44
Eshel, *Yishuvei ha-Yehudim* (1979), pp. 218, 233
Funk, *Monumenta* (1913), pp. 50, 298
Hansman, *Iranica Antiqua* 7 (1967): 21–58 (= *Mélanges Ghirshman*, vol. 2)
Hirschenson, *Sheva Ḥokhmot* (1883), p. 211
Jastrow, *Dictionary* (1950³), p. 1244
Kohut, *Arukh ha-Shalem* (1878–1892), vol. 6, p. 454; *Tosefot* (1937), p. 346
Levy, *Wörterbuch* (1924²), vol. 4, p. 146
Neubauer, *Géographie* (1868), pp. 346, 382
Obermeyer, *Landschaft* (1929), pp. 91, 315
See also the bibliography for "Mesene."

Pərišna/Pašrunya פרישנא/פשרוניא

A. *Sources*

1. Pesaḥim 91a

רמי ליה רב עוקבא בר חיננא[1] מפרישנא[2] לרבא ...

Rav ʿUqba b. Ḥinena[1] of Pərišna[2] contradicted Rava ...

2. Pesaḥim 76a; Ḥullin 112a

.. שרייא רב חיננא בריה דרבא[3] מפשרוניא,[4] אמר רבא מאן חכים למישרא מילתא כי הא אי לאו רב חיננא בריה דרבא מפשרוניא דגברא רבה הוא.

Rav Ḥinena the son of Rava[3] of Pašrunya[4] allowed it, Rava said, Who is wise enough to allow such a thing if not Rav Ḥinena the son of Rava of Pašrunya who is a great man.

3. Pesaḥim 76a (as per the Munich MS)

אמר רב איקא מפשרוניא[5] אמר רב הונא ...

Rav Iqa of Pašrunya[5] said Rav Huna said ...

4. Menaḥot 42a

דתני רב חיננא בריה דרבא[6] מפשרניא.[7]

Rav Ḥinena the son of Rava[6] of Pašrunya[7] taught.

---

[1] The Munich and Oxford MSS have "Rav Iqa son of Rav Ḥinena"; the Munich B MS has "Rav Iqa son of Rav Ḥinena Sava."

[2] The Munich MS has מפרשדוניא, the Oxford MS has מפשרניא, the Munich B MS has מפשרוניא, and see *Diq. Sof.*

[3] The Munich B MS of Pesaḥim has "Rav Ḥinena son of Rabbah," further on as well; the Hamburg MS of Ḥullin has "Rav Ḥama son of Rava," but further on "Rav Huna son of Rava." The Vatican 122 MS of Ḥullin has "Rav Ḥinena" (without "son of Rava").

[4] Rashi, in old printings of Pesaḥim, has מפרשינא, further on as well. The Hamburg MS of Ḥullin has מפרשוניא, further on as well.

[5] The printing does not mention רב איקא מפשרוניא at all. The Munich B MS has רב איקא משורייניא; the Oxford MS has רב איקא מפרשוניא.

[6] The Munich MS has "Rav Ḥinena" (without "son of Rava").

[7] The source has מפשרניא, the Munich MS has מפרשדוניא, the Vatican 123 MS has מפרשניא, the Vatican 118 MS has מפשרונא, and the Cairo MS and Venice printing have מפשרוניא.

5. ʿEruvin 104a

רמי ליה רב איקא[8] מפשרוניא[9] לרבא . . .

Rav Iqa[8] of Pašrunya[9] contradicted Rava . . .

6. Giṭṭin 45b

דתני רב המנונא[10] בריה דרבא מפשרוניא[11] . . .

Rav Hamnuna[10] the son of Rava of Pašrunya[11] taught . . .

B. *Already Proposed Location*

Farāšā, half way between Ḥilla (q.v., D4 on the Tal. Bab. map) and Baghdad (q.v., D2 on the Tal. Bab. map)

C. *Identification*

Obermeyer[12] proposed identifying Perišna with Farāš mentioned by Ibn Ǧubair, which is the Farāšā mentioned by Yāqūt.[13] He also proposed its identification with Bārūs, which he construed to be the first part of the name Bārūsmā[14] (*Bārūs Mata, according to Obermeyer). The former proposal is reasonable (see below) but the latter is not, for Bārūs and Farāš are not identical. They differ not only in their names, but also in their locations, for while Farāšā was half way between Ḥilla and Baghdad, Bārūsmā was closer to Ḥilla, being near Sura (q.v.).[15]
According to Mustaufī, travelers from Baghdad to Naǧaf proceeded as follows[16]: to the village of Ṣarṣar two parasangs, to Farāša (*sic*) seven parasangs, to the Nīl Canal seven parasangs, through the village of Nars (see the entry on "Nareš") to Ḥilla two parasangs. The traveler Ibn Ǧubair likewise followed that route, in the opposite direction[17] (as already noted by Le Strange, Mu-

[8] The Oxford MS has "Rav Iqa b. Ḥanina," the Salonika printing has" Rav Iqa b. Ḥinena"; the Pesaro printing has "Bar Iqa."

[9] The Munich MS has מפרשותא, the Salonika, Pesaro, Venice and Constantinople printings have מפרשוניא.

[10] The Vatican 140 and Oxford MSS have "Rav Ḥinena son of Rava."

[11] The Vatican 140 MS has מפרשרונייא; the Oxford MS has מפרשדוניא. A gaonic responsum from the Geniza has the form מיכשרוניא (*Otzar ha-Geonim* for Giṭṭin, *ha-Teshuvot*, p. 91).

[12] Obermeyer, p. 297, n. 1.

[13] Ibn Ǧubair, p. 215; Yāqūt, s.v. "Farāšā."

[14] See Yāqūt, s.v. "Bārūsmā."

[15] See Yāqūt, s.v. "Bihqubāḏ" (in both editions the name is vocalized "Bārūsamā"); Suhrāb, p. 124. On Bārūsmā and Nahr al-Malik as a single administrative unit, see *Taʾrīḫ Wāsiṭ*, p. 114. Cf. the Bārūsmā mentioned together with Bāniqyā (see the entry on "Tarbiqna"), Ṭabarī, vol. 3, p. 343 (= vol. 1, p. 2017), identical with the Basmā mentioned together with Bāniqyā (*ibid.*, vol. 3, pp. 367, 369 [vol. 1, pp. 2049, 2052]).

[16] Mustaufī, vol. 2, p. 162.

[17] Ibn Ǧubair, pp. 214–217.

staufī's editor and translator): Ḥilla—Nīl Canal—a village called Qanṭara also known as Ḥiṣn Bašīr (see the entry on "Nareš")—al-Farāš (= Farāšā)—Zarīrān across from the palace (Īwān) of Kisrā—before which a short distance away the Madā'in Kisrā[18]—Ṣarṣar—Baghdad.
Farāš was close to Madā'in (see the entry on the "Maḥoza Area") and that provides evidence for the identification with Pərišna, for the Pərišna (or Pašrunya) sages are mentioned in discussion with Rava, head of the Maḥoza yeshiva in the fourth generation of Babylonian amoras. According to Mustaufī, Farāšā was exactly half way between Baghdad and Ḥilla. The distance between it and Zarīrān, which was part of Madā'in, was not great: Ibn Ǧubair stopped at Farāšā at noon, and then proceeded to Zarīrān which he reached in the evening of the same day.

D. *Sages and Pərišna*

The sources above mention a series of sages from Pərišna (or Pašrunya), contemporaries of Rava's. Rav Ḥinena the son of Rava of Pašrunya, Rav ʿUqba (or Iqa[19]) b. Ḥinena of Pərišna, apparently the son of Rav Ḥinena b. Rava,[20] and Rav Iqa of Pašrunya.[21]

Berliner, *Beiträge* (1883), p. 58
Eshel, *Yishuvei ha-Yehudim* (1979), pp. 217, 219
Funk, *Monumenta* (1913), p. 50
Hirschenson, *Sheva Ḥokhmot* (1883), p. 201
Jastrow, *Dictionary* (1950³), pp. 1228, 1243, 1244
Kohut, *Arukh ha-Shalem* (1878–1892), vol. 6, p. 454
Levy, *Wörterbuch* (1924²), vol. 4, p. 145
Neubauer, *Géographie* (1868), p. 396
Obermeyer, *Landschaft* (1929), p. 297, n. 1

Pumbədita פומבדיתא

A. *Sources (a selection)*

1. Rosh ha-Shanah 23b

מאי גולה, אמר רב יוסף[1] זו פומבדיתא.

What is the Exile? Rav Joseph[1] said, It is Pumbədita.

---

[18] Cf. *Marāṣid*, s.v. "Bahurasīr." According to it, Bahurasīr is across from the Īwān, the Tigris flows between them, and Zarīrān lies to the south. See also the Maḥoza Area plan.

[19] See n. 1 above.

[20] If a father and son are meant, reinforcement is provided for the identity of Pərišna and Pašrunya.

[21] Source 6 cites "Rav Hamnuna son of Rava" but the version in the manuscripts, "Rav Ḥinena son of Rava" (see n. 10) is more acceptable. See also the variants of the names of the Pərišna sages in nn. 3, 6 and 8.

[1] The Munich B, Oxford and London MSS have "Abbaye said" as does *Iggeret Rav Sherira Gaon* (Lewin ed., p. 82); the Munich MS does not have "Rav Joseph said" at all.

2. Qiddushin 72a

אמר ליה אביי לרב יוסף להא גיסא דפרת עד היכא, אמר ליה מאי דעתיך משום בירם,[2] מייחסי דפומבדיתא מבירם נסבי.

Abbaye said to him, to Rav Joseph, How far [is Babylonia] this side of the Euphrates? He said to him, What is your opinion [that you came to ask] about Biram?[2] Those of pure lineage from Pumbədita, they marry [women] from Biram.

3. Qiddushin 70b

מכריז רב יהודה בפומבדיתא[3] אדא ויונתן עבדי, יהודה בר פפא ממזירא . . .

Rav Judah expounds in Pumbədita[3] Adda and Jonathan are slaves, Judah b. Papa is a *mamzer* . . .

4. Berakhot 56a

א״ל חזאי אפדנא דאביי דנפל וכסיין אבקיה, א״ל אביי שכיב ומתיבתיה (בכתבי יד פריז ופלורנץ: מתיבתא דפומבדיתא[4]) אתיא לגבך.

He said to him [Rava to Bar Hedya, the interpreter of dreams], I saw Abbaye's house falling and covering him with dust. He said to him, Abbaye will die and his yeshiva (in the Paris and Florence MSS, the Pumbədita[4] yeshiva) will pass to you.

5. Yoma 71a

אמר רבה[5] כי מיפטרי רבנן מהדדי בפומבדיתא[6] אמרי הכי מחיה חיים יתן לך חיים ארוכים וטובים ומתוקנין.

Rabbah[5] said, When rabbis in Pumbədita[6] take leave of each other, they say thus, May He who sustains life give you a long, good and righteous life.

6. Shabbat 148a

רבה בר בר חנה איקלע לפומבדיתא, לא על לפירקיה דרב יהודה, שדריה[7] לאדא דיילא, א״ל זיל גרביה . . .

Rabbah b. Bar Ḥana happened to be in Pumbədita and did not attend the *pirqa* of Rav Judah. He (Rav Judah) sent[7] Adda the steward, Go and pull [his robe].

[2] The Munich MS has ביראם, and בירם further on; the Vatican 111 MS has בים, and בירם further on.

[3] The Munich MS has בנהרדעא, as does *She'iltot de-Rav Aḥai Gaon, She'ilta* 41.

[4] The Paris MS has ואתא מתיבתא דפומבדיתא וסמכי עילווך and see *Diq. Sof.*; the Florence MS has אביי דשכיב בחייך ואתי מתיבתא דפומבדיתא לגבך. The word דפומבדיתא does not appear in the printing at all.

[5] The Oxford MS and *Ein Ya'aqov* have "Rava said."

[6] The Munich and Oxford MSS have בשכנציב מבי רב נחמן (the Munich MS also has the same form as the printing in the margin); the Munich B MS has בשכנציב; see also the entry on "Šəkanṣiv" and nn. 2, 3 there.

[7] The Munich MS has "Rav Judah sent."

7. Yevamot 110b

אמר רב נחמן אשכחתיה לרב אדא בר אהבה ולרב חנא[8] חתניה דיתבי וקמקוו אקוותא בשוקא דפומבדיתא[9] . . .

Rav Naḥman said, I found Rav Adda b. Ahavah and Rav Ḥana[8] his son-in-law sitting and dealing with arguments in the Pumbədita[9] marketplace . . .

8. Bava Metziʿa 38b

א״ל דלמא מפומבדיתא את דמעיילין פילא בקופא דמחטא.

He said to him (Rav Sheshet to Rav ʿAmram), Perhaps you are from Pumbədita, where they insert an elephant in the eye of a needle.

9. Sanhedrin 17b

דייני דפומבדיתא רב פפא בר שמואל . . . סבי דפומבדיתא רב יהודה ורב עינא. חריפי דפומבדיתא עיפה ואבימי בני רחבה. אמוראי דפומבדיתא רבה ורב יוסף.

The judges of Pumbədita, Rav Papa b. Samuel . . . the elders of Pumbədita, Rav Judah and Rav ʿEina; the keen intellects of Pumbədita, ʿEfa and Avimi sons of Raḥavah; the amoras of Pumbədita, Rabbah and Rav Joseph.

10. Bava Batra 142b[10]

בסורא מתנו הכי, בפומבדיתא מתנו הכי . . .

In Sura they taught thus, in Pumbədita they taught thus . . .

11. Horayot 12a; Keritot 6a

ותיבו אקילקלי דמתא מחסיא ולא תיבו אפדני דפומבדיתא.

. . . And sit on the refuse heap of Mata Məḥasya and do not sit in the mansions of Pumbədita.

12. Shabbat 153a

א״ל אביי לרבה[11] כגון מר דסנו ליה כולהו פומבדיתאי[12] מאן אחים הספידא, א״ל מיסתיא את ורבה בר רב חנן.

Abbaye said to him to Rabbah,[11] You for instance whom all the Pumbəditans[12] hate, who will thrill in eulogy? He said to him, You and Rabbah b. Rav Ḥanan are enough for me.

---

[8] The Munich MS has "Rav Ḥama."

[9] The Vatican 111 MS has דפום בדיתא. Various manuscripts of the sources cited in this entry and other sources as well have the name Pumbədita divided into two parts as it is here (see also the entry on "Pum Nahara").

[10] And similarly in many other places.

[11] The Munich and Oxford MSS and *Aggadot ha-Talmud* have "to Rava"; see also *Diq. Sof.*

[12] The Munich MS does not have the word "Pumbəditans."

13. Niddah 67b

אתקין רב אידי[13] בנרש למטבל ביומא דתמניא משום אריותא. רב אחא בר יעקב בפפוניא[14] משום גנבי. רב יהודה בפומבדיתא משום צנה. רבא במחוזא משום אבולאי.

Rav Idi[13] ordained in Nareš to immerse on the eighth day because of the lions. Rav Aḥa b. Jacob in Papuniya[14] because of the thieves, Rav Judah in Pumbədita because of the cold, Rava in Maḥoza because of the gate guards.

14. Bava Metzi'a 86a

אמר רב כהנא[15] אישתעי לי רב חמא[16] בר ברתיה דחסא[17] רבה בר נחמני אגב שמדא נח נפשיה. אכלו ביה קורצא בי מלכא, אמרו איכא חד גברא ביהודאי דקא מבטל תריסר אלפי[18] גברי מישראל ירחא בקייטא וירחא בסתוא מכרגא דמלכא.[19] שדרו פריסתקא דמלכא בתריה ולא אשכחיה. ערק ואזל מפומבדיתא לאקרא[20] מאקרא לאגמא[21] ומאגמא לשחין[22] ומשחין לצריפא[23] ומצריפא לעינא דמים[24] ומעינא דמים לפומבדיתא . . . ערק ואזיל לאגמא . . . נפל פתקא מרקיעא בפומבדיתא[25] רבה בר נחמני נתבקש בישיבה של מעלה.

Rav Kahana[15] said, Rav Ḥama[16] the son of Ḥasa's[17] daughter told me: Rabbah b. Naḥmani's soul expired through persecution. He was informed against at the king's court, and they said, There is a person among the Jews who exempts twelve thousand[18] men of Israel a month in the summer and a month in the winter of the *karga* (= poll tax) of the king.[19] They sent an envoy of the king's after him, and he did not find him. He fled and went from Pumbədita to Aqra,[20] from Aqra to Agama,[21] from Agama to Šaḥin,[22] from Šaḥin to Ṣərifa,[23] and from Ṣərifa to 'Ena Damim,[24] and from 'Ena Damim to Pum-

[13] The Munich and Vatican 111 MSS have "Rav Idi b. Avin."

[14] The Vatican 111 MS does not have "in Papuniya."

[15] The Florence MS has "Ravina."

[16] The Munich, Hamburg, Florence and Vatican 117 MSS have "Ḥama" (without "Rav").

[17] *Ein Ya'aqov* has "Ḥama" which seems to be a garble; see also *Diq. Sof.*

[18] The Munich, Florence and Vatican 117 MSS have תליסר אלפי (= thirteen thousand).

[19] The Hamburg MS has "six months in the summer and six months in the winter" with the word שית (= six) scratched out in both places, and the plural ירחי in both places corrected to the singular ירחא interlinearly. All the manuscripts have מכרגא (= from the poll-tax) without דמלכא (= of the king). See also *Diq. Sof.*

[20] The Munich, Florence, Hamburg, Vatican 116 and Vatican 117 MSS do not have אקרא at all.

[21] The Munich, Vatican 116 and Vatican 117 MSS have אגמא as the last place on the escape route.

[22] The Munich MS has שהי', the Florence MS has שיחא, the Hamburg MS has אפדנא דשוחא, the Vatican 116 MS has אפדנא דשיזהא. The Vatican 117 MS has אפדנא דשיהיא and אפדנא דשיסתנא further on.

[23] The Munich, Florence, Hamburg, Vatican 116 and Vatican 117 MSS have צריפא דעינא. Some printings also have the form צריכא.

[24] עינא דמים appears only in the printing; see the previous note, and *Diq. Sof.* The word *damim* may have been deleted because of the strange meaning the place name would have (spring of blood). But perhaps the name should be vocalized 'Ena də-Mayim or 'Ena də-Maya (the spring of water).

bədita . . . he fled and went to Agama . . . And then a missive fell from heaven in Pumbədita[25]: Rabbah b. Naḥmani was summoned to the tribunal on high.

15. Ḥullin 110a

בסורא לא אכלי כחלי, בפומבדיתא אכלי כחלי. רמי בר תמרי דהוא רמי בר דיקולי[26] מפומבדיתא[27] איקלע לסורא במעלי יומא דכפורי, אפקינהו כולי עלמא לכחלינהו שדינהו, אזל איהו נקטינהו אכלינהו, אייתוה לקמיה דרב חסדא, אמר ליה אמאי תעביד הכי, אמר ליה מאתרא דרב יהודה אנא דאכיל . . .

In Sura they do not eat udders, in Pumbədita they eat udders. Rami b. Tamare who is Rami b. Diqule[26] of Pumbədita[27] happened to be in Sura on the eve of the Day of Atonement. Everybody took out the udders and threw them away. He went and took them and ate them. They brought him before Rav Ḥisda. He said to him, Why do you do so? He said to him, I am from the place of Rav Judah who eats.

16. Qiddushin 70a

ההוא גברא דמנהרדעא[28] דעל לבי מטבחיא בפומבדיתא, אמר להו הבו לי בישרא, אמרו ליה נטר עד דשקיל לשמעיה דרב יהודה בר יחזקאל וניתיב לך, אמר מאן יהודה בר שויסקאל דקדים לי דשקל מן קמאי, אזלי אמרו ליה לרב יהודה, שמתיה. אמרו רגיל דקרי אינשי עבדי, אכריז עליה דעבדא הוא. אזל ההוא אזמניה לדינא לקמיה דרב נחמן . . .

That man from Nəhardəʿa[28] who entered the slaughterhouse in Pumbədita said to them, Give me meat. They said to him, Wait till the steward of Rav Judah b. Ezekiel takes and we will give you. He said, Who is Judah b. Sheviskel (= roast gobbler) that has precedence over me, that takes before me. They went and told Rav Judah. He banned him. They said the man calls people slaves, and he proclaimed him a slave. That man went and summoned him to judgement before Rav Naḥman . . .

17. ʿAvodah Zarah 70a

הנהו גנבי דסלקי לפומבדיתא[29] ופתחו חביתא טובא, אמר רבא חמרא שרי, מ״ט, רובא גנבי ישראל נינהו.

Those thieves that went up to Pumbədita[29] and opened an extra barrel of wine, Rava said, The wine is allowed. What is the reason, most of the thieves are Jews.

---

[25] The Munich MS and *Aggadot ha-Talmud* do not have בפומבדיתא. The Florence and Munich B MSS have the additional words ארישא דאביי (= on Abbaye's head). See also *Diq. Sof.*

[26] Cf. Menaḥot 29b: "Rami b. Tamare that is the father-in-law of Rami b. Diqule." But the manuscripts are like the source from Ḥullin. See also *Diq. Sof.*

[27] The Hamburg and Vatican 121 MSS do not have מפומבדיתא.

[28] The Munich MS and Venice printing do not have דמנהרדעא.

[29] The Spanish MS edited by Abramson does not have לפומבדיתא, and the margin there has דאתו לפום בדיתא.

18. Ḥullin 127a

אמר רב גידל אמר רב [30] נרשאה נשקיך מני ככיך, נהר פקודאה לוייך מגלימא שפירא דחזי עלך, פומבדיתאה לוייך אשני אושפיזך.

Rav Giddal said Rav[30] said, If a Narešan kisses you, count your teeth; if a Nəhar Pəqodan accompanies you, it is because of the fine cloak he saw on you; if a Pumbəditan accompanies you, change your accommodations.

19. Bava Batra 46a

א״ל אביי לרבא תא אחוי לך רמאי דפומבדיתא מאי עבדי, א״ל הב לי סרבלאי, לא היו דברים מעולם . . .

Abbaye said to him to Rava, Come and I will show you what the deceivers of Pumbədita do. He said to him (to the craftsman), Give me my cloak. There was no such thing.

20. Giṭṭin 27a

עבד רבה עובדא בההוא גיטא דאישתכח בי כיתנא בפומבדיתא כשמעתיה . . .

Rabbah acted according to his rule in the bill of divorcement found among the flax of Pumbədita . . .

21. Giṭṭin 38a

ההיא אמתא דהות בפומבדיתא דהוו קא מעבדי בה אינשי איסורא אמר אביי אי לאו דאמר רב יהודה אמר שמואל[31] כל המשחרר עבדו עובר בעשה, הוה כייפנא ליה למרה וכתיב לה גיטא דחירותא.

That female slave in Pumbədita that men did forbidden things with, Abbaye said, If Rav Judah citing Samuel[31] had not said that whoever frees his (heathen) slave disobeys a precept, I would compel her master to write her a deed of manumission.

22. Bava Qamma 93a

ההוא ארנקא דצדקה דאתי לפומבדיתא, אפקדה רב יוסף גבי ההוא גברא, פשע בה אתו גנבי גנבוה, חייביה רב יוסף, א״ל אביי והתניא לשמור ולא לחלק לעניים, אמר ליה עניי דפומבדיתא מיקץ קיץ להו ולשמור הוא.

A purse of charity that came to Pumbədita, Rav Joseph deposited with a certain man. He was careless and thieves came and stole it. Rav Joseph held him liable. Abbaye said to him, But it is taught to keep and not to distribute to the poor. He said to him, The poor at Pumbədita have a fixed allowance, and it is to keep.

---

[30] The Vatican 121 MS has "Rav Papa"; see also *Diq. Sof.*, notes ד, ו.
[31] The manuscripts do not have "Samuel said," nor does Berakhot 47b.

23. Betzah 28b–29a

היכי עביד, כי הא דבסורא[32] אמרי תרטא ופלגו תרטא, בנרש אמרי חלקא ופלגו חלקא, בפומבדיתא אמרי אוזיא ופלגו אוזיא, בנהר פקוד ובמתא מחסיא אמרי רבעא ופלגו רבעא.

What should he do [on holidays]? In Sura[32] they say, [Give me] a third and half a third; in Nareš they say, A half and half a half; in Pumbədita they say, A sixth and half a sixth; in Nəhar Pəqod and Mata Məḥasya they say, A quarter and half a quarter.

24. ʿArakhin 6b

שעזרק טייעא אינדב שרגא לבי כנישתא דרב יהודה, שנייה רחבא ואיקפד רבא[33] . . . ואיכא דאמרי שנייה חזני דפומבדיתא[34] ואיקפד רחבא ואיקפד רבה.

When Sheʿazraq the Arab donated a lamp to the synagogue of Rav Judah, Raḥava changed it from its purpose, and Rava[33] was angry . . . and some say the watchmen of Pumbədita[34] changed it, and Raḥava was angry and Rabbah was angry.

25. Bava Batra 168b

הנהו ערבאי דאתו לפומבדיתא דהוו קא אנסי ארעתא דאינשי, אתו מרוותיהו לקמיה דאביי, א״ל ליחזי מר שטרין ולכתוב לן מר שטרא אחרינא עליה, דאי מיתניס חד נקיטינן חד בידן.

Those Arabs who came to Pumbədita who seized lands of people, their owners came before Abbaye. They said to him, Will the master see our deed and write another deed besides it, so that if one is seized, we hold one in our hands.

26. Ḥullin 46a

ההוא פולמוסא דאתא לפומבדיתא, ערקו רבה ורב יוסף, פגע בהו ר׳ זירא אמר להו ערוקאי . . .

That army that came to Pumbədita, Rabbah and Rav Joseph fled. Rabbi Zera met them and said to them, Running away . . .

27. ʿAvodah Zarah 33b

דבי פרזק רופילא[35] אנס הני כובי מפומבדיתא,[36] רמא בהו חמרא, אהדרינהו ניהלייהו, אתו שיילוהו לרב יהודה, אמר דבר שאין מכניסו לקיום הוא, משכשכן במים והן מותרין.

[One] of the men of the commander[35] Parzaq seized those casks from Pumbədita,[36] filled them with wine, returned them to them. They came to ask him, Rav Judah. He said, It is a thing that was not put in permanently. Rinse them with water and they are permitted.

---

[32] The Munich MS has דבנהרדעא.

[33] The Munich and Vatican 119 MSS have "Rabbah."

[34] The Munich and Vatican 119 MSS do not have the word חזני (= watchmen).

[35] For bibliography on the meaning of the term, see Beer, *Rashut ha-Golah*, p. 25, n. 38.

[36] The Spanish MS edited by Abramson has מפום בדיתאי.

28. Qiddushin 70b

אמר רב יוסף האי בי כובי דפומבדיתא כולם דעבדי.

Rav Joseph said, That Be Kube [in the vicinity] of Pumbədita, all of them are from slaves.

29. Giṭṭin 4a

ואמר רבה בר בר חנה לדידי חזי לי ההוא אתרא והוי כמבי כובי לפומבדיתא.

And Rabbah b. Bar Ḥana said, I myself saw the place and it was as [far as] from Be Kube to Pumbədita.

30. Sukkah 26b

אמר רב אסור לאדם לישן ביום יותר משינת הסוס . . . אביי הוה ניים כדמעייל[37] מפומבדיתא לבי כובי, קרי עליה רב יוסף "עד מתי עצל תשכב מתי תקום משנתך."

Rav said, A man must not sleep by day more than the sleep of a horse . . . Abbaye slept [by day] like a person going up[37] from Pumbədita to Be Kube, and Rav Joseph called at him, "How long, sluggard, will you lie, when will you rise from your sleep?" (Prov. 6:9).

31. Ketubot 111a[38]

אמר רב יהודה אמר שמואל כשם שאסור לצאת מארץ ישראל לבבל כך אסור לצאת מבבל לשאר ארצות. רבה ורב יוסף דאמרי תרוייהו אפילו מפומבדיתא לבי כובי. ההוא דנפק מפומבדיתא לבי כובי שמתיה רב יוסף. ההוא דנפק מפומבדיתא לאסתוניא[39] שכיב, אמר אביי אי בעי האי צורבא מרבנן הוה חיי.

Rav Judah said, Samuel said, Just as it is forbidden to leave Eretz Israel for Babylonia, so it is forbidden to leave Babylonia for other countries. Rabbah and Rav Joseph both said, Even from Pumbədita to Be Kube. A man who left Pumbədita for Be Kube was banned by Rav Joseph. A man once left Pumbədita to Astunya[39] and he died. Abbaye said, If this young scholar wanted it, he could still have been alive.

32. ʿEruvin 51b–52a

רבה בר רב חנן[40] הוה רגיל דאתי מארטיבנא[41] לפומבדיתא, אמר תהא שביתתי בצינתא.[42]

---

[37] The Munich B MS has כדמיזל; see *Diq. Sof.* See also n. 5 in the entry on "Be Kube."

[38] A parallel occurs in *Midrash ha-Gadol* to Leviticus, *be-har*, 25:38 (Steinsalz edition, p. 713).

[39] The Munich MS has לאיסתמא, the Leningrad MS has לבסתנייא, the Soncino printing and *Ein Yaʿaqov* have לאיסתוניא, Geniza fragments have לוסתיניא and לאוסתניא. See also Ketubot in the ICIT edition. The parallel in *Midrash ha-Gadol* has לוס תינייא and the MSS of *Midrash ha-Gadol* have לווסתיניא and לווסתינא.

[40] The Munich and Oxford MSS have "Rava b. Rav Ḥanin."

[41] The Munich MS has מארטוניא, the Oxford MS has מארטביא, the Salonika printing has מארטבינא, and Rashi there has מארטבניא.

[42] The Munich MS has בניזיתא (or בני זיתא), the Oxford MS has בזיתא. See *Diq. Sof.*; see also *Arukh ha-Shalem*, vol. 2, p. 35, s.v. "בזתא."

Rabbah b. Rav Ḥanan[40] used to come [on the Sabbath] from Arṭivna[41] to Pumbədita; he said, My camp will be in Ṣinta.[42]

33. ʿAvodah Zarah 25b–26a

רב מנשה[43] הוה אזל לבי תורתא,[44] פגעו ביה גנבי, אמרו ליה לאן קאזלת, אמר להן לפומבדיתא. כי מטא לבי תורתא פריש. אמרו ליה תלמידא דיהודה רמאה את, אמר להו ידעיתו ליה, יהא רעוא דליהוו הנהו אינשי בשמתיה.

Rav Manasseh[43] once went to Be Torta[44]; thieves met him, said to him, Where are you going? He said to them, To Pumbədita. When he reached Be Torta he stopped. They said to him, You are a disciple of Judah the deceiver. He said to them, You know him. May those people come under his ban.

34. Pesaḥim 52a

רב נתן בר אסיא[45] אזל מבי רב[46] לפומבדיתא בי״ט שני של עצרת, שמתיה רב יוסף.

Rav Nathan b. Assia[45] went from Be Rav[46] to Pumbədita on the second holy day of the Feast of Weeks. Rav Joseph banned him.

35. Bava Batra 90b

רב פפא בר שמואל תקין כיילא בר תלתא קפיזי, אמרו ליה והא אמר שמואל אין מוסיפין על המדות יותר משתות, אמר להו אנא כיילא חדתא תקיני. שדריה לפומבדיתא ולא קבלוה, שדריה לפאפוניא[47] וקבלוה, וקרי ליה רוז פפא.

Rav Papa b. Samuel introduced a measure of three *qefize*. They said to him, But Samuel said a measure cannot be increased by more than a sixth. He said to them, I introduced a new measure. He sent it to Pumbədita and they did not accept it. He sent it to Papuniya[47] and they did, and called it *roz-Papa*.

36. Xenophon, *Anabasis*, I 7, 14–16

κατὰ γὰρ μέσον τὸν σταθμὸν τοῦτον τάφρος ἦν ὀρυκτὴ βαθεῖα, τὸ μὲν εὖρος ὀργυαὶ πέντε, τὸ δὲ βάθος ὀργυαὶ τρεῖς. Παρετέτατο δὲ ἡ τάφρος ἄνω διὰ τοῦ πεδίου ἐπὶ δώδεκα παρασάγγας μέχρι τοῦ Μηδίας τείχους.[48] [Ἔνθα αἱ διώρυχες, ἀπὸ τοῦ Τί-

---

[43] The Spanish MS edited by Abramson, *Ein Yaʿaqov* and *Aggadot ha-Talmud* have רב מנשי. The Munich MS has "Rav Ashi" which is unlikely, for Rav Ashi of the sixth generation of Babylonian amoras could not have been the disciple of Rav Judah, of the second. See also *Diq. Sof.*

[44] *Aggadot ha-Talmud* has תוראתא, further on as well.

[45] The Munich and Oxford MSS have "Bar Nathan Assia."

[46] The Munich MS has מבירם, as does the Munich B MS (corrected, however to מבי רב). The Oxford MS has מבירא. The R-o-s-h has מבירם.

[47] The Munich, Hamburg and Vatican 115 MSS have לפפוניא.

[48] Following the "wall of Media" the MSS contain lines usually considered an interpolation: Here also are the canals, which flow from the Tigris river; they are four in number, each a plethrum wide and exceedingly deep, and grain-carrying ships ply in them; they empty into the Euphrates and are a parasang apart, and there are bridges over them. (trans.: C. L. Brownson, LCL). Cf. *ibid.*, II 4, 12–13, for the "wall of Media."

γρητος ποταμοῦ ῥέουσαι· εἰσὶ δὲ τέτταρες, τὸ μὲν εὖρος πλεθριαῖαι, βαθεῖαι δὲ ἰσχυρῶς, καὶ πλοῖα πλεῖ ἐν αὐταῖς σιταγωγά· εἰσβάλλουσι δὲ εἰς τὸν Εὐφράτην, διαλείπουσι δ᾽ ἑκάστη παρασάγγην, γέφυραι δ᾽ ἔπεισιν.] Ἦν δὲ παρὰ τὸν Εὐφράτην πάροδος στενὴ μεταξὺ τοῦ ποταμοῦ καὶ τῆς τάφρου ὡς εἴκοσι ποδῶν τὸ εὖρος· ταύτην δὲ τὴν τάφρον βασιλεὺς μέγας ποιεῖ ἀντὶ ἐρύματος, ἐπειδὴ πυνθάνεται Κῦρον προσελαύνοντα. Ταύτην δὴ τὴν πάροδον Κῦρός τε καὶ ἡ στρατιὰ παρῆλθε καὶ ἐγένοντο εἴσω τῆς τάφρου.

. . . about midway of this day's march there was a deep trench, five fathoms in width and three fathoms in depth. This trench extended up through the plain for a distance of twelve parasangs, reaching to the wall of Media,[48] and alongside the Euphrates there was a narrow passage, not more than about twenty in width, between the river and the trench; and the trench had been constructed by the Great King as a means of defence when he learned that Cyrus was marching against him. Accordingly Cyrus and his army went through by the passage just mentioned, and so found themselves on the inner side of the trench. (trans.: C. L. Brownson, LCL)

37. Josephus, *Antiquities*, XVIII 315[49]

οἱ δὲ ἐφ᾽ ὕβρει τὴν δικαίωσιν λογιζόμενοι, κατασπάσαντες τῶν ὅπλων πολλὰ ὁπόσα ἦν ἐπὶ τῆς οἰκίας φυλασσόμενα ᾤχοντο εἴς τι χωρίον, διάρρηξιν μὲν ποταμῶν λεγόμενον, νομὰς δὲ ἀγαθὰς παρασχεῖν πεφυκὸς καὶ χιλὸν ὁπόσοι εἰς τὸν χειμῶνα ἀποτιθοῖντο.

. . . they dragged down a quantity of weapons which were stored on the housetop and went off to a certain district called the "Parting of the River." It was capable of providing good pasturage and green fodder in sufficient quantity to be stored for winter. (trans.: L. H. Feldman, LCL)

38. Ammianus XXIV 2, 6–7[50]

Animatus his vincendi primitiis, miles ad vicum Macepracta pervenit, in quo semiruta murorum vestigia videbantur, qui priscis temporibus in spatia longa protenti, tueri ab externis incursibus Assyriam dicebantur. Hinc pars fluminis scinditur, largis aquarum agminibus ducens ad tractus Babylonos interiores, usui agris futura et civitatibus circumiectis . . .

Inspired by these first-fruits of victory, our soldiers came to the village of Macepracta, where the half-destroyed traces of walls were seen; these in early times had a wide extent, it was said, and protected Assyria from hostile inroads. Here a part of the river is drawn off by large canals which take the water into

[49] The story of Asinaeus and Anilaeus.
[50] Julian's campaign, A. D. 363.

the interior parts of Babylonia, for the use of the fields and the neighbouring cities ... (trans.: J. C. Rolfe, LCL)

39. Ammianus XXIV 2,9[51]

Quo negotio itidem gloriose perfecto, ad civitatem Pirisaboram ventum est, amplam et populosam, ambitu insulari circumvallatam.

When this undertaking also had been accomplished with glory, we came to the large and populous city of Pirisabora, surrounded on all sides by the river. (trans.: J. C. Rolfe, LCL)

40. Zosimus III 17,3–5

Ἐλθὼν δὲ εἰς πόλιν ᾗ Βηρσαβῶρα ἦν ὄνομα, τὸ μέγεθος ἐσκόπει τῆς πόλεως καὶ τὸ τῆς θέσεως ὀχυρόν· δύο μὲν γὰρ κυκλοτερέσι περιείληπτο τείχεσιν, ἀκρόπολις δ' ἦν ἐν μέσῳ τεῖχος ἔχουσα καὶ αὐτή, τμήματι κύκλου τρόπον τινὰ ἐμφερές, πρὸς ἣν ὁδός τις ἦν ἀπὸ τοῦ ἐνδοτέρου τῆς πόλεως τείχους, οὐδὲ αὐτὴ ῥᾳδίαν ἔχουσα τὴν ἀνάβασιν. Καὶ τὰ μὲν πρὸς δυσμὰς τῆς πόλεως καὶ μεσημβρίαν περιφερής τις καὶ σκολιὰ διέξοδος εἶχε, τοῦ δὲ πρὸς ἄρκτον μέρους παρασπασάμενοι τοῦ ποταμοῦ διώρυχα πλατεῖαν προυβάλοντο, δι' ἧς καὶ ὕδωρ εἰς χρῆσιν τῶν ἐνοικούντων ὠχέτευον. Τὰ δὲ πρὸς ἕω τάφρῳ βαθείᾳ καὶ χάρακι διὰ σταυρωμάτων ἐκ ξύλων ὀχυρῶν ἐναπείληπτο· πύργοι δὲ εἱστήκεσαν περὶ τὴν τάφρον μεγάλοι, τὰ μὲν ἀπὸ γῆς μέχρι μέσου δι' ὀπτῆς πλίνθου δεδεμένης ἀσφάλτῳ, τὰ δὲ μετὰ τὸ μέσον πλίνθῳ τε ὁμοίᾳ καὶ γύψῳ δεδομημένα.

He came to a city named Bersabora, the size of which he surveyed, as well as the strength of its position; for the city was encircled by two walls, and at its center stood a citadel having its own wall, one that somewhat resembled the segment of a circle. To this citadel a road with a by no means easy grade led from the city's inner wall. In addition, to the west and south of the town there was a turning and twisting way out, while the side to the north the inhabitants had protected with a wide channel diverted from the river; through this channel, too, they drew water for their private use. Finally the side to the east was fenced around with a deep ditch and a palisade made out of stout wooden pales; about the ditch there stood tall towers built, from the ground up to their mid-point, of bricks laid with asphalt and, beyond that point, of the same kind of bricks plus gypsum. (trans.: J. J. Buchanan and A. T. Davis, TUP)

B. *Already Proposed Location*

Anbār, on the east bank of the Euphrates, near presentday al-Fallūǧa (C 2 on the Tal. Bab. map).

---

[51] Julian's siege in 363; see also ibid., 2,12 and 2,22 and Zosimus (Source 40).

C. *Identification*

According to Obermeyer,[52] Pumbədita should be identified with al-Anbār, across from Dimimmā (see the entry on "Damim") which should be identified with Fīrūz Šāpūr.
Both are at the diffluence of Nahr Ṣaqlawīya (ʿĪsā) and the Euphrates, near modern al-Fallūğa. While Obermeyer argued that there were two separate places, Andreas identified Anbār with Fīrūz Šāpūr.[53] Founded as the Sassanian capital on the south bank of Nahr ʿĪsā by Shapur I, or perhaps Shapur II (see below), Fīrūz Šāpūr declined in the Muslim period. The place called Anbār, although mentioned in ancient sources, did not become important until the seventh century.[54] A bishop of the Nestorian Syrians resided there. From about 750 the caliphs established themselves in the place.[55] Ptolemy mentions 'Αγκωβαρῖτις as the name of a region.[56] According to Andreas, this is an indirect reference to Anbār, Persian for "warehouse."[57] As noted by both Andreas and Obermeyer, the place served as a logistic base for the Persian army when it marched against the Romans. In the second century it was on the border, which according to an Arab source was in the neighborhood of Anbār (see the entry on "Aqra də-Tulbanqe"). In the third century, the border was at Circesium, some 400 kilometers upstream (see the entry on "Qarquza"). Earlier sources do not contain any reference by name to the place. Xenophon (Source 36) passed the site.
As pointed out by Obermeyer, Josephus was aware of Nəhardəʿa, but not of Pumbədita, as a center of Babylonian Jewry; in his view, Josephus' expression (Source 37), "the Parting of the River" is a translation of Syriac Pallughtha (Arabic Fallūğa; Aramaic Pum-Bədita). Herzfeld notes that Ammianus' description (XXIV 3, 14) occurs[58] almost word for word in the Syrian Chronicle: "A village named Pallughtha, where the water of the Euphrates divides itself for the irrigation of the land."[59] The verb *mitpalgin* (= divide) explains the name, which is found even in Greek sources.[60]

---

[52] Obermeyer, pp. 215–218.

[53] Andreas, *RE*, vol. 1, cols. 1790–1795, s.v. "Ambara."

[54] The name Anbār appears first in Theophylactus (III 10, 6; IV 10, 4) in connection with Khusro I (573) as 'Αββάρων φρούριον (see *RE*, vol. 1, col. 1793f. for further Byzantine sources).

[55] The ruins of Anbār, called Umburra by the Arabs, are on the west bank of the Ṣaqlawīya canal (Obermeyer, p. 219). Le Strange identifies Anbār with the ruins marked Sifeyra on modern maps ("Ibn Serapion," pp. 52–53) and see also Fransīs & ʿAwwād, *Sumer* 8 (1952): 252–253; Streck, *EI*[1], s.v. "Anbār"; Streck-Dūrī, *EI*[2], s.v. "Anbār." On the pre-Islamic Anbār market, see Ğāḥiẓ, *Ḥayawān*, vol. 4, pp. 369–370.

[56] Ptolemy, V 18, 4.

[57] Andreas, *RE*, vol. 1, col. 1792.

[58] Herzfeld, *Samarra*, p. 13.

[59] Nöldeke, *SAWW phil.-hist. Klasse*, 128, 9 (1893), p. 36.

[60] Appian, *Civil Wars*, II 153; Arrian, *Anabasis* VII 21. See also Strabo XVI 1, 11.

In Source 38 Ammianus mentions Macepracta which he locates north of Anbār. Obermeyer believes the name is derived from *mata bərakta*, "a place of blessing." In Herzfeld's[61] view, the passage refers to Mavrakta (q.v.) near Maḥoza, and Ammianus erred in its location. The Pirisabora[62] that Ammianus mentions in Source 39 does not figure in the Talmud, but only in gaonic literature.[63] Obermeyer's identification of it with talmudic Be Šabur is doubtful.[64] Maricq has taken air photographs and reconstructed the town plan as discernible from them; he was able to identify on his photographs the Sassanian citadel destroyed by Julian in 363.[65]

Maricq and Herzfeld agree on the identification of Misikhe-Mayk (of the Kaʿba inscription of Shapur I) with Fīrūz Šāpūr/Pirisabora (Ammianus)/Βηρσαβῶρα (Zosimus), as refounded by Shapur/Anbār, although they were apparently unfamiliar with each other's work.

Maricq criticizes Obermeyer's suggestion that Anbār and Fīrūz Šāpūr were two different places because they happen to lie on opposite banks of the Nahr ʿĪsā. Maricq points out that Anbār is the usual Sassanian name for the town earlier called Fīrūz Šāpūr, and that the course of the canal changed in post-Sassanian years.

Maricq also states that Obermeyer's identification of Anbār with Pumbədita is hardly defensible,[66] the only basis being an arbitrary correction of the text

---

[61] Herzfeld, *Samarra*, pp. 15–16.

[62] There are two versions of the construction of Fīrūz Šāpūr: One is that it was built by Shapur I (241–272) who called it Fīrūz Šāpūr (= Shapur's victory) to commemorate his triumph over Gordian in 243 (Ḥamza, *Ta'rīḫ*, p. 49; Herzfeld, *Samarra*, p. 12). The other is that it was built by Shapur II (309–379), according to Ṭabarī, vol. 2, p. 57 (= vol. 1, p. 839) as per the correction proposed by Nöldeke, *Perser und Araber*, p. 57. See also Yāqūt, s.vv. "Fīrūzasābūr" and "Anbār"; Dīnawarī, *Aḫbār ṭiwāl*, vol. 1, p. 51; Ṯaʿālibī, *Ġurar*, p. 529. Streck (*EI*[1], s.v. "Anbār") assumed that its construction by Shapur II was actually the fortification and reconstruction of an older place. This assumption has been supported by the survey of remains which provide evidence of the existence of a pre-Sassanian town. Dūrī (*EI*[2], s.v. "Anbār") on the other hand believed that Shapur II did not build the city.

[63] On Firuz Šabur see *Iggeret Rav Sherira Gaon* (Lewin ed., pp. 99–101).

[64] "Rami b. Abba said, Rabbi Isaac said, A person who sees the Euphrates at Gišra də-Bavel says, Blessed is the Doer of the work of creation, and now the Persians changed it from Be Šabur up" (Berakhot 59b). The source thus attests that because the Persians changed the course of the river, the blessing "Blessed is the Doer of the work of creation" could no longer be said at Gišra də-Bavel (see the section on Physical Features in the entry on "Babylon") but only from Be Šabur and further upstream on the Euphrates (the Munich MS, however, does not have the sentence beginning "and now the Persians").

[65] Maricq, *Syria* 35 (1958): 353–355 = *Classica et Orientalia*, pp. 95–97, with figs. 3, 4 and Pls. I–II; *Classica et Orientalia*, pp. 147–156, with figs. 1–5 and Pls. V–VI. Maricq notes that Anbār was described only once, by Ward, *Hebraica* 2 (1885): 79–86.

[66] *Op.cit.*, p. 97, n. 1.

of Benjamin of Tudela.[67] However, he disregards Obermeyer's argument based on the meaning of the name Pum-Badita.[68]
It should be borne in mind furthermore that the identification of Anbār with Pumbədita is not based on an "arbitrary correction" of Benjamin of Tudela. That correction, already proposed by Graetz, is based on the statement in the Letter of Nathan the Babylonian which says *bi-Pumbadita wa-hiya l-Anbār* (= in Pumbədita which is Anbār).[69] Thus there are grounds for Obermeyer's identification, although additional evidence would certainly be welcome.[70]

D. *The Center in Pumbədita*

The importance of Pumbədita is shown in Source 1, as Rav Joseph, head of the Pumbədita yeshiva in the third generation of Babylonian amoras, claims that the term "Exile"—that figures in the Mishnah (Rosh ha-Shanah II 4) as the place which in the Second Temple period received the fire signal announcing the start of the new month—meant Pumbədita. The Pumbədita yeshiva, among the largest in Babylonia, was founded by Rav Judah of the second generation of Babylonian amoras, a disciple of Rav and Samuel, after the Palmyrans had devastated Nəhardəʿa in 259.[71] Following Abbaye's death (in 338) the Pumbədita yeshiva moved temporarily to Maḥoza (q.v.) and functioned there under Rava's direction. According to Source 4, the development was foreseen by Rava in a dream. That source obviously seeks to provide

---

67 *Itinerary of Benjamin of Tudela*, Adler ed., pp. 34, 46.

68 Honigmann and Maricq, p. 114, n. 2, quote the *Iggeret Rav Sherira Gaon* as saying that the members of the yeshiva at Pumbədita fled to Fīrūz Šāpūr during the persecution by Hormizd IV (588); see the Lewin edition of the *Iggeret*, p. 99. If this is a reliable tradition, Pumbədita is not the same place as Fīrūz Šāpūr but somewhere in the neighborhood.

69 Graetz, *Geschichte*, vol. 5, p. 444, n. 1; and see Carmoly, *Notice historique sur Benjamin de Tudela*, vol. 2, p. 18; Friedlaender, *JQR* 17 (1905): 753; Friedlaender notes (p. 756, n. 3) that the words *wa-hiya l-anbār* are missing in the Hebrew version. Cf. Pinsker, *Liquṭei Qadmoniot* (1860), p. 42. See also *Mustaufī* (vol. 2, p. 44): King Luhrasb the Kayaniyan built Anbār for the captives Shapur II brought here from Jerusalem. King Shapur II rebuilt it, and as-Saffāḥ, the first Abbasid caliph, erected many fortified buildings here and made it his capital.

70 de Goeje proposed identifying Pumbədita with al-Ǧubba (on the basis of another version of the name in the *Itinerary of Benjamin of Tudela*) but the proposal is not acceptable. The same is true of his proposal that Pumbədita was located at the diffluence of the Budāt (or Badāt) canal and the Euphrates (de Goeje, *ZDMG* 39 [1885]: 10; Musil, *The Middle Euphrates*, p. 276f.). On linguistic grounds it may well be assumed that Pumbədita lay on a canal, but this cannot have been the Budāt canal which irrigated the land around Kūfa. Pumbədita must have been in the North in the area of Anbār (cf. Musil, *loc.cit.*; Streck, *Die alte Landschaft*, vol. 1, pp. 16, 20, 30; Suhrāb, p. 125; Le Strange, "Ibn Serapion," pp. 16–17, 257–260.)

71 See *Iggeret Rav Sherira Gaon*, Lewin ed., p. 82, and see the entries on "Tadmor" and "Nəhardəʿa."

additional justification for the predominance of Rava, which led to the transfer of the yeshiva from its permanent site to his town. The versions of this source in the Paris and Florence manuscripts have the term מתיבתא דפומבדיתא (= the Pumbədita yeshiva; see also note 4). No other designations of this kind i.e. "a yeshiva of a certain place," occur in the T.B.[72] After Rava's death in 352 the yeshiva moved back to Pumbədita and continued to operate there throughout the talmudic period and in part of the gaonic period as well.[73] During most of the talmudic period the yeshivas of Pumbədita and Sura (q.v.) were the chief ones in Babylonia. They developed independent learning methods and traditions, and in many places in the Talmud their teachings are contrasted, often with the introductory phrases "in Sura they taught thus, in Pumbədita they taught thus" as in Source 10, for example. Source 9 notes various titles and functions of the Pumbədita sages—judges, elders, amoras, keen intellects —and names the amoras who were so designated. The extraordinary cleverness ascribed to the Pumbədita amoras led to a critical tone as discernible in Source 8 which characterizes the Pumbəditans as threading an elephant through the eye of a needle. Deeds and rulings of the Pumbədita amoras are referred to in many sources (among them 13, 15, 20, 21, 22, 23). The teaching and learning activities in the yeshivas and even streets of Pumbədita, as well as the *pirqa* and *yarḥei kallah* are mentioned or implied in Sources 5, 6, 7 and 14, among others.[74]

E. *The Inhabitants*

The Pumbəditans were conscious of the value of the yeshiva in their town, and the sages constituted a social and leadership elite. A clear example of the special privileges enjoyed by the scholars is provided by Source 16 which indicates that the Pumbədita butchers were accustomed to giving first choice to Rav Judah's steward.[75] While the case it deals with concerns a Nəhardəʿan who did not recognize Rav Judah's greatness, or perhaps had never heard of him, the source demonstrates the extra benefits accorded to scholars, and these are confirmed elsewhere as well.[76] The practice of favoring scholars seems to have been a counterpart of the custom that developed in Eretz Israel at the time of allocating "priestly gifts" to scholars,[77] thus recognizing that the scholar's role in community life paralleled that of the priests in the Temple.

---

[72] See Goodblatt, *Rabbinic Instruction*, pp. 83, 265; Gafni, *Ha-Yeshiva be-Bavel*, pp. 67–68.

[73] From the beginning of the tenth century on, the head of the Pumbədita yeshiva lived in Baghdad.

[74] On the *pirqa* and *yarḥei kallah* see the index, and Gafni, *ibid.*, pp. 108–148, and the bibliography there; Goodblatt, *Rabbinic Instruction*, pp. 155–170.

[75] See Beer, *Amora'ei Bavel*, pp. 250–251, 287; Beer, *Rashut ha-Golah*, pp. 92–93.

[76] Cf. Berakhot 44b and Ḥullin 44b on Rava's taking the best meat.

[77] See Oppenheimer, *Sinai* 83 (1978): 282–287.

Sources 2 and 3 treat problems of purity of lineage, a matter that preoccupied the Babylonian amoras a good deal. Source 2, which is concerned with the status of Biram (q.v.) in that respect, mentions "those of pure lineage from Pumbədita." Thus, alongside the scholarly elite, Pumbədita had an elite of wealthy, influential property owners.

The sources also contain pejorative expressions applied to the Pumbəditans, such as "most of the thieves are Jews" (Source 17), or the advice to travelers escorted by a Pumbəditan to move to other accommodations lest they be robbed (Source 18), or designating the local craftsmen as "deceivers of Pumbədita" (Source 19). However, no far-reaching conclusions should be drawn from such sources regarding the ethical standards of the Pumbəditans. A number of those sources deal, not with the Pumbəditan character, but with halakhic questions. One question, for example, is whether wine left in a cask opened by thieves may be drunk, or must be discarded as suspect libation wine. The answer in Source 17—"most of the thieves are Jews"—means merely that in such a densely Jewish area as Pumbədita, the chances are that the thieves were Jewish, so the wine may be drunk.[78] The derogatory expressions in other sources too should be viewed as a reflection of local or inter-city tensions, or run-of-the-mill malice of daily life, rather than as a true portrait of the Pumbəditans. Source 11 too, stating that the refuse heaps of Mata Məḥasya are more desirable than the mansions of Pumbədita, is obviously a case of local patriotism in the rivalry between two major yeshiva towns.

F. *Relations with Gentiles*

The relations between Jews and Gentiles in Pumbədita are connected on the one hand with the administrative center at Fīrūz Šāpūr and on the other with the location of Pumbədita on the Euphrates at the border, which made it vulnerable to forays by the nomadic tribes of the northern Syrian desert.

Source 27 describes an incident involving the appearance in Pumbədita of a commander (*rufila*) who arbitrarily took possession of wine casks.[79] Source 26 mentions a πόλεμος that came to Pumbədita, and whether the term designates a war or a military unit, the reason for it was most likely a confrontation between the Sassanian authorities and the nomads.[80] Sources 24 and 25 refer

---

[78] Cf. the following disagreement between Rav and Samuel: "A barrel floating in the river. Rav said, Found opposite a city mostly Jewish, [it is] allowed; opposite a city mostly Gentile, forbidden. And Samuel said, Even if found opposite a city mostly Jewish, forbidden." (Bava Batra 24a); see the entry on "Ihi də-Qira." Cf. also the problem submitted to Abbaye, head of the Pumbədita yeshiva in the fourth generation of Babylonian amoras, regarding a bird of prey that dropped a piece of meat it had snatched in the market; there too the point is made that most of the inhabitants are Jewish (Bava Metziʿa 24b).

[79] On the place of this function in the hierarchy, see Shevuʿot 6b, and n. 35 above.

[80] See Beer, *Rashut ha-Golah*, p. 212.

to members of nomadic tribes who arrived in Pumbədita, but in quite different terms. Source 25 calls the Arabs land-grabbers, while Source 24 mentions an Arab who donated a lamp to Rav Judah's synagogue.

G. *Economy*

The available information on the economy of Pumbəditan Jews is not very enlightening.[81] Source 20 refers to a flax market; the existence of a special market for flax and flax products indicates the importance of that item in Babylonia in general and Pumbədita in particular.[82] Source 15 mentions a man called Rami b. Tamare or Rami b. Diqule. It seems likely that the last element in his name is not a patronymic, but connected with his business, involving palm trees (*deqel* = palm) and their fruit (*tamar* = date).[83] Source 22 refers to a regular distribution of charity to the poor of Pumbədita, providing some indication of the operation of municipal welfare institutions in Jewish Pumbədita.

H. *The Pumbədita Periphery*

The sources refer to a number of places in the periphery of Pumbədita. Source 32 names Ṣinta (q. v.) which was the permitted Sabbath walking distance (about one kilometer) from Pumbədita, and Arṭivna (q. v.), the same distance from Ṣinta. Be Kube (q. v.) is said to be a neighbor of Pumbədita in Sources 28, 29, 30 and 31. No more than a day's distance from Pumbədita were Be Rav (q. v.) and Be Torta.[84] Places in the Pumbədita area are also listed in Source 14 which describes Rabbah's escape route (see the entry on "Damim"). Another place in the area was Be Ḥarmak̲ (see appendix).
Source 31 refers to Astunya, a place whose name seems to be derived from the Persian *istān*, meaning "district."[85]

ALON, *Meḥqarim* (1958), vol. 2, pp. 298–302
ANDREAS, *RE*, vol. 1, cols. 1790–1795, "Ambara"
BEER, *Rashut ha-Golah* (1970), passim
BEER, *Amora'ei Bavel* (1974), passim
BERLINER, *Beiträge* (1883), pp. 15, 57
ESHEL, *Yishuvei ha-Yehudim* (1979), pp. 208–211

[81] For a general treatment see Yudelevitz, *Pumbedita*, pp. 9–21.

[82] See Newman, *Agricultural Life*, p. 104.

[83] See Hyman, pp. 1103–1104; Beer, *Amora'ei Bavel*, p. 105, n. 65.

[84] Be Torta is mentioned in Sanhedrin 64a, and there too in connection with Rav Manasseh (of the third generation of Babylonian amoras and a disciple of Rav Judah, head of the Pumbədita yeshiva) who goes there. The relative propinquity of Be Torta to Pumbədita refutes Neubauer's identification of the former with a place south of Nahr Malka. See Neubauer, p. 363 and Eshel, p. 71.

[85] Thus it seems reasonable to identify it with Fīrūz Šāpūr (see the section above on Identification) which was the administrative center. See Obermeyer, pp. 228–229. *Iggeret Rav Sherira Gaon* states that there were 90,000 Jews in Firuz Šabur at the time of the Muslim conquest (Lewin ed., p. 101).

FLORSHEIM, *Zion* 39 (1974): 183–197
FRANSĪS & ʿAWWĀD, *Sumer* 8 (1952): 252–253
FUNK, *Juden* (1902–1908), vol. 1, pp. 7, 59, 84; vol. 2, pp. 26, 79, 85, 155–156
FUNK, *Monumenta* (1913), pp. 48, 289, 298, 302
GAFNI, *Ha-Yeshiva be-Bavel* (1978), passim
GOODBLATT, *Rabbinic Instruction* (1975), passim
GOODBLATT, *HUCA* 48 (1977): 187–217
GRAETZ, *Geschichte* (1908–1909⁴), vol. 4, pp. 250f., 319f., vol. 5, p. 444 n. 1
HERZFELD, *Samarra* (1948), p. 16
HIRSCHENSON, *Sheva Ḥokhmot* (1883), pp. 181–184
JASTROW, *Dictionary* (1950³), p. 1142
KOHUT, *Arukh ha-Shalem* (1878–1892), vol. 6, pp. 359–360
KRAUSS, *Qadmoniot ha-Talmud* (1923–1945), vol. 1A, pp. 19, 37, 85; vol. 2B, p. 65
LEVY, *Wörterbuch* (1924²), vol. 4, pp. 14–15
MARICQ, *Syria* 35 (1958): 353–355 (= Classica et Orientalia, pp. 95–97)
MUSIL, *The Middle Euphrates* (1927), index
NEUBAUER, *Géographie* (1868), p. 349
NEUSNER, *History* (1965–1970), 5 vols., passim
NEWMAN, *Agricultural Life* (1932), index
NÖLDEKE, *SAWW phil. hist. Klasse* 128, 9 (1893), p. 37f.
OBERMEYER, *Landschaft* (1929), pp. 218–244, index
STRECK, *Die alte Landschaft* (1900), vol. 1, pp. 16, 20, 30
STRECK, *EI¹*, s.v. "Anbār"
STRECK-DŪRĪ, *EI²*, s.v. "Anbār"
WIDENGREN, *Iranica Antiqua* 1 (1961): 147
YUDELEVITZ, *Yeshivat Pumbedita* (1932)
YUDELEVITZ, *Pumbedita* (1939)

Pum Nahara פום נהרא

A. *Sources*

1. ʿEruvin 24b

ההיא רחבה דהואי בפום נהרא דחד גיסא הוה פתיח למתא וחד גיסא הוה פתיח לשביל של כרמים, ושביל של כרמים הוה סליק לגודא דנהרא . . .

That open space in Pum Nahara, one side of it was open to the town, and the other side to a path of vineyards, and the path of vineyards rose toward the river bank . . .

2. Yevamot 16b; Qiddushin 72b

"צוה ה׳ ליעקב סביביו צריו," אמר רב[1] כגון הומניא[2] לפום נהרא.

"The Lord has commanded against Jacob that his neighbors should be his foes," (Lam. 1:17) Rav[1] said, Like Humaniya[2] to Pum Nahara.

---

[1] The Qiddushin parallel has "Rav Judah said." The Munich and Vatican 111 MSS for Yevamot and Qiddushin and *Ginzei Talmud* for Yevamot have "Rav Judah said Rav said."

[2] The Munich MS for Qiddushin has "כגון הרפני׳ והרמני׳ לפום נהר" as does the Oxford MS, and see the entry on "Nəharpanya" and n. 1 there. The Vatican 111 MS of Qiddushin and *Ginzei Talmud* for Yevamot have המוניא, and the Venice printing of Yevamot has הומנאי. See also the entry on "Humaniya."

3. Yevamot 17a

יתיב רב המנונא קמיה דעולא וקא הוי בשמעתא, אמר מה גברא ומה גברא אי לאו דהרפניא מאתיה, איכסיף, א"ל כסף גלגלתא להיכא יהבת, א"ל לפום נהרא, א"ל א"כ מפום נהרא את.

Rav Hamnuna sat before ʿUlla and was [discussing] tradition when the latter said, What a great man [he would be] if Harpanya were not his town. [As the other] was embarrassed he said to him, Where do you pay poll tax? To Pum Nahara, the other replied. If so, he (ʿUlla) said, you are from Pum Nahara.

4. Berakhot 31a; Soṭah 46b

כי הא דרב כהנא[3] אלוייה לרב שימי בר אשי[4] מפום נהרא[5] עד בי צניתא דבבל, כי מטא להתם א"ל מר ודאי דאמרי אינשי הני צניתא דבבל איתנהו מאדם הראשון ועד השתא.

. . . Rav Kahana[3] escorted Rav Shimi b. Ashi[4] from Pum Nahara[5] to the place of the palms at Babylon. When he got there he said to him, Sir, it is known that people say these palms of Babylon have been here from the time of the first Adam up to now.

5. Qiddushin 81b

רב חנן מנהרדעא איקלע לרב כהנא לפום נהרא חזייה דיתיב וקא גרס וקיימא בהמה קמיה . . .

Rav Ḥanan of Nəhardəʿa happened to visit Rav Kahana at Pum Nahara, and saw him sitting and studying while an animal stood before him . . .

6. Ḥullin 95b

רב נחמן[6] מנהרדעא איקלע לגבי רב כהנא לפום נהרא[7] במעלי יומא דכפורי, אתו עורבי שדו כבדי וכוליתא, אמר ליה שקול ואכול האידנא דהיתרא שכיח טפי.

Rav Naḥman[6] of Nəhardəʿa happened to visit Rav Kahana at Pum Nahara[7] on the eve of the Day of Atonement, and ravens came and dropped livers and kidneys. He said to him, Take and eat them, now that the permitted is more common.

---

[3] Some of the MSS for both parallels have "Rav Huna" which seems to be a garble resulting from the addition of the *waw* and deletion of the *kaf*. "Ravina" too is sometimes given, and see Soṭah in the ICIT edition. The *Midrash ha-Gadol* for Genesis has "רב מרדכי אלוייה לרב שימי בר אשי מפום נהרא ועד ציניאתא דבבל. רב כהנא אלוייה לרב אשי . . ." (= Rav Mordecai escorted Rav Shimi b. Ashi from Pum Nahara to the *ṣiniata* (stone palms) of Babylon. Rav Kahana escorted Rav Ashi . . . [*Midrash ha-Gadol* for Genesis 18:16—Margulies ed., p. 303; cf. *ibid.*, 2:19—Margulies ed., p. 86]). And cf. the testimony on Rav Mordecai further on in the passage in Berakhot and Soṭah. See below and also the entry on "Babylon."

[4] The Vatican 110 MS of Soṭah has "to Rav Sheshet."

[5] The Oxford MS for Soṭah has מפום בדיתא (= from Pum Bədita), and see Soṭah in the ICIT ed.

[6] The Munich and Hamburg MSS have "Rav Ḥanan" and see *Diq. Sof.*

[7] The Vatican 122 MS has לפום בדיתא (= to Pum Bədita); the Munich MS has no place name, and see *Diq. Sof.*

7. Moʿed Qaṭan 27b

והא רב כהנא ספדיה לרב זביד מנהרדעא בפום נהרא . . .

And Rav Kahana eulogized Rav Zevid of Nəhardəʿa in Pum Nahara [on a holiday] . . .

8. Bava Batra 22a

הנהו עמוראי דאייתו עמרא לפום נהרא, אתו בני מתא קא מעכבי עלויהו, אתו לקמיה דרב כהנא,[8] אמר להו דינא הוא דמעכבי עלייכו. אמרו ליה אית לן אשראי[9] אמר להו זילו זבנו שיעור חיותייכו עד דאקריתו אשראי דידכו ואזליתו.

Some wool merchants brought wool to Pum Nahara; the townspeople came and stopped them. They went to Rav Kahana[8] who said to them, It is right for them to stop you. They said, We have a credit[9] [in the town]. He said to them, Go sell enough for your livelihood till you extract your credit, and [then] go.

9. Bava Batra 88a

ההוא גברא דאייתי קארי לפום נהרא,[10] אתו כולי עלמא שקול קרא קרא, אמר להו הרי הן מוקדשין לשמים, אתו לקמיה דרב כהנא, אמר להו אין אדם מקדיש דבר שאינו שלו.

A man brought pumpkins to Pum Nahara.[10] Everyone came and took a pumpkin. He said to them, But these are dedicated to God. They went to Rav Kahana, and he said, Nobody can dedicate something that is not his.

10. Bava Batra 36b

שלחו ליה בני פום נהרא לרב נחמן בר רב חסדא[11] ילמדנו רבנו נירא הוי חזקה או לא הוי חזקה, אמר להו ר׳ אחא וכל גדולי הדור אמרי ניר הרי זה חזקה.

The people of Pum Nahara sent to Rav Naḥman b. Rav Ḥisda[11] [requesting] Will our master teach us whether ploughed fallow land confers *ḥazaqah* (= claim to title) or not. He said to them, Rabbi Aḥa and all the great men of the generation say that ploughed fallow land is *ḥazaqah*.

11. Qiddushin 13a

קשו בה בפום נהרא משמיה דרב הונא בריה דרב יהושע . . .

A difficulty was raised in Pum Nahara in the name of Rav Huna son of Rav Joshua . . .

B. *Proposed Location*

Near Nəharpanya (q.v., C5 on the Tal. Bab. map).

---

[8] The Oxford MS has "to Rava."

[9] The Oxford MS and Lublin printing have in addition the word *bemata* (= in the settlement of), and see *Diq. Sof.*

[10] The Vatican 115 has לפומבדיתא (= to Pumbədita), and see *Diq. Sof.*

[11] The Munich MS and Lublin printing have "to Rav Ḥisda."

C. *Identification*

The sources dealing with Pum Nahara provide a number of indications for its identification but do not pinpoint its exact location. Sources 2 and 3 suggest that Pum Nahara is in the vicinity of Humaniya (q.v.) and Nəharpanya (q.v.).[12] Source 1 indicates the proximity of Pum Nahara to a river bank, and that proximity is inferrable also from its name. The name Pum Nahara (= mouth of the river) shows that the place is situated where a canal branches off from a river (or another canal).[13] As the supply of water was controlled at such a point, it was a natural location for government officials concerned with revenue. Rav Hamnuna of Nəharpanya, of the third generation of Babylonian amoras, paid his poll tax in Pum Nahara,[14] which was evidently the administrative center of the district that included Nəharpanya. The identification of Nəharpanya with Nahr Abān, west of the Euphrates in the Kūfa area, points to the location of Pum Nahara in that same region of southwestern Babylonia.[15]

D. *Sages and Pum Nahara*

A considerable proportion of the sources mentioning Pum Nahara (Sources 4–8) refer to Rav Kahana as the chief sage of the place. The existence of a number of Babylonian amoras by that name makes it difficult to identify the one from Pum Nahara. In view of the sages Rav Kahana was in touch with (see below), he probably belonged to the fifth generation of Babylonian amoras.[16]

The sources report a number of incidents in Pum Nahara on which Rav Kahana was asked to rule. In a dispute between wool dealers of Pum Nahara and outside wool dealers regarding the right of the latter to sell in the local market, Rav Kahana accords the local dealers priority, ruling that outsiders have no right to sell their wares in Pum Nahara. In the specific case considered, how-

[12] The versions of Source 2 in the Munich and Oxford MSS likewise imply the propinquity of Pum Nahara to Nəharpanya, and see n. 2 above.

[13] It should be noted that a name like Pum Nahara probably applied to a number of localities. This entry, however, assumes that all talmudic mentions of Pum Nahara refer to a single place. In the opinion of Sperber (*Iranica Antiqua* 8 [1968]: 71–73) the name Bab Nahara (Sukkah 18a, ʽAvodah Zarah 39a) has a similar meaning to Pum Nahara (*bab* = gate, exit). The name Pum Nahara does appear in some MSS instead of Bab Nahara, and see *Diq. Sof.* for Sukkah 18a, note ל, and Abramson's note, p. 187 in his edition of ʽAvodah Zarah, in the Spanish MS.

[14] Re this episode see the entry on "Nəharpanya." On the payment of the poll tax (= *karga*) in Pum Nahara see Newman, *Agricultural Life*, pp. 169–170; Beer, *Rashut ha-Golah*, pp. 216–217, and *Amora'ei Bavel*, pp. 234–235; Goodblatt, *JESHO* 22 (1979): 260–261.

[15] This refutes Obermeyer's proposal to locate Pum Nahara not far from the bank of the Tigris (pp. 192, 194), which is based on a different method of identification for Humaniya and Nəharpanya.

[16] See Albeck, *Mavo la-Talmudim*, p. 413.

ever, he allows the outsiders to sell their wool locally as long as it takes them to recover a debt some Pum Nahara people owe them.
In Rav Kahana's lifetime, Pum Nahara was a magnet for sages, and the sources report visits by Rav Shimi b. Ashi, Rav Ḥanan of Nəhardəʿa and Rav Naḥman[17] of Nəhardəʿa. Rav Kahana's ties with the Nəhardəʿa sages are indicated as well by the fact (in Source 7) that he eulogized Rav Zevid of Nəhardəʿa at Pum Nahara on a day when eulogies were not customary.[18] Source 10 notes that the Pum Nahara people appealed to Rav Naḥman b. Rav Ḥisda[19] of the fourth generation of Babylonian amoras, who resided in Dəruqart (q.v.).

E. *The Inhabitants*

It appears that most or all of the residents of Pum Nahara were Jewish. Among other things, this is indicated by Rav Kahana in Source 6 when he tells Rav Naḥman of Nəhardəʿa[20] that he is allowing meat dropped by ravens to be eaten, on the assumption that it was ritually slaughtered.[21] That the population was mainly Jewish is shown also by the appeal to Rav Kahana's authority in regard to the wool market in the place. It is suggested also by Source 2 naming Humaniya as the foe of Pum Nahara.

F. *Economy*

As Source 1 refers to a "path of vineyards" going from Pum Nahara to the river bank viniculture and wine-making were evidently among the Pum Nahara occupations. This further confirms the proximity of the place to Nəharpanya (q.v.) for which the sources likewise indicate vineyards and the wine trade. It will be recalled that grapevines were not common in Babylonia but confined

---

[17] According to the MSS and *Rishonim* versions of Source 6, this should also be Rav Ḥanan of Nəhardəʿa and not Rav Naḥman of Nəhardəʿa (n. 6 above), and perhaps so. This is Hyman's opinion in the entry on "Rav Kahana (d)," but in the entry on "Rav Ḥanan of Nəhardəʿa" he suggests that Source 5 should be "Rav Naḥman" as well (Hyman, pp. 847, 472–473).

[18] Rav Kahana held frequent discussions with Rav Zevid of Nəhardəʿa. The statement אמר רב כהנא אמריתה לשמעתא קמיה דרב זביד מנהרדעא (= Rav Kahana said, I said the tradition before Rav Zevid of Nəhardəʿa) appears in a number of places in the Talmud (e.g. T. B. Yevamot 18b, 48b; Bava Qamma 16a, 71b). On the eulogy for Rav Zevid see Neusner, *History*, vol. 5, p. 172.

[19] There is also a variant "Rav Ḥisda" (n. 11 above).

[20] See n. 17 above.

[21] The reason for the permission may have been that slaughtering was concentrated in Jewish hands, or that since the affair occurred on the eve of the Day of Atonement, when considerable quantities of food are prepared and consumed, the likelihood that the meat was ritually slaughtered was especially strong. In either case the ruling is evidence of a predominantly Jewish population in the place.

to particular regions suitable for their cultivation.[22] Further information on the economy of Pum Nahara is provided by Source 8 which indicates the presence of a wool market there.[23]

BEER, *Rashut ha-Golah* (1970), pp. 216–217
BEER, *Amora'ei Bavel* (1974), pp. 92, 168, 234–235, 307–308
BERLINER, *Beiträge* (1883), p. 58
ESHEL, *Yishuvei ha-Yehudim* (1979), pp. 211–212
FUNK, *Juden* (1902–1908), vol. 1, p. 19; vol. 2, p. 85
FUNK, *Monumenta* (1913), pp. 49, 298
GOODBLATT, *JESHO* 22 (1979): 260–261
HALEVY, *Dorot ha-Rishonim* (1897–1939), vol. 5, pp. 515–522
HIRSCHENSON, *Sheva Ḥokhmot* (1883), p. 194
JASTROW, *Dictionary* (1950³), p. 883
JOËL, *MGWJ* 16 (1867): 330–331, 378–387
KOHUT, *Arukh ha-Shalem* (1878–1892), vol. 6, p. 360
KRAUSS, *Qadmoniot ha-Talmud* (1923–1945), vol. 1A, p. 76
LEVY, *Wörterbuch* (1924²), vol. 4, p. 15
NEUBAUER, *Géographie* (1868), pp. 366–367
NEUSNER, *History* (1965–1970), vol. 2, pp. 244, 247; vol. 3, pp. 261, 299–302; vol. 4, pp. 172–173, 238; vol. 5, pp. 146, 172
NEWMAN, *Agricultural Life* (1932), pp. 7, 97, 170
OBERMEYER, *Landschaft* (1929), pp. 192, 194–196, 199, 220, 304 n. 1
ZURI, *Shilton* (1938), pp. 224–226

Qardu קרדו

A. *Sources*

1. Bava Batra 91a[1]

ואמר רב חנן בר רבא אמר רב עשר שנים נחבש אברהם אבינו, שלש בכותא[2] ושבע בקרדו,[3] ורב דימי מנהרדעא מתני איפכא.

And Rav Ḥanan b. Rava said that Rav said, Our forefather Abraham was imprisoned for ten years, three in Kuta[2] and seven in Qardu,[3] and Rav Dimi of Nəhardəʿa taught the opposite.

---

[22] See Beer, *Amora'ei Bavel*, pp. 91–92. On the other hand, it is hard to understand Beer's remark elsewhere in his book that "the residents of Pum Nahara were dependent on the supply of wine brought from other regions" (p. 168).

[23] See Krauss, *Qadmoniot ha-Talmud*, vol. 1A, p. 76; Funk, *Juden*, vol. 1, p. 19.

[1] The parallel in Pirqe de-Rabbi Eliezer has: "נסיון השני נתנוהו בבית האסורים עשר שנים, ג' בכותה וז' בקרדי, ויש אומרים ג' בקרדי וז' בכותה" (= The second trial they put him in prison for ten years, three in Kuta and seven in Qardu, and some say, three in Qardu and seven in Kuta; Ch. XXVI). Cf. also *Yalquṭ Shimʿoni*: "הנס השני, נחבש בבית האסורין עשר שנים, שלש בכותי ושבע בכרדו" (= The second miracle, he was imprisoned for ten years, three in Kuti and seven in Kardu [*Yalquṭ Shimʿoni* for Genesis, § 68, Mossad Harav Kook ed., pp. 257–258 and the note to l. 67 there; see also p. 303, the note to l. 79]).

[2] The Munich MS has "in prison," and see *Diq. Sof*.

[3] The Munich MS has באור כשדים, the Hamburg MS has בקדרו, *Aggadot ha-Talmud* has בנדרו, and see *Diq. Sof*.

2. Yevamot 16a

... אבל מעיד אני עלי שמים וארץ שעל מדוכה זו ישב חגי הנביא ואמר שלשה דברים צרת הבת אסורה, עמון ומואב מעשרין מעשר עני בשביעית, ומקבלים גרים מן הקרדויין[4] ומן התרמודים[5]... ומקבלים גרים מן הקרדויים[6] והתרמודים. איני, והא תני רמי בר יחזקאל אין מקבלים גרים מן הקרדויים, אמר רב אשי[7] קרתויים אתמר, כדאמרי אינשי קרתויים[8] פסולים. ואיכא דאמרי תני רמי בר יחזקאל אין מקבלים גרים מן הקרתויים, מאי לאו היינו קרתויים היינו קרדויים, אמר רב אשי לא, קרתויי לחוד וקרדויי לחוד, כדאמרי אינשי קרתויי פסילי.

... but I call to witness heaven and earth that the prophet Haggai sat on this mortar and said three things: A daughter's rival is forbidden, ʿAmmon and Moab give the tithe of the poor in the seventh [year], and converts are accepted from among the Qarduans[4] and the Tarmodans[5] ... and accept converts from the Qarduans[6] and the Tarmodans. Indeed? For Rami b. Ezekiel taught, Converts of the Qarduans are not acceptable. Rav Ashi[7] said, It said Qartuans, as the people say, disqualified Qartuans.[8] And others say Rami b. Ezekiel taught, Converts from the Qartuans are not acceptable. Are not Qartuans Qarduans? Rav Ashi said, No, Qartuans are separate and Qarduans are separate, as the people say Qartuans are disqualified.

3. T. J. Yevamot I 6 – 3b, 2–3; T. J. Qiddushin IV 1 – 65c, 17–18

רב נחמן בר יעקב אמר מקבלין גרים מן הקרדויין ומן התדמוריים.

Rav Naḥman b. Jacob said, Converts are acceptable from the Qarduans and the Tadmorans.

4. Genesis Rabbah XXXIII 4 (Theodor-Albeck ed., p. 309)[9]

"ותנח התיבה בחדש וגו' על הרי אררט" על טורי קרדונייה.[10]

"And the ark in the seventh month came to rest on the mountains of Ararat" (Gen. 8:4) on the mountains of Qardunya.[10]

5. Pesaḥim 7a; 21b

דאמר רב גידל אמר רבי חייא בר יוסף אמר רב[11] המקדש משש שעות ולמעלה אפילו בחיטי קורדניתא[12] אין חוששין לקידושין.

---

[4] The parallel in Seder Eliahu Zuṭa has "ומקבלין גרים מן הקרדמיים ומן התרמודיים" (Seder Eliahu Zuṭa, I, Friedmann ed., p. 169.)

[5] For variants see the entry on "Tadmor."

[6] The Munich MS has קרויים.

[7] The Vatican 111 MS has "Rav said" here, but "Rav Ashi" further on.

[8] The Munich MS has קרויי.

[9] Cf. the Targum Onqelos and Targum Jonathan of Gen. 8:4 (respectively טורי קדרו, and טורי דקדרון), and that is the form of the translations of other places in the Bible where the Ararat mountains are mentioned.

[10] Versions of Genesis Rabbah have as well קרדוניא; קורדונייה; קרדניא; and see the Theodor-Albeck edition and the notes there too.

[11] The parallel in Pesaḥim 21b has "Rabbi Yoḥanan," but the Munich and Oxford MSS have "Rav" there; see *Diq. Sof.*

[12] The source has קורדניתא. Cf. T. J. Pesaḥim I 4 – 27c, 62.

Rav Giddal said, Rabbi Ḥiyya b. Joseph quoted Rav[11] as saying, If a person is betrothed from the sixth hour on [on Passover eve] even with the wheat of Qardu[12] his betrothal is non-existent.

B. *Already Proposed Location*

The Qardā region, in the area of presentday Kurdistan (on Bab. Env. map).

C. *Identification*

The Qardā district figures frequently in Arabic sources.[13] Bāzabdā too generally appears there along with Qardā or Bāqardā. Bāqardā and Bāzabdā were two districts across from each other near the Ǧazīrat Ibn ʿUmar north of Mosul on the upper Tigris, Bāqardā east of the river and Bāzabdā west of it.[14]

Eshel, *Yishuvei ha-Yehudim* (1979), pp. 227–229
Funk, *Juden* (1902–1908), p. 30, n. 1
Hirschenson, *Sheva Ḥokhmot* (1883), pp. 221–222
Jastrow, *Dictionary* (1950³), p. 1412
Kohut, *Arukh ha-Shalem* (1878–1892), vol. 4, p. 317; vol. 7, pp. 189–191; *Tosefot* (1937), pp. 233–234, 374
Krauss, *Lehnwörter* (1898), vol. 1, pp. 254–255
Krauss, *Paras we-Romi* (1948), p. 25
Levy, *Wörterbuch* (1924²), vol. 2, pp. 455, 536–537; vol. 4, pp. 372–373, 483–484
Neubauer, *Géographie* (1868), pp. 378–379
Neusner, *History* (1965–1970), vol. 3, pp. 31, 343
Obermeyer, *Landschaft* (1929), pp. 8, 131–135

Qarḥina קרחינא

A. *Sources*

1. Berakhot 33a; Sanhedrin 92a

... מתקיף לה רב אחא קרחינאה [1] אלא מעתה גדולה נקמה שנתנה בין שתי אותיות שנאמר "אל נקמות ה'", אמר ליה אין, במילתה מיהא גדולה היא.

---

[13] See examples in Obermeyer, pp. 131–132. Yāqūt, under "Bāqirdā," notes that such is the form of the name "in the books" and that it is pronounced with a "deflection" as Baqerdā, but that its inhabitants say Qardā. In *EI*², s.v. "Ḳardā" and "Bāzabdā," then, Bāqardā should be corrected to Bāqirdā.

[14] See Yāqūt; *ar-Rauḍ al-miʿṭār*, "Qardā" and "Bāzabdā"; "Qardā" and "Diyār Rabīʿa" in Bakrī; *BGA*, passim. Cf. Idrīsī, vol. 6, p. 660, who says both Bāqardā and Bāzabdā were east of the Tigris; Ibn Ḥauqal, p. 219, who says Qardā is Ǧazīrat Ibn ʿUmar; see also *EI*² on "Ḳardā" and "Bāzabdā" and the bibliography there.

[1] Sanhedrin has "Rav Adda Qarḥina'a," the Munich MS of Berakhot has "Rav Adda b. Ahavah Qarḥina'a," and see *Diq. Sof.* The Florence MS of Sanhedrin has "Rav Aḥa Qarḥina," like the standard edition of Berakhot.

. . . Rav Aḥa Qarḥina'a[1] questioned it. That would mean that revenge between two letters (= two names of God) is great, for it is said, "the Lord is a vengeful God" (Ps. 94 :1). He (Rabbi Eleazar) said to him, Yes, at least of its kind it is great.

2. Yevamot 10a

רב אדא קרחינא[2] קמיה דרב כהנא[3] אמר משמיה דרבא לעולם אית ליה לרבי הני כללי . . .

Rav Adda Qarḥina,[2] before Rav Kahana,[3] said in the name of Rava, Rabbi has always had these principles . . .

3. ʿEruvin 86a

. . . אמר ליה לא שמיע לך הא דתני יעקב קרחינאה[4] צריך שישקע ראשי קנים במים טפח.

. . . He said to him (Abbaye to Rabbah b. Rav Ḥanan), Have you not heard what Jacob Qarḥina'a[4] taught, The reeds [forming a partition in a water hole between two courtyards] need to be sunk a handbreadth in the water.

4. Shabbat 139b–140a (as per the Oxford MS)

ונותנין ביצה במסננת: תני יעקב קרחינאה[5] לפי שאין עושין אותה אלא ליגרון.[6]

And an egg is put in a sieve: Jacob Qarḥina'a[5] taught, Because it is done only for coloring.[6]

5. Shabbat 152a

א"ל ההוא גוזאה לרבי יהושע בן קרחה מהכא לקרחינא כמה הוי, א"ל כמהכא לגוזניא.[7]

That eunuch (= *goza'a*) said to Rabbi Joshua b. Qarḥa (= the bald), What is [the distance] from here to Qarḥina? He said to him, As from here to Gozanya.[7]

B. *Proposed Location*

Karḫīnī (actually pronounced Karḫīne), a fort situated between Daqūqā and Arbela (q.v., on Bab. Env. map).

C. *Identification*

Under "Karḫīnī" Yāqūt describes the fort which he himself saw in the course of a visit. Beautiful and strongly built, it was situated on a tell in the valley,

---

[2] The Vatican 111 MS has "Rav Aḥa Qarḥina." (In the Munich MS the entire passage is in the margin.) See n. 9 below.

[3] The Vatican 111 MS has "before Rava" (and not "said in the name of Rava").

[4] The Munich MS has "יעקב קרחאא," and see *Diq. Sof.*

[5] The standard edition and the other MSS have "יעקב קרחה." The Munich MS has "יעקב בן קרחה."

[6] The Oxford MS has ליגרון, but the standard edition has לגוון which seems correct (the Munich MS has לגיאן).

[7] The Munich MS has "to Goza'a."

between Daqūqā and Irbil. In al-Ḥasanī's view, Karḫīnī is Kirkūk, the only place Yāqūt's description fits.[8]
Source 5 mentions the distance to Qarḥina, but the place is named for the purpose of ridiculing Rabbi Joshua b. Qarḥa who was bald (= קרח). In return the sage makes fun of his castrated interlocutor. See "Gozanya" in the appendix.

D. *Sages and Qarḥina*

Three sages from Qarḥina are mentioned in the sources. Rav Aḥa Qarḥina'a appears in Source 1 in a midrashic discussion with Rabbi Eleazar of the third generation of Eretz Israel amoras, who was of Babylonian origin.[9] Rav Adda Qarḥina figures in Source 2, citing Rava to Rav Kahana of the fifth generation of Babylonian amoras. Source 3 and Source 4 (as per the Oxford MS; see note 5 above) refer to Jacob Qarḥina'a. In Source 3 Abbaye of the third generation of Babylonian amoras proffers a *baraita* of Jacob Qarḥina'a's, and a *baraita* of his is cited in Source 4 as well.[10] As the name of this sage appears variously with Qarḥa and Qarḥina'a, he may in fact be Jacob the Bald (= קרח) rather than Jacob of Qarḥina. The resemblance between Qarḥina and the word for "bald" is the basis for the exchange of insults in Source 5 (and see above).

Eshel, *Yishuvei ha-Yehudim* (1979), p. 229
Graetz, *Das Königreich Mesene* (1879), p. 24, n. 1
Hirschenson, *Sheva Ḥokhmot* (1883), p. 223
Jastrow, *Dictionary* (1950³), p. 1416
Kohut, *Arukh ha-Shalem* (1878–1892), vol. 7, p. 193
Levy, *Wörterbuch* (1924²), vol. 4, p. 375
Neubauer, *Géographie* (1868), p. 389, n. 1

Qarquza (Circesium) קרקוזא

A. *Sources*

1. Nedarim 51a

מאי דלעת הרמוצה, אמר שמואל קרא קרקוזאי.

What is *dela'at ha-remuṣah*, Samuel said, Qarquzan pumpkin.

---

[8] al-Ḥasanī, *al-'Irāq qadīman wa-ḥadīṯan* (second printing), p. 218.

[9] The Sanhedrin version, "Rav Adda," seems wrong, because on the basis of Source 2 Rav Adda Qarḥina'a was Rava's disciple, and in any case would not be engaged in a dispute with Rabbi Eleazar. The Florence MS of Sanhedrin has "Rav Aḥa Qarḥina" as Berakhot does, and that seems correct (n. 1 above).

[10] Jacob Qarḥa figures once more in the T.B., in Ḥullin 22b, likewise teaching a *baraita*.

2. Lamentations Rabbah I 53

"... בכרכמיש על פרת," בקרקסיון דעל פרת.[1]

"... at the river Euphrates near Karkəmiš" (II Chr. 35:20) in Qarqəsiun on the Euphrates.[1]

3. Ammianus XXIII 5, 1–2

Ascitis Saracenorum auxiliis, quae animis obtulere promptissimis, tendens imperator agili gradu Cercusium principio mensis Aprilis ingressus est, munimentum tutissimum et fabre politum, cuius moenia Abora et Euphrates ambiunt flumina uelut spatium insulare fingentes. quod Diocletianus exiguum ante hoc et suspectum muris turribusque circumdedit celsis, cum in ipsis barbarorum confiniis interiores limites ordinaret, documento* ... per Syriam Persae ita ut paucis ante annis cum magnis prouinciarum contigerat damnis.

(* e documente VE est d, *BA* ne uagarentur *G* ne discurrerent *Kiessl. lac. indic. Cl.* documento recenti perterritus, ne uagarentur *Her. prob. Gichon* d. ne u. *Češka.*)

After having received the auxiliaries of the Scythians which they offered him with great willingness, the emperor (i.e. Julian, A.D. 363) marched at quick step to Cercusium, a very safe and skilfully built fortress, whose walls are washed by the Abora and Euphrates rivers, which form a kind of island and entered it at the beginning of the month of April. This place, which was formerly small and exposed to danger, Diocletian alarmed by a recent experience,* encircled with walls and lofty towers, at the time when he was arranging the inner lines of defence on the very frontiers of the barbarians, in order to prevent the Persians from overrunning Syria as had happened a few years before with great damage to the provinces.

(* The Latin text is incompletely preserved; trans.: J. C. Rolfe, LCL.)

4. Procopius, *On Buildings* II 6

παρὰ ποταμὸν Εὐφράτην ἐν τοῖς Μεσοποταμίας ἐσχάτοις, ἵνα δὴ Ἀβόρρας ποταμὸς τῷ Εὐφράτῃ ἀναμιγνύμενος τὴν ἐκβολὴν ἐνταῦθα ποιεῖται. τοῦτο Κιρκήσιον μὲν ὀνομάζεται, βασιλεὺς δὲ αὐτὸ Διοκλητιανὸς ἐν τοῖς ἄνω χρόνοις ἐδείματο. Ἰουστινιανὸς δὲ τανῦν βασιλεὺς χρόνου τε μήκει εὑρὼν συντριβὲς γεγονός, ἀπημελημένον δὲ καὶ ἄλλως ἀφύλακτον ὄν, ἐς ὀχύρωμα βεβαιότατον μετεστήσατο, πόλιν τε διεπράξατο μεγέθει καὶ κάλλει περιφανῆ εἶναι.[2]

And there was a Roman fortress beside the Euphrates river on the frontier of Mesopotamia at the point where the Aborrhas river mingles with the Euphrates, into which it empties. This is called Circesium, and was built by the Emperor Diocletian in ancient times. And our present Emperor Justinian

---

[1] The Buber edition, 46a, has בקרקסיון דפרת.

[2] Then follows an extensive description of the fortifications of Circesium, as rebuilt by Justinian.

finding it dilapidated through the passage of time and neglected besides and in general unguarded, transformed it into a very strong fortress and brought it about that it became a city conspicuous for its size and beauty.[2] (trans.: H. B. Dewing, LCL)

5. Procopius, *Wars* II 5, 1–3 (*The Persian War* II 5, 1–3)

Ἐπειδὴ δὲ ὁ μὲν χειμὼν ἤδη ὑπέληγε, τρίτον δὲ καὶ δέκατον ἔτος ἐτελεύτα Ἰουστινιανῷ βασιλεῖ τὴν αὐτοκράτορα ἀρχὴν ἔχοντι, Χοσρόης ὁ Καβάδου ἐς γῆν τὴν Ῥωμαίων ἅμα ἦρι ἀρχομένῳ στρατῷ μεγάλῳ ἐσέβαλε, τήν τε ἀπέραντον καλουμένην εἰρήνην λαμπρῶς ἔλυεν. ᾔει δὲ οὐ κατὰ τὴν μέσην τῶν ποταμῶν χώραν, ἀλλὰ τὸν Εὐφράτην ἐν δεξιᾷ ἔχων. ἔστι δὲ τοῦ ποταμοῦ ἐπὶ θάτερα Ῥωμαίων φρούριον ἔσχατον, ὃ Κιρκήσιον ἐπικαλεῖται, ἐχυρὸν ἐς τὰ μάλιστα ὄν, ἐπεὶ Ἀβόρρας μὲν ποταμὸς μέγας ἐνταῦθα τὰς ἐκβολὰς ἔχων τῷ Εὐφράτῃ ἀναμίγνυται, τὸ δὲ φρούριον τοῦτο πρὸς αὐτῇ που τῇ γωνίᾳ κεῖται, ἣν δὴ τοῖν ποταμοῖν ἡ μίξις ποιεῖται. καὶ τεῖχος δὲ ἄλλο μακρὸν τοῦ φρουρίου ἐκτὸς χώραν τὴν μεταξὺ ποταμοῦ ἑκατέρου ἀπολαμβάνον τρίγωνον ἐνταῦθα ἀμφὶ τὸ Κιρκήσιον ἐπιτελεῖ σχῆμα.

Chosroes (AD 540) did not enter (i.e. the land of the Romans) by the country between the rivers, but advanced with the Euphrates on his right. On the other side of the river stands the last Roman stronghold which is called Circesium, an exceedingly strong place, since the River Aborrhas, a large stream, has its mouth at this point and mingles with the Euphrates, and this fortress lies exactly in the angle which is made by the junction of the two rivers. And a long second wall outside the fortress cuts off the land between the two rivers, and completes the form of a triangle around Circesium. (trans.: H. B. Dewing, LCL)

B. *Already Proposed Location*

Circesium, a Roman fortress city, at the confluence of the Euphrates and the Khabur, identified with presentday Bušayriah (on Bab. Env. map).

C. *Identification*

The Qarquza mentioned in Source 1 may reasonably be assumed to be a place name, and its identification with Circesium is tenable on the basis of linguistic similarity.[3] Samuel, head of the Nəhardəʿa yeshiva in the first generation of Babylonian amoras, explains in that source the mishnaic expression *delaʿat ha-remuṣah* as meaning "pumpkin from Circesium." In Obermeyer's opinion

---

[3] Qarqīsiyā (= Circesium) figures in many Arabic sources. See e.g. Yāqūt, s.v. "Qarqīsiyā'"; *ar-Rauḍ al-miʿṭār*, s.v. "Qarqīsiyā." See also *BGA*, passim, and especially Ibn Ḥauqal, p. 227, who mentions the export of fruit from Qarqīsiyā to Iraq in the winter, of which "*delaʿat ha-remuṣah*" may be an illustration, and see below; Streck, *EI*[1, 2], s.v. "Ḳarḳisiyā."

the explanation is based on the fact that the pumpkin comes from the neighborhood of the Hirmās, a river which has its source near Nisibis and flows into the Khabur near Circesium.[4] Thus Samuel tells the people who were unfamiliar with the Hirmās that *dela'at ha-remuṣah* is simply Qarquza pumpkin, and in fact so called by the Babylonians.[5]

In Source 2 biblical Karkəmiš is identified with Qarqəsiun, apparently Circesium, as the linguistic resemblance suggests. The identification is not, however, correct, as Karkəmiš is far up the Euphrates, presentday Ǧerāblūs, lying a hundred kilometers northeast of Aleppo.[6] There is no justification for Obermeyer's identification of Qurqunya (q.v.), mentioned in 'Avodah Zarah 16b, with Circesium.[7]

D. *History*

Circesium was a strong Roman fortress at the confluence of the Euphrates and the Khabur. The site controlled the Euphrates route northwest of Dura Europos at the point where another road branched off northwards to Nisibis.[8] It has not been explored in recent years, but the ruins have been described by Sarre and Herzfeld.[9]

In the first century it did not exist, for Isidore of Charax (*Parthian Stations*), while indicating the importance of the site, mentions only two villages there.[10] "Then Phaliga, a village on the Euphrates (that means in Greek 'half-way'), 6 schoeni. From Antioch to this place, 120 schoeni; and from thence to Seleucia, which is on the Tigris, 100 schoeni.[11] Nearby Phaliga is the walled village

[4] Obermeyer, pp. 35–36, quotes Le Strange, "Ibn Serapion," p. 12, on this; see also *ibid.* the notes, p. 60. On the Hirmās River, which is the Nisibis River, see also Suhrāb, p. 126; Ibn Ḫurdāḏbih, p. 175; Ibn Rusta, p. 90; Ibn Sa'īd, *Geography*, p. 157 (written "Hirmāš"); Ibn al-Faqīh, pp. 134–135; Abū l-Fidā', p. 47; Bakrī, s.v. "Ṯarṯār"; *ar-Rauḍ al-mi'ṭār*, s.v. "Hirmās." Cf. *ibid.*, s.v. "Khābūr"; *Marāṣid*, end of entry on "Hirmās."

[5] Rav Ashi explains "*dela'at ha-remuṣah*" not as pumpkin brought from a certain place, but as pumpkin cooked over ashes (*remeṣ*). The Mishnah (Kilayim I 2) however, refers to "*dela'at ha-miṣrit* (= Egyptian) *we-ha-remuṣah*" so that obviously a place is meant. Cf. also a question of Ravina's later in the passage about Rav Ashi's view. (On "*dela'at ha-remuṣah*" see Feliks, *Kilei Zera'im*, pp. 63–64.)

[6] This was already pointed out by Obermeyer, pp. 33–34, and see Broshi, *Entziqlopedia Miqra'it*, vol. 4, p. 313, s.v. "כרכמיש".

[7] Obermeyer, p. 33.

[8] For the Nisibis-Circesium road, see Dillemann, *Haute Mésopotamie*, p. 189.

[9] Sarre & Herzfeld, *Archäologische Reise*, vol. 1, p. 172–174.

[10] Musil, *The Middle Euphrates*, p. 334, refers to Michael the Syrian, *Chronicle*, Chabot ed., vol. 4, p. 78. There the founding of "Carcis" is attributed to Seleucus Callinicus. Musil further notes that the present ruins appear to be divided into unequal halves, and he speculates about the relative positions of Phaliga and Nabagath. Cf. Sturm, *RE*, vol. 38, col. 1668, s.v. "Φάλγα."

[11] Musil, *op.cit.* (n. 10 above), pp. 227–228, who visited the place, computes the average length of Isidore's *schoenus* as 4.7 kilometers. He gives the actual distance from Phalga

of Nabagath, and by it flows the river Aburas which empties into the Euphrates; there the armies cross over to the Roman territory beyond the river."[12] (trans.: W. H. Schoff)

Stephanus Byzantius citing Arrian mentions the village of Phalga (second century A. D.) "Phalga, village halfway between Seleucia in Pieria and Seleucia in Mesopotamia. Arrian in Book X of his *Parthica*. Phalga is in the native language 'the middle'."[13]

The existence of a fort of Circesium is attested for the third century. The Emperor Gordian III was buried not far from there.[14] It appears on the Ka'ba inscription among the cities captured by Shapur I in the course of his second campaign (256?)[15] At that time, according to the *Chronicon Paschale*, the eastern frontier of the Roman empire ran "from Arabia and Palaestina as far as the fort of Circesium" (*ab Arabia et Palaestina usque ad Circesium Castrum*).[16]

Ammianus in Source 3 notes that before Diocletian Circesium was small and unfortified,[17] and indeed, although its prior existence is attested in scattered sources, it seems to have become important only after Diocletian rebuilt it as a key site on the frontier.

Bishops of Circesium are attested from 451 onwards.[18]

During the century and a half following Julian's campaign in A.D. 363 the only other references to Circesium are related to the movement of Persian Arabs in the region in 502 and under Justinian.[19] An extensive description of the fortifications is provided by Procopius.

---

to Seleucia in Pieria as 840 kilometers and thence to Seleucia in Mesopotamia as 850 kilometers.

[12] Schoff ed., p. 4. Εἶτα Φάλιγα κώμη πρὸς τῷ Εὐφράτῃ· λέγοιτο δ' ἂν ἑλληνιστὶ μεσοποριкὸν, σχοῖνοι ς'. Ἀπὸ Ἀντιοχείας ἕως τούτου σχοῖνοι ρκ'· ἐντεῦθεν δὲ ἐπὶ Σελεύκειαν τὴν πρὸς τῷ Τίγριδι σχοῖνοι ρ'. Παράκειται δὲ τῇ Φάλιγᾳ κωμόπολις Ναβαγὰθ, καὶ παραῤῥεῖ αὐτῆν ποταμὸς Ἀβούρας, ὅς ἐμβάλλει εἰς τὸν Εὐφράτην· ἐκεῖθεν διαβαίνει τὰ στρατόπεδα εἰς τὴν κατὰ Ῥωμαίους πέραν.

[13] Meineke ed., p. 656. Φάλγα, κώμη μέση Σελευκείας τῆς Πιερίας καὶ τῆς ἐν Μεσοποταμίᾳ. Ἀρριανὸς ἐν ι' Παρθικῶν. ἡ δὲ φάλγα γλώσσῃ τῇ ἐπιχωρίῳ τὸ μέσον δηλοῖ.

[14] Eutropius IX 2; *SHA Gordian* 34. For Circesium see also Zosimus III 12, 3.

[15] Honigmann & Maricq, *Recherches sur les Res Gestae Divi Saporis*, p. 114, no. 27: krksy'; Κορκουσίωνα.

[16] *Chronicon Paschale*, Niebuhr edition, p. 504. Ὁ αὐτὸς Δέκιος βασιλεὺς ἤγαγεν ἀπὸ τῆς Ἀφρικῆς λέοντας φοβεροὺς καὶ λεαίνας, καὶ ἀπέλυσεν εἰς τὸ λίμιτον ἀνατολῆς, ἀπὸ Ἀραβίας καὶ Παλαιστίνης ἕως τοῦ Κιρκησίου κάστρου, πρὸς τὸ ποιῆσαι γενεάν, διὰ τοὺς βαρβάρους Σαρακηνούς. The term "castrum," employed also by *SHA* (n. 14 above) might indicate that Circesium was a fort before Diocletian.

[17] Iohannes Malalas, Dindorf edition, p. 329, even makes Diocletian the founder of Circesium.

[18] See sources cited by Musil, *op. cit.* (in n. 10 above), p. 335. Abraham, bishop of Circesium, was among those who signed the resolutions of the council of Chalcedon, in 451 (Michael the Syrian, see n. 10 above).

[19] Joshua the Stylite, *Chronicle*, Martin ed., p. 58; Michael the Syrian, *op. cit.* (in n. 10 above), p. 270ff.

Circesium appears in the description of the march route of Mauritius (580).[20] In 590, Khusro II, when fleeing his antagonist Vahram, was admitted into the town by the Byzantine prefect.[21]

Berliner, *Beiträge* (1883), p. 62
Eshel, *Yishuvei ha-Yehudim* (1979), pp. 230–231
Funk, *Monumenta* (1913), pp. 51, 299
Hirschenson, *Sheva Ḥokhmot* (1883), p. 225
Jastrow, *Dictionary* (1950³), p. 1426
Kohut, *Arukh ha-Shalem* (1878–1892), vol. 7, pp. 215–216; *Tosefot* (1937), p. 377
Levy, *Wörterbuch* (1924²), vol. 4, p. 390
Musil, *The Middle Euphrates* (1927), pp. 334–337
Neubauer, *Géographie* (1868), p. 354
Neusner, *History* (1965–1970), vol. 1, p. 2; vol. 4, pp. 10, 172, 174; vol. 5, pp. 81, 114
Obermeyer, *Landschaft* (1929), pp. 33–39, 215
Sarre & Herzfeld, *Archäologische Reise* (1911), vol. 1, pp. 172–174
Streck, *EI*¹ ², s.v. "Ḳarḳisiyā"

Qartu קרתו

A. *Source*

Yevamot 16a

ומקבלים גרים מן הקרדויים[1] והתרמודים.[2] איני, והתני רמי בר יחזקאל אין מקבלים גרים מן הקרדויים, אמר רב אשי[3] קרתויים אתמר, כדאמרי אינשי קרתויים[4] פסולים. ואיכא דאמרי תני רמי בר יחזקאל אין מקבלים גרים מן הקרתויים, מאי לאו היינו קרתויים היינו קרדויים, אמר רב אשי לא, קרתויי לחוד וקרדויי לחוד, כדאמרי אינשי קרתויי פסילי.

And accept converts from the Qarduans[1] and the Tarmodans.[2] Indeed? For Rami b. Ezekiel taught, Converts of the Qarduans are not acceptable. Rav Ashi[3] said, It said Qartuans, as the people say, disqualified Qartuans.[4] And others say Rami b. Ezekiel taught, Converts from the Qartuans are not acceptable. Are not Qartuans Qarduans? Rav Ashi said, No, Qartuans are separate and Qarduans are separate, as the people say Qartuans are disqualified.

B. *Location*

None can be specified due to insufficient data.

---

[20] Theophylactus Simocatta, *Historiae* III 17, 5–11. Cf. Musil, *op.cit.* (in n. 10 above), pp. 335–336.

[21] *Ibid.*, IV 10, 4–11. Cf. Musil, *loc.cit.* See also Dan, *Meḥqarim*, vol. 5, pp. 148–149.

[1] For variants see the entry on "Qardu."

[2] For variants see the entry on "Tadmor (Palmyra)."

[3] The Vatican 111 MS has "Rav said," but "Rav Ashi said" further on.

[4] The Munich MS has קרויי.

C. *Attempts at Identification*

In the above source, Rav Ashi distinguishes between Qarduans and Qartuans, converts from among the latter being unacceptable. The distinction is not made just to resolve the contradiction between Rami b. Ezekiel's *baraita*, and what was previously attributed to Rabbi Dosa b. Harkinas (see the passage), but is historically and geographically valid, for Qartu cannot be identified with Qardu (q.v.).[5] Qarduans and Qartuans were located far apart, the former in what is presentday Kurdistan, and the latter, according to Strabo, in southern Persia.[6]

ESHEL, *Yishuvei ha-Yehudim* (1979), p. 231
FUNK, *Monumenta* (1913), p. 21, "קרדו"
HIRSCHENSON, *Sheva Ḥokhmot* (1883), p. 225
JASTROW, *Dictionary* (1950³), p. 1428
KOHUT, *Arukh ha-Shalem* (1878–1892), vol. 7, p. 219
LEVY, *Wörterbuch* (1924²), vol. 4, p. 394
NEUBAUER, *Géographie* (1868), p. 429
OBERMEYER, *Landschaft* (1929), p. 133
WEISSBACH, *RE*, vol. 12, s.v. "Κύρτιοι," col. 205

Qasqəsa קסקסא

A. *Source*

Berakhot 51a

במידי דלא ממאיס נמי לסלקינהו לצד אחד וליברך, תרגמא רב יצחק קסקסאה [1] קמיה דרבי יוסי בר אבין משמיה דרבי יוחנן משום שנאמר "ימלא פי תהלתך".

And a thing that is not loathsome, he could also put it in one side [of the mouth] and bless. Rav Isaac Qasqəsa'a[1] explained to Rabbi Yose b. Avin in the name of Rabbi Yoḥanan, because it is said, "My mouth shall be filled with Your praise" (Ps. 71:8).

B. *Proposed Location*

Aqsās Mālik on the west bank of the Euphrates, southwest of Sura (C4 on the Tal. Bab. map).

---

[5] See Weissbach, *RE*, vol. 12, s.v. "Κύρτιοι," col. 205, and the bibliography there.

[6] Strabo XV 3, 1. See also Strabo XI 13, 3; Polybius V 52, 5; Livy XXXVII 40, 9 and XLII 58, 13.

[1] The Munich MS has **סקאה**, which may be construed to refer to Rav Isaac's occupation (it means sack-maker) rather than to a place (see Jastrow, p. 1397). But all other versions indicate that a place name is meant. The Paris MS has **קטוסכאה**; and the forms **קרקוסאה** and **קטוספאה** (see nn. 9, 12 in the entry on "Ctesiphon" under "Maḥoza Area") are found as well. See *Diq. Sof.*, and n. 6 below.

C. *Identification*

A key to the identification of Qasqəsa appears in Rav Saadia Gaon's exegesis to Berakhot: "קשקשאה: מן אלאקסאסי" (= Qaśqəśa'a: from al-Aqsāsī).[2] A place called Aqsās Mālik is known from Arabic sources. According to Yāqūt, the addition "Mālik" refers to a person (who apparently owned the place).[3] According to Ṭabarī,[4] Aqsās Mālik was on the Euphrates north of Dair al-A'war.[5]

The only scholar who has attempted to identify Qasqəsa is Klein, who quoted Lewin (see note 2 below) but preferred to identify it for no good reason with a place in Eretz Israel, the Arab village of Qusqus in the Sepphoris area.[6]

D. *Sages and Qasqəsa*

The source quoted mentions Rav Isaac from Qasqəsa reporting Rabbi Yoḥanan's comments to Rabbi Yose b. Avin, of the third and fourth generation of Eretz Israel amoras.[7]

Eshel, *Yishuvei ha-Yehudim* (1979), p. 227
Funk, *Monumenta* (1913), pp. 51, 299
Hirschenson, *Sheva Ḥokhmot* (1883), p. 217
Jastrow, *Dictionary* (1950³), p. 1397
Klein, *Sefer ha-Yishuv* (1939), vol. 1, p. 144
Klein, *Eretz ha-Galil* (1967), p. 122

Qimḥonya קימחוניא

A. *Sources*

1. Qiddushin 25b

דרש רב בקימחוניא[1] בהמה גסה נקנית במשיכה.

Rav preached in Qimḥonya,[1] A large animal is bought by *meshikhah*.

[2] See Rav Saadia Gaon's exegesis on Berakhot, Wertheimer ed., 17a; and cf. Lewin, *Otzar ha-Geonim* on Berakhot, *ha-Perushim* (*Liqutei geonim*), p. 114.

[3] See Yāqūt, the entry for "Aqsās." Yāqūt's definition of the location of Aqsās Mālik—"a village in Kūfa or a district"—refers to the vicinity of Kūfa, not to the town itself. On Mālik, who was of the Iyād tribe, see Ibn al-Faqīh, p. 182; *Futūḥ al-buldān*, p. 283. Cf. Balādurī, *Ansāb al-ašrāf*, vol. 1, p. 26.

[4] Ṭabarī, vol. 5, p. 589 [= vol. 2, p. 545].

[5] See the entry in Yāqūt; and see Kister, *Arabica* 15 (1968): 152; al-'Alī, *Sumer* 21 (1965): 236, who notes, re the text in Ṭabarī, that Aqsās was the last station before Karbalā for travelers from Kūfa, that is, it was close to Karbalā. Dair al-A'war was in his opinion halfway between Kūfa and Karbalā. For the location of Aqsās cf. al-'Alī's map, *op. cit.*, p. 253.

[6] See Klein, *Eretz ha-Galil*, p. 122, and see his *Sefer ha-Yishuv*, where he is still unsure and Qusqus is located near Haifa ("קסקסא"[?], p. 144). In n. 1 in that entry Klein explains that Rav Isaac Qasqəsa'a is from Eretz Israel because in the Munich MS the form is "Rabbi" and not "Rav." Klein evidently based his deduction on a mistake in *Diq. Sof.*, for the form in the Munich MS is in fact "Rav" as in the standard edition. In *Eretz ha-Galil* Klein cites Berakhot 51a as if the standard edition had "Rabbi Isaac Qasqəsa'a."

[7] See Albeck, *Mavo la-Talmudim*, pp. 336–337.

[1] The Vatican 111 MS has בקמחוניא.

2. Ketubot 67a

ואמר רב פפי[2] הני שקי דרודיא[3] ואשלי דקמחוניא אשה גובה פרנא מהן.

And Rav Papi[2] said, These sacks of Rodya[3] and ropes of Qimḥonya, a woman can claim her *ketubah* from them.

B. *Already Proposed Location*

In the Sura area, near the diffluence of the Lower Sura (q.v., D4 on the Tal. Bab. map).

C. *Identification*

The location of Qimḥonya is based on the resemblance of the name to Qāmiġān, as the stone bridge near the diffluence of the Lower Sura was called. Obermeyer proffered the opinion that Qimḥonya lent its name to the bridge, which seems reasonable.[4] The bridge spanned the Lower Sura where it flowed out of the Upper Sura,[5] six parasangs from the point where the Upper Sura flowed out of the Euphrates.[6]

D. *Sages and Qimḥonya*

Source 1 mentions Rav, head of the Sura yeshiva in the first generation of Babylonian amoras, preaching in Qimḥonya.[7]

---

[2] The Vatican 113, Vatican 130 and Leningrad MSS as well as the Soncino printing and a Geniza fragment have "Rav Papa"; and see Ketubot in the ICIT edition, and n. 30 there.

[3] For the variants see the entry on "Rodya."

[4] Obermeyer, p. 296. On Qāmiġān see also al-ʿAlī, *Sumer* 21 (1965): 234.

[5] Suhrāb, p. 125; Le Strange, "Ibn Serapion," p. 16. In the opinion of Le Strange (p. 259) that is the only mention of the bridge.

[6] That is the interpretation of the Suhrāb text (pp. 124–125); Le Strange, "Ibn Serapion," p. 16: *wa-yamurru...n-nahru llaḏī yuqālu lahū Sūrā l-Aʿlā...bi-izāʾi madīnati Qaṣr ibn Hubaira...wa-yaḥmilu minhū Nahr Abī Raḥā awwaluhū fauqa l-qaṣr bi-farsaḫ...wa-yaṣubbu ilā Sūrā asfal mina l-qaṣr bi-farsaḫ. wa-yamurru Nahr Sūrā baina l-qaṣr māddan ilā sittati farāsiḫ fa-yaḥmilu minhū hunāka nahr yuqālu lahū Nahr Sūrā al-Asfal.* See already Obermeyer, p. 281, n. 4, who rightly criticized both de Goeje, *ZDMG* 39 (1885): 7, and Streck, *Die alte Landschaft*, vol. 1, p. 29. In any case, Le Strange's translation ("Ibn Serapion," p. 256) which Obermeyer objects to as well, is correct: "The Nahr Sura runs on past the town of the Kaṣr for a distance of six leagues and then there is taken from it a canal called the Lower Sura." The map attached to "Ibn Serapion" likewise proves that Le Strange set the length of the Upper Sura at six parasangs to the point where the Lower Sura begins.

[7] Public sermons by sages of the first two generations of Babylonian amoras are relatively rare; see Gafni, *Ha-Yeshiva be-Bavel*, pp. 123–125 and n. 57 there.

E. *Material Culture*

Source 2 refers to "ropes of Qimḥonya," that is, ropes manufactured in Qimḥonya.[8] According to the halakhah, goods and products are not generally collateral for a marriage settlement or debt. In exceptional cases, however, where some items constitute the main production of the locality, a *ketubah* or debt can be collected from them.[9] The ropes of Qimḥonya figure in such a case, indicating that they were closely associated with the place, probably made there.

Berliner, *Beiträge* (1883), p. 62
Eshel, *Yishuvei ha-Yehudim* (1979), pp. 226–227
Funk, *Monumenta* (1913), pp. 51, 299
Hirschenson, *Sheva Ḥokhmot* (1883), p. 215
Jastrow, *Dictionary* (1950³), p. 1384
Kohut, *Arukh ha-Shalem* (1878–1892), vol. 7, p. 115; *Tosefot* (1937), p. 365
Levy, *Wörterbuch* (1924²), vol. 4, p. 325
Neubauer, *Géographie* (1868), p. 397
Obermeyer, *Landschaft* (1929), p. 296

Qurqunya קורקוניא

A. *Source*

ʿAvodah Zarah 16b

אמר רבי זירא כי הוינן בי רב יהודה אמר לן גמירו מינאי הא מילתא דמגברא רבה שמיע לי ולא ידענא אי מרב אי משמואל חיה גסה הרי היא כבהמה דקה לפירכוס. כי אתאי לקורקוניא[1] אשכחתיה לרב חייא בר אשי ויתיב וקאמר משמיה דשמואל חיה גסה הרי היא כבהמה דקה לפירכוס, אמינא ש״מ משמיה דשמואל איתמר. כי אתאי לסורא אשכחתיה לרבה בר ירמיה דיתיב וקאמר . . . כי סליקת להתם אשכחתיה לרב אסי[2] דיתיב וקאמר . . .

Rabbi Zera said, When we were at Rav Judah's [study] house he said to us, Learn from me this thing I heard from an important person and I don't know whether from Rav or from Samuel, A large beast is like a small animal as to spasmodic movement. When I came to Qurqunya[1] I found Rav Ḥiyya b. Ashi sitting and saying in Samuel's name, A large beast is like a small animal as to spasmodic movement. I said, Conclude from that that it was said in the name of Samuel. When I came to Sura I found Rabbah b. Jeremiah sitting and saying . . . When I went there (to Eretz Israel) I found Rav Assi[2] sitting and saying . . .

---

[8] Newman notes that as rope was made from hemp, presumably hemp was grown in the neighborhood of Qimḥonya; see Newman, *Agricultural Life*, p. 105.

[9] See, e.g. the section on Material Culture in the entry on "Be Mikse." See also the entry on "Rodya."

[1] The Munich MS has לאקרוקוניא, the Spanish MS (Abramson ed.) has לאקרוקניא and see below, while the Pesaro, Venice and Salonika printings have לקרקוניא.

[2] The Munich MS has "Rav Joseph," and see *Diq. Sof.*

B. *Location*

None can be proposed due to insufficient data.

C. *Attempts at Identification*

In Obermeyer's opinion the name Qurqunya (Qarqunya, in his reading, see note 1) should be corrected to Qarquzya, which he identified with Circesium,[3] (see the entry on "Qarquza"). This correction derives from Obermeyer's view, held by others before him as well, that the ʿAvodah Zarah passage reflects stages in Rabbi Zera's journey from Babylonia to Eretz Israel,[4] as follows: Pumbədita (whose yeshiva Rav Judah headed), Qarquzya (which is Circesium), Sura (to his mind, the Sura upstream on the Euphrates), and Eretz Israel.

That identification does not stand up to critical examination for a number of reasons: a) There is no justification for correcting Qurqunya to Qarquzya, particularly since no support for such a correction appears in the MSS or versions. b) As according to the source Rabbi Zera met Rav Ḥiyya b. Ashi in Qurqunya and Rabbah b. Jeremiah in Sura, Obermeyer had to make the unfounded assumption that they too were traveling to or from Eretz Israel.[5] c) There is no reason to conclude that the Sura referred to is not the seat of the great yeshiva which was Rabbah b. Jeremiah's town.[6]

All in all, although Rabbi Zera of the third generation of Babylonian amoras is known to have made the journey from Babylonia to Eretz Israel, the various places he is described in the source cited as having visited are not necessarily connected with that journey.

D. *Aqruqunya* (*the Munich MS version*)

The Munich MS has Aqruqunya rather than Qurqunya (see note 1), and twice has Aqruqanya—instead of Aqrunya in Bava Qamma 7b[7] and instead of Hagrunya in Bava Qamma 88a.[8] That version suggests that the name Qurqunya may be an abbreviated form of Aqra (= fort) də-Qunya,[9] and the place should perhaps be identified with Aqra də-Hagrunya.

---

[3] Obermeyer, p. 33.

[4] Obermeyer, pp. 32–39, and before that Hirschenson, *Sheva Ḥokhmot*, p. 209; Berliner, p. 60; Bacher, *Palästinensische Amoräer*, vol. 3, p. 5.

[5] On Rav Ḥiyya b. Ashi see p. 36, and on Rabbah b. Jeremiah see p. 39.

[6] The version סוריה in Rashi's commentary on the above source cannot serve as proof that the upstream Sura is meant (cf. Obermeyer's implication, p. 39).

[7] See Source 4 under "Hagrunya."

[8] See Source 3 under "Hagrunya."

[9] See *Arukh ha-Shalem*, vol. 7, p. 215.

Bacher, *Palästinensische Amoräer* (1892), vol. 3, p. 5
Berliner, *Beiträge* (1883), p. 60
Eshel, *Yishuvei ha-Yehudim* (1979), pp. 34, 255
Funk, *Monumenta* (1913), pp. 50, 299
Hirschenson, *Sheva Ḥokhmot* (1883), p. 209
Jastrow, *Dictionary* (1950³), p. 1344
Kohut, *Arukh ha-Shalem* (1878–1892), vol. 7, p. 215
Levy, *Wörterbuch* (1924²), vol. 4, p. 390
Neubauer, *Géographie* (1868), p. 398
Obermeyer, *Landschaft* (1929), pp. 32–39

Qurṭava קורטבא

A. *Source*

Yevamot 115b

יצחק ריש גלותא בר אחתיה דרב ביבי הוה קאזיל מקורטבא לאספמיא[1] ושכיב, שלחו מהתם יצחק ריש גלותא בר אחתיה דרב ביבי הוה קאזיל מקורטבא[2] לאספמיא ושכיב, מי חיישינן לתרי יצחק או לא, אביי אמר חיישינן, רבא אמר לא חיישינן.

Isaac Resh Galuta son of Rav Bevai's sister, once went from Qurṭava to Aspamya,[1] and died. They reported from there, Isaac Resh Galuta son of Rav Bevai's sister went from Qurṭava[2] to Aspamya and died. Do we suspect two Isaacs or not? Abbaye said, We do suspect. Rava said, We do not suspect.

B. *Location*

None can be proposed due to insufficient data.

C. *Attempts at Identification*

Obermeyer proposed identifying Qurṭava with Kurdāfād, one of the seven towns in the urban group of Madā'in.[3] The place names in the source — Qurṭava and Aspamya (which Obermeyer believed to be Apamea [q.v.]) — were garbled by a copyist who thought Qurṭava was Cordoba and Apamea was Aspamya (= España), that is, Spain.[4] The similarity of names is not absolute proof of identity, but if that criterion is accepted, the place-name "Qurdābād" resembles "Qurṭava" more closely. In dealing with a village near ʿUkbarā called Šilǧ,[5] Yāqūt reports that the latter, which is situated on the Tigris, has many

[1] The Munich MS has **איספמיא** further on as well.

[2] The Venice printing has **קורטובא**.

[3] Obermeyer, p. 183; Streck, *Die alte Landschaft*, vol. 2, pp. 248, 250, 268; al-ʿAlī, *Sumer* 23 (1967): 51f.; Fiey, *Sumer* 23 (1967): 31. See Ḥamza al-Iṣfahānī, quoted in Yāqūt s.v. "Madā'in"; Ḥamza, *Ta'rīḫ*, pp. 29–30, ("Kurdābād"); cf. also *Futūḥ al-buldān*, p. 275.

[4] Obermeyer, p. 183, n. 5.

[5] See Yāqūt, s.v. "Šilǧ": "a village near ʿUkbarā." *Marāṣid*, s.v. "Šilǧ," adds "above it." See Streck, *ibid.*, p. 229f.

shops selling wine in the neighborhood that is adjacent to the Qurdābāḏ vineyards. Thus Qurdābāḏ is close to Šilğ (and ʿUkbarā) and has vineyards. However, the identification of Qurṭava with Qurdābāḏ is also based only on the linguistic similarity and is not absolutely certain.

D. *The Exilarch and Qurṭava*

The above source deals with the problem of whether a woman may remarry on the basis of information that a man by her husband's name died somewhere else, or whether it must be assumed that the deceased could be a stranger by the same name. The particular case concerns the death in Aspamya (or Apamea) of Isaac Resh Galuta who went there from Qurṭava. The addition of the title Resh Galuta (= Exilarch) to Isaac's name presents difficulties. It is highly unlikely that doubt could arise regarding the identity of an Exilarch who died, so that we can only assume that either the source is garbled, or Resh Galuta in this instance was a nickname and not a title. In any event, it is clear that no Exilarch of Babylonian Jewry is referred to.[6]

Beer, *Rashut ha-Golah* (1970), pp. 23–24
Eshel, *Yishuvei ha-Yehudim* (1979), pp. 224–225
Funk, *Monumenta* (1913), pp. 50, 299
Graetz, *MGWJ* 2 (1853): 196
Hirschenson, *Sheva Ḥokhmot* (1883), p. 209
Jastrow, *Dictionary* (1950³), p. 1412, ("קרדו II")
Kohut, *Arukh ha-Shalem* (1878–1892), vol. 1, pp. 188–189 ("אספמיא")
Krauss, *Lehnwörter* (1898–1899), vol. 1, pp. 254–255
Lazarus, *Die Häupter* (1890), p. 145, n. 5
Neubauer, *Géographie* (1868), p. 355
Neusner, *History* (1965–1970), vol. 4, pp. 184–185
Obermeyer, *Landschaft* (1929), pp. 183–184
Rapoport, *Erekh Millin* (1914), vol. 1, pp. 310–311

Rodya רודיא

A. *Source*

Ketubot 67a

ואמר רב פפי[1] הני שקי דרודיא[2] ואשלי דקמחוניא אשה גובה פרנא מהן.

And Rav Papi[1] said, These sacks of Rodya[2] and ropes of Qimḥonya, a woman can claim her *ketubah* from them.

---

[6] See Beer, *Rashut ha-Golah*, pp. 23–24, and the bibliography there; Neusner, *History*, vol. 4, pp. 184–185.

[1] The Vatican 113, Vatican 130 and Leningrad MSS, the Soncino printing, and a Geniza fragment all have "Rav Papa," and see Ketubot in the ICIT edition, and n. 30.

[2] The Vatican 113 MS has דטמרוקיא (the letter *quf* is scratched out, and the corrected form is דטמרוריא), the Vatican 130 MS has דטמרוריא (or דטמרודיא), a Geniza fragment has דתמדוריא, the *Arukh* version is דאורדיא, and see Ketubot, ICIT ed., and

B. *Location*

None can be proposed due to insufficient data.

C. *Material Culture*

The source refers to "sacks of Rodya," that is, sacks manufactured there. According to the halakhah, goods are not generally collateral for a marriage settlement or debt. But in exceptional cases where a certain item is the main product of a place, a debt or *ketubah* can be collected from it.[3] One of the examples cited refers to the sacks of Rodya, indicating that they were considered typical of the place.

BERLINER, *Beiträge* (1883), p. 39
ESHEL, *Yishuvei ha-Yehudim* (1979), pp. 232–233
FUNK, *Monumenta* (1913), pp. 51, 299
HIRSCHENSON, *Sheva Ḥokhmot* (1883), p. 236
KOHUT, *Arukh ha-Shalem* (1878–1892), vol. 1, p. 274 "אורדיא"
LEVY, *Wörterbfch* (1924²), vol. 4, p. 686

Romai רומאי

See the entry on "Maḥoza" under "Maḥoza Area."

Romqe רומקי

See the entry on "Nihawand."

---

n. 31 there. ʿAvodah Zarah 39a has: "Rav Ashi happened to come לטמדוריא" (the Munich MS has "Abbaye happened to come לטמו בירי'," the Spanish MS edited by Abramson has "Abbaye happened to come לטמרוגיא," and see Abramson's notes, pp. 187–188.) No other references to טמדוריא (= Ṭamdurya) occur, and if the Vatican manuscripts and Geniza fragment are to be preferred, the place is the same one that figures in the source above. Shabbat 20b includes the sentence רבין ואביי הוו קאזלו בפקתא דטמרוריתא (= Ravin and Abbaye went in the valley of Ṭamrurita; the Munich MS has דתרמודיא and the Oxford MS has דטמדירא). The similarity of טמרוריתא and טמדוריא suggests that the same place may be meant, and if for ʿAvodah Zarah the manuscripts are preferred, both there and in connection with the Ṭamrurita referred to in Shabbat, the same amora, Abbaye, is involved.

[3] See, e.g., the section on Material Culture in the entry on "Be Mikse," and see also the entry on "Qimḥonya."

Sabata סבתא

A. *Sources*

1. ʿAvodah Zarah 58b

רבי ירמיה איקלע לסבתא,[1] חזא חמרא דמזגי עובד כוכבים ואישתי ישראל מיניה ואסר להו...

Rabbi Jeremiah happened to be in Sabata,[1] saw wine that a star worshiper poured and Jews were drinking, and forbade them.

2. Pliny, *Natural History*, VI 31, 132

inter has gentes atque Mesenen Sittacene est, eadem Arbelitis et Palaestine dicta oppidum eius Sittace Graecorum, ab ortu et Sabdata, ab occasu autem Antiochia inter duo flumina Tigrim et Tornodatum, item Apamea, etc.[2]

Between these races and Mesene is Sittacene, which is also called Arbelitis and Palaestine. Its town of Sittace is of Greek origin, and also to the east of this is Sabdata and to the west Antiochia, which lies between the two rivers, Tigris and Tornadotus, and also Apamea, etc.[2] (trans.: H. Rackham, LCL)

3. Zosimus III 23, 3

Ἐντεῦθεν ἡ στρατιὰ φρούριά τινα παραδραμοῦσα εἰς πόλιν ἀφίκετο Μείνας Σαβαθὰ[3] καλουμένην· διέστηκε δὲ αὕτη σταδίοις τριάκοντα τῆς πρότερον μὲν Ζωχάσης νῦν δὲ Σελευκείας ὀνομαζομένης· καὶ ὁ μὲν βασιλεὺς πλησίον που μετὰ τῆς πολλῆς στρατιᾶς ηὐλίσθη, προηγούμενοι δὲ οἱ κατάσκοποι τὴν πόλιν | κατὰ κράτος αἱροῦσι· τῇ δ' ὑστεραίᾳ τὰ τείχη ταύτης ὁ βασιλεὺς περινοστῶν ἑώρα σώματα προσηρτημένα σταυροῖς ἔμπροσθεν τῶν πυλῶν.

Thence the army rushed past certain forts en route to a town named Meinas Sabatha,[3] which is thirty stades distant from the former Zochasa, now called Seleucia. While the Emperor encamped nearby with the majority of the soldiery, scouts moved on ahead and took the town by storm. The next day, when the Emperor was making the rounds of its walls, he spied bodies fastened to pales in front of the gates. (trans.: J. J. Buchanan and H. T. Davis, TUP)

B. *Location*

A suburb west of Maḥoza (q.v., D3 on the Tal. Bab. map) on the Nahr al-Malik.

---

[1] The Munich and Spanish MSS for ʿAvodah Zarah edited by Abramson have לסכותא, and Abramson noted there that the Oxford MS too (ʿAvodah Zarah 56b) has סכותא. Evidently the Venice printing should also be read סכתא, and see Sussman, *Tarbiẓ* 43 (1974): 115, n. 158.

[2] See Herzfeld, *Samarra*, p. 33.

[3] Sarre & Herzfeld (*Archäologische Reise*, vol. 2, p. 48, n. 2) derive the name Μείνας Σάβαθα from Sābāṭ al-Madā'in, and deduce that in the fourth century (when Zosimus wrote) Medhīnātha or Medhīne were the forms for Maḥoza (q.v.).

C. *Identification*

Arabic sources confuse Walašpaṭ (q.v.) with Sabata (see below) as does a source from gaonic literature.[4] Source 1 dealing with a ruling concerning wine also allows for the identification of Sabata with Walašpaṭ, where there was a major wine market. However, Herzfeld stresses that they are not identical and must be distinguished for both linguistic and geographical reasons. The reference to wine in regard to both places occurs because the entire region abounded in vineyards.[5] Source 3, combined with Julian's route of march as described by Ammianus (see the entry on "Be Ardəšir-Koḵe") clearly suggests that "Meinas Sabatha" was west of Koḵe (Maḥoza), not quite at the confluence of the Royal Canal and the Tigris, the location of Walašpaṭ (q.v.).[6]

According to Arabic sources, Sābāṭ is an arabization of Balāš Abāḏ. Balāš b. Fīrūz (484–488) built the town and called it Balāšawāḏ (= Balāš Abāḏ) which is Sābāṭ near Madā'in.[7] Sābāṭ was at the confluence of Nahr al-Malik and the Tigris. The stone bridge of Sābāṭ is the Nahr al-Malik bridge and was the southern limit of Madā'in (see the entry on "Maḥoza").[8] Sābāṭ was one parasang from Bahurasīr (see the entry on "Be Ardəšīr").[9] The road between them passed through groves and vineyards.[10] Sābāṭ was the site of a prison of the king of Persia (he had several prisons in Be Ardəšir too). A well-known story extant in a number of versions tells of the death in the Sābāṭ prison of Nu'mān III b. Munḏir (Ḥīra's last independent ruler, 580–602) after offending King

---

[4] ... פרותא דולשפט עיר הסמוכה למחוזא ... ושמה בלשון ערביים סאבאט ... (= port of Walašpaṭ a city near Maḥoza ... and its name in the language of the Arabs is Sābāṭ ...; Assaf, *Teshuvot ha-Geonim mi-tokh ha-Geniza*, p. 11).

[5] See Herzfeld, *Samarra*, pp. 32–34. Influenced by the Arabic sources, modern scholars have reiterated the identity between Sabata and Valāšābād/Vologesocerta (*Valagšāpāt-kirt) but see n. 7 below and the entry on "Walašpaṭ."

[6] Julian's march route will be discussed in detail by Dr. John Matthews in his forthcoming book on Ammianus.

[7] Ṭabarī, vol. 2, p. 90 (= vol. 1, p. 883); cf. Nöldeke, *Perser und Araber*, p. 134, n. 4; Ḥamza, *Ta'rīḫ*, p. 56; Ṭa'ālibī, *Ġurar*, p. 584. Cf. *Kitāb al-ma'ārif*, p. 610; see also Yāqūt, s.v. "Sābāṭ Kisrā": "Balās Abāḏ, and Balās is a man's name"; Qazwīnī, *Bilād*, p. 385: "Balāšabāḏ." For other explanations of the source of the name see Yāqūt, *Marāṣid*, s.v. "Sābāṭ Kisrā." As Walašpaṭ is mentioned by Rava (mid-fourth century), Nöldeke (*ZDMG* 28 [1874]: 59) assumed it was named after King Vologaeses of Persia. Cf. Fraenkel, *Fremdwörter*, p. XIII.

[8] *Aġāni*, vol. 2, p. 31; Ṭabarī, vol. 5, p. 204 (= vol. 2, p. 58); *Marāṣid*, s.v. "Sābāṭ Kisrā"; al-'Alī, *Sumer* 23 (1967): 61. Cf. Fiey, *Sumer* 23 (1967): 12, and the entry on "Gišra də-Šabistana."

[9] *ar-Rauḍ al-mi'ṭār*, s.v. "Madā'in"; Ya'qūbī, *Buldān*, p. 321; al-'Alī, *ibid.*, pp. 52, 61ff. Cf. Fiey, *ibid.*, pp. 13–14. And cf. Sam'ānī, *Ansāb*, s.v. "Sābāṭ" ("Sābāṭ is two parasangs from Madā'in on the road to Kūfa"); and cf. Suhrāb, p. 124; al-'Alī, *ibid.*, p. 62.

[10] Ṭabarī, vol. 2, p. 173 (= vol. 1, p. 990); Fiey, *ibid.*, p. 12; cf. al-'Alī, *ibid.*, p. 62. Another source says that between Madā'in and Nahr al-Malik there was a continuous plain (*marġ*, literally, "meadow") of unfenced groves (Bakrī, vol. 1, p. 72).

Khusro II Parwez of Persia (590/1–628).[11] According to most of the versions, Khusro wished to marry Nuʿmān's sister, but his envoy was told by Nuʿmān that for Arabs marriage with Persians (*ʿaǧam*) was disgraceful and contemptible. That hasty reply, with its inherent assumption of superiority, led to Nuʿmān's death. Nuʿmān's mother, by the way, was the daughter of a Jewish goldsmith from Fadak in northern Arabia, who had been captured by Bedouin of the Kalb tribe.[12]

D. *Sages and Sabata*

Source 1 reports a halakhah that the Sabata people were taught by Rabbi Jeremiah, of the fourth generation of Eretz Israel amoras, who came from Babylonia as an older man.[13] Some of the manuscripts have Sakuta instead of Sabata (see note 1), and the former is connected with another source reporting Rabbi Jeremiah as issuing a ruling to the people of Sakuta (q.v.). "Sakuta" (סכותא) may be a garble of "Sabata" (סבתא). If not, it is possible, in view of the manuscripts referred to, that Source 1 too deals with Sakuta and not Sabata, in which case Sabata does not figure in the Talmud at all.

AL-ʿALĪ, *Sumer* 23 (1967): 50, 52, 61ff.
BERLINER, *Beiträge* (1883), p. 54
ESHEL, *Yishuvei ha-Yehudim* (1979), pp. 193–194
FIEY, *Sumer* 23 (1967): 12–14
FRAENKEL, *Fremdwörter* (1886), p. XIII
FUNK, *Monumenta* (1913), pp. 44, 298
HERZFELD, *Samarra* (1948), pp. 32–34
HIRSCHENSON, *Sheva Ḥokhmot* (1883), p. 172
JASTROW, *Dictionary* (1950³), p. 989, (II סכותא)
KOHUT, *Arukh ha-Shalem* (1878–1892), vol. 6, p. 51; *Tosefot* (1937), p. 165 (וולשפט)
LEVY, *Wörterbuch* (1924²), vol. 3, p. 522, (סכותא), p. 739
NEUBAUER, *Géographie* (1868), pp. 362, (סכותא), 424
NÖLDEKE, *ZDMG* 28 (1874): 59
NÖLDEKE, *Perser und Araber* (1879), p. 134, n. 4
OBERMEYER, *Landschaft* (1929), p. 185
SARRE & HERZFELD, *Archäologische Reise* (1920), vol. 2, p. 48, n. 2

Šabistana שביסתנא

See the entry on "Gišra də-Šabistana."

[11] E.g. Masʿūdī, *Murūǧ*, vol. 2, pp. 224–227 (= vol. 3, pp. 201–208); *ar-Rauḍ al-miʿṭār*, s.v. "Sābāṭ al-Madāʾin"; *Kitāb al-maʿārif*, pp. 649–650; Ǧāḥiẓ, *Ḥayawān*, vol. 4, pp. 375–378; *ibid.*, vol. 7, pp. 112–113; *Šiʿr wa-šuʿarāʾ*, vol. 1, pp. 229–230; *Aġānī*, vol. 2, pp. 29–31; Ṭabarī, vol. 2, pp. 201–206 (= vol. 1, pp. 1024–1029); Fiey, *ibid.*, p. 12. For another version of Nuʿmān's imprisonment and death, cf. Rothstein, *Die Dynastie*, p. 118, but see, e.g. Bakrī, s.v. "Ḫāniqūn"; *ar-Rauḍ al-miʿṭār*, s.v. "Ḫāniqīn."

[12] See in detail Kister, *Le Muséon*, 92 (1979): 321–330. On the Dihqāns of Sābāṭ see Naṣr b. Muzāḥim, *Kitāb Ṣiffīn*, p. 136 (with ʿAlī b. Abī Ṭālib). See also Ṭabarī, vol. 4, pp. 5–6 (= vol. 1, pp. 2426–2427); Morony, *Iran* 14 (1976): 46. On Sābāṭ as a place of exile in ʿAlī's time, see al-ʿAlī, *ibid.*, p. 50. Cf. (on al-Ḥasan b. ʿAlī) *ibid.*, p. 62.

[13] See Albeck, *Mavo la-Talmudim*, p. 340.

Šaḥin   שחין

See the entry on "Damim."

Saḵuta   סכותא

A. *Sources*

1. Moʻed Qaṭan 4b

רבי ירמיה שרא להו לבני סכותא[1] למיכרא נהרא טמימא.

Rabbi Jeremiah allowed them, the people of Saḵuta,[1] to dredge a waterway that was obstructed [on the intermediate days of a festival].

2. T. J. Moʻed Qaṭan I 2 – 80b, 48

כהדא דבני דסכותא איתפחתת במועדא ושרא לון רבי אבהו מעבדינה במועדא.

Such as [the one], of the people of Saḵuta, [that] was spoiled on the festival and Rabbi Abbahu allowed them to do it on the festival.

B. *Location*

None can be proposed due to insufficient data.

C. *Attempts at Identification*

Attempts to identify Saḵuta have been made in three directions:

a. Identifying Saḵuta with Sabata (q.v.) based on linguistic similarity as well as Rabbi Jeremiah's ruling to the Sabata people (ʻAvodah Zarah 58b) which can be related to Source 1 where the same sage issues a ruling to the Saḵuta people.[2]

b. Identifying Saḵuta with a place of the same name referred to in the *baraita* on "Boundaries of Eretz Israel" and in the Rǝḥov inscription, which must be located in Transjordan.[3] Source 2, in which Rabbi Abbahu, of the third generation of Eretz Israel amoras, issues a ruling to the Saḵuta people, supports the hypothesis that Saḵuta was not in Babylonia, a hypothesis strengthened by the fact that Rabbi Jeremiah too left Babylonia for Eretz Israel.

---

[1] The Oxford MS has סכנתא.

[2] Thus already Neubauer, p. 362. However, the contrary is also possible, that the source in ʻAvodah Zarah should also be read "Saḵuta," and see the entry on "Sabata," n. 1 and the section there on Sages and Sabata.

[3] See Hildesheimer, *Beiträge zur Geographie Palestinas* (index, and especially nn. 323–324); Klein, *Sefer ha-Yishuv*, p. 112; idem., *Ever ha-Yarden ha-Yehudi*, pp. 219–232; Sussmann, *Tarbiẕ* 43 (1974): 115, n. 158; idem., *Tarbiẕ* 45 (1976): 237–238.

c. Positing Sakuta as a place in Babylonia at a site which cannot be specified with the data available. This hypothesis is supported by the content of Source 1 (dealing with the course of a river or canal blocked during intermediate festival days) which fits the Babylonian reality of the time.[4] The evidence in Source 2 is too fragmented to allow a determination of whether it deals with the same problem as Source 1.[5]

Berliner, *Beiträge* (1883), p. 54
Eshel, *Yishuvei ha-Yehudim* (1979): p. 198
Funk, *Monumenta* (1913), pp. 47, 298, ("סבתא")
Hildesheimer, *Beiträge zur Geographie Palestinas* (1886), index
Hirschenson, *Sheva Ḥokhmot* (1883), p. 172
Jastrow, *Dictionary* (1950³), p. 989
Klein, *Sefer ha-Yishuv* (1939), vol. 1, p. 112
Klein, *Ever ha-Yarden ha-Yehudi* (1925), pp. 219–232
Kohut, *Arukh ha-Shalem* (1878–1892), vol. 6, p. 51
Levy, *Wörterbuch* (1924²), vol. 3, p. 522
Neubauer, *Géographie* (1868), p. 362
Newman, *Agricultural Life* (1932), p. 87
Sussmann, *Tarbiẕ* 43 (1974): 115, n. 158

Šaliniya שלנייא

A. *Source*

Mo'ed Qaṭan 12b

רב אשי הוה ליה אבא בשלנייא,[1] אזל למיקצייה בחולא דמועדא, אמר ליה רב שילא משלנייא לרב אשי מאי דעתיך . . .

Rav Ashi had a forest in Šaliniya,[1] he went to chop it down during the intermediate days [of the festival week]. Said Rav Shela of Šaliniya to Rav Ashi, What is your view . . .

B. *Proposed Location*

Sanīniyā near Kūfa, evidently on the west bank of the Euphrates (D5 on the Tal. Bab. map).

[4] See Funk, *Monumenta*, p. 298.

[5] According to the Rabbenu Asher version (Mo'ed Qaṭan I 6—first printing), "דבני סכותא איתפחתא מסותא", Source 2 deals with an unserviceable bathhouse, whose repair on the intermediate days of a festival was permitted by Rabbi Abbahu (and see *Ahavat Zion w-Yrushalayim*).

[1] The source has שלנייא; the Munich MS has בשילינ״א, and also "Rav Shela of Šiliniya." The *Arukh* printed editions also have כשלניא explained as יער שנכשלים בו בני אדם (= a forest where people come to grief; see *Arukh ha-Shalem*, vol. 1, p. 3, s.v. "אבא" and nn. 13 and 14 there; see also Beer, *Amora'ei Bavel*, p. 113, n. 40).

C. *Identification*

The single talmudic mention of Šaliniya does not provide enough information for pinpointing its location, though evidently it was not too far from Sura.[2] According to the source above, there was a forest in Šaliniya owned by Rav Ashi, head of the Sura yeshiva, which in his day was located in nearby Mata Məḥasya. While Sanīniyā is not in the immediate vicinity of Sura, its linguistic similarity to Šaliniya, with /š/ being replaced by /s/[3] and /l/ by /n/,[4] supports the identity of the two.
A village called Sanīniyā in the Kūfa district was granted to one of the prophet Muḥammad's Companions by the caliph ʿUṯmān b. ʿAffān.[5]
If this identification is accepted, it appears that Šaliniya was located in the heart of an area of dense Jewish settlement (see the entries for "Tarbiqna," "Nəharpanya" and "Šum Ṭəmaya").

D. *Sages and Šaliniya*

The source above mentions one sage, Rav Shela from Šaliniya, but no other information on him is available.
The source indicates that Rav Ashi, head of the Sura yeshiva, a leading spokesman of the sixth generation of Babylonian amoras, owned a forest in Šaliniya[6] and wished to cut down some trees or branches during the intermediate days of a holiday. It does not say why he needed the wood, but another source relates that Rav Ashi sold wood from a forest he owned to the priests of the fire worshipers.[7] That source does not state where this forest was; it may of course be the forest in Šaliniya.

Beer, *Amora'ei Bavel* (1974), pp. 112–115
Berliner, *Beiträge* (1883), p. 63
Eshel, *Yishuvei ha-Yehudim* (1979), p. 242
Funk, *Monumenta* (1913), p. 300
Goldhaar, *Admat Qodesh* (1913), pp. 86, 89
Hirschenson, *Sheva Ḥokhmot* (1883), p. 235
Jastrow, *Dictionary* (1950³), p. 587
Kohut, *Arukh ha-Shalem* (1878–1892), vol. 1, p. 3 ("אבא"), and n. 13; vol. 8, p. 87
Levy, *Wörterbuch* (1924²), vol. 1, p. 4, ("I אבא"); vol. 4, p. 565
Neubauer, *Géographie* (1868), p. 362 and n. 7
Newman, *Agricultural Life* (1932), p. 45
Zuri, *Shilton* (1938), p. 239

[2] Obermeyer does not mention Šaliniya. Funk identifies it with Bit-Šilanī in southern Babylonia (*Monumenta*, p. 300). See also Neubauer, p. 362 and n. 7.
[3] On the substitution of /s/ for /š/ see Fraenkel, *Fremdwörter*, p. xiii.
[4] On the assimilation of /l/, cf. Yāqūt, s.v. "Nahr Bīl" and "Nahr Bīn."
[5] See Yāqūt, s.v. It was granted to ʿAmmār b. Yāsir, on whom see *Iṣāba*, vol. 4, p. 575.
[6] On Babylonian amoras who owned forests, see Beer, *Amora'ei Bavel*, pp. 112–115 (explicit testimony is available only in connection with two: Rabbah b. Rav Huna and Rav Ashi).
[7] T. B. Nedarim 62b.

Šanwata   שנוותא

See the entry on "Šunya."

Šəḵanṣiv   שכנציב

A. Sources

1. Yoma 18b (= Yevamot 37b)

רב נחמן¹ כד מקלע לשכנציב מכריז מאן הויא ליומא.

When Rav Naḥman[1] happened to be in Šəḵanṣiv he would announce, Who will be [willing to marry me] for a day.

2. Yoma 71a (as per the Munich MS)

אמר רבה² כי מיפטרי רבנן בשכנציב³ מבי רב נחמן אמרי הכי מחיה חיים ''אתהלך לפני ה' בארצות החיים.''

Rabbah[2] said, When rabbis in Šəḵanṣiv[3] take leave of Rav Naḥman's house [of study] they say thus, May He who sustains life "I shall walk before the Lord in the lands of the living" (Ps. 116:9).

3. Qiddushin 70b (as per the Munich MS)

מכריז רב נחמן בשכנציב⁴ . . .

Rav Naḥman announces in Šəḵanṣiv[4] . . .

4. Mo'ed Qaṭan 28b

מאי אמרן, אמר רב ויי לאזלא ויי לחבילא. אמר רבא נשי דשכנציב אמרן הכי ויי לאזלא ויי לחבילא.⁵ ואמר רבא נשי דשכנציב אמרן גוד גרמא מכבא ונמטי מיא לאנטיכי.⁶ ואמר רבא נשי דשכנציב אמרן עטוף וכסו טורי דבר רמי ובר רברבי הוא. ואמר רבא נשי דשכנציב אמרן שיול אצטלא דמלתא לבר חורין דשלימו זוודיה. ואמר רבא נשי דשכנציב אמרן רהיט ונפיל אמעברא ויזופתא יזיף. ואמר רבא נשי דשכנציב אמרן אחנא תגרי אזבזגי מיבדקו. ואמר רבא נשי דשכנציב אמרן מותא כי מותא ומרעין חיבוליא.

What [lament] do they say? Rav said, Woe to the departing, woe to pangs. Rava said: The women of Šəḵanṣiv say, Woe to the departing, woe to pangs.[5]

---

[1] The Munich MS has "Rav Naḥman b. Isaac" in Yoma, and see *Diq. Sof.*

[2] The Oxford MS and *Ein Ya'aqov* have "Rava said," and see *Diq. Sof.*

[3] The standard edition and the margin of the Munich MS have "in Pumbədita take leave of each other" (see Source 5 in the entry on "Pumbədita"). Some of the MSS have two formulas, one on the sages in Pumbədita and the other on those in Šəḵanṣiv, and see *Diq. Sof.* The Munich B MS has "Rav Naḥman said that sages taking leave of each other in Šəḵanṣiv say . . ."

[4] That is the version in *She'iltot de-Rav Aḥai Gaon, She'ilta* 41; the Vatican 111 MS has בשכנסיב. The standard edition has "Rav Judah announces in Pumbədita . . ." and Rav Naḥman and Šəḵanṣiv do not appear at all.

[5] The Munich MS has this sentence only once, cited by Rav, and the next to last saying is missing there too, and see *Diq. Sof.*, and notes ו and ב there.

And Rava said: The women of Šəkanṣiv say, Pull a bone from the teeth and the water will reach Antioch.[6] And Rava said: The women of Šəkanṣiv say, Be wrapped and covered, oh mountains, for he [the deceased] is the son of the lofty, the son of the great. And Rava said: The women of Šəkanṣiv say, The netherworld is a woolen robe for a free [dead] man whose provisions are exhausted. And Rava said: The women of Šəkanṣiv say, He ran and fell at the crossing and takes a loan. And Rava said: The women of Šəkanṣiv say, Our brothers the merchants are searched in their premises. And Rava said: The women of Šəkanṣiv say, One death is like another, it is the pangs that hurt.

5. Pesaḥim 112b

ארבעה דברים צוה רבינו הקדוש[7] את בניו, אל תדור בשכנציב,[8] משום דליצני הוו ומשכו לך בליצנותא.

Our holy teacher (Rabbi Judah ha-Nasi)[7] commanded his sons four things: Do not live in Šəkanṣiv,[8] for they are scoffers and will dispose you to scoffing.

B. *Location*

None can be proposed due to insufficient data.

C. *Attempts at Identification*

Obermeyer locates Šəkanṣiv on the east bank of the Tigris near Dair Qunnā, sixteen parasangs downstream from Baghdad (nine parasangs from Maḥoza and one from Dair al-ʿĀqūl).[9] In his opinion the place name, "Šekunṣib" in his reading, was divided into two names of adjacent places, Askūn and Ṣāfiya.[10] Obermeyer bases that identification on Rav Sherira Gaon's testimony that after the destruction of Nəhardəʿa (q.v.) in 259, the amoras fled from it to Šəkanṣiv, Šilḥe and Maḥoza; from it he deduces that the flight was eastward from Nəhardəʿa,[11] which fits in with the locations of Askūn and Ṣāfiya. Rava's connection with Šəkanṣiv,[12] according to Obermeyer, supports that identification because it suggests that Šəkanṣiv was not far from Maḥoza whose yeshiva Rava headed.

---

[6] The Munich MS has the form **לאנטוכיא** (= Anṭokya), and see *Diq. Sof.*

[7] This is the form in all MSS and versions, but Kohut suggests reading "Rava," and see below (*Arukh ha-Shalem*, vol. 1, p. 290, under "ארם").

[8] The parallel in Pirqe de-Rabbenu ha-Qadosh has "Do not reside in a seat of scorners" (Greenhut ed., p. 72) but Schenblum (in *Sheloshah Sefarim Niftaḥim*, 13b) has "Šəkanṣiv" like the talmudic version.

[9] Obermeyer, pp. 190–192, and many in his wake, e.g. Adams, *Land Behind Baghdad*, p. 74 and n. 27. For other identifications see Neubauer, p. 363; *Arukh ha-Shalem*, vol. 8, p. 73; etc.

[10] See Yāqūt, the entries for "Dair Qunnā," "aṣ-Ṣāfiya" and "Dair al-Askūn."

[11] Obermeyer, p. 190; see also Eshel, p. 241; and see below.

[12] See the section on Sages and Šəkanṣiv below.

Obermeyer's identification is doubtful for the following reasons: a) The division of a place name into two parts each of which became the name of a separate place is a far from usual development. b) The testimony of Rav Sherira Gaon does not contain unequivocal proof of the direction of flight from Nəhardəʻa. Even if we agree with Obermeyer that the Šilḥe referred to there is Sailaḥīna west of Baghdad,[13] we have only two places identified, Šilḥe and Maḥoza—and they do not necessarily provide evidence for the locations of Šəkanṣiv. c) Rava's references to Šəkanṣiv[14] cannot be construed to mean it was in the vicinity of Maḥoza, for Rava had connections with many Babylonian communities, some of them quite a distance from Maḥoza.[15]

D. *Sages and Šəkanṣiv*

Rav Naḥman[16] of the third generation of Babylonian amoras is mentioned in various contexts in connection with Šəkanṣiv. Source 1 indicates that he was frequently there on business, and consequently wished to find a woman who would be his wife on the days he spent there.[17] *Iggeret Rav Sherira Gaon* describes Rav Naḥman's connection with Šəkanṣiv as follows[18]: "In the year 570 (Seleucid era A. D. 259) Papa b. Natzer came and destroyed Nəhardəʻa and Rabbah b. Avuha, our ancestor, and Rav Naḥman went to Šəkanṣiv and Šilhe[19] and Maḥoza." Thus the *Iggeret* does not allow the conclusion that after leaving Nəhardəʻa Rav Naḥman settled in Šəkanṣiv, for it is just one of three places mentioned in that connection.[20] Šəkanṣiv was indeed Rav Naḥman's choice, according to Obermeyer, who specifies further that Source 1 which is definite evidence that Rav Naḥman was not a permanent resident, refers to a time before he left Nəhardəʻa.[21] The Munich MS version of Source 2 supports the assumption that Rav Naḥman resided in Šəkanṣiv at some time or other

[13] Obermeyer, pp. 190, 242. Šilḥe does not appear in the Talmud. In *Iggeret Rav Sherira Gaon*, it appears also as Rav Sheshet's place of residence (Lewin ed., p. 82). Rav Sheshet belonged to the third generation of Babylonian amoras, and the Talmud refers to Nəhardəʻa as his place of residence (Megillah 29a, Nedarim 78a). He may have moved to Šilḥe after the destruction of Nəhardəʻa, just as Rav Naḥman moved to Šəkanṣiv at that time.

[14] See Source 4 above. Obermeyer believed Source 5 too applies to Rava (see n. 7 above), but this seems doubtful, and see below.

[15] See, e.g., the entry for "Nəharpanya."

[16] In the T. J. he is called "Rav Naḥman b. Jacob" and see Albeck, *Mavo la-Talmudim*, p. 298ff., and n. 256.

[17] On this matter see Urbach, *The Sages*, vol. 2, p. 897f., nn. 47, 48; Herr in *Mishpeḥot Bet Yisrael*, p. 40f., n. 16, and the bibliography there.

[18] Lewin ed., p. 82 (the French version; in the Spanish version, Rav Naḥman is not mentiond at all).

[19] An earlier reference and some of the MSS have the usual "Silḥe."

[20] See Weiss, *Dor Dor we-Doreshaw*, vol. 3, p. 157.

[21] Obermeyer, p. 191.

because it refers to his study house there. Further support is provided by the Munich MS version of Source 3, which testifies to Rav Naḥman's presence in Šəkanṣiv (and see note 4 above). If Rav Naḥman did have his study house in Šəkanṣiv, it was presumably the place of residence also of other sages, some of whom arrived there from Nəhardəʿa together with him.[22]

Source 4 testifies to a connection between Šəkanṣiv and Rava, head of the Maḥoza yeshiva in the fourth generation of Babylonian amoras. There Rava cites seven lamentation formulas that were customary among the women of Šəkanṣiv. Source 5 contains a warning by Rabbi Judah ha-Nasi to his sons against residing in Šəkanṣiv, because of the frivolity of the inhabitants. Some scholars have raised the question of what Rabbi Judah ha-Nasi had to do with Šəkanṣiv in Babylonia, and have mostly sought to correct "Rabbi" to "Rava."[23] If so, that is further evidence of Rava's connection with Šəkanṣiv and his familiarity with its populace.[24] The correction, however, is of doubtful validity because the passage in Qiddushin 72a–b lists a number of Babylonian places to which Rabbi referred in his will.[25] In Beer's view, Šəkanṣiv was a T.B. addition to Rabbi's general advice to his sons, which was something like "Do not reside in a neighborhood of scoffers" or "Do not reside in a seat of scorners."[26] Beer bases his view on Pirqe de-Rabbenu ha-Qadosh, but one of the versions of that *midrash* too has "Šəkanṣiv."[27]

It may well be that various comments and admonitions connected with Babylonian communities were attributed to Rabbi Judah ha-Nasi in order to make them more authoritative, and merged with the existing traditions on his death bed instructions to his sons.[28] In any case, there is no specific evidence for attributing the statement to Rava.

Adams, *Land Behind Baghdad* (1965), pp. 74, 178
Beer, *Rashut ha-Golah* (1970), pp. 98–100
Beer, *Amora'ei Bavel* (1974), p. 202, n. 147
Berliner, *Beiträge* (1883), pp. 64–65
Eshel, *Yishuvei ha-Yehudim* (1979), p. 241
Funk, *Juden* (1902–1908), vol. 1, p. 76

---

22 *Iggeret Rav Sherira Gaon* has Rabbah b. Avuha—the Exilarch, Rav Naḥman's father-in-law—as the person who fled with him from Nəhardəʿa (see above). The B-a-ḥ marginal notes for Yevamot 85a have שכנצבו instead of הינצבו as the place of residence of Rav Idi b. Avin of the fifth generation of Babylonian amoras (and see "Hinṣəvu" in the Appendix).

23 Thus Neubauer, p. 363, n. 2; Obermeyer, p. 191, n. 4; and see n. 7 above.

24 If Source 2 cites Rava (see n. 1) this would be an additional testimony by Rava on Šəkanṣiv.

25 Humaniya, Birta (qq. v.), Aqra də-Agama (see n. 16 in the entry on "Damim") and Masgarya (in the Appendix).

26 Beer, *Amora'ei Bavel*, p. 201, n. 147.

27 See n. 8 above.

28 Ketubot 103a–104a; T. J. Taʿaniot VI 2 - 68a; but in connection with Rava too there is a tradition on an admonition to his sons (see Berakhot 8b).

FUNK, *Monumenta* (1913), pp. 52–53, 300
GOODBLATT, *Rabbinic Instruction* (1975), pp. 22, 50, n. 35
GRAETZ, *Geschichte* (1908⁴), vol. 4, p. 270
HALEVY, *Dorot ha-Rishonim* (1897–1939). vol. 5, p. 414
HIRSCHENSON, *Sheva Ḥokhmot* (1883), p. 235
JASTROW, *Dictionary* (1950³), p. 1575
KOHUT, *Arukh ha-Shalem* (1878–1892), vol. 8, p. 73
LEVY, *Wörterbuch* (1924²), vol. 4, p. 554
NEUBAUER, *Géographie* (1868), p. 363
OBERMEYER, *Landschaft* (1929), pp. 190–192, 254
WEISS, *Dor Dor we-Doreshaw* (1904⁴), vol. 3, p. 157

Seleucia

See the entry under "Maḥoza Area."

Ṣərifa צריפא

See the entry on "Damim."

Sikra סיכרא

A. *Sources*

1. Ḥullin 94b

כי הא דמר זוטרא בריה דרב נחמן הוה קאזיל מסיכרא לבי מחוזא,[1] ורבא ורב ספרא הוו קא אתו לסיכרא,[2] פגעו אהדדי, הוא סבר לאפיה הוא דקאתו, אמר להו למה להו לרבנן דטרוח ואתו כולי האי . . .

Mar Zuṭra son of Rav Naḥman was going from Sikra to Be Maḥoza,[1] and Rava and Rav Safra were coming to Sikra,[2] and they met. He thought they were coming to meet him and said, Why did our sages trouble to come all this [way] . . .

2. Ketubot 100b

רבינא הוה בידיה חמרא דרבינא זוטי יתמא בר אחתיה, הוה לדידיה נמי חמרא, הוה קמסיק ליה לסיכרא, אתא לקמיה דרב אשי,[3] אמר ליה מהו לאמטויי בהדן,[4] אמר ליה זיל לא עדיף מדידך.

---

[1] The Munich MS has "from Sikra to Maḥoza" as do other MSS, and see *Diq. Sof.*

[2] The Munich MS has "from Maḥoza to Sikra," and see *Diq. Sof.*

[3] *Halakhot Gedolot* and *Sefer Yuḥasin* under the entry "Ravina" (p. 187) have **אתא לקמיה דרב ששת** (= he came before Rav Sheshet) which would mean that Ravina here was Rav Avina of the third generation of Babylonian amoras, a disciple of Rav Huna's, and see Epstein, *Mevo'ot le-Sifrut ha-Amora'im*, p. 43, n. 85. See also Ketubot with various versions in the ICIT edition, and n. 57 there.

[4] The Munich MS has **מהו לאמטויי מי חיישינן לאונסא דאורחא או לא** (= can I carry it, do we fear accident on the way or not) as do other MSS (see Ketubot in the ICIT edition with variants, p. 413).

Ravina had in hand wine of his orphan nephew Little Ravina, and had his own wine too, which he was about to take up to Siḵra. He came before Rav Ashi[3] and asked him, Can I carry [the wine] together?[4] He answered him, Go, it is not preferable to yours.

3. 'Avodah Zarah 40a

ההוא ארבא דצחנתא דאתי לסיכרא, נפק רב הונא בר חיננא וחזא ביה קלפי ושרייה. אמר ליה רבא ומי איכא דשרי כה''ג באתרא דשכיחי קלפי. נפק שיפורי דרבא ואסר, שיפורי דרב הונא בר חיננא ושרי.

A lighter loaded with ṣaḥanta [fish] came to Siḵra. Rav Huna bar Ḥinena went out and saw the scales in it and allowed them. Rava said to him, Is it possible to permit in that way in a place where scales are common? So Rava's pronouncement forbade, and Rav Huna bar Ḥinena's permitted.

4. Bava Metzi'a 83a

אתקין רב חייא בר יוסף בסיכרא, הני דדרו באגרא[5] ואיתבר נשלם פלגא. מאי טעמא, נפיש לחד וזוטר לתרי קרוב לאונס וקרוב לפשיעה. בדיגלא משלם כולה.

Rav Ḥiyya bar Joseph determined in Siḵra, Those carrying [loads] on a yoke[5] and it breaks pay half. The reason is, it is too much for one and too little for two, like accident and like negligence. As to a pole, [the porter] must pay all.

5. Pesaḥim 31b (= Bava Metzi'a 42a)

אמר ליה רב אחא בריה דרב יוסף לרב אשי הא דאמר שמואל כספים אין להם שמירה אלא בקרקע, מי בעינן שלשה טפחים או לא... וכמה, אמר רפרם בר פפא[6] מסיכרא[7] טפח.

Rav Aḥa son of Rav Joseph said to Rav Ashi, As to what Samuel said—money can only be safeguarded in the earth—do we need three handbreadths or not? ...And how much? Said Rafram bar Papa[6] of Siḵra,[7] One handbreadth.

6. Niddah 36a

אמר ליה רבינא לרב אשי אמר לן רב שמן מסכרא[8] אקלע מר זוטרא לאתרין ודרש, הילכתא כוותיה דרב לחומרא והלכתא כוותיה דלוי לחומרא.

Ravina said to Rav Ashi, Rav Shamen of Siḵra[8] told us, Mar Zuṭra once happened to visit our place and preached that the halakhah is to be restricted according to Rav, and to be restricted according to Levi.

7. Ḥullin 18b

אמר ליה רבינא לרב אשי אמר לי רב שמן מסוברא[9] איקלע מר זוטרא לאתרין ודרש, שייר בחיטי כשרה.

---

[5] The Hamburg, Florence and Vatican 115 MSS have באגדא.

[6] Bava Metzi'a 42a has just "Rafram of Siḵra."

[7] Pesaḥim in the Munich MS has מסתברא instead of מסיכרא, and see Diq. Sof.

[8] The Munich MS has משיכרא.

[9] The standard edition actually has מסוברא, but the Munich and other MSS have Rav Shamen of Siḵra, which seems correct.

Ravina said to Rav Ashi, Rav Shamen of Siḵra[9] told me that Mar Zuṭra once happened to visit our place and preached that leaving some of the gland is fit.

B. *Proposed Location*

Siḵra on Nahr al-Malik (D 3 on the Tal. Bab. map).

C. *Identification*

On the basis of the implication in Source 1, scholars have customarily located Siḵra in the vicinity of Maḥoza.[10] Obermeyer proposes identifying it with Dair al-'Āqūl, on the Tigris fifteen parasangs below Baghdad (and eight below Madā'in/Maḥoza).[11] That proposal seems unacceptable, first of all because Dair al-'Āqūl is not very close to Maḥoza, and secondly because identifications are better made on the basis of a toponymic similarity in Arabic sources. It seems more desirable to identify Siḵra with a place having an almost identical name, Sikra (the Arabic root *skr*, like the Hebrew *sḵr*, has the meaning of "dam"). Sikra was closer to Maḥoza and to the center of Jewish settlement in Babylonia. Sikra is mentioned in a later Arabic geographical treatise which says: "Sikra—a large village containing a mosque (*ǧāmiʿ*) and a pulpit on Nahr al-Malik west (actually southwest) of Baghdad."[12] There were other Jewish settlements such as Disqarta and Parzina (qq.v.) on Nahr al-Malik as well.[13]

D. *Sages and Siḵra*

Various amoras are mentioned in connection with Siḵra throughout the talmudic period. Rav Ḥiyya bar Joseph, a disciple of Rav's, of the second generation of Babylonian amoras, is mentioned in Source 4 as making a determination at Siḵra. The determination deals with the extent of a person's responsibility for goods he is transporting in various ways. From the context of the passage and testimony on the wine market in Siḵra (see below) it appears that the ordinance concerns the transport of casks of wine. Another sage who resided in Siḵra was Rav Huna bar Ḥinena of the fourth generation of Babylonian amoras. Source 3 tells of ṣaḥanta fish that reached Siḵra by boat and which

---

[10] Already Neubauer, p. 361; Berliner, p. 56; and others in their wake. Berliner even insisted that Siḵra was above (= north of) Sura on the basis of the Source 2 statement that people "ascended" from Sura to Siḵra.

[11] Obermeyer, pp. 186–189. Quite similar is the proposal to identify Siḵra with as-Sakr in the Wāsiṭ region made by de Goeje, *ZDMG* 39 (1885): 14.

[12] Yāsīn al-'Umarī, *Maḥāsin Baǧdād*, pp. 48–49.

[13] Testimony from the start of the tenth century states: "Most of the residents of Sura and Nahr al-Malik are Jews" (Ibn al-Qifṭī, *Ta'rīḫ al-ḥukamā'*, p. 194). This information relates to a settlement called Nahr al-Malik on the bank of a river by the same name (see Le Strange, p. 68, and the sources there).

Rav Huna bar Ḥinena declared fit to be eaten on the basis of scales found in the belly of the boat. Of the later sages, Sources 6 and 7 mention Rav Shamen of Sikra, of the sixth generation of Babylonian amoras, and Source 5 mentions Rafram bar Papa of Sikra of the seventh.[14]

Sikra was connected with the yeshivas at Maḥoza and Sura/Mata Məḥasya, and the sources mentioning Sikra refer to prominent scholars of those institutions who appeared in Sikra. According to Source 1, one such was Rava, the head of the Maḥoza yeshiva in the fourth generation of Babylonian amoras, along with Rav Safra. Sikra's ties with Maḥoza and Rava can also be seen from Source 3, where Rava rules contrary to Rav Huna bar Ḥinena and forbids the consumption of the *ṣaḥanta* fish brought to Sikra.[15] Source 2 contains testimony on Ravina, a member of the seventh generation of Babylonian amoras who was a disciple of Rav Ashi's and lived at Mata Məḥasya (q.v.) going up to Sikra to sell wine there.[16] In Sources 6 and 7 Ravina tells Rav Ashi things he heard from Rav Shamen of Sikra.

Another instance of Rava's intervening and ruling in contradiction to Rav Huna bar Ḥinena of Sikra occurred when the Exilarch who then resided in Maḥoza asked Rav Huna bar Ḥinena to issue an ordinance allowing him to carry things in his garden for the purpose of holding a Sabbath feast there. Rav Huna bar Ḥinena tried to solve the problem with a partition of reeds, but Rava came and pulled them out.[17] The garden in question may have been the one in his estate at Disqarta de-Resh Galuta (see "Disqarta"). That would explain why Rav Huna bar Ḥinena was consulted, as both Sikra and Disqarta were on Nahr al-Malik.

E. *Economy*

The combined evidence of Source 2 and 4 indicates that Sikra was the site of a central wine market. Source 2 covers the case of Ravina proceeding to Sikra to sell his wine, and consulting Rav Ashi as to whether he may take along also some wine belonging to the orphaned nephew whose guardian he was.[18] It

---

[14] If the form Rafram alone in Bava Metziʻa and other versions is accepted, the sage involved is Rav Ashi's disciple Rafram, likewise of the seventh generation of Babylonian amoras.

[15] There are a number of instances in which Rava disagrees with the rulings of Rav Huna bar Ḥinena (see below and ʻAvodah Zarah 57b). Evidence of the ties between Rav Huna bar Ḥinena and Rava, and in any case the close connection between Sikra and Maḥoza, can be found in additional sources as well (see e.g. ʻEruvin 67b and Sanhedrin 87a). On the *ṣaḥanta*, see Sperber, *Iranica Antiqua* 8 (1968): 70.

[16] Possibly Rav Avina; see n. 3 above.

[17] ʻEruvin 25b–26a, and see Beer, *Rashut ha-Golah*, pp. 152–153.

[18] On the source of Rava's suspicion see n. 4 above, and see Beer, *Amora'ei Bavel*, pp. 168–169. On the wine trade see also the section on Sages and Walašpaṭ in the entry on "Walašpaṭ," and n. 25 in the entry on "Ctesiphon" under "Maḥoza Area."

appears that the wine involved came not only from the vineyards of Ravina and his nephew: Ravina was a wine merchant. In any case, it was worth his while to take the wine to Sikra and sell it there, an indication that there was an active wine market in the place. Source 4 reports on Rav Ḥiyya bar Joseph's ordinance in Sikra on the transport of wine casks.

ALBECK, *Mavo la-Talmudim* (1969), p. 362
BEER, *Amora'ei Bavel* (1974), pp. 168–169
BEER, *Rashut ha-Golah* (1970), p. 153
BERLINER, *Beiträge* (1883), p. 56
ESHEL, *Yishuvei ha-Yehudim* (1979), pp. 194, 198
FUNK, *Monumenta* (1913), pp. 47, 298
DE GOEJE, *ZDMG* 39 (1885): 14
HIRSCHENSON, *Sheva Ḥokhmot* (1883), p. 179
JASTROW, *Dictionary* (1950³), p. 979
KOHUT, *Arukh ha-Shalem* (1878–1892), vol. 6, p. 55; *Tosefot* (1937), p. 292
KRAUSS, *Qadmoniot ha-Talmud* (1923–1945), vol. 1, p. 208, n. 7
LE STRANGE, *The Lands* (1905), p. 68
LEVY, *Wörterbuch* (1924²), vol. 3, p. 530
NEUBAUER, *Géographie* (1868), p. 361
NEUSNER, *History* (1965–1970), vol. 2, p. 248; vol. 4, pp. 141, 305; vol. 5, pp. 183, 282
OBERMEYER, *Landschaft* (1929), pp. 186–189
ZURI, *Shilton* (1939), pp. 222, 237, 238, 243 n. 34

Šile שילי

See the entry on "Hine and Šile."

Sileq סילק

See the entry on "Seleucia" under "Maḥoza Area."

Ṣinta צינתא

A. *Source*

'Eruvin 51b–52a

רבה בר רב חנן[1] הוה רגיל דאתי מארטיבנא[2] לפומבדיתא, אמר תהא שביתתי בצינתא.[3]

Rabbah b. Rav Ḥanan[1] used to come [on the Sabbath] from Arṭivna[2] to Pumbədita; he said, My camp will be in Ṣinta.[3]

---

[1] The Munich and Oxford MSS have "Rava b. Rav Ḥanin."

[2] For variants see the entry on "Arṭivna."

[3] The Munich MS has בניזיתא (or בני זיתא); the Oxford MS has בזיתא, and see *Diq. Sof.* See *Arukh ha-Shalem*, vol. 2, p. 35, s.v. "בזתא."

B. *Location*

Near Pumbədita (q.v., C 2 on the Tal. Bab. map), between it and Arṭivna (q.v.).

C. *Identification*

On the basis of the above source it may be assumed that before the Sabbath an *ʿeruv teḥumim* could be placed in Ṣinta making it permissible to walk from Arṭivna to Pumbədita (q.v.) on the Sabbath. Thus Ṣinta was between the two, and not more than two thousand cubits (about one kilometer) from either, and see the entry on "Arṭivna."
The name "Ṣinta" means palm.[4] Rabbah (or Rava) b. Rav Ḥanan himself, of the fourth generation of Babylonian amoras, is described as owning palm trees.[5] A distinction must be made between the place Ṣinta and the expression "be ṣanita də-Bavel" (Berakhot 31a; Soṭah 46b) which designates palm groves near the city of Babylon, or a place by that name near Babylon (see the section on Physical Features in the entry on "Babylon").

Beer, *Amora'ei Bavel* (1974), p. 95
Berliner, *Beiträge* (1883), p. 24
Eshel, *Yishuvei ha-Yehudim* (1979), p. 220
Jastrow, *Dictionary* (1950³), p. 1278
Kohut, *Arukh ha-Shalem* (1878–1892), vol. 2, p. 35, "בזתא"; vol. 7, p. 28
Levy, *Wörterbuch* (1924²), vol. 4, p. 203
Obermeyer, *Landschaft* (1929), p. 232
Rapoport, *Erekh Millin* (1914), vol. 2, p. 253

Ṣiṣura ציצורא

A. *Sources*

1. Qiddushin 72a

אמר רמי בר אבא חביל ימא תכילתא דבבל שוניא[1] וגוביא[2] תכילתא דחביל ימא. רבינא אמר אף ציצורא. תניא נמי הכי חנן בן פנחס אומר חביל ימא תכילתא דבבל, שוניא וגוביא וציצורא תכילתא דחביל ימא.[3]

---

[4] See the entry on "Babylon," n. 45.

[5] Bava Batra 26a has Rav Joseph, a resident of Pumbədita who headed its yeshiva for two and a half years, complaining that his orchard is being harmed by the palm trees of Rabbah b. Rav Ḥanan.

[1] The Munich MS has שנייה.

[2] The Vatican 111 MS has גוניא.

[3] The Munich MS has Rami b. Abba's statement and Ravina saying "And Ṣiṣura too is the blue of Ḥavel Yama," and the *baraita* containing the statement by Ḥanan b. Pinḥas does not appear at all. The following *baraita* appears in Seder Eliahu Zuṭa (XVI [Pirqe Derekh Eretz I] Friedmann ed., p. 13): יוחנן בן פנחס אומר הבא ימרו תבליתא דבבל שוניא שרצוניא ואקח סלא ושיצריא תבלותא דהבלא ימא. רבי עקיבא אומר אף אקרוקיא. Obviously the names in that source are garbled, and see Friedmann's remarks on them.

Rami b. Abba said, Ḥavel Yama is the blue of Babylonia, Šunya[1] and Guvya[2] are the blue of Ḥavel Yama. Ravina said, Also Ṣiṣura. It was also taught that Ḥanan b. Pinḥas says, Ḥavel Yama is the blue of Babylonia; Šunya, Guvya and Ṣiṣura are the blue of Ḥavel Yama.[3]

2. T. J. Qiddushin IV 1 – 65c, 26–27[4]

תמן אמרין[5] מישא מתה מדיי חולה, אילם וגבביי גוססות, חביל ימא תכילתא דבבל שנייא וגבביא וצררייא[6] תכילתא דחביל ימא.

There they say,[5] Meša is dead, Media is sick, Elam and Guvai are dying, Ḥavel Yama is the blue of Babylonia; Šunya, and Guvya and Ṣiṣura[6] are the blue of Ḥavel Yama.

3. Genesis Rabbah XXXVII 8, Theodor-Albeck ed., p. 350[7]

ר׳ לעזר בן פפוס[8] אמר מישא[9] מיתה, מדי חולה, עילם גוססת, חבל[10] ימא תכילתא דבבל, צוצירה[11] תכילתא דחבל ימא.

Rabbi Leazar b. Papos[8] said, Meša[9] is dead, Media is sick, Elam is dying; Ḥavel[10] Yama is the blue of Babylonia, Ṣiṣura[11] is the blue of Ḥavel Yama.

B. *Location*

None can be proposed due to insufficient data.

C. *Attempts at Identification*

The sources referring to Ṣiṣura indicate it was in Ḥavel Yama, a region considered superior from the point of view of lineage. In Ravina's opinion, supported by a *baraita* in Source 1, inhabitants of Ṣiṣura along with those of Guvya and Šunya (qq. v.) are considered to have lineage of the highest purity in comparison with even the other Ḥavel Yama residents.

The location of the three depends on the identification of Ḥavel Yama (q. v.) which is not entirely definite. But Obermeyer's proposal to identify Ṣiṣura with the Ṣarṣar canal has some advantages. That canal starts three parasangs below

---

[4] And T. J. Yevamot I 6 – 3b, 10–12 as well.

[5] T. J. Yevamot has "There they call . . ."

[6] The source has שנייא וגבביא וצררייא. T. J. Yevamot has שניות עווניא וגווכייא וצוצרייה.

[7] Similarly in *Yalquṭ Shim'oni*: "ויהי מושבם ממישא', מישא מתה, מדי חולה, עילם וגונבי גוססת, חבל ימא תכלתא דבבל, צור ציירא תכלתא דחבל ימא . . ." (Genesis § 62, Mossad Harav Kook ed., p. 229).

[8] Most versions have "Rabbi Eleazar b. Pinḥas."

[9] For variants see the entry on "Mesene," n. 10.

[10] For variants see the entry on "Ḥavel Yama," n. 11.

[11] The source has צוצירה; the Stuttgart MS has צווציריה; the first printing has צו צייר; the Paris MS has צור צוריה; the Vatican 30 MS has צור צרייה; the Venice printing, Oxford 2335 MS and Yemenite MS have צור צייר.

Dimimmā, the mouth of Nahr ʿĪsā (see the entry on "Damim") and flows into the Tigris between Baghdad and Madā'in four parasangs north of the latter.[12] Obermeyer's identification is linguistically acceptable and, since it sets Ṣiṣura within the area of pure lineage, geographically reasonable but by no means certain.

Berliner, *Beiträge* (1883), pp. 34–35
Eshel, *Yishuvei ha-Yehudim* (1979), pp. 183, 220–221
Graetz, *Das Königreich Mesene* (1879), pp. 39–40
Hirschenson, *Sheva Ḥokhmot* (1883), p. 110
Jastrow, *Dictionary* (1950³), p. 1270
Kohut, *Arukh ha-Shalem* (1878–1892), vol. 7, p. 41; *Tosefot* (1937), p. 350
Levy, *Wörterbuch* (1924²), vol. 4, pp. 216, 224
Neubauer, *Géographie* (1868), p. 327
Obermeyer, *Landschaft* (1929), pp. 119, 125–126, 243–244

Šum Ṭəmaya שום טמיא

A. *Source*

Bava Batra 153a

ההוא דאתא לקמיה דרב נחמן לנהרדעא, שדריה לקמיה דרבי ירמיה בר אבא לשום טמיא,[1] אמר הכא אתרא דשמואל היכי נעביד כוותיה דרב.

There was one who once came to Rav Naḥman to Nəhardəʿa who sent him to Rav Jeremiah b. Abba to Šum Ṭəmaya,[1] who said: This is Samuel's place, how can we act as Rav [decided]?

---

[12] Obermeyer, pp. 125, 243–244. The identification with Ṣarṣar was made earlier by de Goeje, *ZDMG* 39 (1885), p. 14, but he identified Ṣiṣura with a place on the canal bank. Although Obermeyer's contention (p. 125) that the place was founded only in the Muslim period is not reasonable, his view that talmudic Ṣiṣura was the canal and the surrounding area is more likely. Obermeyer refers to Le Strange, "Ibn Serapion," p. 15. See also Suhrāb, p. 124, and the entry here on "Pərišna."

See "Ṣarṣar" in Yāqūt, *Marāṣid, ar-Rauḍ al-miʿṭār*; Abū l-Fidā', p. 48; *BGA*, passim; Idrīsī, vol. 6, p. 668; Samʿānī, *Ansāb* on "Ṣarṣarī"; *Ḥudūd al-ʿālam*, pp. 76, 139; Mustaufī, vol. 2, pp. 162, 202. See also the maps in Ibn Ḥauqal, pp. 206, 232. There Ṣarṣar is on the left bank of the canal. In the map on p. 232, Nahr al-Malik and Nahr Ṣarṣar seem to converge just before the Tigris and flow into it together north of Madā'in. According to Le Strange, "Ibn Serapion," p. 74, the Ṣarṣar canal followed the route of the presentday Abū Ġuraib canal. Muqaddasī (pp. 35–36) makes an interesting suggestion for connecting the place name with traits of its residents: When the letter *ṣād* figures in the place name, the residents are silly, aside from Baṣra ("even in Baṣra and Egypt [= Miṣr]" in another version), "and if there are two, as in Ṣarṣar and Maṣṣīṣa, God help us."

[1] Some versions in the manuscripts have the two parts of the name joined into one word: לשוטמי' in the Munich MS, לשטמיחם (and interlinearly לשמוטי) in the Hamburg MS, and לשיטמיה in the Florence MS.

B. *Proposed Location*

Šumyā on the west bank of the Euphrates, in the vicinity of Kūfa[2] (D5 on the Tal. Bab. map).

C. *Identification*

No attempts have heretofore been made to identify Šum Ṭəmaya except on the basis of the internal logic of the incident mentioned in the only source in talmudic literature in which the place name occurs. Obermeyer does not mention Šum Ṭəmaya at all. Funk claims it is in the neighborhood of Nəhardəʿa, because Rav Naḥman sent a case that applied to him there to Šum Ṭəmaya.[3] Hyman on the contrary argues that the fact that Rav Naḥman sent the case for adjudication in Šum Ṭəmaya indicates it was close to Sura, for Rav Naḥman's intention was to have Rav Jeremiah b. Abba make a decision of the kind Rav would make, and thus Šum Ṭəmaya is in the region of Sura which was Rav's town.[4]
Grounds for the identification with Šumyā[5] include the existence of a Jewish cemetery in the latter place or near it in a place called Nuḫaila. That the two places are contiguous or perhaps even identical emerges from a comparison of two parallel treatments of a place where a battle was fought during the Muslim conquest of Iraq. In one version, the battle was joined after the Persian commander, Mihrān, crossed the Euphrates (from east to west) and camped at a place called Šumyā.[6] In another text dealing with the same battle it took place in Nuḫaila.[7] (On the cemetery itself see the section below on the borders of Babylonia.)

D. *Sages and Šum Ṭəmaya*

According to the source above, Rav Jeremiah b. Abba was a resident of Šum Ṭəmaya. A scholar of the second generation of Babylonian amoras, he was a

[2] On cases of dropped syllables, cf. Yāqūt, s.v. "Ḫusrūsābūr": "the common people say Ḫussābūr"; *ibid.*, s.v. "Rāmahurmuz": "and the common people call it Rāmiz." Hurmuz Ardašīr was called Hurmušīr by the Arabs (see the entry on "Hurmiz Ardəšir"). According to Ḥamza al-Iṣfahānī (*Ta'rīḫ*, p. 46), Bahmanšīr was what the Baṣrans called Bahman Ardašīr: ("They also call it Furāt Maisān."); See Yāqūt, s. v. "Bahman Ardašīr," and also Masʿūdī, *Tanbīh*, pp. 38, 52.

The word "šum" is an inseparable part of the place name, as is clearly shown by the various versions of it found in different MSS.

[3] Funk, *Monumenta*, p. 300; cf. also Eshel, p. 237. In Funk's opinion, Šum Ṭəmaya may be no more than another variant of Samosata (see "Šuṭ Mišuṭ").

[4] Hyman, p. 813. On the basis of the identification with Šumyā, Šum Ṭəmaya would actually be about fifty kilometers from Sura.

[5] See the entry in Yāqūt.

[6] Ṭabarī, vol. 3, pp. 461, 464–465 (= vol. 1, pp. 2185, 2190–2191).

[7] *Ibid.*, p. 472 (= vol. 1, p. 2201), and see the poem there, p. 471 (vol. 1, p. 2200); see also *Futūḥ al-buldān*, p. 254. On the battle in Nuḫaila cf. al-ʿAlī, *Sumer* 21 (1965): 237.

friend and a disciple of Rav's, and yet felt an affinity for Samuel.[8] He is cited by Rabbi Avina,[9] who appears in connection with Nəharpanya (q.v.), as the designated recipient of wine Geniva had there. Nəharpanya too is in the Kūfa region, providing further indirect evidence for identifying Šum Ṭəmaya with Šumyā in the Kūfa region.

E. *The Borders of Babylonia*

A Shīʿite tradition says that Nuḫaila was the site of a large Jewish cemetery slightly west of Šumyā. According to Naṣr b. Muzāḥim, *Kitāb Ṣiffīn*,[10] "... And the funeral passed by ʿAlī (b. Abī Ṭālib) when he was in Nuḫaila. ʿAlī said: What do the people say about this tomb? And in Nuḫaila there was a huge tomb around which the Jews bury their dead. Ḥasan b. ʿAlī said: They say it's the tomb of the prophet Hūd: When his people disobeyed him he came and died there. He said: That's a lie. I know this better than they. It's the tomb of Judah son of Jacob, son of Isaac, son of Abraham, Jacob's first born."[11] In the view of the sages, the eastern border of Eretz Israel was the Euphrates River. Genesis Rabbah quotes Samuel, who said, "To the place where the river goes there is Eretz Israel."[12] According to that conception, Eretz Israel stretched as far as the place in southwestern Babylonia where the Euphrates ends. Burial in Eretz Israel was considered a great merit, averting the torment of rolling there underground for resurrection.[13] That explains the burial of Jews in Nuḫaila and other places west of the Euphrates (see the entries on "Tarbiqna" and "Nəhar Anaq").

Albeck, *Mavo la-Talmudim* (1969), pp. 203, 274–275
Berliner, *Beiträge* (1883), p. 63
Eshel, *Yishuvei ha-Yehudim* (1979), p. 237
Funk, *Monumenta* (1913), pp. 52, 300
Hirschenson, *Sheva Ḥokhmot* (1883), p. 234
Hyman, *Toledot Tanaim we-Amoraim* (1964), p. 813
Jastrow, *Dictionary* (1950³), p. 539
Kohut, *Arukh ha-Shalem* (1878–1892), vol. 4, p. 42; vol. 8, p. 96
Levy, *Wörterbuch* (1924²), vol. 2, p. 166; vol. 4, pp. 521, 688

[8] See Albeck, *Mavo la-Talmudim*, s.v. "Rav Jeremiah b. Abba," p. 203.

[9] See Albeck, *ibid.*, s.v. "Rabbi Avina," pp. 274–275.

[10] Pp. 126–127.

[11] *... wa-marrat ǧināza ʿalā ʿAlī wa-huwa bi-n-Nuḫaila ... qāla ʿAlī: mā yaqūlu n-nās fī hāḏā l-qabr? wa-fī n-Nuḫaila qabr ʿaẓīm yadfanu l-yahūd mautāhum ḥaulahū. fa-qāla l-Ḥasan b. ʿAlī: yaqūlūna hāḏā qabr Hūdi n-nabī (ṣ) lammā an ʿaṣāhu qaumuhū ǧāʾa fa-māta hāhunā. qāla: kaḏabū, la-anā aʿlamu bihī minhum, hāḏā qabr Yahūdā b. Yaʿqūb b. Isḥāq b. Ibrāhīm, bikr Yaʿqūb.*

[12] Genesis Rabbah, XVI 3 (Theodor-Albeck ed., p. 145).

[13] See e.g. T. B. Ketubot 111a.

Šunya שוניא

A. *Sources*

1. Qiddushin 72a

אמר רמי בר אבא חביל ימא תכילתא דבבל שוניא[1] וגוביא[2] תכילתא דחביל ימא. רבינא אמר אף ציצורא. תניא נמי הכי חנן בן פנחס אומר חביל ימא תכילתא דבבל, שוניא וגוביא וציצורא תכילתא דחביל ימא.[3]

Rami b. Abba said, Ḥavel Yama is the blue of Babylonia, Šunya[1] and Guvya[2] are the blue of Ḥavel Yama. Ravina said, Also Ṣiṣura. It was also taught that Ḥanan b. Pinḥas says, Ḥavel Yama is the blue of Babylonia; Šunya, Guvya and Ṣiṣura are the blue of Ḥavel Yama.[3]

2. T. J. Qiddushin IV 1 – 65c, 26–27[4]

תמן אמרין[5] מישא מתה מדיי חולה, אילם וגבביי גוססות, חביל ימא תכילתא דבבל שנייא וגבביא וצררייא[6] תכילתא דחביל ימא.

There they say,[5] Meša is dead, Media is sick, Elam and Guvai are dying; Ḥavel Yama is the blue of Babylonia, Šunya and Guvya and Ṣiṣura[6] are the blue of Ḥavel Yama.

B. *Location*

None can be proposed due to insufficient data.

C. *Attempts at Identification*

The sources referring to Šunya indicate that it was in the Ḥavel Yama district. It was one of the places whose residents were considered to have the purest of pure lineages, even within the Ḥavel Yama district whose inhabitants were all recognized as having impeccable ancestry. The location of Ḥavel Yama (q.v.) itself is not clear. Should it be established that Ḥavel Yama included the

---

[1] The Munich MS has שנייה.

[2] The Vatican 111 MS has גוניא.

[3] The Munich MS has Rami b. Abba's statement and Ravina saying "And Ṣiṣura too is the blue of Ḥavel Yama," and the *baraita* containing the statement by Ḥanan b. Pinḥas does not appear at all. The following *baraita* appears in Seder Eliahu Zuṭa (XVI [Pirqe Derekh Eretz I] Friedmann ed., p. 13): "יוחנן בן פנחס אומר הבא ימרו תבליתא דבבל שוניא שרצוניא ואקח סלא ושיצריא תבלותא דהבלא ימא. רבי עקיבא אומר אף אקרוקיא". Obviously the names in that source are garbled, and see Friedmann's remarks on them.

[4] Similarly in T. J. Yevamot I 6 – 3b, 10–12.

[5] T. J. Yevamot has "There they call."

[6] The source has שנייא וגבביא וצררייא; T. J. Yevamot has "...שניות עווניא וגווכייא וצוצרייה". Probably עווניא is a garble of שוניא, resulting from the splitting of the letter *shin* (ש) into *waw* and *'ayin* (ו + ע). Thus, like the T. B., the T. J. text of Qiddushin deals with three places, and שניות too is Šunya.

Baghdad area as well, and that the vowel following the letter *šin* is *u*,[7] it would be possible to identify the place with Sūnāyā, a village that later became part of Baghdad (see "Sūnāyā" in Yāqūt and *Marāṣid*, and see below). Obermeyer is of the opinion that the names Guvya, Šunya and Ṣiṣura apply to both settlements and waterways. The Nahr ʿĪsā, which flowed between Anbār and Baghdad, joined the Tigris near Sūnāyā, identified by Obermeyer with the Šanwata river mentioned in the Talmud.[8] Obermeyer believes that Šanwata is the "feminine form" of Šunya, so that Šunya/Šanwata are identical with the Nahr ʿĪsā.[9] However, a) the identification of Šunya with Šanwata does not seem sufficiently well-founded; b) the identification of Šunya/Šanwata with Nahr ʿĪsā is incorrect, for the confluence of the latter and the Tigris was not at Sūnāyā. Sūnāyā was also known as "*al-ʿatīqa*" (q.v. in Yāqūt and *Marāṣid*) which went from Ṭāq al-Ḥarrānī (= the Ḥarrānī's arch) to Bāb aš-Šaʿīr (= the barley gate) and the nearby Tigris. It was on the Tigris at the confluence with the Ṣarāt canal, not with Nahr ʿĪsā.[10] Evidently Obermeyer mistakenly believed that Nahr ʿĪsā and Ṣarāt were the same, but in fact Sūnāyā/*al-ʿatīqa* was in the northern sector of Baghdad, where the Ṣarāt joined the Tigris, while the Nahr ʿĪsā joined it further south.[11]

ESHEL, *Yishuvei ha-Yehudim* (1979), pp. 237–238
FUNK, *Monumenta* (1913), pp. 4, 289
HIRSCHENSON, *Sheva Ḥokhmot* (1883), p. 234
JASTROW, *Dictionary* (1950³), p. 1537
LEVY, *Wörterbuch* (1924²), vol. 4, p. 688, ("שנוותא")
NEUBAUER, *Géographie* (1868), pp. 326–327
OBERMEYER, *Landschaft* (1929), pp. 119, 122–125, 227

---

[7] The Munich MS (see n. 1 above) and Source 2 have Šunya without the letter *waw*, so that the pronunciation of the name may be Šanya.

[8] Giṭṭin, 60b, see "Be Ḥarmak̲" and "Aqra də-Šanwata" in the Appendix.

[9] Obermeyer, pp. 122–125.

[10] Cf. Ṭabarī, vol. 7, p. 618 (= vol. 3, p. 277). Actually *al-ʿatīqa* is applied to the village of Baghdad which eventually lent its name to the city, but in vol. 7, p. 616 (= vol. 3, p. 274) Baghdad and *al-ʿatīqa* are mentioned separately. The Ṣarāt canal (not the Nahr ʿĪsā) was spanned by the "old stone bridge" and afterwards by the "new stone bridge" and then flowed into the Tigris a little below al-Ḫuld. See Le Strange, "Ibn Serapion," p. 24; Suhrāb, p. 131; Yāqūt, s.v. "al-Qanṭara al-Ǧadīda" (which was near the Ṭāq al-Ḥarrānī, see above), cf. Yāqūt, s.v. "Ṭāq al-Ḥarrānī"; *Taʾrīḫ Baġdād*, vol. 1, p. 90: and see Ṭabarī, vol. 7, p. 620 (= vol. 3, p. 280); Yaʿqūbī, *Buldān*, pp. 244–245.

[11] See the course of the Ṣarāt canal in Ibn Ḥauqal's maps, pp. 206, 232; see also Iṣṭaḫrī, p. 84, and the map in *Baghdad* (issued by the Iraqi Engineers' Association, Baghdad 1969, Muṣṭafā Ǧawād, ed.), p. 92. On Sūnāyā see Le Strange, *Baghdad*, p. 90; Streck, *Die alte Landschaft*, vol. 1, p. 99f. On the old market, see Lassner, index ("Sūq al-ʿAtīqah").

Sura and Mata Məḥasya סורא ומתא מחסיא

A. *Sources* (*a selection*)

1. Bava Batra 74a

רבי יוחנן משתעי זימנא חדא הוה קא אזלינן בספינתא וחזינן ההוא כוורא דאפקיה לרישיה מימא ודמיין עייניה כתרי סיהרי ונפוץ מיא מתרתי זימיה כתרי מברי[1] דסורא.

Rabbi Yoḥanan related, Once we were traveling on a ship and we saw a fish that raised its head out of the sea. Its eyes were like two moons, and water streamed from its two nostrils like the two rivers[1] of Sura.

2. Ḥullin 111b

רב הונא ורב חייא בר אשי הוו יתבי חד בהאי גיסא דמברא דסורא וחד בהאי גיסא דמברא.[2]

Rav Huna and Rav Ḥiyya b. Ashi were once sitting one on one side of the Sura ferry and the other on the other side of the ferry.[2]

3. Sukkah 26a

הולכין לדבר מצוה פטורין בין ביום ובין בלילה, כי הא דרב חסדא ורבה בר רב הונא כי הוו עיילי בשבתא דרגלא לבי ריש גלותא הוו גנו ארקתא דסורא,[3] אמרי אנן שלוחי מצוה אנן ופטורין.

Those going [to fulfill] a religious duty are exempt [from the sukkah] whether by day or by night, as in the case of Rav Ḥisda and Rabbah son of Rav Huna who when visiting the Exilarch's house on the Sabbath of the Festival slept on the bank of the Sura,[3] saying, We are engaged in a religious duty and are exempt.

4. ʿEruvin 8a

מרימר פסיק לה לסורא[4] באוזלי, אמר חיישינן שמא יעלה הים[5] שרטון. ההוא מבוי עקום דהוה בסורא, כרוך בודיא אותיבו ביה בעקמומיתיה.

Maremar partitioned in Sura[4] with nets; he said, We fear that the sea[5] might throw up alluvium. That crooked alley there was in Sura, they folded up some matting and fixed it in its bend.

5. Ḥullin 110a

ורב בקעה מצא וגדר בה גדר, דרב איקלע לטטלפוש, שמעה להיא איתתא דקאמרה לחבירתה ריבעא דבשרא כמה חלבא בעי לבשולי, אמר לא גמירי דבשר בחלב אסור, איעכב וקאסר להו כחלי . . . בסורא לא אכלי כחלי, בפומבדיתא אכלי כחלי.

---

[1] The Munich MS has מיכרי (or perhaps מצרי; see *Diq. Sof.*). On the meaning of the term here, see below.

[2] The Munich and Vatican 122 MSS have דמברא דסורא.

[3] The Munich B MS has ארקתא דנהרא (corrected to דסורא).

[4] The Munich MS does not have "Sura" at all.

[5] The Munich MS does not have the word "the sea" at all.

Rav found an unguarded field and fenced it in; Rav happened to come to Ṭaṭlafuš, heard that woman say to her friend, A quarter of meat, how much milk is needed to cook it? He said, They didn't learn that meat in milk is forbidden, stopped and forbade them udders ... In Sura they do not eat udders, in Pumbədita they eat udders.

6. Sanhedrin 17b

סבי דסורא רב הונא ורב חסדא.

The elders of Sura, Rav Huna and Rav Ḥisda.

7. Bava Batra 142b[6]

בסורא מתנו הכי, בפומבדיתא מתנו הכי...

In Sura they taught thus, in Pumbədita they taught thus...

8. Giṭṭin 36b

דאמר שמואל לא כתבינן פרוסבול אלא אי בבי דינא דסורא אי בבי דינא דנהרדעא.

Samuel has said, We do not write a *prosbul* except either in the Bet Din of Sura or in the Bet Din of Nəhardəʿa.

9. Taʿanit 21b

בסורא הוות דברתא, בשיבבותיה דרב לא הוות דברתא.

In Sura there was a plague, in the neighborhood of Rav there was no plague.

10. Bava Metziʿa 111a

אמר רבה בר רב הונא הני שוקאי דסורא לא עברי משום בל תלין, מידע ידעי דעל יומא דשוקא סמיכי, אבל משום בל תשהא ודאי עובר.

Rabbah b. Rav Huna said, The market traders of Sura do not transgress [the injunction]. Do not keep [a laborer's wages] overnight, because it is well known that they rely upon the market day, but they certainly transgress Do not withhold.

11. Bava Metziʿa 73a

בסורא אזלי ארבעה, בכפרי[7] אזלן שיתא שיתא.

In Sura they go four, in Kafri[7] they go six [for a *zuz*].

12. Bava Metziʿa 6b

וא"ל רב אושעיא לרבה כי אזלת קמיה דרב חסדא לכפרי[8] בעי מיניה, כי אתא לסורא א"ל רב המנונא...

Rav Oshaʿya said to Rabbah, When you go before Rav Ḥisda to Kafri[8] ask him. When he came to Sura Rav Hamnuna said to him...

---

[6] And in many other places.

[7] The Hamburg MS has בכופרי.

[8] The Vatican 114 MS does not have כפרי at all.

13. Makkot 5a

ואמר רבא באו שנים ואמרו בסורא בצפרא בחד בשבתא הרג פלוני את הנפש ובאו שנים ואמרו בפניא בחד בשבתא עמנו הייתם בנהרדעא, חזינן אי מצפרא לפניא מצי אזיל מסורא לנהרדעא . . .

And Rava said, If two came and declared in Sura on Sunday morning that someone had killed, and two came and said, You were with us at sunset on Sunday evening at Nəhardəʿa, we have to consider, if one can get from Sura to Nəhardəʿa between the early morning and sunset . . .

14. Ḥullin 110a[9]

בסורא לא אכלי כחלי, בפומבדיתא אכלי כחלי. רמי בר תמרי דהוא רמי בר דיקולי[10] מפומבדיתא[11] איקלע לסורא במעלי יומא דכפורי, אפקינהו כולי עלמא לכחלינהו שדינהו, אזל איהו נקטינהו אכלינהו, אייתוה לקמיה דרב חסדא, אמר ליה אמאי תעביד הכי, אמר ליה מאתרא דרב יהודה אנא דאכיל . . .

In Sura they do not eat udders, in Pumbədita they eat udders. Rami b. Tamare who is Rami b. Diqule[10] of Pumbədita[11] happened to be in Sura on the eve of the Day of Atonement. Everybody took out the udders and threw them away. He went and took them and ate them. They brought him before Rav Ḥisda. He said to, him, Why do you do so? He said to him, I am from the place of Rav Judah who eats.

15. Betzah 28b–29a

היכי עביד, כי הא דבסורא[12] אמרי תרטא ופלגו תרטא, בנרש אמרי חלקא ופלגו חלקא, בפומבדיתא אמרי אוזיא ופלגו אוזיא, בנהר פקוד ובמתא מחסיא אמרי רבעא ופלגו רבעא.

What should he do [on holidays]? In Sura[12] they say, [Give me] a third and half a third; in Nareš they say, A half and half a half; in Pumbədita they say, A sixth and half a sixth; in Nəhar Pəqod and Mata Məḥasya they say, A quarter and half a quarter.

Mata Məḥasya

16. Ketubot 4a

אמר רב אשי[13] כגון מתא מחסיא דמפקא מכרך ומפקא מכפר.

Rav Ashi[13] said, Like Mata Məḥasya which is not a city and not a village.

17. Megillah 26a

אמר רב אשי האי בי כנישתא דמתא מחסיא אף עַל גב דמעלמא אתו לה, כיון דאדעתא דידי קאתו אי בעינא מזבנינא לה.

Rav Ashi said, As for this synagogue in Mata Məḥasya, although people come to it from all parts, since they come at my discretion, if I want to I will sell it.

[9] The continuation of Source 5.

[10] Cf. Menaḥot 29b: "Rami b. Tamare who is the father-in-law of Rami b. Diqule"; but the manuscripts are like the Ḥullin source. See also *Diq. Sof.*

[11] The Hamburg and Vatican 121 MSS do not have "of Pumbədita."

[12] The Munich MS has דבנהרדעא.

[13] The Venice printing has "Rav Assi."

18. Shabbat 11a

ואמר רבא בר מחסיא אמר רב חמא בר גוריא אמר רב כל עיר שגגותיה גבוהין מבית הכנסת לסוף חרבה . . . אמר רב אשי אנא עבדי למתא מחסיא דלא חרבה. והא חרבה, מאותו עון לא חרבה.

And Rava b. Məḥasya said Rav Ḥama b. Gurya said Rav said, Every town whose roofs are higher than the synagogue is eventually destroyed. Rav Ashi said, I achieved for Mata Məḥasya that it was not destroyed. But it was destroyed. It was not destroyed as a result of that sin.

19. Bava Batra 3b

כי הא דרב אשי[14] חזא בה תיוהא בכנישתא דמתא מחסיא סתריה ועייל לפורייה להתם ולא אפקיה עד דמתקין ליה שפיכי.

Rav Ashi[14] seeing dilapidation in the Mata Məḥasya synagogue pulled it down and took his bed there and did not remove it until the gutters had been installed [in the new building].

20. Bava Batra 12b

אמר רבי יוחנן מיום שחרב בית המקדש ניטלה נבואה מן הנביאים וניתנה לשוטים ולתינוקות. לשוטים מאי היא, כי הא דמר בר רב אשי דהוה קאי ברסתקא דמחווא שמעיה לההוא שוטה דקאמר ריש מתיבתא דמליך במתא מחסיא טביומי חתים . . .

Rabbi Yoḥanan said, From the day the Temple was destroyed prophecy was taken away from the prophets and given to fools and infants. What is it to fools, like the case of Mar son of Rav Ashi who stood in the Maḥoza market and heard that fool say, The yeshiva head ruling in Mata Məḥasya signs [his name] Ṭavyomi.

21. Bava Metzi'a 68a

אמר רב אשי אמרו לי סבי דמתא מחסיא סתם משכנתא שנה.

Rav Ashi said, The elders of Mata Məḥasya told me that an unconditional mortgage is for a year.

22. Mo'ed Qaṭan 4b

רב אשי שרא להו לבני מתא מחסיא לאקדוחי נהר בורניץ,[15] אמר כיון דשתו מיניה רבים כרבים דמי, ותנן עושין כל צורכי רבים.

Rav Ashi allowed the people of Mata Məḥasya to dredge the river Burniṣ[15] [on intermediate days of a festival], saying because the public drank from it, and we taught, All public needs may be performed.

---

[14] The Munich and Hamburg MSS have "Mar b. Bar Ashi."

[15] The Munich MS has בורנינין (or בורנינץ). The R-i-f has בידן, and בירן in more modern editions, cf. Bava Metzi'a 24b, and see below.

23. Bava Qamma 119b

אמר רב יהודה כשות וחזיז אין בהם משום גזל, באתרא דקפדי יש בהן משום גזל. אמר רבינא ומתא מחסיא אתרא דקפדי הוא.

Rav Judah said, Cuscuta and lichen are not robbery, though in places where people are strict, they would be considered robbery. Ravina said, Mata Məḥasya is a place where they are strict.

24. Horayot 12a; Keritot 6a

ותיבו אקילקלי דמתא מחסיא ולא תיבו אפדני דפומבדיתא.

And sit on the refuse heaps of Mata Məḥasya and do not sit in the mansions of Pumbədita.

25. Qiddushin 33a

רבינא הוה יתיב קמיה דר' ירמיה מדיפתי חלף ההוא גברא קמיה ולא מיכסי רישא, אמר כמה חציף הא גברא, א"ל דלמא ממתא מחסיא ניהו דגיסי בה רבנן.

Ravina was sitting before Rabbi Jeremiah of Difte when a certain man passed by without covering his head. He said, How impudent is that man. He said to him, Perhaps he is from Mata Məḥasya where scholars are very common.

26. Berakhot 17b

אמר רב אשי בני מתא מחסיא "אבירי לב" נינהו, דקא חזו יקרא דאורייתא תרי זמני בשתא ולא קמגייר גיורא מינייהו.

Rav Ashi said, The people of Mata Məḥasya are "stubborn of heart" (Is. 46:12), for they see the glory of the Torah twice a year and never has one of them converted.

27. Giṭṭin 65a–b

... דאמרה ליה התקבל לי גיטא במתא מחסיא וזימנין דמשכחת ליה בבבל וה"ק ליה משקל כל היכא דמשכחת ליה שקליה מיניה, גיטא לא הוי עד דמטית למתא מחסיא.

... She said to him, Obtain my bill of divorcement for me in Mata Məḥasya, but sometimes you will find him in Babylon. And she tells him as follows: Take it, anywhere you find him, take it from him. There won't be a *geṭ* till you reach Mata Məḥasya.

B. *Already Proposed Location*

Near the diffluence of the Nəhar Sura and the east branch of the Euphrates, about fifteen kilometers north of Ḥilla (D4 on the Tal. Bab. map).

C. *Identification*

The accepted location of Sura is near the diffluence of the an-Nīl canal (Nahr Sūrā) and the east branch of the Euphrates, at about the latitude of Tall Abbā (see the entry on "Nəhar Abba") which is between the two branches of the Euphrates.[16]

Nonetheless, a number of sources show Sura as being south rather than north of Ḥilla. Yāqūt states that Sūrā is in the region (*arḍ*) of Babylon, near Waqf and Ḥilla. *Marāṣid* says that Sūrā is a town below (i.e. south of) Ḥilla.[17] Sūrā's neighbor, Waqf, is one of the "daughters" of Ḥilla and is below Sūrā. Similarly Banūrā, which according to Yāqūt is a distance of one parasang from Sūrā, is according to *Marāṣid* south of Ḥilla near Sūrā.[18] Furthermore, Yāqūt asserts that Nahr Ḥilla is Nahr Sūrā, (that is, that Nahr Sūrā came to be called Nahr Ḥilla after Ḥilla was founded).[19] Thus, although the identification of the accepted site of Sura seems well founded, the contention in *Marāṣid* (fourteenth century) that Sūrā was south of Ḥilla does evoke some doubt.

D. *The Center in Sura*

Sura was the site of one of the great Babylonian yeshivas. The yeshiva was established by Rav, whose arrival from Eretz Israel in 219 vitalized independent Jewish life in general, and the study of the Torah in particular, in Babylonia.[20] Rav Sherira Gaon describes developments as follows[21]:

In the days of Rabbi (Judah ha-Nasi) Rav came to Babylonia in 530 of the Greek (= Seleucid) calender we are used to (A.D. 219). And Rabbi Shela was the head of the sages here. And the head of the sages in Babylonia was called the *Resh Sidra*.[22] And we say Rav happened to come to Rabbi Shela's place and

---

[16] For the location of Sura see Kiepert's map (*ZGEB* 18 [1883], map 5) and see already Obermeyer, pp. 283–284, who treats the canal system in detail. See also the entries on "Qimḥonya" and "Dəruqart."

[17] See Yāqūt and *Marāṣid*, s.v. "Sūrā."

[18] See *Marāṣid*, s.v. "Sūrā."

[19] See Yāqūt, s.v. "Furāt."

[20] At the same time, it should be kept in mind that there was community organization and Torah study in Babylonia before Rav's arrival. On its date, see Safrai, *Divrei ha-Qongres ha-Olami ha-Shishi le-Mada'ei ha-yahadut*, vol. 2, pp. 51–57.

[21] *Iggeret Rav Sherira Gaon*, (Lewin ed., pp. 78–80): וביומי דרבי נחת רב לבבל בשנת תק"ל שנה למלכות יון דרגילנא ביה. והוה הכא ר' שילא רישא דרבנן. והוה מקרי ריש סידרא בבבל רישא דרבנן דאמרינן רב איקלע לאתריה דרבי שילא קם עליה באמורא. וכד נח נפשיה דר' שילא הוו רב ושמואל הכא ואדבריה רב לשמואל מקמיה ולא אצטבי רב למהוי רישא עליה ולאותוביה לשמואל קמיה ואף שמואל לא אצטבי למהוי רישא עליה דרב ולאותוביה לרב קמיה דהוה קשיש רב משמואל טובא . . . ומשום הכי שבקיה רב לשמואל בנהרדעא דהוא דוכתיה והוא מקום תורה ואתרחק לדוכתא דלא הוה ביה תורה והוא סורא דהיא מתא מחסיא והוו ישראל נפישי התם ואפילו אסור והתר לא הוו ידעי (בנוסח צרפתי: דאפילו אסור בשר בחלב לא ידעין) ואמר רב איתיב הכא כי היכי דלהוי תורה בהאי דוכתא כי ההוא מעשה דמפורש בפרק כל הבשר רב בקעה מצא וגדר בה גדר וכו' וכי איקלע לטטלפוש אגמרינון ואורינון אסור כחלי . . . והוו בבבל שני בתי דינין גדולים חד בנהרדעא שהיה כבר וחד בסורא דקבעיה רב והיינו דאמר שמואל לא כתבינן פרוסבול אלא או בבי דינא דסורא או בבי דינא דנהרדעא.

[22] On this title see Neusner, *History*, vol. 2, p. 109; Abramson, *Ba-Merkazim u-ba-Tefutzot*, p. 107.

was his speaker.[23] And when Rabbi Shela died, Rav and Samuel were here, and Rav led Samuel, and Rav did not want to be chief over him and seat Samuel before him, and also Samuel did not want to be chief over Rav and seat him before him, for Rav was older than Samuel . . . For that reason Rav left Samuel in Nəhardəʿa that was his place and was a place of Torah, and moved to a place where there was no Torah, and that is Sura which is Mata Məḥasya and there were many Jews there and they did not even know the permitted and forbidden (the French version is: even that meat in milk is forbidden) and Rav said, I will sit here so that there will be Torah in this place, like the case specified in the chapter *Kol ha-Basar* (Source 5): "Rav found an unguarded field and fenced it in"; when Rav happened to come to Ṭaṭlafuš, he taught them and instructed them [on] the prohibition of udders . . . And in Babylonia there were two great courts, one in Nəhardəʿa that already existed, and one in Sura that Rav set up, and this is what Samuel said, "A *prosbol* is written only in the Bet Din of Sura or the Bet Din of Nəhardəʿa" (Source 8).

Rav Sherira Gaon thus reports a large Jewish population in Sura even before Rav arrived there. Source 5, testifying that when Rav reached Ṭaṭlafuš he found the inhabitants unaware that it was forbidden to mix milk and meat, is interpreted by Rav Sherira Gaon as applying to Sura, which before Rav's arrival lacked learning.[24] The phrase "Rav found an unguarded field and fenced it in" recurs a number of times in the sources, and indicates that Rav extended the prohibited areas so that the people who were unfamiliar with the details of the precepts would not err. In the Ṭaṭlafuš instance, Rav forbade the eating of udders—which the halakhah actually allows (cf. Source 14, and see the entry on "Pumbədita")—so that the people would not deduce from the permission that meat and milk in general could be eaten together. Similar rulings were issued by Rav in the course of visits to Damharya (q.v.) and Afsaṭya.[25]

Most of Rav Sherira Gaon's report is devoted to the founding of the Sura yeshiva which from then till the end of the gaonic period was one of the two main yeshivas in Babylonia (see Source 8). The other was the ancient Nəhardəʿa yeshiva which moved to Pumbədita after Nəhardəʿa was destroyed by the Palmyrans (A.D. 259; see the entries on "Nəhardəʿa" and "Pumbədita"). Each of the institutions developed independently, and although in both the main material studied was the Mishnah of Eretz Israel, they evolved different traditions as regards methods of study, and consequently also as regards

---

[23] The speaker (Aramaic: *amora*) transmitted the lessons of the yeshiva head to the students. Cf. Yoma 20b.

[24] Thus Ṭaṭlafuš is in the Sura area but its exact location cannot be specified due to insufficient data. For an attempt at identification, see Funk, *Monumenta*, p. 293.

[25] See ʿEruvin 100b. Obviously Afsaṭya too was in the Sura area but cannot be definitely identified either. For attempts to identify it (outside the Sura area) see Funk, *Monumenta*, p. 288; Kohut, *Arukh ha-Shalem*, vol. 1, p. 222.

halakhic points. This situation is indicated in the sentence "In Sura they taught thus, in Pumbədita they taught thus" (Source 7). Each yeshiva had its sphere of influence in Babylonia, and the people living within the sphere abided by the decisions of the yeshiva they were associated with.[26] The prestige of the two yeshivas varied, depending on the yeshiva heads, the sages connected with them, and the historical circumstances in general.

The Sura yeshiva already reached its apogee in Rav's time, and had hundreds of students. According to one source, "when the sages left Rav's study house (in Sura), a thousand two hundred students remained there."[27] Rav died in 247, and in 254 Rav Huna, one of the outstanding amoras of the Babylonian Talmud, became the new head. The source quoted goes on to say that "Rav Huna preached to thirteen amoras; when the sages stood up at Rav Huna's yeshiva and shook out their clothes, dust would rise and cover the eye of the sun, and in the west (= Eretz Israel) they would say, They have stood up at the yeshiva of Rav Huna, the Babylonian."[28] Rav Huna was succeeded by the eminent Rav Ḥisda, but when the latter died in 309, the Sura yeshiva began to decline, and did not regain its reputation until the time of Rav Ashi (see below).

E. *Physical Features*

A view of life in Sura is presented by Source 2 which mentions the Sura ferry, and describes two of the local sages, Rav Huna and Rav Ḥiyya b. Ashi, of the second generation of Babylonian amoras, sitting at opposite ends of the ferry, apparently in order to keep it level. Source 1 too mentions the Sura ferry, but as the context involves water jetting out of the nostrils of a magic fish, evidently rivers are meant rather than ferries.[29] Source 3 mentions the Nəhar Sura while reporting two sages who were on their way to a *šabata de-rigla* gathering at the Exilarch's house, and considered it the fulfillment of a religious duty, in which case they could sleep on the bank of the Sura, and were not obliged to seek a sukkah.[30]

---

[26] See the entries on "Nəhardəʿa," "Maḥoza" and "Babylon" in regard to the source (Ketubot 54a): "Babylon and all its surroundings acted as Rav, Nəhardəʿa and all its surroundings acted as Samuel."

[27] Ketubot 106a.

[28] Ketubot 106a. While Rav Huna's yeshiva is said to have had only 800 regular pupils remaining after the departure of the temporary ones (those who came in the *yarḥei kallah*?), that does not mean that the yeshiva was larger in Rav's time.

[29] The source may however mean that the form of the jets resembled that of the Sura ferries (see Obermeyer, p. 293 and n. 1 there), or that the streams of water gushing out of the fish were reminiscent of the water spouted by a paddle-ferry. If so, מברי דסורא would have the usual meaning of "ferries of Sura." Another source in which the Sura ferry figures is Ḥullin 95b reporting that as Rav left for the home of his son-in-law, Rav Ḥanan, he saw a ferry approaching and said it augured a fine day.

[30] On *šabata de-rigla* see Beer, *Rashut ha-Golah*, pp. 129–134.

Another river in the neighborhood of Sura was the Burniṣ, in regard to which Source 22 relates that Rav Ashi allowed the people of Mata Məḥasya (see below) to dredge the river on the intermediate days of a festival, so that they could obtain drinking water from it. Obermeyer proposed identifying that river with Barbismā, a district (*ṭassūǧ*) near Sura,[31] but the proposal is not acceptable. While a district and river could have the same name, there is no support in the manuscripts for the substitution of /b/ for the /n/ of Burniṣ.[32]

F. *Mata Məḥasya*

In the days of Rav Ashi of the sixth generation of Babylonian amoras, the Sura yeshiva was transferred to Mata Məḥasya which was close to Sura, evidently bordering on it. Some sources give the impression that Sura and Mata Məḥasya were the same place, but in the talmudic period at least they were definitely two separate places. Thus, e.g. Rav Sherira Gaon says that "the study house of Rav Huna is close to Mata Məḥasya."[33] Source 15 too suggests that Sura and Mata Məḥasya were two distinct localities.

Rav Ashi himself says that Mata Məḥasya was more than a village but not yet a city (Source 16). Yet the Mata Məḥasya yeshiva occupied a central place in Babylonia, and Rav Ashi and Ravina who headed it are credited with the redaction of the Babylonian Talmud. Source 26 indicates the large number of students who came to study Torah at the Mata Məḥasya yeshiva, and the fact that this happened twice a year means that the reference is to *yarḥei kallah*.[34] Rav Ashi expresses his astonishment at the hard-hearted non-Jewish inhabitants of Mata Məḥasya who, despite the impressive stream of students at the yeshiva, refuse to convert. Source 18 and 19 mention the Mata Məḥasya synagogue which Rav arranged to have renovated.[35]

G. *Sura di-Pərat*

Three talmudic sources mention Sura di-Pərat. In two "Ravina happened to come to Sura di-Pərat"[36] and in the third, Rav Ḥaviva of Sura di-Pərat addresses a question to Ravina.[37] According to Obermeyer, Sura di-Pərat was

[31] Obermeyer, p. 297, n. 1.

[32] Obermeyer's addition to Barbīs Mata is not certain. Yāqūt, s.v. "Barbismā" cites a version of the place name with a longer suffix—Barbismiyā—which seems likely as the original form, later shortened.

[33] *Iggeret Rav Sherira Gaon*, Lewin ed., p. 84.

[34] See Gafni, *Ha-Yeshiva be-Bavel*, pp. 138–139.

[35] After Rav Ashi's death, the Sura yeshiva declined, and only became famous again in the tenth century when it had moved to Baghdad (though retaining its original name). The Jewish community continued to exist in Sura and Mata Məḥasya throughout the gaonic period. A unique report states that most of the population of Sura at the start of the tenth century was Jewish (Ibn al-Qifṭī, *Ta'rīḫ al-ḥukamā'*, pp. 193–194: *Sūrā wa-l-ǧālib ʿalā ahlihā al-yahūd* . . .; *akṯaru man bi-Sūrā wa-Nahr Malik* (sic) *yahūd*. See already Obermeyer, pp. 271–272.

[36] Bava Metziʿa 61b; Moʿed Qaṭan 20a.

[37] Bava Metziʿa 106b.

the western section of Sura, and was on the Nəhar Sura as well as the Euphrates,[38] but this assumption cannot be proved and is in fact unlikely. All the sources mentioning Sura di-Pərat involved Ravina, of the seventh generation of Babylonian amoras, who resided in Mata Məḥasya, but Sura di-Pərat may have been a considerable distance from Sura and Mata Məḥasya, for the term "happened to come" is rather surprising if the place was a section of the same town.[39]

ASSAF, *Kiryat Sefer* 7 (1930): 62
BEER, *Rashut ha-Golah* (1970), passim
BEER, *Amora'ei Bavel* (1974), passim
ESHEL, *Yishuvei ha-Yehudim* (1979), pp. 162f., 174–177
FUNK, *Juden* (1902–1908), vol. 1, pp. 35, 45–47, 59
FUNK, *Monumenta* (1913), pp. 40f., 45–47, 54
GAFNI, *Ha-Yeshiva be-Bavel* (1978), passim
HIRSCHENSON, *Sheva Ḥokhmot* (1883), pp. 162–163, 174–177
JASTROW, *Dictionary* (1950³), pp. 763, 969
KOHUT, *Arukh ha-Shalem* (1878–1892), vol. 5, p. 284, "מת"; vol. 6, p. 30; *Tosefot* (1937), p. 290
LEVY, *Wörterbuch* (1924²), vol. 3, pp. 294, 495
MUSIL, *The Middle Euphrates* (1927), pp. 43f., 244, 246f., 274–276
NEUBAUER, *Géographie* (1868), pp. 343–344
NEUSNER, *History* (1965–1970), 5 vols., passim
NEWMAN, *Agricultural Life* (1932), passim
OBERMEYER, *Landschaft* (1929), pp. 283–298 and passim
YUDELEVITZ, *Sinai* 1 (1938): 168–174, 268–275; 2 (1938): 157–162, 317–324, 418–422; 3 (1938): 130–132

Susa (Šušan)* שושן

A. *Sources*

1. Mishnah Middot I 3[1]

חמשה שערים היו להר הבית... שער המזרחי, עליו שושן הבירה צורה...

The Temple Mount had five gates . . . the eastern gate, on which the capital Šušan was drawn . . .

---

[38] Obermeyer, p. 293.

[39] Perhaps the reference is to Sura on the Euphrates 210 kilometers northwest of Circesium (see Bab. Env. map) although that place seems too far from the Jewish centers of Babylonia.

* Talmudic literature abounds in references to Šušan which do not relate to the Šušan of the mishnaic and talmudic period, but to the biblical verses Šušan appears in, mostly in the Book of Esther. The T. B. contains references to Šušan in connection with regulations for the reading of the Book of Esther on Purim (see Source 2 and n. 2 below). There are citations of scriptural verses mentioning "the city of Šušan" and "Šušan the capital" (see Rosh ha-Shanah 3b; Megillah 11a [twice]; 12b; 16b). Biblical Šušan figures in legends (Megillah 12a) and some passages deal with the drawing of Šušan that decorated the east gate of the Temple Mount (see Source 1 and n. 1 below). Šušan is mentioned in similar contexts in other talmudic literature, particularly the *midrashim*.

[1] This mishnah is cited in T. B. Menaḥot 98a, and cf. Mishnah Kelim XVII 9; T. B. Pesaḥim 86a, Bekhorot 40a.

2. Tosefta Megillah I 1 (as per the Vienna MS)[2]

כרכים המוקפין חומה מימות יהושע בן נון קורין בחמשה עשר, ר׳ יהושע בן קרחה אומר מימות אחשורוש. אמר ר׳ יוסה בן יהודה היכן מצינו לשושן הבירה שמוקפת חומה מימות יהושע בן נון,[3] אלא ״משפחה ומשפחה מדינה ומדינה עיר ועיר.״

Cities surrounded by a wall since Joshua bin Nun's days read on the fifteenth. Rabbi Joshua b. Qarḥa says, Since Ahasuerus's days. Said Rabbi Yose b. Judah, Where did we find that Šušan the capital is surrounded by a wall since Joshua bin Nun's days,[3] but "every family, and every province and every city" (Es. 9:28).

3. Megillah 2b

...אמר רבא ואמרי לה כדי[4] שאני שושן הואיל ונעשה בה נס.

Rava said and some say Kedi,[4] Šušan is different because a miracle was worked in it.

4. Sanhedrin 94a

אבל ישראל ספרו בגנותה של ארץ ישראל, כי מטו שוש אמרי שויא כי ארעין, כי מטו עלמין אמרו כעלמין, כי מטו שוש תרי אמרי על חד תרין.

But Israel [when exiled] spoke evil of Eretz Israel. When they reached Šuš they said, It equals our country; when they reached ʿAlmin (עלמין) they said, Like our world (=עלמין); when they reached Šuš Təre (= two) they said, Double.

5. Strabo XV 3,2–4 (727–728)

Σχεδὸν δέ τι καὶ ἡ Σουσὶς μέρος γεγένηται τῆς Περσίδος μεταξὺ αὐτῆς κειμένη καὶ τῆς Βαβυλωνίας, ἔχουσα πόλιν ἀξιολογωτάτην τὰ Σοῦσα. οἱ γὰρ Πέρσαι κρατήσαντες Μήδων καὶ ὁ Κῦρος, ὁρῶντες τὴν μὲν οἰκείαν γῆν ἐπ' ἐσχάτοις που ταττομένην, τὴν δὲ Σουσίδα ἐνδοτέρω καὶ πλησιαιτέραν τῇ Βαβυλωνίᾳ καὶ τοῖς ἄλλοις ἔθνεσιν, ἐνταῦθα ἔθεντο τὸ τῆς ἡγεμονίας βασίλειον· ἅμα καὶ τὸ ὅμορον τῆς χώρας ἀποδεξάμενοι καὶ τὸ ἀξίωμα τῆς πόλεως καὶ κρεῖττον τὸ μηδέποτε καθ' ἑαυτὴν τὴν Σουσίδα πραγμάτων μεγάλων ἐπήβολον γεγονέναι, ἀλλ' ἀεὶ ὑφ' ἑτέροις ὑπάρξαι καὶ ἐν μέρει τετάχθαι συστήματος μείζονος, πλὴν εἰ ἄρα τὸ παλαιὸν τὸ κατὰ τοὺς ἥρωας. λέγεται γὰρ δὴ κτίσμα Τιθωνοῦ τοῦ Μέμνονος πατρός, κύκλον ἔχουσα ἑκατὸν καὶ εἴκοσι σταδίων, παραμήκης τῷ σχήματι· ἡ δ' ἀκρόπολις ἐκαλεῖτο Μεμνόνιον· λέγονται δὲ καὶ Κίσσιοι οἱ Σούσιοι· φησὶ δὲ καὶ Αἰσχύλος τὴν μητέρα Μέμνονος Κισσίαν. ταφῆναι δὲ λέγεται Μέμνων περὶ Πάλτον τῆς Συρίας παρὰ Βαδᾶν ποταμόν, ὡς εἴρηκε Σιμωνίδης ἐν Μέμνονι διθυράμβῳ τῶν Δηλιακῶν. τὸ δὲ τεῖχος ᾠκοδόμητο τῆς πόλεως καὶ ἱερὰ καὶ βασίλεια παραπλησίως ὥσπερ τὰ τῶν Βαβυλωνίων ἐξ ὀπτῆς πλίνθου καὶ

---

2 Cf. T. J. Megillah I 1 – 70a, 17 seq., T. B. Megillah 2b.

3 That is also the form in the standard edition and in the London MS but "since the days of Joshua bin Nun" is missing in the Erfurt MS. This omission is undoubtedly a scribal error for otherwise it would mean that in Rabbi Yose b. Judah's opinion Šušan was always an unwalled city (and see Lieberman, *Tosefta ki-Fshutah*, vol. 5, p. 1122).

4 The Munich MS has "Abbaye"; the Oxford MS has "Rabbah" instead of "Rava."

ἀσφάλτου, καθάπερ εἰρήκασί τινες· Πολύκλειτος δὲ διακοσίων φησὶ τὸν κύκλον καὶ ἀτείχιστον.

Κοσμήσαντες δὲ τὰ ἐν Σούσοις βασίλεια μάλιστα τῶν ἄλλων οὐδὲν ἧττον καὶ τὰ ἐν Περσεπόλει καὶ τὰ ἐν Πασαργάδαις ἐξετίμησαν· καὶ ἥ γε γάζα καὶ οἱ θησαυροὶ καὶ τὰ μνήματα ἐνταῦθα ἦν τοῖς Πέρσαις, ὡς ἐν τόποις ἐρυμνοτέροις καὶ ἅμα προγονικοῖς. ἦν δὲ καὶ ἄλλα βασίλεια τὰ ἐν Γάβαις ἐν τοῖς ἀνωτέρω που μέρεσι τῆς Περσίδος καὶ τὰ ἐν τῇ παραλίᾳ τὰ κατὰ τὴν Ταόκην λεγομένην· ταῦτα μὲν τὰ κατὰ τὴν τῶν Περσῶν ἀρχήν, οἱ δ' ὕστερον ἄλλοις καὶ ἄλλοις ἐχρήσαντο, ὡς εἰκός, εὐτελεστέροις τισίν, ἅτε καὶ τῆς Περσίδος ἠλαττωμένης ὑπό τε τῶν Μακεδόνων καὶ ἔτι μᾶλλον ὑπὸ τῶν Παρθυαίων. καὶ γὰρ εἰ βασιλεύονται μέχρι νῦν ἴδιον βασιλέα ἔχοντες οἱ Πέρσαι, τῇ γε δυνάμει πλεῖστον ἀπολείπονται καὶ τῷ Παρθυαίων προσέχουσι βασιλεῖ.

Τὰ μὲν οὖν Σοῦσα ἐν μεσογαίοις κεῖται ἐπὶ τῷ Χοάσπῃ ποταμῷ περαιτέρω κατὰ τὸ ζεῦγμα, ἡ δὲ χώρα μέχρι τῆς θαλάττης καθήκει· καὶ ἔστιν αὐτῆς ἡ παραλία μέχρι τῶν ἐκβολῶν σχεδόν τι τοῦ Τίγριος ἀπὸ τῶν ὅρων τῆς Περσικῆς παραλίας σταδίων ὡς τρισχιλίων. ῥεῖ δὲ διὰ τῆς χώρας ὁ Χοάσπης εἰς τὴν αὐτὴν τελευτῶν παραλίαν, ἀπὸ τῶν Οὐξίων τὰς ἀρχὰς ἔχων. παρεμπίπτει γάρ τις ὀρεινὴ τραχεῖα καὶ ἀπότομος μεταξὺ τῶν Σουσίων καὶ τῆς Περσίδος, στενὰ ἔχουσα δυσπάροδα καὶ ἀνθρώπους λῃστάς, οἳ μισθοὺς ἐπράττοντο καὶ αὐτοὺς τοὺς βασιλέας κατὰ τὴν ἐκ Σούσων εἰς Πέρσας εἰσβολήν. φησὶ δὲ Πολύκλειτος εἰς λίμνην τινὰ συμβάλλειν τόν τε Χοάσπην καὶ τὸν Εὔλαιον καὶ ἔτι τὸν Τίγριν, εἶτ' ἐκεῖθεν εἰς τὴν θάλατταν ἐκδιδόναι· πρὸς δὲ τῇ λίμνῃ καὶ ἐμπόριον εἶναι.

I might almost say that Susis also is a part of Persis; it lies between Persis and Babylonia and has a most notable city, Susa. For the Persians and Cyrus, after mastering the Medes, saw that their native land was situated rather on the extremities of their empire, and that Susa was farther in and nearer to Babylonia and the other tribes, and therefore established the royal seat of their empire at Susa. At the same time, also, they were pleased with the high standing of the city and with the fact that its territory bordered on Persis, and, better still, with the fact that it had never of itself achieved anything of importance, but always had been subject to others and accounted merely a part of a larger political organisation, except, perhaps, in ancient times, in the times of the heroes. For Susa too is said to have been founded by Tithonus the father of Memnon, with a circuit of one hundred and twenty stadia, and oblong in shape; and its acropolis was called Memnonium; and the Susians are also called Cissians; and Aeschylus calls the mother of Memnon Cissia. Memnon is said to have been buried in the neighbourhood of Paltus in Syria, by the river Badas, as Simonides states in his dithyramb entitled *Memnon*, one of his Delian poems. The wall and the temples and the royal palace were built like those of the Babylonians, of baked brick and asphalt, as some writers state. Polycleitus says that the city is two hundred stadia in circuit and that it has no walls.

Although they adorned the palace at Susa more than any other, they esteemed no less highly the palaces at Persepolis and Pasargadae; at any rate, the treasure and the riches and the tombs of the Persians were there, since they were on sites that were at the same time hereditary and more strongly fortified by nature. And there were also other palaces—that at Gabae, somewhere in the upper parts of Persis, and that on the coast near Taocê, as it is called. These were the palaces in the time of the empire of the Persians, but the kings of later times used others, naturally less sumptuous, since Persis had been weakened, not only by the Macedonians, but still more so by the Parthians. For although the Persians are still under the rule of a king, having a king of their own, yet they are most deficient in power and are subject to the king of the Parthians.
Now Susa is situated in the interior on the Choaspes River at the far end of the bridge, but its territory extends down to the sea; and its seaboard is about three thousand stadia in length, extending from the boundaries of the Persian seaboard approximately to the outlets of the Tigris. The Choaspes River flows through Susis, terminating at the same seaboard, and has its sources in the territory of the Uxii; for a kind of mountainous country intrudes between the Susians and Persis; it is rugged and sheer, and has narrow defiles that are hard to pass, and was inhabited by brigands, who would exact payments even from the kings themselves when they passed from Susis into Persis. Polycleitus says that the Choaspes, the Eulaeus, and also the Tigris meet in a kind of lake, and then empty from that lake into the sea; and that there is an emporium near the lake; ... (trans.: H. L. Jones, LCL)

6. Strabo XV 3, 9–11 (731–732)

... Πάντα δὲ τὰ ἐν τῇ Περσίδι χρήματα ἐξεσκευάσατο εἰς τὰ Σοῦσα καὶ αὐτὰ θησαυρῶν καὶ κατασκευῆς μεστά· οὐδὲ τοῦθ' ἡγεῖτο τὸ βασίλειον, ἀλλὰ τὴν Βαβυλῶνα, καὶ διενοεῖτο ταύτην προσκατασκευάζειν ...
Τὴν γοῦν Βαβυλῶνα ὁ Ἀλέξανδρος προέκρινεν ὁρῶν καὶ τῷ μεγέθει πολὺ ὑπερβάλλουσαν καὶ τοῖς ἄλλοις. εὐδαίμων δ' οὖσα ἡ Σουσὶς ἔκπυρον τὸν ἀέρα ἔχει [καὶ] καυματηρὸν καὶ μάλιστα τὸν περὶ τὴν πόλιν, ὥς φησιν ἐκεῖνος· τὰς γοῦν σαύρας καὶ τοὺς ὄφεις θέρους ἀκμάζοντος τοῦ ἡλίου κατὰ μεσημβρίαν διαβῆναι μὴ φθάνειν τὰς ὁδοὺς τὰς ἐν τῇ πόλει, ἀλλ' ἐν μέσαις περιφλέγεσθαι, ὅπερ τῆς Περσίδος μηδαμοῦ συμβαίνειν καίπερ νοτιωτέρας οὔσης· λουτρὰ δὲ ψυχρὰ προτεθέντα ἐκθερμαίνεσθαι παραχρῆμα, τὰς δὲ κριθὰς διασπαρείσας εἰς τὸν ἥλιον ἅλλεσθαι καθάπερ ἐν τοῖς ἰπνοῖς τὰς κάχρυς· διὸ καὶ ταῖς στέγαις ἐπὶ δύο πήχεις γῆν ἐπιτίθεσθαι, ὑπὸ δὲ τοῦ βάρους ἀναγκάζεσθαι στενοὺς μὲν μακροὺς δὲ ποιεῖσθαι τοὺς οἴκους ... ἐτησίαι τὴν ἄλλην γῆν καταψύχουσιν ἐκκαομένην ὑπὸ τῶν καυμάτων.
Πολύσιτος δ' ἄγαν ἐστὶν ὥστε ἑκατοντάχουν δι' ὁμαλοῦ καὶ κριθὴν καὶ πυρὸν ἐκτρέφειν, ἔστι δ' ὅτε καὶ διακοσιοντάχουν· διόπερ οὐδὲ πυκνὰς τὰς αὔλακας τέμνουσι· πυκνούμεναι γὰρ κωλύουσιν αἱ ῥίζαι τὴν βλάστην. τὴν δ' ἄμπελον οὐ φυομένην πρότερον Μακεδόνες κατεφύτευσαν κἀκεῖ καὶ ἐν Βαβυλῶνι, οὐ ταφρεύοντες ἀλλὰ παττά-

λους κατασεσιδηρωμένους ἐξ ἄκρων πήττοντες, εἶτ' ἐξαιροῦντες, ἀντὶ δ' αὐτῶν τὰ κλήματα καθιέντες εὐθέως.

... Alexander carried off with him all the wealth in Persis to Susa, which was also full of treasures and equipment; and neither did he regard Susa as the royal residence, but rather Babylon, which he intended to build up still further; ...

At all events, Alexander preferred Babylon, since he saw that it far surpassed the others, not only in its size, but also in all other respects. Although Susis is fertile, it has a hot and scorching atmosphere, and particularly in the neighbourhood of the city, according to that writer [unidentified]. At any rate, he says that when the sun is hottest at noon, the lizards and the snakes could not cross the streets in the city quickly enough to prevent their being burnt to death in the middle of the streets. He says that this is the case nowhere in Persis, although Persis lies more to the south; and that cold water for baths is put out in the sun and immediately heated, and that barley spread out in the sun bounces like parched barley in ovens; and that on this account earth is put on the roofs of the houses to the depth of two cubits, and that by reason of this weight the inhabitants are forced to build their houses both narrow and long; ... It is said that the cause of the heat is the fact that lofty mountains lie above the country on the north and that these mountains intercept all the northern winds ...

Susis abounds so exceedingly in grain that both barley and wheat regularly produce one hundredfold, and sometimes even two hundred; on this account, also, the people do not cut the furrows close together, for the crowding of the roots hinders the sprouting. The vine did not grow there until the Macedonians planted it, both there and at Babylon; however, they did not dig trenches, but only thrust into the ground iron-pointed stakes, and then pulled them out and replaced them at once with the plants. (trans.: H. L. Jones, LCL)

7. Pliny, *Natural History*, VI 31, 135

Susianen ab Elymaide disterminat amnis Eulaeus ortis in Medis modicoque spatio cuniculo conditus ac rursus exortus et per Massabatenen lapsus, circumit arcem Susorum ac Dianae templum augustissimum illis gentibus, et ipse in magna caerimonia, siquidem reges non exalio bibunt et ob id in longinqua portant.

The territory of Susa is separated from Elymais by the river Eulaeus, which rises in the country of the Medes, and after running for a moderate distance underground, comes to the surface again and flows through Massabatene. It passes round the citadel of Susa and the temple of Diana, which is regarded with the greatest reverence by the races in those parts; and the river itself is held in great veneration, inasmuch as the kings drink water from it only and consequently have it conveyed to places a long distance away. (trans.: H. Rackham, LCL)

8. Ammianus XXIII 6, 26

His tractibus Susiani iunguntur, apud quos non multa sunt oppida. Inter alia tamen eminet Susa,[5] Saepe domicilium regum.

Neighbors to these lands are the Susiani who have few cities. Conspicuous among them, however, is Susa,[5] often the residence of kings. (trans.: J. C. Rolfe, LCL)

B. *Greek Inscriptions*

Thirty-four Greek inscriptions were discovered at Susa, in secondary use in a Sassanian palace on the Apadana. Most have been published by F. Cumont. Those first found are treated in *Mém. Mission Perse* 20 (1928): 79–98; the others in *CRAI* (1930): 208–219; (1931): 233–250, 278–292; (1932): 238–260, 271–286; (1933): 260–268. The text of the whole series is given in *SEG*, vol. 7, Nos. 1–34 (except for No. 7 which appears in *OGIS*, No. 747 and again in *CRAI* [1930]: 209–210). A short description follows:

a. Letter of A. D. 21 (Cumont, *CRAI* [1932]: 238–260 = *SEG*, vol. 7, No. 1, cf. Tarn, *The Greeks*, p. 27f. and references in n. 2) inscribed on the socle of a statue, from Artabanus III to the citizens of Susa, citing decisions of the polis. The subject is Hestiaeus, one of the king's friends and bodyguards—a purely honorary title accorded to ten men at the Hellenistic courts, but not apparently in the Parthian Empire, as noted by Cumont, *CRAI* (1931): 236–237. Hestiaeus was elected to a second term of office as city treasurer before the legal interval of three years had passed. Differing as to the legality of the election, the magistrates and people submitted to the arbitration of the Parthian king, who confirmed Hestiaeus in office. Susa was a polis with the usual institutions: a council, an assembly, magistrates (*archontes*), two of them eponymous, a quaestor, and presumably others as well.

b. Honorary decrees of the second and first centuries B.C. (*SEG*, vol. 7, Nos. 2–8). Among them is a reference to a gymnasiarch and a stadium (*CRAI* [1933]: 264–268 = *SEG* vol. 7, No. 3), which according to Pausanias (X 4, 1) every Greek polis was supposed to have, in addition to an agora. Many inscriptions refer to Susa citizens who were dignitaries at the court of the Seleucids ("friends and bodyguards") and in the Parthian period. One, or perhaps two, of the inscriptions honor Seleucid *strategoi* at Susiane (*CRAI* [1931]: 288 = *SEG*, vol. 7, No. 5; *OGIS*, No. 747 = *SEG*, vol. 7, No. 7).

c. Dedications. One of the items, *SEG*, vol. 7, No. 9, is a sixth century inscription taken as spoils from Didyma in 494 by Darius' soldiers, and includes a dedication to Ma. There is also a verse dedication to Apollo from the socle of a third-century B.C. statue (*CRAI* [1932]: 274–277 = *SEG*, vol. 7, No. 11)

[5] In the second half of the fourth century. Susa is referred to by its original name, not by the Persian name of Erān-Ḫurra-Šāpūr which it received in 345.

and a hymn to Apollo of the first century B.C. or A.D. (Vollgraff, *Mém. Mission Perse* 20 [1928]: 89–96 = *SEG*, vol. 7, No. 14, Tarn, *ibid.*, p. 39). Line 30 of this hymn contains the vocative Θεέ, a form found only in Jewish and Christian texts. Its occurrence here is thought to be due to such influence (Nock, *JEA* 15 [1929]: 223; *HTR* 27 [1934]: 100; Tarn, *ibid.*, p. 29). The Syriac form *mara* appears in the same line and elsewhere in the inscription (cf. *CRAI* [1930]: 215–216). There are two epigrams dedicated to Zamaspes (late first century B.C. and early first century A.D.; *CRAI* [1930]: 211–220 = *SEG*, vol. 7, No. 12 and *CRAI* [1931]: 238–250 = *SEG*, vol. 7, No. 13, inscribed on the socle of a bronze statue). According to a new reading by Robert (in Le Rider, *Suse*, p. 417) the first was dedicated by Φραᾶτις πόλις, the city of Phraates, as Susa was called in the time of Phraates IV. Zamaspes first fulfilled some function under the stratiarch Tiridates, next he was stratiarch himself, and finally satrap (see Le Rider, *Suse*, p. 756, for the nature of these functions). The second of the two inscriptions was ordered by μεγάλης ἄκρας φρουροί, the guardians of the great citadel, whose κλῆροι benefited from successful irrigation works undertaken by Zamaspes. The guardians thus appear to have been *cleruchs*, as late as the first century A.D., even though the town was a polis.

d. The remaining inscriptions are all manumissions of slaves dating to the second century B.C. (see also Tarn, *ibid.*, p. 68f. and references). These are formal dedications of the slaves to the goddess Nanaia (in one instance to Apollo and Artemis Daïttai, see below).

C. *Location*

The ancient capital of the kingdom of Elam, later capital of Achaemenid Persia, at present Sūs on the Karḫa river (on Bab. Env. map).

D. *History*

The old Achaemenid capital of Persia, Susa, in the Hellenistic and Parthian periods was still a very important town,[6] the capital of a satrapy.[7] The province gradually diminished in size but even so the city controlled a vast territory of great fertility.[8] Susa was an important road station, and played a role in the east-west trade, as emphasized by Le Rider (see below). The great number

[6] For Susa in the earlier periods, see Eliot, *Excavations in Mesopotamia*, pp. 29–33; vanden Berghe, *Archéologie de l'Iran Ancien*, pp. 71–83; Christian, *RE*, Suppl. 7, s.v. "Susa," cols. 1251–1274; Ghirshman, *Campagnes*, vol. 1 (1952); *DAFI* 1 (1971)—9 (1978).

[7] Le Rider, *Suse*, pp. 274–275.

[8] See *Suse* for the extent of the territory (pp. 255–267) and the resources (pp. 271–272). See also the entry on "Be Ḥozai." On Susa in the Arabic sources see Yāqūt, *Marāṣid*, Bakrī, *ar-Rauḍ al-mi'ṭār*, s.v. "Sūs"; *BGA*, passim; Mustaufī, vol. 2, p. 109; *Ḥudūd al-'ālam*, index "Shūsh"; T̠a'ālibī, *Ġurar*, p. 529; and also Streck, *EI*[1], s.v. "al-Sūs"; Le Strange, p. 240; Schwarz, *Iran im Mittelalter*, pp. 313, 358f.

of coins found at Susa provide insights into the economic history of the region (see the entry on "Be Ḥozai").

The town lies in the northern part of the plain between the rivers Eulaeus, Choaspes and Corprates (Karḫa, Šāur and Āb-e Dez). It was excavated by French archaeologists who published their results in *Mémoires de la Mission Archéologique en Iran* and *Cahiers de la Délégation Archéologique Française en Iran*. For the post-Achaemenid period the most important finds are the Greek inscriptions and coins. Together with sparse literary sources, these provide us with all the information available about the history of the town from the Hellenistic to the Sassanian period.[9]

The old Persian capital of Susa, a town of mixed population, was refounded as Seleucia on the Eulaeus by Seleucus I and assigned Greek and Macedonian settlers at that time.[10] Most of the personal names appearing on the Greek inscriptions there are Greek, some of them Macedonian.[11] The Greek texts show that Susa remained a Greek polis with the customary institutions and laws until the conquest of the city by the king of Elymais in A.D. 45. The Graeco-Macedonian population and the Iranian and Semitic inhabitants kept well apart.

It appears from the inscriptions that under Parthian rule (from 140 B.C. on) two officials represented the king in Susiane. One, the strategos, may have been in charge of the administration of the region and of the army, and the other presumably dealt with the affairs of the city in particular.[12] The inscriptions, but not as yet archaeological exploration, indicate the existence of several public buildings: the royal palace, the *chreophylakion* (administrative building), a gymnasium and a stadium.[13] Coinage struck at Susa provides information

---

[9] The coins are published in Le Rider's monograph. For the literary sources and inscriptions, see above. For a brief summary of the archaeological remains of the Parthian period see vanden Berghe, *op.cit.*, (in n. 6 above), pp. 81–82. The Parthian town, the so-called "Royal City," was found on the central hill, east of the acropolis and the Apadana, west of the "town of the artisans." There are indications of violent destruction at an unknown date. Among the structures excavated a bathhouse is noteworthy. Great quantities of Parthian pottery and many other objects were found. Further east, in the "town of the artisans," a Seleucid and Parthian necropolis was excavated by Ghirshman. For Parthian objects from Susa and for bibliography see vanden Berghe, *op.cit.* (in n. 6), p. 174, no. 171.

[10] Σελεύκεια ἡ πρὸς τῷ Εὐλαίῳ; cf. Le Rider, *Suse*, p. 280f.

[11] See the list and discussion by Le Rider, *Suse*, pp. 282–287.

[12] Polybius V 54, 12. For the inscriptions, see above. For the respective functions see Le Rider, *Suse*, pp. 275–276.

[13] For a sketch plan of the group of tells which constitute the site of Susa, see Le Rider, *Suse*, p. 277, fig. 11. For aerial photographs see Schmidt, *Flights over Ancient Cities of Iran*, Pl. 55; Ghirshman, *Village*, Mém. Mission Iran, vol. 36 (1954), Pls. I–III; Le Rider, *Suse*, Pl. I (= Ghirshman, Pl. III). For the *chreophylakion* see Cumont, *CRAI* (1933): 263f. = *SEG*, vol. 7, No. 15; for the gymnasium and stadium see Cumont, *CRAI* (1933): 264–268 = *SEG*, vol. 7, No. 3. These buildings have not been identified by the excavators.

also on the gods worshiped in the Seleucid and Parthian periods.[14] In the Seleucid period all gods represented on coins are Greek: Artemis, Apollo and, less frequently, Athene, the Dioscuri, Hermes, Zeus Ammon, and lightning, the symbol of Zeus.[15] Apollo and Artemis Daïttai are mentioned in an inscription.[16] Some inscriptions also mention the local goddess Nanaia and the Cappadocian goddess Ma, probably introduced by Greek soldiers.[17] Greek gods continue to appear in the Parthian period, but at the same time oriental gods were accepted in the official pantheon of the city, and the image of Artemis was modified under the influence of Nanaia.[18]

In 147 B.C. the Seleucids were expelled from Susa by the Elymaeans under Kamniskires.[19] The Elymaeans had been fighting the Seleucids under Antiochus III and IV, and aside from representing a considerable military force, were reputed to be wealthy.[20] Their region lay to the east of Susiane and Seleucia on the Hedyphon was the capital. Traditionally Susa was in Elam, but in the Hellenistic period Susiane and Elymais were separate entities.[21]

In 141 B.C. the Arsacid Mithridates I conquered Babylonia. The next year he occupied Susa, as appears from Parthian coins issued there.[22] The first three issues show that Mithridates treated Susa, like Seleucia on the Tigris, with special benevolence.[23] Then the usurper Tigraios reigned at Susa (from around 138/7 to 133/2 B.C.)[24] which was retaken for a short time by the Seleucid

---

14 See the treatment by Le Rider, *Suse*, pp. 287–296.

15 *Suse*, pp. 288–293.

16 For Apollo and Artemis Daïttai see Cumont, *CRAI* (1931): 279–285 = *SEG*, vol. 7, No. 17 (manumission of 183 B.C.).

17 Acts of *manumissio* (liberation of slaves) of the third and second century B.C. mention Nanaia and her sanctuary (see below). For Nanaia see Le Rider, *Suse*, pp. 292–293 with bibliography on p. 292, n. 6. Nanaia, originally a Babylonian goddess, was worshiped at Susa since the third millennium. A Hellenistic papyrus based on older material states that Isis is worshiped as Nanaia in Susa (Papyrus Oxy. XI 1380, line 106; cf. Le Rider, *Suse*, p. 292, line 4). Ma appears once on a third century B.C. dedication (*SEG*, vol. 7, No. 10; cf. Le Rider, *Suse*, p. 292 and n. 4).

18 Le Rider, *Suse*, pp. 293–296. See Source 7 (Pliny): *Dianae templum augustissimum illis gentibus*. For Nanaia in Elymais see n. 20.

19 Le Rider, *Suse*, pp. 349ff. Kamniskires presence in Susa is known only from coins.

20 For Kamniskires, see Le Rider, *Suse*, p. 352f.; for the history of Elymais see *Suse*, pp. 353–355. In 187 B.C. Antiochus III was killed fighting the Elymaeans. According to II Macc. 9: 1–2, Antiochus attacked the Elymaean sanctuary of Artemis-Nanaia in 164 B.C. hoping to take possession of its wealth; cf. Holleaux, *Études d'Épigraphie*, vol. 3, pp. 255–280. For the Elymaeans see also Kahrstedt, *Artabanos III. und seine Erben*, pp. 39–47. Their capital, Seleucia on the Hedyphon (the Ǧarrāḥī River) has not been identified. See further Weissbach, *RE*, vol. 5, s.v. "Elymais," cols. 2458–2467.

21 This has been shown by Le Rider, *Suse*, pp. 356 n. 1, 357, who notes that cuneiform texts of the Seleucid and Parthian period referring to Elamites do not make a distinction between the inhabitants of Susiane and Elymais.

22 Le Rider, *Suse*, pp. 355–357.

23 *Suse*, pp. 374–376.

24 *Suse*, pp. 378–380, 385–386.

Antiochus VII.[25] Following their victory over Antiochus VII, the Parthians re-established control of Susa. Hyspaosines of Charax, who in 128/7 B.C. certainly reigned at Babylon and Seleucia, penetrated Media and fought the Elamites, but did not conquer Susa.[26]

Between 31/30 and 27/26 B.C., during the reign of Phraates IV, Susa was renamed "Phraata in Susa" (Φράατα τὰ ἐν Σούσοις) replacing the former "Seleucia on the Eulaeus."[27] According to Le Rider, the renaming was not to be seen as punishment of the town, but rather as a reward. The coinage was still dated according to the Seleucid era, and municipal government was still in Greek hands, as appears from the A.D. 21 letter of Artabanus III,[28] evidence, as are other inscriptions of the period, of the vitality of Greek culture in Susa in this period.

The last Parthian king who struck coinage at Susa was Vardanes I (ca. 39–ca. A.D. 45). In Le Rider's opinion, the Elymaeans returned to Susa in about A.D. 45[29] and from 75 on they issued coinage there. An inscription found at Palmyra indicates that by 138 Susa was the Elymaean capital,[30] perhaps moved there from Seleucia on the Hedyphon in 75. We do not know how long after that date the Elymaeans maintained control over Susa. An inscribed bas-relief found at Susa shows that in 215 the city was part of the kingdom of Artabanus IV. The monument is dedicated by his satrap in old Persian and dated according to the Arsacid era; in it the city is referred to as Susa.[31] In 224 Susa was conquered by the Sassanians. About Susa in the following period practically nothing is known, and no coins or inscriptions have been found. Early Christian sources inform us that in about 345, following an insurrection, Shapur II razed the town (with 300 elephants) and had the inhabitants killed. Excavators found the houses of this period all showing signs of violent destruction. Victims were buried hastily by the survivors, the children among them in jars, some of which are marked with Nestorian crosses.[32] Susa was then

---

[25] *Suse*, pp. 377–378.

[26] *Suse*, pp. 382–383; cf. the entry on "Mesene." [27] *Suse*, pp. 409–415.

[28] Cumont, *CRAI* (1932): 236–238 = *SEG*, vol. 7, No. 1.

[29] Le Rider, *Suse*, pp. 426–429.

[30] Cantineau, *Mél. Syr. offerts à René Dussaud*, vol. 1, pp. 277–279; Seyrig, *Syria* 22 (1941): 255–258 = *Antiquités Syriennes* 3 (1946): 199–202.

[31] Le Rider, *Suse*, p. 430; Ghirshman, *MMFP* 44 (1950): 97–107. Ghirsman argued that the monument he published shows that the Parthians had reason to hope that the satrap of Susa and the city itself would play a crucial role in the Parthian struggle against Ardashīr. It certainly proved that in 221 Artabanus V was in Susa; cf. Nöldeke, *Perser und Araber*, p. 12, and Henning, *Asia Major* 2 (1952): 176. For this inscription see also Altheim & Stiehl, *Ein asiatischer Staat*, pp. 241–243.

[32] Nöldeke, *ibid.*, pp. 58–59, with notes 1 and 2; Ṭabarī, vol. 2, pp. 57–58 (= vol. 1, pp. 839-840). On Ṭabarī see also Altheim & Stiehl, *op.cit.*, pp. 28–29 and n. 33 below. For the archaeological evidence see Ghirshman, *AJA* 55 (1951): 96; idem., *op.cit.* (n. 6 above), p. 18; vanden Berghe, *op.cit.* (n. 6 above), p. 81. For a Sassanian coin hoard (Khusro I, 531–537, to Khusro II, A. D. 590/1–628) see Gijselen, *DAFI* 7 (1977): 61–74.

refounded as Erān-Ḫurra-Šāpūr and rebuilt on quite a grand scale. At least some of the new settlers were Roman captives (see the entries on "Be Lapaṭ" and "Be Ḥozai").

Although it was a bishopric, the metropolitan of the region had his see at Be Lapaṭ.[33] The bishop of Susa ordained Papa, the first bishop of Seleucia (late third century). When the latter attempted to make himself chief of all Persian bishops, the bishops of Susa and Šuštar were his greatest opponents. Bishops of Susa are attested in council acts between 420 and 605.[34]

E. *Jews and Susa*

There was presumably a Jewish population in Susa in the mishnaic and talmudic period, although Susa of the Parthian—Sassanian era is hardly mentioned in talmudic literature, apparently because of its remoteness from the Babylonian centers of Jewish life and creativity.

Most of the instances in talmudic literature refer to biblical Šušan (see note * p. 422). In Obermeyer's opinion, however, the discussions in Sources 2 and 3 and their parallels of the date on which Purim is to be celebrated and the Book of Esther read relate to the Jewish community in Susa at the time of the sages who figure in those sources.[35] Still, although a Jewish community probably existed there, the discussions in the sources may actually be academic ones, unconnected with the situation prevailing in Susa at the time of the sages involved.

Source 4 criticizes the people from the Kingdom of Israel, exiled by the Assyrians in the eighth century B.C., because their new homes appealed to them so much that they compared them favorably with Eretz Israel, and the specific places mentioned are Šušan, Šuštar (qq.v.) and Elam. The interpretation is based on folk etymology of the place names: Šuš, here referring to Šušan, and in fact the Syriac form of it, in Persian means "lovely" or "good,"[36] and Šuštar is divided into two—Šuš and Təre ("two" in Aramaic)—to indicate that it is twice as lovely as Šušan and thus as Eretz Israel as well. It is not likely that the authors of the aphorism noted had an authentic historical tradition on remarks made by the exiles; the story is rather a reflection of the beauty and fertility of Šušan in their own day.

According to *Šahrīnā i Ērān*, a Pahlavi work (*Catalogue*, ed. Markwart). King Yazdagird I (399–420) married an Exilarch's daughter named Shōshīn-duḫt. The source has been extensively investigated and the general view is that the story is authentic, but the later section of the source stating that Susa and

---

[33] Labourt, *Le Christianisme*, p. 20 n. 6, p. 70; Christensen, *L'Iran*, pp. 252–253 267. Susa was surrendered to the Arabs in 642, see *ibid.*, p. 507.

[34] Sachau, *APAW phil.-hist. Klasse* 1 (1919) pp. 38–40.

[35] Obermeyer, pp. 212–214.

[36] Obermeyer, *loc. cit.*; Eshel, pp. 238–239.

Šuštar were built under Shōshīn-duẖt's influence appears to be a popular fabrication.[37] It should be borne in mind that Rav Ashi, head of the Sura yeshiva at the time, describes close relations that obtained between the king and the Exilarch, Huna b. Nathan.[38] Testimony on a favorable policy toward the Jews is available also in regard to Vahram Ğūr (420–438), Yazdagird's son and according to the tradition in the source the Exilarch's grandson as well. An interesting item in *ar-Rauḍ al-miʿṭār* reports that when Sūs was conquered by the Muslims, some books (*kutub ṣuḥuf*) were found in Daniel's grave. They were sold for twenty-four *dirhems* and ended up in Eretz Israel (= Šām).[39]

ADAMS, *Science* 136, (1962): 109–122
BEER, *Rashut ha-Golah* (1970), pp. 47–48
BEER, *Amora'ei Bavel* (1974), p. 84
CHRISTENSEN, *L'Iran* (1944²), pp. 252–253
CONTENAU, *Bull. des Musées de France* (1948): 87–89
ESHEL, *Yishuvei ha-Yehudim* (1979), p. 238
FUNK, *Monumenta* (1913), pp. 51, 299
HIRSCHENSON, *Sheva Ḥokhmot* (1883), p. 234
JASTROW, *Dictionary* (1950³), p. 1543
KOHUT, *Arukh ha-Shalem* (1878–1892), vol. 8, pp. 178–179; *Tosefot* (1937), p. 393
KRAUSS, *Qadmoniot ha-Talmud* (1923–1945), vol. 1A, p. 29
KRAUSS, *Paras we-Romi* (1948), pp. 22, 96
LABOURT, *Le Christianisme* (1904), pp. 20 n. 6, 70
LE RIDER, *Suse* (1965), passim
LEVY, *Wörterbuch* (1924²), vol. 4, p. 528
NEUBAUER, *Géographie* (1868), p. 381
NEUSNER, *History* (1965–1970), vol. 1, pp. 8–10, 14, 17; vol. 4, pp. 380–381; vol. 5, pp. 8–9
NÖLDEKE, *Perser und Araber* (1879), pp. 58–59
OBERMEYER, *Landschaft* (1929), pp. 16, 212–214, 296, n. 4
SCHWARZ, *Iran im Mittelalter* (1969²), pp. 313, 358f.
STRAUSS, *Revue Numismatique* 6/13 (1971): 109–140
STRECK, *EI*¹, s.v. "al-Sūs"
TARN, *The Greeks* (1951), pp. 27–30, 39
WENKE, *Mesopotamia* 10–11 (1975–6): 31–221
WIDENGREN, *Iranica Antiqua* 1 (1961), pp. 139–141

Šuštar שושתרי

A. *Sources*

1. Sanhedrin 94a

אבל ישראל ספרו בגנותה של ארץ-ישראל, כי מטו שוש אמרי שויא כי ארעין, כי מטו עלמין אמרו כעלמין, כי מטו שוש תרי אמרי על חד תרין.

But Israel [when exiled] spoke evil of Eretz Israel. Whey they reached Šuš they said, It equals our country; when they reached ʿAlmin (עלמין) they said, Like our world (= עלמין); when they reached Šuš Təre (= two) they said, Double.

[37] Widengren, *Iranica Antiqua* 1 (1961): 139–141 and bibliography; Markwart, *Catalogue*, § 47 and pp. 97–98; Beer, *Rashut ha-Golah*, pp. 47–48 and the bibliography there; Neusner, *History* vol. 5, pp. 8–9.

[38] See e.g., the description of the meeting between Yazdagird I and the Exilarch Huna b. Nathan in Zevaḥim 19a.

[39] See *ar-Rauḍ al-miʿṭār*, s.v. "Sūs," and cf. also "Tustar" there.

2. Pliny, *Natural History*, VI 31, 136

oppida eius Seleucia et Sostrate adposita monti Chasiro. oram quae praeiacet Minorum Syrtium vice diximus inaccessam coeno, plurimum limi deferentibus Brixa et Ortacia amnibus, madente et ipsa Elymaide in tantum ut nullius sit nisi circuitu eius ad Persidem aditus. infestatur et serpentibus quod flumina deportant.

The towns (of Elymais) are Seleucia and Sostrate, situated on the flank of Mount Chasirus. The coast lying in front, as we have stated above, is rendered inaccessible by mud, like the Lesser Syrtes, as the rivers Brixa and Ortacia bring down a quantity of sediment, and the Elymais district is itself so marshy that it is only possible to reach Farsistan by making a long detour round it. It is also infested with snakes carried down by the streams. (trans.: H. Rackham, LCL)

3. Pliny, *Natural History*, XII, 39, 78

. . . arborem bratum cupresso fusae similem, exalbidis ramis, iucundi odoris accensam et cum miraculo historiis Claudi Caesaris praedicatum: folia eius inspergere potionibus Parthos tradit, odorem esse proximum cedro, fumumque eius contra ligna alia remedio. nascitur ultra Pasitigrim finibus oppidi Sostratae in monte Scanchro.

. . . the wood of the bratum, a tree resembling a spreading cypress, with very white branches, and giving an agreeable scent when burnt. It is praised in the Histories of Claudius Caesar as having a marvellous property: he states that the Parthians sprinkle its leaves into their drinks, and that it has a scent very like cedar, and its smoke is an antidote against the effects of other woods. It grows beyond the river Karun on Mount Scanchrus in the territory of the city of Sostrata. (trans.: H. Rackham, LCL)

B. *Location*

On the Karun river, some sixty kilometers southeast of Susa (q.v.) (on Bab. Env. map).

C. *Physical Features*

Šuštar was one of the strongest natural fortresses in Ḫūzistān. As pointed out by Curzon, most Persian cities are built in plains not far from the mountains from which their water is supplied. Šuštar, on the other hand, is built on a rock at the foot of the hills "and is at once sustained and fortified by the command of a noble river (the Karun)."[1] Curzon further observed that its

[1] Curzon, *Persia and the Persian Question*, p. 370.

position allowed it to control both the nomads of the mountains and the Arabs of the Ḫūzistān plain. Trade between the south and the inland districts of Burūğird, Kermānšāh and Hamadān (q.v.) naturally passed through Šuštar, up to which the Karun is navigable.[2] The great fertility of the plains below Šuštar also contributed to its position as capital of Ḫūzistān.
The major disadvantage of the city is its climate: Šuštar has a mean maximum temperature for July of 47.3° C. which is the highest in the country[3] (see Source 6 in the entry on "Susa"), so that crops must be constantly irrigated. The second disadvantage is the flooding to which the plain is subject in the spring, which may be the reason it was not cultivated in the nineteenth century.[4] However, in the neighborhood of Šuštar are a number of structures designed to solve problems of water supply. Chief among them is a dam known as Band-e Kaiser (see below), a 550-meter long barrage made of dressed stone and cement, which could raise the water level by two meters or more. The river bed is paved with large stones, bonded with clamps, in order to prevent erosion.[5] There are two other barrages in the vicinity, the Band-e Gurgar and the Band-e Miyan or Band-e Muḥammad ʿAlī Mirza.

D. *History*

Very little is known of the history of the town in antiquity. It is mentioned by Pliny and twice by the Ravenna Cosmography (44,20; 52,21) as Sostrate. Ṭabarī states that Shapur I "forced Valerian to built the dam at Šuštar."[6] Since the largest dam there is called Band-e Kaiser (= Caesar's dam), it is quite possible that it was in fact built by Roman prisoners of war settled at Šuštar after Valerian's defeat and capture in 260. The bishops of Susa and Šuštar were the greatest opponents of Papa, the first bishop of Seleucia (late third century) when he attempted to make himself chief of all Persian bishops.[7]

---

[2] *The Cambridge History of Iran*, ed. Fisher, vol. 1, p. 553, notes that in 1887 small steamers could sail up the Karun as far as Šuštar. An old caravan route linked Susa with Isfahan via Šuštar and Malamir. vanden Berghe, *Archéologie de l'Iran ancien*, p. 63, observes that this route explains why travelers in the past, such as Layard in 1840–42 would see ancient monuments which are far from the modern road through Dezfūl, Ḫorram-Ābād and Burūğird.

[3] *Cambridge History of Iran*, p. 232.

[4] *Loc. cit.* In antiquity the Ḫūzistān plain, now a steppe, was densely populated thanks to irrigation.

[5] Dieulafoy, *L'Art antique de la Perse*, vol. 5, p. 60, Pl. XII; van Roggen, *Mémoires de la Délégation en Perse*, 2ième Série, vol. 7; see also the description by Curzon, *op. cit.* (in n. 1 above), pp. 374-379.

[6] Ṭabarī, vol. 2 p. 47 (= vol. 1 p. 827). See also the entry on "Be Ḥozai" for waterworks in Ḫūzistān. On Shapur II's dam, see Dimašqī, *Nuḫbat ad-dahr*, p. 179.

[7] Sachau, *APAW phil.-hist. Klasse* 1 (1919), p. 38f.

Bishops of Šuštar are mentioned in council acts of 420 and later.[8] The lengthy siege of Šuštar and its capture by the Arabs in 638 are described in Arabic sources and in the anonymous Syriac chronicle edited by Guidi.[9]

E. *Jews and Šuštar*

The Israelites exiled in the eighth century B.C. by the Assyrians are criticized in Source 1 for becoming so fond of their new homes that they considered them as good as Eretz Israel, and Šuštar seemed twice as attractive as Eretz Israel (and as Šušan; see the entry on "Susa"). Of course the critics had no authentic historical tradition to support their disapproval, which is based on a folk etymology breaking down the name Šuštar into two words — Šuš Təre — and is intended merely to stress the beauty of Šuštar in the amoraic period.[10]

Eshel, *Yishuvei ha-Yehudim* (1979), p. 239
Funk, *Monumenta* (1913), pp. 51, 299
Hirschenson, *Sheva Ḥokhmot* (1883), p. 234
Kohut, *Arukh ha-Shalem* (1878–1892), vol. 8, p. 180
Kramers, *EI*[1], s.v. "Shuster"
Krauss, *Paras we-Romi* (1948), pp. 22, 96
Labourt, *Le Christianisme* (1904[2]), pp. 68, 102
Levy, *Wörterbuch* (1924[2]), vol. 4, p. 526, "שוש"
Neubauer, *Géographie* (1868), p. 382
Neusner, *History* (1965–1970), vol. 2, pp. xix; 242; vol. 5, pp. 9, 11
Obermeyer, *Landschaft* (1929), pp. 212–213
Schwarz, *Iran im Mittelalter* (1969[2]), pp. 313, 315f.
Weissbach, *RE*, vol. 3A, col. 1199, s.v. "Sostra"

Šuṭ Mišuṭ שוט מישוט

A. *Sources*

1. Qiddushin 72a

ההוא גברא דאמר להו אנא מן שוט מישוט, עמד רבי יצחק נפחא על רגליו ואמר שוט מישוט [1] בין הנהרות עומדת. וכי בין הנהרות עומדת מאי הוי, אמר אביי [2] אמר ר׳ חמא בר עוקבא

[8] Labourt, *Le Christianisme*, p. 102. See also p. 68 for a martyr at Šuštar under Shapur II. In 457 there was a Nestorian bishop from Edessa at Šuštar (*ibid.*, p. 102).

[9] See Nöldeke, *SAWW phil.-hist. Klasse* 129, 9 (1893): 31, 41–42; Īšōdad, bishop of Ḥīra, who had served as mediator between Arabs and Persians, was killed when the town was taken. On Šuštar in Arabic sources see, s.v. "Tustar," Yāqūt, Bakrī, and *ar-Rauḍ al-miʿṭār*; *BGA*, passim; Qazwīnī, *Bilād*, pp. 170–172; Mustaufī, vol. 2, pp. 107–108, 207; *Ḥudūd al-ʿālam*, index "Šuštar"; Dimašqī, *Nuḫbat ad-dahr*, p. 38; see also Kramers, *EI*[1], s.v. "Shuster"; Le Strange, p. 234ff.; Schwarz, *Iran im Mittelalter*, pp. 313, 315f.

[10] For a Pahlavi source reporting the foundation of Šuštar through the influence of Shōshīn-duḫt, the Exilarch's daughter who married King Yazdagird I, see the section on Jews and Susa in the entry on "Susa."

[1] The Munich MS has ששמשוט (ששמישוט in the earlier reference), as does the Oxford MS; the Vatican 111 MS has שוש משוט (שוט משוש in the earlier reference).

[2] The Munich MS has "Rabbi Abbahu."

אמר רבי יוסי בר׳ חנינא בין הנהרות הרי היא כגולה ליוחסין. והיכא קיימא, אמר ר׳ יוחנן מאיהי דקירא[3] ולעיל. והא אמר רבי יוחנן עד מעברתא דגיזמא,[4] אמר אביי רצועה נפקא.

That person who told them, I am from Šuṭ Mišuṭ, Rabbi Isaac Nappaḥa stood up and said, Šuṭ Mišuṭ[1] stands between the rivers. And that it stands between the rivers, what would that be? Abbaye[2] said that Rabbi Ḥama b. ʿUqba said, Rabbi Yose son of Rabbi Ḥanina said, Between the rivers is like the Exile (= Babylonia) in respect of genealogy. And where is it? Rabbi Yoḥanan said, From Ihi də-Qira[3] up. But Rabbi Yoḥanan said, To the ford of Gizma.[4] Abbaye said, A strip extends.

2. Strabo XIV 2,29 (664)

λέγει δὲ καὶ Πολύβιος περὶ τῶν ἐκεῖ μάλιστα δεῖν πιστεύειν ἐκείνῳ. ἄρχεται δὲ ἀπὸ Σαμοσάτων τῆς Κομμαγηνῆς, ἣ πρὸς τῇ διαβάσει καὶ τῷ Ζεύγματι κεῖται· εἰς δὲ Σαμόσατα ἀπὸ τῶν ὅρων τῆς Καππαδοκίας τῶν περὶ Τόμισα ὑπερθέντι τὸν Ταῦρον σταδίους εἴρηκε τετρακοσίους καὶ πεντήκοντα.

But Polybius says that we should rely most on Artemidoros in regard to the places here. He begins with Samosata in Commagene, which lies at the river crossing and at Zeugma, and states that the distance to Samosata, across the Taurus, from the borders of Cappadocia round Tomisa is four hundred and fifty stadia. (trans.: H. L. Jones, LCL)

3. Strabo XVI 2,3 (749)

Καθόλου μὲν οὕτω, καθ' ἕκαστα δὲ ἡ Κομμαγηνὴ μικρά τίς ἐστιν· ἔχει δ' ἐρυμνὴν πόλιν Σαμόσατα ἐν ᾗ τὸ βασίλειον ὑπῆρχε, νῦν δ' ἐπαρχία γέγονε· χώρα δὲ περίκειται σφόδρα εὐδαίμων, ὀλίγη [δέ]. ἐνταῦθα δὲ νῦν ἐστι τὸ ζεῦγμα τοῦ Εὐφράτου· κατὰ τοῦτο δὲ Σελεύκεια ἵδρυται φρούριον τῆς Μεσοποταμίας προσωρισμένον ὑπὸ Πομπηίου τῷ Κομμαγηνῷ.

Commagene is rather a small country, and it has a city fortified by nature, Samosata, where the royal residence used to be, but it has now become a province, and the city is surrounded by an exceedingly fertile, though small territory. Here is now the bridge of the Euphrates; and near the bridge (i.e. on the east bank) is situated Seleucia, a fortress of Mesopotamia, which was included within the boundaries of Commagene by Pompey. (trans.: H. L. Jones, LCL)

4. Pliny, *Natural History*, II 108, 235

In urbe Commagenes Samosata stagnum est emittens limum (maltham vocant) flagrantem cum quid attigit solidi, adhaeret; praeterea tactus et sequitur fugientes. sic defendere muros oppugnante Lucullo, flagrabatque miles armis suis, aquis etiam accenditur; terra tantem restingui decuere experimenta.

---

[3] For variants, see the entry on "Ihi də-Qira."

[4] The Vatican 111 MS has מעברתא דאגמא.

In Samosata the capital of Commagene there is a marsh that produces an inflammable mud called mineral pitch. When this touches anything solid it sticks to it; also when people touch it, it actually follows them as they try to get away from it. By these means they defended the city wall when attacked by Lucullus; the troops kept getting burnt by their own weapons. Water merely makes it burn more fiercely; experiments have shown that it can only be put out by earth. (trans.: H. Rackham, LCL)

5. Pliny, *Natural History*, V 21, 86

a Samosatis autem, latere Syriae, Marsyas amnis influit ... oppida adluuntur Epiphania et Antiochia quae ad Euphraten vocatur, item Zeugma LXXII p.a. Samosatis ...

Below Samosata, on the Syrian side the river Marsyas flows into the Euphrates ... the towns washed by the river are Epiphania and Antioch (called Antioch on the Euphrates), and also Zeugma, 72 miles from Samosata. (trans.: H. Rackham, LCL)

6. Josephus, *Jewish War*, VII 224[5]

τὰ γὰρ Σαμόσατα τῆς Κομμαγηνῆς μεγίστη πόλις κεῖται παρὰ τὸν Εὐφράτην, ὥστ' εἶναι τοῖς Πάρθοις, εἴ τι τοιοῦτον διενενόηντο, ῥᾴστην μὲν τὴν διάβασιν βεβαίαν δὲ τὴν ὑποδοχήν.

For Samosata, the chief city of Commagene, lying on the Euphrates, would afford the Parthians, if they harboured any such designs, a most easy passage and an assured reception, (trans.: H. St. J. Thackeray, LCL)

7. Josephus, *Jewish War*, I 321; *Antiquities* XIV 439ff.[6]

... πόλις δ' ἐστὶν Εὐφράτου πλησίον καρτερά ...

... (Samosata) a strong city near the Euphrates ...

8. Ammianus XVIII 8, 1[7]

... nos disposimus properare Samosatam, ut superato exinde flumine, pontiumque apud Zeugma et Capersana iuncturis abscisis, hostiles impetus (si iuvisset fors ulla) repelleremus.

... We (the Roman troops) planned to hasten to Samosata in order to cross the river from there and break down the bridges at Zeugma and Capersana, and so (if fortune should aid us at all) repel the enemy's attacks. (trans.: J. C. Rolfe, LCL)

---

[5] Caesennius Paetus, governor of Syria, informed Vespasian in A. D. 72–73 that Antiochus, king of Commagene, had plans to revolt and was in touch with the Parthians.

[6] The passage describes Herod's aid to Antony in 38 B. C. during the latter's siege of Samosata.

[7] Referring to A. D. 359.

9. Ammianus XX 11,4[8]

... ipse per Melitenam (minoris Armeniae oppidum), et Lacotena et Samosata, transito Euphrate Edessam venit.

... Going by way of Melitene (a town of Lesser Armenia), Lacotena and Samosata, he crossed the Euphrates and came to Edessa. (trans.: J.C. Rolfe, LCL)

B. *Already Proposed Location*

Samosata (presentday Samsat in Turkey), a fortified city on the west bank of the Euphrates, the ancient capital of Commagene. It was called Sumaisāṭ by the Arabs[9] (on Bab. Env. map).

C. *Identification*

The identification of Šuṭ Mišuṭ with Samosata proposed by several scholars[10] is possible for two reasons: First there is the phonetic similarity between the name Šuṭ Mišuṭ in its various versions to Samosata.[11] Secondly, Source 1 sets the location of Šuṭ Mišuṭ "between the rivers," apparently meaning northern Mesopotamia between the Euphrates and the Tigris, equivalent to the district of al-Ǧazīra (= the island, i.e., the land between the two rivers) of the Arabs (see below). According to the tradition cited by Abbaye (or Rabbi Abbahu; see note 2) in Source 1, the status of the region "between the rivers" is identical, so far as lineage is concerned (see Introduction) with that of Babylonia. As Šuṭ Mišuṭ is located within that region, the lineage of the man in that source who says he is from Šuṭ Mišuṭ is acceptable. Abbaye also settles a seeming contradiction of Rabbi Yoḥanan, who is here quoted as saying that the southernmost point of "between the rivers" is Ihi də-Qira (= Hīt) q.v., but elsewhere stated that the northernmost

[8] Referring to A.D. 360, Constantius II's Persian campaign.

[9] See the entry in Yāqūt, *Marāṣid, ar-Rauḍ al-mi'ṭār* and Bakrī; see also Rossi, *EI*[1], s.v. "Sumaisāṭ," and Le Strange, p. 108. From Sumaisāṭ southwards, the Euphrates is navigable, Ibn al-Faqīh, p. 175; Ibn Ḫurdāḏbih, p. 174; Idrīsī, vol. 6, p. 650; *ar-Rauḍ al-mi'ṭār*, s.v. "Furāt." Cf. Ǧaḥiẓ, *Buldān*, p. 198. And see Ṭabarī, vol. 7, p. 447 (= vol. 3, p. 57); Ibn Ḥauqal, p. 207, the text related to the map on p. 206; see also the map: Sumaisāṭ appears on the right bank (though blurred; see the editor's correction, p. 207, note), and see *ibid.*, p. 227; Iṣṭaḫrī, p. 76; Ibn al-Faqīh, p. 133; Idrīsī, vol. 6, p. 651; *ar-Rauḍ al-mi'ṭār*, s. v. "Sumaisāṭ"; Le Strange, "Ibn Serapion," pp. 49–50; cf. Mas'ūdī, *Murūǧ*, vol. 1, p. 117 (= vol. 1, p. 215). The name Samasṭīya mentioned in connection with a Muslim incursion against the Byzantines at the end of the first century after the Hiǧra (the seventh A. D.) seems closer to the original Samosata, see Ṭabarī, vol. 6, p. 469 (= vol. 2, p. 1236).

[10] See Neubauer, pp. 331, 354; Berliner, pp. 63–64; Funk, *Monumenta*, pp. 299–300; Eshel, pp. 235–236, etc. But see the reservations of Hirschenson, pp. 233–234 and Obermeyer, p. 105, n. 1.

[11] For the various forms of the name see Weissbach, *RE*, vol. 1A, cols. 2220–2221, s.v. "Samosata."

point of Babylonia is the Gizma ford,[12] explaining that a strip of land connected the two border points.

Some difficulty in the identification of Šuṭ Mišuṭ with Samosata arises from the placement of the former "between the rivers" by the talmudic source. First of all, Samosata was west of the Euphrates and thus not strictly "between the rivers." Secondly, Yāqūt cites a district called "between the rivers" (= Baina n-Nahraini) comprising only part of northern Mesopotamia and not including Sumaisāṭ-Samosata.[13] However, the "between the rivers" region of Yāqūt's time (he died in 1229) is not coextensive with the region so named in the Talmud. Talmudic "between the rivers" seems to correspond to the Ğazīra district (on which see the entry on "Ihi də-Qira").[14] According to the Arab geographers, that district also included some places east of the Tigris and west of the Euphrates that were close to the river banks.[15] It seems reasonable to deduce that the same was true in the talmudic period, thus resolving the difficulty of identifying Šuṭ Mišuṭ with Samosata because of its location west of the Euphrates.[16]

That difficulty does not arise at all in connection with another possible identification of Šuṭ Mišuṭ: Šimšāṭ, on the left bank of the eastern branch of the Euphrates on the Armenian border, at a location actually between the rivers. According to Iṣṭaḫrī, Šimšāṭ is the border city (*ṯaġr*) of al-Ğazīra, as it lies west of the Tigris and east of the Euphrates.[17]

---

[12] Qiddushin 71b. The gap between the borders, as well as Abbaye's justification, indicates that the Gizma ford was south of Ihi də-Qira (= Hīt) so there are no grounds for seeking to identify the former with Zeugma (as did Berliner, p. 20; *Arukh ha-Shalem*, s.v. "גיזמא"; Eshel, p. 87; and others).

[13] According to Yāqūt, that district (= *Kūra*) lay "between Nisibis (q.v.) and Baqʿā' al-Mauṣil; sometimes the governor of Mosul (al-Mauṣil) gains control of it and sometimes the governor of Nisibis, and it is closer to Nisibis and resembles its districts more closely." See *Muštarik*, s.v. "Baina n-Nahraini" (mistakenly printed Baʿqā' al-Mauṣil). Baqʿā' is a district near Mosul between Mosul and Nisibis, with its capital at Barqaʿīd, see Yāqūt, s.v. "Baqʿā'" and "Barqaʿīd"; see also Yāqūt, s.v. "Baina n-Nahraini" (where the text is garbled in both editions). (Obermeyer's assumptions [pp. 100–104] in regard to the "between the rivers" region and to Šuṭ Mišuṭ are untenable.)

[14] Still, the epithet "what is between the two rivers" (*mā baina n-nahraini*) does appear; see Ibn al-ʿIbrī, *Ta'rīḫ muḫtaṣar ad-duwal*, pp. 74, 77, 80 (twice). This *ma baina n-nahraini* should not be confused with "Baina n-Nahraini" on the Nahrawān canal east of the Tigris. Mustaufī (vol. 2, p. 48) lists Rāḏān and Baina n-Nahraini together as two districts on the Nahrawān canal. The editor notes that Baina n-Nahraini is not mentioned by any other source. But see Yāqūt, *Muštarik*, s.v. "Baina n-Nahraini."

[15] See Ibn Ḥauqal, p. 209; Iṣṭaḫrī, p. 72.

[16] On Sumaisāṭ as one of the border points of al-Ğazīra see Ibn al-Faqīh, p. 127. According to Yāqūt, s.v. "Šimšāṭ," Sumaisāṭ belonged to Syria (= Šām). Muqaddasī, p. 54, lists Sumaisāṭ among the districts of Aleppo and see *op.cit.* p. 154; cf. *Ḥudūd al-ʿālam*, pp. 76, 141, 148, 393; Bakrī, s.v. "Sumaisāṭ."

[17] P. 75. Bakrī, at the end of the entry on "Sumaisāṭ" notes that Šimšāṭ is a district in the Diyār Muḍar region, which is entirely within al-Ğazīra, and in the entry on "Diyār

D. *Samosata and Its Environs*

Like Zeugma, Samosata controlled one of the important fords across the Euphrates. The roads departing from it provided convenient access to Edessa in Osrhoëne to the southeast, to Melitene in the north from which all of Asia Minor could be reached, to Zeugma in the south along the river, and also southwest to the Syrian capital of Antioch.[18] Samosata was described by a number of nineteenth century geographers.[19] In 1964 Theresa Goell carried out a preliminary survey and sounding on the site.[20]

E. *History*

Although Samosata may have existed in the pre-Hellenistic period, it is not mentioned in any sources before the second century B.C. The Romans besieged it under the command of Lucullus in 69 B.C. and of Ventidius in 38 B.C.[21] Commagene, of which Samosata was the chief town, was annexed by the Romans in A.D. 17. In A.D. 38 Antiochus IV was installed by Caligula as client-king of the province,[22] which he remained, with a brief interruption in A.D. 41,[23] until A.D. 72 when Commagene was reincorporated into the province of Syria.[24] Samosata served as a base for a legion, the sixth (Ferrata) till Trajan's reign, and thereafter the sixteenth (Flavia Firma).[25] Commagene was one of the four eparchies that then made up the province of Syria.[26] Under Hadrian, it

Muḍar" that Diyār Muḍar is identical to al-Ǧazīra. In regard to Šimšāṭ there is a "biblical" interpretation of the name holding that the place was named after Šimšāṭ b. Eliphaz b. Shem b. Noah, because he built it (Yāqūt s.v. "Šimšāṭ"). On Šimšāṭ and its environs see also Suhrāb, pp. 81, 117, 120; Le Strange, "Ibn Serapion," p. 57.

18 Samosata appears as a major crossroads on the *Tabula Peutingeriana* (ed. Miller, XI 3) and in the *Itinerarium Antonini*. Most of the sources cited above refer to armies passing through or trying to gain control of the place. For Roman roads in Commagene, see Dörner & Neumann, *Forschungen in Kommagene*, pp. 102–112; for the country in general, see Honigmann, *RE* Supp., vol. 4, col. 989f., s.v. "Kommagene"; for its kings, see Sullivan, *ANRW*, II 8, p. 732ff.

19 See the references in *RE*, vol. 1A, cols. 2223–2224, especially Humann & Puchstein.

20 The many sherds found there provide abundant evidence of the Byzantine, Roman, Hellenistic and Parthian periods; see Goell, *AJA* 70 (1966): 280.

21 Pliny, Source 4; Josephus, Sources, 6, 7; Plutarch, *Antony*, 34, 2; Cassius Dio, XLIX 22, 1.

22 Tacitus, *Annals*, II 42, 7; 56, 5; Josephus, *Antiquities*, XVIII 53 for the annexation in A.D. 17; for the accession of Antiochus see Cassius Dio LIX 8.

23 Cassius Dio, LX 8; Josephus, *Antiquities*, XIX 276.

24 Josephus, *Jewish War*, VII 220ff.

25 Cassius Dio, LV 24, 3. Evidence from coins (see below) and inscriptions (*RE*, vol. 1A, col. 2222; J. & L. Robert, *REG* [1949]: 190; *AÉ* [1950]: 190).

26 An inscription from Gerasa mentions a priest "of the four eparchies" at Antioch in 119/120 (Welles in Kraeling, *Gerasa, City of the Decapolis*, p. 399, No. 53; *Nouveaux Choix d'Inscriptions Grecques* [ed. Institut Fernand-Courby, No. 32]). These subdivisions of the province are mentioned by name in an inscription of 102–104 which refers to a governor of "Syria, Phoenicia, Commagene and Tyre" (*ILS* No. 8819a).

was one of the two *koinai* in the province; the other was Coile Syria, and their capitals (*metropoleis*) were Samosata and Damascus respectively.[27]
Samosata was the birthplace of the Greek satirist Lucian (c. 125–181) and also of Paul of Samosata, the heretical patriarch of Antioch, who though excommunicated in 269, continued to function as bishop until 272.[28] The town is mentioned as well in connection with the wars between Rome and Persia in the fourth century.[29] During Justinian's reign, the region between Samosata and Edessa was devastated by the Arabs.[30] In 625 Heraclius was at Samosata in the course of his Persian campaign.[31] Thereafter the town was conquered by the Muslims. Under the Roman Empire, Samosata had its own mint.[32]

BERLINER, *Beiträge* (1883), pp. 63–64
BONSACA, *Enc. Arte Ant.*, vol. 6, p. 1102
DÖRNER, *Kommagene, ein wiederentdecktes Königreich* (1967²), passim
DÖRNER & NEUMANN, *Forschungen in Kommagene* (1939), passim
ESHEL, *Yishuvei ha-Yehudim* (1979), pp. 72, 87, 235–236
FUNK, *Monumenta* (1913), pp. 52, 299–300
GETZOW, *Al Neharot Bavel* (1887), p. 19
HIRSCHENSON, *Sheva Ḥokhmot* (1883), pp. 59, 233–234
HUMANN & PUCHSTEIN, *Reisen in Klein-Asien und Nordsyrien* (1890), pp. 181ff.
JALABERT & MOUTERDE, *Inscriptions grecques et latines de la Syrie* (1929), vol. 1, pp. 52–57
JASTROW, *Dictionary* (1950³), p. 1531
KOHUT, *Arukh ha-Shalem* (1878–1892), vol. 8, p. 63
LEVY, *Wörterbuch* (1924²), vol. 4, p. 687
NEUBAUER, *Géographie* (1868), pp. 331, 354
NEUSNER, *History* (1965–1970), vol. 5, p. 116
OBERMEYER, *Landschaft* (1929), p. 105, n. 1
ROSSI, *EI*¹, s.v. "Sumaisāṭ";
Supplementum Epigraphicum Graecum, vol. 7, p. 14, Nos. 47–49
WAGNER, *Seleukia am Euphrat* (1976)
WEISSBACH, *RE*, vol. 1A, cols. 2220–2224, s.v. "Samosata"
WROTH, *BMC*, *Syria*, L–LI

Tadmor (Palmyra) תדמור

A. *Sources*

1. Yevamot 17a

פסולי דהרפניא[1] משום פסולי דמישון,[2] ופסולי דמישון משום פסולי דתרמוד,[3] פסולי דתרמוד משום עבדי שלמה, והיינו דאמרי אינשי קבא רבא וקבא זוטא מיגנדר ואזיל לשאול ומשאול לתרמוד ומתרמוד למישן וממישן להרפניא.

The unfit of Harpanya[1] on account of the unfit of Mešon[2] and the unfit of Mešon on account of the unfit of Tarmod,[3] and the unfit of Tarmod on account

[27] Cf. Rey-Coquais, *JRS* 68 (1978): 53–54. For Samosata as metropolis see the coins, *BMC Syria*, p. 118.

[28] See Millar, *JRS* 61 (1971): 1ff.

[29] Ammianus, Sources 8, 9; Malalas, 328f.; Zosimus, III 12, 1.

[30] Procopius, *Wars I* 17, 22f.

[31] Cf. *RE*, vol. 1A, col. 2223.

[32] Callu, *La politique monétaire des empereurs romains de* 238 *à* 311, p. 162ff.; *BMC Syria*, pp. 1ff.

[1] For variants see the entry on "Nəharpanya."

[2] For variants see the entry on "Mesene."

[3] The Vatican 111 MS has **תדמור**, further on as well.

of the slaves of Solomon. Thus it is that people say, the small *qav* and the big *qav* roll down to the nether-world, from the nether-world to Tarmod, from Tarmod to Mešan, and from Mešan to Harpanya.

2. Yevamot 16a–b[4]

... אבל מעיד אני עלי שמים וארץ שעל מדוכה זו ישב חגי הנביא ואמר שלשה דברים צרת הבת אסורה, עמון ומואב מעשרין מעשר עני בשביעית, ומקבלים גרים מן הקרדויין[5] ומן התרמודים[6] ... רבי יוחנן וסביא דאמרי תרוייהו אין מקבלים גרים מן התרמודים ... מתרמוד מאי טעמא לא, פליגי בה רבי יוחנן וסביא, חד אמר משום עבדי שלמה, וחד אמר משום בנות ירושלים.

... But I call heaven and earth to witness that upon this mortar sat the prophet Haggai and said three things: A daughter's rival is forbidden, ʿAmmon and Moab give the tithe of the poor in the seventh [year], and converts are accepted from among the Qarduans[5] and the Tarmodans[6] ... Rabbi Yoḥanan and Savya both maintain that converts may not be accepted from the Tarmodans ... From Tarmod, why not? Rabbi Yoḥanan and Savya differed on this. One said, On account of the slaves of Solomon; and the other said, On account of the daughters of Jerusalem.

3. Yevamot 17a[7]

יתיב רב יוסף אחוריה דרב כהנא ויתיב רב כהנא קמיה דרב יהודה ויתיב וקאמר עתידין ישראל דעבדי יומא טבא כי חרבי תרמוד. והא חריב, ההיא תמוד הואי, רב אשי אמר היינו תרמוד היינו תמוד ...

Rav Joseph sat behind Rav Kahana and Rav Kahana sat before Rav Judah, and he sat and said, Israel will make a festival when Tarmod is destroyed. But surely it was destroyed. That was Tamod. Rav Ashi said, Tarmod is Tamod ...

4. Shabbat 31a

... מפני מה עיניהן של תרמודיין תרוטות, אמר לו בני שאלה גדולה שאלת, מפני שדרין בין החולות.

... Why are the eyes of the Palmyrans bleared? He said to him, My son, you have asked a great question. Because they live in sandy places.

5. Shabbat 21b

... עד שתכלה רגל מן השוק. ועד כמה, אמר רבה בר בר חנה אמר רבי יוחנן עד דכליא ריגלא דתרמודאי.

[The precept to light Ḥanukka candles is] until everyone has left the street. Until when? Rabbah b. Bar Ḥana said, Rabbi Yoḥanan said, Until the Palmyrans have left.

---

[4] Cf. Niddah 56b; T. J. Yevamot I 6 – 3a, 57ff.; T. J. Qiddushin IV 1 - 65c, 17ff.; Seder Eliahu Zuṭa I, Friedmann ed., p. 169.

[5] For variants see the entry on "Qardu."

[6] Some of the versions (e.g. Niddah 56b) have מתרמוד; others (e.g. T. J. Yevamot I 6–3a) have התדמוריים, further on as well.

[7] Cf. T. J. Taʿaniot IV 8 – 69b, 37–38; Genesis Rabbah LVI 11, Theodor-Albeck ed., pp. 610–611; Lamentations Rabbah II 4.

B. *Location*

An oasis between Syria and Babylonia, about 200 kilometers west of Dura Europos (on Bab. Env. map).

C. *History*

Palmyra[8] lay in an oasis in the Syrian desert and was the most important stop on the shortest caravan route between Syria and Babylonia. It is mentioned in Assyrian texts of the second millennium B.C. and in the Old Testament. The oldest remains date to the end of the third millennium. The city appears in classical sources relating to the first century B.C. To this period belong the earliest archaeological remains of the city.
The first three centuries A.D. were the period of the city's greatest power and prosperity, till its destruction by Aurelian in 273. Palmyra's role in the east-west trade is referred to in the entries on "Babylon," "Mesene" and "Walašpaṭ."[9] Because of the city's political and economic importance, the good preservation of its remains, and the great interest of its culture, there is extensive literature on Palmyra, much of it recent.

D. *Jews and Palmyra*

There is evidence of a Jewish community in Palmyra during the period of its greatest importance. Jewish names appear on Palmyran inscriptions,[10] and a lintel, possibly from a synagogue, has been found, with an excerpt from Deuteronomy engraved on it, as well as "*shemaʿ Yisrael.*"[11]
That the Palmyran Jews kept in touch with Eretz Israel is attested by the "Miryam the Palmyran" incident that took place in the Temple,[12] and by the burial chambers of Palmyran Jews found at Bet Šəʿarim.[13]
Source 1 lists Palmyra among the places with unfit lineage, and Source 2 (which appears in many parallels; see n. 4) dealing with the question of whether Palmyran converts are acceptable, relates to the same problem. For there is a possibility that Israelite *mamzerim* intermingled with the Palmyran gentiles,

[8] The Hebrew name "Tadmor" is proto-Semitic and entered European languages as Palmyra (= city of palms) because of the resemblances of the name Tadmor to *tamar* (= palm).

[9] On Palmyra in Arabic literature see Yāqūt, Bakrī, *ar-Rauḍ al-miʿṭār*, s.v. "Tadmur"; *BGA*, passim; Qazwīnī, *Bilād*, pp. 169–170; Dimašqī, *Nuḫbat ad-dahr*, p. 39; Buhl, *EI*[1], s.v. "Palmyra." The author of *ar-Rauḍ al-miʿṭār*, (13th–14th century) mentions among its inhabitants "a rabble of Jews and runaway slaves."

[10] See, e.g., Frey, *CIJ*, vol. 2, Nos. 820–824.

[11] See Schwartz, *Tevu'ot ha-Aretz*, p. 315.

[12] Mishnah, Nazir VI 11; Tosefta *ibid.*, IV 10; T. B. *ibid.*, 47a.

[13] See Schwabe & Lifshitz, *Beth Sheʿarim*, vol. 2, pp. 4–8; Avigad, *Beth Sheʿarim*, vol. 3, pp. 2–3, 260–261.

which would prevent the conversion of the latter. It is hard to decide whether the discussion arose because of a conversion movement in Palmyra resembling the one in Adiabene (q.v.) or was purely theoretical. Source 3 and its parallels (see n. 7) indicate a negative attitude to Palmyra on the part of the sages. That attitude developed as a result of two events: The first was the destruction of Nəhardəʿa (q.v.) by Odaenathus (identified with Papa b. Natzer) in 259, and the second was the temporary conquest of Eretz Israel by the Palmyrans in 269/270, when they revolted against Roman rule.

Avigad, *Beth Sheʿarim* (1976), vol. 3, pp. 2–3, 260–261
Beer, *Amora'ei Bavel* (1974), p. 354
Ben Hayyim, *Yediʿot* 13 (1947): 141–148
Cantineau, Starcky & Teixidor, *Inventaire des Inscriptions de Palmyre* (1930–1965), vols. 1–11
Drijvers, *ANRW* II 8 (1977), pp. 837–863, bibliography on pp. 899–902
Eshel, *Yishuvei ha-Yehudim* (1979), pp. 244–245
Frey, *CIJ* (1952), vol. 2, Nos. 820–824
Funk, *Monumenta* (1913), pp. 33, 55
Gawlikowski, *Le temple palmyrénien* (1973)
Graetz, *Geschichte* (1908⁴), vol. 4, p. 271
Hirschenson, *Sheva Ḥokhmot* (1883), p. 240
Jastrow, *Dictionary* (1950³), p. 1648
Joël, *MGWJ* 16 (1867): 332–333
Kohut, *Arukh ha-Shalem* (1878–1892), vol. 8, p. 279; *Tosefot* (1937), p. 414
Levy, *Wörterbuch* (1924²), vol. 4, p. 628
Millar, *JRS* 61 (1971): 1–17
Michailowski, *Palmyre. Fouilles polonaises* (1960–1967), vols. 1–5
Neubauer, *Géographie* (1868), p. 301
Neusner, *PAAJR* 31 (1963), p. 171f.
Neusner, *History* (1965–1970), passim
Obermeyer, *Landschaft* (1929), passim
Rostovtzeff, *Caravan Cities* (1932), passim
Schlumberger, *La Palmyrène du Nord-Ouest* (1951)
Schwabe & Lifshitz, *Beth Sheʿarim* (1974), vol. 2, pp. 4–8
Seyrig, *Antiquités Syriennes* (1934–1965), vols. 1–6
Smallwood, *The Jews under Roman Rule* (1975), pp. 518, 531–533
Starcky, *Palmyre* (1952)
Starcky, *Dictionnaire de la Bible*, Suppl. vol. 6 (1960), cols. 1066–1103, s.v. "Palmyre"
Wiegand et al., *Palmyra* (1932)

Talbuš תלבוש

A. *Source*

Yoma 10a (= Soṭah 34b)

"ושם אחימן ששי ותלמי ילידי הענק"... אחימן בנה ענת,[1] ששי בנה אלוש,[2] תלמי בנה תלבוש.[3]

"And there Aḥiman, Sheshai and Talmai, the Anaqites, lived" (Num. 13:22)... Aḥiman built ʿAnat,[1] Sheshai built Aluš,[2] Talmai built Talbuš.[3]

---

[1] The Venice printing of Soṭah has **אנת**, and see Soṭah in the ICIT edition.

[2] The Soṭah parallel has **אלש**, but the Munich and Vatican 110 MSS and *Ein Yaʿaqov* have **אלוש**, as Yoma does.

[3] The Munich MS has **תלביש**, and see Soṭah in the ICIT edition.

B. *Already Proposed Location*

On an island in the Euphrates between Aluš and ʿAnat (on Bab. Env. map).

C. *Identification*

The legend interpreting the verse in the source lists Talbuš together with ʿAnat and Aluš (qq.v.) each built by one of the three Anaqites, i.e., offspring of the *ʿanaq* (= giant).[4] All three are referred to by Arab geographers as places on islands in the Euphrates.[5]
A tradition that resembles the talmudic one mentions three brothers of the ʿĀd tribe, named Alūs, Sālūs and Nāwūs,[6] who fled for their lives and settled on those islands.[7] As Obermeyer already noted,[8] T.l.b.s.—that is, Talbuš—is mentioned in connection with the Muslim conquest of Mesopotamia.[9] The route of the invaders went from Qarqīsiyā downstream through the Euphrates forts (*ḥuṣūnu l-Furāt*) of T.l.b.s.[10] and ʿĀnāt (see entry on "ʿAnat" which is associated with Talbuš in the source), and then Na'usa (q.v.), Alūsa (see "Aluš") and Hīt (see "Ihi də-Qira").

Eshel, *Yishuvei ha-Yehudim* (1979), p. 246
Hirschenson, *Sheva Ḥokhmot* (1883), pp. 186–187 ("ענת")
Jastrow, *Dictionary* (1950³), p. 1670
Kohut, *Arukh ha-Shalem* (1878–1892), vol. 8, p. 231
Levy, *Wörterbuch* (1924²), vol. 4, p. 644
Musil, *The Middle Euphrates* (1927), index
Neubauer, *Géographie* (1868), p. 399
Obermeyer, *Landschaft* (1929), p. 103

Ṭamdurya טמדוריא

See the entry on "Rodya."

[4] There are no grounds for identifying Talbuš with any place in Eretz Israel (see, e.g., Hirschenson, p. 187, or Horowitz, *Eretz Israel u-Shekhenoteha*, p. 46). See n. 9 in the entry on "ʿAnat."

[5] See n. 10 in the entry on "ʿAnat," n. 5 in the entry on "Aluš," and see above.

[6] On this tradition see nn. 11 and 12 in the entry on "ʿAnat."

[7] The place was sometimes called Šālūs; e.g. the entries on "Šālūs" and "Sālūs" in Yāqūt. Of course it does not refer to Šālūs in the Ṭabaristān mountains, and possibly Talbuš (Talbūs?) should be the form.

[8] Obermeyer, p. 103.

[9] *Futūḥ al-buldān*, p. 179. The vocalization is unclear, and it might be "Talbus" similar to the name in the Talmud (Rescher in his German translation of *Futūḥ*, p. 195, vocalized it as Tilbis; Caetani as Talbas, *Annali* vol. 4, p. 222). See Sarre & Herzfeld, *Archäologische Reise*, vol. 2, p. 319, n. 3; Herzfeld, *Samarra*, p. 57, n. 5.

[10] The editor, de Goeje, refers in a note to B.l.b.n. in Idrīsī (Jaubert, *La Géographie d'Édrisi*, vol. 2, p. 150) but in the new edition, vol. 6, p. 661, the text is corrected to "Tunainīr," which see in Yāqūt.

Ṭamrurita טמרוריתא

See the entry on "Rodya."

Tarbiqna תרביקנא

A. *Source*

Genesis Rabbah XVI 3 (Theodor-Albeck ed., p. 145)

שמואל אמר עד מקום שהנהר מהלך שם היא ארץ ישראל, אי זו זו, זו תרביקנה.[1]

Samuel said, To the place where the river goes, that is Eretz Israel; which is it, it is Tarbiqna.[1]

B. *Proposed Location*

Bāniqyā, near Nağaf, southwest of Kūfa (D5 on the Tal. Bab. map).

C. *Identification*

Obermeyer and Rapoport sought to identify Tarbiqna with Aqra də-Tulbanqe (q.v.).[2] The above source, however, asserts that Tarbiqna is at "the place where the river goes," and that description does not fit Aqra də-Tulbanqe, which the Talmud says (Qiddushin 71b) was upstream on the Euphrates, thus clearly indicating that the Euphrates also flowed south of it. It seems reasonable to identify Tarbiqna with Bāniqyā near Nağaf, for the Arab writers report that the Euphrates (that is, a branch of it) went as far as Nağaf and there flowed into what was a kind of extension of the Persian Gulf (see below).[3]

The proximity of Bāniqyā to Nağaf is inferrable from Yāqūt who says that the land in Nağaf was owned by inhabitants of Bāniqyā.[4] Bāniqyā was in the Nağaf region, "behind" (i.e. west or, rather, southwest of) Kūfa.[5] The details of the story associating Bāniqyā with the Patriarch Abraham[6] likewise indicate it was slightly east of Nağaf: Abraham and Lot stopped at Bāniqyā on their way to Eretz Israel, and the earth did not quake that night. The inhabitants went to each other in wonder that they were rid of the affliction. The proprietor of the house, Abraham was staying at, told them, The affliction was

---

[1] The versions of Genesis Rabbah also have the forms תרבי קנה; תרביקנא; תרבקנה; תרבקנא; תרביקני; תרבוקנה.

[2] Obermeyer, p. 96 (in his view the text in Genesis Rabbah is garbled, and see n. 1 there); Rapoport, *Erekh Millin*, vol. 2, p. 11.

[3] Obermeyer did not locate Bāniqyā exactly, see the entry on "Aqra də-Tulbanqe."

[4] Yāqūt, s.v. "Bāniqyā."

[5] Bakrī, *ar-Rauḍ al-miʿṭār*, s.v. "Bāniqyā": *arḍ bi-n-Nağaf dūna l-Kūfa.*

[6] Bakrī, *ar-Rauḍ al-miʿṭār*, *loc.cit.*; see also Yāqūt, s.v. "Bāniqyā."

removed because of the elder (*šaiḫ*) staying with me, who prayed and cried the whole night. They gathered to him and asked him to remain with them, and in return they would collect money and he would be the richest among them. Abraham replied that he was not commanded to do that, but to carry out a *hiǧra*. Abraham set out till he reached Naǧaf, and when he saw it he retraced his steps and asked whose land it was.[7] They told him it was theirs. He asked them to sell it to him. They said it was his, but it grows nothing. He told them he was only interested in buying it, and he paid them with young sheep (*ġunaimāt*) that he had. And sheep are called *niqyā* in Aramaic ("Nabatean"). That tradition is unusual because it is based on the interpretation of an Aramaic place name. In any case, it shows clearly how close Bāniqyā was to Naǧaf.

As noted, a branch of the Euphrates flowed into a sort of extension of the Persian Gulf.[8] According to Masʿūdī,[9] most of the Euphrates water reached Ḥīra and its environs (*bilād al-Ḥīra*) and the Ḥīra river is visible "to the present day," and is known as "the ancient (river)." That river was the site of the confrontation between the Muslims and Rustam, at the battle of Qādisīya. It flowed into the Abyssinian sea,[10] which then reached the place now known as Naǧaf, and boats from India and China used to come there, to the kings of Ḥīra. Masʿūdī then describes a famous conversation between the Muslim commander Ḫālid b. al-Walīd and the extremely old ʿAbd al-Masīḥ al-Ġassānī living in one of the Ḥīra forts, which took place in Naǧaf where Ḫālid camped.[11] Reportedly 350 years old, ʿAbd al-Masīḥ had seen the ships anchored at Naǧaf,[12] bearing goods from China and India "while the waves of the sea struck the ground beneath your feet, and imagine the distance today between us and the sea." Masʿūdī concludes that when the water stopped flowing to that place (*fā-lammā 'nqaṭaʿa l-mā' ʿan maṣabbihī fī ḏālika l-mauḍiʿ*) the sea turned into land, and between Ḥīra and the sea in his day was a distance of many days, "and whoever sees Naǧaf and observes it will realize what we have

---

[7] *ar-Rauḍ al-miʿṭār* mistakenly has *baʿda n-Naǧaf*, which should be *yaʿnī n-Naǧaf* as in Bakrī and Yāqūt.

[8] Yāqūt, s.v. "Ḥīra" at the beginning; Yaʿqūbī, *Buldān*, p. 309, and cf. Bakrī, s.v. "Ḥīra"; Ḥamza, *Taʾrīḫ*, p. 102. On the ancient coast line of the Persian Gulf, see Streck, *EI*[1], s.v. "Maisān," p. 149.

[9] Masʿūdī, *Murūǧ*, vol. 1, p. 117 (= vol. 1, pp. 215–216), and see Nuwairī, *Nihāyat al-arab fī funūni l-adab*, vol. 1, p. 267 (quoting Masʿūdī). See also Dimašqī, *Nuḫbat ad-dahr*, p. 94.

[10] That is, the Indian Ocean (meaning here the Persian Gulf), Masʿūdī, *Murūǧ*, vol. 1, p. 124f. (= vol. 1, p. 230f.); Nuwairī, *ibid.*, has "the Persian Sea."

[11] Masʿūdī, *ibid.*, pp. 118–119 (vol. 1, p. 219). See also *Bayān wa-tabyīn*, vol. 2, pp. 147–148; *ar-Rauḍ al-miʿṭār*, s.v. "Ḥīra." pp. 208–209.

[12] *tarqā ilainā fī hāḏā n-Naǧaf*, but evidently the version in *Bayān wa-tabyīn* and *ar-Rauḍ al-miʿṭār* (but with Naǧaf as in *Murūǧ*) — *tarfaʾu ilainā fī hāḏā n-Naǧaf* (*Bayān* has *l-ǧurf*)—should be preferred. See also *ar-Rauḍ al-miʿṭār*, s. v. "Naǧaf."

described."[13] Ḥīra, which was three miles from Kūfa, was "on Naǧaf" (*wa-l-Ḥīra 'alā n-Naǧaf*) and Naǧaf was the sea shore (literally, "the salty sea") which in antiquity reached Ḥīra.[14]

Bāniqyā is mentioned in the poetry of A'šā Maimūn b. Qais (b. before 570, d. after 625).[15] In one of the two stanzas it appears in, it figures as a border point of the Arabian peninsula. The poet traveled between Bāniqyā and Aden, and also roamed around the Persian countries. Bāniqyā was at the north-eastern corner of the Arabian peninsula toward Iraq, and Aden is the south-western corner.[16]

Bāniqyā was on the bank of the Euphrates.[17] Near by was a ford across the river, close to the site of the famous Battle of the Bridge in which the Muslims were dealt a severe blow. The inhabitants of Bāniqyā helped the Muslim commander, Abū 'Ubaid, construct the bridge.[18]

D. *Eretz Israel and Babylonia*

If we accept the proposal that the Tarbiqna in the source above, is Bāniqyā, the site is located on the border the sages set between Babylonia and Eretz Israel. They contended that the Euphrates was the eastern border of Eretz Israel. As noted above, at Naǧaf near Bāniqyā the Euphrates flowed into an extension of the Persian Gulf that cut deep into Iraq. That is the basis for Samuel's conception that Eretz Israel extended to the place where the Euphrates ended its course in southwestern Babylonia.

Arabic sources report that the Jews used to carry their dead to Bāniqyā for burial because Abraham had said that there seventy thousand of his descendants slain fighting for the sake of the Lord would be resurrected.[19]

---

[13] Mas'ūdī *Murūǧ* vol. 1, p. 120 (= vol. 1, pp. 222–223); and see Abū l-Fidā', p. 169; cf. the verb *inqaṭa'a* with the expression *al-baḥr al-munqaṭi'* in the entry on "Nəharpanya."

[14] *ar-Rauḍ al-mi'ṭār*, s.v. "Ḥīra."

[15] Caskel, *EI*², s.v. "A'shā."

[16] In one stanza the poet compares a man's generosity to the river (*baḥr*) of Bāniqyā when its water reaches the tops of its banks. See A'šā, *Dīwān*, Nos. 25, 3 and 55, 35; and see also Bišr b. Abī Ḫāzim, *Dīwān*, p. 159.

[17] See *Tāǧ al-'arūs*, the end of the entry on "Nqy"; Abū Yūsuf, *Ḫarāǧ*, p. 157, 95 (Lake Burs).

[18] *Futūḥ al-buldān*, p. 251. Balāḏurī adds, "and they say that the bridge was ancient, of the residents of Ḥīra, and they would cross it to their lands." Abū 'Ubaid repaired it because it was damaged and cut. Afterwards "Abū 'Ubaid and the Muslims crossed the Euphrates on it from al-Marwaḥa." See *ibid.*, p. 252: "Abū 'Ubaid crossed at Bāniqyā." On the Battle of the Bridge near Bāniqyā not far from Ḥīra cf. Nöldeke, *ZDMG* 28 (1874): 96; and see Abū Yūsuf, *Ḫarāǧ*, p. 157; Ibn Sa'd, vol. 7, p. 397.

[19] Yāqūt, s.v. "*Bāniqyā*": *wa-ḏakara Ibrāhīm 'alaihi s-salām annahū yuḥšaru min wuldihī min ḏālika l-mauḍi' sab'ūna alf šahīd, fa-l-yahūd tanqulu mautāhā ilā hāḏā l-makān li-hāḏā s-sabab.* And see Bakrī, s.v. "Bāniqyā." See also Obermeyer, p. 323; Klein, *Tarbiẕ* 1 (1930) B: 130–131; see also Gil, *Tarbiẕ* 48 (1979): 51–52 and especially n. 39.

In general, it was in the third century that the practice of sending bodies from the Diaspora to Eretz Israel for burial began to develop. The sages stressed that burial in Eretz Israel helped atone for sins, while burial abroad entailed the torment of rolling underground to Eretz Israel for resurrection.[20] There is evidence of the burial of Jews from Babylonia in the Bet Šəʿarim necropolis, in Jaffa, and in other cemeteries in Eretz Israel proper, but the process involved great expense and bother. Thus burial in the Kūfa region, and indeed anywhere west of the Euphrates that was supposedly included in the borders of Eretz Israel, had the advantages of burial in Eretz Israel without requiring the transportation of the corpse over great distances. (See also the entries on "Šum Ṭəmaya," "Nəhar Anaq," and the section on Connections with Other Places in the entry on "Maḥoza.")

Berliner, *Beiträge* (1883), p. 17
Gil, *Tarbiẕ* 48 (1979): 51–52
Hirschenson, *Sheva Ḥokhmot* (1883), p. 240
Jastrow, *Dictionary* (1950[3]), p. 1653, "תולבנקי"
Kohut, *Arukh ha-Shalem* (1878–1892), vol. 1, p. 260 "אקרא"; vol. 8, p. 273; *Tosefot* (1937), p. 413
Levy, *Wörterbuch* (1924[2]), vol. 4, p. 667
Obermeyer, *Landschaft* (1929), pp. 94–96, 322–323
Rapoport, *Erekh Millin* (1914), vol. 2, pp. 10–11

Ṭaṭlafuš טטלפוש

See the entry on "Sura and Mata Məḥasya."

Tawak̲ תואך

A. *Sources*

1. Bava Qamma 104b; Bava Metziʿa 46a; Bava Batra 77b, 150b

כי הא דרב פפא הוה מסיק[1] תריסר אלפי זוזי בי חוזאי, אקנינהו ניהליה לרב שמואל בר אבא[2] אגב אסיפא דביתיה כי אתא נפק לאפיה עד תואך.[3]

As in the case when Rav Papa was owed[1] twelve thousand *zuz* [in] Be Ḥozai, transferred them to Rav Samuel b. Abba[2] by means of the threshold of his house. When he came, he went out to Tawak̲[3] to meet him.

[20] On the practice of bringing the dead from the Diaspora for burial in Eretz Israel see Gafni, *Cathedra* 4 (1977): 113–120, and the bibliography there.

[1] The parallel versions have הוו ליה (= he had).

[2] The Munich MS and parallels have "Rav Samuel b. Aḥa" which seems correct. See also the section on Sages and Be Ḥozai in the entry on "Be Ḥozai."

[3] The parallels have תווך as does the Vatican 116 MS of Bava Qamma 104b, but the Munich MS of Bava Batra 77b and 150b has תואך; the Hamburg MS has תואך for all the parallels; the Munich MS has תארך in Bava Qamma 104b and תאור in Bava Metziʿa 46a.

2. Niddah 33b

רב פפא איקלע לתואך, אמר אי איכא צורבא מרבנן הכא איזיל אקבל אפיה, אמרה ליה
ההיא סבתא איכא הכא צורבא מרבנן ורב שמואל שמיה ...

Rav Papa happened to come to Tawaḵ; he said, If there is a scholar here, I will go and pay my respects. That old woman said to him, There is a scholar here and his name is Rav Samuel.

B. *Location*

None can be proposed due to insufficient data.

C. *Attempts at Identification*

Source 1 contains an episode involving Rav Papa, of the fifth generation of Babylonian amoras, who sent Rav Samuel b. Aḥa (see note 2) to Be Ḥozai (q.v.) to collect a debt for him, and went out to meet him in Tawaḵ[4] on his return. As Rav Papa's place of residence was Nareš (q.v.), Tawaḵ was presumably somewhere between Nareš and Be Ḥozai. Source 2, however, indicates that Tawaḵ was Rav Samuel b. Aḥa's place of residence, and that makes the general location between Nareš and Be Ḥozai rather doubtful. For it could very well have been that wishing to spare Rav Samuel b. Aḥa a journey back to Nareš, Rav Papa went to the latter's home in Tawaḵ to get his money.

BEER, *Amora'ei Bavel* (1974), pp. 195, 197, 298

BERLINER, *Beiträge* (1883), p. 65

ESHEL, *Yishuvei ha-Yehudim* (1979), p.243

FUNK, *Monumenta* (1913), pp. 53, 300

HIRSCHENSON, *Sheva Ḥokhmot* (1883), p. 238

HOFFMANN, *Auszüge* (1880), p. 273ff.

JASTROW, *Dictionary* (1950³), p. 1649

KOHUT, *Arukh ha-Shalem* (1878–1892), vol. 8, p. 209

LEVY, *Wörterbuch* (1924²), vol. 4, pp. 631, 689

NEUBAUER, *Géographie* (1868), p. 398

NEUSNER, *History* (1965–1970), vol. 5, pp. 170, 173, 232, 248

OBERMEYER, *Landschaft* (1929), p. 208

SARRE & HERZFELD, *Archäologische Reise* (1920), vol. 2, pp. 318–319

Ṭirta   טירתא

Several talmudic passages refer to Rabbi Ḥanina of Ṭirta,[1] and Obermeyer identifies the place with Ṭirastān, located south of Madā'in on the west bank

---

[4] See Beer, *Amora'ei Bavel*, pp. 197–198. For attempts at identifying Tawaḵ see Neubauer, p. 398; Funk, *Monumenta*, p. 300; Berliner, p. 65; Obermeyer, p. 208; Sarre & Herzfeld, *Archäologische Reise*, vol. 2, pp. 318–319; Hoffmann, *Auszüge*, p. 273ff.

[1] Menaḥot 48a, and see *Diq. Sof.*; cf. also "Rabbi Ḥanina Trita'a" (Nedarim 57b), "Rabbi Ḥanina Tirta'a" (ibid. 59b), "Rav Hananiah Ṭriṭa'a" (Temurah 29a), "Rabbi Ḥanina Ṭriṭa'a" (ibid. 31a), "Rabbi Ḥanina Ṭirna'a" (Keritot 9a), "Rabbi Ḥanina

of the Tigris.[2] Rabbi Ḥanina of Ṭirta figures in contexts of discussions with Eretz Israel amoras, citing *baraitot* before Rabbi Yoḥanan, and quoting Rabbi Yannai[3]; it therefore appears that he was a sage of the second generation of Eretz Israel amoras. The fact that there is a Babylonian place bearing a name resembling Ṭirta is not enough reason to assume that Rabbi Ḥanina came from there; it is more reasonable to try to locate Ṭirta in Eretz Israel.[4]

HIRSCHENSON, *Sheva Ḥokhmot* (1883), pp. 120–121
KRAUSS, *Tosefot Arukh ha-Shalem* (1937), p. 165, "וולשפט"
LEVY, *Wörterbuch* (1924²), vol. 2, p. 157, "טירנאה"
OBERMEYER, *Landschaft* (1929), p. 185

Tosəfa תוספא

See the entry on "Ctesiphon" under "Maḥoza Area."

'Ukbara עכברא

A. *Source*

Qiddushin 71 b

עד היכן היא בבל . . . לעיל בדיגלת עד היכא, רב[1] אמר עד בגדא (כ"י ואטיקאן 111: עכברא) ואוונא,[2] ושמואל אמר עד מושכני.[3]

How far does Babylonia extend . . . Upstream, how far on the Tigris? Rav[1] said, To Bagda (the Vatican 111 MS has 'Ukbara) and Awana.[2] And Samuel said, To Moškani.[3]

Tartia" (T. J. Berakhot III 5 – 6d, 28); "Rabbi Ḥanina Tirtiya" (T. J. Pe'ah III 8 – 17d, 22), "Rabbi Hananiah Tirtiya" (T. J. Terumot VII 7 – 45a, 14), "Rabbi Ḥanina Tirta" (ibid. X, 8 – 47b, 33).

[2] Obermeyer, p. 185, on the basis of Ibn Rusta, p. 186. Muqaddasī, p. 114 lists Ṭarāstān (*sic*) among the towns in the Baghdad district. See also *Tosefot Arukh ha-Shalem*, s.v. "וולשפט."

[3] See Albeck, *Mavo la-Talmudim*, p. 183.

[4] It should be noted that many places in Eretz Israel have preserved the name Ṭīra, and several identifications are possible. See Klein, *Sefer ha-Yishuv*, vol. 1, pp. 74, 157; idem, *Eretz ha-Galil*, p. 122 and n. 18.

[1] The Vatican 111 MS has "Rava," but as the difference of opinion is with Samuel, the correct version is most likely "Rav," the former being a scribal error produced by the addition of the letter *alef* to "Rav" under the influence of the initial *alef* in the next word (רב[א] אמר).

[2] The Munich MS has עד נגד' וחוונא; the Vatican 111 MS has עד עכברא ואוינא as does the *Arukh* (see *Arukh ha-Shalem*, vol. 1, p. 45, s.v. "אונא", and *Tosefot*, p. 13 of the entry).

[3] The Venice printing and Vatican 111 MS have משכני.

B. *Location*

'Ukbarā,[4] on the east bank of the Tigris (before its course moved, see below), about fifty-five kilometers north of Baghdad (D 1 on the Tal. Bab. map).

C. *Identification*

'Ukbarā is the Syriac name of Buzurğ Sābūr which was founded by Shapur II (A. D. 309–379).[5] The place is now on the west bank of the Tigris, but up to the thirteenth century, when the course of the river moved, it was on the east bank.[6]
The source deals with the question of the boundary of Babylonia in connection with purity of lineage, and sets 'Uḵbara (or Bagda) and Awana as its northern extremity. The 'Uḵbara alternative is preferable (see note 2) to Bagda. As Obermeyer already pointed out, the Awana that also occurs in the source was ten parasangs north of Baghdad, so that the two could not together mark the northern border of Babylonia.[7] Thus Bagda must be a scribal error. At some point the initial *'ayin* must have inadvertently been dropped, leaving the form כברא which was garbled to בגדא (under the influence of בגדאד?).
The question of the location of 'Ukbarā in relation to the Tigris is especially important. In Obermeyer's opinion, both 'Ukbarā and Awānā were on the east

[4] On this see, e.g. Yāqūt, *Marāṣid* and *ar-Rauḍ al-mi'ṭār*, s.v. "'Ukbarā"; Yāqūt, *Marāṣid*, s.v. "Tall 'Ukbarā"; Muqaddasī, pp. 53–54, 115, 122: "It is a distance of a day from al-Baradān, which in turn is two *barīds* (about eleven kilometers) from Baghdad" (*ibid*, p. 134); "In 'Ukbarā [and in six other places] there were the wisest people in the kingdom of the Persians" (*ibid.*, pp. 257–258); Ibn al-Faqīh, p. 210; see also *Ḥudūd al-'ālam* (index); Šabuštī, *Diyārāt*², p. 93 and Appendix 9 (pp. 360–362); Le Strange, pp. 50–51, 84; and see also Obermeyer, pp. 76, 81–85.

[5] Ḥamza, *Ta'rīḫ*, p. 52 (printed: B.r.z.ḫ. Šābur); Nöldeke, *Perser und Araber*, p. 58, note; Mustaufī, vol. 2, p. 49, reports that 'Ukbarā (or 'Askara; the editor notes that the reading is uncertain) was founded by Shapur II. 'Ukbarā alternates with Buzurğ Sābūr in two versions of a tradition recorded on the authority of a man of the Ṯaqīf tribe who was governor under the caliph 'Alī b. Abī Ṭālib. One version (Abū Yūsuf, *Ḫarāğ*, pp. 16–17) says he was the governor of 'Ukbarā. Another version (Yaḥyā b. Ādam, *Ḫarāğ*, pp. 70–71) says he was the governor of Buzurğ Sābūr. In any case, cf. Ṭabarī, vol. 7, p. 421 (= vol. 3, p. 12) who has separate references to Buzurğ Sābūr and 'Ukbarā. See also Altheim & Stiehl, *Ein asiatischer Staat*, p. 28. See n. 10 below.

[6] Adams, *Land Behind Baghdad*, p. 176, n. 6; Kiepert, *ZGEB* 18 (1883), map. 5; Nöldeke, *Perser und Araber*, p. 500f.

[7] Obermeyer, pp. 81–83 believes Bagda should be corrected to Buṣrā, as Awānā and Buṣrā are mentioned together in Arabic sources (along with 'Ukbarā) from north to south, in the following order—'Ukbarā, Awānā, Buṣrā—on the bank of the Tigris (according to Suhrāb, p. 118; Le Strange, "Ibn Serapion," p. 9). Obermeyer's proposal is unacceptable as no text supports it. In contrast, 'Uḵbara seems preferable as it is not merely an interpretation of the *Arukh*—as Obermeyer says—but also occurs in the Vatican 111 MS.

bank,[8] but it does not seem logical that Rav should mention two adjacent places on the same bank as the northern boundary. It is more likely that if two places on a river are mentioned, they would be across the river from each other, and indeed that is Rashi's interpretation. It appears from the Arabic sources that 'Ukbarā in the talmudic period (and for centuries thereafter) was in fact on the east bank of the Tigris, while Awānā (q.v.) was on the west bank.[9]

D. *History*

Founded by Shapur II, the place was populated among others by captives taken in successful Sassanian raids in Syria.[10] The construction of a canal going from a point north of Ba'qūbā to the vicinity of 'Ukbarā was apparently a central factor in the founding of the latter. There is evidence of what appears to be centrally directed planning and execution of an integrated system of new cities and canals (possibly with supporting villages as part of the comprehensive plan).[11] Literary sources, however, mention only the establishment of the town.[12] The region watered by the canal to 'Ukbarā was deserted by the end of the Sassanian period.[13]

There is no evidence of a Christian community in the Sassanian period, although presumably the Roman captives settled there in the fourth century would have introduced the western Syrian church. Nestorians are not encountered until the ninth century.[14] On the main route leading north from Baghdad, 'Ukbarā and adjacent Awānā and Buṣra were resort towns for Baghdadians in the

[8] Obermeyer, *ibid.*

[9] See Nöldeke, *Perser und Araber*, pp. 500–501; *ar-Rauḍ al-mi'ṭār*, s.v. "'Ukbarā"; Idrīsī, vol. 6, p. 658; Ṭabarī, vol. 7, pp. 410 and especially 412 (= vol. 3, pp. 10, 12); Sam'ānī, *Ansāb*, s.v. "'Ukbarī"; *Ḥudūd al-'ālam*, p. 140; Le Strange, pp. 50–51, 84. See also *Marāṣid*, s.v. "Awānā"; the author (d. 1338) states among other things that Awānā was opposite 'Ukbarā, and the Tigris between them. Then it deviated and flowed at a distance from them. *Marāṣid*, s. v. "'Ukbarā," says 'Ukbarā was on the east bank of the Tigris, and when the river moved eastwards, the part below 'Ukbarā began to be called aš-Šuṭaiṭa, and Awānā was opposite 'Ukbarā west of aš-Šuṭaiṭa. He adds that 'Ukbarā was destroyed and its inhabitants moved to Awānā and to other places; Streck, *Die alte Landschaft*, vol. 2, p. 223f. Cf. Yāqūt, s.v. "'Irāq," p. 94.

[10] Herzfeld rejects the Arabic sources testifying that Shapur II founded 'Ukbarā (see n. 5 above) and prefers the chronicle that credits Shapur I with its founding (*Chronicle of Sa'irt*, ed. Scher, p. 221). In Herzfeld's view, among the original settlers were legionaries captured with the emperor Valerian. Fiey too believes that the city was constructed by Shapur I who settled captives there (despite the fact that Ṭabarī and Ḥamza al-Iṣfahānī ascribe its construction to Shapur II). Herzfeld, *Samarra*, p. 64; Pigulevskaya, *Les Villes*, p. 127; Nöldeke, *Perser und Araber*, p. 57.

[11] Adams, *op.cit.* (in n. 6), p. 76.

[12] Nöldeke, *loc.cit.*

[13] Adams, *op.cit.*, p. 90.

[14] Fiey, *Assyrie Chrétienne*, vol. 3, pp. 127–129.

Muslim period. Muqaddasī speaks of 'Ukbarā as a large prosperous city with vineyards and vegetable gardens.[15] It was abandoned when the course of the Tigris moved eastward in 1230.[16] The remains of 'Ukbarā are known by their original name even today.[17]

E. *The Borders of Babylonia*

The source quoted is part of a passage dealing with the boundaries of the Babylonian region considered pure from the point of view of lineage, and indicates the northeastern extremity of that boundary on the Tigris in the opinions of Rav and Samuel. Obermeyer[18] suggested a connection between the administrative boundaries of the Sassanian period and the places mentioned in this source.[19] The connection, of course, depends on the correlation between the sages' view of the limits of the "pure" area and the Sassanian administrative divisions (see Introduction).[20]

F. *The Inhabitants*

Except for the reference above in some of the versions of Qiddushin, 'Uḵbara does not appear in talmudic literature. In gaonic literature it is mentioned as a place where Jews lived.[21]

---

15 See Adams, *loc.cit.*, and Musil, *The Middle Euphrates*, pp. 135–139, who visited the site.

16 Jones (*SRBG* 43 [1857]: 235) notes that the "tomb of Kef 'Alī, a very venerable building fast tottering to its fall, is the only erect portion of this once magnificent town, whose mounds now cover a space scarcely credible, considering the modern aspect of the country and its dwindled population. The Tigris, as it swept onwards in its ancient bed, washed the walls of this great city . . . 'Akbara itself was divided by a small stream called the Shatayt, or lesser river, whose deep but dry bed is now seen winding to the southeast onwards towards another ruined city, that of Waneh, also a celebrated spot in the more recent history of the country, finally to join the larger bed at a little distance to the south." See also the map relating to this section and n. 9 above.

17 Sūsa, *Rayy Samarrā*, p. 187.

18 Obermeyer, p. 76.

19 The Buzurǧ Sābūr district was the northernmost in the province of Šāḏ Hurmuz. See e.g. Ibn Ḫurdāḏbih, pp. 6, 12; Qudāma, *Ḫarāǧ*, p. 238. Cf. *ibid.*, p. 235; Yāqūt, s.v. "Sāḏhurmuz." The borders of Iraq and the Sawād are a problem in themselves but there is no space here for further discussion.

20 The northeastern border of the Babylonia of pure lineage and the border of the Sawād of Iraq are both demarcated by places across from each other on opposite banks of the Tigris.

21 See *Teshuvot ha-Geonim*, Harkavy, p. 141, § 285, and see Eshel, p. 206.

Adams, *Land Behind Baghdad* (1965), pp. 76, 90, 176, n. 6
Altheim & Stiehl, *Ein asiatischer Staat* (1954), p. 28
Berliner, *Beiträge* (1883), pp. 18, 25 ("בגדא")
Eshel, *Yishuvei ha-Yehudim* (1979), pp. 19, 47 ("בגדא"), 203, 206
Funk, *Juden* (1902–1908), vol. 1, p. 12; vol. 2, pp. 149–150
Funk, *Monumenta* (1913), pp. 4, 277
Hirschenson, *Sheva Ḥokhmot* (1883), pp. 58–60, 65 ("בגדא"), 185
Jastrow, *Dictionary* (1950^{3}), pp. 62, 137 ("בגדא")
Jones, *SRBG* 43 (1857): 235
Kohut, *Arukh ha-Shalem* (1878–1892), vol. 1, p. 45; vol. 2, p. 10 ("בגדא"); vol. 6, p. 197; *Tosefot* (1937), pp. 13 ("אוונא"), 74
Levy, *Wörterbuch* (1924^{2}), vol. 1, pp. 73, 190 ("בגדא")
Musil, *The Middle Euphrates* (1927), p. 139
Neubauer, *Géographie* (1868), pp. 331–332
Neusner, *History* (1965–1970), vol. 2, pp. 241–243
Newman, *Agricultural Life* (1932), p. 6
Nöldeke, *Perser und Araber* (1879), pp. 57, 500–501
Obermeyer, *Landschaft* (1929), pp. 15, 76–85, 81–82 ("בגדא"), 105 n. 1, 121 n. 1, 144, 269

Walašpaṭ (Vologesias) וולשפט

A. *Sources*

1. Bava Metziʿa 73b

אמר רב חמא האי מאן דיהיב זוזי לחבריה למיזבן ליה חמרא ופשע ולא זבין ליה משלם ליה כדקא אזיל אפרוותא דוולשפט.[1]

Rav Ḥama said, Whoever gives his friend money to buy wine for him, and he was negligent and did not buy for him, pays him as it goes in the port of Walašpaṭ.[1]

2. Bava Batra 98a

ואמר רבא האי מאן דקביל חמרא אדעתא דממטי ליה לפרוותא דוול שפט [2] ואדמטי התם זל דינא הוא דמקבל ליה.

And Rava said, Whoever obtained wine for the purpose of taking it to the port of Walašpaṭ,[2] and by the time he arrived the price fell, it is the law that he (the owner) should accept it.

3. Pliny, *Natural History* VI 30, 122

cetero ad solitudinem rediit (i.e. Babylon) exhausta vicinitate Seleuciae, ob id conditae a Nicatore intra XL lapidem in confluente Euphratis fossa perducti atque Tigris ... invicem ad hanc exhauriendam Ctesiphontem iuxta tertium ab ea lapidem in Chalonitide condidere Parthi, quod nunc caput est

[1] The source has זולשפט, the Munich MS has דבילשפט, the Vatican 115 MS has דבי לשפט, the Hamburg MS has דבלשפט, the Florence MS has דוילשפט and the Vatican 117 MS has דלשפט; and see *Diq. Sof.*

[2] The source has וול שפט, the Munich MS has דולשפט, the Vatican 115 MS has דבי לשפט, and the Hamburg MS has דבי אלשפט; and see *Diq. Sof.*

regnorum, et postquam nihil proficiebatur, nuper Vologesus rex aliud oppidum Vologesocertam in vicino condidit.

... but in all other respects the place (Babylon) has gone back to a desert, having been drained of its population by the proximity of Seleucia, founded for that purpose by Nicator not quite 90 miles away, at the point where the canalised Euphrates joins the Tigris ... For the purpose of drawing away the population of Seleucia in its turn, the Parthians founded Ctesiphon, which is about three miles from Seleucia in the Chalonitis district, and is now the capital of the kingdom of Parthia. And after it was found that the intended purpose was not being achieved, another town was recently founded in the neighbourhood by King Vologesus, named Vologesocerta. (trans.: H. Rackham, LCL)

4. Ptolemy V 19

πρὸς δὲ τῷ Μααρσάρῃ ποταμῷ Οὐολγαισία ... Βάρσιτα ...

Along the river Maarsares: Ouolgaisia, ... Barsita ...

5. Ammianus XXIII 6, 23

In omni autem Assyria multae sunt urbes. inter quas Apamia eminet, Mesene cognominata, et Teredon et Apollonia et Vologessia hisque similes multae.

But in all Assyria there are many cities, among which Apamia, also named Mesene, and Teredon, Apollonia and Vologessia, and many similar ones are conspicuous. (trans.: J. C. Rolfe, LCL)

6. Stephanus Byzantius

Βολογεσσίας, πόλις πρὸς τῷ Εὐφράτῃ, ἐκ Βολογεσσοῦ βασιλέως ᾠκισμένη κτλ.

Bologessias, town on the Euphrates, founded by King Bologessos.

7. Sassanian Seals[3]

a. *Nḥl-mlky ZY Wldḥ šp'ty mgwḥ*

In the margin: *Wyḥ-⟨'⟩ltḥštly*

Royal Canal of Valāšābād, office of the *magi*
Vēh-Ardašīr

b. *Wḥ-'ltḥšt(l) štl⟨d⟩st'n mgwḥ.*

In the margin: *Wḥy-'ltḥštl*

Vēh-Ardašīr, city, office of the *magi*
Vēh-Ardašīr

B. *Location*

Vologesias, on the west bank of the Tigris south of Maḥoza (D 3 on the Tal. Bab. map)

[3] Maricq, *Syria* 36 (1959): 267–268 = *Classica et Orientalia*, pp. 116–117.

C. *Identification*

The town of Vologesias is mentioned as an important commercial center in Parthia on a number of Palmyrene inscriptions.[4] One of these, dated in the middle of the second century, refers to Palmyrene citizens in Vologesias and the founding of a temple of the Augusti.[5]
Three place names—Vologesias, Vologesocerta and Walašpaṭ (or Valāšābād)—figure in the sources, which have been understood as referring to either one or two places. At issue are the location of one of the leading trade centers in Mesopotamia, and the interpretation and evaluation of our sources on the geography of that country.

a. Vologesias first appears on inscriptions as an important center for the trade from the Persian Gulf to Palmyra in A. D. 108. Ptolemy in Source 4 makes Vologesias a site on the Maarsares and gives coordinates which place it on the Euphrates, not far from Babylon in the Kūfa region. Stephanus Byzantius in Source 6 says it is on the Euphrates, while the *Tabula Peutingeriana* has a route "Volocesia XVIII Babylonia." The name of the city shows it was founded by Vologaeses I (second half of the first century A. D.).
b. Vologesocerta is mentioned only by Pliny in Source 3 as a town founded by Vologaeses I to replace Ctesiphon.
c. Valāšābād/Walašpaṭ is mentioned in Arabic sources, in the Talmud and on Sassanian seals which place it on the Royal Canal. The Talmud, a source contemporary with the seals, shows (in Sources 1 and 2) that it was a major wine market.

Traditionally it was assumed that Vologesocerta and Vologesias were two different places, the former near Ctesiphon, the latter not far from Borsippa and Babylon. Musil was the first to criticize this view:[6] "As we know from the Palmyrene inscriptions . . . that the merchants of Palmyra used to import their wares from 'Ologesias,' we are inclined to look for this place west of Seleucia-Ctesiphon and west of the Euphrates, thus in the neighborhood of Neapolis. By coming here the Palmyrene pack camels would have avoided the dangerous heat and mosquitoes of Babylonia proper. To Vologaesia-Neapolis the wares could have been brought either on the highroad or on the Royal River." Musil's site west of the Euphrates is entirely speculative, but

---

[4] Palmyrene inscriptions mentioning Vologesias include Dunant, *Museum Helveticum* 13 (1956): 216ff. (cf. J. & L. Robert, *Bulletin Epigraphique* [1958]: 506); Cantineau, *Inventaire des Inscriptions de Palmyre* III 21, 29; IX 14, 15 (A. D. 108); Starcky, *ibid.*, X 112, 124; *SEG*, vol. 7, No. 135. See the general articles by Rostovtzeff in *Mélanges Gustave Glotz*, vol. 2, pp. 793–811; Seyrig, *Syria* 22 (1941): 196ff. = *Antiquités Syriennes*, vol. 3, 196ff.; Will, *Syria* 34 (1957): 262ff.

[5] *SEG*, vol. 7, No. 135.

[6] Musil, *The Middle Euphrates*, p. 277f.

it must be noted that he was the first to point out that the most important trade center between Mesene and Palmyra could be expected to lie on a major caravan route. The search for Vologesias in the Babylon region is based on Ptolemy's coordinates, but as Herzfeld has pointed out, Ptolemy's map of Mesopotamia gives a false picture of the relative position of towns and waterways.[7] Ptolemy places Ouolgaisia at the end of a branch of the Euphrates that flows past Sippar. That would place Vologesias near Seleucia/Ctesiphon (see also "Barṣita" in the Appendix). Ptolemy's Maarsares has been plausibly explained as a mistake for Naarsares (= Nār Šarri, meaning "royal canal"),[8] which would again place Vologesias in the Seleucia/Ctesiphon region. Stephanus Byzantius does not mention any source for his statement that Vologesias lay on the Euphrates and as pointed out by Herzfeld, the *Tabula Peutingeriana*, gives a distorted picture of the road system in the region.[9] From this it has been concluded that Vologesias is likely to have been in the Seleucia/Ctesiphon region. Unaware of Nöldeke's and Herzfeld's similar conclusion, Maricq suggests that Vologesias and Valāšābād are one and the same. Nöldeke cites Arab authors. Herzfeld and Maricq also refer to the Talmud in support of their conclusion. Maricq also published the Sassanian seals cited

---

[7] Herzfeld, *Samarra*, pp. 34, 54ff.

[8] Chaumont, *Syria* 51 (1974): 77–81, criticised Maricq and argued for a southern Vologesias, as indicated by Ptolemy distinct from Vologesocerta = Valāšābād in the Seleucia/Ctesiphon region. This argument is based wholly on Ptolemy whose Maarsares is taken, without further discussion, to be the branch of the Euphrates now called Nahr Hindīya (solely a reference is given to Dillemann, *Syria* 38 [1961]: 153). The identification of Maarsares with Nahr Hindīya again ignores the distortions in Ptolemy's map. Ptolemy's Maarsares branches off at Sippar, surely too far north for the Nahr Hindīya. That is the proper latitude of the Royal Canal, not of the Nahr Hindīya. However, as noted by Musil, *op.cit.* (in n. 6), p. 278, the Maarsares branched of from the right bank of the Euphrates, "but from the same bank also, according to Ptolemy, the Royal Canal branched off, although we know from other writers that the latter issued from the left bank." Furthermore, the only possible help Ptolemy gives us toward identifying the course of the Maarsares is, as observed by Musil, his placement of Vologesias and Borsippa on its bank. This being the case, it is hard to maintain that Ptolemy's Maarsares can help us find Vologesias. Finally, the Maarsares does not appear in any other source. The Marses in Ammianus XXIII 6, 25, if at all connected, is itself unidentified. The most straightforward interpretation of Ptolemy's Maarsares is still that he refers to the Royal Canal twice, once translated as "Royal Canal" and once by the to-him-incomprehensible name of Maarsares (Naarsares — Nār Šarri). Above all, we should be wary of using Ptolemy to provide easy solutions for complicated problems.

[9] Herzfeld, *Samarra*, p. 34. "Die Tabula hat — aus dem Zusammenhang der Routen gerissen, aber mit Sohene-Scene und Balictanor des Ravennaten mit der Tigrisroute von Hatra nach Seleucia zu verbinden —: *Volocesia* XVIII *Babylonia*. Um 50 p. Chr. kann keine Entfernung mehr auf das verlassene und vergessene Babylon bezogen werden, es muß *Seleucia Babylonia* heissen. Im Abstand von 18 mp, 26,7 km, von Seleucia liegt z.B. Baghdad."

above.[10] Herzfeld rejects the notion that talmudic Sabata (q.v.) has anything to do with Valāšābād. According to him, the latter as well as Vologesocerta (in Pliny) derive from *Valagš-āpāt-kirt. Herzfeld states that the same town can be found in Arab authors. Maricq does not attempt to give a precise location for Vologesias, but discusses it in general terms.[11]

Fiey suggests that Vologesias can be identified with ruins called Abū-Halefije on Bachmann's map of Seleucia-Ctesiphon,[12] and notes that the aerial photograph on display in the new Iraqi Museum in Baghdad shows a branch of the Royal Canal joining the Tigris immediately south of these ruins.[13] This identification is certainly possible but cannot be proved.

To sum up, the three towns—Pliny's Vologesocerta which was founded in the first century "to replace Ctesiphon," Vologesias which was a trade center for Palmyra and an important town according to Ammianus, and Valāšābād/Walašpaṭ which was on the Royal Canal according to Sassanian seals and had a wine market in the fourth century according to the Talmud—are most likely one and the same town.[14] This conclusion seems to contradict explicit statements by Ptolemy and the *Tabula Peutingeriana*, but these sources contain internal contradictions and distortions and need to be reinterpreted in any case.

D. *Sages and Walašpaṭ*

The two talmudic sources in which Walašpaṭ figures show the sages referring to its wine market. In Source 1, the halakhah of Rav Ḥama, of the fifth generation of Babylonian amoras, indicates that the prices in the Walašpaṭ wine market served as the criteria in cases of doubt. In Source 2, Rava, head of the Maḥoza yeshiva in the fourth generation of Babylonian amoras, states the

---

[10] The Talmud is cited by Herzfeld, *Samarra*, p. 33f. and by Maricq, *Syria* 36 (1959): 269f. = *Classica et Orientalia*, p. 118f. Both cite Arab authors: Ṭabarī, vol. 2, p. 90 (= vol. 1, p. 883); Ḥamza, *Ta'rīḫ*, p. 56; Ya'qūbī, *Buldān*, p. 321; Yāqūt, s.v. "Sābāṭ kisrā." The Arabic sources ascribe the foundation of the town to the Sassanian king Valāš (484–488), and see the entry on "Sabata." Long mistrusted, this ascription is refuted decisively by the evidence of the seals and the Talmud, cf. Maricq, *op. cit.* (n. 3 above).

[11] He discusses the position of Seleucia/Ctesiphon/Vologesias on the silk route, and see also Neusner, *PAAJR* 31 (1963): 170f.

[12] Reuther, *Die Ausgrabungen 1928–1929*, map; Fiey, *Sumer* 23 (1967): 7, 12; Hopkins, *Topography*, Pl. I (map).

[13] The aerial photograph has not been published and is not accessible to us. See the entry on "Be Ardəšir-Koḵe." Fiey is unaware of Herzfeld's rejection of the identity of Vologesias and Sābāṭ. Even if Sābāṭ was a separate town further west the identification of Vologesias with Abū Ḫalafīya remains possible.

[14] For the historical background of the foundation of the town see the entry on "Be Ardəšir-Koḵe." For linguistic arguments for the identification of Vologesias-Vologesocerta-Valāšābād, see Nöldeke, *ZDMG* 28 (1874): 91–98.

actual conditions applying to the despatch of wine to Walašpaṭ for sale in its wine market.[15]

Beer, *Amora'ei Bavel* (1974), p. 168
Berliner, *Beiträge* (1883), pp. 34, 66
Chaumont, *Syria* 51 (1974): 77–81
Dobiaš, *Listy Filologické* 58 (1931): 11–15
Eshel, *Yishuvei ha-Yehudim* (1979), pp. 112–113
Funk, *Juden* (1902–1908), vol. 1, p. 19; vol. 2, p. 156
Funk, *Monumenta* (1913), pp. 33, 292
Herzfeld, *Samarra* (1948), pp. 33–34, 63
Hirschenson, *Sheva Ḥokhmot* (1883), p. 109
Jastrow, *Dictionary* (1950³), p. 175
Kohut, *Arukh ha-Shalem* (1878–1892), vol. 5, p. 28; *Tosefot* (1937), p. 165
Krauss, *Qadmoniot ha-Talmud* (1923–1945), vol. 1A, pp. 75–76, 212
Levy, *Wörterbuch* (1924²), vol. 2, p 488
Maricq, *Syria* 36 (1959): 264–276 = *Classica et Orientalia* (1956): 113–126
Mordtmann, *SAWM* (1875), vol 2, part 4
Musil, *The Middle Euphrates* (1927), p. 277f.
Neubauer, *Géographie* (1868), p. 392, n. 5
Neusner, *History* (1965–1970), vol. 4, p. 232
Neusner, *Talmudic Judaism* (1976), pp. 121, 139
Nöldeke, *ZDMG* 28 (1874): 93–98
Obermeyer, *Landschaft* (1929), pp. 184–185, 188; Sābāṭ, pp. 163, 165
Widengren, *Iranica Antiqua* 1 (1961): 134
Zuri, *Shilton* (1938), p. 238

Wardina ורדינא

A. *Sources*

1. Soṭah 10a

כתיב "וירד שמשון תמנתה," וכתיב "והנה חמיך עולה תמנתה," ... ר' שמואל בר נחמני אמר שתי תמנאות היו, חדא בירידה וחדא בעליה. רב פפא אמר חדא תמנה הואי, דאתי מהאי גיסא ירידה ודאתי מהאי גיסא עליה כגון ורדוניא[1] ובי בארי[2] ושוקא דנרש.[3]

It is written "Samson went down to Timnah" (Jud. 14:1) and it is written "Your father-in-law is coming up to Timnah" (Gen. 38:13) . . . Rabbi Samuel b. Naḥmani said, There were two Timnahs, one down and one up. Rav Papa said, There is one Timnah, Whoever came from one direction went down, and whoever came from another direction went up, such as Wardunya,[1] Be Bire[2] and the market of Nareš.[3]

---

[15] There was also an important wine market in Sikra (q.v.).

[1] The Vatican 110 MS has **ורדינא**, the Munich MS has **ורדי נאה** and the Oxford MS has **יוריניא**. See also Soṭah in the ICIT edition.

[2] The source has **בי בארי**. For other variations in the name see the entry on "Be Bire."

[3] For variants in this name, see the entry on "Nareš."

2. ʿEruvin 49a

אמר רב יהודה אמר שמואל המקפיד על עירובו אין עירובו עירוב, מה שמו, עירוב שמו, ר׳ חנינא אמר עירובו עירוב אלא שנקרא מאנשי ורדינא.[4]

Rav Judah said Samuel said, If a man is particular about his [share in an] *ʿeruv*, his *ʿeruv* is not an *ʿeruv*: For what is an *ʿeruv*? An amalgamation. Rabbi Ḥanina said, His *ʿeruv* is an *ʿeruv*, but he is called one of the people of Wardina.[4]

3. Giṭṭin 64b

מתיב רב חיננא וורדאן[5] כיצד משתתפין במבוי . . . אמר רב חסדא אישתיק וורדאן.[6]

Rav Ḥinena Warda'an[5] objected, How can an alley be shared . . . Rav Ḥisda said, Warda'an[6] was reduced to silence.

4. Betzah 27a

אמי ורדינאה חזי בוכרא דבי נשיאה הוה, ביומא טבא לא הוה חזי, אתו ואמרי ליה לרבי אמי, אמר להו שפיר קא עביד דלא חזי.

Ammi Wardina'a used to examine the firstlings of the Patriarch's house; on holidays he did not examine. They came and said to him, to Rabbi Ammi. He said, He does right not to examine.

5. Niddah 19b

אמי ורדינאה[7] אמר רבי אבהו כדם אצבע קטנה של יד שנגפה וחייתה וחזרה ונגפה, ולא של כל אדם אלא של בחור שלא נשא אשה, ועד כמה, עד בן עשרים.

Ammi Wardina'a[7] said Rabbi Abbahu said, Like the blood of the little finger of the hand that was wounded and healed and wounded again. And not of any man, but of a young man who hasn't married; to what age, to twenty.

B. *Already Proposed Location*

Tall Wardīya, east of the Euphrates, some five kilometers northeast of Ḥilla (D4 on the Tal. Bab. map).

C. *Identification*

Source 1 indicates that Wardunya was near Nareš in a hilly area. The location of Nareš (q.v.) in the vicinity of Sura not far from Ḥilla has been clarified by Obermeyer and his identification of Wardunya with Tall Wardīya seems well founded.[8] Obermeyer distinguishes between the Wardunya mentioned in Source

[4] The Munich MS has ורדינאה, the Oxford MS has ורדניא; and see *Diq. Sof.* According to the R-a-ḥ "the people of Wardina means the people of Warda'an."

[5] The Vatican 130 MS has וורדינאה, while וורדאן does not appear in the Munich MS at all.

[6] The Munich and Vatican 130 MSS have ורדן.

[7] The Vatican 111 MS has ורידי אנאה.

[8] Obermeyer, p. 308. See also *Ta'rīḫ al-Ḥilla*, vol. 1, p. 154, which refers to a village and canal called Wardīya in the district (= *nāḥiya*) of Nīl. Cf. (*ibid.*, p. 169) a quarter in Ḥilla called Wardīya.

1 and the places of Rav Ḥinena Warda'an and Ammi Wardina'a. He identifies Warda'an with Baradān north of Baghdad.[9] In his view the preferred version for Source 2 is that of Rabbenu Ḥananel which also has Warda'an (note 4), while the Rabbi Ḥanina mentioned there is identical with the Rav Ḥinena mentioned in Source 3, so that Sources 2 and 3 deal with the same sage and the same place. Ammi Wardina'a[10] mentioned in Sources 4 and 5 was according to Obermeyer located in Wardānīya, one of the villages in the area where Baghdad was later built.[11]

There are no grounds for the distinction Obermeyer makes between the Wardunya mentioned in Source 1, whose location near Nareš is clear, and the Warda'an and Wardina figuring in Sources 3–5 (and in Obermeyer's view in Source 2 as well), especially since the manuscripts have Wardina in both Source 1 and Source 2 (see notes 1 and 5). The form Wardunya is not certain, and in any case Wardunya, Warda'an and Wardina (and the other variants in the manuscripts) are evidently the same place.

If it is agreed that the Wardunya of Source 1 is identical with the Wardina and Warda'an of Sources 2–5, it is reasonable to suppose that the place was actually called Wardina or Wardinya in view both of its identification with Tall Wardīya, and of the variety of forms in the manuscripts.

D. *Sages and Wardina*

Two sages from Wardina appear in the sources. Source 3 mentions Rav Ḥinena of the third generation of Babylonian amoras, who disagrees with Rav Ḥisda and Rav Judah and then subsides in the face of Rav Ḥisda's point. Sources 4 and 5 refer to Ammi Wardina'a, of the fourth generation of Babylonian amoras. In Source 4 he is attached to the Patriarch's court in Eretz Israel, and in Source 5 he cites Rabbi Abbahu who headed the study house in Caesarea in the third generation of Eretz Israel amoras. Thus this sage moved from Babylonia to Eretz Israel, or perhaps came to Babylonia from Eretz Israel. In the latter case, presumably there was a place called Wardina in that country as well.[12]

E. *The Inhabitants*

In the course of a discussion of laws on *ʿeruv* in Source 2, Rabbi Ḥanina refers to the well-known miserliness of the Wardina people. In a similar context,

---

[9] Obermeyer, pp. 269–270; cf. also Funk, *Monumenta*, p. 292. On Baradān, see Streck, *Die alte Landschaft*, vol. 1, p. 7; vol. 2, p. 230f.; Streck, *EI*[1] and Streck-Longrigg, *EI*[2] under "Baradān," and the bibliography there; Scoville, *Gazetteer*, p. 395; Herzfeld, *Samarra*, p. 30; Fiey, *Assyrie chrétienne*, vol. 3, pp. 257–261.

[10] Obermeyer for some reason has **ר' אמי וורדנאי** (p. 270).

[11] On Wardānīya, see Ṭabarī, vol. 7, p. 620 (= vol. 3, p. 279); *Ta'riḫ Baġdād*, vol. 1, p. 84. Cf. this entry in Yāqūt as well, and see also Le Strange, *Baghdad*, p. 126; Lassner, p. 67.

[12] See Horowitz, *Eretz Yisrael u-Shekhenoteha*, p. 243; Klein, *MGWJ* 28 (1920): 190.

T. J. ʿEruvin VI 8–24a, 14 mentions "The Bar Dalya people who are not particular about their pennies (= פרוטתן)." According to the R-a-b-a-d this should be read "The Bar Dalya people who are particular about their slices (= פרוסתן) [of bread]" (*Hilkhot ʿEruvin*, V 14). On the basis of that, Lieberman assumes that Bar Dalya is Wardanya (i.e. Wardina), since the contents of the T. J. and Source 2 are so similar, and substitutions of *bet* for *waw* and *lamed* for *nun* are common in the T.J.[13]

Berliner, *Beiträge* (1883), p. 34
Eshel, *Yishuvei ha-Yehudim* (1979), pp. 113–114
Funk, *Juden* (1902–1908), vol. 2, p. 157
Funk, *Monumenta* (1913), pp. 33, 292
Hirschenson, *Sheva Ḥokhmot* (1883), p. 109
Jastrow, *Dictionary* (1950³), p. 375
Klein, *MGWJ* 65 (1920): 190
Kohut, *Arukh ha-Shalem* (1878–1892), vol. 3, p. 258; *Tosefot* (1937), p. 106
Krauss, *Qadmoniot ha-Talmud* (1923–1945), vol. 1A, p. 52
Levy, *Wörterbuch* (1924²), vol. 1, p. 505
Neubauer, *Géographie* (1868), p. 366
Neusner, *History* (1965–1970), vol. 5, p. 205
Obermeyer, *Landschaft* (1929), pp. 269–270, 308–309

[13] Lieberman, *Ha-Yerushalmi ki-Fshuto*, pp. 320–321.

Appendix

This appendix includes communities named in the Talmud which have not been dealt with in one way or another among the entries in the body of the book. As a rule they cannot be definitely identified, are not discussed in classical literature nor illumined in Arabic sources. Most of the names appear only once, and the testimony on them has no true historical significance.
After the source(s) in which the community figures, the main variants of its name are given, followed by bibliographical references to identification attempts (in the main not described since they are no more than hypotheses), and remarks on sages emanating from or associated with the community concerned.

ʿAlmin עלמין

A. *Source*

Sanhedrin 94a

אבל ישראל ספרו בגנותה של ארץ ישראל, כי מטו שוש אמרי שויא כי ארעין, כי מטו עלמין אמרו כעלמין, כי מטו שוש תרי אמרי על חד תרין.

But Israel [when exiled] spoke evil of Eretz Israel. When they reached Šuš they said, It equals our country; when they reached ʿAlmin (עלמין) they said, Like our world (עלמין); when they reached Šuš Təre (= two) they said, Double.

B. *Attempts at Identification*

Neubauer, p. 381; Obermeyer, p. 213; *Arukh ha-Shalem*, vol. 8, p. 180, n. 1; Eshel, p. 207. See also the entries on "Susa (Šušan)" and "Šuštar."

Aqra də-Šanwata אקרא דשנוותא

A. *Sources*

1. Bava Metziʿa 73b

רבינא הוה יהיב זוזי לבני אקרא דשנוותא ושפכי ליה טפי כופיתא, אתא לקמיה דרב אשי . . .

Ravina used to give money (before the grape harvest) to the people of Aqra də-Šanwata, and they poured him a larger measure; he came before Rav Ashi ...

2. Mo'ed Qaṭan 10b

רבינא הוה מסיק זוזי בבני אקרא דשנואתא, אתא לקמיה דרב אשי אמר ליה מהו למיזל האידנא עלייהו . . .

Ravina was owed money by people from Aqra də-Šanwata, came before Rav Ashi [and] asked him, What about going now (in the intermediate days of a festival) to them?

B. *Variants*

The Munich, Florence and Hamburg MSS have אקרא דשנואתא for Source 1; the Munich MS has אקרא דשנרואתא for Source 2.

C. *Attempts at Identification*

Obermeyer, pp. 122–125, 268 (for his view see the entry on "Šunya"); Neubauer, p. 387; Hirschenson, *Sheva Ḥokhmot*, pp. 42–43; Funk, *Monumenta*, p. 289; *Arukh ha-Shalem*, vol. 1, p. 260, s.v. "אקרא"; Eshel, p. 32. See also "Be Ḥarmak̲" below.

D. *Sages and Aqra də-Šanwata*

The sources above testify to the commercial activity of Ravina, of the seventh generation of Babylonian amoras, a disciple of Rav Ashi's. Source 1 deals with his purchase of wine from the people of Aqra də-Šanwata. Regarding Ravina's involvement in the wine trade, see the sections on Sages and Sik̲ra and on Economy in the entry on "Sik̲ra."

'Aravot ערבות

A. *Sources*

1. Berakhot 54a

מר בריה דרבינא הוה קאזיל בפקתא דערבות וצחא למיא, איתעביד ליה ניסא איברי ליה עינא דמיא ואישתי . . . כי מטא לערבות בריך ברוך שעשה לי נס בערבות . . .

Mar son of Ravina was walking in the valley of 'Aravot and was thirsty. A miracle was wrought for him, a spring of water was created, and he drank . . . Whenever he arrived in 'Aravot he said a blessing, Blessed be He who wrought a miracle for me in 'Aravot . . .

2. Ḥullin 106b–107a

אמר להו רבי אבינא לבני פקתא דערבות . . .

Rabbi Avina said to the people of the valley of 'Aravot . . .

3. Mo'ed Qaṭan 15a

ואמר רב זבוני מיא בפקתא דערבות...

And Rav said to sell water in the valley of 'Aravot ...

4. Nazir 43b

א"ל רב המנונא אלא מעתה קאזיל בפקתא דערבות ופסקוה גנבי לרישיה...

Rav Hamnuna said to him, But from now on he walks through the valley of 'Aravot and thieves cut off his head ...

B. *Attempts at Identification*

Eshel, p. 208.

Asporaq אספורק

A. *Source*

Bava Qamma 65b, 94a; Temurah 30b

...ואמר רב יוסף, תני גוריון דמאספורק, בית שמאי אוסרין ובית הלל מתירין.

... And Rav Joseph said, Guryon of Asporaq taught, Bet Shammai forbids, and Bet Hillel permits.

B. *Variants*

The Vatican 116 MS has דמאיספורק in Bava Qamma 65b (as well as 94a); the Florence MS has דמיספורק. The Munich MS has דמן ספורק in Temurah 30b.

C. *Attempts at Identification*

Neubauer, p. 387, n. 7 (citing Ritter) and cf. *Geonica*, vol. 2, p. 243; *Arukh ha-Shalem*, vol. 1, p. 195. See also Eshel, p. 21.

D. *Sages and Asporaq*

Rav Joseph, of the third generation of Babylonian amoras, reports a *baraita* taught by Guryon of Asporaq.

Awirya אוריא

A. *Source*

Shevu'ot 24b

ורב אשי מאוריא אמר רבי זירא...

And Rav Ashi of Awirya said, Rabbi Zera ...

B. *Variants*

The Munich MS does not have Rav Ashi of Awirya and Rabbi Zera at all, but merely the quotation attributed to them in the standard edition. The Florence MS has just Rav Ashi, with מחוורייא added in the margin. The Lublin printing has מאוירא; see also *Diq. Sof.*

C. *Attempts at Identification*

Hirschenson, *Sheva Ḥokhmot*, p. 28; *Arukh ha-Shalem*, vol. 1, p. 47; Eshel, p. 14.

D. *Sages and Awirya*

The source mentions Rav Ashi of Awirya (the only reference to him in talmudic literature) as citing Rabbi Zera. There were several sages by the latter name (see Albeck, *Mavo la-Talmudim*, pp. 233ff., 388ff.).

Bar Hamdak̲ בר המדך

A. *Source*

Mo'ed Qaṭan 4b

אביי שרא לבני בר המדך לשחופי נהרא.

Abbaye allowed the people of Bar Hamdak̲ (on the intermediate days of a festival) to dredge the river.

B. *Variants*

The Munich MS has לבני הרמיך; see also *Diq. Sof.*

C. *Attempts at Identification*

Neubauer, p. 362; some scholars have identified it with Be Ḥarmak̲ (see below), among them Berliner, p. 33; *Arukh ha-Shalem*, vol. 2, pp. 202–204; s.v. "בר שניא". See also Eshel, p. 109.

Barṣita ברציתא

A. *Sources*

1. Mo'ed Qaṭan 4b

והא רב יהודה שרא לבני בר ציתאי למעבד בנכי לכרמיהון...

For Rav Judah allowed the people of Bar Ṣitai to make hollows (on the intermediate days of a festival) for their vineyards.

2. Ptolemy V 19

πρὸς δὲ τῷ Μααρσάρῃ ποταμῷ Οὐολγαισία ... Βάρσιτα ...
Along the river Maarsares: Ouolgaisia, ... Barsita ...

B. *Variants*

The source has בר ציתאי; the Munich MS has בר צרת׳; all the old printed editions have לבי ברציתא.

C. *Attempts at Identification*

Hirschenson, *Sheva Ḥokhmot*, p. 204; Berliner, p. 60; Funk, *Monumenta*, p. 299; *Arukh ha-Shalem*, vol. 2, p. 48, s. v. "בי ברציתא," Eshel, p. 80. Yevamot 21b has בר ציתאי as a family name, so that the place mentioned above may be named for a family living there, or vice versa. *Diq. Sof.*, however, prefers the version of the place name in the old printed editions, and suggests that the form בר ציתאי came into the later printings from Rashi, where it was inserted from Yevamot to Moʿed Qaṭan through a scribal error. The *Diq. Sof.* contention that the place named in Source 1 was Barṣita supports the assumption that it is identical with the place cited in Source 2. Consequently Barṣita was probably in the vicinity of Vologesias (Walašpaṭ, q. v.). Furthermore, Source 1 mentions vineyards which abounded in the Walašpaṭ area.

Be Avyone בי אביוני

A. *Source*

Bava Qamma 117a

רב הונא בר יהודה איקלע לבי אביוני. אתא לקמיה דרבא, אמר ליה כלום מעשה בא לידך . . .

Rav Huna b. Judah happened to be in Be Avyone. He came before Rava who said to him, Did some case come to you . . .

B. *Variants*

The Munich and Hamburg MSS have בי איביוני, the Florence MS has בי אבוויני and see *Diq. Sof.*

C. *Attempts at Identification*

Funk, *Monumenta*, p. 290; *Arukh ha-Shalem*, vol. 2, pp. 45–47, s. v. "בי אבידן"; Berliner, p. 26.

D. *Sages and Be Avyone*

The source reports that Rav Huna b. Judah of the fourth generation of Babylonian amoras went to Be Avyone, returned and came before Rava, who asked him whether a legal problem had been submitted to him which he ruled on.

Be Hadya בי הדיא

A. *Source*

Yevamot 121a

דההוא גברא דטבע בכרמי ואסקוהו אבי הדיא לבתר תלתא יומין ואנסבה רב דימי מנהרדעא לדביתהו.

That fellow who drowned in Karme and was brought up three days later at Be Hadya, and Rav Dimi of Nəhardəʿa allowed his wife to remarry.

B. *Variants*

The Munich MS has אבי חיורי, the Vatican 111 MS has אבי חזרא, and see "Karme" below.

C. *Attempts at Identification*

Arukh ha-Shalem, vol. 4, p. 330, s.v. "כרם (= כרמא)"; Eshel, p. 57; see also "Karme" below.

D. *Sages and Be Hadya*

The source reports the case of a man drowned in Karme, whose body was pulled out three days later at Be Hadya. Rav Dimi of Nəhardəʿa, of the fourth generation of Babylonian amoras, allowed his widow to remarry. See "Karme" below and cf. the entry on "Gišra də-Šabistana."

Be Ḥarmak̲ בי חרמך

A. *Sources*

1. Giṭṭin 60b

הנהו בני בי חרמך דאזול כרו ברישא דשנוותא . . . אתו עילאי לקמיה דאביי . . .

Those Be Ḥarmak̲ people that went and dug a ditch at the top of [the river of] Šanwata . . . Those higher up came before Abbaye . . .

2. Zevaḥim 2b

אמר ליה רבינא לרב פפא לא הוית גבן באורתא בתחומא בי חרמך, דרמי רבא מילי מעלייתא אהדדי ושני להו.

Ravina said to Rav Papa, You were not with us in the evening in the Sabbath limits of Be Ḥarmak̲ when Rava set forth contradictions between lofty things and justified them.

B. *Variants*

The Vatican 140 MS has חרמך alone for Source 1; the Vatican 123 MS has בי הרמך for Source 2.

C. *Location*

Rav Hai Gaon says "Be Harmak̲ is the town near Pumbədita" (*Otzar ha-Geonim*, on Giṭṭin, *ha-Perushim*, p. 241) and that location seems to be suggested also by Source 1, since the case there was submitted to the head of the Pumbədita yeshiva. See Obermeyer, pp. 122–125, 231f. In the case of Bar Hamdak̲ (see above), which is perhaps to be identified with Be Ḥarmak̲, the question was likewise submitted to Abbaye. On the identity of the Šanwata river see the entry on "Šunya," and see "Aqra də-Šanwata" above. (See also *Arukh ha-Shalem*, vol. 2, pp. 49, 202–204, s.v. "בר שניא"; *Tosefot Arukh ha-Shalem*, p. 85; Hirschenson, *Sheva Ḥokhmot*, p. 69; Eshel, p. 60.)

D. *Sages and Be Ḥarmak̲*

Source 1 related an adjudication by Abbaye, head of the yeshiva at Pumbədita (q.v.) in the fourth generation of Babylonian amoras, between people of Be Ḥarmak̲ who had dug a ditch from the Šanwata river, and their neighbors who suffered as a result. Source 2 testifies to a sermon evidently preached at Be Ḥarmak̲ by Rava, head of the yeshiva at Maḥoza (q.v.) in the same period.

Be Kəloḥit בי כלוחית

A. *Sources*

1. Betzah 5b

רב אדא ורב שלמן תרוייהו מבי כלוחית אמרי . . .

Rav Adda and Rav Shalman, both of Be Kəloḥit, said . . .

2. Ketubot 40b

. . . שמעה רב פפא בריה דרב חנן מבי כלוחית אזל אמרה קמיה דרב שימי בר אשי.

Rav Papa son of Rav Naḥman of Be Kəloḥit heard it, went and told it before Rav Shimi b. Ashi.

B. *Variants*

The Munich MS has simply מכלוחית in Source 1. In Source 2 the Munich MS has מרבלוחית, the Vatican 112 MS has מבי כלוחות, and the Leningrad MS has מבי בלוחית. See also Ketubot in the ICIT edition.

C. *Attempts at Identification*

Funk, *Monumenta*, p. 290.

Be Šife בי שיפי

A. *Source*

Giṭṭin 89a

ההיא דנפק עלה קלא דאיקדשה באציפא דתוחלא בעינא דבי שיפי, שלחה רב אידי בר אבין לקמיה דאביי...

On that one who was rumored to have been betrothed with unripe dates in the Be Šife spring, Rav Idi b. Avin sent before Abbaye...

B. *Variant*

The Munich MS has בי שייפו.

C. *Attempts at Identification*

Eshel, pp. 70, 205.

D. *Sages and Be Šife*

Rav Idi b. Avin submits a question to Abbaye, head of the Pumbədita yeshiva in the fourth generation of Babylonian amoras, as to whether betrothal is valid if there is a rumor that the woman was betrothed with something worth less than a cent in the spring of Be Šife. (Moʿed Qaṭan 11a has "Rav happened to come to Be Rav Šafir [בי רב שפיר]" but the Munich MS, Venice printing and others have "Bar Šafir" [בר שפיר]. Qiddushin 71b has "For Rav happened to come to Be Bar Šafi Ḥala [בי בר שפי חלא]" but the Vatican 111 Ms has "Šafiḥala" [שפיחלא] there. The references in these sources may be to families, but that they are place names is also a possibility, in which case note the similarity to "Be Šife." The Qiddushin reference may be to the trade of vinegar maker [see Rashi].)

Dardəšir דרדשיר

A. *Source*

Yevamot 37b, Yoma 18b

רב כי איקלע לדרדשיר מכריז ואמר מאן הויא ליומא.

When Rav happened to be in Dardəšir, he would announce, Who will be [willing to marry me] for a day?

B. *Variants*

Yoma has לדרשיש, as does Yevamot in the Munich B MS. The Munich MS has לדרדשיש in Yevamot; the Oxford MS has לדורשיש and the London MS has לתרשיש, in both places.

C. *Attempts at Identification*

All attempts at identification have contended that the place is Ardəšir. See Neubauer, p. 358, n. 6; *Arukh ha-Shalem*, vol. 1, p. 276, s.v. "ארדשיר"; and see the entry on "Be Ardəšir-Koke" in the "Maḥoza Area." See also Eshel, pp. 100–101.

D. *Sages and Dardəšir*

The source testifies that Rav, head of the Sura yeshiva in the first generation of Babylonian amoras, upon reaching Dardəšir sought a woman that would agree to be his wife for the duration of his stay there. A similar report is made on Rav Naḥman in connection with his visit to Šəkanṣiv (q.v.). Rav's travels to various places in Babylonia are attested by a number of sources. See the section on The Center in Sura in the entry on "Sura."

Dərumata דרומתא

A. *Source*

Mo'ed Qaṭan 27b

רב המנונא איקלע לדרומתא.

Rav Hamnuna happened to come to Dərumata.

B. *Variants*

The Munich MS has לדארו מאתא and the Munich B MS has לדראו מתא; see also *Diq. Sof.*

C. *Attempts at Identification*

Funk, *Monumenta*, p. 291, identifies the place with Dəruqart (q.v.); see also Eshel, p. 101.

Dəwil דויל

A. *Source*

Ketubot 65a, Giṭṭin 81a, Qiddushin 79b, Niddah 26b

רב יוסף בריה דרב מנשיא מדויל.

Rav Joseph son of Rav Menashya of Dəwil.

B. *Attempts at Identification*

Neubauer, p. 389; Berliner, pp. 29–30; Funk, *Monumenta*, p. 291; Eshel, p. 92.

Dihavat דיהבת

A. *Source*

Ta'anit 7b

אמר ליה זעירי מדיהבת לרבינא . . .

Ze'iri of Dihavat said to Ravina . . .

B. *Variants*

The Munich and Munich B MSS have מדהבת, and see *Diq. Sof.*

C. *Attempts at Identification*

Arukh ha-Shalem, vol. 3, p. 28; Eshel, p. 95.

'Ever Yamina עבר ימינא

A. *Sources*

1. 'Eruvin 19a

גן עדן, אמר ריש לקיש אם בא״י הוא בית שאן פתחו, ואם בערביא בית גרם פתחו, ואם בין הנהרות הוא דומסקנין פתחו. בבבל, אביי משתבח בפירי דמעבר ימינא, רבא משתבח בפירי דהרפניא.

Paradise, Resh Laqish said, if it is in the Land of Israel its gate is Bet Šə'an; if it is in 'Arabia its gate is Bet Gerem; and if it is between the rivers its gate is Dumasqanin. In Babylonia, Abbaye praised the fruit of 'Ever Yamina and Rav praised the fruit of Harpanya.

2. Yoma 77b

רבא שרא לבני עבר ימינא למעבר במיא לנטורי פירי.

Rava allowed the people of 'Ever Yamina to cross the water [on the Day of Atonement] to guard the fruit.

3. Bava Batra 40b

דההוא גברא דאזל לקדושי אתתא, אמרה ליה אי כתבת לי כולהו נכסיך הוינא לך ואי לא לא הוינא לך, אזל כתביה לה לכולהו נכסי. אתא בריה קשישא א״ל וההוא גברא מה תהוי עליה, אמר להו לסהדי זילו אטמורו בעבר ימינא, וכתבו ליה, אתו לקמיה דרבא . . .

That man who was about to betroth a woman, she said to him, If you assign me all your property, I will be yours, and if not, I will not be yours. He went [and] assigned her all his property. His eldest son came and said to him, And this man [me], what about him? He said to the witnesses, Go hide in 'Ever Yamina and assign [my property] to him. They came before Rava . . .

4. Berakhot 54a

אניסא דרבים מברכינן אניסא דיחיד לא מברכינן, והא ההוא גברא דהוה קא אזיל בעבר ימינא נפל עליה אריא, אתעביד ליה ניסא ואיתצל מיניה, אתא לקמיה דרבא וא״ל כל אימת דמטית להתם בריך ברוך שעשה לי נס במקום הזה.

Is a blessing said for a community miracle and not for a miracle of an individual? For that man who was going through ʿEver Yamina and a lion attacked him, a miracle was wrought for him and he was saved from it, he came before Rava, and he said to him, Whenever you reach there bless, Blessed be He who wrought me a miracle in this place.

B. *Variants*

In Bava Batra, the Vatican 115 MS has בעבר ימינתא and see *Diq. Sof.* In Berakhot, the Munich MS has לעבר ירדנא, the Paris MS has לעבר ימא, and see *Diq. Sof.*

C. *Attempts at Identification*

Funk, *Monumenta*, p. 298; Berliner, p. 57; Obermeyer, p. 181f.; *Arukh ha-Shalem*, vol. 6, p. 162; Eshel, p. 292f. Obermeyer (and Eshel in his wake) differentiates between the ʿEver Yamina mentioned in Source 1, which is a district around the southern Euphrates, and the ʿEver Yamina in the other sources which he locates south of Maḥoza. His reason is that Rava, head of the Maḥoza yeshiva, is involved in the matters treated in the latter sources. There is no justification for the distinction, however, for Rava is mentioned in Source 1 as well, and furthermore he had a particular connection with Harpanya (= Nəharpanya, q.v.) which was in the southern Euphrates area, and which he suggests (in Source 1) is the gate to Paradise.

D. *Sages and ʿEver Yamina*

All the sources connect Rava, head of the Maḥoza yeshiva in the fourth generation of Babylonian amoras, with ʿEver Yamina. In Source 2 he allows the ʿEver Yamina people to cross a canal on the Day of Atonement despite the prohibition against washing, so that they can guard their fruit, it being harvest time (see the entry on "Be Tarbu"). In Source 3 Rava rules on a case in which a man was interested in concealing a document and sent the witnesses to it away to hide in ʿEver Yamina. In Source 4 Rava stipulates the blessing to be said by a man who was miraculously saved from lions in ʿEver Yamina (on lions in Babylonia cf. the entries on "Parziqiya" and "Nareš"). In Source 1, dealing with the place where "the gate to Paradise" is, Rava extols the fruit of Nəharpanya and Abbaye that of ʿEver Yamina. In view of the probable location noted, there is no drastic disagreement between the two sages, and Nəharpanya is perhaps in the neighborhood of ʿEver Yamina. (The fact that the fruit of ʿEver Yamina figures in both Source 1 and Source 2 is another indication that the same place is concerned.)

Gifte גיפתי

A. *Source*

ʿEruvin 64a

רב מנשיא בר ירמיה מגיפתי.

Rav Menashya b. Jeremiah of Gifte.

B. *Variants*

The Munich MS does not have מגיפתי at all, the Oxford MS has מזיפתי and the Salonika printing has מגובתא; see also *Diq. Sof.*

Gozanya גוזניא

A. *Source*

Shabbat 152a

אמר ליה ההוא גוזאה לרבי יהושע בן קרחה מהכא לקרחינא כמה הוי, אמר ליה כמהכא לגוזניא.

That eunuch (= *goza'a*) said to Rabbi Joshua b. Qarḥa (= the bald), What is [the distance] from here to Qarḥina? He said to him, As from here to Gozanya.

B. *Variants*

The Munich MS has לגוזאה; the Oxford MS has לגו חינא.

C. *Attempts at Identification*

Neubauer, p. 389; Hirschenson, *Sheva Ḥokhmot*, p. 223, s.v. "קרחינא." See the entry on "Qarḥina."

Hinṣəvu הינצבו

A. *Source*

Yevamot 85a

רב פפא ורב הונא בריה דרב יהושע איקלעו להינצבו לאתריה דרב אידי בר אבין.

Rav Papa and Rav Huna son of Rav Joshua happened to come to Hinṣəvu to the place of Rav Idi b. Avin.

B. *Variants*

The Munich MS has להיצניה, the Vatican 111 MS does not have the word להינצבו at all, the B-a-ḥ's marginal notes have לשכנצבו; see also the entry on "Šəkanṣiv," note 22.

C. *Attempts at Identification*

Neubauer, p. 390; Eshel, p. 109.

Ḥuṭra חוטרא

A. *Sources*

1. T. J. Shabbat I 11 – 4a, 45–46

אי זהו מקום קרוב ייבא כיי דמר שמואל כגון מן חוטרה לנהרדעא.

What is a nearby place? It corresponds to what Samuel said, As from Ḥuṭra to Nəhardəʿa.

2. T. J. Shevi'it III 2 – 34c, 33 (and other places)

אמר רבי אידי דחוטרא ...

Rabbi Idi of Ḥuṭra said ...

B. *Variants*

On the name of Rabbi Idi's place, see Lieberman, *Yerushalmi ki-Fshuto*, vol. 1, p. 99.

C. *Attempts at Identification*

Various scholars have identified Ḥuṭra as well as the Ḥatar mentioned in the T. B. (Sanhedrin 5b: Tanḥum son of Rabbi Ammi happened to come to Ḥatar) with Ḥaṭra (see Berliner, p. 37; Hirschenson, *Sheva Ḥokhmot*, p .117. On the identification of Ḥatar alone with Ḥaṭra see Neubauer, p. 392; *Arukh ha-Shalem*, vol. 3, p. 522). Ḥaṭra was an important town lying 50 kilometers west of ancient Assur and approximately 80 kilometers southwest of modern Mosul. It owed its prominence as a caravan city to its position on a major trade route connecting Seleucia-Ctesiphon with Nisibis. The identification of Ḥuṭra with Ḥaṭra is untenable because Source 1 indicates the propinquity of the former to Nəhardəʿa (q.v.). Also, taking into account that Rabbi Idi of Ḥuṭra figures several times in the T. J., a location in Eretz Israel seems more reasonable than one in Babylonia. (Funk, *Monumenta*, p. 293, noted the difficulty Source 1 presents for the identification of Ḥuṭra with Ḥaṭra and identified both Ḥuṭra and Ḥatar with Ḥīra. *Arukh ha-Shalem* [vol. 3, p. 375], although citing Source 1, contends that Ḥuṭra is a place in Eretz Israel.) The identification of Ḥatar (חתר) with Ḥaṭra (חטרא; so spelled in Aramaic texts found at the site) is also disallowed because the replacement of /ט/ by /ת/ is unlikely, and because the names of the sages mentioned in connection with Ḥatar suggest that it was in Eretz Israel (I am grateful to Prof. Joseph Naveh for pointing out the impossibility of the identification).

Idit אידית

A. *Source*

Qiddushin 12b

אמרי ליה רבנן לרב חסדא אמאי, הא איכא סהדי באידית דידעי דבההוא יומא הוה ביה שוה פרוטה...

Sages said to Rav Ḥisda, Why? There are witnesses in Idit who know that on that day it held something worth a cent...

B. *Variants*

The Munich MS has באורית'.

C. *Attempts at Identification*

Hirschenson, *Sheva Ḥokhmot*, p. 32. The *Tosafot* favors the Rabbenu Tam version באורית, and says it means "west," that is, Eretz Israel. Cf. the Munich MS version.

Karme כרמי

A. *Source*

Yevamot 121a

דההוא גברא דטבע בכרמי ואסקוהו אבי הדיא לבתר תלתא יומין ואנסבה רב דימי מנהרדעא לדביתהו.

That fellow who drowned in Karme and was brought up three days later at Be Hadya, and Rav Dimi of Nəhardəʿa allowed his wife to remarry.

B. *Variants*

The Vatican 111 MS has כרמא, and see "Be Hadya" above.

C. *Attempts at Identification*

Neubauer, p. 394; Hirschenson, *Sheva Ḥokhmot*, p. 166; Berliner, p. 38; *Arukh ha-Shalem*, vol. 4, p. 330 s.v. "כרם (= כרמא)"; Eshel, p. 137; and see "Be Hadya" above.

D. *Sages and Karme*

The source reports the case of a man drowned in Karme (by analogy with Be Hadya a settlement, but possibly a river or a canal), whose body was pulled out three days later in Be Hadya. Rav Dimi of Nəhardəʿa, of the fourth generation of Babylonian amoras, allowed his widow to remarry. Cf. the entry on "Gišra də-Šabistana."

Kišar כישר

Source

Ḥullin 134b

לוי זרע בכישר ולא הוו עניים למשקל לקט, אתא לקמיה דרב ששת, אמר ליה "לעני ולגר תעזוב אותם" ולא לעורבים ולא לעטלפים.

Levi sowed in Kišar and there were no paupers to take the gleanings. He went to Rav Sheshet who said, "You shall leave them for the poor and stranger" (Lev. 23:22), and not for ravens and bats.

Margu'an מרגואן

A. *Source*

ʿAvodah Zarah 31b

רב שמואל בר ביסנא איקלע למרגואן, אייתו ליה חמרא ולא אשתי, אייתו ליה שיכרא ולא אשתי . . .

Rav Samuel b. Bisna happened to come to Margu'an. They brought him wine and he did not drink, they brought him beer and he did not drink . . .

B. *Variants*

The Munich MS has מרגוז, and see *Diq. Sof.*

C. *Attempts at Identification*

Neubauer, p. 380; Hirschenson, *Sheva Ḥokhmot*, p. 161; Funk, *Monumenta*, p. 295; *Arukh ha-Shalem*, vol. 5, p. 240; Eshel, p. 148.

D. *Sages and Margu'an*

The source reports that Rav Samuel b. Bisna (the Munich MS has "Rav and Samuel . . ."), of the fourth generation of Babylonian amoras, while on a visit to Margu'an, declined to drink the wine and beer of Gentiles he was offered.

Masgarya מסגריא

A. *Source*

Qiddushin 72a

כי הוא ניחא נפשיה דרבי אמר ... מסגריא איכא בבבל כולה דממזירא היא.

When Rabbi was dying he said ... There is Masgarya in Babylonia entirely of *mamzerim*.

B. *Variants*

The Munich and Vatican 111 MSS and the Venice printing have סםגריא.

C. *Attempts at Identification*

Arukh ha-Shalem, vol. 5, p. 184.

D. *Sages and Masgarya*

Masgarya figures in a series of Babylonian places which Rabbi Judah ha-Nasi considered to be flawed. For details see the entries on "Birta" and "Humaniya" and the section on Sages and Šək̲anṣiv in the entry on "Šək̲anṣiv."

Maške משכי

A. *Source*

Menaḥot 43a

מר ממשכי אייתי תכלתא בשני רב אחאי ...

Mar from Maške brought a blue [thread] in the days of Rav Aḥai.

B. *Variants*

The Vatican 123 MS has ממישכי; the Vatican 118 MS has ממשטי.

Note that the Talmud also mentions places called Moške (see the entry on "Nihawand") and Moškani (q.v.).

Mašrunya משרוניא

A. *Source*

Bava Metziʿa 107b

מכריז רבי אמי מלא כתפי נגדי בתרי עברי נהרא קוצו. רב נתן בר הושעיא קץ שיתסר אמתא, אתו עליה בני משרוניא דפנוהו.

Rabbi Ammi declares, The boat towers cut down [vegetation] on both sides of the river. Rav Nathan b. Hoshaʿya cut sixteen cubits. The Mašrunyans came to him and hit him.

B. *Variants*

The Florence MS has משרינא, the Hamburg MS has משריאתא, the Vatican 115 has שרשוניה, and the Vatican 117 MS has משונייה.

C. *Attempts at Identification*

Neubauer, p. 394; Berliner, p. 45; Funk, *Monumenta*, p. 295; *Arukh ha-Shalem*, vol. 5, p. 263, s.v. "מרשניא"; vol. 3, p. 112, s.v. "דפן 2," n. 1.

D. *Sages and Mašrunya*

The source reports that Rav Nathan b. Hosha'ya, of the third generation of Babylonian amoras, was beaten by the Mašrunyans because he cleared a strip sixteen cubits wide along the banks of the river, felling their trees. (The halakhic question involved is how wide a strip of private land along a waterway can be cleared to make a tow path.)

Našiqiya נשיקיא

A. *Source*

Shabbat 121a

רב יהודה ורב ירמיה בר אבא ורב חנן בר רבא איקלעו לבי אבין דמן נשיקיא.

Rav Judah and Rav Jeremiah b. Abba and Rav Ḥanan b. Rava happened to come to the house of Avin from Našiqiya.

B. *Variants*

The Munich MS has מנשיקאה.

C. *Attempts at Identification*

Hirschenson, *Sheva Ḥokhmot*, p. 172; *Arukh ha-Shalem*, vol. 5. p. 395, s.v. "נשיקאה."

Nazunya נזוניא

A. *Source*

Qiddushin 25a

סבי דנזוניא לא אתו לפירקיה דרב חסדא . . .

The elders of Nazunya did not come to the *pirqa* of Rav Ḥisda . . .

B. *Variants*

The Munich MS has מזוניא, the Vatican 111 MS has נרוניא, and the Venice printings has גיזוניא.

C. *Attempts at Identification*

Funk, *Monumenta*, p. 296; Obermeyer, pp. 298–299; Eshel, p. 187.

Parhaṭya פרהטיא

A. *Source*

Qiddushin 81a

א"ל רב נחמן מפרהטיא לרב אשי...

Rav Naḥman of Parhaṭya said to Rav Ashi . . .

B. *Variants*

The Munich MS has רב רחומי מפרזקיא (see the entry on "Parziqiya"); the Vatican 111 MS has מפרהטיה.

C. *Attempts at Identification*

Neubauer, p. 396, n. 1; Hirschenson, *Sheva Ḥokhmot*, p. 197; Funk, *Monumenta*, p. 298; *Arukh ha-Shalem*, vol. 6, p. 451.

Qalnəvo קלנבו

A. *Sources*

1. Sanhedrin 63b

כי אתא עולא בת בקלנבו, אמר ליה רבא והיכא בת מר, אמר ליה בקלנבו. אמר ליה והכתיב "ושם אלהים אחרים לא תזכירו," אמר ליה הכי אמר רבי יוחנן כל עבודת כוכבים הכתובה בתורה מותר להזכיר שמה, והא היכא כתיבא, דכתיב "כרע בל קרס נבו."

When ‘Ulla came he lodged in Qalnəvo. Rava said to him, And where did you lodge? He said to him, In Qalnəvo. He said to him, But it says, "Do not mention the name of other gods" (Ex. 23:13). He said to him, Rabbi Yoḥanan said, Any idolatry written in the Torah may be mentioned. And where is it written? It says, "Bel bows down, Nebo stoops" (Is. 46:1).

2. Yoma 21a, Zevaḥim 96a

והתניא רב שמעיא בקלנבו...

For Rav Shema‘ya taught in Qalnəvo . . .

B. *Variants*

The Florence and Karlsruhe MSS have בקל נבו in Sanhedrin. In Yoma, the Munich MSS has "Resh Laqish" ("Qalnəvo" does not appear), the Oxford MS has "Rav Simeon" and the London MS has "Rav" ("Qalnəvo" does not appear). Zevaḥim has "Shemaʿya in Qalnəvo" (without "Rav").

C. *Attempts at Identification*

Hirschenson, *Sheva Ḥokhmot*, p. 214; Funk, *Monumenta*, p. 299, who believes the name was Kar Nebo, i.e., the city of Nebo. The element *kar*, which means "city" in Assyrian Babylonian, appeared in other place names as well. If Funk's view is accepted, the Karnəvo mentioned in Bava Batra 91a could be included here: **ואמר רב חנן בר רבא אמר רב אמיה דאברהם אמתלאי בת כרנבו.** (= And Rav Ḥanan b. Rava said Rav said, The mother of Abraham Amatlai daughter of Karnəvo); Eshel, p. 226; *Arukh ha-Shalem*, vol. 2, p. 214, s.v. "בת"; *Tosefot Arukh ha-Shalem*, p. 363.

D. *Sages and Qalnəvo*

Source 1 mentions ʿUlla, who was one of the *naḥote* (sages who traveled between Eretz Israel and Babylonia to bring the law of Eretz Israel to Babylonia), staying overnight in Qalnəvo and being questioned by Rav. The Munich and Karlsruhe MSS have "Rav Naḥman" (not "Rava") which is more logical since both ʿUlla and Rav Naḥman belonged to the third generation of Babylonian amoras. Source 2 mentions a sage named Rav Shemaʿya in (or from) Qalnəvo.

Qalonya קלוניא

A. *Source*

Yevamot 115b

...דההוא גיטא דאשתכח בנהרדעא וכתיב בצד קלוניא מתא...

... that bill of divorcement found in Nəhardəʿa and written near the settlement of Qalonya ...

B. *Variants*

The Vatican 111 MS has קלניא.

C. *Attempts at Identification*

Neubauer, p. 397.

Qaqunya קקוניא

A. *Source*

ʿEruvin 60a

הנהו בני קקונאי דאתי לקמיה דרב יוסף אמרו ליה הב לן גברא דליערב לן מאתין, אמר ליה לאביי זיל ערב להו וחזי דלא מצווחת עלה בבי מדרשא. אזל חזא להנהו בתי דפתיחי לנהרא . . .

Those Qaqunya people who came before Rav Joseph said to him, Give us a man to lay an *ʿeruv* in our city. He said to Abbaye, Go and lay them an *ʿeruv*, and see that there is no outcry about it in the study house. He started out, and saw those houses that were open to the river . . .

B. *Variants*

The source has קקונאי; the Munich MS has קויקוניא (or קוקוניא), the Oxford MS has קקוניא, and the Salonika printing has קנקוני; see also *Diq. Sof.*

C. *Attempts at Identification*

Hirschenson, *Sheva Ḥokhmot*, p. 221; Berliner, p. 60; Funk, *Monumenta*, p. 299; *Arukh ha-Shalem*, vol. 7, p. 215, s.v. "קורקוניא"; Eshel, p. 227. Underlying all attempts at identification is the question of whether Qaqunya is another form of Qurqunya (q.v.) or a separate place (see also Neusner, *History*, vol. 4, pp. 172, 174).

D. *Sages and Qaqunya*

In the source above, Rav Joseph of the third generation of Babylonian amoras, who headed the Pumbədita yeshiva after Rabbah's death, assigns Abbaye the task of laying an *ʿeruv* in Qaqunya at the request of its inhabitants.

Qarmanya קרמניא

A. *Sources*

1. Bava Qamma 21a

ההוא מעיקרא קרמנאי הוו דיירי ביה . . .

There from the outset the Qarmanyans lived there . . .

2. Nazir 31b

בתורא דקרמנאי . . .

About an ox of the Qarmanyans . . .

3. Shabbat 138a

. . . הא דקאמר אף מטה אסורה כדקרמנאי.

. . . as is said that even a bed is forbidden (to be opened on the Sabbath) [means] like that of the Qarmanyans.

B. *Variants*

In Bava Qamma the Munich MS has קדמאי and the Vatican 116 MS has קדמונאי. In Nazir, the standard edition has דקרמונאי further on in the passage. In Shabbat, the Munich MS has בדקמינאי.

C. *Attempts at Identification*

Qarmanya is the name of a region or country inhabited by the Qarmanyans (cf. Source 14 in the entry on "Babylon"). Neubauer, p. 384; Hirschenson, *Sheva Ḥohkmot*, p. 24; *Arukh ha-Shalem*, vol. 7, p. 202f.; *Tosefot Arukh ha-Shalem*, p. 376; Eshel, p. 230.

Qarṭigne קרטיגני

A. *Sources*

1. Menaḥot 110a

אמר רבי אבא בר רב יצחק אמר רב חסדא, ואמרי לה אמר רב יהודה אמר רב, מצור ועד קרטיגני מכירין את ישראל ואת אביהם שבשמים ומצור כלפי מערב ומקרטיגני כלפי מזרח אין מכירין את ישראל ולא את אביהן שבשמים.

Rabbi Abba b. Rav Isaac said Rav Ḥisda said, and some say Rav Judah said Rav said, From Tyre to Qarṭigne they know [the people of] Israel and their Father in heaven, and from Tyre westwards and Qarṭigne eastwards they do not know Israel and their Father in heaven.

2. Berakhot 29a

א"ר יצחק דמן קרטיגנין.

Rabbi Isaac from Qarṭignin said.

3. Ketubot 27b

כי הא דכי אתא רב דימי אמר רב חנן קרטיגנאה משתעי . . .

Such as when Rav Dimi came he said Rav Ḥanan Qarṭigna'a tells . . .

4. Bava Qamma 114b

והא כי אתא רב דימי אמר רב חנא קרטיגנא, ואמרי לה רב אחא קרטיגנא מישתעי . . .

For when Rav Dimi came he said Rav Ḥana Qarṭigna, and some say Rav Aḥa Qarṭigna, tells . . .

5. T. J. Shabbat XVI 2 – 15c, 56

. . . דמר רבי יעקב בר אחא אמר חיננא קרתיגנאה בשם רבי הושעיה . . .

. . . Rabbi Jacob b. Aḥa said Ḥinena Qartigna'a said in the name of Rabbi Hosha'ya . . .

6. T. J .Shevi'it VI 1–36b, 53; Genesis Rabbah XLIV 23 (Theodor-Albeck ed., p. 446)

... רבי ליעזר בן יעקב אומר אסייא וקרתיגני ותורקי.

... Rabbi Liezer b. Jacob says, Asia and Qartigne and Turqe.

B. *Variants*

In Berakhot, the Munich MS has "Rava from קרטגני," and see *Diq. Sof.* The T. J. parallel (Berakhot IV 3–8a, 18) has "Rabbi Abba קרטיגניא" (that sage appears in several other places in the T. J.). For Ketubot, see Ketubot in the ICIT edition. In Bava Qamma the Munich MS has קרתיגנאה both times; the Vatican 116 MS has "Rav Ḥana בגדתאה and some say Rav Ḥanah קרתי גינאה," and see *Diq. Sof.* for additional variants. Genesis Rabbah has קרטגינא, and see the variants in the Theodor-Albeck edition.

C. *Attempts at Identification*

Source 1 makes it clear that the name does not refer to Carthage, but to some region or country east of Babylonia. Obermeyer (p. 134f.) believed Qarṭigne to be Qardu (q.v.). See also Neubauer, p. 411; Hirschenson, *Sheva Ḥokhmot*, p. 233f.; *Arukh ha-Shalem*, vol. 7, p. 219–220; *Tosefot Arukh ha-Shalem*, p. 378; Eshel, p. 229f.

Qašta קשתא

Source

Bava Batra 41b

ההוא גברא דדר בקשתא בעיליתא ארבע שני.

That man who lived in Qašta in an attic for four years.

Qaṭarziya קטרזיא

A. *Source*

Megillah 21b

רב ששת מקטרזיא איקלע לקמיה דרב אשי...

Rav Sheshet of Qaṭarziya happened to come before Rav Ashi ...

B. *Variants*

The Munich MS has מקטרזא, and מקטריא further on; see also *Diq. Sof.*

Qube קובי

A. *Source*

Qiddushin 8a

כי הא דמר בר רב אשי זבן סודרא מאימיה דרבה מקובי...

Such as Mar b. Rav Ashi, bought a scarf from the mother of Rabbah of Qube...

B. *Variants*

The Munich MS does not have the word Qube at all; the Vatican 111 MS has מבי כובי and see the entry on "Be Kube."

C. *Attempts at Identification*

Hirschenson, *Sheva Ḥokhmot*, p. 209; Eshel, p. 224 (there is no connection between this Qube and the Qube in T. B. Sanhedrin 95a which was certainly not in Babylonia).

D. *Sages and Qube*

Mar bar Rav Ashi, of the seventh generation of Babylonian amoras, is mentioned in the source above as having bought a scarf from the mother of Rabbah (or Rava, in other versions) of Qube.

Rabbat רבת

A. *Source*

Sanhedrin 92b

וא"ר יוחנן מנהר אשל עד רבת בקעת דורא.

And Rabbi Yoḥanan said, From the Ešel river to Rabbat [in the] Dura valley.

B. *Variants*

The Munich MS has דוכתי; the Soncino edition has דוכתא; the entire sentence is omitted in the Florence MS. See also *Diq. Sof.*

C. *Attempts at Identification*

Eshel, p. 232.

Šamgaz שמגז

A. *Source*

Giṭṭin 70a; ʿAvodah Zarah 12b

...רביעתא דחלא שמגז.

... A quarter of the Šamgaz vinegar.

B. *Variants*

In Giṭṭin, the standard edition has שמזג, the Munich MS has שמגד and the Vatican 140 MS has שמגזי׳; see also *Diq. Sof.* (Feldblum). In ʿAvodah Zarah the Munich MS has שמגן.

Samqe סמקי

A. *Source*

Yevamot 121a

ההוא גברא דטבע באגמא דסמקי, אנסבה רב שילא לדביתהו...

That man who drowned in the lake of Samqe, Rav Shela allowed his wife to remarry ...

B. *Variants*

The place is mentioned a second time in the same passage. In the Munich MS the form אגמא דסמקא appears in the first instance and אגמה דסמקי in the second.

C. *Attempts at Identification*

Neubauer, pp. 395–396.

Sanwata סנוותא

A. *Source*

Shabbat 17b, ʿAvodah Zarah 36b

אמר באלי אמר אבימי סנוותאה.

Bali said, Avimi Sanwata'a said.

B. *Variants*

In Shabbat the Munich MS has נתוואה, the Oxford MS has ניותאה. In ʿAvodah Zarah the standard edition has נותאה, the Munich MS has simply "Avimi" and the Spanish MS edited by Abramson has ניתואה.

C. *Attempts at Identification*

Hirschenson, *Sheva Ḥohkmot*, pp. 42–43, s.v. "אקרא דשנואתה."

D. *Sages and Sanwata*

Bali, of the fourth generation of Babylonian amoras, cites Avimi Sanwata'a (*Arukh ha-Shalem* maintains it is not a place-name but intended to indicate Avimi's provenance from the land of the Nabateans [vol. 5, p. 324, s.v. "נוותי"; vol. 6, p. 85, s.v. "סנוותאה"]). The Rabbi Eliezer Niyuta'a (ניותאה) mentioned in Giṭṭin 50a may also belong to Sanwata.

Šawire שוירי

A. *Source*

Bava Metzi'a 18a–b, 20a–b; Giṭṭin 27a

דההוא גיטא דאשתכח בי דינא דרב הונא דהוה כתוב ביה בשוירי מתא דעל רכיס נהרא, אמר רב הונא חיישינן לשני שוירי . . .

That bill of divorcement found in the court of Rav Huna that said, at Šawire a place on the Ra<u>k</u>is river. Rav Huna said, We fear there are two Šawires . . .

B. *Attempts at Identification*

Neubauer, p. 398; Hirschenson, *Sheva Ḥokhmot*, p. 234; Funk, *Juden*, vol. 2, p. 149f.; Funk, *Monumenta*, p. 300; Obermeyer, p. 299; *Arukh ha-Shalem*, vol. 7, p. 277, s.v. "רכיס"; *Tosefot Arukh ha-Shalem*, p. 383, s.v. "רכיס"; Eshel, p. 236f.

Səqasna סקסנא

A. *Source*

Niddah 65a

מנימין סקסנאה הוה שקיל ואזיל לאתריה דשמואל, סבר למעבד עובדא כוותיה דרב.

Menjamin Səqasna'a took [his cloak] and went to Samuel's place; he wanted to decide a case according to Rav.

B. *Variants*

The Munich MS has סקוסנא' and the Vatican 111 MS has סכסאה.

C. *Attempts at Identification*

Hirschenson, *Sheva Ḥokhmot*, p. 180; Berliner, p. 57; Eshel, p. 202.

D. *Sages and Səqasna*

The source reports Menjamin of Səqasna going to Samuel, head of the Nəhardəʿa yeshiva in the first generation of Babylonian amoras, and seeking to act according to Rav's rulings. *Arukh ha-Shalem* says that *seqasna'a* does not designate a place at all, but is an epithet applied to Menjamin who was "wily and crafty." T.J. Berakhot (II 6 – 5b, 15) has the same episode, but the name there is Benjamin Ginzak̲ya, that is, Benjamin of Ginzak (see the entry on "Ginzaq").

Ṣiqonya ציקוניא

A. *Source*

Ḥullin 39b

הנהו טייעי דאתו לציקוניא יהיב דיכרי לטבחי ישראל . . .

Those Arabs that came to Ṣiqonya gave rams to the Jewish butchers . . .

B. *Variants*

The Vatican 121 and 122 MSS have לצקוניא; the Vatican 123 MS has לציקניא.

C. *Attempts at Identification*

Neubauer, p. 397; Berliner, p. 60; Funk, *Monumenta*, p. 299; Obermeyer, p. 234.

For the import of the source, see the section on Economy in the entry on "Mavrak̲ta."

Ṣita ציתא

See "Barṣita."

Ṣuṣita צוציתא

A. *Source*

Shabbat 56b

אמר רב יוסף ועוד אחד בדורנו, ומנו, עוקבן בר נחמיה ריש גלותא והיינו נתן דצוציתא.

Rav Joseph said, And there is another (penitent) in our generation, and who is it, ʿUqban b. Nehemiah, the Exilarch, and that is Nathan of Ṣuṣita.

B. *Attempts at Identification*

No proposals for identification have been made, and in the opinion of various exegetes *ṣuṣita* is not a place but a trait; see *Arukh ha-Shalem*, vol. 5, p. 397, s.v. "נתן." Nathan of Ṣuṣita is also mentioned in Seder Olam Zuṭa (Grossberg ed., p. 35). See also Epstein, *MGWJ* 63 (1919): 263; Boyarin, *Tarbiẕ* 50 (1981): 164–175.

Ṣuṣyan צוציין

A. *Source*

Ḥullin 62b

אמר רב יהודה הני כופשני צוצייני כשרים לגבי מזבח ... רבא אמר הני כופשני צוצייני באתרייהו סתמא קרי להו.

Rav Judah said, Those turtle-doves of Ṣuṣyan are fit for the altar ... Rava said, Those turtle-doves of Ṣuṣyan are called simply [turtle-doves] in their place.

B. *Variants*

The Hamburg and Vatican 123 MSS have **דצוציני**; the Vatican 121 MS has **צוצאני**.

C. *Attempts at Identification*

Neubauer, p. 396f.; Funk, *Monumenta*, p. 299. There is also a possibility that it is not a place name at all but designates the kind of dove (crested); see *Arukh ha-Shalem*, vol. 7, p. 40, s.v. "צץ 3"; vol. 4, p. 306, s.v. "כפשני." See also Boyarin, *Tarbiẕ* 50 (1981): 174f.

Tusanya תוסנייא

A. *Source*

Yevamot 21b

שלח ליה רב משרשיא מתוסנייא לרב פפי ילמדנו רבינו ...

Rav Mesharsheya of Tusanya applied to Rav Papi, May our master teach us ...

B. *Variants*

The Munich MS has **מתרבוניא** and the Vatican 111 MS has **מתסיניא**.

C. *Attempts at Identification*

Obermeyer, p. 229, reads this as Astunya, and see Source 31 in the entry on "Pumbədita" as well as the section on the Pumbədita Periphery, and note 85 there.

Zəroqinya זרוקיניא

A. *Source*

Ḥullin 111a

מתקיף לה רב אשי ואיתימא רבי שמואל מזרוקיניא . . .

Rav Ashi objected, and some say Rabbi Samuel of Zəroqinya . . .

B. *Variants*

The Munich, Hamburg and Vatican 122 MSS have מזרקוניא, and the Vatican 121 MS has מאקרוקניא (on this version see the entry on "Qurqunya).”

C. *Attempts at Identification*

Obermeyer, p. 80; Eshel, p. 116; see also Funk, *Monumenta*, p. 292.

Bibliography

Abramson, S., *Ba-Merkazim u-va-Tefutzot bi-Tequfat ha-Geonim*, Jerusalem 1965.

— "Min 'Kitāb al-ḥāwī' (Sefer ha-Me'asef) le-Rav Hai Gaon," *Leshonenu* 41 (1977): 108–116.

Abu al-Soof, B., "Short Sounding at Tel Qalinj Agha (Erbil)," *Sumer* 22 (1966): 77–82.

Abu al-Soof, B. and Es-Siwwani, S., "More Soundings at Tell Qalinj Agha (Erbil)," *Sumer* 23 (1967): 69–75.

Adams, R. Mc., "Agriculture and Urban Life in Early Southwestern Iran," *Science* 136 (1962): 109–122.

— *Land Behind Baghdad, A History of Settlement on the Diyala Plains*, Chicago & London, 1965.

Adams, R. Mc. and Hansen, D. P., "Archaeological Reconnaissance and Soundings in Jundī Shāhpūr," with a historical sketch by N. Abbott, *Ars Orientalis* 7 (1968): 53–73.

Adams, R. Mc. and Nissen, H. J., *The Uruk Countryside*, Chicago 1972.

Adler, N., *Itinerary of Benjamin of Tudela*, London 1907 (repr. New York, no date).

Ahmed, S. S., "Early Parthian Philhellenism as Evidenced in Figurines from Seleucia on the Tigris," *Annales Archéologiques de la Syrie* 17 (1967): 85ff.

Albeck, Ch., "Sof ha-Hora'ah ve-Aḥaronei ha-Amora'im," *Sinai, Sefer Yovel*, Jerusalem 1958, pp. 57–73.

— *Mavo la-Talmudim*, Tel Aviv 1969.

al-'Alī, Ṣ. A., "al-Ḫulafā' wa-quṣūruhum fī Baġdād fi l-'uhūd al-'abbāsīya al-ūlā," *Sumer* 32 (1976): 145–189.

— "Al-Madā'in fī l-maṣādir l-'arabīya," *Sumer* 23 (1967): 47–67.

— "Minṭaqat al-Kūfa," *Sumer* 21 (1965): 229–252.

Alon, G., "M. D. Yudelevitz's *Yeshivat Pumbedita b-Ymei ha-Amora'im*" (review), *Meḥqarim be-Toledot Yisrael*, vol. 2, Tel Aviv 1958, pp. 298–302.

— *Toledot ha-Yehudim be-Eretz Yisrael bi-Tequfat ha-Mishnah we-ha-Talmud*, I–II, Tel Aviv 1954–1956.

— "The Levitical Uncleanness of Gentiles," in *Jews, Judaism and the Classical World; Studies in Jewish History in the Times of the Second Temple and Talmud*, Jerusalem 1977, pp. 146–189.

— *The Jews in Their Land in the Talmudic Age (70–640 C.E.)*, vol. 1, Jerusalem 1980.

Altheim, F., and Stiehl, R., *Ein asiatischer Staat*, Wiesbaden 1954.

Andreas, F. C., "Alexandria 13," *RE*, vol. 1, col. 1390f.

— "Ambara," *RE*, vol. 1, cols. 1790–1795.

Artzi, P., "Kalneh 1" & "Kalneh 2," *Entziqlopedia Miqra'it*, vol. 4, pp. 185–186.

— "Reḥovot 'Ir," *Entziqlopedia Miqra'it*, vol. 7, p. 352.

Assaf, S., "Biqoret al Obermeyer, *Die Landschaft*," *Kiryat Sefer* 7 (1930): 61–62.

Avigad, N., *Bet She'arim*, vol. 3, Jerusalem 1976.

Avi-Yonah, M., assisted by Safrai S., *Atlas Karta li-Tequfat Bayit Sheni, ha-Mishnah we-ha-Talmud*, Jerusalem 1966.

'Awwād, G., "Āṯāru l-'Irāq fī naẓari l-kuttābi l-'arabi l-aqdamīna," *Sumer* 5 (1949): 65–74, 242–253.

— "Taḥqīqāt buldānīya ta'rīḫīya aṯarīya fī šarqi l-Mauṣil," *Sumer* 17 (1961): 43–99.

— "Bābil," *EI*[1]; "Barāṯā," *EI*[2].

Aymard, A., "Une ville de la Babylonie séleucide," *RÉA* 40 (1948): 5–42 (= *Études d'histoire ancienne* [1967]: 178–211).

Bacher, W., *Die Agada der palästinensischen Amoräer*, Strasbourg 1892 (repr. Hildesheim 1965).
— *Agada der Tannaiten*, Strasbourg 1884–1890.
— *Die Agada der babylonischen Amoräer*, Frankfurt a.M. 1913 (repr. Hildesheim 1967).
— *Tradition und Tradenten in den Schulen Palästinas und Babyloniens*, Leipzig 1914 (repr. Berlin 1966).
Barnett, R. D., "Xenophon and the Wall of Media," *JHS* 83 (1963): 1–26.
Baron, S. W., *A Social and Religious History of the Jews*, vol. 3, Philadelphia 1957[3].
Barthold, W., and Boyle, J. A., "Gandja," *EI*[2].
Beer, M., "Rivo shel Geniva be-Mar Uqba," *Tarbiẓ* 31 (1962): 281–286.
— "Li-She'elat Shiḥruram shel Amora'ei Bavel mi-Tashlum Misim u-Mekhes," *Tarbiẓ* 33 (1964): 349–357.
— "Exilarchs of the Talmudic Epoch Mentioned in R. Sherira's Responsum," *PAAJR* 35 (1967): 43–74.
— *Rashut ha-Golah be-Bavel b-Ymei ha-Mishnah we-ha-Talmud*, Tel Aviv 1970.
— *Amora'ei Bavel, Peraqim be-Ḥayei ha-Kalkalah*, Ramat Gan 1974.
Bellinger, A. R., "Hyspaosines of Charax," *YCS* 8 (1942): 51–67.
Beloch, K. L., *Griechische Geschichte*, III 1, Berlin 1904.
Ben Hayyim, Z., "Ketovot Tadmoriot," *Yedi'ot be-Ḥaqirat Eretz Yisrael we-Atiqoteha* 13 (1947): 141–148.
Bengtson, H., *Die Strategie in der hellenistischen Zeit*, I–III, Munich 1937–1952.
vanden Berghe, L., *Archéologie de l'Iran Ancien*, Leiden 1959.
Berliner, A., *Beiträge zur Geographie und Ethnographie Babyloniens im Talmud und Midrasch, Jahres-Bericht des Rabbiner-Seminars zu Berlin, (1882–1883)*, Berlin 1883.
Bevan, A. A., *The Hymn of the Soul Contained in the Syriac Acts of St. Thomas*, Texts and Studies, vol. 3, Cambridge 1897.
Bewsher, J. B., "On Part of Mesopotamia Contained Between Sheriat-el-Beytha, on the Tigris, and Tel Ibrahim," *JRGS* 37 (1867): 160–182.
Birley, A., *Marcus Aurelius*, London 1966.
Blau, O., "Altarabische Sprachstudien," *ZDMG* 27 (1873): 295–363.
Bonsaca, N., "Samosata," *Enciclopedia dell'Arte Antica*, vol. 6, p. 1102.
Bouché-Leclercq, A., *Histoire des Séleucides*, vol. 2, Paris 1914.
Boyarin, D., "La-Leqsiqon ha-Talmudi," *Tarbiẓ* 50 (1981): 164–191.
Brand, J., *Kelei ha-Ḥeres be-Sifrut ha-Talmud*, Jerusalem 1953.
Brok, M. F. A., *De Perzische Expeditie van Keizer Julianus volgens Ammianus Marcellinus*, Groningen 1959.
Broshi, M., "Karkamish," *Entziqlopedia Miqra'it*, vol. 4, pp. 313–317.
Buber, S., "Einleitung und Ergänzungen zum Arukh von Rabbi Samuel ben Jacob G'ama," *Graetz Jubelschrift*, Breslau 1887.
Büchler, A., *Der galiläische 'Am-ha'Areṣ des zweiten Jahrhunderts*, Vienna 1906 (repr. Hildesheim 1968).
Budge, E. A. W., *The Histories of Rabban Hormizd the Persian and Rabban Bar-'Idtā'*, London 1902.
Buhl, F., "'Ād," *EI*[1,2]; "Palmyra," *EI*[1].
Caetani, L., *Annali dell'Islam*, Milan 1905–1926.
Callu, J. P., *La politique monétaire des empereurs romains de 238 à 311*, Paris 1969.
Cameron, G. G., *History of Early Iran*, Chicago 1936.
Cantineau, J., Starcky, J. & Teixidor, J., *Inventaire des Inscriptions de Palmyre*, I–XI, Beirut 1930–1965.
Cantineau, J., "Textes palmyréniens provenant de la fouille du temple de Bél," *Syria* 12 (1931): 116–141.

— "La Susiane dans une inscription palmyrénienne," *Mélanges syriens offerts à M. René Dussaud*, vol. 1, Paris 1939, pp. 277–279.
Carmoly, E., *Notice historique sur Benjamin de Tudela*, vol. 2, Brussels 1852.
Caskel, W., "Aʿshā," *EI*².
Chaumont, M. L., "Études d'histoire parthe III, Les villes fondées par les vologèse," *Syria* 51 (1974): 76–89.
Christensen, A., *L'Iran sous les sassanides*, Copenhagen 1944².
Christian, V., "Susa," *RE*, suppl. vol. 7, cols. 1251–1274.
Conteneau, G., "Monuments parthes provenants de Suse," *Bulletin des Musées de France* (1948): 87–89.
Cohen, G. M., *The Seleucid Colonies* (*Historia, Einzelschriften* 30 [1978]).
Crawford, V. E., "Nippur, the Holy City," *Archaeology* 12 (1959): 74–83.
Curzon, G. N., *Persia and the Persian Question*, London 1892.
Dan, Y., "Yehudim ba-Mishḥar ba-Oqeyanus ha-Hodi Lifnei Tequfat ha-Islam," *Meḥqarim be-Toledot Am Yisrael we-Eretz Yisrael*, vol. 5, Haifa 1980, pp. 147–158.
Debevoise, N. C., *Parthian Pottery from Seleucia on the Tigris*, Ann Arbor 1934.
— *The Political History of Parthia*, Chicago 1938.
ad-Din, A. G., "Muʿǧam ǧuġrāfiyat Wāsiṭ," *Sumer* 13 (1957): 119–147.
Dieulafoy, M., *L'Art antique de la Perse*, I–V, Paris 1884–1885.
Dillemann, L., *Haute Mésopotamie orientale et pays adjacents, Contribution à la géographie historique de la région, du Vᵉ s. avant l'ère chrétienne au VIᵉ s. de cette ère*, Paris 1962.
— "Ammien Marcellin et les pays de l'Euphrate et du Tigre," *Syria* 38 (1961): 85–158.
Dinur, B. Z., *Yisrael ba-Golah*, vol. 1, pt. 1, Tel Aviv 1958².
Dobiaš, J., *Listy Filologické* 58 (1931): 11–15.
Dörner, F. K., *Kommagene, ein wiederentdecktes Königreich*, 1967².
Dörner, F. K., & Naumann, R., *Forschungen in Kommagene, Istanbuler Forschungen* 10, Berlin 1939.
Drijvers, H. J. W., *Bardaiṣan of Edessa*, Assen 1966.
— "Hatra, Palmyra und Edessa," *ANRW* II 8, Berlin-New York 1977, pp. 803–837, 863–896, 902–904.
Droysen, J. G., *Geschichte des Hellenismus*, I–III, Gotha 1977–1978².
Du Mesnil du Buisson, C., *Les Peintures de la synagogue de Doura Europos*, Rome 1939.
Dumont, A., *Revue Archéologique*, nouvelle série 20 (1869): 191–207 = *Mélanges d'archeologie et d'épigraphie*, Paris 1892, pp. 136–140.
Dunant, C., "Nouvelle inscription caravanière de Palmyre," *Museum Helveticum* 13 (1956): 216–225.
Duri, A. A., "Baghdad," *EI*², p. 894.
Eadie, J. W., *The Breviarium of Festus*, London 1967.
*EI*², s.vv. "Bāzabdā," "Ḳardā" (unsigned).
Eisenstein, J. D., *Otzar Masaʿot*, New York 1926 (repr. Tel Aviv 1969).
Eliot, H. W., *Excavations in Mesopotamia and Western Iran, sites of 4000–500*, Cambridge, Mass. 1950.
Ellis, R. S., *A Bibliography of Mesopotamian Archaeological Sites*, Wiesbaden 1972.
Elon, M., *Ḥerut ha-Perat be-Darkei Geviyat Ḥov ba-Mishpat ha-Ivri*, Jerusalem 1964.
Epstein, J. N., „Philologisch-historische Miszellen," *MGWJ* 63 (1919): 253–268.
— "Mi-Diqduqei Yerushalmi: Ketav Yad Leiden," *Tarbiẓ* 5 (1934): 257–272.
— *Mevo'ot le-Sifrut ha-Tana'im*, Jerusalem-Tel Aviv 1957.
— *Diqduq Aramit Bavlit*, Jerusalem 1960.
— *Mevo'ot le-Sifrut ha-Amora'im*, Jerusalem-Tel Aviv 1962.
— *Mavo le-Nusaḥ ha-Mishnah*, Tel Aviv 1964.

Eshel, B.-Z., *Yishuvei ha-Yehudim be-Bavel bi-Tequfat ha-Talmud, Onomastiqon Talmudi*, Jerusalem 1979.

Falkenstein, A., *Topographie von Uruk, I. Teil Uruk zur Seleukidenzeit* (Ausgrabungen der Deutschen Forschungsgemeinschaft in Uruk-Warka 3) Leipzig 1941.

Felix, J., *Ha-Ḥaqla'ut be-Eretz Yisrael bi-Tequfat ha-Mishnah we-ha-Talmud*, Jerusalem-Tel Aviv 1963.

— *Kilei Zera'im we-Harkava, Masekhet Kilayim, Mishnah, Tosefta w-Yrushalmi li-Feraqim I–II*, Tel Aviv 1967.

Feuchtwang, D., "Assyriologische Studien," *MGWJ* 42 (1898): 145–154.

Février, J. G., *Essai sur l'histoire politique et économique de Palmyre*, Paris 1931.

Fiey, J. M., "Auteur et date de la chronique d'Arbèla," *L'Orient Syrien* 12 (1967): 265–302.

— "Topography chrétienne de Maḥoze," *L'Orient Syrien* 12 (1967): 397–420.

— "Topography of al-Madā'in," *Sumer* 23 (1967): 3–38.

— *Assyrie chrétienne*, Beirut, vol. 1, 1965; vol. 3, 1968.

— *Jalons pour une Histoire de l'Église en Iraq*, (*CSCO* vol. 36), Louvain 1970.

— *Nisibe, métropole syriaque orientale et ses suffragants des origines à nos jours*, (*CSCO* vol. 54), Louvain 1977.

— *Communautés syriaques en Iran et Irak des origines à 1552*, London 1979.

Finster, B., & Schmidt, J., 'Sasanidische und frühislamische Ruinen im Iraq,' *Baghdader Mitteilungen* 8 (1976).

Fisher, C. S., *Excavations at Nippur*, Philadelphia 1905.

Fisher, W. B., *The Cambridge History of Iran*, vol. 1, Cambridge 1968.

Florsheim, J., "Yisudan we-Reshit Hitpatḥutan shel Yeshivot Bavel—Sura u-Pumbedita," *Zion* 39 (1974): 183–197.

Fraenkel, S., "Apameia," *RE* vol. 1, col. 2664.

— *Die aramäischen Fremdwörter im Arabischen*, Leiden 1886 (repr. Hildesheim 1962).

Franco, F., "Five Aramaic Incantation Bowls," *Mesopotamia* 13/14 (1978–1979): 233–249.

Frankel, Z., *Darkei ha-Mishnah, ha-Tosefta, Mekhilta, Sifra, Sifrei*, Tel Aviv 1959².

Fransīs, B., & 'Awwād, K., "Nubaḏ ta'rīḫīya fī uṣūl asmā'i l-amkina l-'irāqīya wa-fawā'id hāḏā l-baḥṯ," *Sumer* 8 (1952): 236–280.

Friedlander, I., "The Arabic Original of the Report of R. Nathan Hababli," *JQR* 17 (1905): 747–761.

Frye, R. N., "Hamadhān," *EI²*.

Funk, S., *Die Juden in Babylonien 200–500*, Berlin, vol. 1, 1902; vol. 2, 1908.

— "Beiträge zur Geographie des Landes Babel," *Jahrbuch der Jüdisch-Literarischen Gesellschaft*, vol. 6, Frankfurt 1908–1909, pp. 324–343.

— "Beiträge zur Geographie des Landes Babel," *Jahrbuch der Jüdisch-Literarischen Gesellschaft*, vol. 9, Frankfurt 1911–1912, pp. 198–213.

— *Monumenta Talmudica*, vol. 1, *Bibel und Babel*, Vienna & Leipzig 1913 (= *Monumenta Hebraica*). (repr. Darmstadt 1972).

— *Die Stadt Nehardea und ihre Hochschule, Sonderabdruck aus Festschrift zum 70. Geburtstage D. Hoffmann's*, Berlin 1914.

Furneaux, H., *The Annals of Tacitus*, Oxford 1896² (repr. 1934).

Gafni, I., "Ha'ala'at Metim li-Qevurah ba-Aretz," *Cathedra* 4 (1977): 113–120.

— *Ha-Yeshivah be-Bavel* (Ph. D. Thesis, Hebrew U., Jerusalem 1978).

Ǧawād, M., ed. *Baġdād*, published by the Engineers' Union of Iraq, Baghdad 1969.

Gawlikowski, M., *Le temple palmyrénien, Étude d'épigraphie et de topographie historique*, Warsaw 1973.

Geiger, B., "Mittelpersische Wörter und Sachen," *WZKM* 42 (1935): 114–128.

Getzow, H. N., *Al Neharot Bavel*, Warsaw 1887.

Ghirshman, R., "Un bas-relief d'Artaban V avec inscription en pehlevi arsacide," *Monuments et Mémoires Fondation Piot* 44 (1950): 97–107.
— "Iran," *AJA* 55 (1951): 96.
— *Cinq campagnes de fouilles à Suse (1946–1951)*, Mémoires de la Mission Archéologique en Iran, Mission de Susiane, Rapports préliminaires I, Paris 1952.
— *Village perse achemenid*, Mémoires de la Mission Archéologique en Iran, vol. 36), Paris 1954.
— *Iran; From the Earliest Times to the Islamic Conquest*, Harmondsworth 1954.
Gibson, M., *The City and Area of Kish*, Coconut Grove, Florida 1972.
— "Nippur 1972–1973," *Expedition* 16/1 (1973): 9–14.
— "The Twelfth Season at Nippur," *Expedition* 16/4 (1974): 23–32.
— *Excavations* at *Nippur; 11th season*, with appendixes by M. Civil, J. H. Johnson & S. A. Kaufman, Oriental Institute Communication, Nos. 22-23, Chicago 1975–1977.
— "Excavations in Iraq, 1972–1973," *Iraq* 35 (1973): 189–204.
— "Excavations in Iraq, 1973–1974," *Iraq* 37 (1975): 57–67.
— "Excavations in Iraq, 1976," *Iraq* 39 (1977): 301–320.
— "The Eleventh and Twelfth Seasons at Nippur," *Sumer* 31 (1975): 33-39.
Gijselen, R., "Le trésor monétaire sasanide trouvé en 1976 dans le secteur Est de l'Apadane," *DAFI* 7 (1977): 61–74.
Gil, M., "The Rādhānite Merchants and the Land of Rādhān," *JESHO* 17 (1974): 299–328.
— "Ha-Mifgash ha-Bavli," *Tarbiẓ* 48 (1979): 35–73.
Göbl, R., "Der sāsānidische Münzfund von Seleukia (Vēh-Ardašēr) 1967," *Mesopotamia* 8/9 (1973): 229–258.
de Goeje, M., "Zur historischen Geographie Babyloniens," *ZDMG* 39 (1885): 1–16.
Goell, T., in M. Mellink, "Archaeology in Asia Minor: Addenda," *AJA* 70 (1966): 280.
Goldhaar, I., *Admat Qodesh Hi Eretz Yisrael li-Gevuloteha*, Jerusalem 1913.
Goodblatt, D. M., *Rabbinic Instruction in Sasanian Babylonia*, Leiden 1975.
— "Local Traditions in the Babylonian Talmud," *HUCA* 48 (1977): 187-217.
— "The Poll Tax in Sasanian Babylonia; The Talmudic Evidence," *JESHO* 22 (1979) part III: 234–295.
Goodenough, E. R., *Jewish Symbols in the Greco-Roman-Period*, vols. 9–11, New York 1964.
Graetz, H., "Die talmudische Topographie," MGWJ 2 (1853): 190-201.
— *Geschichte der Juden*, vols. 4 & 5, Leipzig 1908–1909[4].
— *Das Königreich Mesene und seine jüdische Bevölkerung*, Breslau 1879.
Grayson, A. K., *Assyrian and Babylonian Chronicles*, New York 1975.
Guidi, J., "Un nuovo testo siriaco sulla storie degli ultimi Sassanidi," *Actes du 8e Congresse international des Orientalistes*, Leiden 1891, II, 3 = *CSCO*, ser. III, vol. 4.
Gullini, G., "Problems of an Excavation in Northern Babylonia," *Mesopotamia* 1 (1966): 7–38.
— "Trial Trench on the Canal," *Mesopotamia* 3/4 (1968-1969): 39–41.
von Gutschmid, A., *Geschichte Irans und seiner Nachbarländer*, Tübingen 1888.
Hacohen, M., "Toledot ha-Tana Isi b. Yehuda," *Sinai* 33 (1953): 355–364; 34 (1954): 231–240, 325–334, 407–427.
Hadley, R. A., "The Foundation Date of Seleucia on the Tigris," *Historia* 22 (1979): 228-230.
al-Haik, A. R., *Key Lists of Archaeological Excavations in Iraq* (ed. H. Field & E. M. Laird), Coconut Grove, Florida, vol. 1, 1968; vol. 2, 1971.
Halevy, I., *Dorot ha-Rishonim, Sefer Divrei ha-Yamim li-Venei Yisrael*, I–VI, Frankfurt 1897–1939.

Hansman, J., "Charax and the Karkheh," *Iranica Antiqua* 7 (1967): 21–58 (= *Mélanges Ghirsman* II).

Hartmann, R. & Longrigg, S. H., "Didjla," *EI*[1].

al-Ḥasanī, 'A. R., *al-'Irāq qadīman wa-ḥadīṯan*, 2nd pr., Ṣaidā 1375/1956.

Hasebroek, J., *Untersuchungen zur Geschichte des Kaisers Septimius Severus*, Heidelberg 1921.

Haussoulier, B., "Inscriptions grecques de Babylone," *Klio* 9 (1909): 352–363.

Herr, M. D., "Ha-Nisuin mi-Beḥinah Sotzio-Ekonomit le-fi ha-Halakhah," in *Mishpeḥot Bet Yisrael*, Jerusalem 1976, pp. 37–46.

Herzfeld, E., "Untersuchungen über die historische Topographie der Landschaft am Tigris, kleinen Zāb und Ğebel," *Memnon* 1 (1907): 89–143.

— "Der Thron des Khusro," *Jahrbuch der Preußischen Kunstsammlungen* 41 (1920): 17-18.

— "Khorasan," *Der Islam* 11 (1921): 107–174.

— "Awestische Topographie," *Archäologische Mitteilungen aus Iran* 2 (1930): 72.

— *Archaeological History of Iran*, London 1935.

— *Geschichte der Stadt Samarra. Die Ausgrabungen von Samarra*, vol. 6, Hamburg 1948.

— *The Persian Empire*, Wiesbaden 1968.

— "Bābil," *EI*[1]; "Birs," *EI*[1,2].

Hildesheimer, H., *Beiträge zur Geographie Palestinas*, Berlin 1886.

Hill, G. F., *Catalogue of the Greek Coins of Arabia, Mesopotamia and Persia in the British Museum*, London 1922.

Hilprecht, H. V., *Explorations in Bible Lands During the 19th Century*, Philadelphia 1903.

Hiltbrunner, O., "Ephraim," *KP*, vol. 2, col. 301.

Hirschberg, H. Z., "Yosef Melekh Ḥimyar we-Aliyato shel Mar Zuṭra li-Ṭeverya," *Kol Eretz Naftali*, Jerusalem 1966, pp. 139–146.

Hirschenson, Y. Z., *Sefer Sheva Ḥokhmot she-ba-Talmud u-Midrash*, Lemberg 1883.

Hoffmann, G., *Auszüge aus syrischen Akten persischer Märtyrer, Abhandlungen für die Kunde des Morgenlandes*, vol. 7, No. 3, Leipzig 1880.

Holleaux, M., "La mort d'Antiochos IV Epiphanes," *Études d'Épigraphie et d'Histoire Grecques*, vol. 3, Paris 1942, pp. 255–280.

— "Une Inscription de Séleucie de Piérie," *ibid.*, pp. 199–254.

Honigmann, E., & Maricq, A., *Recherches sur les Res Gestae Divi Saporis*, Brussels 1952.

Honigmann, E., "Kommagene," *RE*, Suppl. vol. 4, cols. 978–990; "Ktesiphon," *RE* Suppl. vol. 4, cols. 1109–1119; "Ninos," *RE*, vol. 17, cols. 634–643; "Nisibyn," *RE*, vol. 17, col. 757.

— "Orfa," *EI*[1].

Hopkins, C., *Topography and Architecture of Seleucia on the Tigris*, Ann Arbor 1972.

— *The Discovery of Dura Europos* (ed. B. Goldman), New Haven & London 1979.

Horowitz, I. S., *Eretz Yisrael u-Shekhenoteha*, Vienna 1923.

Huart, Cl.-Sayilī, A., "Gondeshāpur," *EI*[2].

Huart, Cl., "Khūzistān," *EI*[1].

Humann, C. & Puchstein, O., *Reisen in Kleinasien und Nordsyrien*, Berlin 1890.

Hyman, A., *Toledot Tana'im we-Amora'im* I–III, Jerusalem 1964.

van Ingen, W., *Figurines from Seleucia on the Tigris*, Ann Arbor 1939.

Invernizzi, A., "The excavations at Tell 'Umar," *Mesopotamia* 3/4 (1968–1969): 11–27; 5/6 (1970–1971): 13–19.

— "Bullae from Seleucia," *ibid.*: 69–124.

— "Problemi di coroplastica Tardo-Mesopotamica," *ibid.*: 227–292.

— "Ten Years' Research in the Al-Madā'in Area, Seleucia and Ctesiphon," *Sumer* 32 (1976): 167–175.

Institut Fernand Courby, *Nouveau Choix d'Inscriptions Grecques*, Paris 1971.
Jacobs, L., "Ha-Ḥayim ha-Kalkaliim shel Yehudei Bavel bi-Tequfat ha-Talmud," *Melila* 5 (1965): 84–101.
Jalabert, L., & Mouterde, R., *Inscriptions grecques et latines de la Syrie*, Paris, vol. 1, 1929; vol. 4, 1955.
Jastrow, M., *Dictionary of Talmud Babli, Yerushalmi, Midrashic Literature and Targumim*, New York 1950³.
Joël, J., "Beiträge zur Geographie des Talmud," *MGWJ* 16 (1867): 330–343, 375–387.
Jones, J. F.: "Narrative of a Journey Undertaken in April 1848," *Selections from the Records of the Bombay Government* [n. s.] 43 (1857): 34–134.
— "Narrative of a Journey to the Frontier of Turkey and Persia," *ibid.*; 136–213.
Jordan, J., & Preusser, C., *Uruk-Warka nach den Ausgrabungen durch die D.O.G.*, Wissenschaftliche Veröffentlichungen der Deutschen Orient-Gesellschaft, 51, Leipzig 1928.
Jordan, J., et al., "Uruk-Warka," *AAB*, Berlin 1929, No. 7, pp. 1–67.
Kaḥḥāla, ʿU. R., *Ǧuġrāfiyat šibh ǧazīrati l-ʿarab*, Cairo 1384/1964.
Kahrstedt, U., *Artabanes III und seine Erben*, Bern 1950.
Kern, O., *Die Inschriften von Magnesia am Maeander*, Berlin 1900.
Kiepert, A., "Zur Karte der Ruinenfelder von Babylon," *ZGEB* 18 (1883): 1–26, map 5.
Kister, M. J., "Al-Ḥīra, Some Notes on its Relations with Arabia," *Arabica* 15 (1968): 143–169.
— "Some Reports Concerning Mecca from Jāhiliyya to Islam," *JESHO* 15 (1972): 61–93.
— "On the Wife of the Goldsmith from Fadak and her Progeny," *Le Muséon* 92 (1979): 321–330.
Klein, S., "The Estates of R. Judah ha-Nasi and the Jewish Communities in the Trans-Jordanic Region," n.s. *JQR* 2 (1911–1912): 545–556.
— "Hebräische Ortsnamen bei Josephus," *MGWJ* 59 (1915): 156–169.
— "Zur Ortsnamenkunde Palästinas," *MGWJ* n.s. 28 (1920): 181–196.
— *Ever ha-Yarden ha-Yehudi mi-Zeman Bayit Sheni ad ha-Me'ah ha-Aḥaronah shel Yemei ha-Benayim*, Vienna 1925.
— "La-Topografia; Kefar ʿAris Khlakis 'Eretz Yisrael' bi-Bereshit Rabbah XVI 3," *Tarbiẓ* 1-B (1930): 127–131.
— *Sefer ha-Yishuv*, vol. 1, Jerusalem 1939 (repr. Jerusalem 1977).
— *Eretz ha-Galil*, Jerusalem 1967².
Klíma, O., "Mazdak und die Juden," *Archiv Orientální* 24 (1956): 420–431.
Knutstad, J., "A Report on the 1964–1965 Excavation at Nippur," *Sumer* 22 (1966): 111–114.
Koestermann, E., *Cornelius Tacitus, Annalen*, Heidelberg 1965.
Kohut, A., *Arukh ha-Shalem*, I–VIII, Vienna 1888–1892; IX *Tosefot Arukh ha-Shalem* (ed. S. Krauss et al.), Vienna 1937.
Koldewey, R., *Das Wiedererstehende Babylon*, Leipzig 1925.
Kraeling, C. H., *The Excavations at Dura-Europos, Final Reports*, VIII 1, *The Synagogue*, New Haven 1956.
Kramers, J. H., "Shuster," *EI*¹.
Krauss, S., "Die biblische Völkertafel im Talmud, Midrasch und Targum," *MGWJ* 39 (1895): 49–64.
— *Griechische und Lateinische Lehnwörter im Talmud, Midrasch und Targum*, I–II, Berlin 1898–1899 (repr. Hildesheim 1964).
— "Service Tree in the Bible and Talmud and in Modern Palestine," *HUCA* 1 (1924): 179–217.
— *Qadmoniot ha-Talmud*, I–II, Berlin - Vienna - Tel Aviv, 1923–1945.
— *Paras we-Romi ba-Talmud u-va-Midrashim*, Jerusalem 1948.

Kühnel, E., *Die Ausgrabungen der zweiten Ktesiphon Expedition 1931/2*, Berlin 1933.
Kurtz, O., "The Date of the Ṭāq i Kīsrā," *JRAS* (1941): 37–41.
Kutscher, E. Y., *Milim we-Toledotehen*, Jerusalem 1961.
Labourt, J., *Le Christianisme dans l'Empire perse sous la dynastie sassanide*, Paris 1904².
Lacoste, H., "L'Arc de Ctesiphon," *Sumer* 10 (1954): 3–22.
van Lantschoot, A., "Cascar," *Dictionnaire d'Histoire et de Géographie Ecclésiastiques*, vol. 11, p. 1266f.
Lassner, J., *The Topography of Baghdad in the Early Middle Ages*, Detroit 1970.
— "Ḥilla," *EI*².
Layard, A. H., *Discoveries in the Ruins of Nineveh and Babylon*, New York 1853.
Lazarus, F., *Die Häupter der Vertriebenen. Beiträge zu einer Geschichte der Exils-Fürsten in Babylonien unter den Arsakiden und Sassaniden*, Frankfurt a.M. 1890.
Leewenstamm, S. E., "Gozan," *Entziqlopedia Miqra'it*, vol. 2, pp. 450–455.
Legrain, L., *The Culture of the Babylonians from Their Seals in the Collections of the Museum*, U. of Pennsylvania, The University Museum Publication of the Babylonian Section, 14, Philadelphia 1925.
— *Terra-Cottas from Nippur*, ibid., 16, Philadelphia 1930.
— "Coins from Nippur," *The Museum Journal, U. of Pennsylvania* 15 (1924): 70–76.
Lehmann, C. F., "Noch einmal kassu: κίσσοι, nicht κοσσαῖοι," *ZA* 7 (1892): 328–334.
Lenzen, H. J., "Warka," *Sumer* 10 (1954): 86–88, 195–196.
— "Taqrīr awwalī ʿani t-tanqīb fī l-Warkā," *Sumer* 10 (1954): 310–311.
— "Bericht über die dreizehnte deutsche Ausgrabungs-Campagne in Uruk-Warka," *Sumer* 11 (1955): 73–75.
— "Warka," *AFO* 17 (1954–1956): 198–201.
Lepper, F. A., *Trajan's Parthian War*, Oxford 1948.
Le Rider, G., "Monnaies de Characène," *Syria* 36 (1959): 229–253.
— *Suse sous les Séleucides et les Parthes, Les Trouvailles monétaires et l'histoire de la ville* (Mémoires de la Mission Archéologique en Iran, vol. 38) Paris 1965.
— "Un Trésor de petites monnaies de bronze trouvé à Ninive," *Archaeologia Iranica* (*Iranica Antiqua*) 7 (1970): 4–20.
Le Strange, G., "Description of Mesopotamia and Baghdad, Written by Ibn Serapion," *JRAS* (1895): 1–76, 255–315. See Suhrāb in Arabic Literature listing.
— *The Lands of the Eastern Caliphate*, Cambridge 1905.
— *Baghdad During the Abbasid Caliphate*, Oxford 1924 (short title: Le Strange).
Levy, S. J., "Two Cylinders of Nebuchadnezzar II," *Sumer* 3 (1947): 4–18.
Levy, J., *Wörterbuch über die Talmudim und Midraschim*, Berlin & Vienna 1924² (repr. Darmstadt 1963).
Lieberman, S., *Hellenism in Jewish Palestine*, New York 1962².
— "'Kakh Haya we-Kakh Yiheye'—Yehudei Eretz Yisrael we-Yahadut ha-Olam bi-Tequfat ha-Mishnah we-ha-Talmud," *Cathedra* 17 (1980): 3–10.
Lockhart, L., "Ahwāz"; "Ḥulwān," *EI*².
Loftus, W. K., "Notes of a Journey from Baghdad to Busrah," *JRGS* 26 (1856): 131–153.
Löw, I., *Die Flora der Juden*, I–IV, Vienna-Leipzig 1924–1934 (repr. Hildesheim 1967).
Macler, F., *Histoire d'Heraclius par l'evèque Sébéos traduite de l'arménien et annotée*, Paris 1904.
Mann, J., "The Responsa of the Babylonian Geonim as a Source of Jewish History," *JQR* 10 (1920): 121–151, 309–365 (= Mann, *The Collected Articles*, vol. 2, Gedera 1971, pp. 116–146, 148–204).
— "The Responsa of the Babylonian Geonim as a Source of Jewish History," *JQR* 11 (1921): 433–471 (= Mann, *The Collected Articles*, vol. 2, pp. 205–243).

Mannert, K., *Geographie der Griechen und Römer*, Nürnberg 1797.
Maricq, A., "Res Gestae divi Saporis," *Syria* 35 (1958): 295–360 (Pls. XXIII–XXIV).
—"Vologésias, l'emporium de Ctésiphon," *Syria* 36 (1959): 264–276 (= *Classica et Orientalia*, pp. 113–126).
— *Classica et Orientalia*, Institut français d'archéologie de Beyrouth, Publication hors série, No. 11, Paris 1965.
Margoliouth, D. S., "A Jewish Persian Law Report," *JQR* 11 (1898–1899): 671–675.
Markwart, J., *A Catalogue of the Provincial Capitals of Ērānshahr*, Pahlavi Text, Version and Commentary (ed. G. Messina), Rome 1931.
— *Südarmenien und die Tigrisquellen*, Vienna 1930.
— *Ērānšahr nach der Geographie des Ps. Moses Xorenacei, Abhandlungen der Gesellschaft der Wissenschaften zu Göttingen, phil.-hist. Klasse*, n.s. vol. 3, No. 2, Berlin 1901.
Massignon, L., "Explication du plan de Kūfa (Iraq)," *Mélanges Maspéro*, Cairo 1934–1953, vol. 3, pp. 336–360.
McCown, D. E. & Haines, R. C., *Nippur*, vol. 1, Chicago 1967.
McCown, D. E., et al., *Nippur*, vol. 2, Chicago 1978.
McDowell, R. H., "The Excavations at Seleucia on the Tigris," *Papers Michigan Academy of Science, Arts and Letters*, 18 (1932): 101–119.
— *Coins from Seleucia on the Tigris*, Ann Arbor 1935.
— *Stamped and Inscribed Objects from Seleucia on the Tigris*, Ann Arbor 1935.
— "The History of Seleucia from Classical Sources," *Topography* (ed. by C. Hopkins), Ann Arbor 1972, pp. 149–163.
Meier, C.: "Ein griechisches Ehrendekret vom Gareustempel in Uruk," *Baghdader Mitteilungen* 1 (1960): 104–114.
Meier, G., "Opis," *RE*, vol. 18, cols. 683–685.
Meissner, B., "Zu Strabo XVI 1,9," *Klio* 19 (1925): 103–104.
Michailowski, K., *Palmyre. Fouilles Polonaises*, I–IV, Warsaw & The Hague, 1960–1967.
Millar, F., *A Study of Cassius Dio*, Oxford 1964.
— "Paul of Samosata, Zenobia and Aurelian: The Church, Local Culture and Political Allegiance in Third-Century Syria," *JRS* 61 (1971): 1–17.
Minorsky, V., "Roman and Byzantine Campaigns in Atropatene," *BSOAS* 11 (1943–1946): 243–265.
— "Nihāwand," *EI*[1].
Montgomery, J. A., *Aramaic Incantation Texts from Nippur*, Philadelphia 1913.
Mordtmann, A. D., *Sitzungsberichte der philos.-philol.-hist. Classe der k. b. Akademie der Wissenschaften zu München*, Munich 1875.
Mørkholm, O., "A Hoard of Coins from Characene," *Coin Hoards* 4 (1978): 25–27.
Morony, M. G., "The Effects of the Muslim Conquest on the Persian Population of Iraq," *Iran* 14 (1976): 41–59.
Mouterde, R., & Poidebard, A., "La voie antique des caravanes entre Palmyre et Hit, au IIe siècle ap. J.-C.," *Syria* 12 (1931): 99–115.
Müller, D. H., "Birtha," *RE* vol. 3, cols. 498–499.
Müller, K., ed., *Geographi Graeci Minores*, Paris 1885.
Musil, A., *Arabia Deserta, A Topographical Itinerary*, New York 1927.
— *The Middle Euphrates, A Topographical Itinerary*, New York 1927.
Nashef, Kh., *Répertoire Géographique des Textes Cunéiformes*, vol. 5, Wiesbaden 1982.
Naster, P., "Empreintes de sceaux hellénistiques de Warka et monnaies séleucides," *Greek Numismatics and Archaeology. Essays in Honor of Margaret Thompson* (ed. O. Mørkholm and N. Waggoner), Wetteren 1979, pp. 215–219.
Nau, F., *Les arabes chrétiens de Mésopotamie et de Syrie du VIIe au VIIIe siècle*, Paris 1933.

Naval Intelligence Division, *A Handbook of Mesopotamia*, I–II, London 1916–1917.
— *A Handbook of Iraq and the Persian Gulf*, London 1944.
Neubauer, A., *La Géographie du Talmud*, Paris 1868 (repr. Amsterdam 1965).
Neusner, J., *A History of the Jews in Babylonia*, I–V, Leiden 1965–1970.
— "Some Aspects of the Economic and Political Life of Babylonian Jewry ca. 160–220 C.E.," *PAAJR* 31 (1963): 165–196.
— *Talmudic Judaism in Sasanian Babylonia, Essays and Studies*, Leiden 1976.
Newell, E., *Mithradates of Parthia and Hyspaosines of Charax*, *NNM* No. 26, New York 1925.
Newman, J., *The Agricultural Life of the Jews in Babylonia between the Years 200 C.E. and 500 C.E.*, London 1932.
Nissen, H. J., "Südbabylonien in parthischer und sasanidischer Zeit," *Baghdader Mitteilungen* 6 (1973): 79–86.
Nock, A. D., "Greek Magical Papyri," *JEA* 15 (1929): 219–235.
— "A Vision of Mandulis Aion," *HTR* 27 (1934): 53–104.
Nodelman, S. A., "A Preliminary History of Characene," *Berytus* 13 (1959–1960): 83–121.
Nöldeke, Th., "Die Namen der aramäischen Nation und Sprache," *ZDMG* 25 (1871): 113–131.
— "Zur orientalischen Geographie," *ZDMG* 28 (1874): 93–102.
— *Geschichte der Perser und Araber zur Zeit der Sasaniden aus der arabischen Chronik des Ṭabari*, übersetzt und mit ausführlichen Erläuterungen und Ergänzungen versehen. Leiden 1879.
— "Die von Guidi herausgegebene syrische Chronik," *Sitzungsberichte der Akademie der Wissenschaften in Wien, phil.-hist. Klasse* 128 vol. 9, Vienna 1893, pp. 1–48.
— "Delitzsch, F., *Wo lag das Paradies?*" *ZDMG* 36 (1882): 173–184.
Oates, D., *Studies in the Ancient History of Northern Iraq*, London 1968.
Obermeyer, J., "Al Ḥurvot Bavel u-Migdal Dor ha-Haflagah," *Hamagid* 20 (1876): passim.
— *Die Landschaft Babylonien im Zeitalter des Talmuds und des Gaonats*, Frankfurt a. M. 1929.
Oelsner, J., "Kontinuität und Wandel in Gesellschaft und Kultur Babyloniens in hellenistischer Zeit," *Klio* 60 (1978): 101–116.
Olmstead, A. T., "Cuneiform Texts and Hellenistic Chronology," *Cl. Ph.* 32 (1937): 1–14.
Oppenheimer, A., *The ʿAm ha-Aretz, A Study in the Social History of the Jewish People in the Hellenistic-Roman Period*, Leiden 1977.
— "Hafrashat Maʿaser Rishon ba-Metziut she-le-Aḥar Ḥurban Bayit Sheni," *Sinai* 83 (1978): 267–287.
— "Batei Midrashot be-Eretz Yisrael be-Reshit Tequfat ha-Amora'im," *Cathedra* 8 (1978): 80–89.
— "Qishrei Mešan we-Eretz Yisrael," *Zion* 47 (1982): 335–341.
von der Osten, H. H., Naumann, R., et al., *Takht-i-Suleiman, Vorläufiger Bericht über die Ausgrabungen 1959*, *Teheraner Forschungen*, vol. 1, Berlin 1961.
Paschoud, F., "La Naarmalcha: à propos du tracé d'un canal en Mésopotamie moyenne," *Syria* 55 (1978): 345–359.
Pearson, J. D., (ed.) *A Bibliography of Pre-Islamic Persia*, London 1975.
Péres, H., "al-Alusi," *EI*².
Peters, J. P., *Nippur, or Explorations and Adventures on the Euphrates*, I–II, New York-London 1897.
Pettinato, G., "Cuneiform Inscriptions Discovered at Seleucia on the Tigris," *Mesopotamia* 5/6 (1970–1971): 49–66.

Pigulevskaja, N., *Les Villes de l'État Iranien, Époque Parthe et Sassanide*, Paris & The Hague 1963.

— *Byzanz auf den Wegen nach Indien*, Berlin-Amsterdam 1969.

Pinches, T. G., *The Old Testament in the Light of the Historical Records and Legends of Assyria and Babylonia*, London 1903[2].

— "A Babylonian Tablet dated in the reign of Aspasinē", *The Babylonian and Oriental Record* 4 (1889/1890): 131–135.

Pineles, H. M., *Sefer Darkah shel Torah*, Vienna 1861.

Pinsker, S., *Liqutei Qadmoniot*, Vienna 1860.

Plessner, M., "Kutha," *EI*[1].

Pognon, H., *Inscriptions Mandāites des coupes de Khouabir*, Paris 1898.

Pope, A. U., (ed.) *A Survey of Persian Art*, London-New York 1938 (1964–1965[2]).

Pope, A. U., Crane, M., & Wilber, D. N., "The Institute's Survey of Persian Architecture," Preliminary Report on Takhtisulayman, *Bulletin of the American Institute of Iranian Art and Architecture*, December (1937): 71–105.

Posgate, J. N., *Reallexikon der Assyriologie*, vol. 5 (1976–1980): 33.

Putrich, O.W. & Reignard *Die Glasfunde von Ktesiphon*, Berlin 1939.

Ramsay, G. G., *The Annals of Tacitus*, London 1904.

Rapoport, S. J., "Al Devar Matzevah ha-Nimtze'ah ba-I Krim u-Reshimah Aleha," *Kerem Chemed* 5 (1841): 197–231.

— "Hutzal," *Hamagid* 17 (1873): 401.

— *Erekh Millin*, I–II, Warsaw 1914 (repr. Jerusalem 1970).

Rawlinson, H. C., "Notes on a Journey to Takhti-Soleimān and on the Site of the Atropatenian Ecbatana," *JRGS* 10 (1841): 1–158.

— "Notes on the Ancient Geography of Mohamrah and Vicinity," *JRGS* 27 (1857): 185–190.

Rentz, G., & Mulligan, W. E.: "Bahreyn," *EI*[2].

Reuther, O., *Die Innenstadt von Babylon (Merkes)*, Leipzig 1926.

— *Die Ausgrabungen der Deutschen Ktesiphon Expedition im Winter 1928–1929*, Berlin 1930.

— "German Excavations at Ctesiphon," *Antiquity* 3 (1929): 434–452.

Rey-Coquais, J. P., "Syrie romaine de Pompée à Dioclétien," *JRS* 68 (1978): 44–73.

Ritter, C., *Die Erdkunde von Asien*, Berlin 1840–1844.

Robert, L., "Sur Quelques Ethniques," *Hellenica* 2 (1946): 63–93.

— "Inscriptions séleucides de Phrygie et d'Iran," *Hellenica* 7 (1949): 5–29.

— "Décret de Samos," *Hellenica* 11–12 (1960): 126–131.

van Roggen, G., *Notice sur les anciens traveaux hydrauliques en Susiane*, Mémoires de la délégation en Perse, 2e série, VII, Paris 1905.

Rosenthal, E. S., "Rav Ben Aḥi Rabbi Hiyyah Gam Ben Aḥoto?" *Sefer Hanoch Yalon*, Jerusalem 1963, pp. 281–337.

Rossi, E., "Sumaisāt," *EI*[1].

Rostovtzeff, M., "Les Inscriptions caravanières de Palmyre," *Mélanges Gustave Glotz*, vol. 2, Paris 1932, pp. 793–811.

— *Caravan Cities* (trans. by D. & T. Talbot Rice), Oxford 1932.

— "Progonoi," *JHS* 55 (1935): 56–66.

— "Une nouvelle inscription caravanière de Palmyre," *Berytus* 2 (1935): 143–148.

— *The Social and Economic History of the Hellenistic World*, I–III, Oxford 1941.

— "Seleucid Babylonia: Bullae and Seals of Clay with Greek Inscriptions," *YCS* 3 (1932): 1–114 and Pls. I–XI.

Rostovtzeff, M., et al., *The Excavations at Dura Europos. Preliminary Reports*, New Haven 1929–1956.

— *Final Report*, New Haven 1943–1969 & Los Angeles 1977.

Rothstein, G., *Die Dynastie der Laḫmiden in al-Ḥīra*, Berlin 1899.
Sachau, E., *Die Chronik von Arbela, Abhandlungen der preußischen Akademie der Wissenschaften zu Berlin, phil.-hist. Klasse*, No. 6, Berlin 1915.
— *Zur Ausbreitung des Christentums in Asien, Abhandlungen der preußischen Akademie der Wissenschaften zu Berlin, phil.-hist. Klasse* I, Berlin 1919.
Safar, F., *Wasit; The Sixth Season's Excavations*, Cairo 1945.
Safrai, S., *Rabbi Aqiva b. Yosef, Ḥayav u-Mishnato*, Jerusalem 1970.
— "Li-Ve'ayat ha-Khronologia shel ha-Nesi'im ba-Me'ah ha-Sheniya we-ha-Shelishit," *Divrei ha-Qongres ha-Olami ha-Shishi le-Mada'ei ha-Yahadut*, Jerusalem 1975, pp. 51–57.
Sarkis, Y., *Mabāḥiṯ 'Irāqīya*, Baghdad 1367/1948–1374/1955.
Sarkisian, G. Kh., "City Land in Seleucid Babylonia," *Ancient Mesopotamia* (ed. I. M. Diakonoff), Moscow 1969, pp. 312–331.
Sarre, F., & Herzfeld, E., *Archäologische Reise im Euphrat- und Tigris-Gebiet*, Berlin, vols. 1, 3–1911; vols. 2, 4–1920.
Savory, R. M., "Khūzistān," *EI*².
Schaeder, T. H., "Ḥasan al-Baṣrī," *Der Islam* 14 (1924): 1–75.
Schalit, A., "Evidence of an Aramaic Source in Josephus' 'Antiquities of the Jews,'" *ASTI* 4 (1965): 163–188.
Schinaja, P., "A Coin Hoard from Choche," *Mesopotamia* 2 (1967): 105–133.
Schlumberger, D., "Palmyre et la Mésène," *Syria* 38 (1961): 256–260.
— *La Palmyrène du Nord-Ouest, suivi d'un recueil épigraphique*, Paris 1951.
Schmidt, E. F., *Flights over Ancient Cities of Iran*, Chicago 1940.
Schmidt, J. H., "L'expédition de Ctesiphon en 1931–2," *Syria* 15 (1934): 1–23.
Schmidt, J., "Uruk-Warka, zusammenfassender Bericht über die 27. Kampagne 1968," *Baghdader Mitteilungen* 5 (1970): 51–96.
— "Qasr-ī Šīrīn, Feuertempel oder Palast?" *Baghdader Mitteilungen* 9 (1978): 39–47.
Schneid, D., *Tziurei Bet ha-Keneset be-Dura Europos*, Tel Aviv 1946.
Schürer, E., *Geschichte des jüdischen Volkes im Zeitalter Jesu Christi*, III, Leipzig 1909⁴.
— *The History of the Jewish People in the Age of Jesus Christ* (175 B.C.–A.D. 135). A new English version revised and edited by Vermes, G. & Millar, F., I–II, Edinburgh 1973–1979.
Schwabe, M., V Lifshitz, B., *Bet She'arim*, vol. 2, Jerusalem 1974.
Schwartz, J., *Sefer Tevu'ot ha-Aretz*, A. M. Luncz ed., Jerusalem 1900³. (repr. Jerusalem 1979)
Schwarz, P., *Iran im Mittelalter nach den arabischen Geographen*, Leipzig 1896, repr. Hildesheim 1969.
Scoville, S. A., *Gazetteer of Arabia*, vol. 1 A–E, Graz 1979.
Segal, B.-Z., *Ha-Geografiah ba-Mishnah*, Jerusalem 1979.
Segal, J. B., "Mesopotamian Communities from Julian to the Rise of Islam," *Proceedings of the British Academy* (1955): 109–139.
— "The Jews of North Mesopotamia before the Rise of the Islam," *Sefer Segal*, (eds. J. M. Grintz & J. Liver), Jerusalem 1964, pp. 32*–63*.
— *Edessa "The Blessed City,"* Oxford 1970.
Selby, W. R., & Bewsher, J. B., *Survey of Mesopotamia; Sheriat el Beythra to Tel Ibrahim*, London 1862–1865.
Seyrig, H., "L'incorporation de Palmyre à l'empire romain," *Syria* 13 (1932): 266–277 (= *Antiquités Syriennes*, vol. 1, pp. 255–277).
— "Inscriptions de l'Agora de Palmyre," *Syria* 22 (1941): 223–270 (= *Antiquités Syriennes*, vol. 3, pp. 167–214).
— "Trésor Monétaire de Nisibe," *Revue Numismatique* 17 (1955): 82–122.
— *Antiquités Syriennes*, I–IV, Paris 1934–1965.

Sherwin-White, S. M., "A Greek Ostracon from Babylon of the Early Third Century B.C.," *ZPE* 47 (1982): 51–70.

Simon, H., "Die sāsānidischen Münzen des Fundes von Babylon," *Acta Iranica* 12 (1977): 149–337.

Simonetta, B., "Considerazioni sull'inizio dell'anno pratico nella monetatione di Seleucia sul Tigri," *Schweizer Münzblätter* 28 (1978): 2–8.

Smallwood, E. M., *The Jews under Roman Rule*, Leiden 1976 (repr. 1981).

Smith, S., *Babylonian Historical Texts Relating to the Capture and Downfall of Babylon*, London 1924.

Sorek, Y., "Mi Heḥeriv et Nehardea?" *Zion* 37 (1972): 117–119.

Sourdel, D., "Irbil," *EI*².

Sperber, D., "Bab Nahara," *Iranica Antiqua* 8 (1968): 70–73.

Starcky, J., *Palmyre*, Paris 1952.

— "Palmyre," *Dictionnaire de la Bible*, Suppl. 6, cols. 1066–1103, Paris 1960.

Stein, A., *Old Routes of Western Iran*, London 1940.

Stein, O., "Tylos," *RE*, vol. 7A, col. 1732f.

Steingass, F. J., *A Comprehensive Persian-English Dictionary*, London 1963 (repr. of 1892 ed.).

Stern, M., *Greek and Latin Authors on Jews and Judaism*, vol. 2, Jerusalem 1980.

St. Martin, J., *Recherches sur l'histoire et la géographie de la Mésène et de la Characène*, Paris 1838.

Strauss, P., "Un trésor de monnaies hellénistiques trouvé près de Suse (2ᵉ partie)," *Revue Numismatique* 6/13 (1971): 109–140.

Streck, M., *Die alte Landschaft Babylonien nach den arabischen Geographen*, I–II, Leiden 1900–1901.

— "Seleucia und Ktesiphon," *Der alte Orient* 16 3/4 (1917): 1–64.

— "Diakira," *RE*, vol. 5, col. 317.

— "Ktesiphon," *RE*, suppl. 4, cols. 1102–1109.

— "Anbār," "Ahwāz," "Barāṯā," "Irbil," "Karkīsiyā," "Madā'in," "Maisān," "Niffar," "al-Sūs," "al-Warkā," "Wāsiṭ," *EI*¹.

— "Hīt," "Karkīsiyā," *EI*².

Streck, M.-al-'Alī, S. A., "Baṭīḥa," *EI*².

Streck, M.-Duri, A. A., "Anbār," *EI*².

Streck, M.-Lassner, J., "Karkh," "Kaskar," *EI*².

Streck, M.-Longrigg, S. H., "Baradān," *EI*¹,².

Sturm, J., "Nisibis," *RE*, vol. 17, cols. 714–757.

— "φάλγα," *RE*, vol. 38, col. 1668.

Sukenik, E. L., *Bet ha-Keneset shel Dura Europos we-Tziuraw*, Jerusalem 1947.

Sullivan, R. D., "The Dynasty of Commagene," *ANRW* II 8, Berlin-New York 1977, pp. 732–798.

Sussmann, Y., "Ketovet Hilkhatit me-Emeq Bet She'an," *Tarbiẓ* 43 (1974): 88–158.

— "Baraita di-Teḥumei Eretz Yisrael," *Tarbiẓ* 45 (1976): 213–257.

Syme, R., *Tacitus*, Oxford 1958.

Tarn, W. W., *The Greeks in Bactria and India*, Cambridge 1951².

Thompson, R. C., & Hutchinson, R. W., *A Century of Exploration at Nineveh*, London 1929.

Timothy, L. D., "A Cuneiform Tablet from Tell 'Umar," *Mesopotamia* 13/14 (1978–1979): 96–97.

Tkač, J., "Gerrha (2)," *RE*, vol. 7, cols. 1270–1272.

Townsend, P. W., "Bur, Bure and Baris in Ancient North African Place Names," *JNES* 13 (1954): 52–55.

Treidler, H., "Dura," *KP*, vol. 2, cols. 179–181; "Hatra," *ibid.* col. 957.
Tscherikower, V., *Die hellenistischen Städtegründungen von Alexander dem Großen bis auf die Römerzeit*, Leipzig 1927.
Umansky, J., *Ḥakhmei ha-Talmud*, Jerusalem 1949.
Urbach, E. E., "Hilkhot Avdut ke-Maqor la-Historia ha-Ḥevratit bi-Yemei ha-Bayit ha-Sheni u-vi-Tequfat ha-Mishnah we-ha-Talmud," *Zion* 25 (1960): 141–189.
— "Al Iyun Histori ba-Sipur al Moto shel Rabbah b. Naḥmani," *Tarbiẓ* 34 (1965): 156–161.
— *The Sages—Their Concepts and Beliefs*, I–II, Jerusalem 1975.
U.S. Board on Geographic Names, *Official Standard Names Gazetteer*, Baḥrain 1976.
Vollgraff, G., *Mémoires de la Mission Archéologique de Perse* 20 (1928): 79–98.
Walbank, F. W., *A Commentary on Polybius*, vol. 2, Oxford 1967.
Ward, W. H., "Sippara," *Hebraica* 2 (1885): 79–86.
Waterman, L., *Royal Correspondence of the Assyrian Empire*, Ann Arbor 1930.
— (ed.), *Preliminary Report upon the Excavations at Tel ʿUmar, Iraq*, Ann Arbor 1931.
— (ed.), *Second Preliminary Report upon the Excavations at Tel ʿUmar, Iraq*, Ann Arbor 1933.
Weiss, I. H., *Dor Dor we-Doreshaw*, I–V, Vilna 1904[4].
Weissbach, F. H., *Die Inschriften Nebukadnezars II in Wadi Brisa*, Leipzig 1906.
— *Die Keilinschriften der Achämeniden*, Leipzig 1911.
— *RE*: "Charakene" (vol. 3, cols. 2116–2119); "Charax" (vol. 3, col. 2122), "Elymais" (vol. 5, cols. 2458–2467): "Gazace" (vol. 7, col. 886f.); "Is" (vol. 9, col. 2047f.); "Koche" (vol. 11, col. 943f.); "κύρτιοι" (vol. 12, col. 205); "Mesene" (vol. 15, cols. 1082–1095); "Samosata" (vol. 1A, cols. 2220–2224); "Sostra" (vol. 3A, col. 1199).
Welles, C. B., "The Inscriptions," in *Gerasa, City of the Decapolis* (C. H. Kraeling), New Haven 1938.
Wenke, R. J., "Imperial Investments and Agricultural Developments in Parthian and Sassanian Khuzestan: 150 B.C. to A.D. 640," *Mesopotamia* 10–11 (1975–1976): 31–221.
Wetzel, F., Schmidt, E., Mallwitz, A., *Das Babylon der Spätzeit*, Berlin 1957.
Widengren, G., "The Status of the Jews in the Sassanian Empire," *Iranica Antiqua* 1 (1961): 117–161.
Wiegand, Th., et al., *Palmyra*, Berlin 1932.
Wiesner, J., *Scholien zum babylonischen Talmud*, I–III, Prague 1859–1867.
Wilber, D. N., "The Parthian Structure of Takti Sulayman," *Antiquity* 12 (1938): 389–410.
Will, E., "Marchands et Chefs de Caravanes à Palmyre," *Syria* 34 (1957): 262–277.
Williams-Jackson, A. V., *Persia Past and Present*, New York 1906.
Winckler, H., "Kasiphja-Ktesiphon?" *Altorientalische Forschungen* II vol. 1, pp. 509–530, Leipzig 1898.
Wright, W., *Catalogue of the Syriac Manuscripts in the British Museum*, I–III, London 1870–1872.
Wroth, W., *Catalogue of the Greek Coins of Galatia, Cappadocia and Syria in the British Museum*, London 1899.
Yudelevitz, M. D., *Ḥayei ha-Yehudim bi-Zeman ha-Talmud, Sefer Nehardea*, Vilna 1905.
— *Yeshivat Pumbedita bi-Yemei ha-Amora'im*, Tel Aviv 1932.
— "Ha-Ir Sura," *Sinai* 1 (1938): 168–174; 268–275; 2: 156–162, 317–324, 418–422; 3: 130–132.
— *Ḥayei ha-Yehudim bi-Zeman ha-Talmud ba-Ir Pumbedita*, Jerusalem 1939.
— "Ha-Ir Naresh (be-Bavel) bi-Zeman ha-Talmud," *Sinai* 14 (1943–1944): 94–98; 16 (1944–1945): 93–98, 226–229.

— *Maḥoza, me-Ḥayei ha-Yehudim bi-Zeman ha-Talmud*, Jerusalem 1947.
Zadok, R., "Two Talmudic Notes," *JQR* 68 (1977–1978): 255–256.
— "The Nippur Region during the Late Assyrian, Chaldean and Achaemenian Periods Chiefly According to Written Sources," *IOS* 8 (1978): 266–322.
Zambelli, M., "L'ascesa al Trono di Antioco IV," *Rivista di Filologia* 38 (1960): 363–398.
Ziegler, C., *Die Terrakotten von Warka*, Berlin 1962.
Zunz, L., *Ha-Derashot be-Yisrael we-Hishtalshelutan ha-Historit* (ed. and completed by Ch. Albeck), Jerusalem 1974[3].
Zuri, I. S., *Toledot Darkei ha-Limud bi-Yeshivot Darom, Galil, Sura u-Nehardea*, Jerusalem 1914.
— *Shilton Rashut ha-Golah we-ha-Yeshivot*, Tel Aviv 1938.

Maps Consulted

The following maps, among others, have been consulted: Bartholomew's map of the Near East, 1 : 4,000,000; the various sheets of the British quarter-inch and one-inch maps of the area; the Map of Ancient Sites of Iraq of the Iraqi Department of Antiquities.

Particularly helpful for the identification of ancient sites are the maps which appeared in various works in the last century: J. F. Jones, "A Plan of the Ruins of Babylon and of the Surrounding Country, drawn from the Surveys of Selby, Bewsher and Collingwood," 1 : 253,440 = 1 inch to 4 miles (1874); re-edited by H. Kiepert on a scale of 1 : 500,000 (see bibliography).

For Seleucia and Ctesiphon, Bachmann's map in Reuther (see bibliography), partly republished by Hopkins (in English, see bibliography).

For the Diyala area, the detailed archaeological maps in Adams, *Land Behind Baghdad* (see bibliography).

Obermeyer's book (see bibliography) contains a sketch-map of the area which is helpful for the identification of a number of sites.

Arabic Literature

(with short form references)

'Abīd b. al-Abraṣ, *The Dīwāns*—*The Dīwāns of 'Abīd b. al-Abraṣ*, ed. Ch. Lyall, Leyden, 1913.

Abū l-Fidā'—Ismā'īl b. al-Malik Abū l-Fidā', *Kitāb taqwīm al-buldān*, Dresden, 1846.

Abū Dāwūd, *Sunan*, Cairo, 1371/1952.

Abū 'Ubaid, *Amwāl*—Abū 'Ubaid al-Qāsim b. Sallām, *Kitāb al-amwāl*, ed. M. Ḫ. Harās, Cairo 1389/1969.

Abū Yūsuf, *Ḫarāǧ*—al-Qāḍī Abū Yūsuf, *Kitāb al-ḫarāǧ*, Cairo, n. d.

Aġānī—Abū l-Faraǧ al-Iṣfahānī, *Kitāb al-aġānī*, Būlāq, 1285 A.H.

Ansāb al-ašrāf—al-Balāḏurī, *Ansāb al-ašrāf*, vol. 1, ed. M. Ḥamīdullāh, Cairo, 1959; vol. 4a, ed. M. Schloessinger, revised and annotated by M. J. Kister, Jerusalem, 1971; vol. 5, ed. S. D. Goitein, Jerusalem, 1936.

al-A'šā, *Dīwān*, ed. M. Husain, Cairo, 1950; ed. R. Geyer, London, 1928.

Bakrī—Abū 'Ubaid al-Bakrī, *Mu'ǧam mā sta'ǧama*, ed. Muṣṭafā as-Saqqā, Cairo, 1364/1945–1371/1951.

Bayān wa-tabyīn—al-Ǧāḥiẓ, *al-Bayān wa-t-tabyīn*, ed. 'Abd as-Salām Hārūn, Cairo, fourth printing, 1395/1975.

Dimašqī, *Nuḫbat ad-dahr*—Šams ad-Dīn ad-Dimašqī, *Nuḫbat ad-dahr fī 'aǧā'ib al-barr wa-l-baḥr*, ed. A. Mehren, St. Petersburg, 1866.

Dīnawarī, *Aḫbār ṭiwāl*—Abū Ḥanīfa ad-Dīnawarī, *al-Aḫbār aṭ-ṭiwāl*, ed. V. Guirgass, Leiden, 1888–1912.

Farḥat al-ġarī—'Abd al-Karīm b. Ṭāwūs, *Farḥat al-ġarī fī ta'yīn qabr amīr al-mu'minīn 'Alī b. Abī Ṭālib 'alaihi s-salām fī n-Naǧaf*, Naǧaf, 1368 A.H.

Futūḥ al-buldān—al-Balāḏurī, *Futūḥ al-buldān*, ed. M. de Goeje, Leiden, 1866; translated into German by O. Rescher, Leipzig, 1917.

Ǧāḥiẓ, *Buldān*—Ch. Pellat, "al-Ǧāḥiẓ rā'id al-ǧuġrāfiya al-insānīya," in *al-Mašriq* 60 (1966): 169–205.

Ǧāḥiẓ, *Ḥayawān*—al-Ǧāḥiẓ, *Kitāb al-ḥayawān*, ed. 'Abd as-Salām Hārūn, 2nd printing, Cairo, 1389/1969.

Ġāyatu l-iḫtiṣār—Tāǧ ad-Dīn b. Muḥammad al-Ḥusainī, *Ġāyatu l-iḫtiṣār fī l-buyūtāt al-'alawīya al-maḥfūẓa mina l-ġubār*, ed. Muḥammad Ṣādiq Baḥr al-'Ulūm, Naǧaf, 1382/1963.

Ḫalīfa b. Ḫayyāṭ, *Ta'rīḫ*—ed. Suhail Zakkār, Damascus, 1968.

al-Ḫalīl, *Kitāb al-'ain*—al-Ḫalīl b. Aḥmad, *Kitāb al-'ain*, Baghdad, 1914.

Hamdānī, *Ṣifat ǧazīrat al-'arab*—ed. D. H. Müller, vol. 1, Leiden, 1884.

Ḥamza, *Ta'rīḫ*—Ḥamza al-Iṣfahānī, *Ta'rīḫ sinī mulūk al-arḍ*, ed I. Gottwaldt, Leipzig, 1884.

Harawī, *Ziyārāt*—'Alī b. Abī Bakr al-Harawī, *Kitāb al-išārāt ilā ma'rifat az-ziyārāt*, ed. Sourdel-Thomine, Damascus, 1953.

Ḥudūd al-'ālam—*Ḥudūd al-'Ālam, The Regions of the World*, ed. V. Minorsky, London, 1970.

Ibn al-Aṯīr, *Kāmil*—Ibn al-Aṯīr, *al-Kāmil fī t-ta'rīḫ*, Beirut, 1385/1965.

Ibn al-Aṯīr, *Lubāb*—*al-Lubāb fī tahḏībi l-ansāb*, Beirut, n.d.

Ibn Baṭṭūṭa—*Voyages*, ed. C. Defrémery & B. R. Sanguinetti, Paris, 1853–1859.

Ibn Biṭrīq—Eutychius (Sa'īd b. Biṭrīq), *Kitāb at-ta'rīḫ al-maǧmu' 'alā t-taḥqīq wa-t-taṣdīq*, ed. L. Cheikho, Beirut, 1905.

Ibn al-Faqīh—Ibn al-Faqīh al-Hamadānī, *Kitāb al-buldān*, ed. M. de Goeje, Leiden, 1885 (*BGA* V).

Ibn Ǧubair—*The Travels of Ibn Jubayr*, ed. W. Wright, Leiden, 1907.

Ibn Ḥabīb, *Kitāb al-muḥabbar*, ed. I. Lichtenstaedter, Hyderabad, 1361/1942.

Ibn Ḫallikān, *Wafayāt al-a'yān*, ed. Iḥsān 'Abbās, Beirut, 1968.

Ibn Ḥauqal—*Kitāb ṣūrat al-arḍ*, ed. J. H. Kramers, Leiden, 1938 (*BGA* II).

Ibn Ḥazm, *Ansāb*—Ibn Ḥazm al-Andalusī, *Ǧamharat ansāb al-'arab*, ed. 'Abd as-Salām Hārūn, Cairo, 1382/1962.

Ibn Ḫurdāḏbih—*Kitāb al-masālik wa-l-mamālik*, ed. M. de Goeje, Leiden, 1889.

Ibn al-'Ibrī, *Ta'rīḫ muḫtaṣar ad-duwal*, ed. Sāliḥānī, Beirut, 1890, 2nd printing, Beirut, 1958.

Ibn Kaṯīr, *Bidāya*—*al-Bidāya wa-n-nihāya*, Beirut, 1974.

Ibn al-Qifṭī, *Ta'rīḫ al-ḥukamā'*, ed. J. Lippert, Leipzig, 1903.

Ibn Rusta—*al-A'lāq an-nafīsa*, ed. M. de Goeje, Leiden, 1892 (*BGA* VII).

Ibn Sa'd—*aṭ-Ṭabaqāt al-kubrā*, Beirut, 1380/1960–1388/1968.

Ibn Sa'īd, *Geography*—Ibn Sa'īd al-Maġribī, *Kitāb al-ǧuġrāfiyā*, ed. Ismā'īl al-'Arabī, Beirut, 1970.

Ibn Serapion, See Le Strange, "Ibn Serapion."

Ibn Ṭaifūr, *Baġdād*—Ibn Abī Ṭāhir Ṭaifūr, *Kitāb Baġdād*, Baghdad, 1368/1949.

al-Ibšaihī, *al-Mustaṭraf*—*al-Mustaṭraf fī kull fann mustaẓraf*, Cairo, 1379 A.H.

Idrīsī—*Kitāb nuzhat al-muštāq fī iḫtirāq al-āfāq* (*Opus Geographicum*), Naples, 1970f.

Iṣāba—Ibn Ḥaǧar, *al-Iṣāba fī tamyīz aṣ-ṣaḥāba*, ed. 'Alī Muḥammad al-Biǧāwī, Cairo, 1392/1972.

Iṣṭaḫrī—*Kitāb masālik al-mamālik*, ed. M. de Goeje, Leiden, 1927 (*BGA* I).

Kitāb al-ḥayawān—al Ǧaḥiẓ, *Kitāb al-ḥayawān*, ed. 'Abd as-Salām Hārūn, Cairo, 1389/1969.

Kitāb al-ma'ārif—Ibn Qutaiba, *Kitāb al-ma'ārif*, ed. Ṯarwat 'Ukāša, 2nd printing, Cairo, 1388/1969.

Kuṯayyir 'Azza, *Dīwān*, ed. Iḥsān 'Abbās, Beirut, 1391/1971.

Le Strange, "Ibn Serapion"—"Description of Mesopotamia and Baghdad, written by Ibn Serapion," *JRAS* (1895): 1–76, 255–315, see Suhrāb.

Lisān—Ibn Manẓūr, *Lisān al-'arab*, Beirut, 1374/1955–1376/1956.

Marāṣid—Ibn 'Abd al-Ḥaqq al-Baġdādī, *Marāṣid al-iṭṭilā' 'alā asmā' al-amkina wa-l-biqā'*, ed. 'Alī Muḥammad al-Biǧāwī, Cairo, 1373/1954.

Masālik al-abṣār—Ibn Faḍlallāh al-'Umarī, *Masālik al-abṣār*, vol. 1, ed. Aḥmad Zakī Bāšā, Cairo, 1342/1924.

Mas'ūdī, *Murūǧ*—al-Mas'ūdī, *Murūǧ aḏ-ḏahab wa-ma'ādin al-ǧauhar*, ed. Ch. Pellat, Beirut, 1966–1974. The references in brackets are to the edition of E. Barbier de Meynard & Pavet de Courteille, Paris, 1861–1877.

Mas'ūdī, *Tanbīh*—al-Mas'ūdī, *Kitāb at-tanbīh wa-l-išrāf*, ed. M. de Goeje, Leiden, 1894 (*BGA* VIII).

Munammaq—*Kitāb al-munammaq fī aḫbār Quraiš*, ed. Ḫūršīd Aḥmad Fāriq, Hyderabad, 1384/1964.

Muqaddasī—*Aḥsan at-taqāsīm fī ma'rifat al-aqālīm*, ed. M. de Goeje, Leiden, 1906 (*BGA* III).

Muštarik—Yāqūt al-Ḥamawī, *Kitāb al-muštarik waḍ'an wa-l-muftariq ṣuq'an*, ed. F. Wüstenfeld, Göttingen, 1846.

Mustaufī—Ḥamd Allāh Mustaufī, *The Geographical Part of the Nuzhat al-Qulūb*, ed. G. Le Strange, Leiden, 1915–1919.

Naqā'iḍ—*Naqā'iḍ Ǧarīr wa-l-Farazdaq*, ed. A. A. Bevan, Leiden, 1905–1912.

Naṣr b. Muzāḥim, *Kitāb Ṣiffīn*, ed. ʿAbd as-Salām Hārūn, 2nd Printing, Cairo, 1382 A.H.
Nuwairī, *Nihāyatu l-arab fī funūni l-adab*, Cairo, 1342/1923.
al-Qāḍī at-Tanūḫī, *Ǧāmiʿ at-tawārīḫ*—al-Qāḍī at-Tanūḫī, *Kitāb ǧāmiʿ at-tawārīḫ al-musammā nišwār al-muḥāḍara wa-aḫbār al-muḏākara*, Damascus, 1348/1930.
al-Qāmūs al-muḥīṭ—al-Fīrūzābādī, *al-Qāmūs al-muḥīṭ*, Cairo, 1371/1952.
Qazwīnī, *ʿAǧāʾib*—*ʿAǧāʾib al-maḫlūqāt wa-ġarāʾib al-mauǧūdāt*, Beirut, 1978.
Qazwīnī, *Bilād*—*Āṯār al-bilād wa-aḫbār al-ʿibād*, Beirut, 1380/1960.
Qudāma, *Ḫarāǧ*—Qudāma b. Ǧaʿfar, *Kitāb al-ḫarāǧ*, ed. M. de Goeje, Leiden, 1889 (*BGA* VI).
al-Qurṭubī, *Tafsīr*—Abū ʿAbdallāh al-Qurṭubī, *Tafsīr al-ǧāmiʿ li-aḥkām al-qurʾān*, Cairo, 1372/1952–1387/1967.
al-Qurṭubī, *al-Masālik wa-l-mamālik*, MS. Nur Osmaniya.
ar-Rauḍ al-miʿṭār—Muḥammad b. ʿAbd al-Munʿim al-Ḥimyarī, *ar-Rauḍ al-miʿṭār fī ḫabar al-aqṭār*, ed. Iḥsān ʿAbbās, Beirut, 1975.
Ṣābī, *Wuzarāʾ*—Hilāl aṣ-Ṣābī, *Kitāb al-wuzarāʾ*, ed. H. F. Amedroz, Leiden, 1904.
aš-Šābuštī, *Diyārāt*, ed. Ǧurǧīs ʿAwwād, Baghdad, 1951; 2nd ed., Baghdad, 1386/1966.
Samʿānī, *Ansāb*—as-Samʿānī, *Kitāb al-ansāb*, ed. D. J. Margoliouth (Gibb Memorial Series, 20), Leiden, 1912.
Šarḥ nahǧ al-balāġa—Ibn Abī l-Ḥadīd, *Šarḥ nahǧ al-balāġa*, Cairo, 1329 A.H.
Šiʿr wa-šuʿarāʾ—Ibn Qutaiba, *aš-Šiʿr wa-š-šuʿarāʾ*. ed. Aḥmad Muḥammad Šākir, Cairo, 1386/1966–1387/1967.
Suhrāb—*Kitāb ʿaǧāʾib al-aqālīm as-sabʿa*, ed. H. v. Mžik, Leipzig, 1930.
Sūsa, *Rayy Sāmarrā*—Aḥmad Sūsa, *Rayy Sāmarrā fī ʿahd al-ḫilāfa al-ʿabbāsiya*, Baghdad, 1948–1949.
Ṯaʿālibī, *Ġurar*—Abū Manṣūr aṯ-Ṯaʿālibī, *Ġurar aḫbār mulūk al-furs wa-siyarihim*, ed. H. Rotenberg, Paris, 1900.
Ṭabarī—Abū Ǧaʿfar Muḥammad b. Ǧarīr aṭ-Ṭabarī, *Taʾrīḫ ar-rusul wa-l-mulūk*, ed. Muḥammad Abū l-Faḍl Ibrāhīm, Cairo, 1380/1960–1387/1967. References in brackets are to the edition of M. de Goeje, Leiden, 1879–1901.
Ṭabarī, *Tafsīr*—*Ǧāmiʿ al-bayān fī tafsīr al-qurʾān*, Būlāq, 1321–1330 A.H.
Taḏkirat al-ḥuffāẓ—aḏ-Ḏahabī, *Taḏkirat al-ḥuffāẓ*, Hyderabad, 1376/1956.
Takmilat taʾrīḫ aṭ-Ṭabarī—Muḥammad b. ʿAbd al-Malik, *Takmilat taʾrīḫ aṭ-Ṭabarī*, ed. A. Y. Kanʿān, Beirut, 1961.
Ṯaʿlabī, *Qiṣaṣ al-anbiyāʾ*—aṯ-Ṯaʿlabī, *Qiṣaṣ al-anbiyāʾ* (= *ʿArāʾis al-maǧālis*), Beirut, n.d.
Taʾrīḫ Baġdād—al-Ḫaṭīb al-Baġdādī, *Taʾrīḫ Baġdād*, Cairo, 1349/1931.
Taʾrīḫ al-Ḥilla—Yūsuf Kerkūš al-Ḥillī, *Taʾrīḫ al-Ḥilla*, Naǧaf, 1385/1965.
Taʾrīḫ al-Mauṣil—Abū Zakarīyā al-Azdī, *Taʾrīḫ al-Mauṣil*, ed. ʿAlī Ḥabība, Cairo, 1387/1967.
Taʾrīḫ Wāsiṭ—Baḥšal, *Taʾrīḫ Wāsiṭ*, ed. Ǧurǧīs ʿAwwād, Baghdad, 1387/1967.
Ṯimār al-qulūb—Abū Manṣūr aṯ-Ṯaʿālibī, *Ṯimār al-qulūb fī l-muḍāf wa-l-mansūb*, ed. Muḥammad Abū l-Faḍl Ibrāhīm, Cairo, 1384/1965.
Usd al-ġāba—Ibn al-Aṯīr, *Usd al-ġāba fī maʿrifat aṣ-ṣaḥāba*, Cairo, 1280 A.H.
ʿUyūn al-aḫbār—Ibn Qutaiba, *ʿUyūn al-aḫbār*, Cairo, 1343/1925–1349/1930.
Yaʿqūbī, *Buldān*—Aḥmad b. Abī Yaʿqūb al-Yaʿqūbī, *Kitāb al-buldān*, ed. M. de Goeje, Leiden, 1891 (*BGA* VII).
Yāqūt—Yāqūt al-Ḥamawī, *Muʿǧam al-buldān*, Beirut, 1957.
Yāsīn al-ʿUmarī, *Maḥāsin Baġdād*—Yāsīn Ḫairallāh al-ʿUmarī, *Maḥāsin Baġdād*, Baghdad, 1388/1968.
Yaḥyā b. Ādam, *Ḫarāǧ*—*Kitāb al-ḫarāǧ*, ed. A. M. Šākir, Cairo, 2nd printing, 1384 A.H.
Zuhrī—Abū ʿAbdallāh az-Zuhrī, *Kitāb al-ǧuʿrāfiya*, ed. Muḥammad Ḥaǧǧ Ṣādiq, in *Bulletin d'Études Orientales* 21 (1968): 7–312.

Index of Sources

Greek and Latin Texts Quoted or Discussed

Inscriptions Quoted or Discussed

General Index

Boldface indicates that the place is an entry in the body or appendix (A) of the book

Chronological Table of Amoraitic Generations in Babylonia

Generation (Approximate Dates)	Leading Amora	Academy
First Generation A.D. 220–250	Rav	Sura
	Samuel	Nəhardə'a
Second Generation A.D. 250–290	Rav Huna	Sura
	Rav Judah	Pumbədita
Third Generation A.D. 290–320	Rav Ḥisda	Sura
	Rabbah b. Huna	Sura
	Rabbah b. Naḥmani	Pumbədita
	Rav Joseph	Pumbədita
Fourth Generation A.D. 320–350	Abbaye	Pumbədita
	Rava	Maḥoza
Fifth Generation A.D. 350–375	Rav Papa	Nareš
	Rav Zevid	Pumbədita
Sixth Generation A.D. 375–425	Rav Ashi	Sura (at Mata Məḥasya)
Seventh Generation A.D. 425–460	Mar b. Rav Ashi	Sura (at Mata Məḥasya)
	Rav Geviha of Be Katil	Pumbədita

TALMUDIC BABYLONIA

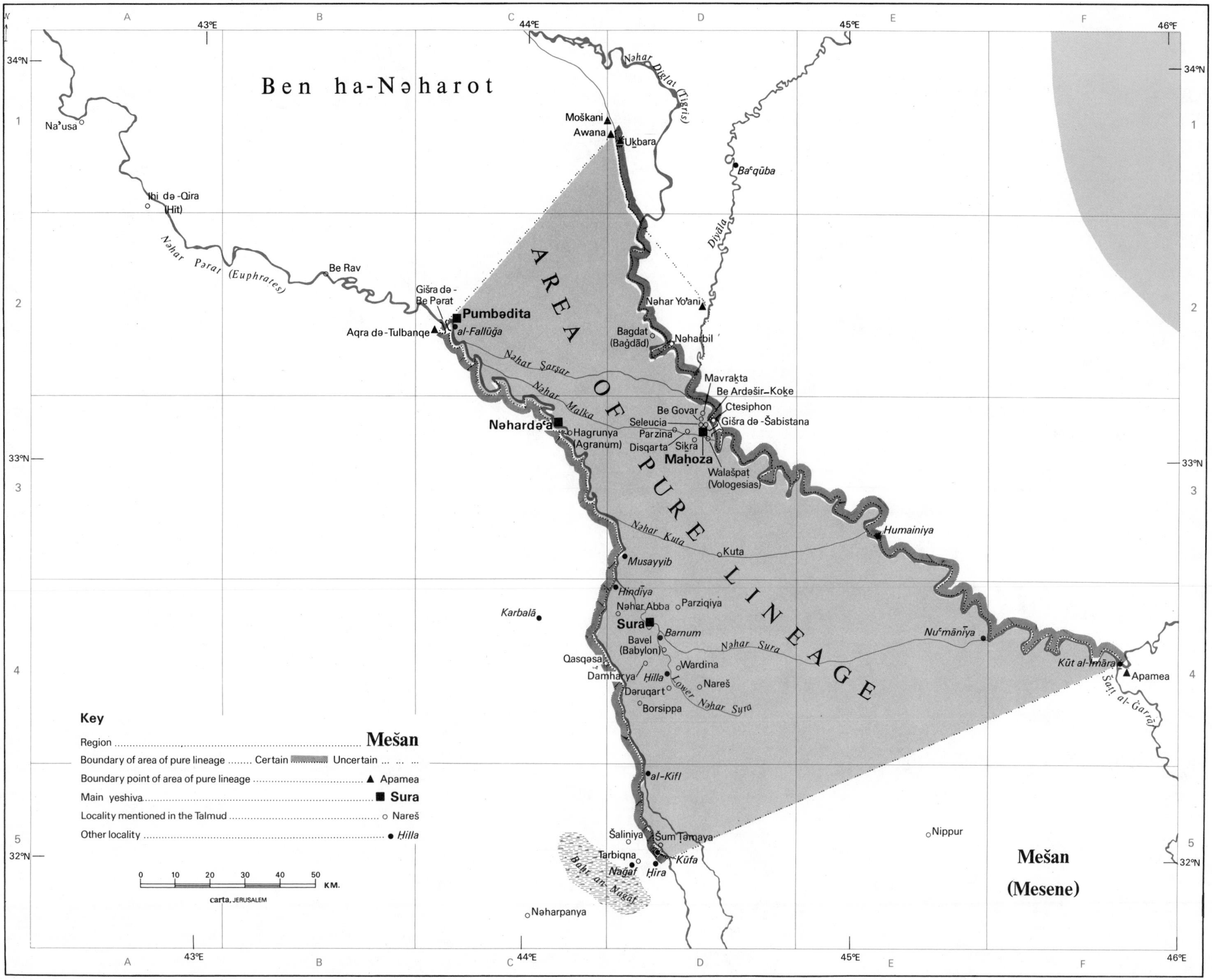

Ben ha-Nəharot
AREA OF PURE LINEAGE
Nəhar Diglat (Tigris)
Nəhar Pərat (Euphrates)
Diyāla
Nəhar Şarşar
Nəhar Malka
Nəhar Kuta
Nəhar Sura
Lower Nəhar Sura
Šaṭṭ al-Ġarrāf
Baḥr an-Naǧaf
Na'usa
Ihi də-Qira (Hīt)
Be Rav
Gišra də-Be Pərat
Pumbədita
al-Fallūǧa
Aqra də-Tulbanqe
Moškani
Awana
Ukbara
Ba'qūba
Nəhar Yo'ani
Bagdat (Baġdād)
Nəharbil
Mavrakta
Be Ardəšir-Koke
Be Govar
Ctesiphon
Seleucia
Gišra də-Šabistana
Parzina
Disqarta
Sikra
Maḥoza
Walašpat (Vologesias)
Nəhardə'a
Hagrunya (Agranum)
Humainiya
Kuta
Musayyib
Hindīya
Nəhar Abba
Parziqiya
Karbalā
Sura
Barnum
Bavel (Babylon)
Nu'māniya
Kūt al-Imāra
Apamea
Qasqəsa
Wardina
Damharya
Ḥilla
Nareš
Dəruqart
Borsippa
al-Kifl
Šaliniya
Šum Ṭamaya
Tarbiqna
Naǧaf
Ḥira
Kūfa
Nəharpanya
Nippur
Mešan (Mesene)
Key
Region .... Mešan
Boundary of area of pure lineage .... Certain ... Uncertain ... ...
Boundary point of area of pure lineage .... ▲ Apamea
Main yeshiva .... ■ Sura
Locality mentioned in the Talmud .... ○ Nareš
Other locality .... ● Ḥilla
0 10 20 30 40 50 KM.
carta, JERUSALEM
43°E 44°E 45°E 46°E
34°N 33°N 32°N
A B C D E F
1 2 3 4 5